Reflections from Gavea
My Epic Journey Home

Reflections from Gavea
My Epic Journey Home

Marianne Campagna

To Donny
with wishes for
a life filled with wonder!

Marianne Campagna

Reflections from Gavea
My Epic Journey Home

Gavea Press
1993 Wexford Dr.
Ypsilanti, Michigan 48198
reflectionsfromgavea.com

ISBN: 9780988910805
Library of Congress Control Number: 2013932320

Book Design: www.StorytellersFriend.com

Dedication

In memoriam for my mother, father, and son

For Lisa, Michelle, Suzy, and Sara

For all children who have lost parents and homeland

Acknowledgments

This book was written over a period of thirty years due to the input and encouragement of so many family members and friends who believed in me and wanted me to tell my story. I am grateful to my father who sowed the initial seed and imagined me gathering my memories in separate pieces of paper and placing them in a box to be later bound in a book as a gift to humanity. It did not happen in this simple way, but the words were gathered in longhand in loose and bound paper and in notebooks and diaries and then typed and retyped and finally shaped in the current form. To my daughters, Lisa, Michelle, Suzy, and Sara, my love and appreciation. They urged me on to complete the book, showing me over the years how proud they were of me and how happy they were to be part of my story. Early on, my good friends Carl and Marilyn Wagner read the first manuscript, and Carl penciled in corrections of usage and spelling; to them I am so very grateful. To my creative writing teachers, Art Lindenberg and Vicky Diaz at Schoolcraft College, my many thanks for being enthralled with my story in 1984 and encouraging me to publish. Thanks to Jane Saylor and members of the memoir weekly class at the Plymouth Library for patiently listening to some chapters of the book and giving me suggestions. Thanks also to the late Neil Shine, editor of the *Detroit Free Press* for taking the time to read a few chapters and seeing potential for a book. To my friend and editor of the first few chapters, Marybeth Dillon, my heartfelt gratitude for her untiring enthusiasm and often referring to me as "an author." I am grateful to Victor R. Volkman, publisher and senior editor of Loving Healing Press Inc. for publishing a chapter of my book in the journal *Recovering the Self*, and for referring me to Tyler Tichelaar, Ph.D. as a wonderful editor. To my editor par excellence, Tyler Tichelaar, I owe the realization of this book. He embraced the task of editing my book with diligence, enthusiasm, and a clear vision. He helped me forge a clear path through the lengthy and meandering narrative to deliver a more enjoyable and readable book. I am forever grateful to him. And thanks again to all those mentioned and not mentioned who wished me well and were eager to see the fulfillment of a lifetime, the completion of this book.

Table of Content

I've heard it said that the soul is neither white nor black, neither feminine nor masculine. It is a rising plume in search of God. And I've been searching. It hasn't been easy, but somehow I manage to get up and move forward in this journey we call life. I identify with the homeless, the orphan, and the abused. But I also identify with those who dance and cheer in triumph over daily battles and contests. For me, there are no borders. Due to my international background, I find myself in the face of every person, the native and the foreign. My immigrant status opens doors for me to reveal my story as I lived it on different soils. For a long time, I have been trying to find the connection between suffering and truth, between what gives pleasure and what binds; in essence, what gives me identity and authenticity in this world, in the human family.

— Marianne Campagna

Reflections from Gavea

A place, more than any other entity or belief, has defined me, and captured my soul. Even after decades of absence and longing, nothing has replaced it or come closer to "home" than Gavea, Sao Conrado (St. Conrad) in the city of Rio de Janeiro, Brazil. It lies in a narrow valley on the outskirts of Rio, where the granite mountains of the "Serra do Mar" meet the sea, or more specifically, the Atlantic Ocean. I came here in 1950, at the age of five, from Shanghai, China with my German mother and Russian stepfather. We sailed across oceans to Brazil, as refugees, fleeing the Communist takeover of China in 1949. My stepfather and mother established an *Escola de Equitacao* (riding school) not far from the beach, adjacent to the Gavea Golf Course at the foot of Pedra da Gavea (Gavea Mountain) as it is known by the locals. My father and brother stayed behind in China, an event that marked my life and gave me much pain, and no doubt, prompted this book.

Because of its proximity during my childhood, the sea has always held a special attraction for me. In the neighborhood where I grew up, they called me the "Princess of the Sea." The locals had seen me dive without hesitation into the curl of the bottle-green wave and emerge unscathed from the waters of this place I called home—Gavea, Sao Conrado.

I had spent the formative years of my life in this sun-bathed valley where the mountains met the sea. On weekends, I loved to go to the beach with my mother or with some of the riding school's guests, and on weekdays, I would go with whomever would take me—a maid, the neighbors next door, or sometimes, alone. I remember, at the age of five, running along the shore with my panties glued to my buttocks and someone laughing and asking whether I was a girl or a boy. Apparently, my mother, on a stroll by the shore, had come unprepared for my dip, but I had no embarrassment.

In the end, she would let me run naked since I was just a small child, enjoying the sea. I loved the wetness and the stinging of salt water on my skin on hot days. I had seen this beach in all kinds of weather: when the waves were huge and washed up the clay road, and when the sea was calm and the water had created pools in the sand. I saw it when it was crowded with bathers in the summer and deserted on rainy or cold winter days.

In the year 2000, I returned to Rio, Brazil for two weeks and stayed with my childhood friend Harumi, who still lived at the base of the Gavea Mountain. I met Harumi, the youngest girl of the Uratas family and a couple of years older than I, in 1952 at the end of the school day by the bus stop when I was in first grade. On one occasion or more, she paid my bus fare since I had spent mine on candy during recess. Now during the current visit, I had so many invitations that I had no time to go swimming. But on the eve of my departure, I told Harumi, "I am going to the beach, rain or shine." The forecast was rain for the coming days. I rose early, put a shift over my bathing suit, and carried only a towel. The sky was overcast, but the walk along the road and over the footpath bridge to the Atlantic was invigorating. I crossed a couple of busy thoroughfares and soon I was on the black-and-white mosaic sidewalk so characteristic of Rio, dotted with food cabanas, which run the beach's whole length.

It was winter in Rio and the beach was rather deserted, except for a few fishermen fishing with bamboo poles. I looked up and down and soon realized there was only one place for me to go swimming—right in front of where our riding school used to be, and where a towering luxury apartment building now stood. I climbed down the retaining wall and crunched my feet into the damp, coarse sand. Leaving my things near the water, I felt a sense of disbelief that I was here.

I walked toward the fisherman and asked him in Portuguese, "What kind of fish are you catching?"

"I myself don't know the name, Senhora," he replied, "but I have taken many a fish from here."

He was a simple man from the surrounding foothills, and I felt a natural kinship with him as with other Brazilians I met along the way.

I returned to my chosen place and ventured into the water, near the edge where pools were formed by rippling waves that had first crashed far into the sea. At this time, I did not dare to walk the full length of the shallow bed into the deep since I was just getting reacquainted with these waters. When I splashed my face, I had a taste of the salt I had not tasted in years. As I thrashed my arms and legs gleefully in the water, I looked up and saw that the gauzy clouds had turned into a transparent mist that soon evaporated, leaving the sky a limpid blue. Relishing the sun's warmth on my face and shoulders, I felt a desire to stay here forever. I looked about and remembered the good times I had experienced here as a child. How often I had gazed far into the horizon and thought, "My father and brother are in China, beyond these waters, and I wish I could reach them."

As I had few belongings (bathers are encouraged to bring just the necessities because the beaches are canvassed by thieves who do not miss many opportunities), I felt free to leave them behind and go up and down the shore, collecting shells and rocks, examining them carefully to see whether they were keep-worthy, just as I had done as a child. When I had a handful, I placed them in a clear plastic bag I had filled earlier with sand. I intended to take it to America with me, just pieces of the sea and land I had longed for over the years.

I sat there on the edge of my towel and looked far and wide. The air was balmy and fresh with an ever-so-slight breeze. In front of me, I watched the undulating waters that shimmered a translucent turquoise to emerald green. I saw a ship in the distance. To my right, I looked up at Pedra da Gavea and followed its rocky contour. I could see the old man lying on a pillow with folded hands, all in granite. I could even see his brow, the hollow of his eyes, his nose, and chin. At the summit, I saw a single bird floating like a kite in the azure sky. A few moments later, I saw another one, and then a third, all with dark wings doing their slow paper dance. They too wanted to linger here a little longer and enjoy the weather.

Two men stopped by, fully clad and in sandals, and armed with a digital camera. They told me they were friends, one from Pakistan and the other from India. They had arrived yesterday and were staying at the International Hotel, built where once I rode on horseback in a wild field. I told them I had lived here, and we shared our stories. One was a pilot for an airline, who had brought his friend here for vacation. They were enthralled with this place and asked whether I'd mind if they took a picture. I obliged, knowing full well I would not get a copy, as I would not see these gentlemen again.

I looked up the road and saw a middle-aged woman waving at me as she tried to descend the broken cement steps. I soon recognized Harumi. I went to meet her.

"I walked all the way to the other end of the beach because I saw a small figure there and I thought it was you, but it turned out to be a fisherman," Harumi said.

"Haru, I can't believe you came to search for me. You knew I would be in front of my old house."

"Oh! I should have known," she said.

I saw she was flushed from all the walking. She was not a young woman, but she had boundless energy and a generous heart. She took care of me like an older sister and understood my longing.

"Do you have a swimsuit on?" I asked, hoping she could refresh herself in the water.

"No. It's just like me to wear a black t-shirt and dark slacks to come to the beach. I came to take a few pictures of you. Go ahead and get into the water."

I let the shallow waves crash on me, hoping she had captured the foam and the spray of the moment. Then I walked farther and farther, negotiating each wave and seeing the myriad shades of green revealing the water's depth. I had decided to swim beyond the breakers. It was wonderful to be past the aquamarine shallows and dipped in liquid emerald. Harumi waved again and summoned me back. After a few rolls with the waves, I let one of them take me to shore.

"Do you want to return now?" I asked, concerned she was getting too hot.

"No, take your time," Haru said. "I was worried you were going too far. The current can be very strong. There's no hurry!"

We sat there together and watched a few colorful hang-gliders approach the beach from the lush mountainside, but we did not see them land since the landing strip was beyond our sight.

A jogger, a Brazilian local man who was lean, tanned, good-looking, wearing a faded Speedo suit, and holding his worn flip-flops, stopped by and asked, "Senhoras, do you speak Japanese?"

Harumi, a little more suspicious of strangers than I, answered, "Why do you want to know?"

The man continued, "Well, the reason I ask is that I am studying Japanese. Every day, I meet a little Japanese lady, Dona Margarida, walking early in the morning. I often greet her and say a few words in Japanese."

"She is my mother; she's been walking for years to meet the sunrise," said Harumi.

"I know. I'm a tour guide and take many foreigners of all nationalities by van to the nearby favelas (the slums in Rio, most of them located on the mountain foothills). You'd be surprised how many tourists are interested in seeing how the poor live in our favelas. I've learned German, French, English, but now I'm interested in the Oriental languages. I'm careful to learn one at a time, or else I may mix them up."

"Marianne is visiting from the U.S. She used to live here. Her family ran a riding school over there," Harumi explained.

"Yes, I did hear there were horses here. All that is gone. Some polo horses remained for a while."

"I remember visiting the polo horses at the stables nearby. We kids liked to see the rabbits they kept in the empty stalls," I said.

"You see, I was a small boy then," the jogger said. "My mother was a domestic for some of the rich families, and we lived in one of the houses in the woods behind the golf course. I am only in my forties so I can't remember that far back," the man said apologetically.

Then I inquired, "Do you remember the Russian golf course manager? He used to play chess with my stepfather. One day I saw him storm out of our house chased by loud Russian curse words. One of them had won the game and the other was not happy."

With some laughter he said, "No I don't remember him. You ladies have a good day." And he continued his jog.

I took another refreshing dip, and then told Harumi I was ready to go. I had been at the beach for three hours, and it had been simply wonderful. I had been replenished.

As we walked up the steps, Harumi said, "They repair these walls every year, but sometimes the sea is so violent, the waters come up to the road and break up all the cement, no matter how strong they build them."

"I do remember watching the towering waves crashing and pounding the surf and covering the whole beach."

Yes, I have remembered this place and many of its aspects. The sea determined our seasons. It has witnessed the good and the bad. People have come and gone, carrying with them their memories. I was one such person. I had been gone for many years, but after 1988, I did return often. Rio was a place that provided me a sense of identity, continuity, and belonging, and I often went there in search of healing from life's woes. My life in America for over forty years had been very much that of an exile, a Teflon existence. I had been dipped into a different culture, and I was unable to find the same enthusiasm and passion I felt for Brazil. Because of the history of my life, I was a nomad, often going home to reclaim my past and my identity. Along the way, I had created many homes and mothers and fathers for myself who loved me and took me into their bosoms when I was young, and who were always ready to shelter this stray sparrow, who had wandered far and wide.

We walked down the street where we used to play as children, and we saw some of the houses of the families we had known who no longer lived there. We called out to a young man who was about to enter the courtyard of a house. He told us the house had been transformed into a rustic seaside restaurant, but it was closed now.

I was so grateful Harumi still lived here in Sao Conrado, in the house her father built in the '50s. He was a stone sculptor who had come with his family from Japan in the 1930s. His intention was to make stone lanterns to line the streets. During one of my visits, he retrieved the original blueprints from his office and showed them to me. However, he ended up carving tombstones with the help of laborers in his workshop under the large overhang of his house. Above the overhang was the terrace where the family gathered and where we youngsters met. Harumi was a couple of years older than I, and we did not see each other often as children because we lived almost a mile apart. But we met often as teenagers, and we knew the same people both from the neighborhood and the Stella Maris School. She was now a retired lawyer who had worked for years in the Treasury Department.

She often joked, "The smart ones from our school did not amount to much, but I, who had terrible grades, made something of myself!"

Her mother would tell me, laughing, that all eyes were on her when I got up to receive awards during end-of-the-year ceremonies at our school. People thought I was her daughter, all decorated in medals, and she was not about to dissuade them.

This prompted Harumi to retort, "Yes, that's because I didn't get too many medals then."

Harumi's mother, Dona Toki, as I knew her, said, "I remember helping you cross...." She helped me cross the big street after the ceremonies to catch the bus back to Sao Conrado. My mother was not very eager to come to these school ceremonies then. It is fair to say I acquired several mothers along the way, as will be apparent in the unfolding of my story.

Dona Toki enjoyed my visits. She had a chance to reminisce and tell me things that were important to her. She was now in her late eighties and her husband had passed away a few years earlier. She remembered that she and her husband had come from the city to the Sao Conrado area to fish. He liked to fish off the rocks and gather mussels. He became acquainted with the owner of a banana plantation at the base of the Gavea Mountain. In time, the owner asked him whether he would like to mind the plantation. In return, he could stay in the simple, rectangular house on the premises. He accepted and the family had lived there ever since, except for the time when Senhor Hurata was placed in a concentration camp during World War

II for being Japanese. He told me this story during my visit to Brazil in 1967. There wasn't much rancor in his voice, only the realization that your nationality defines you, no matter how long you have resided in the country of your choice. Brazil, like America, interned people of Japanese descent during the war.

Dona Toki captivated me in many ways. She would take me to the back of the house and show me the rock that protruded from the steep rise of the almost vertical terrain.

She would say, "I have here Pedra da Gavea and the Botanical Gardens," and then proceed to point to all the plants gracing the terrace that Harumi had collected over the years from the vicinity.

She loved this place as much as I did. For years, every day at sunrise, she would walk the length of the beach as if it were a prayer to greet the day and the Creator. She kept the house very much like it always had been. Her room was very simple with very little clutter. More than once, she took out a carefully folded tissue paper with an ink imprint of a large fish her husband had caught. I saw some of her poems in Japanese lettering and wondered what thoughts went through her mind. Harumi wanted to move back to the city into an apartment building where they would be safe from intruders. But Dona Toki refused to budge; this place was too much a part of her soul.

Harumi and I continued our walk and crossed a square studded with palm trees. Near the curb, I found a paper Brazilian flag, most likely dropped by a school child at an Independence Parade in anticipation of Independence Day (September 7th). We stopped in front of the little white church, Sao Conrado, which gives the region its name. It is perched on a hill overlooking the square and was the gathering place for poor and rich alike. We children liked to sit in the front pews on Sunday and listen to the kind priest who often gave us treats on special holydays. In this little church, bathed in sunlight and open to the breezes of the sea, I had sat listening to sermons, trying to comprehend the world.

As we approached the Sao Conrado Square, I saw the man from the hills with the faded swimsuit and worn flip-flops board the bus stationed there. He turned his head over his shoulders with a momentary furtive look, and I wondered whether he was a marginal person from the favelas who might pose danger to others. The slum dwellers in Brazil had increased exponentially, and much mistrust exists between those who have and have not. Much of the population lives in fear of assault and robbery. The rich live in compounds enclosed in walls with security and dogs. But I considered this man lucky and I envied him. He was a man with roots who had the fortune to live in this beautiful place of his birth.

We walked up the main road, ever closer to the lush base of the Gavea Mountain. We turned right onto a cobblestone street where the houses were hidden behind tall interesting stonewalls and gates adorned with overgrown tropical plants and vines. At the bend of the road, on an island in the cul-de-sac, we saw some uniformed public school children at recess, playing marbles. They appeared to be fourth grade boys dressed in white shirts and black shorts, each rolling marbles onto shallow holes in a dirt patch. Because I played marbles as a child, I knew the object of the game was to have your marble fall into all three holes, after which you could take out your opponents and continue the game if you made a hit, and keep as many marbles as possible. The boys invited us to play with them, and I almost did for old time's sake. After learning all their names, we proceeded to Harumi's house.

Across from her house, we saw a large fallen tree over a broken stonewall, its network of roots exposed. Harumi said, "That tree has lost its principal root; therefore, it could not withstand the storm. I learned this when I took a Bonsai class."

"How funny you should speak of the principal root," I said. "It's a little like people. We too have our root system and some have been shattered and need to be restored. You know I'm going to see my father soon."

"It's wonderful that you are going to see your father in China. Is your brother going with you?" my friend asked.

"My brother and I have been talking about it for some time," I answered. "He intends to go, and he thinks it would be a good idea for me to go as well, since father is getting old. When I get back to Detroit, we will make the final arrangements. We might leave mid-October or the beginning of November. I'll let you know as soon as I find out."

It rained that afternoon and the next day, the day of my departure. I said goodbye to friends who had been part of my childhood, and whom I always carried in my heart.

Harumi said to me later during a phone call, "After you left, it rained for a straight week. It was as if Brazil were crying because you were gone."

Part I

Family Beginnings

Chapter 1

My Parents' Meeting and Background

The principal root is as important for a person's life as it is for a plant's. It is the life force that passes from parents to child.

On a visit to Germany with my mother in 1965, I learned how my mother and father met. The story came from an old woman whose name escapes me now, but I shall call her Elena. My mother, Aunt Eva, and I went on an excursion through the Bavarian Hills and stopped at the village where this woman lived. We knocked at the door of her first floor apartment, situated in an old stone building with a throughway that led to an interior courtyard where chickens roamed. We peered through the windows and saw a teapot on the table and some family pictures on a bureau. Neighbors said she lived there but had gone for a walk in the nearby woods.

We drove to the edge of town, and in a meadow, some distance from the forest, we saw a good-sized matronly old woman wearing a printed dress, a straw hat, and walking with a swaggering gait and using a cane; a bouquet of wildflowers was in her hand. We walked down the path, waving at her. She soon recognized Eva and my mother and approached us with great enthusiasm. After greeting my mother and Eva, her effusiveness spilled over to me; she embraced me warmly, saying, "Ein kleiner stuck von China" ("A small piece from China"). I was touched with delight. Now in my twenties and still not knowing of my father's whereabouts, I was glad to meet someone who knew my father and was instrumental in my parents' meeting.

My parents met at the beginning of World War II in 1940, in the city of Munich, Germany. My father, Wang Fu Shih, was a doctoral electrical engineer student at Munich's Institute of Technology, and he had been in Germany for about eight years. He could speak German with a perfect Bavarian accent. I was told he was given a free mug of beer in a Bavarian Inn because he could speak the dialect so well. One evening, he and his friends were having dinner at a Chinese restaurant and talking animatedly. At the next table were my mother, Aunt Eva, and Elena. The young men caught Elena's attention and she began to talk with them in Chinese. She was of Russian descent but had lived in China for over twenty years, where her family ran a movie theater in the Chinese city of Tiensin. Before long, the two groups were intertwined in conversation and sharing stories. Elena had a chance to practice her Chinese and my father a chance to work his charm. Before the night was over, my father had invited the three of them to an authentic Chinese dinner at his apartment, which they accepted without hesitation.

In the ensuing weeks, my father became enamored with my mother, a beautiful blue-eyed, blond woman, with the look of an actress, and a genuine soul, who loved Nature and adventure. They went on many mountain hikes and rides on my father's motorcycle. I have some pictures of those outings. In the few references to my dad that my mother made during my years growing up, she would say that he could jump one meter on one leg. Soon, my mother, who worked as a secretary in the city, began typing my father's doctoral dissertation. I have a picture of my handsome young dad given to my mother with an inscription in his handwriting, "In memory of our work together and hoping for a Summa Cum Laude." Another picture of my dad in a tuxedo and bow tie also has writing on the back, which translated from the German, said, "Conceited and immature, this fellow knows only Agi." (Agi in German is the endearing nickname for Agnes.) The romance began, and soon my father learned a little more about my mother's background.

My mother, Agnes Viktoria Anna Schuetzinger, was born in Tirschenreuth, Bavaria on April 20, 1916. According to my Aunt Fe—the family historian who always tried to keep us in touch and informed—my mother's parents, Joseph Schuetzinger and Karoline Schuetzinger, nee Penzkofer, were married in the full style of that time in 1907. After their wedding, her parents moved to Moosburg near Munich where they operated a printing, bookbinding, and stationery shop, and her father published a newspaper, the Moosburger Tageszeitung. They kept this establishment from 1907-1912. My mother's oldest sister Caroline, her twin brothers Joseph and Ernst, and her sister Eva were born in Moosburg.

In 1912, her father bought the Tirschenreuther Volksbote, another newspaper, and the whole family moved to Tirschenreuth, a lovely little city north of Regensburg and east of Nuremberg, close to the Czechoslovakian border. There her sister Maria, my mother, and her sister Hildegard were born. The family stayed at this place from 1912-1919. In the meantime, Grandpapa Schuetzinger, who ran the Donau Post, a newspaper he founded, and a printing shop at Wurth a.d. Donau (on the Danube), died in 1918. Pushed by his mother, Great-Grandmama Schuetzinger, my grandfather Joseph Schuetzinger took over the business of Great-Grandpapa in Wurth near Regensburg.

The move brought my grandmother closer to her family, as Grandpapa Penzkofer, who had run an inn and brewery in Falkenstein, on the Bavarian hills, had bought a large house with an expansive garden and orchard on one of the hills in Wurth. This was a choice location, romantically situated near the old eleventh century castle in Wurth, in which the Emperor Barbarossa had once stayed overnight. The famous German artist Albert Dürer painted the same castle.

However, my grandfather's move did not bring much prosperity to the family since the business fell into bad times after World War I, and most of the money was consumed by the big inflation of 1923. By then, the family had grown to nine children with the birth of my mother's sister Felizitas (Fe) and her youngest brother Erich. In 1924, her father fell ill with throat cancer, most likely caused from exposure to the printing inks used at that time, which were stored in large drums and present everywhere in the shop.

On January 24, 1925, Papa, as he was called by the children, died. My mother was eight years old, but she always had some fond memories of her dad. She remembers going with him by train to the big city, Regensburg. In the city, held by his secure hand, she was taken to the best establishment and treated to the best chocolate in town. It certainly was a special occasion to have been singled out from a brood of nine brothers and sisters and treated to the nectar of the gods. No wonder my mother loved good chocolate and always celebrated special occasions by giving us bars of European chocolate!

Here is an unfolding of my mother's family in more detail.

The first child, Caroline, died as an infant after tumbling out of a carriage precariously parked on a hill. The second child was also given the name Caroline after her mother, Karoline Penzkofer, and moved to Wurth to be raised by her paternal grandparents, after the birth of the twins Joseph (Seppy) and Ernst. At age five, Caroline was returned to the family home in Wurth, which was above the publishing house. She never quite felt at home there and did not get along with her mother or her siblings. She tells of how the boys broke her exquisite china doll given to her by her beloved Schuetzinger grandparents, who pampered her with affection and fine clothing.

Nevertheless, she adored her Papa, so she was devastated when he passed away in her early teens. Bright and studious, she was sent to study with the English nuns. Later, she transferred to the boarding school of the Dominican Sisters in Niederviehbach, where all the other sisters joined her, including her youngest sister Felizitas (Fe), who was only four at the time.

Aunt Fe told me that Caroline, who by then had entered the convent, did not want her in the school, often avoiding her. Aunt Fe felt hurt and rejected—a feeling that lingered all her life. Caroline, who died at the age of ninety-three, spent her last years in the Wurth castle in the city of Wurth, where she had lived with her grandparents and parents. Today, part of the castle has been transformed into a home for the elderly. My husband Tony and I visited her in 1994 and again in 1997 when she was placed in the Wurth Castle. To test her mind, I asked her, "Where are you, Linchen?" (A long time ago, she had asked me not to address her as aunt but preferred I use her favorite nickname.)

She answered me from across the table at the nursing home's dining room, "I am at my grandparents' house, and I receive many visitors from all over the world." I did not have the heart to tell her otherwise. Even though she had been a philosophy professor at Mercy College in Detroit, and been retired in Germany for over twenty years, she was touched with dementia that made some twists and turns in her mind. She recognized us and often held lively discussions about the course of history and men's hunger for power, from the Roman exploits to the Nazi regime. She would say, "But all will end in the heart of God. And before Truth, all are silent." I asked her whether she would like us to bring her additional clothes from her apartment in Pfaffenberg. She said, "No. When one is on a journey, one does not take very much. It becomes a burden." One day we offered her some maltzbeer, which she did not refuse, exclaiming, "How can a granddaughter of a Bavarian brewer not take a sip of beer? But not too much so I won't get tipsy! Ha!..Ha!" She was happy in the castle and felt the staff took good care of her, and she could order whatever she wanted, just like in a hotel.

It is well to say here that while their father Joseph Schuetzinger was alive, the family held a respectable position in the town of Wurth. Grandfather Schuetzinger even had a special table at the fine restaurant Butz where the family dined often on Sundays, and which still exists today. After my grandfather's death, grandmother was unable to manage the publishing business, which was bought out. A small fund was established for maintenance of the family and the children's education. Those were depression years, not only for the family, but also for the whole of Germany. The children were all sent to boarding school in different Bavarian cities and uprooted from their beloved Wurth on the Danube.

The twin boys, Joseph and Ernst, and the youngest child, Erich, were sent to schools run by Catholic Monks. Of my uncles, I heard little, except that they all died on the front in World War II—one in Monte Casino, Italy, another in France, and the youngest in Russia at the age of twenty-one in 1944. Aunt Caroline published a collection of Erich's letters from Russia and called it The Grüss Gott Camarade because he so signed his letters, which means, "God's Greeting, Comrade." Grüss Gott was and still is a daily greeting among Bavarians. Before going to war, Seppy and Ernst had fathered my cousins, Utte, Marile, and Rudi.

Eva, the second oldest of my mother's family, never married. She was a virtuoso on the piano and became a baby products representative before retiring early. My mother and she had a special bond, perhaps because of their love of music and adventure. As for my mother's other sisters, Maria and Hilde, I know little of their childhood. Maria married an architect, but she did not have any children. She worked in antiques and was a motherly, enterprising lady. When I met her in Nuremberg in 1965, she was very welcoming, self-assured, and attentive to our needs, and often bestowed small gifts upon us. I remember her saying, "Always cream your skin so it will be smooth and silky in your old age." To the end of her days, she continued to visit spas every year.

Hilde was a rebel, whom I heard called the black sheep of the family, with some suspect political affiliations. In 1965, when I first went to Germany with my mother, we stayed at Eva's apartment. Hilde would often visit and accompany us on our excursions through the Bavarian countryside. However, Eva and Hilde did not get along; once, while in the process of crossing a bridge, Eva insisted that Hilde get out of her Volkswagen—she was just too heavy a load, and the two had a heated argument. My mother and I chuckled at the hilarious scene and chose to get out of the car with Hilde. We watched Eva go over the bridge alone. Even though it was a "Folkswagon," it could not carry so many hefty folks on winding roads and precarious bridges.

Hilde had three children: Rainer, Helmut, and Hildegard. They were left under my grandmother's care in Wurth during the war and the early post-war years, as were Fe's children, Roland, Ilse, and Erich, so the mothers could pursue whatever work was available in Munich. Hilde's husband was killed in the war, leaving the young family to fend for itself. When Fe was expecting her youngest child, Erich, in 1945, she was destitute, roaming the streets for any morsel of bread. Aunt Caroline had heard of Fe's imminent delivery and begged officials at various hospitals to accept her, but none would take her. Caroline even confronted a high commander in the Nazi party, but her defiance only earned her a demotion, and her religious order asked her to leave because it feared for her life. Caroline did help Fe deliver a healthy baby in her cramped apartment in Munich.

The war's devastation and the people's suffering in Bavaria and Germany as a whole are unfathomable to me. I know Aunt Caroline did leave the order of the Dominican nuns and sought shelter with a baroness friend; the two sheltered several Jewish families. Caroline immigrated to the United States in 1950 and worked her way up to becoming a psychology and philosophy professor. Aunt Fe married an American electrical engineer, a specialist in radar, whom she met in Munich. The two lived in Europe during the 1950s with Fe's three children. Eventually, her children immigrated to Canada to join their father, a painter, who had moved there earlier. Aunt Fe and Poncho moved permanently to the States in 1965 and settled in Mobile, Alabama. It was then that I met her for the first time while she was passing through Detroit. I also met all my German cousins over the years.

As for my mother, I know she had fond memories of her childhood in Wurth on the Danube, a typical Bavarian village. It had a main street with various essential shops, including her father's Donau Post publishing company. The business and the house above still stand today. One of the largest buildings on the street, it often was referred to by townspeople as the "Schuetzinger House."

Mother remembers the special holidays when a piglet was roasted and brought to the table with an apple in its mouth. Then the family had servants and everything was scrubbed spic-and-span, including the children. Linens were ironed in a big press and sauerkraut was made in large vats that the children were allowed to stomp in with great glee—of course, after having their feet sanitized to the maximum.

My mother's adventurous spirit and fierce independence were put to the test when she was sent to the public kindergarten on the edge of town. She did not like the crowded room, or the confinement. So, during recess, she walked all the way home on a dangerous road to the surprise of her mother, who took her in her arms and did not send her back. She did, however, spend her early elementary school years in this public school in Wurth by the Danube.

My mother especially liked the surrounding countryside. On holidays, she swam in the Danube with its swift currents, and one time, she almost drowned but for the quick hand of a classmate. She also liked the Bavarian Forest. Once, she told me, her mother and father had a huge argument at night, probably about in-laws.

Grandmother gathered all her children at midnight and took them for a walk in a pitch-black forest. The last one always ran to the front of the pack to be close to mother because they were petrified.

Whenever possible, my mother liked to play in her maternal grandmother's house, with its huge orchards and gardens very near the medieval castle, which in her time was abandoned. During the lean war times, grandmother could always provide the family with a batch of fresh vegetables or a bushel of fruits. Sometimes, the children played hide-and-seek in the castle grounds, skirting with danger. As a matter of habit, my mother liked to gather fruits and flowers during her many walks, whether given or stolen, a habit she might have acquired in childhood. She said to me, "We make a wonderful pair because with you I can steal horses."

The regiment was severe at Niederviehbach, the girls' boarding school run by the Dominican Sisters where most of my mother's school years were spent. Rain or shine, the children took walks around town after lunch. They rose early and washed their faces with frigid water given to them in basins. My mother was a happy child there, not so much rebellious as mischievous. In order to break the monotony, mother joined the troublemakers in some serious pranks. Once they substituted the holy water, which the nuns used to bless themselves on the way into chapel, with writing ink. The girls could hardly contain their laughter as they saw the nuns file by with blotches on their faces. I wonder what punishment they received for this prank.

Mother excelled in gymnastics and the German language. She could tumble and do pirouettes with ease. Needless to say, mother was a tomboy with great love for the outdoors. She also loved to sing. Mother learned to play the guitar and could entertain friends with folk songs. She made many friends during this time, some of whom she kept for a lifetime.

When my mother graduated from high school, she joined a Christian youth group that included many idealistic thinkers and promising musicians. Hilde Wust, my mother's best friend, had a lovely voice, and for a time, she sang ballads on the radio and even cut a few records. Hilde's brother, George Wust, played for Munich's Philharmonic Orchestra and remained my mother's faithful pen pal for life. Once my mother told me he had asked her to marry him, but it was not to be. She had a few other suitors as well, and went on some fun outings, including, on occasion, skiing trips to the Alps, which were nearby. I have a few pictures of my mother and her friends singing, playing the guitar, flute, or violin along the Bavarian countryside.

On her twenty-first birthday, my mother and Hilde went on a European tour, traveling as far north as Norway and Denmark, and as far south as the Vatican. The two slung over their shoulders a few pots and pans, a blanket, and a change of clothes, as well as a guitar. They headed for the high road, staying in youth hostels and convents. They often hitchhiked. Once, while in Italy, a man who picked them up got fresh with them. They promptly took care of him by bopping him on the side of the head with their guitar. Whether the guitar survived, I do not know, but I know they remembered their trip with fondness. I met the Wust family in Munich, and I have a set of antique dishes they sent my mother.

It appears that my mother led an almost idyllic life, but it was not to last. While in Munich in her late teens and early twenties, she had to make a living and support herself. At first, she lived with Tante Anni, a single teacher, but they had a falling out, so my mother had to find her own apartment. She had completed secretarial school and needed to find a permanent job. She told me there were times when she walked the streets for days without eating anything in search of a job. She finally landed a job with the German government.

In 1939, Hitler invaded Poland and the Second World War began. All women of age were employed at the service of the Third Reich. My mother worked in Munich for a while until she was transferred to Le Haag, Holland. There, I heard, if she knew of any Jewish families who were going to be targeted, she quietly sent out warning in whatever way she could. Once, when I was an adult, I asked her whether Jews in Germany had been disliked and experienced prejudice before the war. She answered, "Yes." She said no more because it weighed heavily on her heart.

It was during this time that she met my father, Wang Fu Shih. My father wrote my mother numerous letters, begging her to return to Munich from Le Haag, and promising abiding love. His persistence paid off, for my mother returned. Little did they know the two of them would soon be making the journey of a lifetime.

Chapter 2

━━━━━━━ ❀ ━━━━━━━

The Odyssey

It was July, 1941. World War II was raging in Europe, and Germany was fully engaged in its horrors. My father, Wang Fu Shih, age twenty-eight, had just completed his doctorate degree in electrical engineering from Munich's Technical Institute, graduating Summa Cum Laude, a fact that did not go unnoticed by my mother who had helped type his dissertation. (Here is perhaps where his conceit came in—a quality inherited by his daughter.) My mother, Agnes Schuetzinger, age twenty-five, had returned from Le Haag, Holland, where she had been working as a secretary for the German Government and taken up household with my father in Munich, Bavaria's main city. My father, who had been sponsored by the Chinese Government for studies in Germany, after excelling in the electrical engineering field at Tungchi University in Shanghai, was ready to pursue his career. He had some money from the sale of a radio part he had patterned and sold to the Siemens Company.

Now, at this time, my father was very much in love with my mother and proposed marriage, but it was not possible since Germany was under Hitler's hegemony laws that prevented the mixing of the races. Besides, my father, who had spent eight and a half years in Germany, was there on a student visa. The two decided to flee Germany and find their destiny elsewhere. My father packed his books, research papers, and clothes; my mother packed her dresses, hats, medications, toiletry, photos, and paraphernalia. They did not say goodbye to anyone except my mother's mother, Karoline Schuetzinger. My mother had taken my father to see her earlier, and they made her aware of their plans. They must have met at the Schuetzinger House in Wurth a.d. Donau (at the Danube) where my grandmother rented a room in the former family's house till her death in 1957. My father told me later that my grandmother had been a very good person and he had grown fond of her.

It is hard for us to reach back in time and relive life as it was experienced by our parents or grandparents. One is a child of one's own time, and that boundary separates us from the generations before us and the generations that come after us. But we must bend backwards and find the sap that flows in our veins, that will give us understanding and wisdom, and from which we can nourish our own offspring and any who would hear our story. I have to recreate my parents' journey from anecdotes, documents, photos, letters, and especially from a tattered passport that was in my mother's possession all her life.

My parents had their trunks packed and they headed toward Munich's Train Depot, which was packed with military personnel, civilians, and foreigners, all trying to leave the War Zone. They boarded the Orient Express, acquired a coach cabin, and headed toward Istanbul, Turkey, a neutral country during World War II. It was a long journey—they had to traverse the mountainous and flat regions along the river Danube, through Austria, Yugoslavia, and Bulgaria, and finally arrive at the Bosphorus Strait between the Black and Aegean Seas, a much-celebrated area known as the gateway to the Orient.

They stopped in Istanbul, Turkey, formerly known as Constantinople, once the Emperor Constantine's Christian Stronghold, and the former seat of the Ottoman Empire. After such a long journey, they needed rest and took up lodging in one of the city's hotels after paying a luggage handler for his help. Surely they saw the famous church Hagia Sophia, now a mosque flanked by palaces where the Ottoman rulers had resided and organized their campaigns to conquer the world. They also took a boat ride along the Bosphorus Strait, so often painted by famous artists because of its shoreline and silhouette of the city with its memorable buildings. My mother was filled with hope and expectations and was taking in all the new sights and sounds. She often told me that she loved Turkey, its geography, people, and customs, so different from the world she was accustomed to in Germany. In the streets, she saw crowds gathered, about to watch the Whirling Dervish dancers who twirled about almost in a trance in praise of God. They ate in typical restaurants where the food was spicy and tasty. My father said he especially liked the sweet olives, something he commented that only the rich could afford.

They proceeded east on to the capital city of Ankara, Turkey, where they went to The Legation of the Republic of China, a type of Chinese Embassy. Here, my father met a colleague, the minister, who was the brother of a fellow student who had studied engineering with my father at Tongshi University in Shanghai in the early 1930s. On August 21, 1941, my parents got married, witnessed by the distinguished minister. My mother at this time became a Chinese citizen. I have to wonder how my mother, brought up in traditional Bavarian towns, decided to uproot herself completely from Germany. In her papers, she explains that she was motivated to become a Chinese citizen and to give up her German citizenship due to her great interest in China and a desire to put some distance between herself and the current situation in Germany with its Third Reich ideology. In an official document of the time, my mother declares her desire to become a citizen of the Republic of China by the act of marriage to Wang Fu Shih, a Chinese citizen, and to obey thereafter all the laws of the Republic of China and to forego all connections attached to her former nationality. From then on, my mother would be known as Agnes Wang.

There was no white veil or religious ceremony, but my parents were well-groomed—my dad in a suit and tie, and my mother with a white blouse and broach; they looked dapper and absolutely charming, and I'm sure they celebrated with a dinner in town, accompanied by the Chinese Consul.

On August 27, 1941, also in Ankara, Turkey, my father was issued an Official Chinese Passport, granting him diplomatic status together with my mother. My parents look so happy on the passport picture. My father is described as Dr. of Engineering, Chief of the Department of Electrical Engineering of the Central College of Officers of the Police, Chungking with his wife Mme Agnes Wang. It states that the Ministry of Foreign Affairs of the Republic of China requests all civil and military authorities of Foreign States to let pass freely the porters of this passport and afford assistance in case of necessity. The Turkish authorities give them a permit for travel for 100 days in transit through Turkey. Their destination was China via Iraq and India. But they made a grand detour because my dad had other plans.

On August 28, 1941, at the British Embassy in Angora, they were given a Special Visa to journey to Palestine, Syria, and India en route to China. So they traveled southeast to Damascus, Syria where they stayed for a couple of days. They went through some French checkpoints in Meidan-Ekbes (August 30, 1941) and left Nakoura on September 1, 1941. During the war, the border patrols and the bureaucracy of visas and permits to enter and pass through a determined region were intense. My parents chose to travel through countries that were friendly to the Allies.

They arrived in Haifa, Palestine, a British Protectorate, on September 1, 1941. Even though there were already many Jewish settlements in Palestine, the State of Israel was not founded until 1948. Here, they met some German friends, university colleagues, as well as some Chinese colleagues at the Chinese Consulate. My father decided to stay for a while in this charming sea resort on the Mediterranean's eastern shores, so my parents registered in a pleasant and comfortable, two-story hotel with striped awnings, veranda, and airy rooms. He took a few pictures of my mother sleeping; she certainly needed her rest because she was expecting a child. The days went by quickly. They had a social life and intellectual discussions with their friends. My mother felt somewhat at home in this milieu and enjoyed her new status of wife to a distinguished Chinese engineer. I have pictures of them seated on a park bench with friends and also aboard the deck of a ship, where my mother is sporting a fashionable broad-brimmed hat and appears very happy.

In consultation with a friend in the Chinese Consulate, my dad had plans to seek a position in London, England. My mother later told me that she believed he had a diplomatic mission that was not revealed to her, so the journey was partly funded by the Chinese Government. A route through Europe or North Africa would be too dangerous due to Rommel's campaign there as well as the various German incursions and World War II fronts in that area. The Palestine Government, on October 18, 1941, gave my parents a return visa good until April 18, 1942. They were also permitted to proceed to Cairo, Egypt and given thirty transit days. The Egyptian Consulate in Haifa also issued a visa permitting my parents to stay one month in Egypt and to travel through the Sinai Desert.

In the port of Haifa, Palestine, my parents boarded a ship on October 18, 1941 with a destination to Cairo, Egypt. They passed through Kantara, Suez Canal on October 19, 1941, and via the Sinai Desert, arrived in Cairo, Egypt, a bustling metropolis where the population spilt onto the roads and pavements dressed in kaftans. Donkey and bicycle carts got out of the way of motor vehicles and buses. There were many bazaars where merchants hocked their wares of metal and cloth, ceramics, rugs, and tunics. The Western influence could also be seen, with many businessmen wearing suits and ties. My parents stayed in a reputable hotel, and during the next few days, they went to the various embassies to obtain transit passes and visas. I know my parents visited the Sphinx and the pyramids and were in awe of these ancient structures in the desert. And of course, they rode the camels. But it is unclear whether they visited the pyramids during this visit to Cairo, or on their return when they had more time.

On October 22, 1941, my parents were seen at the Chinese Consulate in Cairo, and given permission to travel to the British Empire, Sudan, Portugal, and Palestine. At the British Consulate in Cairo, on October 23, 1941, my parents were given permission for entry into the United Kingdom by air—valid for thirty days. On the same day, in the Portuguese Consulate in Cairo, my parents were given a special official visa per request of the Embassy of Great Britain in Cairo to land in Portugal in transit to England by air. On October 24, 1941, my parents left Cairo aboard MISR Airlines and landed in Khartoum, the Anglo-Egyptian Sudan, where they rested for a couple of days.

Now my parents were in Central Africa, where the faces were darker and the customs and language were stranger, although in the airports and custom offices, either English or French were spoken. The climate was warmer and my father observed servants fanning clients with large grass woven fans that were also useful in clearing the flies. From the Central African Republic, my parents landed in Apapa, Nigeria, on the West Coast of Africa, on October 26, 1941. Here again, they rested for a couple of days. They proceeded up the African Coast by air and arrived in Bathurst, Gambia on October 28, 1941. The next day, they proceeded to Portugal via S-ASCB airline and arrived in Lisbon, the capital, where they stayed overnight. On October 30, 1941, via the same airline, they left Portugal and arrived in Shannon Airport, Ireland on October 31, 1941. They rested one more night and arrived at their final destination, England, through the airport of Bristol on November 1, 1941. Here they were permitted to land on condition that they register at once with the police and not remain in the United Kingdom longer than two months.

It is well to note here that England had already gone through the German Blitz from September 1940 to May 1941 when my parents arrived. Many cities had been heavily bombed, including Bristol, Liverpool, and London, the cities my parents visited. I'm sure they must have seen vestiges of these attacks, and they must have felt very torn and devastated. My mother, in one of her personal papers, explained that she had felt the effects of the war very deeply, having lost her fiancé to the war before she met my father. This detail I only know through an outline of her life that

I recently came across. Until then I did not know my mother had been engaged; nor did I know the name of her fiancé. Now in London, she felt the full impact of her nationality. My father learned that China had declared war on Germany, Japan, and Italy. His country was on the Allies' side, yet he had ties with Germany since he had been a doctorate student for many years and had grown to love the country.

My parents arrived in London and settled in a hotel. They were exhausted, but they dutifully registered with the police. The atmosphere was somewhat tense. My parents' luggage was carefully searched, and in my father's suitcase was found Karl Marx's Das Kapital. That would not have looked good for him, except that my father was an academic who had purchased the book in Germany out of intellectual curiosity, wanting to be knowledgeable about the philosophical currents of the times.

My father presented himself to the British Broadcasting Company for a job with his proper credentials and a recommendation from the Chinese Government. The BBC almost gave him a broadcasting position, but he refused it because he did not want to speak out against Germany; he had great fondness for the country and its people and had many good friends there. He applied to other companies and was hopeful to get a research position in Canada. In the meantime, my parents waited in London for a reply to my father's job applications.

My mother had much time on her hands. As it was her custom to take daily walks, so she visited some of London's famous sights, such as Westminster Abbey, Big Ben, and the Tower of London on the Thames. One day when she was walking, she noticed a secret service agent was following her. She felt suspect. When she entered the hotel room, she found my father looking for wires and implanted devices. She had a wave of paranoia and feared that my father also believed she was a German spy. But this moment passed and mutual trust was restored. Later, a routine was established and my mother felt more relaxed and able to enjoy her time in London. Since she was pregnant, she decided to do some knitting. She also read some English books and polished up her fluency in the language. I believe my parents always tried to speak to each other in English, especially in public. When they spent their first Christmas together, I'm sure it brought much longing to my mother's heart as she reminisced about her home in Bavaria. I do not know whether my mother wrote any letters to her family and friends in Germany from England, but she must have written many in her mind.

No answers were received from my parents' queries for work in Canada. I do not know whether Karl Marx's book in my father's luggage, or having a German wife, had anything to do with my father's failure to obtain a position in the English Commonwealth, but my parents' visas were running out, so they had to make preparations for their departure. The world was in turmoil, and this young couple, from opposite ends of the conflict, were trying to set a foothold somewhere. But no one would have them. The only answer now for my father was to return to his motherland and take with him his foreign wife. For my mother, the decision had already been made. She had relinquished her nationality, her place of birth and upbringing, and was ready to follow my dad wherever he would take her. They made plans to return to China. The English gave them exit visas on January 27, 1942, stating that husband and wife could depart for one journey only, and the route was optional. To leave by air from England was dangerous; the Germans could bomb them and the English could not give them any assurances. They chose to leave by ship from the city of Liverpool on the west coast of England, even though the German U-boat submarines had already torpedoed several merchant ships sailing in the Atlantic. My parents took a chance and boarded for Lagos, Nigeria on January 29, 1942.

The journey from then on would be by air. My mother had already complained of nausea during earlier flights, and it was very tiring for her to fly in the later months of her pregnancy. They crossed the continent of Africa and arrived in Cairo, Egypt around March 10, 1942. At that time, they did most of their Egyptian sightseeing since they did not leave Cairo until March 25, 1942. They boarded Imperial Airways and flew over Iraq, Iran, and arrived in Karachi, now in Pakistan. From there, they boarded another plane and flew to Bombay, India, and then another plane to Calcutta, India. Now they were in the Far East, and one last flight took them to Chungking, China, their final destination after traveling for eight months. They arrived in mid-April 1942. For my dad, it was a return after eight and a half years of absence. For my mother, it was a whole new world.

Chapter 3

═══════ ✿ ═══════

Chinese Episodes in My Mother's Voice

Before my mother died in 1986, she left this essay about her life in China:

It was in the spring of 1942 that we flew to China from Calcutta. Chungking was our destination. Finally, we had landed on a makeshift airport. Chinese officials were swarming all over the place. They looked strange in their military outfits, with bandaged legs, padded coats, straw shoes. If ever before I had any hope that our entrance would be painless and swift, this was the moment. I knew that not the smallest object in my luggage would remain untouched. With exemplary eagerness, the officials did their duty, and I wondered how on earth I ever would be able to pack the things back into the trunks. After endless hours, we were through. By then, my watch showed 2:00 a.m., a ghastly hour to get accommodations for the night in a town like Chungking, war torn as it was. Fu Shih, my husband, after having been absent for many years from China, had to readjust himself. Even for him, who had stayed for so many years in Germany and England while studying engineering, the moment demanded a quick orientation. With one look, he evaluated the situation—a most precarious one. He deposited the big luggage, called for two sedan chairs, and, after finding out that the Chaling Bingwa (Chaling House) was perhaps the best possibility to find accommodation for the night, he gave the coolies his instructions.

At this point, I have to say something about sedan chairs in general and Chungking in particular:

A sedan chair is a basket-like seat with a "roof" fastened to two long rods. To be transported in a sedan chair requires two coolies. They lift the sedan chair shoulder-high and carry it, one in front and one in the rear. When they carry, the coolies make a certain singsong, which, as far as I could find out, is to help their breathing. And for Chungking, with its inclined curved roads and alleys, the sedan chair was the best mode of transportation at the time.

Chungking is a town built in terraces on the Chaling and Yangtse Rivers. It must be thousands of years old. Slippery, curved stone stairways lead up to the city. The city is rat-infested to such a degree that cats are looked upon as a treasure. They hardly ever stay alive. In Chunking, the rats eat the cats.

So, there we were with the coolies and the sedan chairs we were about to occupy. Fu Shih accommodated himself, and I followed his example by boarding a chair. It was a stormy dark night. Up we went; slowly, ever so slowly the coolies in their cautious way tried to get a foothold around the slippery curves. From afar, dogs howled. Some flicker of very dim lights in the distance could be seen. We went on, it seemed to me, forever. As we ascended practically all the time, my bodily posture in the sedan chair was several feet high up in the air and my body in a lying position with my head rather low. Finally, I thought I could not stand it any longer, as I was sitting practically on nothing, not having any support from underneath, only hanging between two wooden fixtures. I called Fu Shih who, however, asked me to be patient. So on we went and went. I was pregnant, so for me, this modus of sitting on nothing, only being suspended so to say for hours, became unbearable. I became firm, called my husband who was transported in front of me in his sedan chair, and unmistakably demanded a stop. It surely was granted. I asked my husband, "How are you able to endure such hardships?"

"Hardships?" he asked puzzled. "What are you talking about?"

"I cannot sit any longer in this makeshift," I answered.

"Now how is that?" he asked and strode to examine my sedan chair. To his amazement, he found that the seat was missing from it. The coolies had forgotten to put it in. He told them and they roared in boundless laughter. After the seat was put in, the ascension was tolerable enough.

After what seemed an eternity, we were catapulted on the sidewalk of a building-complex, the contours of which we could not make out, as there were no lights. Fu Shih paid the coolies who lit a match and then took off. There we stood in the darkest possible night, on top of a hill in a strange country. Since it was wartime, the Japanese fighting the Chinese, everything was blacked out for the Chinese were afraid of air raids. It was so pitch black I shuddered. I was overtired, desolate, pregnant, and uncertain of the future. Fu Shih started to awaken someone in the house by banging on the door. For long, nothing stirred. As he did not let up, finally a window was opened on the first floor and out peeped a head asking in Chinese, "Ni jau soma tongshi?" ("What do you want?") Now started a conversation between Fu Shih and the person at the window. I did not understand Chinese and had to judge from the intonation what our chances of finding a night's lodging would be. Somehow, I saw myself as Mary, with Joseph, her husband, pleading with the innkeeper for accommodation. Fu Shih used all his power of persuasion, and after mentioning a couple of influential names with which he supposedly linked his own, the person at the window disappeared and a hustling descending shuffle could be heard from inside. The door opened. We entered. That very moment, some shadows were rushing from the lobby. Probably some servants of the house had found their sleep that night on the couches of the entrance hall, which were then offered to us as preliminary accommodations. I was too tired to give it a second thought, and after we were motioned by the thin, gentle-eyed man to take up our night's rest, we began to settle down. Soon the oblivion of a deep sleep took hold of us.

In the morning, I discovered I had been mercilessly bitten by innumerous fleas. I felt terribly itchy all over my body and found I was covered with enormous red spots. Since we had slept in the lobby, we had to get up early. Meanwhile, a room was prepared for us on the upper floor. It is worthwhile to describe our then temporary domicile: There were no walls between the rooms; only bamboo mats separated the different quarters. I went upstairs to take a look at our "hotel room." There was no bed in the ordinary sense of it, only a square frame over which ropes were spanned, and no mattresses or the like. The bedding had to be furnished by ourselves, consisting of one or several so-called pugais (cotton padded covers). We were in a haste to acquire them. Well, it was a place where we could stay until further arrangements could be made with the well-to-do in-laws in Chengtu (capital of the province of Szechuan). I was due to deliver my baby in the first half of May.

Chaling Bingwa was considered the "Hilton Hotel" in the badly bombed-out Chungking of 1942. Many foreigners lived there—reporters, government officials, and the like. It was a most interesting thriving atmosphere, which prevailed in Chaling Bingwa (Chaling House). Every morning, I was awakened by the singsong of coolies who pulled sampans and junks up the river by ropes attached to their bodies—an extremely hard work. The meals, which we took in the big dining room, were excellent, well prepared and very graciously served. I made efforts to acquire day-by-day some knowledge of the Chinese language that would be useful to me on a daily basis. Fu Shih busied himself to get in touch with government officials to get a job.

One Sunday morning, I awoke to find Chaling Bingwa steeped in quiet. I felt myself dipping into it. It seemed to me like bathing in some cool, sheltered pool after a long tread in parching sun. I went outside into the garden. The grass was wet with dew. The hedges were hung with mist, and so were the long brilliant strands of the willow that swept down, nearly touching the ground. Around me was the garden wall. The black iron gates in the back of the building stood open. A coolie came slowly up the steps with two dripping pails of water hanging from the ends of the pole on his shoulder. I could see the river covered with bits of floating mist. Mirrored in the water were shreds of white mist and streaks of amber sunlight, little mauve clouds, and beyond was the great green mass of a mountain range. The mist was burning up and the subtropics sun was beating down on me, and when I went back to our room, I felt it had enfolded me like a blessing.

The next day, there came a change over the smiling face of Chungking and its surrounding. The soft spring wind rose into a hint of menace. The sailboats scudded by like fugitives fleeing. Junks huddled to the shore. By night, the houses of Chungking were caught in one of the sudden storms common in the Yangtze valley. The wind was beating in terrifying blasts at Chaling Bingwa's walls, and the city seemed swallowed up in wind and water. As I lay in my bed and listened to the roar of the wind and the sound of the river, like the dash of the ocean against the house, it came to my mind how small Chaling House really was. Its personality had shrunken in the face of the roaring wind and water, and I too had shrunken and felt alone, here in the midst of China, and far away from my homeland of Germany.

The doctor had told me that my baby would be due on or around May 5th, so my husband packed me off to Ko-Lo-Shan, the place where the central hospital of Chungking was located. The Ko-Lo-Shan hospital was typical in Chinese style and material. The hospital's walls were of bamboo plastered with mud and whitewashed. The furniture in the different wards was very primitive. Comfort in the Western sense was unavailable. But this lack was greatly made up by the kindness, humor, and compassion of the hospital staff. I got a single room after we had gone through the routine of registering. Shortly afterwards, my husband had to leave. I inspected the room with its bamboo bed and the net suspended from the ceiling, the night table, the oil lamp with the cotton wick swimming in it, the floor, and so on. I came to the conclusion that some cleaning had to be done if I were to avoid an infection. And so I set to work with the few means at my disposal.

The meal, consisting of rice, chicken, and vegetables, was served in my room. It was very tasty and steaming hot. The shadows on the walls grew larger, and soon night set in. I lit the oil lamp and tucked myself in bed with the net drawn over me. Mosquitoes swarmed all over, and then came the rats. I was stunned; I could not believe it. There were rats of all different sizes, small, medium, and big ones. I noticed something, which was impossible: the rats were running up the vertical walls, apparently defying every kind of gravitational law. The rats are about the worst aspect I remember of my Chinese episodes. But then one gets even used to them. Anyway, I was sleeping under the net, and therefore, thought I was safe. One night, still before my son was born, I awoke around 1:00 a.m., having felt some very strange sensation on my left foot, which, because it was so hot, I had uncovered. Sure enough, I soon discovered what the case was: a rat had tried to gnaw on it. From then on, I kept all my limbs "indoors."

In the hospital, the newborn babies were watched day and night on account of the rats. Once, a nurse had left the baby ward for just a few minutes after having fed the babies with their formula and before her replacement arrived. As everybody knows, babies sometimes burp after being nursed and leave some milk on their lips. A rat, which must have smelled the milk, attacked a baby. The baby was terribly injured. Had I not been acquainted with conditions in China's interior, I never would have believed it.

It was May 4, 1942 when I awoke at 4:00 a.m. with pain. I knew then that it would be the day of my delivery. The pains came regularly, first in long intervals, then increasingly stronger and in shorter intervals. Ten o'clock passed, then noon, then two o'clock, by which time I was almost out of my mind. But the doctor told me the baby was not yet due for a couple of hours. I kicked the doctor with my foot when she tried to examine me because I felt such excruciating pains. I wondered how the Chinese ladies in labor in the hospital could keep so still, with only an occasional moaning I heard through the doors. The doctor told me I should scream if I felt like it. I felt terribly ashamed, but scream I did. My door stood ajar, and now and then, a Chinese visitor unknown to me, peeped in and I overheard her remark to others,

"Ta shi weige ren, to ju siau har" ("Look, she is a foreigner and gets a baby."). I put a towel into my mouth and screamed. Giving birth to a first child seemed to me the most unbelievable pain on earth. But every time I screamed with all my might, the pain would let up. Unfortunately, the hospital had no anesthetics except for ether, which was also in short supply. Finally, my husband came and held my hands, trying to comfort me. The hours went by so slowly, and I had sweated through my gowns a couple of times. At 5:00 p.m., I was at the point of almost complete exhaustion. The doctor then ordered the nurses to take me to the delivery room. My lady doctor had marvelous fine hands and worked very skillfully. It was then that I received some ether and dozed off.

The cry of a little baby awoke me. It was my boy! They showed him to me. He was a sturdy little fellow of seven and a quarter pounds. Although completely exhausted, I was unspeakably happy. Soon I was rolled back to my room and fell asleep. However, before long, I was awakened again. Two nurses stood at my side with a lot of bandages. I wondered what they were going to do next. Since we could not communicate in Chinese, they made signs and made me understand that I had to be bandaged around the belly so the uterus would contract and I could keep my slim figure. Of course, I immediately agreed. They bandaged me so thoroughly that I could no longer take a deep breath. But then I was to endure this "cast" only for a day. The nurses were awfully nice and very concerned with all their patients. I felt very grateful. In no other hospital have I ever received such kind and efficient attention as in the Chinese hospital in Ko-Lo-Shan.

I was blessed with a lot of milk for my baby. As a matter of fact, he could not drink it all. A Chinese woman in the hospital at the same time was very frail and had no milk. She also was very poor and could not afford a wet nurse. One of the nurses came to me and showed me her little baby—the cutest thing on earth. She asked me, "Would you consider nursing this little one along with your baby boy?" I did not hesitate a moment and was very glad to oblige. It was one of the greatest satisfactions of my life to watch how the other baby grew stronger day-by-day together with my own son. The Chinese woman's gratitude was boundless. This act of kindness was very much to my advantage once everybody in the hospital learned of it. Everyone showed great appreciation. I think I was a precedent. Everyone became my friend, it seemed. It is amazing how a little kindness can break down barriers. I lacked absolutely nothing of those things the hospital could provide, most of all care. Meanwhile, some of the nurses also approached me to teach them some English or German. It was great fun, the more so since they in turn taught me some of the badly needed Chinese. When I left the hospital eight days after the delivery, I had acquired a considerable repertoire of Chinese, which was very useful after my return to Chungking.

My husband had made arrangements for me to live with his sister, Pei Tan, in Chengtu. One day, I flew alone with the baby to Chengtu where my sister-in-law awaited us with two rickshaws. Off we went to her house that became my home for almost a year. The welcome was cordial, and the curiosity of my English speaking Chinese in-laws was tremendous. We had altogether a jolly good time, not that I did not have to make some adjustments.

The most marvelous thing for me was to have all the time I wanted at my disposal. I had to do nothing but look after my baby. There were so many servants: Lao Tang, the doorkeeper; Tzu-Ching-Ming, the fat cook and her entourage of helpers; and the strong coolie for the rickshaw. All became my friends, and every one of them was eager to teach me some more Chinese. In due course, I became almost fluent in the daily usage of Chinese.

My sister-in-law's home consisted of several buildings: the main house for the immediate family, wife, husband, and two children, and now myself the newest sensational acquisition. There were servants' quarters and the doorkeeper's tiny house. It was quite a compound, with a tennis court and a flower and vegetable garden. All was walled-in, as is the custom in Chengtu and other Chinese cities. The doorkeeper did all the shopping. Milk was brought to the big entrance door, or rather, the cow was brought there and milked in front, with Lao Tang watching so no dirty water would be poured in to increase the quantity. Sometimes, I ventured out only a few steps; that was in the beginning. Every time, I saw quite a few beggars in most deplorable conditions camping on the doorsteps. There were women with trachoma whose watery eyes were terribly inflamed. There were those poor creatures who, in their infancy and early childhood, still had their feet bound to prevent them from growing because it was then considered pretty for a girl to have tiny feet and to wiggle her behind, which was inevitable after such a procedure. When I saw those old women hobbling along in their threadbare blue ishangs (cloth shoes), emaciated bodies, with outstretched hands begging for a pittance, my heart was pierced by compassion. Whenever I had some small change in my purse, I would distribute it. Never can I forget the moment when a woman literally fell on her knees before me because I had given her the equivalent of five cents. "My God," I thought, "what have you done to this humanity?" From then on, whenever I could, I stole out through the entrance door with some little change or a bowl of rice. But word seemed to get around, and soon, the crowds became larger. Finally, my sister-in-law got wind of it and told me sternly, "I do not want you to continue distributing alms; Chengtu is full of beggars and is very dangerous."

I asked, "Does anyone take care of them?" She shrugged it off, but I had no alternative except to stop. I was heartbroken for all those poor, malnourished, and sick people.

Since I breastfed my baby, I had a terrific appetite and quite a sweet tooth. Not too far away from our compound was a bakery that produced the most delicious cookies. One day, I remember vividly, I made up my mind to do my own candy shopping. It was again a day of extreme heat. To protect myself against the sun, I put on a wide rimmed felt hat; it was the dernier cri—the last fashion before I left Germany. However, it was most uncommon here in the interior of China, where the ladies ventured out, usually with a sun umbrella. I left the house, trying to find my way through the narrow streets. Soon I noticed a couple of children behind me making fun of me, pointing at my hat and chanting, "Ni kan kan weigo ren, kan kan ta-di mautse" ("The foreigner, the foreigner, she has a funny hat"). In no time, I had quite a procession of children behind me, apparently very amused by my head gear. Somewhat hastily, I reached the bakery. By then, grown-ups had mingled with the children and a whole mob swarmed around me. None of them was malicious; they were just very curious. I did my shopping, and as fast as I could, I went home. Never again did I wear my wide brimmed felt hat; instead I got myself a sun umbrella made of oilpaper and bamboo. Slowly but surely, I transformed myself outwardly into a Chinese lady with silk gowns and other paraphernalia. I did not, however, give up my daily excursions, and the novelty of seeing a foreign woman soon wore off for the children.

One terribly hot day in August, 1942, I was at my in-laws' house and we were busy discussing the latest political developments, the family of Chiang Kai-shek, Chiang Ching-kuo, Chiang Wei-Go, Madame Chiang Kai-shek, Dr. Sun Yat-sen, and Madame Sun Yat-sen. My in-laws were very sophisticated and well informed. When the discussion became very controversial and heated, I suggested we go swimming in the river to cool off tempers. My proposal was accepted, and after getting ready, we marched for a long stretch on the edge of the rice paddies, where the Chinese not only grow rice but also fish (fish being a very good fertilizer). I had never seen this kind of agriculture, which had been perfected over the centuries. In Szechuan, a general had installed an irrigation system in the seventeenth century by means of bamboo pipes. It works very efficiently to this day. Most of the people in this part of China were farmers and they tended their fields very carefully. They set out every day from their houses in the village along narrow paths to reach their scattered fields. I could see them pushing wheelbarrows full of manure, or carrying a hoe, and sometimes driving their water buffaloes—a very interesting sight for me at that time. Much of the work was done by hand. Rice was first planted in a seedbed and later moved to a larger field or paddy. When the rice was knee high in the seedbed, men, women, and children pulled up each plant by its roots. Several plants were tied together, and then the bundles of rice plants were taken to the paddies and planted on evenly spaced rows. The paddies were kept filled with water much of the time. When the sun shone on the water-filled paddies, the valleys and terraced hillsides glistened like mirrors. These were for me very interesting experiences.

We marched swiftly to reach the river, panting in the terrible heat. The humidity was also unbearable. On the water's edge was a teahouse, completely made of bamboo, along with its furniture, and it looked terribly inviting. There, the bearded and unbearded Chinese sat, sipping the fragrant Chinese green tea. No one was swimming. The Chinese stirred when they saw us coming. A foreign white woman in the remote interior of Szechuan—what a sight! I became inhibited as I was looked over and sized up by many of the Chinese gentlemen. I quickly disappeared into the house to change into my swimming suit. When I reappeared, I became once more the focal point. It was unpleasant for me, but I thought, "You have to get used to such things."

I was a good swimmer. With my brother-in-law, Wang Fu Ming (my husband's brother), I entered the river, which had quite a current and was pretty wide. Wholeheartedly, I pushed myself away from the riverbank and into midstream, with

Fu Ming following. I had trained in Germany, often times getting into the Danube, which can be very tricky. Looking back at the tea house and its many visitors, I noticed something unusual: all the people had gotten up from their chairs or benches and were now lining the shore, pointing at me, expecting me to go under. Apparently, never before had a woman dared to entrust herself to these waters. Everything went well for a while until suddenly I noticed Fu Ming having trouble. He was drawn into an inconspicuous whirlpool. I became very agitated, motioning to him to try by all means to push through. Finally, he made it. From then on, I kept very near to him. I thanked God when we reached the river's other side. Then we went back over the bridge to join the others. Fu Ming did not enter the river again—I was glad.

Fu Shih, my husband, had joined me at his sister's house for an interval. He was an idealist at heart and had invited some of his countrymen for tea and some snacks. A conversation got under way. From gestures and some words spoken in English, as well as from some Chinese phrases I had learned, I gathered the conversation was about Germany, Hitler, China, Japan, and of course, that great inexhaustible topic, the war. What impressed me most was the genuine politeness of the people, their broadmindedness, and their wit. I think nobody can laugh so wholeheartedly as the Chinese. Their laughter was unbounded.

It was only this once that we went swimming in that river, as later we learned it was not safe, the waters being very polluted. On our way back, Fu Shih hurt his big toe very badly, and we were afraid it would get infected, which it promptly did. The next day he had a high fever and we had to call a doctor. Those were still the days of no antibiotics! But eventually, the toe healed. It took three weeks!

The years 1942 and 1943 in Chengtu went by almost unnoticed. I was busy raising my baby boy, Paul. I had a lot of interaction with the immediate and extended family. Reunions were celebrated in grand style with the obligatory delicious, multicourse meals.

Chinese cooking was one thing that interested me to no end. Often, I would go into the kitchen and watch the expert cook. She prepared the most delicious foods from the simplest raw materials. The way she prepared vegetables was as follows: she washed, dried, and shredded them into small pieces. Meantime, lard was placed in the frying pan and the vegetables were added. In China, two kind of fats were used: lard and vegetable oils. The cook knew exactly how to proceed to bring out the specific flavor in every dish—no "accent" or monosodium glutamate was needed. Vegetables and meat were never overcooked or underdone; she always knew the exact point of doneness. Almost every dish was improved by soybean sauce and other kinds of Chinese spices. In preparing fish, no one could surpass her art. She would marinate the fish sufficiently long to give it a sweet and sour flavor and turn it into a delicacy, and everything, even the bones, could be eaten. She knew hundreds of ways to prepare all kinds of meat—beef, pork, chicken, duck, lamb, veal, and so on. Even certain kinds of snakes, properly prepared, were a source of food, unlikely as it may sound.

She knew at least a dozen ways to cook eggs. With the large eggs of geese, for instance, she would proceed in the following manner: she would wash them thoroughly, then work a lot of salt into a light brown regular mud and kneed it through and through. Then she would plaster the mud in a thick layer around the eggs and bury them in the ground for about half a year and sometimes longer so the eggs would absorb all the salt from the mud. When the cook dug them out and removed the hardened wrapping, the eggs had undergone a chemical change that made them translucent. They looked like hardboiled eggs, but the yoke had an aspic, dark green color with a slight sulfur odor. Such eggs were eaten with soybean sauce, the ever present, food improver.

The cook also knew how to prepare shark fins, a high protein food of glassy, jelly substance. Sometimes, she would prepare "bird's nest," also made of a jelly substance of unknown origin; this dish was considered in China one of the most expensive foods and could only be prepared by a real gourmet connoisseur. At every meal, the main dish in China is, of course, rice, which is prepared over steam, unsalted, and without fat. It is always served separately, the other dishes being placed in the center of a round table where the family would be seated. A bowl and chopsticks made of bamboo, wood, ivory, horn, silver, or other metals served as eating utensils. Everyone would use their chopsticks to pick up food from the center bowls and transfer it to their own rice bowl. Soup is served as the last dish. Sweets are not usually served after regular meals; instead, tea and perhaps fruits are served.

The usual portion the Chinese eat at the principal meal is one or two bowls of rice with an adequate amount of meats and vegetables. In the morning, they rarely drink coffee. What they have, instead, is a bowl of rice porridge, sometimes enhanced with beans, peanuts, or peanut butter, perhaps some smoked soy cheese (most delicious stuff), and some kind of buns cooked in oil.

On a few occasions, my sister-in-law asked me to prepare a German meal, and I always complied with her wishes. To this "famous" German meal, she would invite several friends, one of whom was a Chinese gentleman who had studied criminology in Vienna, Austria, and who, therefore, could speak good German, with an Austrian accent. He always did great honor to all the dishes I prepared. He was a tremendous eater and especially loved my German layer cakes. He was a very friendly and jolly fellow while he was entertained at my sister-in-law's house in the interior of China. Unfortunately, I had to change my opinion of him later in 1946, when we had moved to Shanghai after the war. At that time, with everyone returning from the interior to the big cities in the east, it was extremely difficult to get a flat or an apartment. One had to have connections. Meanwhile, our expert in criminology had become the police commissioner of Shanghai, and thus, held a very high position. I approached him to give me some kind of recommendation, but he would not give it to me. He, apparently, refused to recall that at one time we had been very well acquainted. It was then, I realized, how easy it was for one to be friendly while eating another's German layer cakes and quite another thing when the German layer cakes had vanished without leaving a trace of memory behind. Our gentleman friend had no recollection of bygone pleasant times in Chengtu. To the credit of the Chinese people, I must say that such incidents were rare in my experience. Usually, friends or family members would go out of their way to comply with requests. Unfortunately, this man had become a snob.

About this time, May of 1942, Fu Shih, who was working for the National Resources Commission, was transferred to Kweilin in the province of Kwangsi, in the south of China where the center for the manufacture of radios was located. Fu Shih was employed at the research laboratory as an expert in electronics. I stayed behind in Chengtu with Paul. In the beginning, my husband's letters would reach me regularly, but gradually, they became less frequent. Then came an interval of no news from him at all. As the weeks went by, I became very worried. My letters remained unanswered and he stopped writing and sending me money altogether. I was, so to speak, at the mercy of my sister-in-law. It is interesting to note how relationships can deteriorate. My sister-in-law became fussy and even nervous with me at times. I wanted to get to the bottom of the problem. Suddenly, it dawned on me: I was without my own family, had no income of my own, and was entirely dependent on my in-laws; in other words, I had no face. To remedy this situation, I recruited some students who were interested in studying German. My sister-in-law's husband assisted me in this process. He was the friendliest person one could imagine. Later on, I supplied him with all kinds of patterns and modern designs for cushions, which he greatly appreciated. Our mutual collaboration was a great success. I gave individual lessons to the students, instructing them in German grammar, vocabulary, and conversation. I had about ten students who not only paid their tuition regularly, but also showered me with presents. I discovered that I was to them, after all, a rarity: a white woman who spoke fluent German in the interior of China. With money thus earned, I could put part of it at my sister-in-law's disposal. Earlier, I had given her a ring to pay for my stay. She accepted all graciously, and soon our relationship was based again on solid, friendly terms. I was then in better spirits.

My husband's silence, however, was inexplicable. Since he was working at Kweilin's radio plant, I thought I would get in touch with him via radio, the distance being about 2,000 miles. I applied at the local radio station, and the radio communication was scheduled for the next afternoon. I arrived early and nervously waited for my turn. Finally, Fu Shih came on the air. I asked him, "Why the long silence? Why have you not answered my letters?"

He explained, "The letters got lost on account of bandits plaguing the country. I have been ill with typhoid fever, but will be soon in Chengtu. I will stay only a short while, but we will return to Kweilin together. Although I have been sick, I am quite happy here."

And so it came about that we settled on the outskirts of Kweilin, where the radio factory was located. The scenery was gorgeous! Massive mountains rose unexpectedly from the comparatively flat land, making needlelike bizarre formations, reflecting in the wide river and often creating gushing streams with the surrounding lush vegetation, painted in various shades of greens, yellow, and brown, and all under a constantly bright sun. Kweilin was subtropical in climate.

We occupied a small house put at our disposal by the factory management. A huge garden surrounded the house, which consisted only of two big rooms and a large veranda, but no bathroom or WC. Nowhere in the interior of Szechuan or Kwangsi province were "water closets" installed in houses. The substitute for the WC was the so-called ma-tung, a big pot in a wooden frame with a seat, and of course, a cover. The servant was in charge of keeping it clean. Later on, Fu Shih installed something like an outhouse and also a bath. He made a high wooden stand with a staircase and a platform for a metal drum. A pipe with a shower fixture was connected to the high standing drum. If one wanted a shower, the only thing to do was to fill the drum with heated water. Of course, there was no way to regulate the water's temperature. All the water had to be brought by coolies in buckets hanging from the ends of poles on their shoulders. No one could imagine our pride and joy after installing our own private bath.

In Kweilin, I was very happy. I had all the time I ever wanted at my disposal. I did not do the cooking because we had hired a very good servant. She was very loyal and a much better cook than I. We had a huge garden, and I decided to plant all kinds of vegetables with the help of a coolie who, of course, did the main work. My husband, all of a sudden, became very enterprising, and became enchanted with the idea of raising goats, pigs, chickens, and bees. Soon all became a reality, and so we had goat milk, cream and butter, eggs and meat, all home grown. With the bees, we were less lucky; I don't remember ever getting any honey, but quite a few stings. Soon, I discovered how clean pigs are and how dirty goats are. You had to clean forever after the goats, whereas the pigs would go exactly to the same place for their business. Pigs would also develop a lot of camaraderie among themselves. Once I fed a pair of pigs out of a wooden bucket. Both were eating heartily, when all of a sudden, the bottom fell out and one pig had the rest of the bucket with the metal band around its neck. I was apparently very frightened. The other pig banged against this artificial neck decoration and finally the pig got rid of it. It was quite a sight!

Our small male piglets had to be "clipped." A Chinese "veterinary," whose sole business probably was the clipping of pigs, came. He did it expertly and in the nick of time. He would grab the little pig, place it sideways on the ground, hold its head down with his foot, make an incision on the lower part of the pig's abdomen, insert his finger, pull out some kind of tube, cut it, disinfect the cut, and sew it up, having a helper for the latter part of the operation. The piglets would, of course, squeal terribly and immediately run off when the veterinary removed his foot. The whole procedure for one clipping lasted about two to three minutes. For two or three days, the piglets would be rather limp, but then recover speedily from the operation. We fed them with crushed soybeans, boiled potatoes, rice, and all possible leftovers. Within half a year's time, they were rather fat. Whenever one of our piglets was to be slaughtered, it was a sad day for me. I never could eat any of the meat. The way the Chinese slaughter a pig is rather unique. A couple of men would enter the backyard. The pigs would be let out from their sty. The men determined which pig to get hold of. They would separate it from the others, approach it swiftly from behind, and try to grab a hold of the tail, which was sometimes very difficult, as the pig realized it was in mortal danger. As soon as one of the men grabbed the pig's tail, it would twist, and within a split second, the tail's end was a knot, onto which the man would hang with all his strength, thus bringing the pig to a halt with his counterweight. Then followed the terrible procedure of cutting the animal's throat and bleeding it. Cruel as it may seem, I daresay the whole thing is less frightening than a Spanish bullfight I witnessed last year in Spain, which literally made me sick. Afterward, the pig was placed in a huge tub, and boiling water was poured over it. The bristles were shorn or shaved off with an extremely sharp knife, and every part of it scrubbed thoroughly. Thereafter, the whole pig was suspended from a pall. One of the men would take one foot of the pig and cut a hole between the tendon and the toe, and then blow air from his own mouth into this hole, inflating the pig like a balloon. Then the pig would be cut open, intestines and lard taken out, likewise the liver, kidneys, bladder, and so on. Nothing was ever thrown away—neither bristles nor gall bladder, the latter being used for pharmaceutical purposes.

We made some money on our pigs, having had twenty at a time. But I never was really very happy with it, as some of the pigs became so friendly with me. Thinking in evolutionary terms, I almost ended up with a guilt complex. Eventually, we discontinued the thriving pig business.

We remained in Kweilin for about eighteen months. My boy had grown into the most loveable little toddler, happy, healthy, and droll. I myself adjusted very well to the demands of the Chinese living conditions. Often, I took my little Paul for a walk accompanied by our most esteemed goats. We would walk sometimes for hours. Later on, I heard what people said, "Ta ju sen-shing bin" ("She is crazy"). Crazy because I took walks alone, for none of the ladies took such walks. But coming from Germany, I could not suppress the habits of a very Spartan upbringing. I must have been the only lady venturing beyond the factory grounds out into the endless landscape.

According to Chinese astrology, 1944 was the year of the monkey, and rumors reached Kweilin that the Japanese were on the march and approaching the city. Bombings were inevitable. The terrible massacres of 1938-39 in Nanking were too vividly in the minds of the Chinese for them not to fear the Japanese. Unfortunately, the news came at the eleventh hour so nothing was organized for such a calamity. People were fleeing in panic. To stay meant the greatest of risk-taking. Fu Shih was very worried, so we had to leave. We gathered together whatever necessities we could carry in our hands—it was very disheartening to leave behind our books, our marvelous garden that had large ripe tomatoes, all the furniture, and so on. The goats and chickens were sold. Whatever was left in the house would, of course, be looted.

It was a very hot afternoon in June when we made our way to the train station together with a multitude of other people. I was pregnant again and not feeling too well. I was convinced that in that onrush of people, we would never be able to board the train to Do-Shan. Fu Shih, however, had worked out a very clever plan. He had hired six strong boys who, when the train entered, pushed their way and us through the crowd and pulled us up on the train. Of course, part of our luggage got lost, but it mattered now so little in the face of so much danger. In droves, the people would hang on the train's steps and hold fast to every tangible board. They were up on the roofs, filling every inch of the train corridor, sitting on windowsills with children hanging out from luggage nets. The confusion was unimaginable, the noise deafening, and the air so hot, dusty, and smelly that I became sick.

Finally, the terrible overcrowded train set itself slowly into motion. "At least," I thought, "we are on it." But this thought would soon prove to be futile. The train had left Kweilin and the station slowly behind, traveling only about two or three miles, when the conductor and other train personnel commanded everybody out of the train after sounding the alarm signal. The locomotive was defective and had to be repaired. I don't know whether or not this claim was true; I never found out. We had, however, to get off the train, losing more of our luggage. The great question was, "What to do now?" We trudged back to Kweilin Station—with a stream of utterly disillusioned people. Fu Shih had studied the train schedule the night before and told me that another train would have to come through soon, and we could perhaps make it if we would quickly move over to the other rail.

The train was to stop only a very short time. But we would try to board it by all means. Fu Shih saw the train coming in and pulled Paul and me after him. The train did not stop but went very, very slow. It was a dangerous undertaking as the train was well guarded and terribly overcrowded. But Fu Shih was just marvelous. He always had been an outstanding athlete, and in this hour of danger, his strength and circumspection doubled. He pulled us onto the moving train while some people helped from the inside. At last, we were on the train and on our way to Do-Shan.

It took us eight days to reach Do-Shan. As the train was so terribly overcrowded, we had no possibility to stretch our limbs, let alone lie down and sleep. At every station, more and more people wanted to come on. Finally, the train did not stop anymore except in the open fields. Almost no water was to be had. Sanitary conditions were beyond description. Children would wail; women would become hysterical and scream. It was a nightmare! After eight days, we arrived in Do-Shan, halfway between Kweilin and Chungking, then the capital of national China. By this time, Paul and I had become ill. Fu Shih was lucky enough to arrange for a quick transport to Chungking via a ferryboat over the Yangtze River. Fu Shih had brought a revolver with him and stood up in the boat to protect us. I learned later that many passengers had been tossed in the stream before. He was a brave man. Only two boatman and we were on the ferry.

We arrived in Chungking very late in the afternoon. The sun was setting in the west, and we could see the city in the distance. Before long, we had crossed the river. We left the ferry and went to town to our temporary quarters. Paul and I were very sick. We had dysentery and I was pregnant. It was then I realized something like Providence existed. We had brought a lot of medicines from Germany such as quinine and Yatrin, a very strong medicine against dysentery. In Kweilin, I had thought of throwing them out, but somehow they had found their way into our luggage. This Yatrin saved our lives. After taking it for two weeks, we were out of danger. Still, I felt very weak and not at all healthy. One day I would have a high fever, and the next day, none at all. This pattern went on for some time. I made up my mind to go to the Hong Shi-tse Kwai, (Foreign Red Cross) to see a doctor.

When I arrived there, I had one of those fever attacks and pulled myself up on the railing. The Red Cross, unfortunately, had no dyes, which were indispensable for identifying certain strains of germs, but the doctor recognized my sickness anyway. It was malaria, the good-natured, tertiary kind where only every third day would a person have an attack. The doctor pricked my earlobe, took some blood, and had his diagnosis confirmed. Well, at least I knew what was wrong. The doctor gave me a lot of quinine, Plasma-quinine, Atabrine, and other medicines, most of which I could not take because I was pregnant. He acquainted me with all the rules of fighting malaria. I weighed about ninety pounds then and was in the ninth month of my pregnancy. Nobody believed I would soon give birth. Contrary to my own fears, I had a healthy little baby girl of four-and-a-half pounds on November 15, 1944.

It is not easy to relate in proper order all that happened in those turbulent years between 1944 and 1949. As everyone knows, the year 1945 meant the end of World War II. In October of that year, we were still in Chungking, trying desperately to take a flight to Shanghai. All of a sudden, everybody was in great haste to go to Shanghai, but it was extremely hard to book a flight. Thousands and thousands of people were on the waiting list. Finally, we made it.

I shall not go into detail about what life was like in that big metropolitan city of the Far East, except to say it was most colorful, with tremendous hectic social activities, carried on not only by the Chinese, but also by the French, English, Russians, and Germans, many of the latter having been expatriated and placed in concentration camps by the Chinese by the end of 1945. American G.I.'s were swarming all over the place, turning their heads after every girl, which earned them the nickname "vultures." There were even pockets of Japanese leftover personnel from the days of the Shanghai occupation; they were awaiting repatriation in Hong-Kew, the place where, formerly, the Japanese forced the Jews to live. The Russians looked down on the American G.I.'s. I do remember that the Russian waitresses in the famous Kavkas restaurant were openly hostile to them. Because there were many drunken soldiers, I often witnessed an unpleasant scene. Foreign advisors of all sorts were everywhere. And finally, there was The United Nations' headquarters for the Far East, with its numerous departments and a tremendous staff, a typical United Nations assortment.

Despite all these changes, life seemed to go on as usual. Only the politically interested and informed sensed that there was plenty of change in the air. The situation was far from stable. Chiang Kai-shek and sons were in Shanghai. Chiang Ching-kuo, the mastermind of the monetary reform, had hoaxed the members of the Chamber of Commerce into exchanging their foreign values with the newly printed Chinese paper dollars, which were declared equivalent in value to one U.S. dollar. There was, as everybody knew, no basis for such assumption. Nevertheless, the people, still dealing with outdated Chinese paper money, expected and welcomed the currency reform. In November 1948, shortly before that reform, all of a sudden all goods disappeared from the shops; nothing was to be had anymore for old money. One had to pay in foreign exchange or go away empty-handed. Soon then, the reform took place. Of course, the foreign firms, and foreigners in general, knew what it was all about. They were clever enough to exchange only a small fraction of their foreign money against the newly printed paper Chinese yuan. It really was all a trick because after that exchange had been going on for some time and the firms had declared dutifully their compliance with the government requests, one night Chiang Kai-shek and company, with all the gold reserves and foreign exchange from the Hong-Kong China Bank, and all the rest available in Shanghai, left Shanghai overnight for Taiwan (the island of Formosa). I believe the Chamber of Commerce had bought Chiang and company out. They wanted Shanghai to be declared an open city.

Weeks before, we had heard rumors that the Communists were approaching; they were so and so many miles north of the Huangpu River. It was a development no one could stop. Many foreigners left Shanghai long before the Communist occupation; everyone was desperate to get out because they were so afraid of the Communists. Hair-raising stories were in circulation. The new currency in Chinese paper money was still in operation, but, of course, a terrific inflation had set in.

At that time, I was working for a Swiss firm dealing outwardly in hog casing while, in reality, operating the most thriving black market in gold ingots. With the approach of the Communists to Shanghai, these firms, many of which dealt in illegal operations, became frantic. I was not Swiss, and therefore, had to be discarded, confidence being only extended to members of the Swiss' own nationality. At that time, I really despised the Swiss businessmen who seemed so philanthropic and gentlemanly in social circles, but inwardly, were whitewashed tombs. Absolutely nothing else but their own profit was in their minds; they were not even interested in politics, except for how to find a way to protect their loot. It was a very hard time for me.

Shortly after we had come to Shanghai in 1946, Fu Shih and I agreed to a divorce. We still were very good friends, but to live together had its great disadvantages. The Chinese became very anti-foreign minded. Foreigners could be expected to be spat at when walking on the street. Communists were trying to prepare the soil by influencing people's attitudes. The Chinese all of a sudden seemed to become aware of how much they were exploited, dating back many decades. It was a national awakening, some aspects of which took on sinister significance. Soon after the war, some Japanese war criminals would be dragged through the streets of Shanghai, such as Nanking Street, to be executed. Such spectacles occurred almost every day.

In May 1949, the Communists finally crossed the Huangpu River, giving them access to Shanghai. Chiang Kai-shek had already left. All shops, days before the Communists occupied the city, had closed their shutters. Nothing whatsoever could be bought. The common people seemed to know well in advance what would happen. Apparently, the so-called "bamboo telephone" had worked perfectly well. Many Chinese tried to go to Formosa during this last week before the Communist occupation. Some succeeded. The general atmosphere was sickening. Of course, everybody was afraid with so many rumors of executions and atrocities circulating. Nothing seemed to be of value any longer. It was a very tough time. We lived on the last of our reserves.

When the Communists entered, however, no battle was fought. The corrupt National troops had fled with all the gold available; the civilian population was left to its own fate, which turned out to be better than expected. One night, we heard shooting. The noise came from various directions at the same time. Apparently, not much resistance was put up. To me, it seemed to be only a face-saving gesture on the Nationals' part. The next morning, it was all over. People were lining the streets to watch the columns of Communists soldiers enter the city. The entrance was a most ordered one. The Communists had their rifles, were clad decently, and even sometimes sat down to eat their rice meals, producing from one of their pockets, the indispensable chopsticks. It was an astonishingly peaceful sight. I, like everybody else, was on the street watching the spectacle. When I looked into some of the soldiers' faces, I was surprised by the good-humored expressions on their solid peasant faces. No looting occurred anywhere. Apparently, the troops had strict orders to behave their very best, which they did.

During those days, my daughter Marianne, because I was working, stayed in a boarding school for preschool children in Hung Qiao. It was a very nice place for her, managed by a lady from Hamburg, Germany. Unfortunately, when the Communists came, the lady was deported to Germany. All the mothers had to take their children out of the boarding school. We were, however, promised that the school would operate again in about a week's time. So in a week, I tried to bring my daughter back to the boarding school. There was, however, no free movement yet between Shanghai and Hung Qiao, or the other suburbs for that matter. But I had to try anyway. So I hired a rickshaw, proceeding into the direction of Hung Qiao. Some of the people stared at me. I had reached the city limits with many soldiers gathering there. My rickshaw coolie asked me, "What should I do?" I instructed him to go on and that we would find out in time whether we could go through. Soon, we were stopped by a soldier pointing his rifle into our faces. I stepped out of the rickshaw with my daughter, explaining to the Communist soldier in Chinese that I had to bring my daughter back to the boarding school because I had to go to work. He was very friendly then, telling me, "Today, it is not possible because of certain troop movements, but tomorrow at the same time, you can try again and probably all will be clear." I thanked him for this information and asked the rickshaw coolie to drive us back again. The Communist soldier had expressed some laudable remarks to me that I could converse with him in Chinese. The next day I tried again; again the soldier was standing there. This time I could pass. The soldier waved at me and I waved back. We had become friends.

Chapter 4

—— ❁ ——

In My Own Voice

Commentary and Additions to My Mother's Chinese Episodes

Thus, I was born in the city of Chungking on November 15, 1944. By a turn of fate, I was born in the same city and in the same hospital as my brother, Wang Qian, to whom my mother gave the Christian name Paul and nickname, *Goggeli* ("small rooster" in German). For some reason unknown to me, my mother did not mention that my aunt, Pei Yan, a doctor at the Ko-Lo-Shan hospital in Chungking and half-sister to my father (daughter to my grandfather's Japanese wife), delivered my brother and provided the only birth certificate which, much later, became instrumental in proving my brother's filial bond to my mother. I believe I also was delivered by Aunt Pei Yan, who also provided my birth certificate in the war torn city of Chungking, which I would not have had otherwise and which gave proof to my parentage, date, and place of birth, as well as my first name, Marianne Wang. My mother told me that while she was in the hospital, awaiting my birth, several times when sirens sounded to announce possible Japanese bombings, she had to be carried on a cot to the basement. My brother recalls seeing a burst of light and afterglow during these events.

My father told me that our family was very poor in Chungking. He could buy only one cigarette at a time. My parents rented a room in a compound and ordered their meals from outside or cooked them in a makeshift stove. My mother, always the gemutlichkeit (cozy/comfort maker), cut up some of her dresses to make curtains for the window, and I'm sure she washed the place from top to bottom with the help of an ama (maid and nanny). Because I weighed only four-and-a-half pounds, my mother initially had to place me in the bed with her to keep me warm. My father told me he recalled rocking me in a bamboo cradle at night when I cried. At that time, my mother did not work, so she nursed me for over a year. The process was painstaking for her because I would take one swallow and then fall asleep and forget

I was nursing. For this reason, my mother had more pleasant memories when she cared for my brother, who was more robust and agile and stayed with her for a longer period of his infancy. She was also healthier and better off at that time.

My parents stayed in Chungking for one year. In October 1945, after the end of World War II, the family moved to Shanghai, the Nationalist Headquarters at the time. My brother flew there with Uncle Fu Ming, my father's younger brother. I followed with my mother, and I believe my father preceded her since it was very hard to find multiple seats on the plane to Shanghai. Once in Shanghai, my parents occupied a room in my grandfather's house. On one occasion, my grandfather's third wife, Pei Ron, was walking the floors with me to put me to sleep when my mother looked over and noticed I was not making any sound and was turning blue. She immediately grabbed me from Pei Ron's arms and resuscitated me. Apparently, I had some of these fits after a cry. The family became aware of this problem and exercised proper vigilance.

At that time, the situation between my parents began to deteriorate. My mother, who was a very independent woman, could no longer tolerate living in a family clan. She had always longed to have her own household and means of sustenance, but my father could not provide it for her. It appears he also had a few dalliances with women, including with one of the maids. I learned this detail from my mother, much later in my life, just before my return to China. So my mother sought a divorce. According to my brother, my father first agreed, but later regretted the decision. He pleaded with my mother to reconsider, but the papers were already underway. My mother told me his pleas had a religious fervor. He promised to become a Christian while still remaining a Buddhist. My brother remembers going to a Christian Church with my father.

Regardless, my parents were divorced on September 21, 1946. The papers decreed that my brother would stay with my father and I would stay with my mother. Only later, I found out that this arrangement was my grandfather's wish. An influential figure in the family, he followed the Chinese precept of preference for sons. Shortly thereafter, my mother had my father sign a paper, promising to provide for me until I was sixteen years old.

My grandfather, Wang Siao-Ao, was a prominent figure in Chinese politics during the Communist Regime. As a young man, he was stirred into public service and politics by his mother, who had told him countless stories of national heroes and steeped him in Chinese history and philosophy. He also heard a story that one of his ancestors during the Ming dynasty was an advisor to the emperor. His job was to travel with the emperor and point out any mistakes the emperor made. Needless to say, one day the emperor did not like his advice and ordered the Wang official executed. Later, the emperor realized that the Wang official was correct and ordered a large memorial to be constructed in his honor. This memorial exists to this day and can be seen in the region of Tong Li.

My grandfather had lost his father as a young man, and therefore, was not rich. The family, which included a sister, lived in the Wang compound (today it is a museum) in the city of Tong Li, from where my father's family comes. After primary and secondary school, my grandfather wanted to go to Japan to study political science and economics. However, he did not have enough money for such studies. His mother tried to help by selling some land, but it was not enough. Driven by his strong desire to study in Japan, he approached a richer Wang relative, who at first denied help but later was impressed by the young man's discourse and persuasion and gave him the remainder of the money for his studies.

My grandfather completed his studies in Japan and even married a Japanese wife while still married to his first Chinese wife. At that time, it was legal to have more than one wife. His first wife bore him three children: my aunt Pei-Tan (my father's sister with whom my mother stayed in Chendu and the only aunt I never met), my father Fu Shih, and my uncle Fu Ming (who also became an electrical engineer). My grandfather's second wife (Japanese) bore him a daughter, my aunt Pei Yan (the doctor who delivered my brother and myself). Both of his wives died due to complications in childbirth. Later, my grandfather married again and had a daughter, Pei Ron, who was theatrical and involved in the Shanghai Theater. His third wife became his lifetime companion. After the Second World War, my grandfather became very concerned about China's future. He saw the workings of Dr. Sun Yat-sen's government and admired the leader's tenacity. At that time, my grandfather was part of the Nationalist Movement. Now during the Chiang Kai-shek years, he became disillusioned with the power of the Nationalist Movement to transform China. He was seeing too much corruption and the rampant misery of the people. He is said to have locked himself in his room in Shanghai for two years to study the Communist philosophy and political strategy. He emerged convinced that Communism could save China, and he joined the Communist Party. In the 1950s, he moved to Beijing and became China's Vice Minister of Finance.

My mother cites her incompatibility to assimilate the Chinese way of life as reason for the divorce. In those years after the divorce (1946-1949), my mother worked in various capacities. To supplement her income, she taught German and English in Shanghai to graduates of the Tungshi University. From November 1, 1946 to August 20, 1947, my mother was employed as a secretary-steno-typist for the Import and Hospital Department of the Kofa American Drug Company. From August to October 1947, my mother obtained a temporary job at Dr. A. Grossmann, Attorney and Counselor-at Law, by way of replacing an absent secretary. Then from January to June of 1948, she was employed as a secretary/stenographer for the Import/Export House of G.R. Coleman and Co. Dr. Grossmann's office, I believe, is where my mother befriended a fellow secretary, Elizabeth von Ulrich and her husband, Baron von Ulrich, both Russian immigrants with aristocratic German ancestry. This couple was instrumental in introducing my mother to my future stepfather, another aristocratic Russian, Prince Valerian Tmiro Khan Chestohin. To complete my mother's work history in Shanghai, it is worthy to note that she worked for the United Nations as a steno-typist/translator in the Language Section (comprising English and French) of the United Nations' ECAFE (Economic Commission for Asia and the Far East) from August 23, 1948 to December 18, 1948, and only was terminated due to ECAFE's curtailment in Shanghai. As can be seen, it was not easy to keep a job for very long during these turbulent times in Shanghai.

As noted before, my mother longed for family stability. She had lost her father at age eight, and after that, had spent most of her school years in a boarding school. During her young adult life in Munich, she supported herself, and through her writings, it is known she lost a fiancé in the war prior to meeting my father. These last years in China, she had experienced constant change and deprivation. After divorcing my father, she was again in a large metropolitan area, trying to support herself and her young daughter. Of course, she needed companionship. As a beautiful European woman, she began dating and was drawn to my stepfather, Prince Ismael-Bey Valerian Tmiro Khan, with his gallant ways, riding expertise, and an interesting Russian history. She learned he had lived for many years in Tiensin, China with his Russian wife, a theater actress of exceptional beauty, and their two children, Helen and Peter. His wife had died of cancer many years earlier. He had migrated from Russia after fighting the Bolsheviks as a captain in Czar Nicholas II's Imperial Cavalry.

My stepfather's family came originally from Daghestan and were from the sovereign house of the Tmiro-Khans. During the Russian subjugation of the Caucasus, many Mohammedan mountaineer tribes rallied bravely round the Tmiro Khan's banner. My stepfather's grandfather was seized by the Russian forces, and refusing to capitulate, was led, with other members of his family, into captivity to the Transbaikal Region (Siberia), in the Cossack settlement known as Chindant II. The clan's survivors were installed in spacious and comfortable quarters, but guarded as Cossack hostages. Here, my stepfather's father, Prince Ismael-Ghemir, son of the captive general, eventually organized and operated a stud-farm on an imposing scale, supplying thoroughbreds to the Russian Imperial Government, and being secretly commissioned by the latter, experimenting with novel high-pedigree crossbreeds. In this settlement on November 14, 1896, Valerian Tmiro-Khan Chestohin was born. His baptismal certificate cites his father as Ismael-Ghemir Tmiro-Khan, captive Caucasian Prince, direct lineal descendant of the sovereign princes of Daghestan and Chechnia, and his mother, Princess Fatima, his lawful wife, both Mohammedan. My stepfather, per request of the Russian Czar, was baptized as a Christian and took on the surname of his baptismal sponsor, Peter Chestohin. He was raised in a Mohammedan environment and became versed in the Koran. Later, Ismael Valerian came to embrace the Christian Orthodox faith consciously and deliberately. After a high school education in the adjacent provincial capital of Chita, the young Khan was summoned to St. Petersburg to a private, in fact secret, audience with Czar Nicholas II, who received him with the utmost graciousness, proffering to the Tmiro-Khans his pardon, and to Ismael himself, a commission in any regiment of his guards or army, on condition that he content himself with remaining in permanent obscurity and identifying himself with his baptismal sponsor's name of Chestohin. The young khan gave his assent and allegiance wholeheartedly, having been raised in the finest Russian tradition and assimilated the specific culture of the Russian aristocracy.

In St. Petersburg, my stepfather studied painting and worked under the eminent Russian painter of battle-scenes, Professor Samokish. He became an accomplished artist, excelling in human and equine portraiture. He also graduated from the Nikolayevsky Cavalry School in St. Petersburg, and elected to serve in the Argun Cossack Regiment, stationed in the vicinity of his childhood home. World War I broke out and afforded him numerous opportunities to distinguish himself as an officer of matchless valor and keen initiative. He would bear scars of many a hot action, having been wounded in a cavalry attack upon a German infantry regiment that his platoon literally hacked to shreds. In this encounter, a German bullet pierced and partly shattered his lower jaw, carrying off part of his tongue and causing temporary loss of speech. By tenacious determination, however, he subsequently overcame his infirmity, so that his articulation was but slightly affected, and his facial scars enhanced the virile charm and distinction of his features. Constitutionally anti-Red, he took active part in the ensuing struggle against Bolshevism, and after the final defeat of the White Cause, settled in Tientsin, China, where he kept and trained race horses and was known as the best horseman and connoisseur in town. Like many others, he moved to Shanghai after Japanese incursions into China's mainland.

Much of what I have written thus far about my stepfather was provided by a brief biographical outline by Elizabeth von Ulrich, whom my stepfather befriended in China, and who later became my mother's friend and "matchmaker." Even though Valerian Tmiro Khan Chestohin was twenty years older than my mother, Agnes Schuetzinger Wang, the two were married in Shanghai, on the 17th of January 1949, and their mutual friends, Baron von Ulrich and his wife, Elizabeth von Ulrich, known affectionately as "Lizochka," witnessed the marriage certificate. Perhaps, for my mother, my stepfather symbolized a father figure and a means out of the chaos that was China. My mother, who was without a country at the time, was able to acquire proper immigration papers through the use of my stepfather's solid Russian credentials and passport. At age four, I was adopted by him, and I became, in 1949, Marianne Tmiro Chestohin.

Chapter 5

━━━━ ✿ ━━━━

My First Two Moments of Consciousness

My Parents' Separation in Shanghai

I am lying on a large bed in a small room. The light is on and I hear some strong sounds. I see my mother first and then my father in a doorway. He is trying to embrace her, but she is pushing him away. (I am in my grandfather's house at the approximate age of eighteen months.)

In my next memory, I am standing in a large white crib, crying for my mother. She does not answer. The room is filled with a gray light and I look through some paneled glass doors that open to the outside. There is a small garden pond, but nothing more. (My mother is staying here with a friend and searching for a job.)

Chapter 6

China: Early Years

My mother lived in an apartment at the top floor of a four-story building that was referred to as the "Penthouse" because it had a huge terrace. There, I remember a swing-set, some potted plants, and sightings of a black cat.

Inside was a bedroom, living room, bathroom, and kitchen. I don't remember the furnishings, except for two green stuffed chairs that were put together to make a bed for my brother during his occasional visits. I suppose I slept on the sofa. On the armchair was a knitted green crocodile—a familiar object that became my friend during countless hours of play.

The stairwell was off the living room door; it had a large window toward the bottom landing that shed a grayish light. The stone stairs with iron railings and wood banister led to a door that opened into a large courtyard surrounded by tall and short buildings. To go to the main street, one would walk across the courtyard and through an archway directly across from our building where a wooden booth was occupied by a watchman.

I'm sure there was a kitchen table and a food cabinet or icebox. On one occasion, perhaps when I was home from the boarding school, I stole a carrot and ran to the terrace. When my mother spotted me eating the carrot, she comforted me, saying, "It's okay, *pupperly* ("little doll" in German); you can always take anything you want to eat. Carrots are good for you." Since that time, I never hesitated to help myself and my mother always furnished me with plenty of treats: chocolates, sugarcoated peanuts, and hazelnut cookies, which I found in my drawer to take to boarding school (in Brazil).

An *ama* (a type of nanny) was taking care of me while my mother was at work. We were in the kitchen, and the *ama* might have been seated on a stool; I beat at her chest, demanding she make me rice and fish. I believe she obliged as I still remember the good taste of the food. I could speak Mandarin Chinese fluently, which regrettably I have since forgotten. Initially, my mother spoke German with me and then English, and occasionally, switched back to German.

Before the boarding school experience, I went to a neighborhood kindergarten for a few days, but I only remember one day. I was seated around a large dark adult-size table surrounded by other children. We had jars of paste, paper, and scissors, and we were all busy cutting and gluing paper. I was totally absorbed and had a wonderful time. I think my love for making things began there, but it was short-lived.

I remember one time my brother Goggeli was carried down the four flights of stairs by a couple of men. It was late at night and I felt very sorry for him. I heard he had an earache and had to be taken to the hospital. The next day, I feigned an earache with great persistence until my mother had no alternative but to take me to the doctor, who promptly said I was fine.

One evening, I saw a couple of men carrying barrels of hot water up the semi-lit stairwell and dumping the water in the bathtub. My brother was visiting for the weekend and my mother made sure we got a good scrub-down bath. We both enjoyed the wet extravaganza.

Once I was awakened in the middle of the night by my mother. She swooped me in her arms and carried me to the window, saying, "Come; see the fire." In the distance, I saw a raging fire; the flames were all engulfing; it was an exciting spectacle, but I did not know its significance. Later through this same window, I saw the marching of troops. The Communist Regime had occupied Shanghai. It was May, 1949.

My mother could not keep me at home; she needed to have me cared for while she worked in the city as a secretary and translator, so she placed me in a boarding school run by Germans in an area called Hungqiao in the city's outskirts, near the current airport. I must have been four at the time. She had told me she would come and visit me on horseback as she went riding nearby with my stepfather, but she never came.

I remember swinging, quite alone, in the playground and feeling worried because I had wet my pants. I also remember being stung by a bee near the building's side entrance where there were some bushes and being carried inside by a strange lady.

Another memory I have is of Christmas Eve when I was told by the ladies that Saint Nicholas was coming in the morning to drop off a red bag at the foot of the bed. We slept in a large dormitory, and I was filled with expectations. I saw St. Nick at the foot of my bed with his red bag early in the morning, and I remember retrieving something, but I was more fascinated by this kind, goodly character whom I had never seen before than by the gift itself.

I was in the Hungqiao boarding school when a typhoon hit Shanghai. I remember people talking about the coming storm, but I had no idea what it was, so I was filled with curiosity. When I was able to go outside, I saw overturned fences and some ice on the ground, which blended in my mind with the blocks of ice which had been predicted, but I didn't know where they came from.

I have memories of watching some Turkish people through a fence adjacent to the boarding school. They appeared to be cooking something outdoors; the food scent was not quite familiar. I believe I had heard from the other children in the boarding school that the Turks were strange and different, so I wondered whom they really were and why they dressed differently.

I did not like to be separated from my mother at this tender age, but neither did I put up much of a fight. I did not know what normal life was, so I accepted the inevitable. Once, however, I staged a protest. I was home from the boarding school and delighted to be once more in a familiar and safe place. One morning, I woke up eager to see my mother. She was not there; only the maid was with me. In the afternoon, I heard my mother coming up the stairs. I ran to the door to greet her. But when she opened the door and I saw her, I turned my back and stomped away, relinquishing the embrace. I imagine these demonstrations of temper must have hurt her, for she was trying her best to support us during those hard times.

As mentioned earlier by my mother in her memoir, she hired a rickshaw and we went toward the direction of Hung Qiao, where I went to boarding school shortly after the Communist takeover of 1949. I remember the trip and feeling excited to be with my mother in the rickshaw when we were stopped by the soldiers who had formed a barricade. This was the first time I bore witness to my mother's courage in the face of civil difficulties. They did not let us go through that day, and I was so glad to return home with my mother instead of going to the boarding school. I did return thereafter, but I do not remember the details.

I loved being home. I delighted in my mother playing hide-and-seek with me, and we shrieked with joy when I found her or she found me hidden behind a chair or sofa. Sometimes, I would sit on her lap and she would tell me fairy tales such as Little Red Riding Hood or the Seven Kids and the Wolf. She would dramatize the stories, pretending to be the mother, the grandmother, or the wolf, and I loved it.

We also went downtown a few times. My mother was a very beautiful and elegant lady who was fond of the European styles. I remember going with her into fashionable shops, especially a lady's hat shop. I became fascinated with the red, green, and black hats displayed on individual stands. We walked along the street like it was a holiday. Not far from downtown, we went into a Catholic Church. I remember my mother bowing and kneeling in a pew. I saw candles flickering in the distance and altar boys dressed in white robes. It gave me a sense of the mysterious as a haze of incense hung in the air.

One weekend, my mother had some guests in the apartment while I played at the courtyard's entrance. I looked out and saw a bearded robed man dismount a bicycle. My heart pounded and I ran upstairs as quickly as I could, and almost without breath, I burst through the door and exclaimed, "Mommy, Mommy, I saw Jesus Christ on a bicycle!" The guests and my mother had a good laugh, but this did not shatter my conviction.

I remember a few other outings. My mother had been invited to a country club, so she took my brother and me to swim in the pool. We were having an uproarious good time. I watched my brother jump into my mother's arms in the deep end. My mother kept encouraging me to jump, "Come, Marianchen! See, Goggi jumps!" But

I had no courage; I was afraid and ended up tugging at the wall around the pool.

I have a vague recollection of visiting my grandfather. My mother must have taken me there. It seems he was somewhat bald with a rounded head, and I remember him gazing at me. Later, I saw a picture of him and he wore something of a crew cut. Family members have told me that he was fond of me and that he kept a family picture in the living room that included my mother and myself. He was a powerful family patriarch, and much later, I found out that he had ordered that my father keep my brother and that my mother keep and raise me after the divorce in 1946.

The best of times was when my brother came over. He would run up the stairs calling, "Mariaha! Mariaha!" We would go to the terrace and he would push me as high as he could on the swing. We would sail paper boats in a basin or engage in making a kite with paper, bamboo, and rice paste. Sometimes, we would go to the courtyard and play conductor. He would climb onto a long bamboo stick and I would lead him all around, pretending we were on a bus.

Behind the buildings adjacent to our apartment house were some poorer dwellings. My brother and I went there to play in an old abandoned automobile. As we approached one day, some tough kids bullied my brother and a fight broke out. I thought I was very strong and I could save my brother, so I got into the middle of the rolls and punches. Needless to say, I got a good beating and began to holler. My brother, who felt he should have protected his younger sister, took me home with great concern and explained to my mother in an excited fashion what had happened. She consoled us and dissipated our fright and tears.

In May 1949, my mother had a birthday party for my brother. He had turned seven and I was four-and-a-half. It was a sunny day, and children and festivities filled the apartment. I believe we were around a table on the terrace, and I wanted to try some of the toys my brother had received. I spotted a toy cannon that worked with a roll of paper explosives. I tried to snap one in the shutter, but it caught my finger and I went running to my mother with a blood blister.

Another time, we went to the open street market nearby. It was a warm and bright day, and it felt wonderful to walk freely with my brother and watch the people milling about and occupied in the stands with a myriad of things. He bought me a long piece of sugarcane that I thoroughly enjoyed. I held the cool wet cane with a firm grip and sucked on its sweet juice; it was heaven. On the way back, we had to pass through the archway and in front of the watchman's booth. I was terrified to pass in front of this booth because I thought the man inside was mean and would do us harm. I hid behind the sentinel's booth, afraid to budge. My brother came over and took my hand and carried me through bravely. Nothing terrible happened, and my trust in my brother increased a hundredfold.

Also in this main thoroughfare in front of my mother's apartment house, I witnessed the celebration of Chinese New Year. The long colorful paper dragons with their menacing heads and jaws would undulate their bodies at the beat of loud drums and cymbals. The display of color and light fascinated me. I don't think I realized walking men moved the dragons; they had a force of their own, more like mythical figures I did not understand.

I saw my father less frequently. On one occasion when I was walking down the street with him, I saw a child pushed in a stroller. I turned to him and said, "Daddy, give me a stroller; I want to be pushed like him." He turned to me and said, "Okay." Little did I know about the financial difficulties and the rampant inflation occurring in China at that time. My father wanted to do his best, but I never got a stroller.

Once, my father brought my brother to spend the night. I saw him try to give my mother a wad of paper money, but she refused. My mother put the two armchairs together and covered them with a sheet for the two of us to sleep on. My brother was picking on one of his sores and some blood got on the sheet. My father got angry and reprimanded him. I remember defending my brother and getting a slap. The tension of my mother's rejection and my insolence got the better of him. I don't remember him ever striking me again.

One weekend, my father took my brother and me to the zoo. We boarded a bus and I kept sticking my arms out the window. My father warned me not to do that, and I instantly obeyed. I had great respect for my father. At the zoo, while being carried piggyback style on my father's shoulders, I saw monkeys behind iron grates. I was still on my father's shoulders in the busy street before we went home.

Only once do I remember staying at my father's house. It was a gray house nestled between some buildings with an open courtyard in front. It was tall, spacious, and had very few pieces of furniture. My father did not work too far from the house, so my brother and I decided to visit him at his office. I remember climbing a tall flight of stairs, each step measuring half the length of my body, and thinking how happy my father would be to see us. When we got to the top, my father was there, and he was annoyed. He quickly ushered us away. At the time, I did not understand why he didn't receive us with more kindness, especially after our effort at climbing the stairs. However, the world of adults and the world of children do not always mesh. He had to work at the engineering office and we had to play.

While staying with my father, my brother took me to his school. I was placed in the first grade, a small classroom with windows near the ceiling. The teacher was enthusiastic and welcoming. When I learned to write a Chinese character on the blackboard, I was very proud of myself. At the end of class, no one was outside the door to take me home so I began to cry. I waited by the cement steps outside the classroom that faced the playground. My brother, accustomed to walking home alone, had forgotten me. After a great while, he and an *ama* showed up and took me home.

One day, my father sent a barber with a barber's case to the house. The barber propped me up on a chair, and after washing my long hair, proceeded to cut it. When I returned to my mother's apartment, she was very surprised to see me with a short haircut and did not like it. I, on the other hand, loved it. I was also very enthusiastic about what I had learned in school and began to show my dad how I could write Chinese characters. Before he left, he watched me patiently draw a square with a cross inside. I was convinced I could write Chinese.

Aside from the times mentioned above, I saw my father very little. I took everything as a natural occurrence, for I did not know what life should really be like.

I wasn't especially unhappy. My mother loved me and so did my father and brother. I did, however, see my brother and father less frequently than I would have liked, and that created in me a tremendous longing that has extended itself into my whole life. I have jotted down almost everything I can remember about my last year in Shanghai because it is the only tangible aspect of my early life that gives me a sense of roots and belonging.

Chapter 7

=== ✿ ===

Shanghai Departure

Our childhood joys were soon marred by an intruder: my stepfather. Prince Valerian Tmiro Khan Chestohin was a thin man of normal stature, with deep set dark eyes, a mustache, thinning gray hair, inscrutable perked lips set above a triangular chin, and scarred cheeks from being pierced by a bullet during the Bolshevik Revolution while he was fighting as a captain in the Czar's cavalry.

I called my stepfather "Uncle" and never found myself able to call him "Father." My brother and I were deadly afraid of him. He was a man twenty years older than my mother and had a chronic cough. When we heard him come up the apartment building's stairs, we would freeze and hide. Once I remember quickly gathering our paper boats and a basin of water and hiding. Fortunately for me, I did not see my stepfather all that much. I was either at the boarding school or he was away.

I met my stepfather's children at the apartment once. They were young adults. Helen was about seventeen and Peter about twenty. They were seated in chairs, statuesque style, and were very quiet and somber. It was a farewell. They were moving to Australia, like many other foreign refugees in China at the time.

Preparations were also being made for us to emigrate from China to Brazil. Through a United Nations charter, a ship would be provided. It was bound first for Europe, and then another would take us across the Atlantic to Brazil, one of the nations besides Australia that was prepared to receive refugees from Communist China. Documents had to be prepared for our departure. At this time, my stepfather adopted me officially, and I lost the family name Wang, exchanging it for the surname of Tmiro Chestohin. My mother was without a country, having lost her German citizenship by marrying my father, and her Chinese citizenship by divorcing him. My mother and I had no alternative but to travel under my stepfather's Russian passport and credentials.

My mother recounts that the process of getting the proper documents to satisfy the Chinese and international officials was very difficult, due to the chaotic but strict state of the Chinese Communist Government, and also, because my stepfather had lost some essential papers. While at an official office crafting a new document, my mother grabbed a couple of passersby in the street to witness the signatures. I remember going with my stepfather to a photo studio for passport pictures. He was especially nice to me that day, holding my hand amicably while we strolled down the street. Perhaps it was a gesture to impress my mother who had just recently married him; I don't know. Strangely, I felt protected by this tall adult and had no sense of fear during this outing, something I could not say about him much of the time.

On our terrace were huge trunks for my mother to fill with our belongings. I loved to play hide-and-seek in them. I was amazed that my whole body could fit so easily in them. My stepfather, as a joke, once locked me in one of the trunks for a short while. I was terrified and glad when he let me out. It was the beginning of his sadistic pleasures.

I was quite happy with the prospect of our journey. I knew we were going by ship to another world, not one made of earth and people, but a magical world that was going to be fantastic. The day before our departure, I went around the neighborhood bidding the neighbors a boastful farewell. I was going to another world. They all looked at me with quiet wonder.

In late October, 1949, the Wooster Victory was docked on the Huang Pu River, awaiting our arrival. Early in the morning of our departure, my father and brother arrived at the courtyard of my mother's apartment house in a dark green van to take us to the Shanghai port. I don't remember the luggage. I think the trunks might have been sent ahead of time. I sat in the front seat on my father's lap, not very much aware of the moment's significance. I could not foresee that beyond that day, we would not see each other again for thirty-two years. The van sped through Shanghai's streets, propelling us toward the inevitable. We traveled in silence. The gray of the morning gave way to patches of sunshine. We were ushered into a huge covered area where scores of refugees of various ethnic backgrounds stood alongside their bundles, awaiting the call to board the ship. A certain headdress worn by a man nearby intrigued me—he might have been a Sikh. I believe my father and brother waited with us, but I don't remember interacting with them; I just had a feeling of protection from being close to my family. Then the crowd began to move and we were allowed to board the ship. It must have been late in the afternoon, for the sun no longer shone. I went up the iron stairs, well aware that my father and brother did not follow us. We stood by the ship's railing to wave to the crowd of onlookers. My mother called to my father, indicating that she had forgotten the thermos. As the ship was ready to push away from the pier, I saw my father standing tall, but very serious, and my brother on his left, with his head hung low. He would not see his mother for another thirty-four years. My mother told me that in those last moments, my father shoved a handgun into her hand for our protection, but she later threw it into the sea.

Chapter 8

— ✿ —

Journey at Sea

We were at sea, about to begin anew elsewhere. When I was an adult, my mother told me that when the ship had pulled away from the Chinese shore, a sense of relief had overcome her. She had been immersed in the struggle of divorce, of making a living in a country torn by the Sino-Japanese war as well as the Civil War between the Nationalists and the Communists. The country's economy and social system were in chaos; she saw misery and suffering among all classes, so she was glad to escape. If my mother had a salient quality, it was her courage to make order and function out of seemingly nothing. She had packed away some Chinese scrolls and porcelain figures, which would come in handy to provide for us during the journey.

The experience aboard the Wooster Victory was great fun for me. I met a great many Russian children, and we played all day on deck, which afforded me an elementary knowledge of Russian. The adults had their own entertainment, quite apart from the children. The men and women's quarters were separated, and I slept on the lower bunk while my mother slept above me. Once, my mother noticed I was playing with a stuffed monkey near my bunk. She said, "Where did you pick this up?" By the tone of her voice, I realized I had done something wrong, so I said quickly, "I will 'pick' it back." Due to the Shanghai influence and the recent marriage to my Russian stepfather, my mother mainly spoke English with me, as it was the only language in common among us. German was left in the background of my infant years or when my mother was really mad at me. And from here on, I never spoke Mandarin Chinese, which I had known quite well.

On November 15, 1949, I turned five. I remember a small birthday party for me aboard the ship. The children sat around a table on wooden benches, and there was a cake, laughter, and fun, all engineered by my mother; I can still see her beautiful smiling face above the children's heads. And I remember other festive moments in the days to come. The captain organized relay games. The children were separated into teams, and I ran in the sack and spoon run, eager to win, although I did not. However, I excelled in one game: jam eating. The children were lined up before bowls filled with jam, and at the sound to begin, I buried my face in the jam and finished first. Still with my nose and face covered with jam from ear-to-ear, the captain lifted me up on his shoulders above the crowd and gave me my prize, which I don't remember, but from that day on, I liked the captain and savored the recognition.

We had traversed the South China Sea and cruised a long time across the Indian Ocean before reaching our first stop in Cape Town, South Africa. It was a bright sunny day, and I saw men in light suits and hard hats hanging around the plank, giving or relaying orders. We were only there to refuel and restock, so our stay was short. I do not remember leaving the ship. We then headed up the Atlantic Ocean along the African Coast and stopped at Las Palmas, one of the Canary Islands. As we disembarked, I saw many vendors on the pier and my eyes were drawn to a beautiful Spanish doll I could not resist. I ran to my mother and implored her to buy me this doll. When I saw that she might refuse, I cried out loud, "Mommy, I beg to God, please give me this dolly." She capitulated before such a request and bought me this beautiful slender doll with combs in her dark hair and a printed skirt, even though her funds were very limited.

Proudly, I carried the doll on deck and showed the children the beautiful gift I had received. Some were happy for me, and we played dolls in an outside corner of the ship. However, some boys were jealous and tried to take the doll from me. They pulled on one arm while I held onto the other, and before long, the arms came apart and the doll was broken. The boys abandoned the idea of appropriating my doll and scurried away with some delight over their mischief. With the broken pieces in my hand, I ran to my mother. She tried to connect the rubber bands that connected the arms, but I don't think she was successful since I do not remember playing with this doll again.

The ship then passed through the Strait of Gibraltar and entered the Mediterranean, making its way to our final destination of Naples, Italy. We arrived there at the end of 1949 and stayed for six weeks. All passengers disembarked and were taken to special refugee headquarters sponsored by the United Nations. These were warehouse buildings with cement floors, outfitted with many rows of bunk beds. My mother took one look at the place and decided she did not want to stay there. Armed with some Chinese porcelains and scrolls, she headed for downtown Naples where she registered us in an old hotel, which was affordable and comfortable. I remember the hotel had wide stairs rising out of the lobby, very tall ceilings, and a restaurant on the side serviced by men in suits and ties, and some sported mustaches. My stepfather was not yet in my sphere of awareness, although I heard later that he and my mother went to a restaurant where my stepfather choked on a chicken bone and had to be hauled to the emergency hospital and nearly died, costing my mother more money and worries. I too accompanied my mother on trips to the city. Once she bought me a red helium balloon. As we walked along the street, my eyes were drawn to the sky by that tall balloon, and I could also take in all the buildings and the occasional palm tree. When we got to the hotel, I was somewhat careless and let go of the balloon's string; my balloon floated to the top of the lobby's ceiling, and I cried, thinking it was lost for good. One of the waiters in uniform and mustache climbed the stairs, and with a pole, he retrieved my balloon. I was so happy and touched by this man's kindness. I also remember eating spaghetti at the hotel restaurant and being fascinated by its long strands. One detached memory is going in a small boat toward a larger vessel where my mother made a social visit to an acquaintance and appeared to enjoy herself. What stayed with me was the effort of climbing the boat's ladder from the dinghy in the middle of the water.

Our stay in Naples soon came to an end. Papers had been drawn by the United Nations Charter to give us the "go ahead" for our trip to Brazil. My mother received a visa for Brazil in the Brazilian Consulate in Naples in January of 1950. We boarded a train for Genoa, where a ship was waiting to take us to Rio de Janeiro, Brazil. En route, the train stopped at a station and we were able to walk outside. I remember walking by the tracks and touching the snow and being amazed, as I had never seen snow before. Then, we had to take an elevator to reach the intended platform, for this train station was built on the side of a cliff. The Genoa Port was not too far away, and before long, we were at the narrow pier trying to find our ship. We ended up boarding the wrong ship, but we were quickly ushered out. In the confusion, our thermos bottle from China was broken. Finally, we boarded the right ship. It was more crowded and less pleasant than the Wooster Victory.

I have less fond memories during this last leg of our journey to Brazil. We were in the Atlantic in the high seas, and the ship was tossing to and fro, weathering a storm. Most of the passengers became sick and were running toward the deck's railing to vomit. My mother was deathly sick. But the seas did eventually calm, and before long, we were crossing the equator. A ritual celebration was performed during this time. A king and queen rose miraculously out of the sea and took their place on thrones by the ship's small swimming pool. I was watching the festivities from an inconspicuous corner, filled with fear and reluctant to meet this queen and king, for I saw how they were throwing people in the pool. I saw too, that they were giving people special breads, which were supposed to make them rich and famous. Someone came to the hallway where I was standing and encouraged me to take a bite of the "sacred" bread. Immediately when I took a bite from this bread, my tongue began to burn, and I cried uncontrollably. The bread was filled with hot pepper and was suppose to test your audacity and bravery. Needless to say, I had failed, being only five years old and not able to understand adult jokes.

Three months had already passed since we had left Shanghai, and now we were fast approaching Brazil's shores. We entered Rio de Janeiro's Guanabara Bay, at night. In my mother's personal papers, I found the arrival documents that stated we entered Rio on February 16, 1950, and that the ship's name had been Campana, a version of my later married name, a strange coincidence. Once we entered Rio's port and had docked, my mother asked the captain whether we could spend the night onboard and venture out in the morning. When he consented, we spent our last night on the ship, while anticipating the future.

Part II

Brazil

Chapter 1

The First Three Months in Rio

On a sunny morning, we stepped for the first time onto Rio's pier. I was disappointed. I had imagined our destination to be a make believe world, and yet curiously, everything seemed the same: men, buildings, and cars. My mother took a hotel room in downtown Rio in an area called Gloria. Our arrival coincided with the Carnival weekend, when the population dresses in costumes and en masse celebrates the Brazilian Mardi Gras. Businesses close for four days before Ash Wednesday and revelers flock to the streets, dancing in parades and ballrooms and generally having a good time. On our first Sunday afternoon in Rio, to escape the summer heat, my mother took me for a walk in the park outside our hotel where the trees were huge and the roots stuck out of the ground like snakes. As we walked, a man in a costume and mask stuck his long red tongue out at me. I quickly hid behind my mother's skirt, petrified. It was an exciting time to be in Rio, but quite incomprehensible for me.

Our life at this point was very tentative. My mother was running out of money and could hardly buy us food. We survived on milk and yogurt for many weeks. One day, my stepfather, mother, and I went out to the local butiquim (neighborhood restaurant) in an inner city street for our ration of yogurt. While my mother stayed behind to pay the bill, my stepfather, in what I thought was a generous gesture, invited me to go with him. We walked to the end of the street, and there he left me. I quickly caught on that he wanted to lose me, and with tears in my eyes, I ran back to my mother outside the restaurant. I do not know whether she knew about his evil intent, and I was too young to express my fears to her.

When Easter came, we were still in the hotel. My mother bought some chocolate eggs and hid them about the room to mark the occasion. I found one in a tall boot and was very happy. However, my mother could not continue to entertain me for long. She needed to find a job and a place for us to live. She thought the best solution would be to put me in another kindergarten boarding school. She found one in the mountains behind the city in a region called Santa Teresa. I remember riding there in a streetcar with its tracks partially suspended over the city's rooftops and seeing houses and streets below. I sat snugly on the wooden bench near my mother, in my red coat, fearful I would fall, for the only thing separating us from the precipice below was a wire mesh along the tracks. The train meandered through the mountains, and soon, we were in front of a lovely house converted into a kindergarten. It had stone steps leading to a porch and a large garden surrounded by stonewalls. Here, I was to be imprisoned for a while.

I don't think I ever stopped crying from the moment I arrived at the boarding school. Everyone was a stranger to me: the big lady who put me on the tricycle on the porch to stop my tears, the children with whom I played "Ring Around the Rosy." Everything familiar had been taken away. The attendants tried to do everything to appease me, but it was in vain. I would not eat, so a woman sat me on her lap and spooned big portions of food into my mouth. They put us to sleep early in the evening. I was lying in the top bunk while most of the children had already fallen asleep. Dusk's light was filtering through the window, and I had an urge to pray. It was the first time I consciously petitioned God. I said, "Dear God, please bring my mommy tonight or tomorrow morning, but I prefer tonight." To my surprise, the next day, while I was given a bath in the same water in which other children were bathed, my mother arrived to take me home to the hotel.

I was much happier in the hotel, even though my mother was not always there. I developed a kinship to the servant class there that persists to this day. Because the hotel was not an institution or a boarding school, I had no strict structure to follow, so there I found freedom and enjoyment. I followed the bellboys on their errands, moving large white wicker chairs from one place to another, climbing wide stairs, and quickly learning the Portuguese language from them because they welcomed me in their midst as their mascot.

It was around this time that my mother found a job as a bilingual secretary in an international firm. She was also interested in an ad in the paper for the lease of an equestrian riding school, which would provide a job for my stepfather as a riding instructor, and a place for us to live. Seeing a golden opportunity, she immediately responded to the ad.

On a weekend, together with some other people, we were driven to the riding school, a forty-minute ride from Rio's center. It was located on the outskirts, outside the business district and beyond the skyscrapers, and also beyond the popular beaches of Copacabana, Ipanema, and Leblon. After traversing the city, we had to take the road cut into the granite mountain where it met the sea. On one side could be seen the ocean endlessly expanding, and on the other side, a towering wall of granite, softened by some vegetation and an inhabitant or two along the way. Mountain and sea were part of one another for a long stretch; then the road moved away from the sea and cut across a small valley where lovely houses were built along the mountain's crest. Also in this valley, called Gavea/Sao Conrado, was the American golf course with its manicured lawns and large clubhouse. The riding school was across from the golf course, and we had a view of the mountain, which rose out of its lawns. Beautiful flamboyant trees lined the road leading to the riding school, and shortly thereafter, the tall granite mountain, Pedra da Gavea, touched the sea once more. Behind the riding school was the white sand beach of Sao Conrado, nestled between the granite mountain road and the rocks and caves at the foot of Pedra da Gavea, which was so much a part of my childhood.

That day, several black 1950 Chevrolets were parked in front of the riding school. In my haste to take another car ride, I entered the wrong car. A lady quickly pointed out my mistake. Embarrassed, I slid out and went in search of my mother. Immediately, I found her and we were on our way back to town. I believe the riding school's owner had arranged for this caravan to view the property. I do not know whether it was because my mother had acquired a job, had some Chinese artifacts, or whether the owner was impressed by my stepfather's credentials as a Russian prince and captain in the Russian Imperial Army's cavalry, but needless to say, my mother and stepfather were granted the lease. We moved to the riding school soon after.

Chapter 2

Chapter 2

Beginning at the Riding School

All was not so idyllic for me at the riding school. Although, it certainly was a lovely two-story stucco house with ivy growing on the outside walls and an archway through the center, which led to the grounds and the stables behind. On each side was a separate garden with its own gate, where pink oleanders grew freely. At the archway was a short, green, wooden gate trimmed with brass, which allowed for the reading of *Escola de Equitacao* (Riding School) on a stucco rafter in the center.

At first, we lived in the riding school's lower level, in one of the guest rooms. The people who had leased the riding school prior to us were still living upstairs. One night, I was fast asleep when my mother woke me up in a hurried manner, put on my red coat over my pajamas, and said, "Let us go from here!" She'd had a fight with my stepfather and had decided to leave. She wanted to make a phone call in the office across from our room, for a taxi I suppose, but my stepfather blocked the way. I could see his implacable expression and his immovable arms stretched out across the doorway, impeding my mother's escape. She ultimately desisted and I went back to sleep.

Shortly after our arrival, the people upstairs began to take their leave. A heated exchange of hostilities took place between my stepfather, mother, and them because they were being displaced, and taking more than they should. When they left, we moved to the apartment upstairs and life began to take on a more routine appearance, except for my stepfather's abuse. From then on, I became the object of my stepfather's pranks and malice.

My mother would wake up early and catch two buses to work downtown while I was left behind with my stepfather, who took care of the riding school's affairs, including the care of several boarded horses left by the previous manager. From the start, he was bent upon tormenting me. Once, because I liked sugar, he made me eat a whole glass of it, enjoying his sadistic act. I can still see myself seated at a table, staring at the full glass of sugar I had to ingest under his watchful, malicious eyes. Another morning, when my mother had gone to work and I was still in bed, he came near with a tablespoon of pepper that he made me eat, and then he ordered me to masturbate myself while he paraded back and forth, nude from the waist down, watching me. I pretended to please myself. When my mother came home, I believe I told her most of what had occurred, but I'm not sure. I was around six at that time so it is hard to remember. I know my mother was aware of his malice toward me, however the worst incidents occurred when she wasn't around and I was at his mercy. Surprisingly, I felt brave when I was with my mother, and I would accuse him even in his presence. He would grin and she would be enraged. On one such occasion, I saw her throw a hot cup of coffee in his face, something that pleased me and made me feel vindicated. I would have demanded she leave him, but I was too young, so I accepted what occurred as the inevitable. The impact of the horrendous abuse, which would continue, did not have an immediate disabling effect. It did, however, play havoc in my adolescent and later years. For now, I had an indomitable spirit, nourished by my mother's love. Of course, I no longer could stay home, so my mother began looking immediately for an appropriate boarding school.

Around this time, my mother heard of a convent school run by Dominican nuns in Petropolis. I remember the bright sunny morning when my mother was standing with me on the granite flagstones in front of our riding school, waiting for the bus to take me to the boarding school. My mother turned to me and said somberly, "Marianchen, your father died." Death was incomprehensible to me, but I knew he was no longer on earth and had gone somewhere God and the angels lived. I turned to her with a single tear rolling down my cheeks and asked, "Is he in Heaven?" She answered, "Yes, he is." She did not say much more, and we were both lost in our thoughts during the trip.

We took the first bus down to the city and another downtown to the main bus terminal. There we boarded the tour bus to Petropolis, a fashionable resort town in the mountains, two hours from downtown Rio. We rode this bus for a very long time, but I could not see much since the window was above my head. Finally, we arrived at the school where a nun in a black and white habit ushered us into a parlor and closed the glass pane door. I remember it being very quiet while the nun spoke to my mother very politely. After speaking with the mother superior, we left, and I got news in the interim that I had not been accepted. I was very car sick down the mountain on the way back. My mother had to ask the bus driver to stop the bus so I could vomit on the roadside. When we arrived home in the dark, I only had thoughts of my father being in Heaven. I asked my mother as she tucked me in, "Are there bicycles in Heaven?" She answered positively. Then I went to sleep, wanting to be in Heaven with my dad, and glad that there, I could ride bicycles.

My father's death was a lie. I did not discover the truth until years later. My mother and I never discussed this lie, but I surmise she told it to me then because she had been divorced from my father, and I was about to enter a Catholic school; Catholics forbade divorce, so my chances of entering the school would be diminished. As it was, I did not get in, but not knowing differently, from then on, I told everyone my father had died.

Chapter 3

Protestant School

Afew English ladies came riding at our riding school. One of them, Mrs. Flanagan, who had a dachshund, rented the lower room from us. She took to me and I took to her dog, resulting in many lovely photos at the time. I believe she and her friends suggested that my mother place me in the Protestant School *Joao Batista* (John the Baptist). My mother accepted the suggestion gladly, especially since the ladies would help her with my wardrobe and registration. The school was on the north side of town at the foot of a mountain and far from the sea, in a borough of Rio called Tijuca. After underwear, blankets, and a uniform were purchased, I was shipped off to this school, and picked up on occasional weekends and holidays to visit home. Just before entering, however, I saw my first movie at the invitation of one of these sweet ladies. It was Disney's *Snow White and the Seven Dwarves*. On my way to the movie theater, I saw an advertisement for a movie on the life of Christ, which invoked in me a feeling of a sacred presence; I guess we were close to Easter of 1951.

The prospect of being separated from my mother brought me some sadness, but I adjusted to the new school's surroundings and routine quite well. By then, I spoke Portuguese fluently and had forgotten Chinese and the colloquial Russian I had picked up on the ship on our journey to Brazil. The dormitory at the John the Baptist school had rows of beds placed against walls that had open archways every so often to lead to the adjacent room. At night when I became lonely, I hugged my pillow and imagined it to be a very dear friend. During the first few weeks, I attended kindergarten in a large house separate from the main school. There, I learned to write the alphabet very quickly so the teachers thought I was ready for first grade since I was six. However, it was a mistake. I was placed in the room of a teacher who wore light frame glasses and had her gray hair in a bun. The learning process was no longer amusing to me, for we had to sit quietly in desks, all in a row, and listen to the teacher while she talked. I lost all interest and concentration and did not do well or learn much.

The study hall was supervised by a black lady who wore her black curly hair combed back, had crimson lipstick, and long fingernails painted in a lovely shade of red. Since I was the youngest child in the study hall, she would let me go out to the playground to play. She could not see how I could sit for two hours in the afternoon and study. I still feel a sense of gratitude toward this lady who understood a child's passion and need for play.

I had some good times in this school. On Sundays, we were taken to the church dressed in our best outfits. While the services were taking place in the main hall, we sat in the corner of the building for Sunday School. The teacher asked, "Who of you is Protestant? Raise your hand." Of course, I felt I was Protestant and raised my hand. At that time, I did not know about the divisions in Christianity, nor that Brazil was mainly a Catholic country and that my mother had been raised a Catholic by Catholic nuns in Bavaria. I felt perfectly at home in this setting as in any other.

One evening, we were taken to an auditorium to see a lovely puppet show. I sat in front and saw the lights illuminating the puppetry stage as well as the curtains that zipped back and forth, hiding the puppets' presence. Enacted were a few fables by a famous Brazilian writer, involving animals such as ants, crickets, and cicadas. The audience, composed mainly of children, laughed hard and were perfectly delighted with the puppets' antics.

On June 24, the Feast of Saint John the Baptist (for whom the school was named), we were taken to a roaring party in someone's backyard with a huge bonfire, many typical Brazilian homemade sweets, and much dancing and music. The yard was strung with lanterns and colorful paper flags. Holding hands, children began to dance around the fire, singing typical songs for the day. A spark from the fire flew onto my aqua coat and singed it; that gave me a small reason to worry, for I had been given the coat and a bonnet from home as part of my initial wardrobe.

Some of my less pleasant memories from 1951 were that I contracted pleurisy, an inflammation of the lungs' lining. I had to cough thick mucus and was quite embarrassed when I had no place to spit it out. I was grateful to the study hall lady who let me out to the grounds. I was very lethargic and was running a fever; it felt good to lie in the sun on the playground's benches. After my mother was called, she took me to the doctor for treatment. I was given a shot and then put on an electric bed where pads were put on my chest. The nurse would kindly warn me and then turn on the voltage dial, giving me an awful shock, together with some heat.

My mother took me back to the riding school to recover. The Russian doctor who treated me also operated on my stepfather who had tuberculosis and had one of his lungs removed. Dr. Guegorin came riding one weekend and my mother asked him to give me the usual streptomycin shot. I submitted myself bravely; however, he had a very bad needle and apologized repeatedly for not being able to insert the needle in one try, which gave me a sore rump.

While I stayed home during this illness, "Uncle" (my stepfather) was asked to administer some compresses on my chest. He had to heat this medicated putty that I recall had a smell of camphor and place it under my ribs on a washcloth. He skipped the washcloth and placed the hot matter directly on my skin. Needless to say, I jumped and screamed with pain. I would visit the doctor's office a few more times to undergo the warm shock treatment before I slowly recovered.

As was in my nature, I went exploring. My mother was home, but she gave me ample room to discover the neighborhood. One day, I went behind the stables to the paddock that opened to a fenced field. I opened the gate and was on the mud road that ran along the beach. I began walking far and found many vines and grasses growing in the crevasses of the sinewy mud that often had been washed by the sea. I began collecting flowers that I found along the way, and I ran back home delighted to have a bouquet for my mother, who scooped me in her arms, glad to see me well and happy.

When it was time for me to return to school at John the Baptist, my mother and I rode the bus there late on a Sunday. To my surprise, darkness began to envelop us when we were riding the bus toward the school. I had taken a nap that afternoon, so it seemed we were plunged into the night prematurely, and I felt very sad, for I did not want to be left alone once more. The school was situated near a business district, so my mother stopped at the bakery and bought me a can of cookies and some chocolates. Then we walked on the pavement toward the school, which was surrounded by a wrought iron fence that had a very somber and dark quality. The lady received me at the front room and whisked me away inside after I had said goodbye to my mother very reluctantly. That night, the young children were given warm milk in white enamel mugs and biscuits that softened the blow of separation for me.

Besides dorm students, the school also had a large body of daytime students who came well-dressed and well-prepared for class. I remember, when it was teacher's day in our classroom that I did not have a present to give the teacher. I watched the students hand the teacher wrapped presents and saw her smile in appreciation. I thought long and hard and was determined also to give her a present. I had a small bare plastic doll with movable arms and legs the size of a finger. I thought my teacher would be so happy to receive this doll. When I passed by her desk in the morning, I placed this doll on her desk. She was pleased, but not as ecstatic as I had thought she would be. She did not take much notice of the doll for the rest of the class, and I was disappointed, considering my sacrifice.

Before long, I made friends with a lively young girl my age, with lots of curls and freckles. One evening during recess, we lay on the cement near a gazebo, looking up at the stars. The sky was lit with flickering diamonds. As we watched the palpitating stars, we told each other funny jokes and laughed with abandon while deciphering the mysteries of space. I believe I made acquaintance with her shortly after I returned from home and was telling children that I knew how babies were brought into the world. Amused and laughing, the older children had me tell the story again and again to other children. Relishing the attention, I obliged and said to all who would hear, "The stork flies up in the sky with the baby in its beak and then comes through a window and puts the baby in the mother's tummy." This explanation was inevitably followed by much laughter from the older children who knew the truth of the matter.

At the beginning of December, summer vacation arrived. (In the Southern Hemisphere, the seasons are reversed.) I remember the day I was to return home that most of the children left before me and a handful of us waited to be picked up by our parents. There were no classes, so we spent the day in the front yard trying a variety of fruits from large trees along the front path and garden. It was then I became familiar with many tropical fruits and their tastes—the sourness of kumquats, the sweetness of mangoes, and the tartness of a variety of berries. While I was playing, I saw my mother through the iron-gate. My heart thumped with happiness. She had come to bring me home.

Chapter 4

==== ✿ ====

The Armazem and Stella Maris:

My First Year at Home

Next door to our riding school was a general store we called the *Armazem* ("General Store" in Portuguese). The family who ran it and the children whom I came to call the boys and girls from the Armazem, lived in the back of the store. I had made acquaintance with the two older girls in the family, Vera (nicknamed Nega) and Augusta (nicknamed Bisuca), who was my age, when they stood outside in their starched sailor uniforms and hat, waiting to take the bus to school. Later, I met their mother, Dona Linda, father Senhor Joao, and a host of younger siblings and an older brother named Paulo. They had eight children at that time, and almost every year, they added a new brother or sister until they eventually were twelve, not to include the maid and her child and a number of visiting relatives and friends. The store was the neighborhood hub, and I grew accustomed to running next door and inserting myself into their family. I told them I had come from China by ship. To them, China was as alien a place as the moon. One Sunday, the store was closed and their father was relaxing on the interior veranda, listening to a soccer game on the radio. He asked me, "Are you 'Vasco' or 'Flamengo'?" I replied, "I am Chinese," not realizing he was asking me for which team I was rooting. Of course, from that day, on I was Vasco, the family's team.

Above the store lived another family who had one daughter, older than us. The father worked as a waiter at the American golf course, so I hardly saw him. One day, the mother called me and said, "Can you arrange to have these vines that hang over your wall cut because they block the sunlight on my porch." I thought it was a very reasonable request since I could see the shadows on her porch. I approached the groom at our riding school and asked him to cut the vines. He did so, and in one afternoon, the vines' bare stalks were the only things on the wall between the neighbor and us. Upon learning of what had happened, my stepfather went into a rage. He began to yell obscenities at the neighbors and managed to show his anger with his broken Portuguese. I knew I was in trouble, but he did not blame me; perhaps the groom protected me by stating the neighbor had demanded the vines be trimmed. I remember a few buckets of water were thrown back and forth. After this event, not much was said between my stepfather and the neighbors, and he gained a reputation of being a mean old Scrooge.

The enjoyment Uncle received from frightening me did not cease. One day, I was in the archway that ran through the first floor of our house from the street to the front garden when I saw my stepfather with a pair of scissors in his hand. He proceeded to chase me, gesturing with the scissors that he was going to cut out my tongue. I ran as fast as I could out the front gate and around the corner to the alley beside the store that led to the storekeeper's house. I was crying, laughing, and shaking at the same time. I was met by Dona Linda, and I told her what had happened. She tried to calm me down with a glass of sugar water, a remedy she used to calm nerves. It worked, and it would not be the last time; I found solace with this family so many times when threatened by my stepfather.

On another occasion, I was still sleeping in bed when I heard some banging on the downstairs door that led to our upstairs quarters. My mother had gone to work and I was alone in the house. At first, I didn't pay much attention to the banging and continued to sleep. Later, I got dressed and was ready to go next door to play when I found that the door leading out had been nailed shut. This time I outwitted him. I called my next-door neighbors and asked them to bring a ladder, explaining the situation. Sebastiao, their servant, came promptly and propped the ladder on the front balcony. I descended in triumph. When my stepfather came back from the paddock to take the nails out, much to his surprise, his prey was gone.

On occasion, my mother kept a maid to take care of me and clean the house. Most of the maids did not last long, either because of our lack of money or other commitments. During the time I was in the Protestant boarding school, my mother had a white maid named Iracema, who had a daughter about my age. I do remember being home from the boarding school, eager to play with my dollhouse that a client from the riding school had left for me. My mother disappointed me by saying, "Schatzy, I gave it to Iracema's daughter." Needless to say, I became friends with Iracema's daughter, and that summer when I was home from school, Iracema took me to her house in the slum, named Rocinha, which today is a sprawling metropolis. We walked a distance along the main road, past the golf course, and toward a roundabout where one road climbed the mountain and the other went along the sea. Halfway up the mountain, and just past the serpentine curves, we veered off the narrow paved road onto a mud path that was smooth and well-packed and where wooden huts were stacked at either side. Soon Iracema took me into her *barracao* ("barracks" in Portuguese), also made of wood and with a pounded earth floor. There was but one room, but we sat outside near the door on benches made of planks. I remember a young man helped to serve us by putting a piece of *jaca* fruit ("jackfruit" as it is known in English), on another bench. I was familiar with this fruit since I had tasted it and seen poor women carrying it on their heads in a rolled up rag. It was a very large fruit, weighing up to twenty pounds, and inside it were hundreds of meaty white tongues bearing a slippery seed. When ripe, the fruit was very sweet and would render many days of food. It grew wild on large trees in the surrounding woods in the mountains. This particular jaca was of the butter type: soft, slippery, and sweet. Each person helped himself by retrieving one of the tongues and drinking some water from mugs made of empty cans, whose handles were hammered from their lids. I enjoyed this visit and was able to see the breathtaking view of the sea from this height.

By this time, Dona Linda considered me one of her daughters; one more or less didn't matter. The twins, Grande and Miuda (nicknames for Maria Celia and Celia Maria), were always rocking to and fro on the interior porch. Joaozinho, the little one, was most of the time in his wooden playpen naked, stepping in his mess that was washed out once or twice a day with a hose. Senhor Joao was always in the store attending to the customers. They sold all kinds of dry goods such as rice, black beans, and corn meal kept in bins at the back, as well as *chorizo* (dried sausage) and *carne seca* (salted meat). They also had potatoes, onions, margarine, *mortandela* (pork meat sausage), and an assortment of fresh breads brought by the baker each day. The children's favorite was the glass case that had typical Brazilian sweets made of sweet potatoes, pumpkin, and coconut. We also liked the soft drinks that came ice cold from the refrigerator such as Grapete, Crush, Coke, and lemonade, but these were seldom affordable to us. On the store's left side was a counter that served liquor or *cachaca* (a kind of clear Brazilian rum) to local patrons, mostly poor people from the slums who worked at the golf course as caddies, or servants for rich folks in the surrounding area. Some of them were fishermen or peddlers. At times, a brawl would start and Senhor Joao would run to the back and call the police. Once, I witnessed such a brawl as I was running toward their house in the back. One man threw a glass at his opponent, cutting him severely in the arm with the blood gushing out. Later, the same man who was hurt came back with a crowbar for revenge. Seldom were we allowed in front of the store. We always played in the back or on the side in the dirt path. We played house with old wooden crates and used real food in empty cans that Maria, the half-black cook and maid, would give us.

Maria was an integral part of the family. Once or twice, she tried to work for somebody else, but she always came back. The Armazem parents did not pay her anything, but they gave her free room and board. She had a small child whom she kept most of the time in the dispensary (the store's storage room) where she slept. This room had no sunlight, and as a result, this little girl grew to be very small and developed rickets. Maria was ashamed to bring her child out. I spoke with Maria sometimes in the kitchen and became aware of her need. I left some of my mother's old clothes by the outside steps that led to the apartment above the store. Later, Dona Linda, not quite happy with my donation, told me Maria used the clothes to pad the infant child. They named this child Ximbica, after a chicken character on the radio. Maria had one protégé in the family: the twin Maria Celia; however, she would not speak to some of the older children. This phenomenon puzzles me to this day. Maria was not married, but she had a clandestine boyfriend whom she met at night. By him, she also had another child whom she boarded with a woman who raised pigs and lived in the woods behind the golf course. On one occasion, I accompanied Maria to visit her daughter. We had to go into the golf course grounds and follow a path in the back. The lady lived in a modest wooden house with various rooms and the pigs roamed freely outside. The child, already seven, with dark long curly hair, appeared well-nourished and well-groomed.

One Sunday, my mother was away, visiting friends. I was at my friend Marlene's house, a half a block away, playing with neighbors, including the Armazem kids. We decided to race in the backyard. I took my shoes off and challenged Paulo, who took me on. We ran with all our might, and only at the finish line did I notice blood trickling down my foot. I had stepped on a sharp can and cut deeply the front of my left foot above the big toe. I only cried when I saw the blood, for I had not felt any pain. The family who lived in this house propped me up on a chair and washed the wound with peroxide. They also called the ambulance, which took two hours to arrive because we lived outside the business district. Marlene's sister's fiancé accompanied me in the ambulance. The sirens sounded all the way to Miguel Couto, the emergency hospital in Leblon. At the hospital, I was placed on a stainless steel table, and a friendly doctor proceeded to fix me up. He said he would have to wrap my eyes with gauze if I cried. I watched the whole procedure bravely: the shots and the stitching. Then the doctor wrapped my foot in gauze and told me I could walk on it if I wanted. Once I put my foot on the ground, it felt heavy, so I was afraid to burst the stitches. The gentleman who brought me in helped me walk to the bus stop and we arrived home after nightfall. My mother greeted me with great concern, and for the next few days, I was bedridden.

At first being stuck in bed was okay. My mother bought me an abacus, a child's flute, and an accordion, and I slept in her big bed while she was at work. But after a while, I became utterly bored and was determined to go to school. I put on some galoshes on a plain sunny day because I could not find my other shoes (my stepfather had hidden them). I boarded the local bus in front of my house and had heart palpitations when I had to pull the string at a bend flanked by rock walls to signal the driver to stop at Vidigal where my school was located. I arrived at my class a few hours late, but the teacher and students applauded when I walked in, which made me feel very welcomed and acknowledged for my efforts.

In 1952 for first grade, I went to Stella Maris School as a day student and did not return to the Protestant boarding school because I implored my mother to put me in the same school that the Armazem children attended. They went to Stella Maris School, about a twenty-minute ride along the coast on Niemeyer road and perched on the mountain overlooking the sea. Catholic nuns of the order, Daughters of Jesus, which had originated in Spain, ran it. So one Sunday, my mother dressed me up and led me to the school of my choice to be matriculated. We met with the mother prefect in the reception area, and this time, I was accepted. I would be placed in the first or second grade, depending on my achievement. I was glad because I would be a daytime student, taking the bus back and forth with my neighbor friends.

When the first day arrived, I went to school with Nega and Bisuca. I took my place in line with the first graders on the cement patio since I was not too confident about being with the second graders. We marched to class, and soon a nun, the second grade teacher, came to test me for second grade. She took me to the second grade classroom across the hall and asked me to write *boneca* ("doll" in Portuguese) on the blackboard. I went to the blackboard and wrote, *bone...* and could not go further. So I was taken back to first grade, much to my pleasure.

Our teacher, Madre ("mother" in Spanish) Diva, was excellent! She was the best teacher I had in grade school. Our lessons came in scrolls, not in books. Each week, she had a new scroll under her arm that developed the story of a family in different circumstances. The characters were hand-painted and the story was written in large enough letters for the whole class to see. Each week, we were given a copy of the story so we could cut out the words and place them in a small box. Then Madre Diva would come around and help us reconstruct the story and listen to our reading while the other children finished their lesson. It was an atmosphere of enjoyment and learning.

In first grade, I made friends with a little girl named Martha Lucia Gomes. We stood in line together because she was about my height, and we also sat next to each other in class and worked on our lessons together. Often, we would amuse ourselves while we were kneeling at our desks for beginning or end prayers by lifting our skirts over the seat and showing our underwear. We were able to laugh together, and she remained my friend till fourth grade when she was transferred to another school.

We arrived at school around 12:30 p.m. and left around 5:00 p.m. At the end of the school day, I descended the steep road to join the other children who lived in Sao Conrado, Gavea to wait for the bus. The children who lived in the city were taken back home by school bus, whereas we had to go home on our own. We felt a little like outcasts because the children and nuns who descended the ramp on Stella Maris school buses saw that we mingled with the poor people from the *favelas* (Rio slums) on the street and city buses. A *favela* named Vidigal was behind our school, and another large one in the mountain behind the valley where I lived, that I already mentioned, was named Rocinha. Most of the time, I had the two *cruzeiros* (the currency of that time) for bus fare, but on occasion, I would have to borrow it because I had spent my own on candy or just plain lost it. Somehow, I made it home each night, even though I was only seven. I would spend the evening with the Armazem children until my mother called me, "Marianne...!" when she arrived home from work.

Paulo and Nega were often amazed by how quickly I could memorize a lesson without much effort. First grade was a breeze for me because I enjoyed it and the lessons were relatively easy. On occasion, my absentmindedness caught up with me and I would forget my school bag, on the wall ledge in front of our riding school where we caught the bus, and show up at school empty-handed. Madre Diva would reprimand me in a joking way, remarking, "You must have eaten too much cheese and softened your brain to be so forgetful." On the whole, my first year at Stella Maris School was a happy one. I had a friend, I went to school with my neighbors who gave me a sense of belonging and companionship, and I was spared the loneliness of boarding school.

The galoshes incident soon repeated itself. My stepfather hid my new black patent leather shoes that went with my uniform. Because I had to wear galoshes, I was prevented from participating in a small skit for the mother provincial. As kind and understanding as Madre Diva was, she could not allow me on stage without the proper shoes. Also in May, the first graders carried basket of flowers to put at the altar for Mary, the Mother of God. I was sad because I had no basket and not even petals to throw at the feet of the statue. I began to realize that some children had more than I had.

I became quite accustomed to the school's routine. After a short recess at the time of arrival, we all lined up at the sound of a bell. We stood in line according to height at an arms' distance, with our hands folded together by our waists. Then we marched to the chapel to recite the rosary. At first, I mimicked the Hail Mary's and Our Father's, and I was quite amused with the singsong quality of the voices and the repetition. Madre Diva would then march us to the back building, where we would enter our classroom at the end of the hallway where the desks were smaller and painted green, giving the room a cheerful atmosphere. Sometimes to initiate the day, the mother superior, Madre Gloria, would speak through the P.A. system. For me, it was almost like hearing the voice of God. This segment was called, "The Voice of Truth." Along the way, we were indoctrinated with the life of Jesus and Mary and especially with anecdotes about the mother founder, Madre Candida Maria de Jesus. At three o'clock, we had a half-hour recess where the day students ate their *merenda* ("snack" in Portuguese) brought in lunchboxes, and the dorm students were given a piece of bread with *goiabada* (guava paste), a banana, and some Kool-Aid at the refectory door. At five o'clock, the bell rang and we marched out, some to waiting school buses, and others like me, to the street to await the city bus.

Chapter 5

Summer Days and Then School: 1953

Summer came around again. The days were long and hot, and I had ample amusement with the Armazem children. Next door to the riding school's paddock, behind the Armazem children's house, and very near the beach, was a small white house used by its owners as a summer home. Vani, a boy of eleven, was spending the summer at this house. We made friends with him very quickly and played some of the wildest games. Cowboy and Indians (in Portuguese the game was called *Bandido e Mocinho* or "Bandits and Gentlemen") involved climbing on the rooftop of our stable as well as the large fica trees on each side of the stables. I would hide on our house's second story ledge, so I seldom got tagged because none of the other children would dare go up there. Vani would imitate a horse's stampede by beating on his chest with his fists while he ran around the paddock. I liked him very much and he liked me. He always chose me to be on his side for games. I remember the boys built a cart from odds and ends, and to have a ride in this cart, we had to pay with cigarette paper we found in the street. American cigarette paper was the most valuable and Vani found some. To make it go further, he tore it in half and folded it a certain way so no one could detect, and he gave it to me so I had many extra rides. Vani was very protective and kind to me, and I considered him my boyfriend long after he returned to the city, never to come back again.

Christmas came in the summer, and my mother made sure I had a happy one. I went to the city with my mother to a children's Christmas party in a high rise in Copacabana, arranged by one of her friends. Once in the apartment, I saw a large Christmas tree surrounded by gifts, and my eyes fell on a doll I very much wanted. Shortly, it was announced that Santa Claus would come by plane to the top of the building. I awaited his arrival anxiously. To my surprise, he arrived with very little noise, but I was given my preferred doll. At home, my mother urged me to make a list for Santa Claus. Then she told me to get on the phone at the paddock to speak with Santa. With trepidation, I heard his voice when I put the phone to my ear. I believe I told him the few things I wanted for Christmas. Only many years later did

I find out that my mother had used the phone in the house to speak to me as Santa.

Now Christmas Eve had arrived. My mother sent the groom to cut some twigs from a tree and placed them in a bucket. While I was out of the house, she hung chocolates on the twigs and placed all my presents around it. Soon she called for me, saying that *Kristkindel* ("the Christ child" in German) had arrived and brought me all these presents. I was delighted to see I had received a black doll with three braids tied with red ribbons, a sewing machine with a hand wheel that really sewed, some frocks, and denim rope moccasins. I could not wait to show these presents to the Armazem children. I ran next door, swinging the doll joyfully, and hit her head on the wall and broke it (at the time dolls were made of china). But I still had the sewing machine that amused the children for days.

We had a black maid that summer, named Sebastiana, who took care of me. She was very gentle and kind, but she did not stay long with us. Carnival time was approaching in mid-February, so she promised to bring me a Hawaiian costume, complete with grass skirt. Although she was not able to do so, I appreciated the effort. Once she took me to the *favela* where she had her hair straightened with a hot iron, a procedure I found most interesting. This *favela* was in the city, in the borough of Leblon; it was on flat ground and not perched on the mountainside like most others. I found out later that this *favela* was eradicated due to the valuable real estate on which it sat, and the residents were transported to a far location and housed in buildings they called *Cidade de Deus* (City of God). On another occasion, I went with Sebastiana to the beach behind our riding school to watch the local residents pull in a fishing boat and fish net teeming with fish. In Portuguese, this process was called *arrastao* (the big drag). Once the nets are on the sand, the fish are sorted out, and those who helped pull the rope are each given a handful of fish. These sea rituals in my neighborhood pleased me very much. On one occasion, a kind local man gave me a string of crabs. I ran home and boiled them in a pot and have been hooked on crabs ever since.

Around the beginning of March 1953, I returned to Stella Maris School to begin the second grade. I remained a day student for a while. My sailor uniform had to be starched and there was no one to do it or to clean me up to go to school. My appearance was rather shabby and dirty to say the least. To aggravate the situation, the mosquito bites I had acquired in the riding school had turned into unsightly wounds that would not heal. I put soap on my legs to prevent the bites and wrapped them in gauze, but the damage was done. My second grade teacher, Madre Ligia, a kindly nun, gave me a uniform to improve my appearance. She was very proud of me when I came to school one day all cleaned up and shiny. I had dragged the maid from the beach and asked her to starch my blouse with gooey cornstarch cooked in a pan and to iron it like the uniforms of the children next door. The nun took me out of class with a beaming smile and said I looked perfect, except for the shoes that she would help me shine. And she showed me around to the other nuns who passed by and who agreed with her about my improved appearance.

However, we could not keep up this daily effort. It was around this time that my stepfather began to abuse me sexually. It is hard for me to write these things because it brings back the shame and inadequacies I have felt all my life. But the truth is, while I was home for the winter vacation in July, my stepfather invited me to the main bedroom where he was lying naked in the big bed. While I stood by the bed, he told me to hold his penis and move it up and down several times. I complied with an automatic submission, and then he told me to sit on him, saying, "Your mother does it." This I did not do. That weekend, I sat on my mother's lap in the front room and told her about what had happened. Some other things happened of which I'm not sure my mother was aware, but she might have suspected since many years later she asked me some questions.

My mother had taken in a couple from Hungary to help out at the riding school. The man carried me on his back in our garden and proceeded to fondle me, something I enjoyed. One day, he took me to the small house where he had moved. I remember hiding under the table, cowing in the corner and refusing to give in to him. When he lived in the room downstairs with his wife, I placed my leg on his crotch when we were playing a game at the table, and one day, I walked in on him and his wife when they were having sex. I did not see much, but I realized they were engaged in something private. At that time, I had no knowledge of human sexuality. A few years later, my mother told me the mechanics of how children are made. I did not find the topic very pleasant and the conversation was rather short.

I could no longer remain a day student at Stella Maris and be exposed to my stepfather's daily abuse. My mother talked to a nun at Stella Maris School who said they would give her a discount if she put me in their boarding school. I remember one evening when it was dark and the stars were out, my mother took me for a walk in the golf course along the beach, and said, "Schatzy, it is best you go to the boarding school…." She knew how much I had resisted separations from her when I went to boarding school before, but I acquiesced. My bags were packed and I was sent to Stella Maris Boarding School for the remainder of second grade. Martha Lucia, my friend, was also a dorm student there, as well as other students from the second grade. They all had their peculiarities. One of them wet her pants and carried a doll. Another picked her nose and ate the boogers, so no one wanted to sit next to her, yet she wrote poetry. Some were athletic and pretty. Some told fibs, while others were very rebellious.

The very first day around five o'clock when all the day students had gone home, I was introduced to a relay team coached by a very energetic and enthusiastic nun, Madre Violeta. She was nice to me and I joined in her enthusiasm. We practiced every day until six o'clock and were either on the blue or red team. The older dorm students, who were not engaged in playing volleyball or other games, cheered us on. The day soon came for us to compete before the community of nuns. Madre Violeta had prepared us very well, and woe to us if we made a mistake. The older children helped comb our hair and place large red and blue bows on top of our heads. I do not remember who won the relay team, but everyone had a lot of fun, including the nuns who gave us hugs and prizes. Some days, all the boarders, elementary as well as secondary levels, engaged in the game of *queimada* (Portuguese for "the burning," and known as "dodgeball" in English). The captains chose their teams, and a center and back lines were drawn on the cement. I was too small to catch the ball, but I loved running back and forth to avoid it. Those hit by the ball would stand on the back line in the opposing team's camp and throw the ball to their team or try to hit a player in the field. I remember one time I was the last one standing in my camp because no one could hit me with the ball. With rosy cheeks and sweat running down my face, I was carried on the shoulders of the older girls, who were exuberant with their win due to my performance.

Madre Violeta was real dynamite. One year, she played tricks on the students on April Fools Day. She sliced soap and placed it on dessert plates and covered it with a pink sauce, making it look like custard. The girls filed in for lunch at the refectory and stood by their seats, awaiting prayers. Some could not wait to eat the dessert and proceeded to run out the door to wash out a soapy taste in their mouths. I was one of them. Another time, she sold Coke out of the snack bar, but had replaced it with coffee. We kids did our share by plugging the bells with cotton, tying the teacher's chair to the desk, or hiding ourselves in the backroom before the teacher arrived to see an empty classroom. Some of our antics got us in great trouble.

On the whole, the school was a very structured place that did not condone leisure fun. We got up very early in the morning to the sound of a bell, said prayers, brushed our teeth in the lavatory, and made our beds in silence. Then we lined up and marched over to the chapel for Mass. The priest who said Mass most mornings was Frei (Friar) Jose, a tall, lanky fellow who did not have much patience for ceremonies. He would ride his motorcycle from Santa Monica Parish in Leblon, so we would know he had arrived from his motorcycle's loud rumblings and the skid on the gravel on the patio adjacent to the chapel. While standing in full vestment in front of the altar, he once turned abruptly toward the organ in the back and yelled, *"Como e que e? Nao vai comecar nao?"* ("How is it? Aren't we going to start?"). This amused the children, but mortified the organist/nun who had delayed the opening song for the Mass. On another occasion, the children were filing out of the chapel when we heard a loud thump and wondered what had happened. Apparently, the sacristy nun had forgotten to put a chair in the confessional, and Frei Jose hit the floor with his legs protruding out of the booth in plain view of the girls who were passing. Needless to say, no confessions were heard that day.

While I am on the subject of Frei Jose, I must tell a short anecdote. At the Feast of Corpus Christi (which honors the Body of Christ in the form of the bread or bread wafer, known as the Host), the boarders were invited to join the Santa Monica religious procession around town near the parish. I remember walking behind Frei Jose, who was quite drunk and entertained the girls with his unsteady gait and foolish sayings. The scene was right out of the film *La Dolce Vita*—a drunk priest, nuns in full regalia, and uniformed girls following the monstrance, carrying the Host on a hot day in Rio, while bathers in skimpy bathing suits lined the beach avenue where we were passing. Many years later, I heard that Frei Jose left the priesthood, even though he had come from a large Catholic family from the state of Minas Gerais whose children had all entered religious life. In actuality, he was a kind and amusing fellow—a breath of fresh air in those strict regimented times—and we all liked him.

The daily schedule remained unchanged. The secondary students had their class in the morning and study time in the afternoon and vice versa for the primary students. We had four or five recesses a day when the students could mingle and play and sign out game equipment from the playroom. At meal time, we had an older student sitting at our table to make sure we ate. The mother prefect at the time, Madre Zeni, was especially nice to me. Once when the mother prefect approached our table, the older girl asked us how much we liked Madre Zeni. One of the girls replied, "I will love her till the day I die." Then I replied, "I will love her even after I die." Apparently, Heaven was a reality for me since I had been told my father had died.

Second grade was not as interesting for me as first grade. Madre Ligia, although with much good will, could not keep order or the students' interest. But I do remember that a lady came to our class to teach us some English rhymes. I was asked to teach one side of the classroom while she taught the other. It involved the number rhyme: "One, two, three, let me see/four, five, six, count the sticks/seven, eight, they are straight/ nine, ten, give me them." Nega, who was in the other classroom, said that my voice was so loud it resounded in the hallway and into her classroom. The teacher was very proud of my knowledge of English.

We only went home every other weekend. The weekend we stayed in school, we were taken out on an excursion. The nuns prepared our lunch in brown paper bags, and we were allowed to sit with a friend whom we chose carefully beforehand. When the driver was about to take off, we would say our customary prayers and invoke the protection of Our Lady as well as the Mother Founder, who had promised that her institute would be guarded from accidents. We sang all kind of songs. The ban of silence was lifted, and we frolicked and laughed at will. We had great fun watching the nuns eat, for at school, they ate at their own refectory, never in front of the children. They were human after all. During these outings, we came to know the nuns as persons, and we enjoyed their company. We visited shrines high up on hills (Nossa Senhora da Penha), Rio city parks, the zoo, other convent schools, and places of interest such as a remote beach in an area called Recreio dos Bandeirantes.

When we came back to the school, we were all very exhausted and ready for bed. Silence was once more imposed, and a nun called out the rows in the old dormitory for us to brush our teeth. Night prayers were said and the light was shut off. We were supervised for the first few hours. A nun would march back and forth in the aisles between the rows of beds, making tingling noises with her rosary and the scores of medals under her vest. Sleep came soon and we were lost to the world of dreams.

The first few years that I attended Stella Maris, the school was housed in an old one-story building that ran in a T-shape from the mountain's base to the hill's edge overlooking the sea. The horizontal bar housed the classrooms and the refectory or lunchroom. The vertical bar housed the dormitory that doubled as an auditorium, as well as the nun's quarters (forbidden to students), the chapel, reception area, and the balcony, which had a beautiful view of the ocean and the areas in Rio called Leblon and Ipanema. Between these two sections was a large covered area with a hallway that had small cubicles for piano lessons and a series of steps that led up to the refectory and classrooms. In this upper level were two rooms, one with a dentist chair and medical cabinets, and next to it, a room to store sports equipment and games. On either side of the T were two large playgrounds: one called the Patio of Cement and the other the Patio of the Trees. The latter was cooler because it had four or five large fica trees, similar to those in our riding school. Beyond the short cement walls that encircled this playground was an incline that opened to an unpaved road that curved around the building to the school's back gate. We were never allowed to play beyond the walls, nor at the front entrance where there was a graveled landscaped garden. The school's front gate was far below at the mentioned dirt road. To get to the school's front entrance, a series of cement steps had to be climbed. At the last stage of the steps was a lovely cement rink where we could play if accompanied by an adult. Some classes were taken there to eat lunch.

Sometime toward the end of 1953, I made my First Communion in the little white church in Sao Conrado where we lived. It was a lovely whitewashed church with a steeple bell tower and windows on either side. Built in the early twentieth century, oil paintings of it from 1917 or 1918 show it just beyond the beach's sand dunes. Before my First Communion, Madre Ligia, my second grade teacher, took me in her charge and prepared me for the event. She would have liked me to make my First Communion at the school chapel with the other Stella Maris students, but I expressed to her my wish to receive communion from Frei Luiz at my Sao Conrado Church. She taught me how to pray the rosary and all the common prayers, including the Apostles' Creed and the Act of Contrition, and arranged for a private confession with Padre Barros who came to the school to hear the nun's confessions. He was a Jesuit who had a retreat house in the Gavea region where I lived. When it was time for me to enter the confessionary booth, I trembled in fear and shame. Some sexual images as well as sexual experiences muddled my mind, and it was hard for me to distinguish between sin and what was childhood misfortune. Somehow, I got through the confession, wondering what the priest thought of me as he lived in my neighborhood and might have known me. I know he visited the Armazem family and was very fond of Dona Linda; once in a talk, he cited her as a dynamic personality much like Saint Peter. At the time, he was explaining the different types of temperaments and used her as an example of the sanguine type. I don't remember what I said in the confessional, but I know it was an anxious experience because I had to reveal many secrets I had harbored in my heart and that gnawed at me like a cancer.

The day of my First Communion was fast approaching so my mother sewed some sheer sleeves on a white dress she had bought for the occasion; she had forgotten that at that time, one did not enter a church with a sleeveless dress. She accompanied me to church, but I don't think she stayed for the whole ceremony. Bisuca, my next-door neighbor, also made her First Communion that day, and she had a big party with many relatives and friends, true to the Brazilian tradition. I joined her party since there was no party for me, my mother living outside the conventions of the time. A kind lady, who often rode at our riding school, gave me a change purse in the shape of a hat. So I was grateful to have at least that one present.

Chapter 6

———— ✿ ————

Teddy and Family

Mid-year 1953, the Von Ulrich family arrived from China. My mother helped them emigrate from China to Brazil and arranged for them to stay at our riding school. I anticipated their arrival with great excitement. I knew they had arrived by ship, but I was unable to meet them because I was at school. The next morning, while the sun was shining brightly, I stood outside the window of the room of our house where the Von Ulrichs were staying and peeked through the shutters to get a glimpse of the new family. I saw Teddy and May fast asleep, and I had to wait a long time before they woke up.

The Von Ulrichs had been instrumental in introducing my mother to my stepfather when we lived in Shanghai. At that time, the family was experiencing great hardship due to the scarcity of jobs and the general state of civil war and economic depression in China. My mother took Lizochka (the mother, Elizabeth von Rosen) into her apartment for a while. Teddy was sent to an orphanage run by Catholic nuns, whom she described later to me as very unhappy women. The other children—May (Maysie), Cyril, and Andrew—were sent to acquaintances or other schools. The family had aristocratic roots and was very cultured. Teddy (Theodora) was the youngest and came to Brazil at the age of sixteen. Andy was twenty-four, May was twenty-two, and Cyril was nineteen. They all befriended me, but I had a special relationship with Teddy because she took a special interest in me.

Teddy's bright sunny nature and her deep convictions about life impressed me very much. We spent countless hours together in July, my winter vacation. She shared with me parts of her diary that she had kept since she was thirteen. I came to know that she had a boyfriend in Shanghai who had taught her judo. He was married, but she loved him very much. He reciprocated and gave her a jade ring that she wore. She felt great despair when the family packed to leave China. She told me she had thoughts of throwing herself on the railroad tracks on their way to Hong Kong. However, by the time I met her, she had recovered from her broken heart. I believe the sunshine, the mountains, and the sea made her forget her homesickness.

She had long golden silky hair and bright blue eyes; she was petite, but very athletic. She was filled with an eagerness to live and make her dreams a reality. Her nurturing spirit made her love all living things. She had a deep respect for animals. Once we found a cat that was badly diseased. She nursed it for a while inside the gates of our side garden, but it was so filled with maggots and too ill to survive. Mercifully, she put it to sleep. Nevertheless, Teddy made me feel that life was filled with promise, and wonderful things would come to pass. Once she asked me how I would like to look when I grew up; when I told her I would like to have long curly hair, she sketched me that way. Sometime before she came to Rio, she joined the Christian Science faith and shared with me many tenets of her religion. She prayed every day and read sometimes from a small black book she considered her daily nourishment. I would often share in her prayers, and at that time, I had a dream where an angel appeared to me, saying her religion was true. Apparently, I was weighing unconsciously her beliefs with the Catholic beliefs I was getting from school.

Every night, Teddy put me to bed with a story. She was a storyteller *par excellence*! I heard about princes and princesses, forbidden gardens, mean stepmothers, and faraway adventures. I went to sleep enriched and filled with dreams and possibilities. The story that touched me most profoundly was the story of *The Little Princess*, which I thought Teddy made up and only later learned was a famous book. I identified with the little girl whose father went to India on a military assignment and left her in a boarding school. Before he left, he went to town with his little daughter and bought her a most beautiful doll. He was wealthy, so he put his daughter in an exclusive English boarding school in London where she had her own room and many other privileges. She was treated like a princess until news came that her father was killed. Payment to the boarding school stopped and she was reduced to a mere maid. She took a room in the establishment's servant quarters, which were located in the attic. Dreary days followed when she had to rise very early to pick up bread at the bakery and spend most of her time in servitude, scrubbing floors and helping in the kitchen. The madams at the school were not very nice to her, demanding more than she could give, resulting in her punishment. Her only friend was another young girl, a servant, who roomed next door to her in the attic. When she was sad and lonely, she sometimes threw her beloved doll on the floor to show her anger at her father's betrayal. However, her plight was ended with a stroke of luck and fortune. An Indian man in the vicinity found her and related to her that her father had left her great wealth. She was able to redeem herself and her friend from the dreary life in the boarding school. In my case, my father too was gone and perhaps dead, and I had to spend so many years of my life in boarding schools.

But that summer, with Teddy there, we had carefree days when the Gavea sun inundated our lives, the sea beckoned, and the mountains uplifted our gaze. We were filled with the promise of life. In the evening, we would go to the beach to watch the sunset. One Saturday afternoon, Teddy and I took the *lotacao* (a small local bus) to the end of the line and back. We enjoyed the ocean view as the bus meandered through the serpentine road cut into the granite mountain. The bus driver was surprised to see us remain in our seats for the ride back. In these surroundings, it did not take much to amuse us. Another day, Teddy invited me to go for a walk with her to a grocery store some twenty minutes away toward Rocinha. Even though I was playing with the Armazem children, I quickly agreed to go with her. She needed some alcohol for the stove that was very much like ours: four nails on a board with a tin receptacle for the alcohol. We went along the golf course, lined by rows of flamboyant trees, passed in front of large houses hidden behind stucco walls, and crossed some streets that led into the mountain where some rich people lived in myriad beautiful homes.

One dark summer evening, Teddy, May, and I decided to go to a nearby restaurant. I later found out it was a lover's motel. Most of the time the restaurant was empty since the owners drew their main income from the rooms they rented in the back for clandestine lovers. The restaurant itself was large and pleasant with marble floors and white wrought iron furniture in a charming interior courtyard. Since we were the only customers in the place, we were served with much courtesy and no rush. As we sipped our lemonade, Teddy noticed that the Portuguese *garçon* serving us had a familiar face. He also recognized Teddy because he had come on the same ship with the Von Ulrichs from Portugal to Brazil. Everyone lightened up from this coincidence and the celebration went on. We were in such a wonderful mood, and we had a fit of laughter going home about something I do not recall. All I know is that we had to go to the bathroom all at once, but the riding school only had one changing room. We stormed in, wondering who would go first, bawling in laughter, which was intensified when I let out an air biscuit.

Once, Teddy joined my friends and me in an exercise of judo. She taught us to do somersaults by leaping over each other's body. A boy named Ricardo challenged her to a judo match at the paddock. Teddy approached him very slowly, and when he was near at hand, she lay on the ground, and as he darted upon her, she very skillfully flipped him in the air. He landed on his behind, very much surprised by what had happened to him. Neither I, nor the others, could forget his look of astonishment. Privately, Teddy taught me how to stand on my head. I remember once she was trying to keep me balanced and held me by the rip of my pants; the moment she touched the rip, I let out a loud fart, which sent her laughing hysterically.

May was six years older than Teddy, so I saw her less often. She was gone most of the time because she had found a job in town. I do remember her joining us at the beach on the weekends. She was a brunette with light eyes and a chiseled profile; she was slender, taller than Teddy, and very charming. She brought around a handsome boyfriend or two. Cyril, too, I seldom saw. He was very much into electronics and busy repairing radios, which I watched him do on occasion. At the time, he was engaged to Laura, of Russian descent, who had come from Shanghai, shortly after the Von Ulrichs' arrival. They had known each other since their early youth and had courted each other in my mother's Shanghai apartment, he later told me. Laura was of exceptional beauty, with long dark hair and blue eyes, very demure, and self-possessed. Cyril was energetic, debonair, and charming, but he only had eyes for his Laura. They made a beautiful, romantic couple, the stuff of which books are written.

Andy was the older brother, more laid back and easygoing. He enjoyed swimming and strolling about the area. Once, on a very sunny Sunday afternoon, I was walking up the dirt road beside our riding school to go swimming when I saw Andy waving at me from the water. I waved back, not realizing he was in distress. He continued to wave and some onlookers charged into the water to help. A neighbor of ours, who ran an auto repair shop, provided a long rope and Andy was pulled to safety, gagging and in a collapsed state. He was turned face down on the sand and his back was massaged to cause him to vomit volumes of water. People were standing all around, and the ambulance came to take him to the hospital. By that time, he had recuperated somewhat and refused to go. That day, I saw him retire to his room, very pale and ill indeed.

The Von Ulrichs spent approximately three months with us. They occupied the first floor of our house, which had rooms on each side of the entrance archway. They lived very simply. The mattresses were made of dried grass that my mother had ordered the groom to fashion before their arrival. Their stove, as I already mentioned, was made of nails and lit with alcohol. The scarcity of materials did not dampen their spirits. They moved about with a great zest for life and love for people. Soon Baron Von Ulrich and his wife Lizochka rented a large apartment in a tall round building in Niteroi, the city across from downtown Rio on the left arm of Guanabara Bay and opposite Sugarloaf Mountain. This location was convenient for the family because they just had to take the ferry across the bay to be in the heart of the downtown district, where most of them worked. Lizochka worked for Air France as a multilingual secretary. Once, she was able to provide a free ticket to her husband to go to the United States to try to sell his airplane propeller he had modeled out of wood. I saw the propeller, but I do not know whether he was able to sell it. Cyril and Andrew worked in electronics in city factories and May worked as a secretary somewhere downtown.

The Von Ulrichs' comings and goings were not always apparent to me since I only spent part of my vacation with them at various periods during my preteen years. I spent most of my days with Teddy or alone when she was gone. She and I would go shopping in the morning and do housework in the afternoon; she was disciplined and organized. She explained to me how every family member chipped in with the household expenses and she kept house for them. I remember walking with her one morning when the sun was shining brightly, making the walls of residences whiter and the streets friendlier. We passed the residence of a dentist whom Teddy visited once. She told me she was not in the custom of visiting doctors nor dentists, save in grave emergencies. She followed the Christian Science belief that God's healing power would make one well. I admired her reliance on God and learned so much about life with her. We had a great rapport, and even though she was eight years older than I, she treated me like a little sister. We talked about important matters as well as trivial girlish things. In the evenings, I would take a shower and splash myself with cologne. It felt so good to be so fresh in the hot summer air. It did not matter that I had to crawl on a mattress placed on the floor that was sprinkled with flea powder. It was the same mattress from the riding school that had become infected with fleas, perhaps from the cat? I could not tell. Anyway, Teddy was meticulous about her grooming. She told me I should brush my hair with one hundred strokes to make it healthy and shiny, something I found myself, at times, doing on my own.

During my stay, Teddy also dated. I remember she was being courted at the time by a tall, fairly good-looking Englishman with curly hair. But, as fate would have it, her heart was with a Brazilian fellow who worked for the airlines and was away on a trip. This Englishman and Teddy sat on the floor in the living room discussing their relationship. I was to stay away, so I occupied myself in the kitchen, ironing her brothers' shirts, hoping to be of help. However, I interrupted them every five minutes to show them my progress on the shirt and get their approval, which of course did not please them very much.

Since her favorite boyfriend was gone, Teddy had a great deal of time for me. We went to the beach on the bay. All we had to do was walk along a canal and soon we were at Icarai Beach, the most popular in Niteroi. It was a busy place with traffic, bathers, and many vendors. Once in the water, which was usually calm, Teddy invited me to hang onto her back as she swam toward the deep. There she let go of me and taught me how to swim. On one occasion, some rough boys began to play with us and let us use their inner tube. One of them held me down under the water for some time, which frightened me a great deal. I believe Teddy scolded them. We soon went home.

We occasionally went to a movie in Icarai Beach. I remember seeing Leslie Caron in *Lili*, and I sang "Hi-Lili, Hi-Lo" animatedly. Teddy wanted to introduce me to art and culture, so she would relate to me the story of *Swan Lake* when we heard Tchaikovsky's music. Once she told me the story of a black movie where the family lived secluded from the whites and the beautiful black heroine suffered very much. The name Carmen comes to mind as associated with this story. She told me life was like that in America for the blacks. I was puzzled because that was not my experience in Brazil; there were no "black only" enclaves. Sometimes, I heard some modern music, such as "Jambalaya" or "Luna Rosa," which I began to learn by heart. I had seldom listened to the radio or heard music on a record player before this time.

One day, Teddy took me to downtown Rio to attend a Christian Science service. We took the trolley along Icarai Beach to the ferry station where we boarded a small ferry toward Rio. Once at the square by the Rio dock, I saw vendors selling mangos, watermelon, sugarcane juice, and a myriad of sweats and homemade foods. I believe Teddy bought me a treat, and we proceeded to the service. However, we did not attend it because the schedule was different than we had thought, so we returned home. In this case, the journey was more important than the destination.

May also took me along with her a couple of times to Niteroi's Yacht Club. It was built on a hill in the Sao Francisco area, just beyond Icarai. I had a delicious Coke while I perched on a bar stool in the rustic clubhouse. Then we descended the stairs toward the dock where her boyfriend Johnny (an Englishman she later married) was preparing his small sailboat for our voyage. Once in the sailboat, we went off in a considerable clip against the wind, piercing the deep green undulating waters. We dropped anchor by a secluded beach and had a delicious ham sandwich.

I could sit on the side of the boat and drag my legs in the water and feel the hot sun on my back. Without reservation, I can say it was the most memorable sailing I have ever done. In bigger boats, I always felt seasick and miserable. Andy (Teddy's older brother) also took me on an outing. He took me to the Sao Francisco Beach by trolley where we bathed and then came back. I mention all these outings because they were important to me since this family was the closest I came to having relatives.

Around 1956, Cyril got married to Laura. I watched all the preparations. I had a special three-tiered striped green dress a neighbor had made for me, and I planned to wear it for the wedding. Cyril invited us to see his apartment in a two- or three-story building in a pleasant area in Niteroi. It had hardwood floors and French doors opening to a balcony, but no furniture. One day, he invited me to hop on his motorcycle and check out an armoire for his apartment. My long hair blew in the wind and I felt a strong breeze on my face. It was exhilarating to speed along and bend with the motorcycle along the curves.

The day of the wedding came. The religious ceremony was going to take place in a Russian Orthodox Church in Santa Teresa, Rio's mountainous district where I had spent a week in kindergarten boarding school. I remember traveling by taxi with the family; Lizochka paid the fee but needed some change, which I had in my purse. The bride and groom were beautiful in the center of the sanctuary with crowns placed over their heads. The bearded Russian Orthodox priest read prayers in Russian and the couple exchanged vows and placed their wedding bands on each other's finger. At dusk, the party was in full swing on the church's terrace overlooking a panorama of Rio. Champagne glasses were in everyone's hand, including the priest's, and I was allowed a sip. My mother and stepfather were in attendance, but I went home with the Von Ulrichs. In the Neteroi apartment, we continued to celebrate by putting records on the record player and someone played the guitar on the balcony. That night, I was allowed to stay up after nine o'clock.

But soon after, I began to feel homesick. I would be alone in the apartment more frequently as Teddy was engaged in a course or work. Teddy sensed my loneliness and tried to introduce me to some children in the apartment building; we played in the courtyard, but I did not bond with them. I wanted to go home so Teddy decided to take me on the long trip back to Gavea. We arrived sometime in the afternoon and knocked at our fourth floor apartment. By then, late 1956, we had already relinquished the riding school and were living in an apartment building in the Sao Conrado/Gavea area. In his underwear, my stepfather opened the door and greeted Teddy pleasantly and they began talking in Russian. Soon we left and took the fifteen-minute walk toward the Armazem. Along the way, I told Teddy how much I hated my stepfather, and in general terms, I told her about the abuse. She understood and expressed her sorrow for my predicament many times hence. She left me with the Armazem family, who were so happy to see us. Later, I took the bus home. Incredibly, I loved Gavea more than any other place. At this time, I began to sift all my experiences through the soil of my soul, which was inextricably bound to the soil of this place, Gavea, Sao Conrado, which I came to call home despite the difficulties.

Chapter 7

═══════ ❀ ═══════

Uncle and Life in the Riding School

However much of an evil figure Uncle was in my childhood, he was an interesting man. Most of his friends, acquaintances, and riding students called him *O Capitao* ("Captain" in Portuguese) because of his title in the Russian army. He was educated in fine art and had gone to the military academy in St. Petersburg. I was in the room one day when he told a group of friends in the riding school a story of his military experience. He was fleeing from the Russian Army (Bolsheviks) by horseback when he encountered a river. He could not swim so he did the next best thing. He held on to the horse's tail and in this manner got safely across. He found this story amusing and laughed as he told it.

To pass his time, my stepfather had a habit of hunting bats in the evening. He would whirl the training whip that had a long rope at the end until it made a high-pitched sound. A bat would fly into it, and then he would nail it to the wall of the wooden stables that lined the right side of the property on the back. He would often show visitors this trophy collection, as if the bats were prizes of war. Perhaps the bat population had to be reduced since we would find a horse bleeding from the neck after a bat had latched onto it. The stables had a capacity for about seventeen horses: ten housed in the main brick stables that opened to both sides of the property and seven in the wooden stable I've mentioned.

My stepfather was not a good businessman. If people were his friends, he would let them ride for free. Once my mother set up a system in which the rider could purchase a ticket for a series of lessons that would be punched each time he/she came. These tickets were kept in the office on the first floor. It worked for a while but not for long. My mother would often have to support us as well as the horses to buy grass and grains.

Uncle had a small circle of intimate friends, most of them Russians, who knew his identity and were very fond of him. He had a magnetism that attracted people to him. Often, women who came to our riding school fell in love with him, and he had ongoing affairs with many of them. Once, I remember, I was coming home from the boarding school and found the door to the upstairs quarters locked. When I knocked at the door, a pretty blond woman opened it and asked, "Who are you?" I answered, "I am my mother's daughter." Recognizing the oddity of her presence in our home, I went next door to the Armazem family to wait for my mother. Another beautiful Russian woman named Tatiana came riding on occasion and established a friendship with my stepfather. I believe he was very fond of her, not only because she was beautiful and Russian, but because she also was a painter. They talked on the phone quite often. I once saw her painting the sea by the rocks. She was married to an American who worked in the American Embassy, and I remember going to a dinner there with my mother. She had a daughter also named Tatiana, in her twenties, who took me with her to their apartment in the city; there I saw a large parrot on its perch. Later, she took me riding at the prestigious Hippica Club where we changed our clothes in the locker room, a first for me. When we came home, we went swimming, and in the dressing room of our riding school, I stepped on a wasp that stung me with a vengeance. Tatiana felt sorry for me as if it were her fault and tried to help me, but I went hopping away in pain.

For many people, our house was the center of entertainment. Horses had to be saddled for so and so, and my stepfather would take his place in the middle of the paddock, yelling out instructions to the submissive students with whip in hand and dressed in his customary breeches and tall black boots as well as his captain's hat. After their lessons, however, the students would come to the living room for drinks and cordial exchanges. Some of the visitors would greet me with a smile and befriend me, but I tried to keep a low profile because I felt like an outsider when my mother was not around, and my stepfather regarded me as a nuisance.

Nonetheless, I did make some friends. A lady named Helena Santos Valle, who was very rich and had two beautiful horses in our establishment, took a liking to me. Her horse, Tobiano, was a black and white stallion that pranced rather than walked. Once when I tapped on his left leg in the customary fashion to look at his shoe, he let his leg down and stepped on my foot, so I had to call for help. Her other horse was Madre Selva, a red thoroughbred my stepfather often used for riding lessons. One Sunday, a Brazilian couple came to ride and they took Madre Selva and another horse off the stable grounds. While in the open field, they tied her to a bush. Madre Selva got loose and ran to the street where a car hit her, causing severe lacerations to her legs. Someone brought her back to the stable, spooked and bleeding. My mother called a vet and the owners, and that night Madre Selva had to be sewed up. Before all this happened, Dona Helena came riding and once took me by car to an open market in town and bought me some trinkets. Later, she had me spend several weeks in her estate in Teresopolis where an elderly German housekeeper knitted me a multicolored sweater.

I also befriended an American girl named Ann, a few years older than I, who came riding quite often the summer I was home. She came one morning and decided to ride Madre Selva. I met her in the cemented area behind the stables where the horses were saddled and where there was a huge water tank. Ann was already on

Madre Selva and invited me to get on the horse behind her. I climbed on the water tank, and the instant I was bareback on the horse, she bucked violently and threw me off. I hit my forehead on the latch of a door on the side stables. While I was still on the ground, an enormous egg grew on my head. Immediately, Jose, the groom, and his common law wife who lived in the servant quarters in the back of the riding school, came to my rescue. His wife was a practical nurse and decided to press a cold knife against my forehead. Soon I was back to my old self and Ann thought I should be rewarded so she took me to the Golf Club for lunch and some swimming in the pool. We ate on the clubhouse's second-story wraparound veranda where the garçons wore white uniforms and bowties. I had the best club sandwich and a "black cow" (coke and vanilla ice cream), something I enjoy to this day. I also swam with delight in the pool. Several days later, Ann presented me with a collection of English storybooks and a beautiful slender dark-haired doll with a suitcase filled with a raincoat, roller-skates, various outfits, and a blanket. I played with this doll until I was thirteen, bestowing on her all my fantasies, and then I gave her to a young child in our apartment building in Gavea, who broke her since she was made of china. I had such great attachment to personal belongings that it pained me when I heard she was broken.

The riding school provided a nucleus for us to make friends and acquaintances. It often was a forum for philosophical discussions for a variety of people mostly of European background. Once, I remember being around when the question, "What is love?" arose, and each person took a turn answering the question with a glass of brandy in his/her hand. I don't remember the answers, but the question stood sharply in my mind. I also remember touching the brandy with my tongue and feeling it burn. I probably stood around because my mother was home and part of the group. That year, my mother invited a group of friends for my birthday party. The children had a garden party while the adults ate inside. I wore a white organdy dress embroidered with flowers. At this party, I first met my future godmother, Dona Vera Elcock. She came down from upstairs to talk to me and asked me what I wanted for my birthday. Without hesitation I told her, "A bicycle!" I did not get the bicycle, but we became friends. She came often to the riding school because she boarded her horse Brinquedo (Toy) there. She was a dynamic woman of small stature, with long reddish blond hair in a perm, a bony structure with masculine traits, and husky voice from smoking. She could outtalk almost anyone. Underneath all that steel was a kind person who gave me attention, so I asked her to be my Confirmation godmother, which she promptly accepted.

Because Dona Vera was also fond of my stepfather, our friendship prompted my stepfather to be kinder to me. One day, a small white horse arrived in a trailer at our riding school called Borboleta (Butterfly). As I watched her come out of the trailer, my mother and Uncle told me she was mine. I was so happy to have a horse and I did ride her occasionally. At this time, Uncle also bought me a pair of jeans (the only gift I remember receiving from him) and began training me to jump on a horse named Domino, a brown Morgan horse, who was gentle-natured and could swim in the ocean, Spanish dance, and do various other equestrian movements. But if you brought a whip near him, he would balk and retreat. Once I was riding on Domino with my mother and some friends in a grassy plane at the end of the beach when my reins broke. Any other horse would have taken off, but Domino halted with my mother's prompting, so she was able to lead us home with the remaining rein. Domino was my favorite horse as well as my mother's. Once, he was very sick with a kind of influenza and lay dejected in his stable and refused to eat. When my mother put his head on her lap, he moaned to complain of his illness. She was able to give him a carrot or two. Besides jumping, my stepfather also trained me to do other feats on Domino in anticipation of the Spring Games that would take place at the Flamengo Club in town. I remember standing on Domino while he walked; I only did it a few times, not enough to be a pro. Anyway, I did not participate in the Spring Games or jumping competition in the horse clubs in town because my stepfather's kindness was short-lived and soon he was back to his old ways.

At one time we had a groom, Antenor, who was from the interior of Brazil and lived in the servant quarters with his wife and two small children. He had a repertoire of ghost and folk stories he had learned in his native state. In the evenings, the local children would gather around him on the front garden's lawn, and totally captivated, listen to his mystic stories. After the story, I would go to our top floor and lean over the central window overlooking the interior garden. One such evening, I was perched on the window when I saw a figure appear before me that frightened me to death. I ran screaming to my mother. Around the corner came my stepfather, laughing. He had dressed up a wooden measuring device for horses, complete with jacket and hat, knowing he would scare me. That night when my mother put me to bed on the anteroom's sofa, I asked her to keep the window closed because I was afraid ghosts would come in.

My first encounter with death happened at the riding school when I was nine. Antenor and his wife, both of mixed race, had a healthy boy of three and an eighteen-month-old boy who was long and pale and had to be in his mother's arms constantly. While I saw the healthy boy run about and watch the activities in the riding school close to his dad or mom, the sick boy remained in the room with his mom. I did not know he was sick at the time, so it alarmed and saddened me when I heard he had died. I went to the back room in the servants quarters to pay my respects and saw the boy laid out on a table dressed in a white gown. His mother cried uncontrollably, trying to take the boy from the table while guests restrained her and tried to console her. I dressed myself in my best clothes and asked my mother whether I could go to the burial with the family. Her answer was, "No," so I just lingered about and watched the movement from afar. I guess my mother was trying to protect me from the painful reality of death, but it did not work since the image of this mother crying stayed with me for a long time.

Another violent drama occurred in the riding school when I was there. I was preparing to go to bed when my mother came in from the stables to get some flat couch pillows. She said the groom, Enrique, had been assaulted and was lying on the ground bleeding. She forbade me to come out, but I noticed a great deal of commotion with the police and the ambulance's arrival. The next morning, I heard the full story at the Armazem where so many grooms and servants gathered for drinks. A group of these men had been in the back with our groom when a feud developed between Enrique, a balding, chubby, white man, and Manuel, a lean tall black man. Manuel vowed to kill Enrique. He waited for him in the dark that night in a corner of the stables. He was armed with a hoe, and when Enrique appeared, Manuel whacked him on the head. I don't know what they quarreled about, but I suspect it might have been related to an insult or a job at our stable. Manuel went to jail for several years, and I later saw him working as a groom at the Flamengo Horse Club. I also saw Enrique many years later, and by a strange feat of nature, he had a full head of dark hair and was much thinner.

Many grooms came and went, but Jose, whom I mentioned earlier, was one who remained for some time. He was a tall, slender, black-haired white man who exhibited a great deal of loyalty to our family and had a very gentle nature. I don't know whether he was always paid, but he stayed to occupy the servant quarters. Once, I refused to go to school because it was Thursday, usually the elementary school's day off, but that day it had been mandated that we go to school. Instead, I hung out with Jose and some others at the loft where alfalfa was kept for the horses, and I remember him condoning my behavior of skipping school. His benevolence made me spend some time at the back with him and his "wife." They cooked outdoors on a makeshift wooden stove in an area adjacent to their quarters in the very back that was surrounded by bushes. His wife told me that the best way to keep their pots shining was to scrub them with ashes. Jose told me that they also used ashes to clean their teeth with their index fingers. I found their secret very revealing and thought for sure I would use it someday. One day, I was washing my feet after a swim at the faucet in the front garden when Jose approached me. He said he and his wife were separating because she drank too much. I had heard rumors that he beat her up sometimes. He also said he was sick with syphilis and proceeded to open his pants and show me the lesion. I saw some kind of wound, but I do not know whether it was connected to his genitals. I know I was filled with compassion and asked him what he was going to do. He didn't know, and I watched him go away distraught and pale. I don't think I ever saw him again.

Around the age of nine or ten, I became very curious about sex. One time, I was rummaging around the downstairs office when I found a condom pack. I opened it up, thinking I had found a balloon. I blew it up and placed a small plastic doll inside, and then I ran next door to show my find. Dona Linda immediately whispered to Landa, her cousin, who was there helping, for me to put it away because it was not nice. I gave it up, not knowing why. At the stables was a large, teenage mulatto boy who helped the groom. Jose had warned me about him. However, some children and I played a game with him by looking through the large keyhole of the servant quarters' middle room, and watching him expose his large penis. That went on for a while. Later, he approached me and asked, "Do you want to have my penis? Men and women do it." We marked a time to meet at the loft. So I went to the loft and he told me to lower my panties and sit straddled across from him on a bench. When we were about to touch, the maid called me and I took off running. Later, I sat at the lower steps of our staircase and told Marlene, a neighborhood friend a little older than me, what had happened, saying, "He said men and women do this." She agreed and told me it was very natural. The maid who had called me out of my sexual predicament, an older white lady with glasses and her hair in a bun, listened to my conversation with Marlene and gave me a sermon, saying, "Good girls do not engage in this kind of behavior, and you should beware of bad boys." I often felt myself sandwiched between sex and religion.

But opportunity abounded in my environment. My stepfather was a painter who often had women pose in the nude in the bedroom for him to paint. One of his models was a black, well-endowed maid named Malvina. She was the model for a satirical painting he did portraying a black woman carrying a large can of water, the theme of a popular Carnival song at the time. I remember hanging at the back of her skirt and following her around while she sang. She later disappeared, but I did see her brother walking by on the street playing the mandolin. My stepfather had a drawer full of nude watercolor/pencil drawings and paintings of nudes and genitalia in various poses of copulation. I did rummage his desk several times and saw these paintings. He was definitely a man obsessed with sex. He walked around the house nude, wearing only a T-shirt, not minding that I was present, and he enjoyed teasing me. He had a strange grin on his face when he would tuck his penis behind his legs and tell me, "You see, I am a woman." He repeated this scene several times. He would be nude in this manner for long periods, leaning on a buffet in the room where I slept while talking on the phone in Russian to a lady friend. Once when he punished me, he forbade me to leave the small veranda in the front of our second story. He closed the veranda shutters and checked intermittently whether I was still there. Luckily, I had a doll and a pot to play with. When he took me out of confinement, he led me to the bedroom and had me lean over the bed; then he whipped me with a long blade used to dry the horses. I did not know why he did this, but I showed the red welts on my bum to the neighbors at the Armazem and later to my mother when she came home. I think it was around this time that I saw my stepfather, nude from the waist down, cut a papaya fruit from the second-story window with a knife tied to a bamboo pole. I told him I had planted the tree in the side garden when I was five years old from seeds I carried in a bucket. He adamantly denied that I was the one who had planted the tree. He went to the kitchen to enjoy the sweet succulent reddish fruit, saying, "I planted it." While in the kitchen barefoot, he tried to light our makeshift stove with alcohol when the alcohol bottle caught on fire and he dropped it in the sink with some flames dropping to the tile floor. Luckily, he didn't even get burnt.

As I think of my mother's relationship with my stepfather, the word that comes to mind is "resistance." She was in my camp, and when we were together, we formed a united front. On Saturdays, my mother liked to clean house and insisted Uncle take off his boots when he came from the paddock, to which he reluctantly complied. I never saw my stepfather raise a hand or voice to my mother. He took the verbal lashings, as if they were a joke. One afternoon, I came into the house in the afternoon when they were in the bedroom. I peeked through the slat in the door and saw my stepfather seated on the edge of the bed next to my nude mother. He was fondling her and asked her what felt good. This act of voyeurism on my part caused me some shame when I was older. Later when we moved from the riding school, they did not share the same bed.

My mother never assigned anyone in particular to take care of me. She knew I would spend most of my time at the Armazem, so she did not bother. This caused me to feel abandoned often, but I enjoyed the freedom to come and go as I pleased without the constraints of Dona Linda's supervision since she tended to be very protective of her children, never letting the little ones wander too far out of her sight. At times, I would watch them eat while I was quite hungry. I could go home and prepare something for myself, but I dreaded meeting my stepfather. Dona Linda sold plates of black beans and rice to the locals; however, no arrangement had been made for me to receive food. Once, Dona Linda remarked to me that I belonged in a juvenile home since there was no one to take care of me. I told this to my mother, who definitely did not like this remark about her parenting. However, my mother liked Dona Linda and one evening invited her for tea, which delighted Dona Linda, who hardly went out. She took this opportunity to dress up and wear her glamorous short wide coat. Later, she told me how she'd had such a good time and that she was very fond of my mother.

One day, after I returned from the beach with the neighbors, I noticed that my house key, which I always carried around my neck on a string, was missing. When I told my mother, she became very angry. She scolded me very sternly and told me I had better come up with the key. She feared I might have given it to one of the men who frequented the bar next door or a man who wandered around the back of the riding school. I was very shaken, worried, and had a heavy heart. I did not like to disappoint my mother, and it hurt me that she doubted my story. I decided to go back to the beach where we had swum. The beach was deserted since the day was now overcast, and I began looking for the key in the sand. Nothing. Looking up to the sky, I began to pray, first to Christ, then to all the saints. I begged them to please let me find the key. Then I walked to the water's edge and looked down. To my utter astonishment, I saw the key sunk in the wet sand with the string trailing. I grabbed it at once, believing it was a gift from heaven. I ran home and gave the key to my mother, who continued to think I had given the key to someone. How else could I have retrieved it so quickly?

My times with my mother at the riding school were brief. While she cooked in the kitchen, I set up house behind a chair in the bedroom with the flat pillows and played with my doll and pots endlessly. Then I would run to the kitchen and my mother would put cooked rice in my pot. That culminated my play enjoyment. Sometimes, I would stay in the kitchen with her. Once, I remember kneeling on a chair looking out the kitchen window when a boiling pot of water fell on my legs and I sustained a bad burn. She was boiling the water on a hot plate and the electrical cord hung across the window. My mother took me to the bathtub and rubbed oil on my legs, but the pain persisted. I ended up running to the tub where the horses drank water and immersed my legs in it for a long time, which brought me immediate relief. That afternoon when I went to the beach with my mother, she carried a black umbrella to protect my legs from the sun. Sometimes, I helped her clean the house on Saturdays and wash dishes standing on a chair. Once when she was at work, I cleaned the whole house, even sweeping the stairs. I thought she would be very surprised and delighted. She thought the maid had come and forgotten to clean the toilet, which disappointed me. But she did sing my praises when she asked me to clean my drawer in the buffet. I put all my rocks and shells as well as books and trinkets in order, and she was delighted when she came home. It made me happy to please my mother.

One weekend, my mother decided to cut my hair and give it a Toni perm. I remember the distinct smell of the perm, but I enjoyed being fussed over. The perm did not come out so well and soon washed away, leaving my hair stringy with some uneven waves. Then my mother decided to cut my eyelashes, saying it would make them come in longer and stronger. Needless to say, they never did, and to this day, I have flimsy eyelashes. I played with my mother's makeup in the bathroom. I would put lipstick on my lips and rub it on my cheeks. I did not know what to do with the black powder for eyeliner, so I rubbed it under my eyes, which gave me a scary look and caused a rash, even though I washed it off quickly. Once when I was looking at myself in the mirror, my mother said, "Never mind what people say; your eyes are getting bluer every day." Perhaps people thought I was adopted and she worried that I might be concerned that I looked so different from her. In reality, it did not occur to me that I looked so different; I was oblivious of my Chinese heritage. When I went shopping with my mother to Leblon for groceries, I would often stare at people on the street and sometimes even look backwards when my eye caught the sight of a beautiful woman, but my spell was broken when my mother corrected me. I thought I looked like everyone else, and most especially like my mother, because I had internalized her inside. I liked when she would show me off to riding school visitors, pointing out how well I could do cartwheels and somersaults on the grass, but she sometimes cautioned them not to give me too much praise, less I grow a big head. She demanded I show guests respect and wanted me to greet them with a curtsey from the knees. When I ate lunch with guests, table manners were a must. She would send me to the kitchen if I touched the food with my hands or made rice and bean balls, something I had learned next door.

My mother had a special way of ingratiating herself with others, which caused me some jealousy. In the mornings, she would often hitch a ride with one of several gentlemen who lived in the vicinity, even if he were married. On one occasion, her good friend Ludmilla and her husband invited my mother to a ball at a fancy club in Rio. I remember she wore her jade necklace and an elegant black strapless long gown. When she came to kiss me, she looked beautiful, but I felt abandoned and angry by her leaving me to go to the ball. These feelings would repeat themselves several times in the future. My mother belonged to me, and I did not like to share her with anyone else, especially when I had to be left with Uncle.

By this time, I had been instructed in school about many of the Christian gospels' tenets. But my stepfather wanted to take even that from me. He would ask me, "Where does Jesus Christ live?" And I would have to answer, "He lives at Estrada da Gavea 841," which was our address. I do not know why I gave him the answer he expected from me. Perhaps I felt defenseless as a child and he loomed like a large monster in my life. However, I knew he was not Christ, and I held dear to many of the gospel stories I heard. I liked when Jesus said that even if you give a glass of water to someone, you have given it to Him. So when a beggar came knocking at our gate, I wanted to feed him. He was a tall, dignified black man who held a walking stick, and when I looked down, I saw he had a very large foot, a condition I later found out to be elephantiasis. I went to the kitchen, but I could not find any food, so he went away empty-handed. Then I returned to the kitchen and found a couple of oranges, so I went running after him to give him the fruit, for which he was very grateful.

Life was not boring at the riding school. That summer, Nega, Bisuca, Marlene, and I had an agreement that we would take turns and provide for the hot chocolate and bread around three each afternoon. Somehow, I forgot when my turn came around, but I agreed to have it anyway, even if a little late. The only problem was that my house was locked and no one was home since my stepfather had gone to town. We looked for a way to go in and saw some long water pipes lying around in the garden. We brought two pipes into the small office on the first floor. An opening in the panel separated the office from the stairs that led to our second floor. With the help of the pipes and a push on the buttocks from the girls, I leaped over the boards and onto the stairs and was safely inside the house. I was in the kitchen getting the sugar, the powdered cocoa, and milk when I heard the girls whistling outside. My stepfather had just stepped off the bus and was on his way up. I put everything away the best I could and hid behind a bedroom door. Through a crack, I could see his figure going from room to room, looking for me. He knew I wasn't far away since the girls were waiting in the garden for me. He never found me, or he pretended not to see me. When he went down and began talking with the girls, I had time to arrange for our cocoa engagement. That day I was not harassed by the Capitao with his hard hat and whip, and we girls had our cocoa picnic on the garden bench, complete with buttered French bread, sprinkled with sugar, under the illuminated tile picture of Saint George at the top of the ivied stable wall.

Chapter 8

Later Elementary Years

March 1954 was the beginning of third grade for me. I had a very stern nun for a teacher, Madre Nise. She wore thick glasses and had an attachment dark lens when she was out in the sun. We were very much in fear of her. She expected complete cooperation, neatness, and total submission to the rules, especially silence. We were only allowed to talk at meals when the signal was given, and during recesses, which were interspersed throughout the day. The long hours of study hall did not suit me very well. I wasted a great deal of time because I did not have an ounce of self-direction. Memorization of words and the reading of textbooks bored me to death. So I played with the inkbottle, filling my pen countless times, or I sharpened my pencils to the point that my hands changed color.

The big thing in third grade was the skeleton in the closet of the science room. Once, we were brought to this room to study the skeleton bones. Its dangling movements sent a chill through our spines, and we would conjure up all kinds of stories, attributing this skeleton to some person in the past who would get out of the closet and frighten us at night in our beds. Our fears and skirmishes did not prevent us from having to memorize every bone in the human body—quite a feat for a nine year old.

Often, I would get in trouble for not having learned my lesson or for being untidy with my books and assignment. I had a passion for play and did not acquire the serious habit of work and study. Thursday, as usual, was a day off for the elementary school children. The dorm students, therefore, had long hours of study hall. One Thursday, my friend Martha and I cuddled up in one seat and began reading a comic book. All was well until Madre Nise spotted us through a window in the adjacent room. We were called in for such frivolity and our comic book reading ended there. Once Madre Nise called me aside and admonished me to be like Elizabeth, who was neat and orderly with her belongings. I tried but failed to be like her. The only subject I did do well in that year was math. It did not require much memorization, and I became so good in division that I could instruct others on the blackboard.

In 1954, I remember an incident that introduced me to a person who would have great bearing on my life. We were all sleeping in the old auditorium (it doubled as a dormitory) when we heard a couple of people shouting at the gate. Because we were at ground level, we were scared to death. We thought there was an invasion of the school, most probably the Russians with their red boots. There was some talk at the time about a Communist takeover. A nun assured us that all was well. The next morning at Mass, we saw a couple of new faces: two nuns who had arrived from the U.S.A.—Madre Euridyna and another nun whose name I don't recall. I was introduced to Madre Euridyna during an evening recreation session of the nuns in the Patio of the Trees. They were seated in a circle when I was brought into their midst. Madre Euridyna asked me, "Where did you learn to speak English?" I told her I had learned it on the ship. Many years later, she told me she saw me in braids, playing with pots, and too immersed in cooking leaves to engage in any kind of conversation. Little did I know that this sister would become a second mother to me in the years to come and that we would maintain a friendship to this day.

Some time during third grade, I received the sacrament of Confirmation. We were told that we would become soldiers of Christ spurred on by the Holy Spirit, whom we would receive that day. The bishop came dressed in his red garb, ring, and hat, and during the ceremony, he would slap each of us on the face in the presence of our godmother. I had chosen Dona Vera Elcock, whom I met at the riding school, for my godmother. However, there was a problem; she had not worn a skirt in years and would have to buy one for the Confirmation. She showed up dressed in a skirt and dying to have a cigarette because she was a chain smoker. She refrained, however, considering the religious atmosphere. That day, she presented me with a lovely gold ring with a ruby and two small diamonds that I wore throughout my teens.

When the school year of 1955 rolled in, the new building of five stories was ready for use. The completion of the building's roof called for a special celebration. Mother Superior called the dorm students to the building's attic to toast the new building with the workers. Usually, we were kept away from the workers and even the servants at the school named "auxiliaries." But today, we could mingle with the grubby individuals who were grateful to the nuns for the free beer and humbled by the students' presence. Big smiles of appreciation were on their faces. For us girls, too, it was very exciting. We could look down to the cement playground from way up high, and we had a new building in which to live, study, and play. We would now sleep in large airy dormitories with sliding glass-paneled windows and Venetian blinds. The lavatories were modern and convenient. The older children stayed on the fourth floor while the younger ones occupied the third floor. We were exempt from going to Mass on weekdays and an older student watched us during the early morning hours. With the new building also came new rules, more in keeping with the times. From now on, we would be going home every Sunday rather than every other week. However, we could not see our parents if they happened to visit us during the week. To this day, I don't understand the reasoning for this rule. We were already traumatized children separated from our parents, so why intensify our pain? One Saturday afternoon, my mother came by to bring me some goodies. I saw her from afar while I was playing ball. I waved to her, but I could not speak to her. Nevertheless, it made me very happy to see her and show my beautiful mother to my friends, who paid special attention to me on account of that visit.

When fourth grade began, my friend Martha became a day student. I missed her a great deal since we were not in the same class. As a token of our friendship, she gave me a silver napkin holder that I later had to return because she had given it to me without her parents' knowledge. My mother once took me on a Sunday to Martha's apartment in Copacabana to play. We stayed mainly in the servant quarters, but I did meet Martha's mother for a short while. She was an elegant woman with a kind disposition. Martha and I kept in touch during our brief recess during the school day, and I called her from the riding school on weekends, but we drifted apart due to our separate schedules.

My fourth grade homeroom teacher was the very dynamic Madre Violeta, whom I introduced earlier. She had an imposing stature, a shuffle kind of walk, and made sweeping turns when called upon. She was a very physical and aggressive woman, with a milky white complexion, and when she got mad, she thundered. She was great at sports and all kinds of competitions, and her enthusiasm was contagious. Because of her vivacious spirit, she was in charge of the volleyball teams, the game room, and the snack bar. She was a take-charge kind of person, and there was no monkey business with her. She made us memorize our catechism backwards and forwards. Even in the classroom, we were organized in teams to see who could answer the most questions. Once when we goofed in geography class, the whole class was punished during the late afternoon recess. When Madre Violeta came into our classroom, we shook in our seats. The first one called on the stand was a girl named Elvira. She stood on the platform trembling, unable to answer the questions. Every time she would plead for mercy, she would raise one of her legs. We were all tied up in a mixture of laughter and fear.

Now and then, the lights went out in the school. One evening, the lights were off for a considerable time. In the beginning of the blackout, the nuns let us out on the patio because it was a starry moonlit night. Some of the girls pranced back and forth, singing Carnival songs, and we made a parody of a nice song about the city and sang instead, "Rio de Janeiro marvelous city, during the day it has no water and at night it has no light." Soon all the girls joined in and it became a real celebration. We enjoyed the freedom and not having to study. During another blackout, the dorm students were in the study hall. The prolonged darkness put all the smaller children in a spooky mood. Some of us got together and started to tell frightening stories. We imagined our mothers stabbed to death by robbers. The children began to cry, one after another. During this hysterical fit, Madre Violeta appeared on the scene. She called the culprits, including me, out onto the patio. She stood each one of us against the wall, where by this time a light was shining. No one dared utter a word. As she talked, she grabbed us by the shoulders and shook us violently, one at a time. We went to bed cured of our ailments.

One of the happiest times I can remember was when Madre Violeta decided to take the dorm students of the primary grades to the beach on Thursday, our day off. We were dressed in our checkered apron dresses, and we took the shortcut instead of the main road that weaved around the mountain. We walked straight down an embankment. The first part of the descent was relatively easy. We hopped down a steep stairway that led into the back of an apartment building. Then we crossed the main road and took a natural path toward the beach. Some fishermen were sitting by a boat shack, mending their nets. Madre Violeta came down in full habit plus a straw hat, sunglasses, and a suitcase filled with supplies. Another sister helped her carry other equipment, a black umbrella, a long rope, and an insulated container with homemade popsicles. The children were delighted to be walking on the sand. Soon Madre Violeta bound each of us by the waist on the same rope and held it while she stood just beyond the water's reach. She enjoyed watching us spatter in the water. We never went beyond the water's edge. Some kids lay in the sand, allowing the waves to cover them. The worst part was trying to stand all at one time. Someone was always trying to pull the other one down, and oh, the pain on the waist. Even Madre Violeta was amused when one little girl's dress had lifted, uncovering her buttocks glued to her transparent panties. We all laughed at the sight. Then it was time for us to go up to the dry sand and eat our lunch. But before this could be done, we had to be unfastened from each other. When it was my turn to be loosened from the rope, Madre Violeta was unable to undo the knot. My partner Sandra and I went to the fishermen to ask whether they had a knife to free us. They sure had one and we were on the loose in no time. As a gesture of gratitude, the Sisters sent us back to the fishermen with a couple of popsicles. They were very pleased with their cool treat, considering they were sitting in the hot sun for a long time. They asked us whether we were orphans. We told them we were boarders from the Stella Maris School above the road. We could not have spent a better day off!

In fourth grade, I began playing with a definite group of girls and continued to do so for the next few years. They were all boarders and the more animated ones in my class. The leader of the group was Adelma. She was an attractive well-developed girl with soft brown hair and natural curls. She was good in all sports and carried herself with grace and self-assurance. I wanted so much to be her best friend, but I was a run-of-the-mill child in appearance and short in stature. I had enthusiasm and above average intelligence, but my emotional deprivation made it hard for me to get close to others. But Adelma was able to keep the group together, and we rallied behind her, following her like a magnet and playing all kinds of games. We were the first ones at the ping-pong table, most of us playing the game quite well. Sometimes, we would play hide-and-seek in the building when we were supposed to be in the playground. There was never a dull moment with us.

Only once did my group get in serious trouble; one Thursday during recess, we were playing dodgeball in the cement playground. Adelma got the ball and struck me with it rather hard, or so I thought. After dodgeball, the group decided to play volleyball in a circle. When the ball came to me, I held it and then aimed it at Adelma, striking her hard and saying, "You think you are everybody's princess, but you are not mine." Then I ran, knowing the group would chase me. I went around the building and was tempted to go into the chapel, but I thought it might be a desecration of the premises. Instead, I ran to the front of the building, the school's main entrance. By this time, I was attacked from both sides. Everyone on the playground came to witness the fight. I was kicking and biting at everyone who came near me, but I was overpowered. My former second grade teacher, Madre Ligia, stopped the fight and ordered all of us to go to the green room—a classroom reserved for first graders. I lingered in the back, begging the sister not to suspend me. Then Madre Marina, the fifth grade teacher and prefect of the primary grades, came in to see us. She was very calm and very objective about the situation. She told us it was a serious matter to be fighting at the school entrance, and that we would be punished. When the admonishing was over, she called me aside and said, "Marianne, play with the good girls and stay away from the rowdy kids. Sheila is a nice girl; why don't you play with her?" I did sit with Sheila for one play period. She was too good, too quiet, and too boring. I was in for some excitement and some daring. Adelma and I made up when we sat punished in the back of the classroom that day. For a short while, I was considered her closest pal, but it never quite remained that way. The others took over and I was more on the perimeter, enjoying the feverish dodgeball and volleyball games.

Since we had very little outside amusement, we enjoyed taunting certain nuns. Madre Conceicao was an elderly stout nun who wore dark-rimmed round glasses and was not altogether in touch with the kids. The grade school study hall was separate from the secondary students. We continued to occupy the old building for classes and study. That day, we were in a classroom that had windows that opened up to a service area in the back where students were not allowed. Here the servants washed clothes, kept a vegetable garden, and took care of some animals. That evening, we heard a continuous squeal of pigs, which sent a ripple of laughter throughout the room. We thought someone was slaughtering the pigs. The hilarious atmosphere continued, and when it was time to line up to go to bed, the pandemonium continued. Madre Conceicao, who was in charge of us, would not take us to the dormitory unless there was perfect silence. But there was a continuous stir somewhere in the line. The mother prefect had been awaiting us at the dorm in the new building for some time, so she sent someone to inquire about our delay. Madre Conceicao did not budge. Unless we were quiet, she would not march us to bed. So after a prolonged resistance, we finally made it to bed. This same nun taught us Portuguese, and no one got more than 60 percent on her tests and essays. Madre Conceicao did not believe anyone could achieve 100 percent excellence, save God.

At the end of 1955, my mother planned a visit to Germany to visit her mother and family. At first, she hoped to take my stepfather and me along. We went downtown for smallpox shots and passport pictures, but finally, the funds were not sufficient and she went alone by ship. She was away for about three months, and I was under the care of my godmother, Dona Vera. Before my mother left, she went to Dona Vera's apartment in Leblon to hand her some documents. While I was playing in the hallway, I heard my mother tell Dona Vera, "Marianchen's father is alive in China, but she was adopted by the Captain." This was a new revelation to me. I had considered my father dead now for years. I don't recall ever discussing the matter with my mother or asking her why she had lied to me. But after that, I acted like my father was alive when speaking to my mother, talking about him in the present and the past tense, and my mother accepted this change without question until it just became understood between us that he was alive. The desire to see him again simmered quietly inside me. Still, I continued to tell everyone else my father was dead, and so I kept his being alive a secret for now, feeling unable to discuss it with others.

I had a good time during this period. On Sundays, my godmother would take me on excursions around the city of Rio. Once we went to an area behind Gavea Mountain called Barra da Tijuca. There we took a boat ride on a large lake adjacent to the sea. On our way back, we ate some oysters doused with lemon. It was the first time I had eaten oysters, and I liked them very much, especially because of the lemon. Sometimes, she would take me to the Sunday morning matinee of *Tom and Jerry* cartoons in Copacabana. I also went to a tent circus for the first time where she bought me some colorful balloons. At her apartment, her mother and her Aunt Martha would take special care of me. Every Thursday, I would come from boarding school, the day designated for a dental appointment, whether I had a dental appointment or not. Dona Vera did take me to her dentist to put a crown on a lower front tooth I had broken while barrel racing with the children in the Armazem. For lunch, I was treated to a succulent pork chop, fries, and a Coke in a special mug designated for me. Aunt Martha served me as if I were a princess. I always had to have a huge napkin draped around my neck to prevent stains on my uniform. The meal was delicious; a real change from the bland boarding school food.

Because Dona Vera was an avid horse person, I would also visit the Flamengo Horse Club with her. She kept her horse, Brinquedo, there now because our riding school was soon to be liquidated, as I will explain later. I rode sometimes, and at other times, I roller-skated at the horse club's rink. My stepfather also came there once in awhile to give riding lessons. Once when I met him at the club, he tried to have me jump obstacles with his horse, Achmed, which he also loaned to a Brazilian rider, Nelson Pessoa, who competed in the Olympics for Brazil. The horse was huge and heavy set, light brown with a white patch along its profile and lower legs. I felt like a mouse on its back. Try as I might with my whip and legs, the horse would not gallop. Finally, I got him to gallop, and as I approached the obstacle, he made a sudden stop and I went flying over his head, landing on the obstacle bar on my fanny. It was useless for me to continue to try. My stepfather was nice to me during this time, and I even visited our riding school with Dona Vera. She also took me to the prestigious Hippica Club where she had bought a membership title and was a permanent member. She had brought a horse from Rio Grande do Sul in the south of the country to board there. I loved to watch the jumping and dressage competitions. Once while watching a competition at Hippica, the president of Brazil, Juscelino Kubitschek, came in with his motorcade, and I could see him in the stands. He was the president who built the city of Brasilia to open the interior of the country, and in 1960, Brasilia replaced Rio as the new capital of Brazil.

Dona Vera's family background was never entirely clear to me. I know she had European ancestors on her father's side, and well-to-do Brazilian ancestors from the state of Rio Grande do Sul in the south on her mother's side. Once Dona Vera pulled out a sword from a closet that had belonged to a general who was related to her. He had fought in border wars with Paraguay and Argentina in the south. The family owned a substantial amount of land in the state of Rio Grande do Sul and was living on its dividends, leasing them to *rancheros* (cattle farmers). So I can say that Dona Vera was rather rich and did not need to work. Her mother was in poor health and mostly lay in bed, seldom leaving the house. Her aunt, a woman of exceptional beauty despite her years, had very delicate manners and liked to pamper me. She always wore a turban in the house and seldom left the house, except once in awhile when a male caller took her out.

Dona Vera enjoyed leaving the house to get away from these old ladies who nagged her with their illnesses. When we were home, I watched them listen to the daily *novellas* (South America's equivalent of soap operas) on the radio or play with the dog Ming Ming, a Pekingese, who ate chopped up filet mignon and carrots. His bath and meals were a real ritual. Dona Vera's mother would sit at the kitchen table and chop up his meat by hand that the butcher delivered. Since Dona Vera did not marry, her horses and Ming Ming were an extension of her life. For Christmas, Dona Vera bought the tallest tree she could find. She found one that reached the ceiling and was a monstrosity by Brazilian standards since Brazil was a tropical country and few people could afford a real tree. She had thousands of ornaments her family had saved for decades that she placed on the tree with great care and the help of a ladder.

Frankly, I did not miss my mother while she was in Germany. Dona Vera provided great entertainment, so I was having a splendid time. When I returned to school, she would give me spending money to buy chocolate and ice cream at the snack bar. On a festive day, the snack bar was open just before the student assembly. When I went to the window, Madre Violeta, my homeroom teacher, gave me an extra helping of homemade wine-soaked prune ice cream. It was the best! I went to the assembly hall, our old dormitory, licking this delicious ice cream. Madre Julieta, our mother prefect, saw me and ushered me out of the hall by my ear and had me stay in the bathroom. I was embarrassed and humiliated and felt an instant dislike for this nun, even though she was popular with some of the girls.

Madre Julieta also wanted to remove me from a dance number that Tilda, our student instructor (the same student who watched us in the morning when the nuns were at Mass), was choreographing for a celebration. Tilda was a wonderful dancer and she was especially fond of me. She refused to remove me, despite the mother prefect's complaint that my dress was inadequate. At that time, I had written to my mother, complaining to her that I would not be able to participate in the ballet dance because my organdy white dress was sleeveless. Aunt Martha read the letter and was cross with me because I had not told her about the situation earlier. For two days, she was busy in her room sewing sleeves on my dress. When I brought the dress to school all ironed and pretty, I had it placed on the rack with the other girls' dresses. When Madre Julieta saw it, she said to me, "This must be the only party dress you have." All the effort was for naught anyway because I was also in a missionary skit just prior to Tilda's dance number where I had to wear a Chinese silk pajamas costume brought to the school by a missionary nun. Earlier that evening, Madre Violeta had me walk around in it and sell candy for the missions to the guests from a wicker basket strapped to my shoulders. To change, I had to go to a room in the back of the auditorium. I rushed as much as I could, but I was too late and ended up watching the other girls dancing on the illuminated stage from the stage wings. It was a disappointment, but I lived through it.

When my mother returned from Germany, a week or so before Christmas, I went to meet her at the port. When I spotted her amidst an immense crowd on the deck, I waved to her from the pier with great enthusiasm. She was surprised that I had gained so much weight and looked so well. I asked her whether I could stay a little longer with Dona Vera because she intended to take me Christmas shopping downtown. When she refused adamantly, that night my mother and I had one of our first riffs. She scolded me severely when I was going to bed on account of my "betrayal." I went to sleep with a heavy heart, not knowing what she meant, but later, I reckoned that she thought I had chosen Dona Vera over her after her long absence.

I did visit Dona Vera again and we went Christmas shopping in a very crowded city. The buses hardly moved in the streets and the shops were bulging with people. At New Year's Eve we were once more invited to visit Dona Vera and her family. After a champagne toast, Dona Vera fired her gun up in the air from the veranda of the third floor apartment. This was the first time Dona Vera's mother, a matronly woman with a kind disposition and refined manners (but somewhat of a hypochondriac) met my stepfather, the much spoken of Captain of Russian background. He presented them with a watercolor picture of a laughing horse flying over Rio. Dona Vera liked it very much and said, "It looks just like my horse Brinquedo." Later, she framed it and hung it in the living room.

That summer I went with Dona Vera to spend some time at her friend Dona Maria's mountain cottage in Teresopolis. Dona Maria was a matronly woman with short straight hair, bold manners, and a farmer's gait, whom Dona Vera had met at the Flamengo club. They made an odd couple, but they shared a love for horses. Dona Maria came from somewhere in Europe and spoke Portuguese with an accent. She was married and had a son named Tom, two years older than I. I only met her husband once; he pretended to be some kind of former count, but years later, a story in *A Manchete*, a Brazilian magazine, came out revealing his story was false. I only know that he could roller-skate very well. Dona Maria and he led very independent lives; he seldom accompanied her to the riding clubs or their cottage.

The cottage was in a remote area in the mountains surrounding Teresopolis, some three hours from Rio. I remember the kerosene lanterns and the pitch darkness of the nights. The two women were always busy making plans and checking on the duck in the icebox, which some mysterious power kept running. While the women gossiped and talked about everything under the sun, Tom and I played. He was a chubby fellow with a good-natured disposition. One night, he wanted to kiss me under the covers, but I kept him away, and nothing inappropriate ever did happen between us. I was grateful to him for teaching me how to ride a bicycle. He took me to a country road where he would hold the bike while I held my heart in my throat, trying to keep clear from the ditches. After several trials and spills, I finally managed to stay balanced and get in a pretty long ride.

That Saturday, a great picnic was planned. A peasant helper was hired to clear a path to the summit where we intended to have our picnic. The journey was disappointing as we walked over sticks and didn't see much, except bushes. When we reached the summit, the view did not improve. There was only a round clearing surrounded by trees. There, all sweaty, bitten by mosquitoes, and pricked by all kinds of ticks, we sat and ate our sandwiches. I think the garden outside of the house would have been prettier. But it didn't hurt us to share in a pioneering spirit by blazing a new trail.

After that visit, I continued to see Dona Maria and Tom at various riding stables. One Sunday, as usual, a large group of people were at our riding school, including Tom and his mother. The adults went riding in the large open field nearby, while we kids went swimming and played in the sand in front of the riding school. Tom and I had built a marvelous sand castle and were fantasizing about princes and princesses when my mother rode by with her horse. She ordered that I go home immediately. I hadn't noticed that most of the people had already gone home from the beach since it was getting late. Tom and I took our time going home because we were lost in our imaginings. By the time I got home, my mother was very cross with me. That was the first time I remember her punishing me. She sent me to the large bedroom where I stayed, feeling humiliated because guests were still in the house. Only after Dona Vera pleaded my case was I allowed to come out. I think my mother was just trying to be protective of me now that I was getting older, so having me be around boys was maybe making her a little nervous.

It was in late 1956 that my mother and stepfather had to give up the riding school. The lease was up, and the owners, the Mirandas, wanted to claim the place for themselves. We moved to the fourth and highest floor in a studio apartment in the first multi-level building in the Sao Conrado/Gavea valley. It sat much further back from the sea, which could be seen across a large expanse of field from the wide-paneled window and where earlier we sometimes rode on horseback. Surprisingly, while I did miss the Armazem children, I did not miss the riding school very much since I was glad we did not have the stream of local laborers coming and going and sleeping at the servant quarters at will, a form of trespassing we were unable to control that made us feel violated.

I began fifth grade in 1956 and continued to play with the Adelma group that was now solid and closer than ever. We were all part of a self-contained fifth grade class of mainly boarders. Study times were interrupted with lessons throughout the day and Madre Marina, the prefect of the primary grades, was our main instructor. I enjoyed her gospel stories when she taught religion and I joined the Crusaders, a group she led. I was proud to wear the yellow sash with a cross over my shoulder and chest when we went to Mass. She handled us quite well, preparing us for state exams given to every fifth grader at the end of the year for admittance to *ginasio* (secondary school).

Our homeroom teacher was Madre Euridyna, the nun who had come from the U.S. and whom I later befriended. She was very stern, but a couple of times, I managed to win her praise. The first time was when she was handing back a set of corrected papers and commented that my handwriting had improved. Later, on a special feast day, Madre Euridyna had the fifth graders write a poem to Our Lady. She was very impressed with my poem, which surprised me since I thought I had only expressed common sentiments found in the many songs we sang to the Mother of God. It pleased me to be so recognized, but it did not make me study harder or become a teacher's pet; instead, I continued to play with the kids who were somewhat anti-establishment.

The following year, 1957, we all were promoted to secondary school. Our classroom was in the new building and Madre Euridyna continued to be our homeroom teacher. We had a classical curriculum that included Latin, English, French, world history, Brazilian history, geography, design, music, math, and last but not least, Portuguese. For each subject, we had a different teacher. Just before our Easter recess, Madre Euridyna gave each one of us a handwriting notebook to complete before returning to school. The notebook escaped my attention the minute it was given to me. I remember I went to Jacarepagua, a northern section of town, by bus to see Dona Linda and the Armazem children who had moved there earlier that year. They too were forced by the owners to relinquish the grocery store. I no longer could run to their house from mine as I had done before, but I managed to visit them a couple of times during the holidays. There, I had a splendid time riding bikes along the streets and never gave one thought to homework. When I returned to school, Madre Euridyna came to our class and went up and down the aisle to collect the notebooks. I told her I had thrown mine out after completion—a logic that was acceptable to me but not to her. Those of us who had failed to do the homework got an extra load of handwriting assignments. I can't say I either liked or disliked Madre Euridyna, but I knew she was very demanding.

My trials and tribulations in school continued. Sometime during my first year in what we considered "high school," (sixth grade in the U.S.) our uniforms were changed. The seamstresses, housed in the old kindergarten building at the entrance gates, were pumping the pedals of their old-fashioned Singer machines, making the new uniforms for everyone. We would no longer wear the sailor suits, and we were anticipating the change. When the day came for the dorm students to be fitted, eight or so girls, including myself, were called out of the study hall. Madre Caridad escorted us to the fitting room across the playground behind the auditorium in the old building. I was filled with excitement. At last I would have my new uniform, and I felt privileged to be one of the first fitted for one. When we got to the fitting room, Madre Caridad singled me out. She said out loud, "Marianne can sew this button on this skirt." I readily obliged, sitting down near a table while the others were fitted. Soon the room was empty of all persons, except the nun and myself. She turned to me and said with a heavy Spanish accent, "You see, Marianne; your mother did not pay for the uniform, so you cannot be fitted; nor can you have it." I walked out of the room in silence, as though my whole world had collapsed. My heart was filled with sorrow. While the patios were filled with laughing children, I walked to the hallway of the empty classrooms in the old building and sobbed uncontrollably.

Nor did the humiliation end there. On the day the new uniforms were first worn by the whole student body, a special Mass was held to celebrate the event. Seated in the back of the chapel and wearing street clothes were the five of us who could not pay for our uniforms. My friend Beatrice and I consoled each other. Madre Violeta gave us some compassionate looks, but nevertheless, we stood out in disgrace.

At this time, small sorrows seemed to mark my life. Madre Diva, my first grade teacher whom I liked very much, told me that one night I had sat up in bed and screamed. Apparently, I was having nightmares, but I did not recall any of it. I also wet the bed one morning, and out of embarrassment, I decided to stuff my nightstand with the sheets. Sister Pilar, a Spanish nun (she did not carry the title of Madre because she was not a teacher) found the sheets and told me, "You Chinese people are very dirty." In later years, she paid deference to me because the prefect had high regard for me. But at that time, I was starting to realize people had mentally placed me in an inferior position because I did not pay full board. Therefore, I had no right to complain about the food or the regimentation. A sense of rebellion was awakened in me, and I resented the many hours of silence we had to observe and the punishments we had to suffer for small infringements. I sided with the children whose parents could not pay full tuition. And at night, we would walk under a starlit sky and share stories. One of the girls told me the nuns had accepted her grandmother's ring for payment. Whether the stories I heard were true, I do not know. I know we did often exaggerate the situation. On the whole, we were well treated by the nuns. We never received corporal punishment (except a shaking by Madre Violeta) and I cannot remember any kind of cruelty performed other than the humiliations mentioned here. Nevertheless, a sense of restlessness began to overtake me, and I became bored with the overly regimented life.

This kind of restlessness spread among my friends. They began to plan an escape. At the appointed time, they would go down the secret service stairway of the new building, leave the school gates, take the bus, and go home. Two or three girls carried out the plan. Sandra, my friend from the group, was one of them. A mother in the town, however, saw the girls walking down the winding road along the sea and called the school. They were quickly retrieved by the school bus and severely punished with a suspension.

Well, it wasn't long before I got into trouble again. Now that we were in secondary school, we no longer wore the checkered apron dresses of the boarders in primary grades. The secondary dorm students wore white short-sleeve blouses with a pleated blue skirt during the week. On Sunday, however, we wore the full uniform with long-sleeve shirt, pleated blue skirt attached to a vest, as well as a tie and hat. Unfortunately, I forgot my hat at home one week so I asked Nega, who was a grade above me, to contact my mother and retrieve my hat. She lived with her grandmother in town in order to be able to attend Stella Maris School, but she was unable to bring me the hat. There I was on Sunday without a hat. We were all sitting by our beds, awaiting the signal to rise and form a line to go to Mass when Madre Euridyna spotted me. I explained to her the situation. She ordered me to stay in school that Sunday. It happened to be Mother's Day. The girls had prepared a short program for the mothers who came to pick up their daughters. One of the girls, Ana Maria, while reciting a poem about motherhood, broke into tears because her mother had died in a plane crash in the Andes a few years earlier. But all was corrected with some songs and refreshments. Then parents and children paired off and went home. I thought to myself, "This is Mother's Day and I'm not going to stay in school," so I mingled with the crowd and then went home on the bus as I was accustomed to doing on Sundays.

It was a glorious sunny day, and my mother thought it normal that I should come home. We went to the beach, and later that afternoon, to the movies in town. I gave her an embroidered towel, a gift I replicated each year, but she was always very pleased by it. When Monday morning came, I showed up at school unaware of what would be the consequences for my having skipped out the day before. When I went to my classroom, Madre Euridyna was awaiting me in a furor. She told me that I might as well pack up my belongings and leave. She had searched for me the day before all over the school and I was nowhere to be found. I was to stand outside the classroom and wait for the mother prefect, Madre Julieta (the one who disliked me and pulled my ear). I thought for sure I would be expelled. As students passed me by out of malicious curiosity, I stuck my tongue out at them. During the first recess, the prefect came. She had a sort of smile on her face. Somehow, the situation amused her. She informed me that I was to remain in school the following Sunday. I stayed in school two consecutive weeks. That year, I was sure glad when summer came.

Chapter 9

Celebrations, Rituals, and Social Life in Gavea

Christmas was a special time in the Armazem household. The children would put their shoes under the living room window, hoping for a gift from Papai Noel (Santa Claus). Senhor Joao would go to town and make sure he bought a toy for each child, all ten of them. Sometimes, he would dress up as Santa and pass out the gifts. Once I slept over at their house during the holiday because my mother did not come home; where she was, I don't know. I was so astonished to see so many people in the same bed. The children occupied one bedroom and the parents with the babies occupied the room on the other side of the living room. I was in a single bed with three other children and had to be careful not to bump into anyone, which kept me awake. I noticed they were oblivious to each other, not caring whether arms or legs overlapped. In the morning, the chamber pot under the bed was filled from us all using it. I was glad when my mother called me back in the morning.

One time before Christmas, Landa, Dona Linda's cousin who often came to help and received a small stipend from Dona Linda, decided to take all the kids, except the baby, Tadeu, to visit Papai Noel at the Sears building in downtown Rio, overlooking the Guanabara Bay and Sugarloaf Mountain. First, we stood outside the Armazem, all ten of us, and took the small bus to town. Once we were dropped off at the cobbled stone road of Ataulfo de Paiva, Leblon, where many avenues from the city converged, Landa, a petit energetic lady with much "chutzpa" and a brew of kids to escort, waved to the policeman conducting traffic. When he approached, she explained our predicament. He hailed a taxi and we all climbed in—Paulo, Nega, Bisuca, the twins Grande and Miuda, Ana, Wanda, Joaozinho, Landa, and myself— all sitting on one another's laps, and the driver could do very little about it. We arrived at the Sears building and marveled at the escalator, the only one in existence in Rio at the time. We went up it and saw Santa on his throne. Each child had a chance of sitting on Santa's lap and making last minute requests. It was fabulous! I believe we returned by taxi via the Jockey Club, often having to duck down, so the

~ 99 ~

driver would not get a ticket from a policeman.

A word must be said about our celebrations at Sao Conrado Church. From our house, I could hear the church bells resound through the valley around eight o'clock in the morning, beckoning us on holidays and weekends. The Armazem children and I would walk the short distance to the church and sit in the front pews, reserved for the children. The men would sit on the right and the women on the left. Most people were of humble origins, but sometimes a rich person would come as well. I remember an heiress, whose family produced a notable Brazilian newspaper and who had a house on the beachfront, who would attend Mass on occasion. She was rather eccentric and had a reputation for being crazy. She wore a large straw hat and took communion twice from the priest, but no one made much of it. We were all just glad to be in church to hear the kind, charismatic, and gentle priest, Frei Luis, an Augustinian, who came from the Santa Monica Parish in Leblon. We children would stay after Mass for some lessons, and around Christmas, we would receive a bag of goodies that included sugar, fabric, and a few toys. Once when Nega brought her bag home, her father, Sr. Joao, yelled angrily at her, "Take this right back. We are not poor! I sell sugar and rice and don't want handouts!" My mother, however, appreciated the bag and even used the fabric to fashion a gypsy costume for me to celebrate Carnival.

I liked Frei Luis very much. He was gentle and kind, especially to the children. On a special feast of Our Lady, he had some of the children dress as angels, complete with feathered wings. We stood in special nooks of the tiered altar, eager to participate in the ceremonies. He chose me to recite a poem, which I carried around on a paper that was almost in tatters after much rehearsing with anyone who would hear me. He was pleased with my perfect delivery at the appointed time. Many years later, I heard from my history teacher, Dona Aglae, that Frei Luis was a holy and spiritual man who guided her and others in the parish.

Another great celebration was Festa de Sao Joao (Feast of St. John). Family, neighbors, and friends would be invited. A big bonfire was built in the back and the festivities began at dusk. People came dressed as country bumpkins with straw hats, patched pants, and long flowing skirts. We danced around the fire singing songs for the feast. Sweet potatoes were roasted on the fire, and people were served a myriad of *doces e salgados* (sweet and salty treats) placed on the outside table. The frying of *bolinho the bacalhau* (fish patties) and *pastel* (meat turnovers) continued in the covered veranda while guests were arriving. Dona Linda's sister-in-law (Senhor Joao's sister), who was of Portuguese descent, would join in with Dona Linda's family who were of mixed race. At the evening's end, the colorful hot air balloon made of tissue and wire was sent off into the sky. Sebastiao, the Armazems' servant, would climb the painter's ladder and light the kerosene-soaked burlap wired at the balloon's mouth, and we would watch it ascend slowly in the night sky, becoming smaller and smaller and disappearing. Today, it is forbidden to send off these balloons because of the fires they might cause, but in my time, we would see scores of these balloons, like earthstars in the dark sky. Dona Linda loved these parties, and she would throw similar ones for birthdays, First Communion, and other church celebrations. Often, there was dancing in the living room where she had one of the first *vitrolas* (phonographs), and I learned to dance a simple shuffle to the samba, bolero, and tango, as well as the *frevo* and *baiao* (typical music of northeast Brazil).

Dona Linda herself did not attend Mass on Sundays, but unfailingly at 6:00 p.m., she would stop everything to listen to the radio play the "Angelus" or Gounot's "Ave Maria." She would sit by the radio in a prayer stance and listen to the meditation offered by a popular priest. She had a special devotion to certain Catholic saints such as Sts. Cosmas and Damian, St. Judas Tadeu, St. Rita de Cassia, and St. Tarcisius. She named her last three children after these saints. She would often light a candle to Our Lady, Nossa Senhora Aparecida, patroness of Brazil, as well as to the Christ Child. She also had some primitive beliefs related to African rituals, such as macumba. When a child was sick, she would call a well-known healer, who would come with certain herbs and pray over the child while it was held in its mother's arms in the interior veranda. The healing was then attributed to the healer who had spiritual powers. It was not uncommon in Brazil to see Catholic rituals mixed with African devotions and lore. I myself found at the riding school a buried earthen bowl that had been used as an offering to the gods or a saint. Sometimes, we would see such offerings at the beach or in a nook in the mountains near a waterfall surrounded by candles. Lighting candles was a natural accompaniment of prayer and big in Brazil, and it could be compared to lighting incense in the East. Once I saw an old white poor man, carrying fish, drop dead in front of the Armazem. He had froth on his mouth and a vacant look. Out of respect they placed candles around his body while awaiting the morgue truck.

It was wonderful when Landa or some grown-up would take us swimming at the beach. Then we felt an uproar of happiness. I would call my mother at the office and receive her permission to go. Most of the children stayed close to shore, but I loved to swim at the waves' formation, beyond the breaking point. It was so refreshing and thrilling to jump high, meet the waves at their peaks, and join the other children in the game of "beat the waves." Sometimes, a wave got the better of us and would roll us head over heels into the sand. We would get up with our hair matted in sand and our eyes and nose burning with salt water to try again. When we returned to the Armazem, we all had to take a shower. Three of four girls would pile up at the back of the store—in the small cubicle with a cement floor that also served as a bathroom—to wash off all the sand and salt water. When we were all bathed and dressed, some of the adults and older girls would pretty up the smaller ones, so we would all look, smell, and feel clean like the afternoon breeze. Then hot coffee and sweet buttered bread were served to everyone on the veranda.

Some of the neighborhood's usual occurrences that brought people out of their homes were the appearance of: the milk truck, the bread man in his bicycle-wheeled cart, or the pots and pans and knife sharpener man. I would run to the milk truck with a liter bottle and have it filled to the brim with fresh milk. The bread man would bring freshly baked French rolls, but our favorite was a sweet long roll with a thick sweet egg custard glaze sprinkled with large crystallized sugar. The ice cream cart would come on rare occasions. The poor man would have to push his yellow

Kibon cart (Kibon was the best name brand of ice cream at the time) from the city along the winding coastal road to reach us at the Sao Conrado Beach. Mostly, he would come on a Sunday when the beach was crowded. Once, I remember standing at where the beach sand met the road to watch small racecars zip by. Other times, we ventured further from home to the beach's opposite end, below Pedra da Gavea to watch the boys play soccer, including Cazu and Nao, brothers to my school friend Harumi. I myself played *futebol* (soccer) with Paulo and friends in the Armazem family's backyard, and they would often make me the goalie because I was fast. I would also barrel race with them, and once, I went home crying because I fell on the barrel and broke a lower tooth.

Nega and I were friends even though she was a couple of years older than I. Bisuca and I were the same age, but once she stole some of my doll's clothes and placed them in a dry goods bin in the Armazem (store). I liked to watch Nega prepare the formula for the babies from Nestle powder and place it in a Coke bottle with a rubber nipple. She often baked cakes from scratch. I was always around when sweets were made or saltwater taffy. I saw Maria, the maid, stretch the white taffy until it acquired a frosty sheen. Nega would choose me to go to the dressmaker in Gavea along the Rocinha slum. After she would get measured for a dress, she would take me to her grandmother's meat market on the mountain's other side, near the botanical gardens, and there I would meet many of her father's relatives.

At home, we made a solid group with the other girls and boys. However, we had adversaries—the Adriano family's children, who lived on the other side of the riding school and operated a service garage. My mother let them use our phone, which was placed in a wooden box on the fence at the paddock, in exchange for use of a piece of land directly behind the paddock, which faced the ocean. When relations between my family and the Adrianos became strained, this agreement was cancelled and we children also became their enemies. We found them to have a mean streak, even though we had played with them earlier. Our feud grew, and one day we agreed to meet at the paddock for a fight to settle the score. We went to the riding school and got sticks from the trees. At the appointed hour, we met at the paddock. All the other children froze while I was the only one who approached the enemy. Needless to say, my stick broke and I got some good lashes. So much for bravery!

That was not the only time the Armazem children let me down. One time, the group decided to go to the movies in town. When I asked my mother whether I could go, she gave me twenty cruzeiros. The group did not want to take me, but I climbed on the bus anyway, believing I had the right to go if my mother had approved. Most of the time I was included, however. We would meet for hours at the steps to the upper flat over the store and exchange songs we had heard on the radio. I copied one in Spanish called, "Una Noche Tibia Nos Conocimos" (One Sad Night We Met) that was a Guarani (South American Indian Tribe) song from Paraguay. It became my favorite love song and I learned it by heart; later, I learned to accompany it with the guitar. Many years later in the U.S., I heard a tape by Julio Iglesias on which he sang the song. Hearing it felt like my childhood had been dormant and now come back to life. We also did all sorts of arts and crafts, like painting on tile and making macramé bags out of yarn or rope. I loved the Armazem family, and I felt so much at home with them. I balked when my mother brought me to play with some richer children in the area, who were not much fun. On one such visit, I sat at the dining room table for lunch while the lady of the house bossed the maid to serve us. Once lunch was over, the children, two boys and a girl, went to the back and climbed on some construction dirt and rubbish and tried to antagonize each other. I definitely did not feel any connection with them or other families to whom I was brought.

Nega and Bisuca were the oldest girls and Paulo the oldest boy of the Armazem family. It was customary for us to meet with the other children in the neighborhood. We met at the unpaved street, Henrique Midosa, which led to the beach, and sat under the streetlight. The funny thing was that the boys would congregate on the opposite side of the street to whisper and tell tales about the girls. Paulo was in love with Gloria, who also liked him, but she would not admit it. We played Berlinda, a game in which an individual's true feelings would be revealed. One of us would sit in a special place and all the others would make remarks about that person. It was up to the person at stake to guess who had made what remark.

By this method, I discovered that Nilson, a neighbor boy of fourteen, liked me very much. He said nice things about me, but I played hard to get. I let him know that I was still loyal to Vani, the boyfriend I had when I was eight, but had not seen in years. Yet something happened inside me once I knew how Nilson felt. When I awoke the next morning, the leaves outside my window were lit with a glow of sunshine. And in me there was an inexplicable joy. I leapt out of bed with a desire to live, to embrace this day, and above all to see Nilson again. He had been Laura and Bisuca's boyfriend, so I couldn't imagine he could be mine. Nevertheless, he continued to court me. Dona Linda had the only television set in the neighborhood, so we all gathered there on Thursdays to watch television. On occasion, Nilson and I would sit together on the living room floor, under the big middle table, and watch *Show Lux* or *Circo Bom Bril* (Circus Brillo). Nilson was slender, with a shock of undulated black hair. He was a quiet boy, but intense—he was gentle in manner and very thoughtful. Since I was now officially his *namorada* (girlfriend), he bestowed on me special favors. Once he gave me a brown paper bag filled with *carambola* (star fruits) he had gathered from the trees by the golf course. He lent me his bicycle that I took to the riding school to ride an entire day. I really did love him very much, but something in me would not allow this relationship to grow. I teased him by telling him that soon I would be going on a vacation elsewhere when I was only going to the dentist. This hide-and-seek game saddened him and he grew frustrated with me. He recognized that my upbringing was higher. He was three years older than I, but attended the same grade as me in the humbler public school. He lived with his sister for reasons I never found out. They were of the servile class, and in Brazil, these distinctions were keenly felt. So one day I heard him tell Paulo, his best friend, that he would study very hard in hopes of being a good match for me. In one of my escape schemes, I realized I had hurt him as well as myself. When we met that evening, I gave him a medal I had in my pocket, hoping this gift would soothe his pain.

Nilson and I acted as boyfriend and girlfriend for some time, and nothing inappropriate happened between us. Once, the group decided to meet at night on the clay road in front of the beach to kiss our respective boyfriends. We planned to chew guava leaves to take the smell away from the one cigarette we smoked. The meeting never did take place, but I did go to the Miramar Theater with Nilson and the others in Leblon, and I sat next to him while we watched a movie. After the movie, we got a gelato along the main busy avenue. We were so happy together. I continued to love him for a long time. Even when I moved to the apartment, I made every effort I could just to pass in front of his house; it made my heart palpitate in my chest. I began to see him less and less as I went back to boarding school, and later that year (1956), the riding school was liquidated. We sent each other some messages through Nega, but it was not enough to maintain the relationship.

Chapter 10

━━━━ ❀ ━━━━

High School Years

Madre Euridyna became my homeroom teacher during my first year in high school. One day when she was dismissing the class, she called on me to stay behind. She approached me kindly and said, "Marianne, I think I can get a scholarship for you. I need to call your mother to come see me." Needless to say, I ran out of the classroom with leaps and bounds, jumping over students' briefcases (the book bags at the time), so happy that someone was paying special attention to me. My mother came in with the necessary documents: my birth certificate and proof of adoption by my stepfather. Madre Euridyna and she then had a discussion, but I was not present. I was not able to get the scholarship because I was not Brazilian. However, Madre Euridyna continued to bestow upon me special attention. When the winter vacation came, she arranged for me to visit Mato Grosso, an interior state of Brazil that was remote and underdeveloped, with two boarding sisters, Eladir and Leslie Correo. I believe Madre Euridyna had an inkling of my situation at home, although I had not discussed it with her.

Eladir was one year younger than I, and Leslie, two years older. Eladir was a very quiet girl with whom the nuns encouraged me to play. Leslie was a very studious girl who was beautiful and had won beauty pageants in her state. They agreed to take me to Corumba, Mato Grosso, where their parents lived. I packed my small suitcase and book bag with necessities and my mother took me to the airport, Santos Dumont, in Rio. There I met the sisters who were all smiles and eager to take me to their hometown. We boarded a small plane. We were free to walk around the plane and even visit the cabin. When we passed over the city of Bauru, Sao Paulo, someone remarked, "Pele (the famous soccer player) was born here." When the plane landed in the town of Campo Grande, Mato Grosso, we were at the cabin talking to the pilot. We braced ourselves tightly, but there was such a loud vibration with violent shaking that it caused us to laugh hysterically. My first ride by plane was great fun!

We arrived in Corumba in the afternoon. It surprised me to see that most of the roads from the airport to the city were unpaved. The mother, a simple lady with medium wavy blond hair and one eye glazed with cataracts, ushered us through the front yard gate into a stucco one-story house with a large back veranda and yard. I soon got acclimated and rather enjoyed my stay, shedding my large city prejudices. The meals were fantastic. For breakfast, we got the canon bread (large Italian-style bread) accompanied with an over-easy steak seasoned with salt and garlic. For beverages, we either drank mate tea or coffee. In the afternoon, we had a snack of freshly made *sequilhos* (cookies) and Guarana, a typical Brazilian soft drink.

Leslie and Eladir's mother treated me very well, and I had ample amusement. During the day, I would take rides with Leslie in the Model-T Ford parked in the yard. We had to dodge the police because she was only fifteen and not allowed to drive. Sometimes, we would play cards, and I noticed Leslie was less scrupulous than I and cheated. Leslie's father, a dark, robust man, came from the farm on occasion, and he would then take us for rides in the country in his '50s black Chevrolet. Once we visited a manganese mine owned by Americans. It was interesting to see the iron ore in the red clay soil in the surrounding hills. I met a young American connected to the mining who had come from the West Coast on a ship that docked on the river. Corumba bordered Bolivia, but I didn't go with the family to the Indian open market, which was held once a week across the border. They told me the Bolivian Indians wore colorful long broad skirts and would do their business in the street, seldom changing their clothes. In the evening, we would be freshly bathed and dressed to promenade up and down the main street with the other families in town. It was an unfailing ritual and I rather enjoyed it. Sometimes, we young ones would break away to the newly built juice bar by the river, complete with table and umbrellas. The mother took us once to a concert and had me sit next to her, prompting some jealousy from Eladir. In the evening, we would sleep in a net covered bed with windows opening to the back veranda that was also the kitchen and dining area. It spooked us once when we saw candlelight shadows from the servant quarters. The maid, who was a mixture of black and Indian and who had some kind of mental illness, would sometimes roam back there with her head covered, carrying a candle. I saw her iron with a charcoal iron, but she never spoke. The best thing about my trip to Mato Grosso was that I placed a green *fruta de conde* (tropical fruit with thick outer segments and sweet core) in my book bag wrapped in newspaper. The airline lost my bag, and when my mother retrieved it a few days later, the fruit was ripe to order, with succulent sweet white segments.

During my second year of high school when I heard that Madre Euridyna had been made prefect of the student body, I jumped for joy! I remember taking a shower at home, feeling the light of day caught in myself and in the water beads running down the glass door.

Around this time, I had a religious conversion. I was about thirteen years old. Madre Euridyna arranged for a retreat for the secondary students and invited Padre Barros (the same Jesuit to whom I had made my first Confession) to give the conferences. He talked about how people had different personalities, some more introspective and others more outgoing, but all could give themselves to Christ. I took the whole thing very seriously and stayed utterly silent, praying and reading the religious books given to me. I decided to be a model student, obeying the rules and studying more than I had before. I became so good that Madre Euridyna cited me as an example. I joined a religious student group named Congregadas Mariana, and Madre Euridyna had me lead the group in the rosary many times. We had certain rules of conduct, such as not participating in Carnival dances and an opportunity to make a vow of chastity. Sex had been always an area of turmoil for me. I now became very scrupulous. I had read somewhere that masturbation was a sin, so I decided to confess it and cut it out from my life. My mother herself had told me that masturbation was bad for your health. I remember waking up one morning and telling the student next to me that if she saw me touching myself at night, it was because I was sleeping. She had a very dismayed look; lucky for me, this student immigrated to Canada shortly thereafter.

I now changed from being a rambunctious young girl to a more pensive and quiet one. I left behind my troublemaker friends. Adelma had become a day student. When Madre Marina asked me about our friendship, I told her I did not play with Adelma anymore, and Adelma accepted this. But I did make a new best friend, a boarder who had come from Espirito Santo, a coastal state north of Rio. Her name was Alzira Abreu Judice and she interned in Stella Maris School together with her cousin Etelvina (one year older than I) because it was close to the orthodontist who was putting braces on their teeth. On weekends, they went to their aunt's house in the city. Alzira shared my sensibilities and I liked her very much. We were in the same class and together all the time. At school recess, we would sit together and dream about the future, revealing to each other what we would like to be. I had religious aspirations, but she did not. During school celebrations, she would trim my hair and curl it. Once, I was going to recite a poem at school that I had written, so Alzira decided that my hair needed special care for this event. She had heard that beer would make the curl hold longer, a very good idea for my straight hair. We had a friendly nun provide us with a cup of beer and Alzira proceeded to plaster my hair. All I know is that when performance time came, my hair had not dried, and it felt heavy and sticky. But this did not dampen my trust in her sense of fashion and style, and she likewise admired my scholarship, brightness, and religious fervor. Once we went together to the Municipal Theater to hear an opera singer. We both found the lady's high notes very funny and had to hold our noses to keep from bursting in laughter. On the weekend, we did some excursions such as to Paqueta Island, or we went to the movies with Etelvina and Virginia to see a funny Jerry Lewis feature. We also saw *The Ten Commandments* with Charlton Heston. On my birthday, my mother invited my friends to go to the beach in Sao Conrado and come to lunch at our apartment later. Nega and Eladir also came, and I have a photo with them.

At this time, Madre Euridyna selected a group of fifteen boarders she trusted to occupy a study room by themselves. We would not have an attendant watching us. We moved to this classroom adjacent to the large study hall in the new building. We did not have to observe the strict rule of silence, and we could move around the room and help each other during study. Alzira, Etelvina, Virginia, and I, as well as some of our other friends in our classes, were part of this group. When we returned to school after the weekend, one of the girls, whose father had a liquor factory, brought a couple of bottles to school. She gave one to the nuns, who gladly accepted, and she kept the other bottle for herself. When the evening study time came, she passed around the bottle, and each of us had a capful of this sweet, delicious caramel color liqueur. It was June and cold, and I didn't think we were doing anything wrong. That evening too, we had watched the movie *Roman Holiday* with Audrey Hepburn and Cary Grant in the old auditorium across from the cement patio. Madre Euridyna was working the movie projector and would put a cardboard on the lens when there was a kissing scene. All was well until the next day when she heard we had been drinking the liquor in the private study room. She cried her eyes out and called each one of us privately to witness to what had happened. I told her the truth. Needless to say, we all lost our weekend pass home and the special study room was eliminated. However when the weekend came, I asked her whether she would allow my friends (Alzira, Etelvina, Virginia) and I to visit my mother. Surprisingly, she said yes, so my friends and I took the bus to our apartment in Gavea. When we told my mother what had happened, she thought Madre Euridyna had taken the matter too seriously. Later, I would restore Madre Euridyna's trust in me and come to realize that she held me very dear as I did her.

I did well in school, excelling in most subjects, but I liked math, music, art, and gymnastics the most—anything that did not require too much study. I loved to sing and exercise. Our physical education uniform was hilarious by today's standards. It was a black pair of puffy pants gathered with elastic on the waist and legs. We did all kinds of gymnastic movements as well as play volleyball. Once in the third year of high school, Madre Violeta, who became my homeroom teacher for the remainder of my high school years because only she could handle our class, wanted me to be part of the class volleyball team as a setter. I was so happy to be chosen, but I had no money to buy the aqua team uniform. I had earned some money for giving English lessons to Michelle, a younger French student, but Madre Euridyna and I both agreed it would be better spent on shoes I very much needed because mine were developing holes. Madre Violeta was not very happy with the arrangement. However, my enthusiasm for volleyball did not wane. I loved to go to the intramural games with the other high schools in the area. Once I remember we were going to play Imaculada High School, our arch competitor, at the Catholic University. We loaded up a school bus and began practicing all kind of cheers. Once at the volleyball court, we never stopped yelling and cheering for our team. Unfortunately, the other team had a girl, whom we named "Moby Dick," who had killer spikes, so in the end, we had no one to match her, and we lost. We were all hoarse that night.

While at school, "the group" (Alzira, Etelvina, Virginia, Martha, and others in the Mariana student congregation) continued to have its privileges. Madre Euridyna gave us a recreation room we stocked with magazines and games. We collected sweets and desserts from the girls in a special plastic canister for the poor children to whom we taught catechism in the slums behind the school. I wanted to be especially effective and placed a pebble in my shoe as a sacrifice for the poor children. We went there once a week in the afternoons, and at first, we met in a room above a grocery store whose owner was the leading catechist. It was great talking to the poor children about Jesus, who was also poor and loved them. Despite the smell of sweaty, dusty poor children squeezed tightly on wooden benches, we appreciated their enthusiasm to learn, and they especially liked the treats we brought them. Later, we were able to teach in the new public elementary school erected behind our school. There the classrooms were ample and filled with light from broad windows and the children wore uniforms. I had much success with the children because I was one of them and spoke their language, having lived in Sao Conrado so close to the slums. The first grade teacher marveled at how quiet and attentive the class was when she returned to take it over.

At the end of the year, 1959, both Alzira and I turned fifteen. The school was going to have a special end of the year party for us debutantes. I went to a dressmaker in a building across from the school with a pattern I drew and fabric my mother had bought. It was a silky beige material with small button roses that I had the dressmaker form into a short-sleeve dress with French collar and belt that formed a bow in front. Alzira also had a beautiful dress, but we both needed shoes. Her Aunt Hortensia took us to Copacabana to shop. I found my first high heels in the first shop. Alzira could not find hers. We went to all the shoe stores in Copacabana and then downtown, and she finally settled on a pair because it was late and she had no alternative. The day of the party, we looked smashing, using makeup for the first time.

When summer came, Alzira invited me to go to Guarapari, a beach resort town in her home state of Espirito Santo where her family had a house. Her cousin Etelvina also went, along with Etelvina's friend, Virginia. The night before the trip, we all gathered in her aunt's apartment in Leme (a borough next to Copacabana) to sleep and then proceed to the bus station. It was a twelve-hour bus ride from Rio to Guarapari along the coast and parallel to the mountains, one of which was called The Monk and the Nun; the roads were not always paved. Midway, we stopped in a town and sucked a few oranges that had been peeled and sold from a cart near the town bridge over a river. We also passed through the city of Cachoeiro de Itapemirin where Alzira lived and where her father held his law office and where he stayed to tend his coffee farm. We had a carefree and relaxed feeling, anticipating our beach vacation.

In Guarapari, the family had a small stucco house on the main street. We all shared a bedroom that was stacked with beds. Our routine was to spend the day at the beach, then come home, take a shower, have lunch, and then a siesta or girlish grooming. Sometimes, we lay in hammocks on the front veranda. In the afternoon, we walked along the main road, meeting people and even going to a dance hall in an open patio with lanterns. It was called Boate Azul (Blue Nightclub). A boy there asked me to dance, but I refused. By then, I had the idea that I was going to be a nun, and therefore, I couldn't be involved with boys. The other girls danced and Alzira even got an early morning serenade under our bedroom window. Etelvina also found a boyfriend whom she kissed at the rocks by the beach. Even though I got up early and went to Mass daily at the nearby Anchieta church (built in the 1600s and named for José de *Anchieta, a sixteenth century* Spanish Jesuit missionary to Brazil who protected the Brazilian Indians from the Portuguese settlers), I did not miss out on any other family fun and excursions.

After I came home from Guarapari, my mother told me we would be moving to Eli's apartment in Copacabana. Eli, like the Von Ulrichs, was like family to us. She was a German lady who had lived in China. After her divorce from her Chinese husband, she had immigrated to Brazil with her son Peter, leaving her other son, Didi, behind with his father. Shortly after our arrival in Brazil, my mother left a trunk of belongings on Eli's veranda, and unfortunately, lost some pictures that were exposed to the rain. Eli and my mother, however, kept their friendship throughout the years, and I accompanied my mother on visits to the family many times, considering Peter like a brother since he was a Eurasian like me.

I was so happy to be moving in with Eli and her son, since I had a palpable hatred for my stepfather, who on various occasions still tormented me. He was, to me, the devil incarnate. Once, around this time while parading in his underwear, he spat on my face and called me bastard. When I was sleeping in my mother's bed (he slept on the couch beyond the partition while I shared the big bed with my mother), he put his hand under the covers and tried to molest me. Another time he pulled my covers toward a burning mosquito spiral on the floor with some kind of evil intention. He would hide small presents I received and prized such as a ballpoint pen or wallet behind the refrigerator. Once due to some quarrel, my mother and I got a hairbrush and began hitting him while he lay on our bed, laughing. The commotion was not unnoticed by the neighbors. The notion of living elsewhere would liberate me from this monster.

We visited Eli and her son the weekend after my mother's announcement. Peter, who was about six years older than I, enjoyed my company and was very eager for our move. He and I talked about our similar circumstances in life, and he couldn't wait for us to join him. That evening, he asked whether he could accompany my mother and I home, and my mother reluctantly agreed. When we arrived below our apartment, my mother bid him adieu without inviting him in. I felt so sorry that he had to take two buses to go home. Unconsciously, I felt she had turned away a person who could understand me and shared my roots. But then I thought, "She is protective of me when it comes to boys, even this boy who is like a brother to me."

After weeks went by, my mother changed her mind about moving. While we were walking near the apartment house, my mother told me she could not move, but she would give me a bicycle instead. What a trade off! My monster stepfather vs. a bicycle! There was nothing I could say. I believe my mother was attached to Gavea and could not bear to live in the congested city. I did receive my green bicycle, which I named Esmeralda. I kept it in a utility closet on the first floor where the building porter and manager, Senhor Vincente, kept it safe; he even showed me how to repair a leaky tire. I rode it around the neighborhood, around the canal with the big houses, and also to visit Harumi's family at the foot of Gavea Mountain. By then, the Armazem children had already moved to Jacarepagua, about ten miles away, which for us, since we had no car, was considerable.

Also down the road from my apartment building was a large wooden house where a mixed black family lived. The grandmother, who was more than ninety years old, also lived there and liked to sit under the large shade tree. I was told she had been a slave. Brazil's abolition of slavery didn't come until 1888, so she must have been a child at that time. The young daughter was a beautiful girl who was engaged to my school's white bus driver, Tonico. She could sew very well, so my mother asked her to make me a series of petticoats and nightgowns for school because I hadn't had any new ones since first grade, and the petticoats were more like blouses, so I felt ashamed when I had to wear the gala uniform and my legs could be seen through it. The new petticoats and nightgowns came out beautifully. I even had a blue nightgown for feast days. It was at this neat house that I saw magazines that printed a series of novellas or love stories in pictures that were very enticing. I began reading them with much delight, but I gave them up later due to my religious inclinations and stuck to comic books. Love stories did appeal to me, and I do remember going to the movie by myself five times to see the movie *Sissi* with Romy Schneider; I even kept the postcard from the movie under my pillow.

Chapter 11

Last Year in Rio

Alzira did not return to Stella Maris for our last year of high school because her orthodontic treatment was complete. Consequently, I returned to school with a kind of empty feeling. I was like a butterfly, talking to this friend and then another, not knowing where to anchor myself. I spent recess time talking to Madre Luiza, my math teacher, who admired me and was a good friend of Madre Euridyna, who continued to single me out as a model student. She sensed that I did not have many close friends, and I was particularly pale. At meals, she would bring me an extra cup of milk and greet me with an "*Oi moleza, vamos comer mais depressa. O dia esta passando e temos muito que fazer!*" (A comment about how slow I ate and that the day was passing by.) I found it hard to open up to her, even though I wanted to.

One evening after supper, Madre Euridyna was walking through our recess with her characteristically energetic light step when I stopped her and told her I needed to talk with her. She took me to the front patio overlooking the sea where the lights of the Ipanema beach could be seen. I said, "My father is alive in China and not dead. My parents were divorced when I was very young." She responded with enormous compassion, "It is okay. Divorce is sometimes the natural outcome of life. But you are here now. Go to chapel and thank God for all your blessings!" I did so and felt a weight lifted off my shoulders. I still had a hard time talking to Madre Euridyna, but gathered around her when other children were conversing with her during recess. I had with me a small tattered leather box with a couple of pictures of my young father as well as pictures of my brother and me when we were young. Everyone looked attentively at them. After that, I no longer told anyone that my father was dead.

When it became known that *Dom* Hélder *Câmara*, a holy and charismatic bishop in the city known to help the poor, was going to give a talk to Rio's youth, Madre Euridyna chose Virginia and me to represent the school. When we went to the talk, I was completely mesmerized by Dom Hélder. With trepidation, I raised my hand to ask a question and he came right over to where I was seated and leaned over the empty chair in front of me. He had such magnetism and made me feel like the only person he cared about. After this visit by Dom Hélder, Virginia and I became good friends, although she was a year older and not in my class. When we exchanged stories about our lives, I learned that she too had a stepfather and not such an easy life. Madre Euridyna also liked Virginia very much and chose her to be on the yearbook cover because she was tall, blond, and beautiful.

Even on weekends and holidays, Virginia and I would meet at her house and make our way back to the school to visit Madre Euridyna. She was our beloved sister, so we would miss her when away. Instead of taking the bus from Leblon, we would walk on the parapet of Avenida Niemeyer that was carved from the rock rising from the ocean. I always had a sense of fear that I might fall down the precipice to the sea. Virginia, having studied ballet, negotiated her way around the wall with great ease. On vacation, I would visit Virginia at her house in Leme on Princesa Isabel Avenue. Her mother also worked, so we had plenty of time to cook up some adventure. Once, we decided to visit her old boarding school, Santa Marcelina, in the mountain of Santa Teresa. We took the tram up the mountain and stopped in front of her old school. A nun ushered us in and showed us around. She asked, "Why do you want to come to this school?" We said that we were looking for a change from the ocean dampness and the mountain air would be very beneficial. Once out of the premises, we laughed at our ruse.

My last year of high school, my stepfather became very ill. He spat in his can a lot and my mother feared the worst. His cough had turned to advanced tuberculosis as was confirmed when she took his sputum into the clinic. She arranged for him to be interned in a government-run sanitarium for T.B. patients. After he received this bad news, I saw him seated at the edge of the bed with his head buried in his hands and his elbows on his knees, dejected, like a general after defeat. Seeing him broken and suffering, I was filled with pity. The same man who had tortured me as a child and made my life miserable was for me now an object of love and compassion. He did not want to go to the hospital, but my mother was unwavering. Before his internment, my mother and he decided to have a family dinner in the Russian restaurant in Copacabana. For the first time, he and I took the bus to meet my mother in the city. We met her in the street where we discovered the Russian restaurant was closed on Mondays. So we took the bus and went to a famous Chinese restaurant in Leblon, close to the beach. We sat there together and had a good meal in the restaurant's interior, even though this restaurant was inside a house with a balcony overlooking Atlantic Avenue. There was not much to say—we could only await what was to come.

Once my stepfather was in the hospital sanitarium, my mother and I would take a taxi on weekends to visit him and bring him some goodies from home. He was mostly in bed with a spiral binder where he wrote some poetry and jotted some thoughts. I read in it a poem he called "Jesus, the Greatest Gentleman on Earth." His writing revealed aspects of his soul I had never known. My mother told him she had bought a Siemens turntable, and we were listening to music by Beethoven, Mozart, Tchaikovsky, and Strauss. He felt jealous and wished he were home. The Von Ulrichs and some of his other riding friends also came to visit him. Once, my mother stopped at the nearby Russian Orthodox Church to ask the bearded priest to come visit my stepfather in the sanitarium and he agreed.

One time on the way home, my mother and I went via the mountain crest with Uncle's English friends to whom he had taught riding for many years. They lived in a beautiful home nestled in the mountains with a brook and an orchid hothouse. We were served on the veranda by a waiter dressed in a white tux. The contrast of these moments could not be starker. I had an occasion to see our old horse Domino at the Flamengo Club; the owners had bought him for their children. In fact, this old horse was only good to amuse children. He was now spent and his back sagged. It was sad to see him led by others. He was no longer ours. It was another sign of the passing of time.

My stepfather had stashed away a small amount of money from his lessons and the sale of horses. He told my mother to buy me the *Encyclopedia Britannica* and a gold watch. She did not buy me the encyclopedia, but she did buy me a self-winding Omega watch that I wore for years to come. At first, I told her I would prefer it if she gave the money for the watch to a poor family in the slum behind the school because their children were eating mud. She said she would give me the watch and also money for this poor family. I went to school with a note for 1,000 cruzeiros in a plastic wallet. I asked Madre Euridyna whether I could go to the slum to deliver the money. She said it was too dangerous for me to go alone, so I should leave the money with her. Later, she approached me to ask whether I had sent word to this family. She told me the mother of the family came to the school saying that someone had called for her. I don't know how the message got to her, but I was sure glad she got the money. Perhaps it was a miracle!

In summer, Madre Euridyna thought it a good idea for her, the mother superior, and me to visit my stepfather in the hospital. I agreed, so we took the school bus up the mountain with great difficulty around the curves. Once at the hospital, I went to see my stepfather in the usual room on the second floor. He was not there and the bed was empty. I thought he had died, and Madre Euridyna noticed my consternation. Immediately, we asked an attendant who told us my stepfather was in a private room downstairs. Later, I realized it was one of the rooms where people were placed to die. I saw him in bed, wrapped in a white sheet. He tried to lift his head and talk, but no voice could be heard. Then slowly, some sound came out. He asked, "Where is Mommy?" I told him, "She is in the city working." Madre Euridyna then gave me a holy card with the picture of Our Lady painted by Murillo. I said, "Sister wants you to have this picture so you can see something beautiful by your bed." He replied, "I have my own concepts of beauty in my head." Then Madre Euridyna asked him whether he prayed. He nodded yes, and then slowly began to recite the Creed in Russian. He went on and on, and Madre Euridyna whispered to me, "He can die now," meaning his soul was prepared. When we said our goodbyes, I asked him whether he would like anything from home. He said, "Tell Mommy to bring me a sandwich." This was the last time I saw him alive.

Plans were for me to go to Guarapari for the summer on the next day, so I packed my things and went. I had a good time and a couple of weeks went by without my hearing anything from my mother, so I sent her a telegram. She responded by saying that my stepfather had died on the Monday following my visit. I took the bus home and my mother waited for me at the bus stop. She told me that she and her friends, Eli, Jackie, Edda, Ludmilla and her husband, and Lucia and Krisha Friedlander had buried my stepfather. She presented the Friedlanders with some of his pictures. He had died on January 19, 1960, and was buried in the Cemetery of Inhauna a few days later.

I don't know why my mother excluded me from the funeral. I suppose she wanted to do it alone since he had been a torturous figure in my life. However, I decided to honor his death anyway. I wore a black band on my left arm as many people do in Brazil when a relative dies. I never did go to the cemetery.

When I got home, it was now just my mother and me. On the weekends, we went to the beach to cool off. The summer heat was unbearable, especially when there was no breeze. My mother would close all the windows and shades and place wet cold towels below the door and at the base of the windows. We got some relief when she opened the refrigerator door, but needless to say, it soon went kaput. For dinner, sometimes we each had half a brick of ice cream. It was too hot to cook. To be comfortable, we would run in the cold shower and go to bed wet. After a few days of this suffocating heat, the rains finally came.

One evening, we were home enjoying the quiet. It had rained a great deal that day, and we had gone to town shopping. Our fourth floor apartment was clean and tidy. As I sat there in the dark, I was feeling the coziness of this place when I heard a whistle coming from the street below. After I ran to the window, I saw a group of soldiers marching on the wet shiny tar pavement, whistling to the theme song from the movie *The Bridge on the River Kwai*, and carrying a dim lantern to illuminate the way. The darkness of the pavement matched that of the night. Only that steady whistle broke the silence and made me feel good inside. It was as if I were watching a movie right at my doorstep, and I was the only spectator. This scene stuck in my mind for a long time.

My mother and I did things together now more than ever. We went to the movies—American Westerns such as *Shane*, which in Portuguese was titled, *Os Brutos Tambem Amam* (*The Brutes Also Love*), and romances like *Pillow Talk* with Doris Day and Rock Hudson. We visited the beach, or we visited her friend Eli and son Peter who had a lovely apartment in Copacabana on the tenth-plus floor, overlooking Lake Rodrigo de Freitas. Eli always had a group of people over, all longtime friends, and they would discuss current books and engage in office gossip. One of their favorite books was by psychologist/philosopher Carl Jung. Most of the time, their discussions went right over my head.

We went there for the fireworks display over the lake to celebrate the inauguration of the Guanabara state when Rio was no longer the national capital. It was an amazing display of fireworks with panels of words and bursts of color. At the time,

Eli was living with Jackie, a lady of about sixty, who was very glamorous and wore her white/gray hair short and flipped up; she had been married to an American pilot. Jackie invited my mother and me to her country retreat in Teresopolis. We had great difficulty reaching it, taking various buses and a taxi in the end. My mother, Jackie, and I went swimming in a rustic pool in the mountain neighborhood. We thoroughly enjoyed the refreshing dips. The ladies talked in the living room under lantern light about their many romances formed over the years, which is when I came to know of my mother's many dalliances while she worked as a secretary. I occupied myself by taking many walks around the mountains; I loved to see the many purple and yellow flowered trees in bloom.

Now that my stepfather was gone, my mother became more involved in my life. She took me for the first time to an amusement park in the District of Flamengo in the city. The rides were very hard on my mother because she was hemorrhaging a great deal, and shortly thereafter, she underwent a hysterectomy. When I visited her in the hospital, her spirit was brighter. She told me that on those days before the operation, she would be extremely tired after work at the Sao Conrado/Gavea bus terminal. While waiting in the back of a long line for the bus in this state of exhaustion, she hoped she would be in the front of the line ready to board the next bus. Suddenly she found herself in the front of the line and she believed it was a miracle.

Sometimes we lay in bed and she told me about her family in Germany and how I had five aunts. She told me she had gone to boarding school in a town called Niederviehbach. When I heard the word Niederviehbach, I could not stop laughing. With my Portuguese sense of sound, some German words, especially the long ones, sounded hilarious. My mother joined in the humor and told me of some of her antics in school. We would laugh when she would offer me anything at all to eat, but what I chose, we did not have in store.

We traveled to some mountain resorts together that were recommended by some of her German friends. We went to Muri and Maua, where we took long walks in nature, a habit she had never forgone since her youth in Germany, sometimes in pouring rain or the pitch darkness of the night. Once we went to hear a local man play the guitar in his hut and returned home without being able to see a foot in front of us. We walked also in Gavea in the open fields, even when it was raining, picking flowers and branches that would make a lovely bouquet. Along the way, we would sing some German songs she had taught me; we had become pals! She would say to me, "With you I could steal horses…!"

On weekends, we went to the beach, taking a good fifteen-minute walk along the road and then into a wild path to the shore. That particular day, I was not swimming, so I sat on the sand and watched my mother negotiate the waves. A man who had come from afar also began to jump the waves near my mother. I noticed he had a large machete tucked into the front of his swimming trunks. I froze in fear. When my mother came to dry herself, I told her I wanted to leave, indicating the man's presence. She brushed it off as nothing and continued to swim. I knew she was courageous, but inwardly, I felt very angry that she had disregarded my feelings of fear.

Once my mother went to the beach alone, carrying only a towel and our apartment keys. After arriving at her usual spot, she deposited the towel, the keys, and her slippers, and went swimming. When she returned to the sand to retrieve her things, they were nowhere to be found. She was frantic. She observed some youth in the area and told them, "I will give you a reward if you return my things to my apartment." Then she walked home barefoot on the burning pavement, wondering whether she would ever see her things again. A few hours later, a youth came with all her items and told her to be careful because he had heard the others had plans for her life. The youth got his reward, and my mother a heavy burden of worry. But my mother was brave, and she continued to carry on her life as usual. She loved Gavea, the beach, and the sound of samba music that came from afar at night in the flickering hills of the Rocinha slum.

However, Gavea was becoming very dangerous. Even when we had lived at the riding school, I had seen the body of a robber who was shot by a man parked with his girlfriend on the road in front of the beach. People said the body belonged to a man from the Rocinha slum who combed the beach day and night, looking for items to steal. I was apprehensive when I had to walk in the dark alone. Once, a man with a bare torso jumped out of the bushes when my mother and I were walking home one night. He was a black man, with shiny skin, who barred our walk for an instant, but then let us go.

Despite my fears, I had sympathy for the people who lived in the slums. My mother had hired a black maid to come twice a week to wash clothes and do some cleaning. She was very efficient and did an excellent job. She and I had many conversations. She told me she had a two-year-old son who was very sick, with lung problems. He was the son of a bus driver with whom I was familiar. During the week, he stayed with a woman in the city. She was working to save 2,000 cruzeiros to buy a hut in the Rocinha Slum. She said, "Life there is not very good. There is so much noise and people are constantly yelling obscenities and swearing at each other. But one of the doctors, the son of the Soto bar owner (restaurant/love motel) next door to your building, donates his free time and has seen my son. They are good people." My mother liked this woman's work but could not tolerate her absences. The day my mother fired her, I asked the maid to go to the movies with me. I don't believe she did, but I understood her plight.

On weekends and holidays during my last year of high school, I also had a need to be with friends. Even though I missed my best friend Alzira, who lived in another state, I went to visit other school friends in the city. We would go to the beach, to the current movies (such as *Modern Times* with Charlie Chaplin), and walk the main avenues with an ice cream in hand. While on vacation, I visited Virginia at the Villa St. Isabel in Leme near Copacabana. I would stay till dark and then cross a tunnel to the St. Therese of Lisieux Church in Batafogo for the six o'clock Mass. I had great reverence for the presence of Christ in the Eucharist at the time and made it a point to attend daily Mass. After Mass, I would pass the patio of candles, and then I would walk through the tunnel once more to take a bus to Leblon. There I would walk toward the beach to the bus terminal for the Sao Conrado bus. People admired my courage to walk and travel in this area alone. Once I ran out of money and asked the old popcorn man (always there with his lantern illuminated cart), who was always very nice to me, if he could lend me the fare, promising I would return it the next day. The generally amiable man turned wooden and only gave me the money after my repeated pleas. When I did return his money, he smiled again.

These forays into the city gave my mother some worries. Once I did not come home until late. I had walked up and down the main avenue in Copacabana, eyeing a porcelain coffee set I wanted to buy for my mother in a china store. Finally, I summoned the courage and went in. The lady behind the counter was most gracious and wrapped the coffee set for me in a box so I could carry it. In the midst of getting a scolding, I handed my mother the gift. Another time, I was invited by Nega to go to a birthday party at a cousin's house in the city. As was always the case with Nega's family, the party was very animated and lasted beyond midnight. It was too late to go home, so the family invited Nega and me to spend the night, and I thought nothing of it. We did not have a phone, so my mother was not notified. When I showed up the next afternoon, my mother was in tears. She had searched for me everywhere, calling those we knew to ask whether they had seen me. I never thought my mother would worry that much about me since I was most of the time away from her.

At school during this time, I felt very distracted and had no desire to study. I was glad whenever I could leave the study hall and go to the Patio of Trees to practice guitar. I had just begun taking lessons and liked to sing familiar folk songs and *Bossa Nova*, strumming them with chords. I looked over to the sea, the sea I had gazed on so many times, knowing that beyond those waters were my father and brother. But the future was nebulous to me. I admired Madre Euridyna so much. I liked to listen to her when she spoke in the evening to us. She would say, "I don't need to go to the chapel to pray. I am in the presence of God right here with you. God is in you." These words resonated in me. I watched her rise early before everyone from the cubicle where she slept in our dorm. I saw her take Communion and then walk the students to the refectory for breakfast. She rang the bell for classes from a podium in the Patio of Cement, sometimes wearing sunglasses. She wore the full habit with the starched bib and medallion of the order inscribed with "I.H.S." (Jesus Man Savior). She had prominent teeth like Eleanor Roosevelt, but what was most striking were her sparkling blue eyes. I loved her, but I could not express it. Once I sat next to her on the train that took us to the Corcovado Summit, she wearing her customary sunglasses, but it was a hazy day, so we did not see the famous statue of Christ, nor the panoramic view of Rio. She gave me some religious books to read: one on Our Lady and the other *The Imitation of Christ*. I read them regularly and meditated. I was very pious then, and once when I prayed in the chapel alone, I went up to the altar and knocked on the small door where the Eucharist was and made a petition to Christ: "I'm here, Lord." Madre Euridyna gave me a medallion to wear with the image of the Immaculate Conception of Murillo, and on the back, the same initials "I.H.S." used by the Daughters of Jesus Order. When I asked her during study hall what Immaculate Conception meant, she explained it in simple terms. I was so proud to wear that medallion. I thought of it as a prelude to one day dedicating my life to God in the same order of my beloved sister, Madre Euridyna.

When Madre Euridyna sent me on a school excursion to visit the Mother House in Belo Horizonte, Minas Gerais, I met the Mistress of Novices and was enchanted with the prospect of one day entering the order. While in Minas Gerais, the precious metal and gem capital of Brazil, I also visited a gold mine. I saw how gold was extracted from the rock, crushed, and then laid in beds that vibrated, separating the gold from the rock. The gold would then be melted and placed in large drums for further refinement. The end product came out of a spigot, but what could be seen was a small mound of pure gold. Then we were marched into a safe with hundreds of bricks of gold. The English manager said, "If you can hold the brick on your pinky, the gold brick is yours." Some of us tried, but it was in vain.

One concern I had was that my mother had not attended church in years. When I invited her to attend the Easter services at our school, she agreed. Madre Euridyna was beside herself when she saw my mother at the chapel. We attended Mass together sometimes and even went to the midnight Mass in the little white Sao Conrado Church for Christmas. We also attended the beautiful Easter Liturgical Ritual at the Benedictine Monastery in downtown Rio the next year. Madre Euridyna had been grooming me to enter the convent, so I decided to ask my mother one weekend. I approached her bed and said, "Mami (I spelled it this way), I would like to become a nun. I do not want to go to America." She looked at me with utter alarm and said, "Absolutely not. You do not belong in a convent. You will go to America with me and further your education." That was that. I was not the master of my destiny. She was.

My aunt Caroline Schuetzinger, my mother's oldest sister, had written earlier that year to my mother and me, inviting us to come live in America with her. She lived in Detroit and was a professor of philosophy at Mercy College, where I would get a scholarship. She wrote beautiful letters to me with a postcard of the college next to a pond with swans and drooping willows. I became almost enticed, but I knew I did not really want to leave Brazil. Madre Euridyna accepted my mother's dictum and helped me fill out applications to attend Mercy College. My Brazilian credits in secondary school were accepted as equivalent to a four-year American high school. So plans were made for us to leave some time the next year, once my mother had our German passports ready and the permanent visa from the U.S. Embassy.

I attended school as usual, benefiting from the special events arranged by Madre Euridyna. She once invited a Marist Brother to come and demonstrate paranormal states he had studied in Belgium. Once in the auditorium, we witnessed many extraordinary events. He called some people on stage and touched them on the spine and they were as stiff as boards and placed in a horizontal position, supported only by their head and feet between two chairs. Then he put some people in a trance just by repetition of drumbeats. I went up when he asked for some volunteers. He touched my spine and I felt a tingling sensation. Then he put his finger on my eyeball and I couldn't feel a thing. He hypnotized a few girls and made them digress to early childhood. In the last experiment, he placed six girls on stage in a trance state. He then turned to the audience and asked a volunteer the name of his mother. When he repeated the mother's name to a girl on stage, she began to moan and indicate a spot in her abdomen. He proceeded to use other names with the other girls, all getting a particular response. Later, this brother, who was also a doctor, talked with the man who had provided his mother's name and told him she appeared to be suffering from cancer, which was later verified. We were all very astonished and began to believe the paranormal phenomenon without having to abandon our Catholic faith or to join the Spiritist religion or macumba (voodoo), so prevalent in Brazil.

At the end of November, 1960, I had already turned sixteen. With the end of year convocation, the school was in a bustle of activity. I had taken a shower and was looking down at the patio from the fourth floor of the new building when I saw Madre Euridyna escorting her parents. A great sadness overtook me and I began to cry. I did not understand my emotions at the time. It appeared that I felt distanced from Madre Euridyna, who had parents and family (she was the eldest of nine children) while I had none. It was all very irrational but very real. It was akin to the feeling I'd had when I was sick and stayed all day in the dorm alone and no one came to visit me, not even Madre Euridyna, except for the sister who brought me tea for the meals.

That year, I earned the "Non Plus Ultra" ("princess") title for my class for excelling in math, music, and design. The next day was the high school graduation ceremony. My mother invited Eli to come and witness my graduation. Later that evening, we had dinner at the Chinese restaurant in Leblon at the edge of the ocean, and my mother invited Harumi and Terumi, my good friends from Gavea/Sao Conrado, whom she met so often while taking the bus to work. We sat in the balcony, and my mother ordered a whole fish, which was most delicious. There was plenty of laughter and joy. They were like family, but I was preparing to leave Stella Maris and Gavea.

The next year, 1961, I returned to school as usual to attend the first year of Colegial (at that time, after four years of secondary school, one could attend three more years of Colegial, which was more specialized and varied: scientific, literary, or normal for those pursuing a teaching career). My school only offered Colegial of Letter (Literary) so I enrolled in this class even though I had a more scientific bent. Since I was not going to complete the school year, it didn't really matter. In class, I met a dorm student, Maria Clara, who was most colorful and dramatic. She would often have arguments with Madre Luiza, our math teacher, to the point of making us all laugh. She was excellent in poetry and writing, but lousy in math. In study hall, I sat toward the back in front of Maria Clara and loved to watch her do calligraphy or fix her nails. Next to us sat two sisters, and with them, we shared crackers and *doce de leite*. I did not study much and was mildly reprimanded by Madre Euridyna for my poor grades in Latin and French. In some ways, I was already disengaging. Madre Euridyna had given my number fourteen to another boarder, a number I had had since second grade. I now felt like a guest. When Easter came, I asked my mother to buy Madre Euridyna a beautiful flower arrangement and a cheesecake that was out of this world from the German deli. She was most willing to oblige, even though she had some flares of jealousy regarding my attachment to Madre

Euridyna. I was so grateful to be able to give Madre Euridyna some presents she could share with her community.

For my journey outfit to America, my mother took me to an *atelier* (workshop) in town where I was fitted with a rust red corduroy suit with corrugated wooden buttons of the same color and a matching hat. I had a large navy blue purse and shoes I chose from a store in the fashion district in Copacabana. At home, I had packed my large soft plaid vinyl suitcase with my belongings; my mother threw out the gold rocks I had collected from the mine in Minas Gerais. We were only allowed forty kilos. I would travel in style.

I chose to sleep at school my last day, May 18, 1961. After breakfast, Madre Euridyna came for me and took me to see the mother superior, who gave me a crystal rosary and a frame with a picture of Our Lady of Guadalupe. Madre Euridyna and I parted, scarcely saying a word. She walked away sadly about her business, and I exited the school to take the bus to my apartment. My mother greeted me nervously because I was late. We had arranged for the furniture to go to the Santa Monica Church and some to Landa, Dona Linda's cousin. It was a bright sunny day, and we took our last ride down Avenida Niemeyer on the edge of the sea toward Santos Dumont Airport. When we arrived at the airport, a group of students from Stella Maris, including Harumi and Terumi, as well as some of my mother's friends, were there. Her friends gave my mother a bouquet of roses. The students gave me an orchid in a transparent vinyl box.

Soon we were on the tarmac and approaching the Pan American plane. As I ascended the plane's steps, I turned and waved to my friends, who were on the airport balcony, and I noticed a photographer snap a photo. I thought we would get this memory of a last wave in a picture that sealed this chapter of my life.

Part III

America

Chapter 1

Arriving in America

Little did I know that the colors of my life would change so completely when we moved to America. By the time our plane landed in New York, the city was a sea of flickering lights against the night darkness. As we were waiting against a wall with our heavy carry-on bags, we were approached by two gentlemen in suits and hats who inquired of my mother, "Are you Princess Chestohin?"

"Yes," she replied.

I thought these men were inspectors, so I was about to caution my mother not to let them carry our bags with our keepsakes, some from China. They had spotted us because we were wearing two fur coats we had brought from Brazil. They turned out to be Pan Am representatives who helped us through Customs and were most gracious. The Customs agents said my mother's roses had to be tossed out, but I got to keep my orchid, and nothing else in our luggage was disturbed.

The Pan Am gentlemen then ushered us to the Pan Am pressroom where a man with a large round plate flash camera, chewing gum, and talking a mile a minute, began taking our picture against the Pan Am logo. After the photo session was finished, the Pan Am representatives told my mother that a limousine was waiting for us outside to take us to the International Hotel near the airport where we would be guests of Pan Am Airlines. My mother, however, told them we already had reservations at the Sheraton. So we stepped out from the lobby to the street and into a large black limousine. I continued to be distracted by the newness of the experience. I was amazed by the smoothness of the ride through a deserted freeway a little past midnight. I noticed a black phone in the limo and ample room for our legs. Then I noticed a button that when pressed made the glass between the driver and ourselves move up or down. All this I pointed out to my mother, exclaiming, "Look at this, Mami!"

When we arrived at the Sheraton, the driver, in white gloves, opened the door for me and extended his hand. I thought he was greeting me, so I said, "How do you do?"

We were then taken to our room in an upper floor of the hotel. I did not know how to operate the shower or how to make the water run out of the tub, but after some trial and error, I found out how everything worked and showed it to my mother.

The next day, Friday, we made our rounds through New York City. I found the skyscrapers darker than in Rio, for many were made of dark brick. People were walking faster, with more serious expressions; some ladies wore hats and had ankle bracelets. It was hard to decide which person to approach for directions because they were all so focused in their own pursuits. When we approached Central Park, I saw tulips in bloom for the first time. They did not look real; they were so erect and perfect, like planted plastic flowers. When I saw the horse drawn carriages and saw the humbly clad men tending to them, I remarked to my mother, "Look, they have poor people in America too." We climbed into a carriage and were covered with a blanket due to the crisp air; then we took a lovely ride through the park. While walking through the city, we visited a restroom, where I was surprised that we had to pay ten cents to a lady attendant, but the bathrooms were immaculate with a decorated foyer. It was harder to find a reasonably priced restaurant offering homemade food, so we settled for fries. In the afternoon, we visited the Empire State Building. In the elevator, I saw many students who were very loud and talkative, recounting their experiences in the city. On the top floor, we had a picture taken and looked through the periscopes. When we took the bus, I did not know which coin to throw in the receptor, so I showed the driver all the coins in my hand and he pointed to the quarter. After a quick tour through the Metropolitan Museum, we returned to the hotel. After a short rest, my mother invited me to go back into the city for dinner. I refused and planted myself crosswise on the bed and began to sob. I told her, "You will find gangsters out there." I had heard about gangsters from the movies. So she left without me.

By then, it had dawned on me that I had left Brazil for good and there was no return. The light had been extinguished in my soul. I longed to tell my friends about my experiences, especially Madre Euridyna. I continued to cry with abandonment. When my mother returned, I talked her into sending a telegram to Madre Euridyna, saying I had arrived well. To our surprise, our expenses were covered by Pan Am. Aunt Caroline had sent a press release via the German Consulate in Detroit to Pan Am, prior to our departure, and therefore, we were receiving this kind of preferential treatment, perhaps in the interests of advertising the airline.

Saturday, May 20, 1961, we headed for Detroit. The limo was waiting outside to take us to the airport. It was a sunny day, contrary to the overcast day before. At the airport, I noticed cigarette and soda machines and pointed them out to my mother. I was amazed that just by inserting a coin, you could push a button or pull a lever and your choice of merchandise would fall to the bottom. The plane ride to Detroit was uneventful. I looked out the window and saw a vast flat territory dotted with houses. I wondered where the city was? When we landed, my aunt, Caroline Schuetzinger, and her Lithuanian landlord couple, the Mikailas, were there to greet us. Mr. Mikaila drove us on the expressway and mentioned that it was one of the first freeways that led to downtown Detroit, but we veered off before approaching the city.

My aunt lived on the first floor of a brick house and the Mikailas lived on the second floor. It was a quiet neighborhood with residential homes in a spread of parallel streets dotted with trees, near the University of Detroit. My aunt was a very organized person who liked to keep her apartment spotless and host formal teas and breakfasts. On the very first day, I noticed the large strawberries and cakes she served. She showed me my room, complete with a desk and taffeta bedspread with matching curtains. It was the first time I had my own room. My aunt's initial kindness began to wear off when I became involved in the cleaning of the house. I tied the curtains in a knot to elevate them from the floor. My aunt was horrified and said, "We do not live in the slums of Brazil." She would demand my mother and I join her for breakfast early in the morning, even though we were often quite tired and could have used some extra sleep. The breakfast table was beautifully set, and there I was first introduced to cornflakes, strawberries, and grapefruit. Soon we visited friends of my aunt, the Steuyers from Bavaria, which gave my mother a social outlet. I, on the other hand, felt quite alone.

Within a few weeks, a reporter from the *Detroit Free Press* newspaper came to interview my mother and me. This interview followed an article in the *Detroit News* announcing the arrival of Princess Chestohin and her daughter in Detroit with the photograph of us taken in New York. It did not please me that we were getting notoriety from our relationship with my stepfather. I said to my mother, "He is not my father. I know who my father is." She understood, but the interview went on. The photographer took a picture of me in front of the house, and the paper reported that I had visited an elementary school as a guest and attended my first baseball game, but shed many tears for friends and for my hometown of Rio, Brazil. It was true I was getting acclimated to life in Detroit, but I carried Brazil in my heart. My aunt took me to Mercy College where I met the registrar and director, both nuns of the Mercy Order, who were impressed that I could speak English. I attended a lawn tea, served with a silver tea set, and I wore my gala school uniform with a cream woolen jacket to match with an emblem on the pocket. I did have the airs of a princess, which pleased my aunt, but not a matching heart, and that did not please her.

I soon realized how involved my aunt was in creating a spectacle of her own importance. She liked to be seen rubbing shoulders with the high and mighty, especially those in academic and religious circles. She had been instrumental in informing the German Consulate in Detroit that my mother was a princess by virtue of marriage to Prince Valerian Tmiro Khan Chestohin of Russia; the consulate in turn informed Pan American Airlines. All this attention led to my mother receiving a job offer to be a hostess for high society parties, but not feeling comfortable in that milieu, she declined.

My aunt was going to spend the summer at Harvard University to work on her doctoral dissertation, so she decided to take me with her so I could study English before I began my freshman year at Mercy College. We took the Greyhound bus to Cleveland, then Philadelphia, and changed buses in New York to reach Boston, and finally, took a taxi to Cambridge. The journey was at night so I did not see any remarkable scenery. I was very tired when we arrived in New York.

We rented two rooms in an upper flat with Mrs. Morris, a lady in her mid-seventies who gave us the run of her kitchen. She herself slept in the broom closet, which had enough room for a cot. I liked to spend mornings with Mrs. Morris when my aunt was busy doing research at the library. We would watch *The Price is Right* or other TV programs. She would often have rollers in her hair, and she would water the petunias in flowerboxes on her upper porch. When I returned to Detroit, I received a postcard from her, saying she was tanning at a beach near Boston.

When it came time for me to register for the English class for foreigners, I went alone because I had a spat with my aunt, who did not like my carefree behavior. It took me longer than expected to go through the registration lines because I had never had to fill out forms by myself, but I succeeded. During the time I was studying there, I longed for companionship. Once when I was walking through the campus, my hair comb fell on the curb and a gentleman, a Canadian student I had met at an office for foreign students, picked it up and handed it to me. This momentary contact made me wish I could meet him again. When I did meet him later at a tea given for the foreign students, he quickly vanished from sight. I spent a lot of time alone, learning how to type and sometimes taking walks through the campus. Once when I was sitting by the river, two Indian or Pakistani fellows approached me and said, "We have been debating what nationality you are? We cannot place you either in China, Japan, or the Philippines." I told them I was Eurasian with a German mother and a Chinese father. They went away satisfied. I had answered their riddle.

That summer, Viktor Frankl, the author of *Man's Search for Meaning* and *The Will to Meaning: Foundations and Applications of Logotherapy*, was a guest lecturer at Harvard. My aunt had corresponded with him prior to our trip and attended his morning lecture. He invited my aunt and me for tea at his house to meet his current wife and his daughter, Gabby. When he made a trip to the supermarket with us, I could see how he was overwhelmed by the abundance of food at the market and was very careful to pick only what was absolutely necessary. I became friends with his daughter, Gabby, and we went swimming together at the school's gym and dared to dive from the high platform. Once after his lecture, Viktor Frankl and I walked side-by-side through Harvard Square. We talked about what constituted sainthood, and I, without hesitation, said, "It is a person who loves completely." He was impressed with my answer. I had not read his books and was unaware of my arrogance in speaking to a scholar who had lived in the concentration camps and was much more aware than I about the meaning of life. I later met him again when he lectured in Detroit. He did not remember me, but his wife did, and she said that Gabby was married with children and living somewhere in Europe.

I went to classes everyday in a building in Harvard Square. Our teacher was a woman with encyclopedic knowledge. She knew the etymology of every word and was a little too advanced for foreign students who just wanted to construct a proper sentence. But we plowed through it. At the end of the class, we were assigned a report about our country that we would have to present to the class. I learned how to use the library and do some research, and I finished well in the class.

I didn't have a lot of homework to do so I had time to write my letters to Brazil, go to a concert, or attend an exhibit. I remember attending a memorable string quartet concert in an old wooden concert hall at the campus. I heard one of Beethoven's Sonatas for strings with an *andante cantabile* movement that I will never forget. I attended a beautiful exhibit of glass objects that was also very memorable. Often in the evening, I would go to Mass at the Catholic church off Harvard Square, where I heard some beautiful sermons given by a very spiritual and eloquent Jesuit priest. I joined an Ecumenical group that met after Mass on Sundays for breakfast at the rectory. I helped there to make orange juice from frozen concentrate. A little can could make a whole pitcher—something I found quite remarkable after being accustomed to squeezing oranges. My aunt joined me for our Sunday devotions. I remember meeting there a Jewish man who had converted to Catholicism and was fascinating to talk with.

My relationship with my aunt was very much that of a child with a teacher. She was very concerned with manners and would scold me for such things as deciding to eat a steak right from the frying pan rather than on a plate. But sometimes, we had fun. She did become more affectionate toward me, calling me *Mousi*, a nickname my mother had given me long ago. Once on a Sunday, I went to her room and she began to read excerpts from her dissertation that had a long title dealing with Nicolai Hartmann's theory of knowledge. She would say to me, pointing to the landlady's dog, "You see that dog?"

"Yes, I do."

"Well, the dog you see is not the dog that is there."

"How come?"

"Because what is in your eye is only an image of that dog."

Then I would begin to laugh, and she would join in, realizing the absurdity of it all.

Because I was only sixteen and a half, I could not relate very well to my aunt and her life. Later, I heard about the hardships she had endured when she was a nun, and her horrifying experiences in Germany during World War II. In America, I heard she had worked as a housekeeper for a bishop in New York, and then in a flower nursery before obtaining a Master's in Psychology and then beginning work on her doctorate in philosophy, which she was concluding when I arrived in the United States. She had lived in San Antonio, Texas, and then St. Louis, Missouri, before landing the position of professor at Mercy College. She was definitely a self-made woman who had learned to discipline herself and demanded the same discipline from others, including me. Hers was an academic and European world. She did not understand my homesickness and why I cried into my pillow every night, longing to be back in Brazil. But she did admire my religious fervor and respected my attachment to Madre Euridyna. She could see that I could tolerate long separations from my mother since I wrote to her so seldom, preferring to write letters to my friends. I did get a few letters from Brazil. One friend told me Madre Euridyna walked around sad, as if her right hand had been cut off. I got a clipping from a newspaper article with our departing picture taken on the steps of the plane that appeared in *O Diario Carioca,* a Rio newspaper. My girlfriends were very surprised and in admiration of my status as princess. But now I had only their words while their presence was gone.

My aunt tried to lighten my homesickness by planning some trips. I kept comparing everything with Brazil, and of course, Brazil was always better. We went one Sunday to Revere Beach in Massachusetts by subway. It was interesting to ride sometimes above the city of Boston and then through tunnels underground. Once we got to the beach, I did not see much of the water because of the haze. The ocean front street had a carnival aspect with many storefronts offering different kinds of games and quick snacks and neon signs with young people milling about. I believe we had an ice cream, and shortly thereafter, boarded the subway home because it was getting dark. This feeling of steel, dust, concrete, and haze, with anonymous people coming and going with glum faces and drab clothing, followed me until we arrived in Buffalo on our way back to Detroit. Then it lifted when we took a side tour to Niagara Falls. My aunt arranged for us to stay in a motel and we had a whole day to marvel at the falls. It was beautiful to see that massive soft undulating water break at the edge and plummet in a white torrent. We boarded the *Lady of the Mist* and experienced the spray from up close wrapped in protective raincoats.

While I had seen the beauty of Niagara Falls, it did not help that my first introduction to America was done on a bus trip where I saw the endless cement stretches of highways with little remarkable scenery, and often stopped in crowded, dank depots. The Brazilian curtain had been drawn, making Rio's mountains and sea disappear. I was dropped in a new environment, where I had to confront new realities, so different, and often demanding much responsibility, giving me little time to nurse my homesickness.

Chapter 2

==== ❀ ====

College Years

While I was at Harvard, my mother had obtained a secretarial job and could now support us. Once I returned to Detroit, we found a flat a few blocks away off the main business street of McNichols or Six Mile. It was the first frame house on San Juan Street with a view of the Larcos restaurant's parking lot. The landlord, Doug Marsh, was a truck driver, and he and his wife Helen lived on the first floor. They had four boys; the oldest, being only eight, ushered us in to view the flat while his parents were out. We decided to take the flat without much hesitation. It had one bedroom, a dining room, a living room, kitchen, bathroom, and a small front porch. It was ideal for us and reasonably priced. My mother bought some essential pieces of furniture on credit at a bargain furniture store and my aunt gave us a sofa bed I could use. When we prepared our first meal of round steak and salad, my mother and I celebrated our freedom and new beginning with glee.

My aunt's demands and criticism had strained our relationship with her, but now that we had our own place, she gave us parting gifts. She knew I was very religious so she gave me a book about the life of St. Francis of Assisi, the first book in English that I read, and I enjoyed it very much. She also bought me an aquarium with a multitude of fish. She marveled at how I made a pull-string net to catch the fish so I could empty the aquarium for cleaning. To prepare me for college, my aunt bought me a new wardrobe and two winter coats. When we got home, I wore one coat over the other, thinking that was the only way I could ward off the winter cold. However, the greatest gift she gave me was to introduce me to a Jesuit priest, Jules Toner, with whom she had taught philosophy at the University of Detroit. The night she invited him for dinner, I saw him ambling down the street in his priestly garb and hat and wondered what kind of a man he was. He was in his mid-forties, of average height and weight, with sparse black hair, bushy eyebrows, dark welcoming eyes behind glasses, and a pronounced reddish nose. He seemed serious but attentive. During dinner, my aunt remarked to him that I was very devout, had an interest in the subject of love, and had once desired to enter the convent. I frowned on her revelation, but he found it sincere. I would not see him again until a year later when I needed some counseling for the emotional upheaval I would begin to experience by then.

My mother and I continued to take walks. We found a golf course, surrounded by beautiful mansions, a mile or so east on McNichols, beyond the University of Detroit campus and past the Gesu Parish. We walked in and out of the golf course many times, pretending it was our private garden. It was during this time that my mother told me she had a dream about my stepfather. She said, "He came to me in a dream and said he was sorry." We did not elaborate, for I knew what he was sorry about. We went to the Wrigley supermarket on the corner, a block away, and returned by crossing the street and passing a deli and fruit market with an awning that had fruits piled up in crates in front of the store. When I accidentally bumped into the strawberries, a couple came rolling down. I quickly rescued them and placed them back, but the manager saw it from inside the store, and thinking I was stealing, he yelled at me. My mother quickly came to my defense, saying sternly, "My daughter was just putting the fruit back. We will never come and buy in your store!" We never did.

In my college entrance exams, I scored low. I had to write an essay on the subject, "My Country, Right or Wrong." My knowledge of written English and American history was so elementary that I did not understand the topic. In any case, I was placed in a remedial English class and in a less advanced algebra class. However, I carried eighteen credit hours with classes also in world history, French, and chemistry. I found the books enormous, and they weighed a ton. I could not keep up with it all. My mother would type up the answers to the history questionnaires, and in this manner, helped me to prepare for the quizzes and tests. I did not have time to read the chapters. Luckily for me, the history tests were mainly multiple-choice, unlike the ones in Brazil that were only essay tests. In chemistry, I got a D on the mid-term exam, which horrified me.

Because I thought I liked math and science the best, I enrolled in a very difficult class worth five credit hours for medical technologists and nurses. The teacher was Sister de Paul, who had just earned her Ph.D. in chemistry. She filled the board with formulas and lectured at a dizzying speed. I sat in the back, trying to take notes. As I wrote the first sentence, she was completing her explanation of a topic. I tried to copy the notes of the student next to me, but she could not wait; she had to take the bus for her next class in Marian Hall. In the lab, we were doing experiments unrelated to the class. I felt very disorganized and frustrated. Once I burned the ring that held the test tube and ended up throwing away the substance we were trying to identify. The teacher did not think I would pass the class, especially after correcting quizzes I could not finish. But I applied myself and explained to her that I knew the answers but did not have time to complete the quiz. Once during class when we were going over homework problems, she asked whether anyone had come up with the answer to the first question. No one raised her hand except me. When she called me to the board, I worked out the problem related to volume and pressure. Algebra had saved me, and from then on, and to the teacher's surprise, I scored better on the tests. Since I had no friends, I spent Thanksgiving break studying algorithms at the kitchen table so I could work problems with multiple decimal points. In the end, I got a B in the class.

Life was a solitary affair for me in college. I remember sitting alone in the student lounge after taking the school bus to the Mount Carmel Campus. I watched life go by all around me and could not relate to any of it. However, I did meet with an occasional kindness. Patricia Fairbanks, a Native American student, who was a dorm student at the Mount Carmel Campus and with whom I had chemistry and English class, escorted me a few times to the bus stop on Six Mile. We talked about how difficult chemistry was and our progress in writing essays in English class. I managed to write a good essay by bringing to life a picture of Gavea placed on my desk at home. Patricia also improved, but she quit chemistry and gave up the idea of a career in medical technology for one in medical records. In time, I abandoned my interest in math and the sciences and chose to major in English because I liked to read poetry and stories, much to the chagrin of the math teacher who had tutored me in calculus and wanted to keep me as a math major, one of only two in my class.

My first two years, I took the city bus to and from school. My mother would wake me up gently from the sofa in the dining room while it was still dark outside and say, "Mousy, you still have five minutes to sleep." Then she would prepare porridge and slices of oranges for breakfast and send me off with my canvas carry-on bag, filled with books, and a brown paper lunch bag with a slice of French bread, Swiss cheese, and an apple. Occasionally when I misplaced my lunch as well as my purse, Jeannie Milkovie, a student I met in Sodality (a religious club) would run after me and say, "You forgot your purse again. The lunch I recognized immediately as yours. Only you bring Swiss cheese and a chunk of bread for lunch."

I liked Jeannie very much. She was energetic, smart, and had a roly-poly kind of figure. She began to treat me like a younger sister. She had been the president of her class in high school, and she thought I probably should have been placed in high school rather than college due to all the difficulties I was experiencing. I, however, did not want to go backwards and face another strange place; the one I was currently facing was enough. Jeannie and I were in French class together, and with another student, we devised a time saving routine. We divided our translations into three parts, and each of us would take one part and write the translation on carbon paper to make three copies. The teacher never suspected our ruse and we aced the class.

Even with Jeannie, however, I had difficulty communicating, mostly because of my emotional state. She was a couple of years older than I, and we had come from vastly different worlds. Yet she understood my unhappiness and showed me real affection. She lent me an English term paper on T.S. Eliot to help me out with my class. Around Christmas, she took me to her house and I helped her wrap some Christmas presents. Then we went for a ride in her father's shark-finned Chevrolet. She asked me, "Do you want to go for an ice cream?" I thought she was kidding. I could not imagine anyone would have an ice cream in winter. But it was no joke; we came out of the drugstore with ice cream cones. She brought me home and admired our cozy place (we used boxes covered with cloth for corner tables) and the Christmas tree my mother had planted in a bucket and decorated with golden-sprayed apples.

Jeannie had had a difficult life. Her mother was an alcoholic and had schizophrenia; she also had a husky voice from much smoking. Most of the time she was interned at Northville, a long-term mental hospital in the area, but once I saw her momentarily on the stairs at Jeannie's house. Jeannie did not speak about her mother very much, but she was devastated when her mother died of pneumonia at the above-mentioned hospital a couple of years later. We visited her grave and she knelt by it and wept.

My first winter in Detroit, I had been looking forward to the first snowfall, but it did not come until after Thanksgiving. When it came, I was walking back from the supermarket with my mother and began to slide on the powdery stuff with glee. I could not imagine that the pond at school would be frozen. I thought everyone would be out there playing in it. I got my coat and bundled up and went out to the pond, but there was no one in sight. I walked on the ice and bent down to touch it, amazed that the water, which had been flowing a few weeks earlier, had turned solid. My aunt told me she had watched me from the chemistry lab and was touched by my childlike amazement. She commented that she thought I had great intellectual and spiritual development, but was retarded in my emotional growth. Perhaps she was right. The trees that winter also stunned me, having lost all their leaves to reveal the very last tentacle of their branches against the withering light of day. Sometimes the cold bit me hard, especially when I had to wait for the bus. By the time I came home, my toes were frozen and painful so I would place them in a basin of warm water. Later, I found out it was better to thaw them in cold water rather than warm.

Waking up in the morning, taking the bus to school while it was still dark, studying and doing homework, all became a great weight for me. It was as if the silence and darkness of winter penetrated my soul. I began to experience shame, confusion, and an inability to concentrate. If someone talked to me or addressed me in any way even at the bus stop, I blushed.

I began to have chest pains. Although the pain was psychological, my soul felt like it was aching. I remember lying in my sofa bed in the middle room of our flat, unable to fall asleep because of the pain. I sat up in bed to relieve the pain with my knees tucked under my arms and my head low, and I begged God to take my life away. I wished I could die. But I carried on, as if all were normal. My mother noticed the change in me—my confusion, withdrawal, as well as internalized anger. At one point, she thought I was possessed by the devil. She turned to an Austrian friend, Frances Wagner, who was a friend of Aunt Caroline and who liked my mother very much, so the two of them would often meet. My mother thought Frances might be able to help since she was a teacher and understood childhood development. She was married to Walter Wagner, a colleague of my aunt, who taught chemistry at the University of Detroit. I went to see this lady at her house near the university. She tried to understand my conflict with my mother, but she couldn't because I was mostly silent.

Finally, during my sophomore year when I was eighteen, it was decided that I should see Father Toner, whom I had met at my aunt's apartment, as I mentioned previously. My mother called him for an appointment. He lived at the Jesuit Residence Hall at the University of Detroit and met me in one of the parlor rooms to the right of a long entrance hallway. I sat across the table from him and briefly outlined my difficulties. He told me he had a psychologist friend who could give him a test that he would administer to me. Then he asked that I release him from the secrecy bonds of confession so he could discuss the test with the psychologist. I agreed and came the following week to take the test, which consisted of a thick booklet with two hundred questions. He asked me to answer them as best I could and said he would be back in a couple of hours. He came back earlier than that to see how I was doing. When I asked him the meaning of "brooding," he told me it was like a hen sitting over her eggs. I don't know whether I was able to extrapolate the figurative meaning, but I did finish the test. Father Toner told me to come back the next week for the results. When I came, he told me that the test showed I was experiencing some neurosis and that I needed some counseling. I asked whether he could counsel me and he agreed, so we set up weekly meetings.

Father Toner and I began to delve into my past. I remember sitting across from him with my head on the table, unable to tell him about the sexual abuse and other sexual events in my life. He sat there, patiently waiting for about an hour, until I told him I would tell him next time. When I came the following week, the scene repeated itself, so I told him I would write to him. Then he sent me a typewritten note: "You come here and say you will say it next time and then you will write me. Which will it be?" I told him I would tell him in person.

I mustered all my strength, held a crucifix tightly in my hands, and while I sat across from him, I went through the events one by one, sometimes with embarrassment, sometimes as if I were suspended and outside of myself, sometimes in a halting staccato mode, like a laundry list, but I got it out. When I finished, I was perspiring with sweaty palms. Father Toner congratulated me. He said in a soothing way, "All these ugly, terrible things are not you. They are a part of the puzzle of your life and the whole picture is beautiful. What happened is not your fault. You were but a child with curiosity."

After that, I continued to see Father Toner and elaborate on my past as well as my current difficulties. Sometimes, I called him, using the phone in the front closet, so my mother would not hear me. Father Toner and I developed an easy banter, and we laughed a lot. My mother, however, became angry with me because she thought I had revealed too much to him and she accused me, by saying, "You told him I was a *loose woman.*" I tried to tell her that nothing of that sort had happened, but she would not hear it. For the first time, she struck me on the face with a book, causing my lips to bleed. I also felt she was intruding into my privacy when she read a letter Madre Euridyna had sent me before I had a chance to read it. I felt smothered by my mother and contained in a dark place. I wanted to break free from this container.

Relations with my other elders were not much better. My aunt thought I defied her and embarrassed her among her colleagues. When I went to ballet class with house slippers (I had chosen this class to satisfy physical education requirements), the teacher admonished me, not believing I couldn't afford ballet shoes, which was the case. My mother and I were on a very tight budget and she barely could afford the bus fare of twenty-five cents to school since she was still repaying the one thousand dollars to the Mikailas, my aunt's landlords, for our plane tickets to the U.S. The history teacher was not very pleased with me because I asked her whether I could keep the history books she had lent me because my mother wanted to read them. Once when I drove my aunt to school (I had learned to drive and my mother had bought a blue Falcon), I said something that prompted my aunt to strike me in the head, causing me momentarily to lose control of the steering wheel. When we got to school, I proceeded to the McCauley Auditorium at the back of the campus and sat in a seat for the general convocation. There I had a strange experience, as if I had been placed in a bubble and heard everything coming from very far away. I knew something had to change.

Seeking a solution to my situation, I went to see Sister Lucille, president of the college, who liked me very much. She agreed to sponsor me as a dorm student; in return, I would work in the library and at the switchboard in Marian Hall, where the dorms were located. This new situation would begin in my junior year.

Once during this time, I remember entertaining Sister Lucille's niece, who had come from the East Coast; we were driven by a chauffeur to a shopping mall and to the Sisters of Sacre Coeur School in Grosse Point, a very affluent Detroit neighborhood. I saw so little connection between these religious organizations and the poor that my desires to become a nun began to vanish.

Sometime in 1962, during this family upheaval, I started to feel a great desire to go to China to visit my dad and brother. I wanted to find and be in contact with them, so I wrote two identical letters to my father's cousin, Jane Yuan, and mailed them to two different addresses in Hong Kong from where she had written to my mother in Brazil, in the late '50s. In both letters, I included my passport photo, which showed me in my school uniform and wearing a religious medal on my chest, indicating to her that we had moved to the United States. One letter came back. The other never returned, but I got no response. My mother thought I should go to Germany to spend a few years there, but with the help of Father Toner, she was dissuaded and I moved into the Mercy College dorm.

My junior year of college, I roomed with Marilyn Valere, a student from Trinidad, whom I had met in an English literature class. She was a vivacious girl who loved to sing, dance, and have fun, a good antidote to the school's somber atmosphere. People knew when we were around because there was plenty of laughter, and we were notoriously tardy for the bus that took the students to the college's main campus. Mr. Clapper, the bus driver, a portly elderly gentleman with white hair who usually stuck to the schedule to the second, would wait for us when he heard us running down the hall with our shoes in hand.

Marilyn and I signed up to be in the chorus of a play and would walk back to the dorms in a residential area on Outer Drive, an island divided boulevard lined with beautiful trees and houses, while she taught me some beautiful English songs.

We also took a philosophy class together entitled *The Philosophy of God* and taught by Sister Paul Mary, a brilliant teacher who later assumed her given Christian name of Margaret. We and other students teased Sister Margaret one day by wearing hats and asking her challenging questions in class. One time, we missed class because we stayed up all night, typing a term paper, due the next day, on the stage of Marian Hall Auditorium in our pajamas. When we finished in the early morning hours, a dorm student kept us up talking, so we slept in, unable to wake up for the class. Sometimes on weekends, Marilyn and I would walk to Cunningham's, a corner drugstore on Six Mile Road near our dorm where there was a soda fountain. My mother gave me twenty dollars a month to do my laundry, and there was just enough left over for our soda escapades. I usually got a black cow that I had learned to drink at the Gavea Golf Course as a child.

Marilyn and I engaged in plenty of discussions about her life in Trinidad, and I would fill her in on my life experiences in Brazil. Inevitably, we would talk about the beaches, the tropical fruits, the love of dancing, and sometimes, we had a heated discussion whether British or American English was better. She told me how she would go dancing at the clubs in Trinidad after she finished a day working at the bank. We both agreed that kind of life was nowhere to be found here.

I met Sister Margaret Farley in Sodality when she became its moderator. She held regular counseling sessions with the Sodality students, so one day, I met her in her office and told her that I had psychological difficulties but was seeing a counselor. She asked whom I was seeing. When I told her, "Father Toner," she was surprised and told me she knew him well. Later, I found out he was her beloved priest who had taught her at the University of Detroit where she had a 4.0 average and who had been instrumental in her entering the Mercy religious order. I saw her often and shared with her the progress of my counseling. Once I shared a particularly tender letter, written in longhand, that I had received from Father Toner. When I told him I had shared the letter, he asked, "Why?" But I knew they were good friends and I did not want to be selfish with my letters.

About this time, Father Toner was transferred to a Jesuit Seminary in Aurora, Illinois. In writing a letter to him once, I paused, and wrote in the middle of the letter, *I love you.* He was touched by it even as I explained to him that I did not want to disrespect him because I knew he was a priest. He wrote back, saying there was no need to give a name to my love; it was okay. When I received a letter from him at my dorm mailbox, I was filled with joy and ran to my room where I knelt down in gratitude before opening the letter carefully with a letter opener. His letters were filled with spiritual admonitions and admiration and seldom had any direct display of affection. When some affection was expressed, I was beside myself with contentment. Early on when he wrote, I complained to him that he had typed the letter. From then on, he always wrote in longhand, for which I was very grateful.

I actually felt a little jealousy toward Sister Margaret because I knew he sent her roses on May 31, and she and Joan Wilder, another of Father Toner's protégées, had visited his mother before she died. When I confessed my jealousy to him, he thought it was childish. But I know he held me in great esteem. Our relationship was unique, very direct and personal, and not mired in philosophy or teaching. Whenever he visited at Christmas or other holidays, I would always see him.

I settled quite well into my school routine, following my class schedule, working a few hours a week at the main campus library, and in the evening, helping the switchboard operator connect calls to the various dorm floors and offices. I even became friends with the very serious and proper telephone operator who handled the old fashioned cables to connect calls.

While on the exterior it seemed that my life was going well, inside I was still suffering. I sent Father Toner a poem about a sunflower that had been yanked from its garden and planted elsewhere, only to become wilted and prostate on the ground, unable to turn its face to the sun. I also compared myself to a tree bare of its leaves and exposed to the winter cold. When Father Toner came back from Aurora for a visit, I went to see him and told him I felt terrible. Sometimes, I felt it would be best if I went to the mental hospital. That way I would not need to pretend that I was well, and the burden of my studies would be lifted from me. In a letter, I told him that my pain was as if my very soul were aching. He did not think that going to a mental hospital would be a good idea, but he put me in touch with a psychologist, Mrs. Shea, who was a friend of his. I went to see this lady several times and she was very compassionate and kind. After many weeks of counseling, she thought that my pain would only go away once I formed a family of my own. I kept my pain very much to myself and would share it sometimes with Sister Margaret. None of the students knew about it, but one particular dorm student who was in the field of social work noticed it and wrote me an anonymous letter which she left on the bulletin board. In it, she said I did not need to suffer in silence; I could write to her anonymously, and she would be my angel. I considered writing to her, but I never did. I feared the impersonal nature of this communication. What I wanted was closeness, immediacy, and intimacy.

When summer came, I did not go back to live with my mother. Mrs. Shea arranged for me to stay with Mrs. Prague, a Jewish woman who wanted company because her husband, a dentist, spent long hours at the office. I would help with the dishes and do some dusting. I also got a summer job at a dry cleaner's where I earned one dollar per hour. There the owner yelled at me in front of the workers for not doing something correctly. I was in charge of pinning a tag on shirts and brushing and folding sweaters. The working conditions were terrible. The black women ironed in unbearable heat and nobody complained. Later when I was summoned to the office, I courageously confronted the owner and said, "You may correct me if I'm doing something wrong, but you do not need to yell at me in front of the others." I believe the owner appreciated my honesty; however, I was dismissed.

I spent the rest of the summer with Mrs. Prague. When my mother invited Mrs. Prague to our flat, they visited together and became fond of each other. I too liked Mrs. Prague. I enjoyed watching her do the Sabbath prayer covered in a veil on Friday at sundown. She took me to lunch with her sister and to other family gatherings. She had two married daughters and an unmarried son who shared with me Salinger's *The Catcher in the Rye*.

Father Toner once came to visit and we met at Mrs. Shea's house. When it was time to leave, I offered to walk with him, but he refused. I had not realized until then that it was inappropriate for a young woman to be walking with a priest. My feelings were hurt, but I understood it was impossible, and our love remained deep and platonic. Once when I mentioned my love for Father Toner in confession, the priest was taken aback and thought it might be a subject for counseling. I left there, knowing that it was not necessary. Our love was pure and spiritual.

While I was living with Mrs. Prague, I would go to Mass in the evenings at the University of Detroit. Once a young security guard who worked there approached me. He said he was a medical student at Wayne State University and would like to meet me again. We exchanged phone numbers and agreed to meet at Mrs. Prague's house on Friday. Mrs. Prague was very excited for me and allowed us to visit in the lovely gathering room in the basement for privacy. Later, this gentleman invited me to go for a ride around an affluent neighborhood. We were talking about houses and I said, "I would like to have a small house with plenty of nature and a lawn around it." He retorted, "But who would cut all the grass?" It was obvious I was the dreamer and he the practical fellow. He made an off-hand remark, "You seem to have had a very sheltered life." We returned to Mrs. Prague's house and bid adieu without a kiss. He said he would call me over the weekend. I waited Saturday and Sunday by the phone, but there was no call. I developed a kind of fever because I was attracted to this young man. *C'est la vie*—life went on.

During college, I did manage to have a few dates. I consulted with Father Toner regarding a date with a nephew of my mother's friend, Frances Wagner, who had come for a visit from the Boston area. Father Toner encouraged me to go and forget about my previous intentions to enter a convent. I met this handsome, articulate young man at Mrs. Wagner's house. We walked to the movie theater nearby and saw *West Side Story*, which we both enjoyed. Then he walked me home on a beautiful summer evening. But it was a one-time experience since he returned to the East Coast. From my summer job, I had saved enough money to buy a prom dress, so I decided to invite a young man I had met at Mrs. Shea's house. He was tall, dark, and debonair, and a few years older than I. He picked me up at Marian Hall and we danced away at the ball; he even did the Tango dip. I was swept away and told Marilyn and the girls at the dorm that I even liked the way he turned the steering wheel. But it wasn't to be. He already had a steady girlfriend, a beautiful blond lady who was a hairdresser. I used the same prom dress to go to another ball with a young man named Charlie. He was kind of a nerd, with slightly protruding and overcrowded teeth, who never stopped talking. I went to the dance with him more out of sympathy than true attraction. In truth, when I went to the dances either at Mercy College or the University of Detroit, I always waited on the sidelines since no one asked me to dance. This experience made me feel awkward and unattractive, and I wondered whether being Oriental had anything to do with it.

Finally, the last semester of my senior year arrived. Marilyn, with the guidance of Sister Margaret, had decided to enter the convent of the Sisters of Mercy. She did not move far since the novitiate was housed in a building right on Mercy College's main campus. When I visited her a few times on visiting days, it was strange to see her in a postulant habit. She was cheerful but in some ways remote, adjusting to her new surrounding and the companionship of other postulants whom she did not know very well.

Since I needed a new roommate, I was asked to share a room with a Bolivian student who was going through great difficulties. She had developed a case of paranoia toward American students, but we were able to communicate because my Portuguese gave me a working knowledge of Spanish. I was able to sympathize with her since I also felt a sense of alienation and aloneness in the United States. In the evenings, she would make hot soup for us, either instant or from a can, and I understood then what she missed: the comfortable conviviality with friends and family that could not be found here.

I was swarmed with term papers for my English and philosophy courses. I remember sitting in an empty classroom trying to write a term paper for metaphysics class and still feeling the inner pain that only much later was identified as a smoldering depression or dysthymia, where one can function, but barely. I wrote that paper about the essence of the sunflowers in Van Gogh's painting *The Sunflowers*. The young teacher, Donald Yarnevic, a friend of my aunt (who was now chairman of the philosophy department), gave me an A and thought my paper was deep and poetic. I had met him a few times in a social context at my aunt's house and he found me amusing. In his class, I sometimes waved a white handkerchief to signal him to stop because he would go on and on and no one would understand what he was talking about. He asked me out once, but I was not attracted to him in a romantic way since he tended to be fastidious and too intellectual. I found out later that he tried to enter the priesthood. As for my other papers, I managed to complete all of them, except the one for an independent study I took from my aunt. It was a paper focused on the unity of all things as presented by Teilhard de Chardin, one of my aunt's favorite writers. Because I could not summarize his theory by the deadline, my aunt at first became very angry with me, but then she allowed me to dictate my paper into her recorder (a cumbersome machine with large cellophane reels) and she ended up giving me a B for it.

At Easter, Father Toner came home from Aurora. I went to see him, which gave me a sense of joy. Our visit was brief because he did not want me to miss my contemporary literature class. Later in a letter, I sent him an invitation to my graduation; he said he was honored but would have to be there in spirit.

When graduation came, we all piled up in our caps and gowns in McCauley Auditorium. As I sat down, I saw a lady with a large Kelly green brimmed hat trying to get into her seat in front. I turned to the student next to me and said, "I hope that is not my mother" because in that large hat she would definitely embarrass me. Well, it was my mother. She saw me get my college diploma with a certificate for *Who's Who in American Colleges and Universities* among 100+ graduates. She was brimming with pride, this mother who failed to see me grow up, but who bestowed upon me great affection and care, as one would give a ten-year-old child. She would often come by the dorm with vitamins and iron fortified syrup for her daughter, and once she climbed the stairs to reach me when everyone else was going down because of a fire in the basement and the alarms going off. My mother and aunt and I joined the rest of the seniors and their families afterwards for a celebratory luncheon at a country club. For a graduation present, my mother gave me a trip to Europe, and my aunt gave me a camera to take pictures. I was twenty and wondering what lay ahead for me.

Before I went to Europe, Marilyn left the convent. I went to pick her up and brought her to my mother's flat. In the convent, she felt that she was among a bunch of teenage lesbians who entertained themselves by making religious scenes to decorate their quarters. It was summer, but it struck me that she felt cold in her arms because she was so used to wearing the long sleeves of her habit. A friend of hers, Betty, with whom she had roomed earlier in college and who lived in an affluent neighborhood of Bloomfield Hills, took her in for the summer. Upon my return from Europe, Marilyn and I intended to rent a flat and live together. I wrote her from Europe to be on the lookout for a reasonable flat in the Six Mile area. Both of us had graduated in liberal arts, which was only good for finding a teaching job in a Catholic school with a very meager salary. Marilyn obtained a position in a Catholic School in a distant suburb, and I got a position to teach fourth graders at St. Michael School in Southfield, a nearby suburb of Detroit.

Chapter 3

— ❁ —

Journeys, Teaching, and Grad School

My mother and I were off to Germany in a plane chartered by the Carpathians, a German Club in the Detroit area. We sat next to a young lad of fourteen, who was going to visit his grandparents and could not speak a word of German. To our amusement, by the time of our return six weeks later, he had forgotten how to speak English. We took a night flight, so because of the six-hour time difference, we landed in Frankfurt at 11:00 a.m. I was dead tired, but I watched the scene at the airport in the morning sun with amazement. We were in another country and everyone was speaking German. My mother quickly booked two tickets on a train going to Cologne. She had a cousin in Bonn, a nearby city, whom she wanted to visit. In our train compartment, I watched the scene along the Rhine River pass by, wondering how my mother felt, being home, while all was very strange to me.

When we got to the hotel, I fell asleep in the big bed, but I was awakened to go to cousin Bruno's house for dinner. We were picked up by his son in a Mercedes and taken to a respectable neighborhood where my mother shared her world exploits with the family, while we ate cheeses, cold cuts, fresh bread, and drank wine in a good old-fashioned German high tea. In the morning, Bruno's son picked us up to tour the beautiful Gothic cathedral in Cologne and then take us to the train station where we boarded a train toward Stuttgart where we would join a tour group for two weeks to visit the main cities in Italy. The first evening in Stuttgart we dined in a restaurant near the hotel and were serenaded at our table by gypsy violins.

The next day, we boarded a large tour bus with thirty other tourists, mostly Germans, and headed toward the Austrian Alps. It was beautiful to see the white-capped peaks and the small blue lakes nestled between the mountains with an abundance of green pastures. We stayed in a quaint Austrian inn in the Alps where we were served a delicious breakfast. Then we proceeded to northern Italy where we stayed in an old hotel painted white with very tall ceilings.

That night, I slept next to my mother and had an awful experience. I felt hatred for her surge in my chest and an iron wall of resistance between us. I suppose I felt as if I were being led on a leash like an esteemed pet. I did not tell her about this experience, and she continued to treat me like a child, making sure I wore my sweater to ward off the cold on the bus, even though I was not cold.

As we traveled through lanes of cypresses and olive groves toward Rome, the German tour guide seated in front never stopped talking, in German, of course. I understood most of what he said, but I wanted to turn him off sometimes when he went on and on about every small village and region we passed, even though he was a wealth of historical information.

We arrived in Rome mid-afternoon and stayed in an old hotel in the central city. The place was replete with old architecture, buildings, and fountains, but it was a little suffocating and made me long for green and space. In the hotel, we heard echoes coming through the inner hollows and courtyards, a voice singing opera, loud exchanges of women making comments, and birds cackling away. Yes, Rome was noisy but exciting! The next morning, I rose early to go to Mass and passed a priest on the street. I used my Portuguese to ask him where was a church, "*Igreja*?" He did not understand since the word for church in Italian is *chiesa*. He understood when I put my hands together in prayer and pointed me to one of Rome's oldest churches, Santa Maria Majore, near the hotel. The church had a wooden staircase where people climbed on their knees because it was purported to have been brought there from Jerusalem and that Jesus himself had climbed these stairs.

My mother and I visited St. Peter's Basilica and saw Michelangelo's *Pieta* before it was encased in Plexiglas, due to the hammer of a madman in 1972. I also went to confession in a booth where confession was held in many languages in front of the Basilica. I was amazed by the Sistine Chapel with its vault and ceiling paintings by Michelangelo. Then we proceeded to the Vatican Museum where I saw Egyptian mummies and artifacts from antiquity. Next, we went to the Catacombs, where I left my clutch purse with my passport on a bench at the entrance; the tour driver kindly maneuvered back through Rome's one-way streets to the Catacombs. Luckily for me and to my mother's relief, the purse was still on the bench. We also visited the Church of St. Paul, the Pantheon (I enjoyed the quiet light coming through the large opening in its dome), the Coliseum, the Trevi Fountain, and various ruins. In one church near the ruins, there was a gargoyle on the sidewall with a hole; it was said that if you placed your hand in the hole, an evil creature would swallow your hand. Few of us dared to challenge the evil spirit. We even had an enjoyable spaghetti dinner alfresco at a restaurant in town.

Because I was so fond of St. Francis, my mother decided to forego the visit to Pompeii and Naples with the tour group while the two of us went by train to Assisi. The Central Station in Rome was a microcosm of the world: crowded, loud, with vendors selling watermelon outside, and inside a melee of people. We bought our ticket to Assisi and rode the train there. When we arrived, we had lunch at the small train station in Assisi where there was a quaint family run restaurant, complete with red-checkered tablecloths. Here I bought a couple of small rounded flasks covered with wicker of *Lacrima Christi* wine. Then we took the bus up the hill to the main square overlooking the Perugia valley. Inside the Basilica of Saint Clara, my mother and I decided to split since my rhythm of sightseeing differed from hers. I wanted to linger about to pray and attend Mass and see St. Clare's body, which was preserved in the crypt, so we agreed to meet at the train station at the end of the day. After I left the basilica, I walked about the cobblestone narrow streets and bought small clay pots and Franciscan crucifixes at door fronts along the way.

I ended up going to the city outskirts where I found the picturesque Convent of St. Clare. It had a lovely courtyard and a room with a balcony where St. Francis composed his "Canticle of the Sun," a poem that pays homage to God through Nature. St. Clare and he had a great love for each other, and he visited her and the Sisters of St. Clare (which he helped to found) many times. Everything was in a smaller scale, the refectory where they took their meals, and the rooms, still made from the bare rocks of the countryside, but intimate and lovely. I sat outside on the roadside curb with open fields surrounding me, and enjoying the sun. Here I wrote a postcard to Father Toner because we had a kind of love similar to St. Clare and St. Francis, and I felt like he was with me on this journey.

Then I looked at the map and realized I had not gone to the Basilica of St. Francis, the main attraction that was at the very top of the hill. I ran up as fast as I could, cutting across alleyways with stone steps to reach a higher road, and finally, I arrived at the church breathless. It was a large formal church, crowded with people, and in a haze of candles and incense smoke. I saw the crypt of St. Francis and the famous Franciscan Crucifix and many red flickering lights inside glass globes hanging from the ceiling. I did not linger long because I had to catch the bus and meet my mother. I managed to catch the last bus to the train station and even saw the setting sun against the parapet of the square where Italian women dressed in black with veiled covered heads sat on benches.

When I arrived at the train station, my mother was up in arms, but relieved. "This was the very last bus," she told me. "I have been waiting for you for a long time. Our train will be here any moment." We stepped onto the train at dusk, and I sat down exhausted. As we approached Rome, more people boarded the train; perhaps they were commuters. A handsome middle-aged man in a white suit and shirt with expensive watch sat next to me. I don't remember whether my mother exchanged any words with him, but I did feel his presence. I think he noticed the pain in my countenance as I sat there silently because he stroked my face. He left shortly thereafter.

We attended a dinner concert at the Piazza where Michelangelo's *David* was displayed. A couple of young men there made eyes at me, but my mother was very reluctant to let me out of her sight to give in to these flirtations. Next, we visited the tower of the Palazzo Vecchio. When we entered the door of the spiral staircase leading toward the tower, the attendant below locked the door behind us. My mother and I looked at each other, wondering whether we had been locked in for good. There was no other way but to go up, and it was a very long way up. Once out at the terrace of the turret, we found another staircase leading to the bell tower. This staircase was an iron frame with chicken wire on either side, giving me a sensation of being suspended in air without any tangible support. I experienced acrophobia, viewing the city below and having a sense I could fall at any time. I was glad when they let us out of the tower and we were off to explore other attractions. I rushed through the Medici Galleria of famous paintings since at age twenty I was not too fond of museums and would much rather be in the open fresh air. I did enjoy seeing Dante Alighieri's house with the front yard where they tied the horses. In college, I had read some of the love poems Dante wrote about Beatrice, a young woman with whom he had fallen in love, but who was unaware of his love or his poems. Beside *The Divine Comedy,* these poems made Dante more human to me.

On our return journey toward the Alps, we stopped briefly in front of the famous gothic Milan Cathedral with its spindly peaks, where I was offered a trained white pigeon a man was carrying on his shoulders. I smiled apologetically, puzzled with his offer; perhaps he was trying to get our attention to sell us something or for us to toss him a coin. Then we proceeded to the Great St. Bernard Pass in the Alps between Italy and Switzerland and dined in a German restaurant in the city of Lausanne, Switzerland. People there spoke German with a Swiss accent. We stayed there in a lovely inn.

Before long we were in Munich, Bavaria's main city and where my parents had met. My mother made arrangements for us to meet two of her living aunts, Tante Annie and Tante Lisa. Tante Annie was the youngest of my grandmother's sisters, with whom my mother had lived in Munich in her youth, and with whom she did not get along; she was a teacher and never got married. She was more reticent about meeting us, compared to Tante Lisa, who was most affable. Yet Tante Annie came, guiding Tante Lisa, who was blind and in need of assistance. Later, as the oldest member of the family, Tante Lisa would send me greetings and blessings for my wedding, and I named my oldest daughter Lisa after her.

While in Germany, we stayed with Tante Eva, my mother's second oldest sister who lived on the seventh floor of a high rise apartment building in Regensburg. From there, we went in Eva's Volkswagen through the Bavarian Forest and visited many quaint towns and villages, sometimes accompanied by Tante Hilde, who did not always get along with Tante Eva. We took our meals together, which sometimes included wild mushrooms the sisters gathered in the forest after a swim in a small lake. Eva found almost all of them and I none. To test whether they were poisonous, my aunt inserted a silver spoon while cooking them, and if it did not turn black, they were safe to eat. They were cooked with cream or sour cream and quite delicious. Tante Eva did not like me very much, and I was not too fond of her either. I found her quite bossy and demanding.

On one occasion, we went to a famous Bavarian shrine of Our Lady of Altotting, a Black Madonna that was spared from a fire and is said to bestow miracles. When we got there, I saw people walking around the church, carrying wooden crosses. I inquired where one could get a cross, for I intended to carry a cross around the church as a way to do penance and ask for blessings for my upcoming teaching year. When my mother and Eva spotted me, they said I was carrying one of the largest ones, and they chuckled and hid behind a pillar with embarrassment.

Another visit we made was to my cousin Utte, who, with her husband Kurt, raised pigs in a farm near Wurt a. Donau, the town where the Schuetzinger family had their printing business and where my mother spent her childhood. It was a beautiful farm nestled in the hills of the Bavarian Forest, but at the time, they were living in a garage because the main house was under construction. Utte had many small children and a baby in a cradle that gave the place an air of the Christmas story. The cramped quarters did not dampen the hospitality; coffee was served with fresh German bread and cake by Lucy, Kurt's mother, who lived with them. Later, Utte took us to the lake nearby to see the horses and the suckling pigs, carefully indicating the mud puddles to avoid. I enjoyed visiting this cousin who treated me with great affection.

Before leaving Regensburg, we also visited my mother's birthplace of Tirchenreut where an old man in my grandfather's printing business recognized my mother, having known her as a young child. And, of course, we toured my mother's famous boarding school of Niederviehbach where all the Schuetzinger girls got their education. My mother even recognized some of the old nuns as we walked around the premises.

Another cousin we visited was Helmut, one of Hilde's sons who lived in the vicinity of Regensburg with his wife. One weekend, he took my mother and me to Munich on the autobahn so I could visit with his sister Hildegard, who was single and lived in an apartment there. I was ushered into Hildegard's lovely apartment and allowed to sleep in her feathered bed while my cousin talked to me in German about old times. She had visited my aunt Caroline (Linchen) in the U.S. while I was in college, and we had made a two-week trip across Michigan with my mother and a friend, Dorothy Hitchcock, who taught microbiology at Mercy College and was my aunt's colleague. We laughed about Dorothy's frugal ways and her witchy appearance when she wore a hat and glasses while seated in a rowboat in the lake by our rented cottage. Hildegard also talked to me about her current dating experiences and some outings she took with friends. During the day, we took a tour of Munich via the city tour bus and I saw some of the devastation of World War II since some of the ruins had been left as a memento. We walked around the main square and saw the Glockenspiel (clock) marking the hour on the main tower of the city hall, with figurines coming out on the stage of the clock. In the evening, we joined Hildegard's brothers, Rainer and Helmut, and their wives to tour the city's beer halls and taverns. I drank much beer and ate bratwurst, and at one point, the men tossed me about from man to man as their Chinese cousin. I had a wonderful time with these cousins.

My mother took the opportunity to stay with her friend Hilde with whom she had traveled around Europe when both were twenty-one; unfortunately now, Hilde had been diagnosed with stomach cancer and did not have long to live. Hilde was living with her sister Leni and was in a wheelchair with an extended stomach. She was divorced, and I believe only her children came to visit her. I traveled there by bus the next day, passing the famous English Gardens that my mother and father liked to visit while living in Munich. At Leni's apartment, I also met George Wust, Hilde and Leni's brother, with whom my mother kept a lifelong correspondence, and who in his youth had asked my mother to marry him. He played for the symphony and was happily married with kids. He walked us at night to the bus stop that would take us to the main train station. There we would take the train to Frankfurt and join the Carpathian group for a banquet and some dancing. My mother and I did some polkas, and I was amazed by her agility and enthusiasm. The next afternoon, we left to return to the U.S.

Once in Detroit, I went to see Father Toner armed with a small flask of *Lacrima Christi* wine and some dried heather I had picked from the Bavarian Forest. To my surprise, he wanted to drink the wine right then and there. He opened the flask and we shared it, toasting the upcoming school year. Then I handed him the flowers; when he returned some to me, I said, "I have much more at home." But then I realized it had become a gift from him to me, so I took it. He was to depart to Aurora, Illinois shortly, and I knew I would miss him. In fact, I was completely absorbed in my love for him in such a way that he was in my thoughts constantly. He was a priest and I respected that, but at times, I felt I could not move forward and try to make new relationships. I went to see him again and told him I would stop writing to him for a while. I ran out of there in sobs and went to see Sister Margaret, who was a very good friend of his and counseled me at times. I told her about my decision and she witnessed my sobbing. A few weeks later, I received a letter from Father Toner with this admonition, "No news is good news." Needless to say, I wrote him back. I visited him at Aurora Jesuit Seminary on occasion, and when he came to Detroit for the holidays and sometimes to give a seminar, he would give me a call. Our close ties remained. Once at Aurora, he said to me, "You came thirty years too late."

Marilyn and I found an ad in the paper for an upper flat apartment on Mendota Street near Puritan in Detroit. We called and the landlord met us with a lantern because the electricity was turned off. We saw that the apartment had two bedrooms and was perfect for us. The landlord was reluctant to give it to us because we were so young and single and might not stay for very long, but when we begged him to hold it for us, he did. The next day, we went to Sears and opened a credit account and bought a bunk bed, two card tables with chairs, two red shag rugs, and long gray curtains for the living room and dining room. Then we went to the dime store to buy pots and pans and dishes. We were ready to set up house with sectional brown couches given to us by the downstairs tenants, a married couple with children. Both Marilyn and I obtained cars. I got a tan Volkswagen Beetle that sometimes gave way on me on deserted roads in winter. But we managed to set up a household, dividing the grocery bills, rent, and utilities with the money we got from our teaching jobs.

Teaching at St. Michael's School was no picnic. I still suffered from that low-grade depression that just would not go away. I was given a class of fifty fourth graders. The nun took the academically superior fourth graders while I had a class with mixed ability and a retarded girl with a 60 IQ. I often prayed the retarded girl would not come to school so I would not have to deal with the other children running away from her and not wanting to sit next to her because she was so unkempt and distracting. It was very hard for me to keep discipline and teach.

When I taught language arts to the better class, we made some headway. I was even able to be creative and have the students compose a group poem on the board. A nun, a visiting superintendent, sat in the back of my class and watched the class compose a poem. She called me aside into an empty classroom and chastised me. She said I was teaching the students as if they were in high school by having them write poems. Then she looked at me and said, "I hope you do not tell the students you're *Chinese*." This was the first time I had experienced prejudice because of my race. I did not know what to make of it and it undermined my self-esteem, which was in a fledgling state.

Marilyn and I had enrolled in a Master's of Education with an English cognate program at the University of Detroit, and asked our "The Psychology of Education" instructor, Joan Wilder (also a friend of Father Toner), to come out to my classroom to assess the situation. She told me that having fifty students in the classroom with mixed abilities was an astronomical problem. Even an experienced teacher would have found it difficult. So I decided I could no longer teach at St. Michael's. At the end of the year, I said goodbye to Melinda Wiggle, whose name fit her well because she was very restless and inattentive, and Mount Spoutz who had very low ability but gave me a golden-rose broach at the end of the year.

I landed another job for the next year, teaching second graders at Sts. Peter and Paul School. Instead of fifty students, I had forty. It was a great improvement, but nevertheless taxing. I had a few discipline problems and a few exceptional students. I had to put little Robert outside of the classroom because he broke other students' pencils and was most disruptive. However, he would come right back in, so I had to slide him out in his desk and lock the door. One student was a genius. His mother said he read the encyclopedia for fun, yet he was failing math class taught by my partner, a nun. In religion class, he told me he was an atheist and that nuns were wolves in sheep's clothing. That certainly made him a memorable student for me. The regimentation the nuns required from the students and teachers was inhuman. In calligraphy class, all the students had to write and rest their pencils simultaneously with one another. I taught in this school for two years and then chose to proceed to high school teaching.

Meanwhile, my dating was sporadic. Marilyn and I went to a few dances, but I was seldom asked to dance. Once, Marilyn got a date with someone from Yugoslavia. When she was picked up on a Friday night, he had a friend in the car who needed a date, so Marilyn came upstairs and asked whether I would like to go. He was my first blind date, and I must say it was interesting because he did not speak English. We went to see *Dr. Zhivago* in a theater in downtown Detroit. He tried to touch my thighs, but I soon put a stop to his moves. When we came back to our flat, Marilyn and I and our respective dates sat on the two brown couch sectionals. We proceeded to do some pretty heavy kissing. I stopped for a moment to ask my date, "By the way, what is your name?" This question prompted a laugh from Marilyn. Before he left, my date attempted to take me to the bedroom, and I could see he had an erection that showed through his pants. I definitely was not about to go to the bedroom with this perfect stranger, so I said, "No" and led him to the front door and down the stairs where he said, "You good girl."

I also dated three Chinese fellows, all of whom asked me to marry them. The first one was Frank, with whom I was hooked up by a middle-aged fellow teacher. He was an engineer, short and scrawny with glasses, who took me to Thanksgiving dinner at a fellow teacher's house, a football game, and the movies. He held my hand, but I was not attracted to him. He gave me a string of pearls, and one day, when I walked him down the flat stairs, he asked me to marry him. While he had tears in his eyes, I told him I was not in love with him. He told me to keep the pearls and I never saw him again.

Mathias was a very handsome Chinese engineer who had been engaged in Italy to an Italian woman, and who had lived in Italy several years. When we went to Mass together, he slipped me a paper saying, "*Te amo*" (I love you). Then one morning, he came running to my room, saying he had made me the beneficiary of his bank accounts and that I should take care of his mother who was still back in China in case of his death. He was a good French kisser, but I did not fall in love with him. My heart was still filled with Father Toner.

Around this time, I went to see Father Ellis, pastor of St. Cecilia's Church in Detroit (my mother worked as his secretary). I revealed to him my feelings for Father Toner. When I wrote to Father Toner, telling him of my encounter with Father Ellis, he sent a special letter, forbidding me to talk about our relationship to anyone for fear it might be misconstrued.

As for the last Chinese fellow I dated, I cannot remember his name. He was good-looking and had beautiful sisters in Taiwan. At a restaurant, I told him I could not marry him because I did not have romantic feelings for him. He was very despondent and said he wanted to commit suicide. I don't know what became of him after we parted.

Despite being in a large city, I felt more like I was on the sidelines, watching the American way of life. Marilyn and I led rather secluded lives centered on the routine of teaching and going to school at night. One gentleman who came to our apartment could not believe we did not have a television. We told him we did not miss it.

The Vietnam War was now going on, and I was completely opposed to it. Sometimes, Marilyn and I would be invited to a neighborhood backyard barbecue where the young people drank too much and told horror stories about those who returned from the war and those who didn't. I heard of young people going to LSD parties and having psychedelic hallucinations. The United States did not feel like a happy country. My depression and unhappiness over being uprooted from Brazil coincided with the country's malaise, and I did not find solace in this milieu.

Marilyn and I listened to music that tended to be popular, classical, and folk, missing the rock scene altogether. We had records by the Ray Conniff Singers with songs such as: "This is My Song," "Strangers in the Night," "Cabaret," "Georgy Girl," "Born Free," and "What Now, My Love?" We listened to Noel Harrison with songs such as, "Suzanne," "Just Like a Woman," "Woman," "Lucy in the Sky with Diamonds," and "Strawberry Fields Forever." We heard Simon and Garfunkel in "The Sound of

Silence." We also listened to Joan Baez; Peter, Paul, and Mary; Ed Ames; as well as music and poetry by Rod McKuen. Our favorites also included Barbra Streisand's "People," Petula Clark's "Downtown," and The Seekers' version of "Georgy Girl."

When I got a summer job at a dairy near where my mother lived, she came to see me one night with a tray of ice cream and cookies (mind you I worked in a dairy that sold ice cream). She was opposed to my working there and said, "I wish your father could see you working here." I did not know why she mentioned my father, except to make me realize that this job was beneath my status. Anyway, I gave up the job because it was too difficult to keep up with graduate summer school classes and then take inventory in a dairy until midnight.

When Father Toner came for Christmas, he marveled at our Christmas tree. We had obtained it from a lot that had closed, but I was able to pull it over the fence, holding to its top, and I left a few dollars at the door. We decorated it with newly sprayed golden apples that I quickly told him not to touch.

My life was moving along, but I was still searching for fulfillment. Was I to get married here in the U.S., or was I to enter the convent in Brazil? I decided I wanted to go back to visit Brazil, so I saved enough money from my teaching salary to buy a round trip ticket to Brazil in the summer of 1967.

Chapter 4

❦

Summer in Brazil

Soon, I was boarding a plane at Kennedy International Airport on my way to Brazil, the place where I had left my childhood. I was so excited since it was the first time I was returning to the country I considered so much my own and hadn't seen in six years. I could see the moon for a long time and some stars. It was not so dark after all. I hoped light would shine all the way through. It was dawn when someone remarked, looking at the huge vastness of the Amazon, "Rough country down there." The topography changed to wrinkled lands. This was the country I came to because I loved it.

My first stop was in Brasilia (the current capital of Brazil), where Virginia and her husband, Edson (in military uniform) were waiting for me, much to my surprise because it was so early in the morning. Virginia had not changed much, only become much more mature. We drove to her house and met her two boys (ages one and two) who were under the care of a maid. I could see how she was a wonderful mother. We spent the whole day talking of old times. My Portuguese was rusty so Virginia carried the conversation pretty much by herself, as she well could, by being exuberant and loving, and helped me to recover my fluency. It was good to be back. I experienced a kind of peace and enjoyed the vast spaces as we drove around the city (the brand new ultramodern city built by the famous Brazilian architect, Oscar Niemeyer, to be the seat of the Brazilian government in 1960). The next morning, I flew to Rio.

Madre Euridyna, some students from Stella Maris, and my good friend Maria Clara greeted me at the airport. Madre Euridyna and I embraced, and it seemed that she had shrunk, but she was still the same graceful person. I was received so well by all, yet I had such trouble with the language that did not flow as naturally as English did. At school, I found everything the same, but smaller. Madre Euridyna housed me in the old house in front of the school that used to be the first kindergarten and watched me unpack. I felt a little strange, especially because of the language. It seemed funny to me that I had been there once upon a time. The bell was the same and the nuns were so friendly.

Madre Euridyna and I walked on the cement patio playground. The moon was beautiful, the sea shimmered, and I still loved her, but I could not unburden myself to her. I wished I could speak English with her. The next few days, I spent some time with Madre Euridyna, talking, while she escorted me around the school, and I participated in some school activities. I played with some children I had taught when they were three years old. I found them so beautiful and with such good manners. Madre Euridyna and I had a wonderful talk. I found her so wise and experienced. She understood how homesick and estranged I felt, and she told me she wanted me to know happiness, but I had to find it either *here* or *there*, one way or the other. I prayed to God to show me the way.

The next few days, I went out to visit old friends. I went to see Dona Vera, my godmother, who took me horseback riding and swimming at Hippica Equestrian Club where I met Tom and his mother Dona Maria, and then we went to the movies in the afternoon. The following days, I went to see my mother's friends, Lucia and Grisha Friedlander. They were happy to see me and receive news from my mother. I had dinner and spent the night there. In the morning, Lucia showed me some of her artwork and ceramics. I learned she came from Latvia and had lost all her relatives in the Holocaust. Then I stopped in Copacabana at Eli's apartment; by then her son Peter had died from brain cancer. She had moved from the beautiful apartment overlooking the lake, Lagoa Rodrigo de Freitas, and was now in a small apartment with a terrace packed with plants. She and I had a good talk about life, and on our way to the elevator, she told me that during a Spiritism meeting, she found out through a medium that Peter's job in Heaven was to escort the souls of the children who had died in Vietnam. She was now very much involved in her church and had taken a few old ladies under her wings whom she visited regularly. Jackie, my mother's mutual friend, did not live with her anymore; she lived with Vera, Peter's widow, and did not see visitors because of her appearance. One last friend of my mother's I visited was Edda, a German lady who worked in the American Consulate. She was the youngest of the group who had been newly married and lost her husband in a plane crash while the plane was attempting to land in Rio. She never quite recovered and immersed herself in drinking. She invited me for lunch at a restaurant on Atlantic Avenue, overlooking Copacabana Beach, and we had a *cozido* (pot roast) with cabbage, sweet potatoes, and corn. It was most enjoyable. Later, we went to a French movie in the pouring rain, and then she invited me to her place for a drink. She revealed to me that she had had an abortion, which had caused her much pain.

When I returned to school, Madre Euridyna introduced me to one of her friends she counseled, Maria Carmen, who took me to her apartment in Copacabana for lunch and then we walked on Nossa Senhora de Copacabana Avenue, window-shopping. I found the fashions there to be tremendous. Also, even though we were in one of the densest populated areas in the world, I found the pace of life much slower. One could find groups of people talking on the sidewalk, and no one seemed to be in a hurry. My time clock was still wound up according to American time, so I found it hard at times to relax. Maria Carmen bought me a gift: a wooden box with Rio's scenery on it, made from butterfly wings. Her generosity touched me since I had just met her. While at Stella Maris School, I also went to the movies with Michelle and Suely, who were a few years younger than I, and we saw *The Gospel According to St. Matthew*. I had taught English to Michelle when I lived in Brazil. She had curly blond hair and was of French descent. She took us to her mother's apartment, where her mother prepared a beautiful lunch for us. Before we parted, she asked us to tell the nuns to look out for a reliable maid for her as she was having a hard time finding one.

The next few days were sunny and balmy. I accompanied a third grade class on a picnic at the city park and watched Brazilian children play familiar games that brought back childhood memories. I continued to have talks with Madre Euridyna, and I accompanied her through her rounds in the school. On June 29, I attended a Mass honoring St. Peter and St. Paul with the poor of the *favelas* in the mountains near the school premises. Madre Euridyna was happy when I gave her flowers I had purchased in the city. It was strange that I felt the pain within as before. I was homesick. I felt confused because I felt estranged. I asked myself, "Where will I feel at home? Where will I make a home?" Madre Euridyna was somewhat sad when I told her I was leaving on Thursday for a trip to the state of Bahia with Harumi. She felt that I was running away.

When Harumi picked me up from school, I was able to do some clothes washing at her house. I had lunch with her family and met Terumi, her sister. We played guitar with some friends. One of them could play very well! That afternoon, we went riding around the mountains with Cazu (Harumi's brother) as our chauffeur. He bought us a bunch of mini-bananas, still on the vine, and we munched away while penetrating a beautiful forest, which opened to beautiful scenes of Rio; all the way, we were laughing and singing. The good old times had returned! Cazu took me back to school to retrieve the rest of my belongings and I spent the next few days at Haru's house. In the morning, I watered the plants on the terrace, read in the sun *Song of Sixpence* by A. J. Cronin, many of whose books I had read in the States, and I thought a great deal to settle my mind over the question of being in two worlds. The day was radiant. I was at the foot of Gavea Mountain, and the sea was just a look beyond. I marveled at the different kinds of trees and plants and felt at home here. Harumi and I went to the hairdresser in the afternoon, and I called Dona Vera, my godmother, and Madre Euridyna. Then I discovered I had received a letter from Father Toner. He told me he was staying at the Mercy College campus with Sister Margaret Farley and did nothing but write and work. A tinge of jealousy passed over me, but I was so glad to receive a letter from the person I loved most at the time.

We arrived in Salvador, Bahia, by plane to participate in an excursion Harumi had enrolled us in; plenty of young people were on the excursion, including some from Sao Conrado, our neighborhood in Rio. We were very glad to be there in Salvador, a terraced city that had been Brazil's first capital, which abounded in examples of Portuguese and African cultures. In the morning, we went to the marketplace and found many interesting crafts to buy, including a *berimbau*, a musical instrument used in the *capoeira* (martial arts) dance first practiced by African slaves. In the afternoon, we hitchhiked to one of the long beaches, and traveled along the sea, singing and having fun on an open truck. At night we went to an African ritual, part of the *Candomble* religion, which included a type of voodoo dance performed in a house where ladies in long white skirts and turbans dance to the beat of drums played by men. As the ladies follow each other in a circle, singing lyrics about lost heroes and journeys to Brazil, some fall in a trance; then their breasts are tied with a white sachet and they are carried to the side. The scene is frightening and it caused me much internal pain.

The next few days, we went on a trip to Mataripe where we saw a petroleum refinery with the dark liquid spewing out of the ground. We also went to visit the industrial center of Aratu—a place of hope for Brazil's future—where we saw the plans for the erection of many different buildings and machinery. We came home very tired and glad we had no formal programs to attend. In the evening, we went to a performance of *capoeira,* an African dance for men, a type of rhythmic fight. It was fantastic and the singing was most interesting. I also had a chance to visit a fabulous progressive school for the arts sponsored by the United Nations. There were five different pavilions specializing in theater, music, dance, and arts and crafts. It was a great project, the only one of its kind in the world, and I was happy to see that it was located in Brazil. At night, we had a drink at a terrace bar by the seashore and learned some more about Brazil's history. Later, we attended a madrigal of Brazilian folkloric music that was hauntingly beautiful!

At times, I was surprised to feel myself somewhat lonesome for my home in the United States. It was not easy to integrate myself completely once again. I continued to think about Father Toner and felt he was in my heart. We made more visits to churches and museums, popular and sacred, and I took a photograph of a sorrowful looking statue of St. Peter. We collected some shells at a beach and saw some interesting abandoned boats by the seashore. One night, I felt very sick, so I ate nearby and then went to bed. The girls went out with a young man we had met, Ray Torres, for whom I had some attraction; together, they serenaded each other on a terrace where they said they had great fun.

A few days later, we made an interesting excursion by bus to the city of Santana where there was an amazing open market. All of us on the tour had seats, but those who caught the bus along the way had none. The poor people packed the bus like sardines in a tin can. I felt pity for these poor primitive people, moving like they were in a beehive, dirty and sick. The market was primitive but with an abundance of things to buy, from animals to fruits and leather goods, much of it laid out on cloths or paper on the ground or on makeshift booths. For sale were salted sheets of meat, dried in the sun and very typical of the Brazilian diet. I bought some leather trinkets and had a delicious lunch at a storefront restaurant, but the poor made their presence felt by coming to the restaurant's edge to beg. My heart went out to them! The bus was super full! We had some relief at the end when many of the passengers were dropped off at their destinations along the dusty roads. We approached the city in the evening, singing songs together. For our last event in Salvador, Bahia, we visited the School of Medicine at the University of Bahia and saw many corpses lying on tables, which was somewhat upsetting.

In the evening, I spent some time with Raymond Torres, the architect we had met earlier. We spoke about art and social relations between the classes and countries. I found him to be fascinating. When it was time to go back to the hotel, it was late, and with all the packing and chatting, we only slept from 3:40 a.m. to 7:30 a.m. Then it was time to leave the Hotel S. Bento (a memory to remember and to forget since it was so shabby and my pearl ring that my mother had bought me before I left Brazil was stolen) and head for the airport.

Our plane was so late, however, that we had to wait at the airport for eight hours. Finally, we were on our flight to Rio. We were very tired. While half asleep and half awake, we had to land in Vitoria for maintenance. Everyone was exhausted. The pilot told us that we might have to overnight in Vitoria while the plane was fixed. Luckily, the plane was fixed in time for us to begin our flight to Rio at 2 a.m. It was a very hazardous flight through thunderstorms. We thought for a while that the plane would fall. Bebel, one of the youngest in the group and Harumi's neighbor, reached out to me, and we hugged and prayed while the plane bounced in the storm. We landed safely at 6 a.m. after a twenty-four-hour ordeal for a flight that should have taken three hours.

Cazu, Harumi's brother, took us home. We slept the whole day and night. The next morning, I washed clothes and then went to Stella Maris where I met with Madre Euridyna and told her about the trip. The school was all decorated for the arrival of the mother general from Rome. However, I did not feel I belonged in this world anymore. I decided to pack the rest of my clothes and stay the remainder of the time with Harumi since I felt more comfortable there. I did not always want to be dependent on the school or on Madre Euridyna. Sometimes, I felt kind of lost, not knowing whether I was really altogether welcome, since I did not feel completely at home. During this week, I went to school often to talk with Madre Euridyna and was very disappointed that I had not received any letters from "home," either from Father Toner or my mother.

The next few weeks there were more visits with friends. I went to see Nega and all the Armazem family. Dona Linda welcomed me with an open, magnanimous embrace. I saw Senhor Joao by the door on a chair. Tears rolled down his cheek and he extended his hand, showing the height I was when he knew me at age five. I was touched! These people were my family. Senhor Joao could not talk much as he was in the late stages of kidney failure. With the brood of brothers and sisters, I talked about old childhood memories with much joy and tears while munching on snacks prepared by the twins, Grande and Miuda. When I saw Joaozinho, I remembered how I held him on my lap, but now he was a grown man.

There was so much to do and so little time. I found out Alzira was in town and went to meet her, but I was sad she had to leave the next day for her hometown of Cachoeiro de Itapemirim. Then I found out that Virginia was in town as well. I met her at her mother's house in Jardim Botanico and had lunch with her and her

English grandmother and aunt. Afterwards, we decided to pack the children with the maid in the car and go visit Madre Euridyna at Stella Maris School. We talked all afternoon with Madre Euridyna and the mother general, who had arrived, and they both enjoyed the children's antics. Over these few days, I had countless talks with Madre Euridyna, who wanted to give me a vocational test. She thought it would be a good idea for me to visit the order's novitiate in Belo Horizonte to give me a better perspective. Harumi brought me my suitcase, and Madre Euridyna was happy that I was going.

The next day, I traveled through the mountains toward the city of Belo Horizonte for twelve hours on a bus with two nuns, Madre Marina, who had taught me in grade school, and the mother provincial. We had much fun reminiscing about funny incidents that had happened in school. Occasionally, we heard a fat man snoring behind us. As we approached the city at night, I could see it illuminated, sleeping among the hills. The novitiate itself was perched high on one of the hills. I was greeted by many nuns and then went to sleep.

The next day, I talked with the Mistress of Novices, Madre Benita, and a novice, Eliana, who greeted me with much kindness. I also met a Jesuit priest, Father Agero, who was giving a retreat to the nuns and was very much loved by the community. While there, I did feel a spirit of joy and a simple love for Christ. Later that day, I went with the novices, postulants, and juniors (young ladies who intended to enter the convent) to their country house in an orange grove by a lake. It was sunny, with a country air, and the girls exuded happiness. I had a wonderful time! In the evening, as I said goodbye to the sisters, I met Madre Bertha, who had spent more than twenty years in China as a missionary until she had to flee to Formosa, current day Taiwan. She was so glad to meet someone who had been born in China, and she told me countless stories with much affection.

On my return to Rio, I was traveling alone through the mountains on a clear sunny day. Many thoughts were going through my head—some happy and some very painful. When I met some Americans on the bus, I learned there had been a major race riot in Detroit and many buildings had been burnt or looted. Only then did I understand why earlier my mother had sent me a telegram with the message, "Don't worry; all is well with us."

On my way to Stella Maris School by taxi, I argued with the driver about the fee because it did not coincide with the price on the meter. He told me he had to add to the price because of the steep road leading up to the school. I paid reluctantly, and in the confusion, forgot on the back seat the woolen coat Madre Euridyna's friend, Maria Carmen, had lent me. Needless to say, I had to replace it. Later, I shared in a note to Madre Euridyna my thoughts expressing my trepidation about religious life, even though I had had a wonderful time at the novitiate. When I prayed, I told God, "Thy will be done."

Cazu came to pick me up so I could spend a few days in Sao Conrado with Harumi and her family before I left once more on a journey to Cachoeiro de Itapemirim in the state of Espirito Santo to visit Alzira. While in Sao Conrado, I went to Mass in the little white church perched on the hill that brought back so many memories.

Later, I went to the beach with Terumi and her little cousin. The clear water, bright sun, mountains, and sand were absolutely delightful. I was so happy to be on the beach of my childhood.

July 31st was the Feast of St. Ignatius. I thought of Father Toner with much love and wished him a happy feast day in my heart. I was again on a bus traveling alongside mountains on my way to see Alzira. With all the comings and goings of the last few weeks, I was glad to be alone with my thoughts and to "be with" those I loved, gathering all the moments in one in an attempt to be present to myself and to God. I arrived in Cachoeiro in the late afternoon. Alzira and I had pleasant days, dressing up and helping each other with makeup and baking a cake. We went by foot on a tour of the town and took some pictures in the square. Alzira and I talked, and she played wonderful pieces on the piano. The following day, we toured a Guarana soft drink factory and made a trip to the majestic mountains. The trip back to Rio was wonderful; the weather was clear and a great part of the journey was along the sea.

In Rio, Cazu came to pick me up at the bus station and took me to the lake in Rio called Lagoa Rodrigo the Freitas, to see the slum that was burnt along the mountainside. The government wanted to clear certain picturesque tourist areas from the blight of the slums. I had always felt special affection for the poor, and the disregard the city had for them brought me sadness. The city's beauty was placed as a higher priority, so the poor had no place to live here.

In the evening of my last day, I took a walk alone around the school, knowing full well that I would leave this place of my youth that I loved so much. Lights flickered in the distance along the shoreline of Leblon and Ipanema. I had no idea what my future held and what life I would embark on. At breakfast the next day, Madre Euridyna came to see me and said her last words, "The Holy Spirit will guide you." Yes, I wanted to have a clear path, but all was unclear. We said goodbye at the door and I left the woman I most loved. I could not stay because I needed to finish my Master's degree and return to the country where my mother, the only person who had followed me my whole life, was. Soon Harumi and family drove me to the airport, and then I was in the plane alone. To all, I disappeared through the clouds. At this moment, it was a comfort to me to know that at least God could be everywhere.

Chapter 5

Marriage

In August, 1967, I met Tony Campagna. My mother, who worked with him at St. Cecilia's Church in Detroit, introduced us. Father Ellis, the pastor, had met Tony in the seminary in Providence, Rhode Island (Tony's hometown) while giving a retreat to the seminarians. When Tony came to Detroit to join his parents after leaving the seminary in 1965, Father Ellis gave him a job as an assistant maintenance man. Since my mother was Father Ellis' personal secretary, she met Tony many times and thought he was a wonderful, educated young man. With Tony and another fellow, Donald Yarnevic, a professor at Mercy College, she went on a vacation to visit the Montreal Expo at the end of the summer of 1967 while I was still in Brazil.

When I returned home, my mother invited me to join Tony and her on a visit to the Michigan State Fair, the weekend before Labor Day. When I met Tony that afternoon at my mother's place, I thought he was very good-looking, with beautiful eyes, but with a serious demeanor. He only showed some interest in me when I felt nauseated on the Ferris wheel, and he did not seem to be enjoying himself. When we walked through the pavilion, a person in the Catholic booth gave him some pamphlets on the missions, which he promptly threw in the trash on our way out. This moment was the first time I witnessed him display anger toward the Church. Apparently, he had not been treated very well in the seminary, became sick, and had to leave.

On Christmas Eve that year, my mother held a small party and invited Tony. As was customary, I gave all the guests a small gift, and Tony received an ashtray. I had decided to go to Midnight Mass that night, so before I left, I gave all the guests a kiss on the cheek since I had come from the Brazilian culture where people were more demonstrative and showed their affection readily. I know Tony was surprised by my display of affection.

Later during the holidays, Marilyn and I decided to have a co-ed party, so we invited an equal number of male and female friends and Tony was included. When

~ 158 ~

some wine was spilled in the kitchen, Tony owned up to the mishap and his honesty touched me. After that party, Tony and I began dating and we were together almost continuously until our marriage on November 29, 1968.

Our courtship was difficult because I was suffering from a chronic depression (later diagnosed as dysthymia), which I disguised but felt deeply; it was due to the many losses and separations I had experienced, and the abuse I had endured from my stepfather. The monumental separations and distance from loved ones and places from my youth complicated my task of finding happiness and integration. I was very vulnerable, feeling I had lost my past and had no one to share my language and my customs. I had hoped Tony would understand my desires and longings; he seemed to have some compassion for me. We went to a seminar on the power of women where I believe the lecturer was Isaac Stern, who commented on the meaning of suffering. I thought Tony understood the meaning of suffering and his Christian formation seemed to help create a bond for us.

Yet I was not certain that I wanted to marry him because I did not feel an overwhelming love for him. I wrote to Sister Margaret Farley, stating I did not want to marry Tony since I did not love him enough. She questioned what I meant by "enough." It was a question with me as well. I found Tony's irritability and anger over minor things kind of surprising and could not explain it. He wanted to be close physically, but because of my Catholic upbringing, we stopped short of intercourse. We almost broke up once, with many tears on my part, when we both decided our cultural differences were too great. Perhaps, he wanted to rescue me because he pursued me and asked me to marry him over forty times. In July 1968, Father Toner called me and asked me what my answer would be for Tony and I said, "Yes." Thus it was that we became engaged. Tony wrote me a beautiful poem about the oak tree and the lotus that made me think his love was true. In poetic terms, our love was idealized, but when it came to the realities of daily living, it deteriorated.

The bottom line was that Tony and I did not bond emotionally. Both of us were staunchly rooted in our backgrounds, neither yielding to the other. Because we both hungered for acceptance and understanding, neither of us could give them to the other. I was now a bored, isolated, suburban wife.

Nevertheless, I became pregnant a few months after our wedding, and our daughter Lisa was born on November 7, 1969. A year later, I gave birth to Michelle, who was born on November 24, 1970. The domestic workload was overwhelming for me, even though my mother came everyday to help me after Michelle's birth.

On September 2, 1974, I lost my three-month-old baby boy Paul, who was born (May 28, 1974) with an incorrigible heart defect. Needless to say, it was devastating to Tony and me. It took me at least four years to regain a degree of consolation and peace. We lived through those years unable to be a source of comfort to each other.

On June 13, 1976, I gave birth to Suzy, and that fall, we moved to Canton. Tony, who was a pharmaceutical representative, was always very involved with his work, spending much time in the basement office in our home, talking to his boss or colleagues, complaining to them about his workload and the treatment he received. That summer, he became even more involved with his work because he was promoted to district manager. Now that we had moved, we also had the added chore of landscaping, taking care of the kids and the house. Therefore, we found little time for companionship with each other.

The years that followed were very hard for me. I remember visiting a lawyer to find out about my rights, but I did not have the nerve to divorce Tony since I had four children, the youngest being only a few months old (Sara was born November 27, 1978), no income, and a sense of inadequacy and dependence.

Once when I complained to Tony's mother about his enraged behaviors and treatment of me, she replied, "You know, Tony travels a lot, and he can have any woman he wants." For much of our lives, Tony and I were like two rivers traveling side-by-side but never merging. Sometimes, I referred to it as oil and vinegar.

Sometimes, I would say that Tony and I were engaged in rice and spaghetti wars. He molded in his Italian/American ways, and I, my Chinese/Brazilian ways. Despite these difficulties, we did have good times, especially some pleasant summer vacations in Northern Michigan where we went camping or rented a cottage with the whole family, my mother sometimes accompanying us. Shortly after baby Paul's death in 1974, we packed Lisa and Michelle in the car and went to an Indian Reservation, Cape Croker in Canada, where we camped for over a week. It was very soothing to take walks on the ledge of an escarpment formed by Nature, bathe in the lake, and watch the girls play with the clay they found at the bottom of a lake estuary. In Michigan, we spent several summers camping in Ludington where the children had fun diving from a bridge into a river off Lake Michigan. In later years, we rented a place in Elk Rapids and had fun exploring the many beautiful scenes in Michigan, including the dunes in Sleeping Bear National Park, Tahquamenon Falls, and the many lighthouses along the shoreline. Once again, I took refuge in Nature.

By comparison, at home, I felt disconnected and isolated. I lived like a hermit, with no one to share my deepest thoughts, but I resigned myself to living this unhappy life. To distract myself, I decided to enroll in some art classes at Schoolcraft College (they would count toward my teaching certificate). In a ceramic class in 1980, I met Fadia Jabbour, who had come from Lebanon a few years back. She and I managed to cover ourselves with clay while working the potter's wheel; we found we had so much in common, including being messy, while working with clay. She and her family became my friends and made my life less lonely. That same year, I met Vera Dias, a Brazilian lady, while I was shopping at Kmart. She was holding a sleeping baby for a friend and I heard her say, "*Ele esta dormindo.*" ("He is sleeping.") Her accent gave her away. When I asked her whether she was from Brazil, she said, "Yes." These two have been my friends to this day, and with them, I eventually shared my burdens.

I was involved in my children's lives as much as possible even though the atmosphere in our home was not pleasant. They enrolled in many activities (swimming, skating, sports, Girl Scouts) and I threw birthday parties, took them on trips, and to the movies with their friends. In fact, I stayed home fifteen years so they would have a stay-at-home mom and a sit down hot meal for dinner. Once, I drove my youngest daughter, Sara, to a baseball practice and stayed in the car waiting for her while she trained. As I looked at the field, I felt so alien to it all. Even when she played soccer and I was on the sidelines rooting for her, I did not have the same passion for the soccer games that I had in Brazil, and I could not relate to the soccer moms who talked about enrolling their sons and daughters in the best universities, often bragging in a competitive tone. Around this time, I was in the car alone, driving at dusk on a country road when I heard on the radio the musical poem "Desiderata." Among the lines I heard, "You are a child of the universe, no less than the trees and the stars; you have a right to be here." These words resonated in my heart, piercing it with affirmation. Yes, I belonged in this world and was part of it. I needed to find myself in it.

It was then I decided to try to find my father and brother in China once again.

Interlude

On the Threshold: Pause Before China

I like the scent of a rainy breeze; I can smell the
Earth and feel the soft spray coming through the window.
I hear the rumblings in the sky, which culminate in a loud burst.
The pouring intensifies and I wish I could run outside and
Get soaked with my face washed in the rain and my breath
Filled with the goodness of the Earth.
— Marianne Campagna

I have always felt close to the earth, perhaps because I grew up in a sun-bathed Brazilian valley of Gavea between the mountains and the sea that has left a lasting impression in me. I have felt one with the Earth, but despite some wonderful friendships, I have never felt at one with the people. I have always felt like an onlooker to a life that was never really my own. I had been uprooted from China and then Brazil, and separated from my father and brother when I was age five, something that fragmented my very core. I had been forced to come to grips with my mixed parentage, and to integrate myself with the various cultures that were part of my life. For many years, I had almost denied my Chinese heritage. Even though I looked Chinese, I had known very few Chinese people throughout my life, and I was ignorant of Chinese culture and history. My ethnic background, the moves from one country to another, and the lack of an extended family made me feel like a guest in someone else's house. I always had to explain myself to others, telling them where I had come from, to justify my presence among them.

Yet, my father and brother were Chinese living in China, and somewhere deep within me, I longed to be with them and share their heritage. Their absence had created a vacuum in me; they were part of my blueprint and I could not feel whole until I accepted that side of myself.

Part of my sense of isolation, especially after coming to America, was caused because my inner world was not in tune with the outer world that I encountered. I tried hard to belong; yet, the nagging sense of being different followed me.

To a great extent, after some years in America, I succeeded in bridging the gap between myself and the world around me. Slowly, the beauty of the northern landscape became apparent to my eyes, and I began to enjoy the sky as if it were a canvas, so often painted with the sunset's vibrant colors. I noticed that almost everyone cultivated a garden, and I was fascinated by the abundance of flowers and trees everywhere. I watched the huge oak and elm trees shed their leaves, exhibiting the very last tentacles of their branches, only to be rejuvenated in the spring with fresh green buds, an experience that was very new to me, having come from the tropics. This imagery in Nature mirrored the change in my soul. I, too, was growing and shedding the illusions of childhood and learning to accept the responsibilities that would prepare me to lead a productive life. I learned the principle of self-reliance the hard way: it was a painful reaching out for independence when I really never had a lasting threshold to begin with.

Gradually, I wove myself into American society. After graduating from college, I taught in elementary and high schools. The children I taught gave me a part of America I had missed in my own childhood. I learned about Halloween, the raking of leaves, Thanksgiving, Christmas carols, and the indomitable Mr. Snowman. In 1968, I got married and raised four beautiful daughters. Along the way I made some wonderful friends who have given me much joy and understanding. To them, I will always be grateful.

Yet with all these accomplishments and friendships, I moved into adulthood with a void, for I still missed my father and brother, whom I had not seen since I was five.

When America established diplomatic relations with China in 1979, I seized the opportunity to begin searching again for my father and brother. I wrote to the American Embassy in Peking, and it in turn referred me to the Chinese Embassy in Washington, D.C.

So I wrote to the Chinese Embassy, and then I waited....

Children's feet
One generation after another
Running on different soil
Yet mother and father to a child
Never the same is the offspring
A new set of images
A new story
A link with new vistas
The heart, the heart
Here is where it all meets
The secret of unity.

— Marianne Campagna

Part IV

China

Chapter 1

=== ✿ ===

First Letters

It was an ordinary Thursday very much like the other cold, dreary, and wet days we were having that October of 1981. The rains had washed the pavements and the waters were running in a steady stream into the street gutters. A freshness was in the air, but I knew that the soggy grass was for naught. It was the end of the summer season, and all I had to look forward to was my children's busy school schedule. After picking up my daughter Suzy and a neighbor boy from their kindergarten, I walked over to the mailbox while the children scurried into the house awaiting their lunch. I opened the mailbox latch and noticed among the other mail a small white envelope with Chinese stamps, addressed to me in longhand. On the upper left hand corner was the name Wang, my father's name. I recognized the handwriting. My hands began to tremble and my heart to pound. I was sure I held my first letter from my father, which had come from Hangzhou, China.

With wet eyes, I walked into the house and said, "Children, be very quiet. I will give you lunch later. I just received, for the first time in my life, a letter from my father." I did not want to tear the envelope in a haphazard fashion, so I looked for a knife and made a clean cut through the edge of the envelope, then ran to my bedroom upstairs still holding my breath. I stood by the window and took out a couple of folded pages that read:

Hangzhou
12. Oct., 1981

Dear Marianne,

One month ago, we know that you search our existence through the Embassy in U.S.A., that gives us a very great joy. But until today we get your address through some official channel. It set us in the position to write to you. My English is very poor, but I will learn it very hard.

My dear younger sister, how is our mother? Urgently I hope you can tell me about that. We have many times tried through Aunt Yun to get your address but all failed. It is a special joy that you come to search our existence. Now I am working in the Shipbuilding Co. mostly for the painting.

I have two children, one daughter and one boy. My wife is a teacher for the elementary school. Please tell us something about you and your family!

We all hope that you can come here to see us. Let us forget the longing for the thirty years separation. Best regards to the whole family!

Your older brother,

Wang Qian

The words rushed through my mind like a vision. How long had I waited for them, and they were now here in my brother's own handwriting, a brother I had been cut off from for more than thirty years.

But where was my father's letter? Anxious thoughts filled my mind. Had he died and was, therefore, unable to write to me, or had he relied on my brother for the correspondence? My doubts were quickly appeased when inside the same envelope I found a single sheet of paper and recognized my father's handwriting (as a child I had seen a letter he had written to my mother while we still lived in Brazil). With my eyes transfixed on the paper I read:

Hangzhou

12.Oct., 1981

Dear Marianne,

Here writes your dear father to you after more than thirty years separation. The longing after longing must come after so long a separation between daughter and father. I sincerely hope that you can come here to see me and your brother.

I have worked in the Chekiang University as a Mathematician, but now I don't go to the school. Your brother works now as a painter in a Shipbuilding Co. So long until I hear something from you.

Best regards to your mother
to your husband

Your father,

Wang Fu Shih

Note: Please fast one of this small notes to the envelope, it contains the address in Chinese.

The words resounded in me like a voice. I sat on the edge of the bed and read and reread the letter. *"The longing after longing must come after so long a separation between daughter and father."* These words went through my mind many times, and I was touched by their poetic tenderness. It surprised me that my father had deep feelings for me. I had been a mere child when I left, and my parents had been divorced when I was a year and a half. I had not spent a long time with my father, and I only remember an occasional Sunday outing or visit in Shanghai. I had thought that it was easy for him to give me up because I was so young. The subconscious feeling that I had been abandoned by my father slowly dissipated. Now I read the words of a caring man, and I was deeply moved. I shed tears of joy. At last, I had found my real father. The buried affection I had for my father all my life came to the surface and I began to care for a real person.

My father's perceptiveness had resulted in his making address labels in Chinese for me to place on the letters I was going to send him. These were four little squares of tissue paper with Chinese writing on them, which I also found in the same envelope. He knew then that I could neither speak nor write Chinese.

As was customary, my mother would come to the house that afternoon to sit with the children while I went to a painting class at the community college. When I heard her opening the front door, I ran down the stairs and stopped midway; leaning over the banister, I said, "Mami, I got a letter from my father and my brother today!"

She froze in place and looked at me with a penetrating, disbelieving stare and said, "What? You got a letter from your father and brother!"

I gave my mother the letters to read. She was utterly stunned by the reality of it all. Many times she had tried to contact them, but all attempts had failed. My father and my brother had been for us faint images far in the deep past. My mother and I hardly ever engaged in conversation about them, except when she told me an occasional anecdote about her life in China, and these came in intervals few and far between. She had, however, helped me to prepare a fact sheet—i.e. my father's name, profession, various jobs he held, and the possibility that he might be in Hangzhou— all facts she gathered from the last letter she received from my father's cousin Wang Yuan in 1958 while in Brazil; so all this collecting of information brought about this turn of events. Now we were both confronted with their existence not as they were thirty years ago, but as they were now, living in the '80s in China. Our search had finally materialized.

My mother stood by the kitchen counter reading the letters. She remained in utter disbelief. Her son, her first-born, had written and also her ex-husband for whom she still bore some tender feelings, despite their marriage difficulties in China. She wanted to take the letters home with her, but I would not part with them, so I told her I would make a Xerox copy of the letters on my way to painting class.

At class, I shared the good news with the students and the teacher, who happened to be a Chinese-born American. They were so aghast at my good fortune that they wondered what I was doing in class on such a day. I felt it was a day for celebration and for sharing. So I went about spreading the news to everyone I met, even the cashier at the checkout counter in the supermarket. Everyone was very happy for me.

That night, I sat down and wrote long letters to my father and my brother. I could not let them wait another unnecessary day. I gave them a brief sketch of my life to fill them in on where I was and what I did throughout the thirty years of our separation. I remember writing to my brother: *"The pain and suffering I experienced in life was due to the lack of family."*

I meant what I said. Almost immediately, I began experiencing a feeling of belonging. I looked at people around me with greater clarity, as if a veil marring my true identity had been lifted from my eyes, and a mark of authenticity was engraved in me. I felt a new bond with the ordinary man and woman in the street, for I too had a father, a family, a birthplace, and a background. The isolation, the uprootedness, began to give way to a new relationship, and so I began to discover my bond with this world that made me feel more a part of it. I could finally call something my own and tug on my corner of the earth's blanket.

When my mother came over a few days later, I asked her, "Have you been able to sleep?"

She answered in an emotional weary state still filled with excitement, "No, I haven't been able to sleep for days. So much is coming back to me, whole sections of my life. I have written Goggeli (my brother's nickname) and your father long letters and I have included some photos."

With my mind totally wrapped up with my family in China, I said, "I wonder what they will feel when they receive our letters. I am preparing to send them a parcel as soon as possible. From what I hear, conditions in China are very difficult. As soon as I have some information on what one can send and not send to China, I will let you know." Not long after, my mother and I sent my father and brother two separate boxes that contained toiletry items, chocolate, games, and some clothes. I sent my box separately as I wanted to establish my own separate and unique relationship with my father and brother.

A few weeks later, I received a second letter from my brother. He was experiencing the same intensity of feeling as I. He wrote:

Nov. 19, 1981

My dear sister,

I am very glad to receive your letter. It is beyond my capacity to describe my excitement when your letter came to me, especially when I know some information about my mother's situation, really I kept awake all night. I am longing to go across the Pacific Ocean to be with you—your happy family and those loving children. The reception of your letter and pictures put us in such high spirit that we simply want to dance.

My dear sister, just as you put in the letter, we suffered a lot from our separation—

the separation from my mother and from you.

During my childhood I was abused by my stepmother. When I graduated from high school I applied for the Institute of Arts. Though I had a deep interest in this line yet failed because of want of tutorship. Next year grandfather managed to get me a position as an auditor in the Institute of Fine Arts. The year after that I was engaged as an elementary school teacher during which period I got acquainted with Lou Su Juan with whom I was married in 1965. We had a baby boy who died because of the fact that he took wrong medicine (at that time we also had a baby daughter). All of us were in depressive mood until we again had a baby boy whose name is Wang Yung, about two years old now. He knows more than thirty Chinese words. We all like him very much.

Later I left Elementary School and came into the Shipbuilding factory as a worker. During that period I attended amateur University of Fine Arts and also gave some lessons in oil painting. Now I serve as an artistic worker in designation of toys for children.

I want to avail myself of this opportunity to tell you something. My grandfather died in 1970. Uncle Wang Fu Ming suffered from lung cancer. He underwent an operation and now is in good situation. My father now retired and in poor health, physically weak. His second wife gave birth to a baby daughter called Wang Jia Ming (27). I have no dealing with her. My cousin Low Xi Cheng now is studying at Massachusetts Institute of Technology and is going to apply for Ph.D. through his mother Wang Pei De (our aunt). He knew that we communicated with each other. Perhaps he will write you or give you a long distance call.

Our dear mother once and again wrote to my third Aunt (Wang Pei Yan) hoping to know our situation and she did not tell us, otherwise we had come into contact with each other long ago.

At the end of this letter I want to know what kind of painting is most promising in your country. Is it possible to be once a part time worker and a part time student?

I have a lot of words to say. Because of limitation of the paper and my difficulties in expression in English I want to stop here. But I am sure such things including the distance between you and me will be overcome. Enclosed are a few pictures.

Embrace you and kiss your daughters,

Your elder brother

Wang Qian

P.S. I ask a friend of mine to write this letter. Personally speaking I can't write a letter in this way.

One Sunday afternoon, while still euphoric about the discovery of my family, I received a call from a Chinese gentleman whom I at first thought was someone from the Chinese Embassy in Washington. It turned out to be my cousin Lou Xi Cheng who was studying at M.I.T. At the time, I had not yet received my brother's letter advising me of this cousin's stay in the U.S.; nor did I know I had a cousin named Lou Xi Cheng. I was thrilled to hear from a first cousin who had firsthand knowledge about my father and brother. No one who knew them well had ever spoken to me about them. Over the phone, he gave me some details about my aunts and uncles in China, their names and occupations. Before we concluded our conversation, I asked him whether he would like to come visit us during the Christmas holidays. He seemed pleased with the idea. We would work out the details later. He also gave me a clue that my father was not well, but I could not determine what was wrong with him. Xi Cheng also called my mother who remembered him as a baby in Chentu, when she lived with his mother, Wang Pei De, my father's older sister, for nearly a year.

Xi Cheng did come for Christmas and stayed with us for a few days. He was a tall handsome Chinese man with a youthful appearance despite his forty years. During the course of his visit, he told me that a few years earlier he had gone to Hangzhou to see my father and brother. My father took him to a restaurant and told him about his days as a student in Munich, Germany. That evening, he saw tears roll down my father's cheeks as he reminisced. He also told me that my brother was a very good artist; in their childhood, they had occupied the same room while my brother was staying in Peking with our grandfather.

One evening, I sat on the couch with Xi Cheng and showed him some pictures I had of my father and brother. He looked at them with amusement and even recognized himself in one of the photos. "Don't you think my father was a handsome man?" I asked him with childlike pride. I saw him make a sad expression, as if to tell me something about the passage of time and its wear on the human body and spirit. Perhaps I was holding on to an illusion, so I said, "But he must be much older and different now." How much older and how different I did not know. I wanted to see it all for myself.

We continued to learn more about my family in China through my cousin. He told us that both my father and brother had humble dwellings, that my brother cooked with coal, and that they shared a common lavatory with other families in the compound. He made a drawing of the compound and pointed out where my brother lived in relationship to my father's room. When Xi Cheng was in Hangzhou, he had met my niece Wang Qion, whom everyone thought looked very much like me, when I was a child. I also learned that my brother as well as my father had suffered in the Cultural Revolution, but Xi Cheng was very cautious in elaborating on this subject.

After much conversation, we found out Xi Cheng himself had been purged during the Cultural Revolution. Because of his family name and because he was an intellectual, he was sent to Inner Mongolia to work in a shoe factory. He remained separated from his wife and children for six years. It took a great deal of persuasion on his part to convince the authorities to transfer him to Peking, even after he had found a job there. But he managed to be reunited with his wife and children. He showed me pictures of his wife and that of his son and daughter. He was very proud of them. During the many lonely nights in Inner Mongolia, he was able to study English. It made him very happy and proud when he was chosen to study electrical engineering at M.I.T. He was planning to complete his dissertation in the next few years. After he affirmed that he had adjusted well to life in the U.S., I asked him whether he found American life overly saturated by technology and electronic gadgetry, and he quickly answered, "But how convenient."

By the time my cousin left, I had decided to go to China as soon as possible. My original plan was to go in the fall to give myself sufficient time to absorb the new discoveries in my life and to save some money for the trip. But my father's deteriorating health would change that plan. I had received a few hints about his condition, but I was not aware of its gravity until I received this letter from my brother:

10 Dec. 1981

My dear sister,

I want to write to you after receiving your letter, but now I have to write to you because of my father's bad physical condition. It is for this reason he can't write to you personally.

Now, he is suffering from dropsy, often falls on the ground and what is more, he can't stand up without any support of others. He has lost control of evacuation of bowels and urination, and can't digest what he eats and also can't walk.

He even cannot take off his clothes and go to bed by himself if without help.

Doctors paid visit to him, but he refused to take any medicine after only taking one dose. He has no confidence in doctors. To be frank, his inclination in this respect really is something beyond our capacity to understand.

He told us these days before he underwent the dangerous situation physically, however, he survived, but he said his days are numbered. Now only I and my family take care of him. My stepmother and her daughter (whom I mentioned last time) do not take care of him, so my father's life is a sad one.

So, I think if it is possible, perhaps you are still in time to see him while he still lives, but time is very pressing and my father also hopes to see you while he is alive.

Please give me a letter.

Remember me to my brother-in-law and your darlings.

With best regards and wishes,

Your brother,

Wang Qian

P.S. Because of limitation of time, I ask my acquaintance to translate this letter from Chinese into English. I don't copy it again.

This letter made my joy turn into sorrow. I had to reach my father before it was too late. When I read the letter to my mother-in-law, Madeline Campagna, over the phone, she was deeply moved. The issues of her jealousy over my relationship with Tony had dissipated some. The next day, she called me back and offered to loan me the money to go to China, making me recognize her generosity.

Now I understand why my father had not written me another letter. He had been much too ill, and as my brother described it, practically on his deathbed. A few days after Christmas, however, I did receive a note from my father, written in a labored fashion:

Hangzhou

15.12.1981

Dear Marianne,

I am not very well but every day get better, you don't be in worry about me.
All about me and your brother you can ask the son of my sister. I write only a very short letter to you because I am not well, excuse me please.
Best regards to all your family and wish you all a very happy new year.

Your dear father

I took this note to the bathroom to be alone, and with my head buried in my hands, I cried. "Why did I have to find my father when he was dying? Why was everything I loved taken away from me?"

The next few days, I frantically prepared for my trip to China. We had talked about Tony getting a passport, just in case the opportunity presented itself for him to go with me, but the finances and the children made it difficult for him to accompany me, so he resigned himself to my going alone. Because finances were tight, my mother also chose not to go so she could save the money to bring my brother to the States. Of course, it was a great disappointment for both of them because they so much wanted to share in this reunion, and accompany me.

Two days before New Year's Eve, Tony and I drove to Chicago late at night and went to the passport office first thing the next morning. The passport was ready at noon, so after consulting a Pan American World Airways office downtown concerning flights to China, we drove home. We bypassed a visa agency that had offered to handle my visa application to China because, at this time, most people who traveled to China went in tour groups and their papers were handled by such agencies. I decided to handle the visa request myself because I thought it would be more personal.

In the meantime, I received a letter from my brother notifying me that my father's health had improved and it was not necessary for me to come to China right away. But plans were already underway, and I was determined to go. A Chinese lady in the neighborhood helped me fill out the visa application (I had obtained it by calling the Chinese Embassy) in Chinese with the help of my Chinese birth certificate and other papers with my father and brother's names and address. The very same day, I sent the visa application, passport photos, my brother's letter, and stamped self-addressed envelope via Federal Express. The following week, I received the passport with the visa, which allowed me to visit the cities of Beijing, Hangzhou, and Shanghai. The passport office was also kind enough to return my brother's letter. In the same envelope were some instructions on how to obtain accommodation in China through China Travel Service and about duty tariffs imposed on certain items, all written in Chinese. My Chinese lady friend helped me translate all of it.

I went to a travel agency and purchased all my plane tickets, including the ones I needed for flying between cities in China. Xi Cheng, my cousin from M.I.T., had convinced me to visit Beijing for a few days. His wife would take time off work to show me the city. Even though I was drawn to seeing my father straightaway, I thought my going to Beijing for a few days would give me an opportunity to become acclimated to the Chinese way of life. As it turned out, Pan Am's flights to China at the time were only going through Beijing, so the decision was in essence made for me to visit China's prestigious capital before going to the city of Hangzhou, where my father lived.

Another relative of mine, Aunt Wang Yuan, also known as Aunt Jane, my father's first cousin, who lived in San Francisco, also contacted me at this time. She had been my mother's friend in Shanghai and had been the sole person with whom my mother communicated regarding my brother during our early years of separation. When Aunt Jane had moved to Hong Kong around 1958, my mother had lost contact with her. It was through her that we had known my father and brother had moved to Hangzhou from Shanghai that same year. This small piece of information had been instrumental in my finding them again.

Aunt Jane was very interested in my trip to China and wrote a battery of letters concerning my Chinese family. I learned that she and the family were very much afraid to contact us in the West due to the social conditions in China. My grandfather, Wang Sao-Ao, had been active in politics most of his life, becoming China's Vice Minister of Finance for a period. My father, she thought, was wrapped up in his philosophical world and too advanced in thought for any of the family members to understand him. Now more than ever, he needed my love and care, especially because of his poor physical condition due to deficiency in his diet and cigarettes. My brother, she thought had his whole life ahead of him, and I should, therefore, concentrate my attention on my father. She advised me to bring him some vitamin B. Her admonitions made me realize that she too wanted me reunited with my father.

The second week in January, just as I was making all the preparations to go to China, I received a longer letter from my father, a sign of his improved health. I read the letter very slowly, trying to unfold its meaning:

My dear Marianne,

Your letter of 11.Dec. I have received day before yesterday. It is really a happy emotion that some tear come out from my eye.

I am really everyday better. Day before I received your letter I went out to buy some fruits and biscuits, of course the distance is not very long. So I am certain that I can be in sound condition to bid welcome to you.

As you say we have been separated for most of your life, that is more than thirty years. As I remember how heavy were in my heart to let you go, but God's will be done. So many years I was sick in heart as I had lost part of my heart.

As my health is really improved you don't need to ask the doctor who is your friend. Anyhow I thank you from my heart.

I were retired from the University after more than 20 years service.

Also (thus) you are very busy for the preparation of Christmas. Lou Xi Cheng will be very happy to have a Christmas holiday in your family (the time tense as I write is present, because otherwise is very difficult to write!)

My brother Fu-Ming has had a lung operation, but now everyday he rides a bicycle to some place in Nanking to have gymnastic training. Thus you can be entirely happy and not worry about that. I will write to him to tell him regards and good wishes from you.

Now let me make a close of this letter and wish you and your family happy holiday through the season.

Your dear father

In a short space of time, I would be seeing this man, my father, who by now was very dear to my heart.

Chapter 2

Departure to China

The evening before my departure to China, my suitcases were spread out on the bed. I noticed my three-year-old Sara watching me pack, her face barely clearing the paraphernalia scattered everywhere. She grabbed the large Teddy bear I had bought for my brother's two-year-old son, and hugged it with loving possessiveness.

"Can I keep it, Mommy?" she asked. "It is so soft."

She could not understand how I could bring coloring books, crayons, markers, toy cars, and quilted nylon jackets to children she had never seen. I understood her bewilderment. There was a dreamlike quality to it all. I was returning to China, my birthplace, after an absence of more than thirty-two years.

I bent down and took Sara in my arms. "Mommy is going away for a long time," I said, "but I will be back, and I will bring you a beautiful Chinese doll and many other presents. I am going to China to see my father, your grandfather. He was very sick around Christmas. Remember?"

Sara, then a pudgy little girl with curly hair, looked at me through her hazel eyes with an ocean of affection. I worried about leaving her for a month because I knew firsthand the experience of separation from one's parents at an early age, and I did not want to cause her the same pain. Tony, my husband, would be with her, though, as would her older sisters, Lisa (twelve), Michelle (eleven), and Suzy (five) her constant friend and companion. "Mama," however, was her sustenance—the person who could soothe her fragile feelings best, and in whose arms she felt most secure.

However, the trip to China was inevitable for me. For many years I had felt my life was a jigsaw puzzle, which destiny had tossed in the wind. I knew it was my job to find the pieces at all cost and fit them together for a completed picture. Now was my chance; the tickets were bought and arrangements made for me to spend the next four weeks in China. By 2 a.m., I was able to shut the suitcase by kneeling on it and squeezing the contents with my bodyweight. I went to bed, numb and exhausted. A feeling of suspension overtook me, partially from fatigue and partially because I was embarking on a journey to an entirely new and unknown world. China was for me, for all practical purposes, a foreign land, shrouded in mystery. Because of my Western upbringing, I'd had little contact with Chinese people and did not know their language or their customs. I was leaving my comfortable suburban home and going to a country that, until recently, had been closed to visitors such as myself. I wondered whether I would be a stranger to my father and my brother.

I had a fretful sleep. The morning of my departure, Saturday, February 6, 1982, Michelle, Suzy, and Sara had traces of chickenpox. They had contracted it from Lisa, who was recovering from the disease. What a way for Tony to be introduced to household demands! I wondered whether he thought I had ordered the ill-fated conditions, so as to give him a good taste of domestic burden. But he had totally accepted my trip by now, and gone were the nagging and self-pitying remarks made earlier. This morning, as he attended to our children's needs, I was assured he was fully in charge. He had taken two weeks off work to stay with the girls, and my mother and a neighbor would fill in the rest of the time.

Several snowstorms recently had hit Detroit, so the ground was covered with a thick blanket of snow. Another storm had been forecast for that weekend, but fortunately, the weather was calm. I was glad the ride to the airport would be unimpaired. The suitcases were by the door and I was ready to leave. Lisa offered Tony and me some tea, which she had thoughtfully prepared. She loved to bestow little acts of kindness at times of need, and she had a special concern for the physical well-being of others. It was no wonder she hoped to be a nurse one day. Michelle had made a plastic token for me, which said, "Dear Mom, I hope you have a good time. Always remember I love you! Say hi to grandpa! Remember to take pictures."

I embraced and kissed each of my children, and then Tony and I got into the car. Michelle took Sara in her arms in a self-confident manner. It pleased me to know Sara had older sisters to look after her. My sweet Suzy was standing by the door. Her long brown hair and beautiful, expressive eyes were filled with childhood wonder as she pondered the moment. This trip was as important to them as it was to me. I caught Lisa's smile and wistful expression. I saw them all looking through the glass storm door as the car pulled away. I carried them in my heart. The snow was piled high on either side of the road, delineating our path, as we drove on soft tracks toward the expressway.

When we arrived at the airport, we learned that the United Airlines plane to San Francisco would be an hour late. Tony and I sat quietly in the plastic chairs near the departure gate. I showed him the black notebook I was taking to China, with all the pertinent addresses and information taped to the pages, such as my flight schedule, addresses written in Chinese given to me by my cousin Lou Xi Chen, and hotel listings for the cities of Beijing and Hangzhou.

Tony marveled at how prepared I was. "I wish I could be going with you," he said. "But now, it is too late to think about it. It's certainly going to be an epic journey for you to go to China to see your father again."

I knew he shared my apprehensions, my hopes, and my dreams about this trip. We waited and mused about what would take place.

When my flight to San Francisco was called, Tony and I embraced, and then I walked toward the plane. He stood there, tall and handsome, with his dark hair parted on the side, looking almost like he did when we had gone to Bermuda on our honeymoon, only a great deal more robust due to the hearty meals I had prepared for him over our thirteen years of marriage. I was grateful he was generous enough to let me go on this trip, which would take me some 10,000 miles away. For the first time since our marriage, I would be on my own, free from household chores and children, a world traveler going to a country where few ventured to go alone.

Once in the plane, I settled in a seat next to a tall, elegant, middle-aged executive man. Although he was dressed in sports clothes, he had an air of good breeding and gentle authority about him. He was pleasant, but he had the reserved demeanor of an aristocrat. Through some sparse conversation, I learned he was returning to San Francisco after taking care of some business in the Midwest. He had clients in the Detroit area and flew around the country often, he told me.

During the flight, I took the opportunity to write some Valentine's Day cards to Tony and the children. I knew they would be pleasantly surprised that I had not forgotten them on this most important day of love. Since I was seated on the aisle, I seldom looked out the window, but I did look out when we flew over the snow-capped Rocky Mountains. The captain, at one point, told us we had taken an alternate route westward toward Wisconsin in order to avoid turbulent weather on the southern route. We did fly over Reno, Nevada, and before long, were in the San Francisco area, and I could see the green hills overlooking the bay. The skies were clear and the warmth of the sun beckoned us to this picturesque city, especially after the cold and snow in Detroit.

I looked at my watch. It had taken approximately four hours for us to arrive in San Francisco, and I was worried I would miss the plane going to Tokyo, which was due to leave in a half-hour. I expressed my concern to the gentleman seated on my right and he promptly hailed the stewardess, explaining my predicament. The stewardess immediately took me to the front of the plane where I sat in the first class section, near the exit door, during the plane's descent. I was grateful to the man who had helped me. How wonderful to be able to accomplish things with the wave of a hand, I thought.

When we landed, I was the first person off the plane, and I immediately spotted Aunt Jane (Wang Yuan), who was elegantly dressed in a beautiful, black quilted silk coat. She was slim and glamorous in spite of her years. I waved to catch her attention and to confirm that I was, indeed, the niece for whom she was waiting. As mentioned before, Aunt Jane was my father's first cousin with whom my mother corresponded while we lived in Brazil regarding my brother. She smiled at me and seemed to know me immediately.

As we walked hurriedly toward the outside of the building, Aunt Jane looked at me with wonderment. "Do you remember when your mother brought you and your brother to visit me in my apartment in Shanghai?" she asked.

I shook my head.

"Your brother remembers," she continued. "You were such a beautiful child with an impish expression. I see traces of that face now."

It pleased me that she found me attractive and intelligent (she had commented on my sensitivity and wisdom in letters received prior to this meeting), but we had little time for a leisurely talk. Long before I arrived at the airport, she had been aware of the tight schedule and had mapped my way to the Pan Am gate with utmost precision. Without her help, I do not think I would have made it on time.

Quickly, we took the shuttle bus, and while I was enjoying the momentary warmth of the day, she gave me an envelope that contained a number of presents: scarves for the aunts, a set of colored marking pens for my brother (an artist), and Scotch tape for me. As I tried to fit the envelope into my flight bag, she remarked, "I had to think of something light for you to carry. Tell Aunt Pei Yan (my father's sister who lived in Shanghai) that these scarves belonged to my mother. She adored my mother and she will be very happy to have them." With a nervous laugh, she added, "I thought you might need the Scotch tape. I never travel without Scotch tape. By the way, Tony called and wants you to call home."

When we were inside the International Terminal, I reached for the nearest phone. Soon Tony answered excitedly. "Uncle Fu Ming, your father's brother, wrote you a letter, which we received this morning. He has sent some photos of himself and his family," he said. "He was surprised that you have decided to come to China so soon after you found your father and brother. After his trip to Shanghai for a post-operative examination, he expects to go to Hangzhou to meet you."

"Okay, darling," I said. "Thanks for letting me know. I have to rush. The plane is leaving in fifteen minutes. Love you."

Aunt Jane waited for me outside the telephone booth. When I was finished talking with Tony, she and I walked in haste along the side ramp leading to the departure gate. I had so many questions about my family in China that I wanted to ask her. I wanted to know more about my grandfather, whom she had written was a Communist revolutionary leader, and had participated in most of the political movements of his time, living to the ripe old age of eighty-six. She had given me some information about my father's sisters and brother, and some of the conditions I might find in China, but it was all very sketchy in my mind. I knew she thought my trip to China was very timely because it might have a healing affect on my father, preventing him from further health deterioration and loneliness. I had little time to share my thoughts with her at this moment, but I hoped to have ample time to talk with her on my return.

At the Pan Am counter, I asked for a seat near the window, something I did at every stop because I loved to view the scene beneath me. My aunt observed my assertiveness and remarked, "I always take the outside seat so I do not have to trip over people's legs on my way to the lavatory." Here was the older generation telling the younger generation what to do, I thought. I took her advice in stride and loved her for it, but I did as I pleased. In a moment, I bid her adieu, and soon, I was inside the plane.

With coat and bags in hand, I settled in a window seat a few yards behind the plane's wing. I was soon joined by a wiry, middle-aged gentleman of small stature, who had an intense disposition. He put his flight bag and coat in the overhead compartment, and after he had organized himself, neatly sat down. While we waited for the plane to take off, I introduced myself and told him a bit of my life story and reasons for going to China.

I noticed as I talked that he listened attentively to everything I had to say, and when I finished, he remarked, "This is very interesting. It is strange the course which some people's lives take."

By talking to him, I could see his understanding of life was neither commonplace nor ordinary. He told me he was Jewish, so he understood full well how the ravaging events of history could sweep through and destroy people's lives. I was glad he did not take lightly what I had told him, and I was encouraged to show him some pictures of my family. I pulled out a small, tattered, leather box from my purse, which I had kept all my life. It contained an assortment of pictures of my mother, father, brother, and myself taken in the 1940s. This little box was one of my most treasured possessions, for it held the only pictures I had of my father and brother, my only tangible link with my past. The gentleman held in his hand a picture of my mother and father taken in Germany a year or so before their marriage. "You look just like your mother in this picture," he said. This statement took me by surprise. I did not think I looked like my mother, who is blond and blue-eyed while I am brunette with slanted, dark eyes. How different people's perceptions can be of whom you look like and who you are.

The gentleman then took two pictures from his wallet and showed them to me. One was a picture of his wife, a beautiful redhead with a dazzling hairdo, and the other was a picture of his twelve-year-old son, celebrating his bar mitzvah. "I am a Canadian United Nations delegate," he said. "And I am going to Tokyo and to Sidney, Australia for meetings dealing with different aspects of International Finance. My wife accompanies me quite often on these trips, but we did not want to take our son out of school this time."

As we talked, the plane stayed on the ground for more than an hour. We waited for other passengers to board who were coming from other parts of the country. All the rush at the San Francisco airport had been unnecessary, I thought. Finally, the stewardess asked us to place our hand luggage under the seats or in the overhead compartments. The seatbelt and other signs went on. We were all glad to be on our way. The plane took off at 1:30 p.m.—an hour late—but now we were flying into the azure skies over the Pacific.

Chapter 3

━━━━ ❀ ━━━━

Flight to Beijing

I had been flying for almost fifteen hours since I had left home, and I was filled with anticipation for my arrival in China. My thoughts wavered between the home I had just left and the *home* I was to find in China with my father and brother. I had the curiosity of a child, and I felt the freedom of a bird that gained the world after spending a long time confined in a domestic cage. In the semi-lit atmosphere of the cabin, where some people were sleeping while others were reading or watching a movie, I continued to think. A lifetime had passed between my family in China and myself. Would I be able to bridge the gap of thirty-two years? Would I be an outsider looking in? Such thoughts flashed through my mind, yet I felt determined to re-establish my relationship with my father and brother, whatever the sacrifices involved. I had the desire to embrace their people and their customs, so that I could be a part of them as I once was.

The sun had never set. I lifted the window shutter to see that the sun continued to spread its golden rays over the horizon. It was strange to have lost one complete night. We had crossed the International Time Zone, and we had to set our watches to 4:00 p.m. My watch registered 2:00 a.m., Detroit time. So far I'd had three delicious meals, but I could not eat anymore because this was nighttime for me. I mused to myself, "If one would continue on this journey indefinitely, traveling with the sun, one would lose all sense of balance, and time, relatively speaking, would be shortened. Just imagine that after this trip I will have gone around the world twice, clockwise and counterclockwise. The first time by ship when I was a child of five, and the journey took several months. Now I am in a Boeing 747, and the trip takes less than a day."

I saw a dignified, elderly Chinese gentleman mention to the stewardess that he was going to Beijing. He had silvery hair, was dressed in a dark, woolen suit, and had a long woolen overcoat. I was happy to know that I was not making this trip to China alone.

Often I was filled with emotion, and tears came to my eyes when I thought that in a matter of days, I would be with my father and brother. Thirty-two years! A dream come true. The possibility of my traveling to China had always felt remote. For me, China was a hazy reality far in the past. I remembered driving alone one late afternoon on a country road in Michigan, gazing into the distance, when the images of my father and my brother flashed through my mind. "Wouldn't it be wonderful if I could see them again," I had thought. But the thought was only a faint hope then, and it seemed quite absurd at the time because China maintained its isolation, and I had no clue as to my family's whereabouts.

At one point the captain informed us that we would arrive in Tokyo at 5 p.m., as expected because he had gained some time during the flight. I would be able to make the connection with Pan Am Flight 15 to Beijing, leaving at 6 p.m. It was not possible for me to sleep in the seated position—my legs or arms got numb, and I was not able to secure a pillow or a blanket—I think they had all been taken. I would make up for lost sleep in Beijing when I would arrive late at night, around 10:10 p.m. Luckily, I had my pile-lined jacket over me and I used my sweater as a pillow.

The gentleman seated next to me was amusing. He reminded me of an engineer friend of mine with a logical mind concerned with minute details. He had the biggest flight bag I had ever seen. It was a blue, rectangular-shaped box made of heavy nylon, with many compartments, which he placed in the overhead compartment with great difficulty. He had gotten up several times to go to the lavatory to wash, I thought, for he dug a huge towel out of this bag. He had two watches, and every now and then, he would take one out of his pocket to compare the time in Toronto with the time in Tokyo. Several hours into our trip, he wrote a carefully thought out letter to his wife. Sometime after our last meal, this gentleman and I resumed our conversation. "You know, when I arrive in Tokyo, the business men with whom I will be dealing will most certainly ask me out to dinner, and I cannot refuse, even though I had three meals on this plane," he said. We laughed at his unwarranted ordeal.

I replied, "It must be very heavy for you to carry your flight bag around."

"The last time I was in Tokyo, my luggage was lost together with all my business files. I was dressed in jeans and a sports shirt and had to be completely outfitted from underwear to overcoat in one evening," he explained. "The airline footed the entire bill, which came close to 1,000 dollars, and I must say they were very courteous in this respect. But now I carry my oversized bag, which contains all my U.N. files right on board with me, just in case of another mishap, and I always dress in a suit," he concluded.

The sun kept shining. "It must be the middle of the night for my family in Detroit," I thought. I looked out the window and saw that we were flying above a scattered formation of dense clouds at an altitude of 41,000 feet, as mentioned by the captain earlier. The Pacific Ocean was not very visible from this distance; it all seemed part of the sky. I did not feel that time dragged because I was well entertained. I purchased an earplug for three dollars, and listened to Segovia for a while. The movie *Rich and Famous* was shown and I watched a short section of it.

Then I tried to sleep, and I was able to catnap some.

Soon there was some movement in the cabin, and people were beginning to talk and tidy up to prepare themselves for the descent. Some people were lifting their chairs to the upright position and opening the window shutters. The sleepy and dozing atmosphere we had earlier was replaced by a sense of arrival. The plane was lowering its altitude, so as I looked out the window, I was able to see Japan's coastline, which looked like a large crocodile protruding from the sea. As we approached Tokyo, I began to see small cars moving along a mountain road and I recognized a gasoline sign.

The Canadian gentleman to my left told me about Japan during our descent. "Japan is topping all industrial nations with their products, such as cars, watches, and computers. They are providing fierce competition for the U.S. and European countries, and in many cases, are pushing them right out of the market. Look at the Seiko watches and the Toyota cars; they can be found everywhere. Nowhere else in the world have I seen such discipline and dedication among the workers. Most of the people have to live along the coastline because of the uninhabitable rugged mountains of the interior. There are 100 million people, so it is very crowded."

I listened attentively to everything he had to say, for I was eager to learn about Japan, a country on the gateway to China. As I have said before, my Asian experience was limited, but now I was about to see Asia for myself.

The plane landed and we were flagged before a round glass building, Pan Am's section of the airport. It was late afternoon, and the lights inside the building could be seen from the plane. The Jetway tunnel was attached to the aircraft, and soon we were inside Pan Am's waiting pod.

Once at the airport, I realized the arrival and departure gates for Pan Am's flights were next to each other, so I did not have to walk a long distance in search of my next flight. Since I had left San Francisco, I had been seeing more and more Oriental faces, each with its particular individuality. The clerk at the Pan Am desk was very friendly and efficient; it seemed like he was accustomed to dealing with large groups of people. He assigned each person in line a new seat on the next Pan Am flight to Beijing with the aid of a computer tucked under the counter, all the while exchanging animated remarks with his fellow workers who were all wearing ear phones and communicating with unseen centers.

Evening was upon us and it was dark outside. I walked over to the waiting pod and took a seat. Waiting with me was a scattered group of passengers who looked very tired, and who, like myself, might have lost a night's sleep. Seated across from me on a bench was a grandmotherly Chinese woman of humble appearance who was straightening something inside her plastic shopping bag. She looked as if she were waiting for the bus rather than going on an international flight.

While I was waiting for the plane, two Chinese gentlemen stood near me. When one of them looked my way, I knew he was curious why I was going to China, so I began to talk to them. "I'm going to China to see my father whom I have not seen in thirty-two years. He lives in Hangzhou and taught mathematics at Zhejiang University for twenty years," I explained.

In a restrained but polite manner, the elderly gentleman I had seen earlier on the plane asked, "And may I ask your father's name?"

"His name is Wang Fu Shih, and he studied in Germany before the war," I said, wondering whether I was treading on dangerous grounds. Were these men my enemies or my friends? I honestly did not know. China's social conditions in the last three decades made it unwise to trust strangers. However, we continued our conversation.

The younger man, dressed in a Western suit, was more ebullient and spoke to me about his experiences in America in an animated fashion. "I finished some medical studies at the University of San Francisco. This man is my boss," he said, pointing to the elderly gentleman with him. "We both work at a Beijing hospital, and he is the chief of staff," he concluded with an excited smile.

After waiting twenty minutes in the holding area, a Pan Am official ushered us through a gate where a small shuttle bus was waiting to take us to the aircraft. Less than twenty passengers were aboard the bus. The darkness, the silence, and the fresh air filled me with excitement and with a feeling that I was plunging into unknown territory.

Soon, I was on the plane and we were airborne once more. The moon was shining in its fullness against the dark sky. I had a window seat on the plane's left side, just in front of the wings. The plane was rather empty so no one sat next to me. But I could feel an atmosphere of curiosity and quiet apprehension among the passengers. A variety of people were on board, some dressed very simply. I later found out there were a group of women, Chinese doctors, who were returning home from a seminar held in Japan. I was struck by how emaciated some of them looked. They wore no makeup and many had a blunt haircut held back by bobby pins. Behind me was a young man from the States who, I found out, was studying at the University of Beijing. In front of me was another American, tall and bearded, who later during the flight told me he was going to China on business.

The trip was very quiet and the lights within our compartment were subdued; only an occasional reading light was on. The stewardess offered me some dinner, which I refused, considering all the meals I had taken so far. After having some orange juice, I coiled within my blanket and tried to rest and embrace within me all that I was experiencing. I felt I had come with a mission, and that this trip was not a mere pleasure trip for me. I had come to find my father and to find myself.

The lights were turned on when the plane was an hour away from arriving in Beijing. The stewardess handed out forms from the Chinese Customs Bureau for everyone to fill out. We had to declare all our valuables and our destination in China. Unfortunately, my father's address was written in Chinese in my black notebook, so I asked a Chinese lady seated in the middle row to write it in the form for me, which she did in an obliging manner. I was subtly beginning to feel like a foreigner because I could neither write nor speak Chinese.

We had been flying over China's mainland for some time, but nothing was visible below. An incredible sense of where I was going overtook me. I could not believe that we were about to land at Beijing's airport. As the plane began to descend over the city, I could see thousands, maybe millions of very dim tiny lights flickering endlessly into the distance. From my window, I saw an illuminated runway, and before long, we touched ground and cruised toward a large modern structure, the Beijing airport. As we stood in the aisle, waiting to disembark, the American bearded gentleman turned to me and said, "Make sure you leave before your visa expires." His tone was serious. I appreciated his fatherly concern and took his warning on a wait-and-see basis.

At the terminal, everyone was for himself. As we stepped off the Jetway, I saw along the wall close to the arrival gate several uniformed officials, including some very young ladies with very serious expressions, who added to the ominous feeling of our arrival. The large cavernous building was virtually empty, and it seemed as if we had to walk for miles to reach the immigration booth. For those of us too tired to walk, a people mover conveyor belt was operating, but I chose to walk, glad to feel the ground beneath me again.

As I reached the processing window, the Chinese official took my passport, looked at it carefully, stamped it, and gave it back to me in a manner of grave importance I translated to mean, "You will be okay, but only because we allow you to come in."

In an open area, I claimed my luggage from a revolving belt, and then I went to a table set up in front of the luggage checkpoint, where a number of male and female Chinese officials were helping the newly arrived passengers. I approached a friendly young man who could speak English very well. "You go to that window to pay duty," he said to me with a broad smile, reminiscent of a coach conducting a winning game.

At the duty booth to my left, I pulled out the tape recorder and the watches from my shoulder bag, which I was going to present to my family, and handed them to a young lady perched on a tall stool. Her demeanor was docile, but I could tell she would not deviate from the just assessment of taxes rendered by the items, especially after I saw her consult a fellow lady worker. She wrote the items and the amount to be paid on a form about as thick as tissue paper, then gave it to me, and told me to pay at the bank.

I walked toward a large booth with a wide counter situated in front of this hall, bearing the title, "Bank of China," in large letters. I was amazed to find the furnishings of this bank very antiquated. In the room's center were two large wooden desks behind which two workers were seated, dressed in Mao suits. Against the wall were two cabinets also bearing signs of age. One worker exchanged all the money from a large metal box on the bench beside him. He had a skillful way of folding the money around his fingers and counting it very fast in a fanlike fashion. Then he gave the money to the fellow next to him, who rechecked the amount in the same manner. The only modern piece of equipment in this room was a large electrical calculator used to figure out the foreign exchange of given amounts. These two workers were very officious and serious; it seemed they could not speak English, but they could understand my request to cash in some American Express checks. At the time, the

Chinese yuan was worth 75 percent of the American dollar. I got receipts for all the transactions I made at the bank, which I placed in my large canvas zip-around wallet, just in case I needed to present them to the custom officials on my return to the U.S.

After I took care of my business at the bank, I looked around and saw that most of the passengers were already processed, and only a few lingered about. One of them was the Chinese doctor, dressed in a Western suit, whom I had met at the Tokyo airport. He was the only passenger beside myself who had to pay duty on a valuable item. I saw him dragging the carton of a television set, smiling nervously but looking relieved that the ritual of customs was over. When I finally went through the final checkpoint, a female official asked me to open my large suitcase. In it, she found a couple of transistor radios I had forgotten to declare. I thought I would have to go through the whole process of duty paying again; however, she let me go after consulting a fellow official. Now, I was at last free. All I had to do was sit on my suitcase and hope it would close. Fortunately, it shut.

At this late hour, over-packed and alone, I entered the airport's front lobby in search of solace. On my way into the airport, I remembered seeing a group of Chinese citizens dressed in their customary blue and gray suits, pressed against a large glass pane, eagerly awaiting their relatives and friends. It was as if they were crowded inside a glass bottle and were only able to catch a short glimpse of the outside world before nightfall. I was hoping that Kwang Yi, my cousin's wife, would be among them. Before I left Detroit, my cousin Lou Xi Cheng had told me over the phone that his wife was planning to meet me at the airport and would be waving a large sign. I did not see such a lady, and I soon realized I would have to find lodging myself because no one was waiting for me. "Kwang Yi lives far away, and she does not have the means to come to the airport at this ghastly hour," I thought.

I parked my belongings next to the empty counter of the China Travel Service agency and approached the American university student I had met earlier on the plane. I had heard him speak Chinese very well, so I thought he might be able to help me.

"Have you been in China before?" I asked, sensing his familiarity with the place.

"Yes. I have been studying for almost four years at the University of Beijing, and I am just returning from my winter break a little early, so I can see some of my friends," he said.

I looked at this tall, blond youth with rimless glasses and thought him handsome in an aloof way. I asked him, "Could you tell me where I could make a phone call? I need to find a hotel room."

He pointed to a blue phone resting on a ledge behind the counter. "You can use this phone without charge, only dial 9 for an outside line."

I scrambled in my purse for the black notebook and dialed the number of a Peking hotel, which I thought had a reservation made in my name by the China Travel Service, which I had written to earlier. On the line's other end, a short brisk voice answered. I inquired, "Do you have a room reservation for Marianne

Campagna?" The man did not understand me, and after a few more short words in Chinese, he hung up.

So I sought out the university student once again and asked him to make the phone call for me. I watched him speak in Mandarin and hoped he would meet with success. After several attempts, he returned the notebook to me and said in an unsurprised fashion, "There are no reservations and all the hotels in town are booked solid." His expression led me to believe that it was the normal course of events for someone like me to find herself in this predicament while traveling in China. I felt stranded in this large and empty human warehouse. While I looked at the darkness outside, which enclosed us in a patch of light in the lobby, I began to wonder whether there was indeed a city out there where the masses lived.

A handful of people were waiting for a taxi, but none were in sight. Another plane had arrived, and the doors to the lobby were opened by a line of Chinese passengers walking excitedly with all sorts of luggage and roped boxes (TV, stereos). They were soon met by relatives and acquaintances who drove them to the city in vans and cars. The airport was deserted once again, and I stood by the entrance wondering what to do.

A young Japanese gentleman, who was well-dressed and had courteous manners, came to my rescue. I sensed he was pleased to make my acquaintance and enjoyed speaking English. With a smile he said, "Why don't you come and stay at the airport hotel? My companion and I are staying there tonight. I'm sure they will have a room for you until you contact your relative tomorrow."

"I don't know if it is possible. I thought China Travel Service alone could assign hotel rooms," I said with uncertainty. "Well, I guess I am taking everything too seriously," I reasoned. "There is no alternative for me, so I might as well join you."

He was happy with my decision. We continued to stand around and chat into the night. In a musing way, I said, "I would love to see the Great Wall. Do you know whether there are bus tours to the Great Wall this time of the year?"

The American student laughed and said sarcastically, "The last time I went to the Great Wall in winter I caught pneumonia. Sure, you can take the train or go by bus."

This pessimistic remark made me begin to wonder whether all my plans were going to be dissolved, and I would remain quite lost in this strange land. But I was not so easily dissuaded, and I knew I would plod on, facing each moment bravely.

An American lady, who was a librarian and missionary type, had come on the last plane. She now approached our small group with a personal telephone-address book in one hand and a small suitcase in the other. She asked, "Where can I find a phone to call my friend?" I pointed to the same phone we had used earlier, which was placed rather obscurely behind the counter. Soon, she returned distraught and said, "I could not reach anyone; there was no answer." We had forgotten to tell her to dial the outside line. She did finally reach her friend, and before long, she too was gone.

As we waited for a taxi to appear, I noticed a young porter dressed in a sloppy baggy suit. He was humble looking with sad eyes and big hands and feet. I felt there

My grandparents Karoline and Joseph Schuetzinger's wedding, 1907

My mother kidding around with her best friend Hilde Wust with whom she toured Europe, 1936

My mother singing in her youth group, Bavaria, circa 1936

My parents, Wang Fu Shih and Agnes Wang, Passport picture, 1941

My dad in Munich Germany, circa 1938

My handsome dad in white tuxedo, Munich Germany, 1940

My mother applying make-up in Haifa Palestine, 1941

My dad Wang Fu Shih in Haifa Palestine post marriage, 1941

My mother aboard ship from Haifa Palestine to Cairo Egypt, 1941

My brother with parents on a swing set that my father built_Guilin China, 1944

Uncle Fu Ming with my brother in Chungking, 1945

This is one of my earliest photos Shanghai, 1946

My mother and I in Shanghai,
circa 1947

My mother with my brother and
me, Shanghai China, circa 1947

My brother Wang Qian
and I in Shanghai, 1949

Passport type
picture, Shanghai,
1948

My mother and I at the Wooster
Victory ship that took us to Naples
Italy, 1949

Me at the Riding
School in Rio, 1950

My mother, stepfather and I at back of riding school, 1950

Riding Borboleta, 1950

Me at the outer paddock of the Riding School with part of Gavea Mountain in background 1952

At the beach on my birthday, 1953

School picture at end of year recital, 1954 (third grade) - I am in the front row from left

Jumping on Domino, 1955

*Stepfather, me, Dona Vera riding at the
beach with mother in water, circa 1955*

*The family watching riders at the paddock,
circa 1954*

*My mother and I at S. Conrado
beach, 1956*

Me on left front row, Alzira 4th in back and Virginia 6th in back with dorm students at Stella Maris School, 1959

Me, Bisuca, and Laura at the S. Conrado Beach, 1956

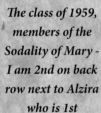

The class of 1959, members of the Sodality of Mary - I am 2nd on back row next to Alzira who is 1st

My passport picture, 1960

Visiting Harumi's family, 1960 - from left -Harumi, cousin, friend, mother Toki, cousin, Terumi, me, another friend

Press Picture taken at New York Airport, May 18, 1961 for article in the Detroit News re - Princess Chestohin and her daughter Marianne arriving in Detroit

My mother and I at a Mercy College tea party, 1961

Graduating from Mercy College, 1965

Mercy College graduation picture, 1965

The Lopes family (Armazem) 1967(same year as Brazil trip) - back - Paulo, Nega, Bisuca, M. Celia, Celia Maria, Wanda, Ana - middle- Rosaria, Rita - front - Joao, Tadeu, and Tarcisio

At my brother's kitchen - from left - my brother,   niece Joan(Qion), my father, and I, Hangzhou, China, 1982

With my dad in the kitchen, Hangzhou, 1982

Pondering all of it at West Lake, Hangzhou, 1982

At West Lake with Uncle Fu Ming, 1982

My dad by the family compound, 1982

Walking at the beach and visiting Gavea Mountain, Rio, 2000

A postcard of the Gavea Valley - S. Conrado Beach taken in the early 1900s

Current view of the Gavea-S. Conrado valley with S. Conrado Church, 2000

My mother and I at the top of the Empire State Building upon our arrival in New York, 1961

Me on the front patio of Stella Maris School during my visit to Brazil, 1967

Tony and I with Lisa and Michelle, 1973

My mother at a birthday party for Lisa and Michelle at our house in Detroit, 1975

I am in the sand dunes with Sara by Lake Michigan near Ludington State Park, 1979

At our house in Canton, MI - Lisa, Tante Maria, myself with baby Sara, and my mother, 1979

My family with cousin Xi Cheng Lou, Christmas, 1981

Me at the Great Wall, 1982

Kwang Yi and her family at the Forbidden City, Beijing, 1982

My brother, his wife Su Juan, and daughter Qion at his in-laws, Hangzhou, 1982

Su Juan and my brother in their kitchen, 1982

Su Juan's mother and family at dinner, 1982

My dad with his brother, Uncle Fu ming, 1982

My father's 2nd family - from left - Wang Jia Xing (stepsister), my father, his wife, Jia Ming (my half-sister) and her husband Wang Shing Juan

Sunday excursion at Hangzhou West Lake district with Su Juan's family, 1982

My father and I posing at a bridge in a park near the family compound, Hangzhou, 1982

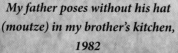

My father poses without his hat (moutze) in my brother's kitchen, 1982

My brother and I in front of my mother's building in Shanghai, 1982

My brother and I at the door of my mother's penthouse in Shanghai, 1982

My brother and I at Shanghai's port by the Huang Pu River where our family parted 32 yrs. ago, 1982

With Aunt Pei Yan and brother in Shanghai, 1982

The Shanghai excursion - from left - Liu Yun Yun, Liu Tzu, Qian Ji Jun, my brother, me, Henry Lu, Yi Dien, 1982

Before leaving Shanghai, 1982 - from left - Uncle Liu Tzu, cousin Yi Dien, my brother, me, cousin Liu Yun Yun, Aunt Pei Ron, Aunt Pei Yan

At the kitchen with my father and brother

Christmas - back row from left - Michelle, Lisa; front- Sara, Suzy, 1982

My family 1983

Sara with cat Smokey, 1983, around the time I composed poem, The Magic of Your Day

My mother and my brother at the time of their reunion, Ann Arbor, MI, 1984

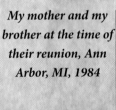

Celebrating my brother's arrival, Aug. 1984- mother, brother, Aunt Caroline and cousin Erik

My brother with his newly arrived family at my house - nephew Yun, my brother Qian, Su Juan, and niece Qion, Canton, MI, 1987

Father Toner with me and my daughters Sara (her first communion) and Suzy, 1985

My father and I at our house in Canton, MI, 1987

Suzy with Buddy, 1988 - the riding tradition goes on

Tony and I at the grounds of our Riding School in Rio, Brazil, 1988

Me in front of Riding School house, 1988

My daughters and I visiting Dona Linda's family (the Armazem children) with friends, Rio, 1997

Visiting Madre Euridyna at Stella Maris School - me, Madre Euridyna, Harumi, and Maria Clara, 1997, Rio

My daughters Suzy, Michelle, Lisa, and Sara at the Sugar Loaf Mountain with Rio's panorama in background, 1997

My father, Tony and myself in Hangzhou, China, 2000

The last picture I took of my father in his green striped lawn chair with bookcase and Great Wall hat in background, Hangzhou, 2000

Mom and daughters 2007

Sara and I at her wedding 2011

Me parasailing off the Gavea Mountain, Rio, 2006

Halloween with grandchildren - 2011- from left - Sawyer, daughter Michelle, Cole, Marlo and me

might be a kinship between us, so I said to him, "I have come to China to see my father. He lives in Hangzhou and I haven't seen him in thirty-two years. Do you think you can call a taxi for us?" There was sympathy in his face, but he did not speak. He led me to the bank window that opened itself to the lobby. There I met the two officials I had dealt with earlier in the evening. I told them once again my story and stressed that I was born in China, whereupon they smiled. Their passivity puzzled me, but I think I managed to convince them that I was one of them.

When a taxi did arrive after more than two hours of waiting, the Japanese gentlemen and I carried our luggage to the curb outside the airport lobby. The taxi was a red, fairly new Japanese model sedan, but the driver was not quite sure whether he should take us; I think he might have been committed to another group. But a young, cheerful, Chinese student who had just arrived from the States appeared on the scene and convinced the taxi driver to take my Japanese friends and me to the hotel. With a huge smile on his face, the agile and elegant student said to us, "I have been in your position in a foreign land. It is my turn to help you." Then he bid us adieu with a magnanimous wave, happy to have been of assistance.

We packed into the compact car, the two gentlemen in the backseat with a television carton and suitcases on their laps, and I in front with my hand pieces, while the rest of the luggage was placed in the trunk. Soon we arrived at the airport hotel, a solitary structure standing at the junction of the circular drive, leading to the airport, and the long straight avenue, leading to the city. The taxi driver helped us carry the suitcases to the door, and I offered to pay, but the Japanese gentleman did the honors. The street was deserted, the lobby was dark, and it looked like the hotel was shut for the night. However, an attendant emerged from the shadows and ushered us into the lobby of this modern hotel that promised to be quite comfortable. At the counter, under subdued lighting, each of us showed our passport and paid for one night's stay: forty yuans or thirty dollars. The clerk wrote my name and passport number onto a registry and I was given a receipt and issued room 618. A young attendant dressed in a white lab coat helped us to the sixth floor via the lobby elevator and assisted us with the suitcases. In the sixth floor's hallway, the friendly Japanese gentleman said, "Would you like to meet us at eight in the lobby for breakfast?"

"Okay, I'll be up then," I said, not quite expecting this invitation. Considering that my day had been turned into night, it did not matter what time I got up. I might as well join these gentlemen in the morning.

Shortly after I went into my room, I heard a rap on the door, and a young attendant with a humble posture, also dressed in a white lab coat, walked in with a soft shuffle and put something in a tin can on the table by the stuffed chair. It sounded like he said, "Keys," so I did not bother to look. Later, I found out it was an envelope of tea that I could have used had I known.

When I found myself alone in the room, an empty hollow feeling came over me, but I summoned the courage to continue with this journey. As I looked around the room, I noticed a single bed covered with a green silk spread. The walls were painted white and the floor was parquet wood. Against the wall beside the bed was a glass-topped desk with a lamp that had a pleated red and white shade made of silk and a colored glass base. The furniture was made of pine and had a simple structure, very much like one would find in a U.S. college dormitory. There was even a laced doily under the glass that covered the table near the reclining chair, where a large thermos bottle with a flowered design and a covered teacup stood. The private bath was clean and adequate. I went to sleep under the thick cotton sheets and heavy blankets.

My wristwatch's alarm rang at 7 a.m. I awoke and stood by the large double-paned window watching the scene behind the hotel. It was dawn, and gray, somber human figures moved in foreboding silence. A couple of people pedaled on bikes down a road behind the hotel. Some scattered individuals were on foot, and all seemed to be headed for their workplaces. Not too far away, a small beige, old-fashioned bus unloaded a group of workers who walked to their destination the rest of the way. Someone was being admitted through the hotel's back gate by an attendant who had apparently just had her breakfast since she was carrying an enamel bowl. Directly below me were cubicle-like rooms opening to a small courtyard that seemed to be the servants quarters. Smoke was coming out from a smokestack of a sand-colored brick building in the distance. Slowly, the daylight was intensifying. I took a shower, put on a set of fresh clothes, took from the suitcases the items my cousin Xi Cheng sent to his wife, and placed them on an armchair. Then I went down to the lobby.

I asked the girl at the front desk whether she had a plastic bag or some paper for me to wrap Kwang Yi's belongings, sent by her husband. She stood up from her seat and tried to understand what I was saying. From her blank look, I knew I could not make myself understood, so I went to the post office booth. There, with the help of my *Chinese for Travelers* guide, I asked once more for wrapping paper, but the girl attending the booth either did not understand me or there was none.

My Japanese companions arrived shortly after, and we entered a large, airy dining room with a high ceiling, tall paneled windows, and large round tables covered with white tablecloths. We sat at a table near the entrance and a young waitress, wearing a white apron speckled with food stains, took our order. We had bacon, eggs, and toast with butter and jam—a typical American breakfast, except the bacon was undercooked. Very few people were breakfasting at the time, but I recognized the Pan Am crew at a table further in front of us. As we ate, the Japanese gentlemen and I talked about our destinations in China. The older, shorter man remained silent throughout because his English was not fluent. The young man said, "We are going to the north of China to teach the people in some villages how to make shoes, which our company in Japan would import. We have come to China three times before, and we have traveled extensively by train. Conditions in the country are very primitive and poor. It usually takes us two months to get our visa to come here."

To which I added, "It took me one week to get my visa, but then, I was born in China and my father was very ill when I applied."

Then I took out a couple of small albums from my purse and showed them some pictures of my husband and daughters taken in recent years. They were surprised to know I had four daughters, for they thought I looked very young. I later showed them pictures of my mother, father, and brother taken in China and Germany during the '40s that I kept in that old leather box. As they looked at the pictures, I could tell they were interested and moved by my story, and I detected an expression of sympathy on the young man's face.

"Isn't my father handsome in this picture?" I asked, after showing them a picture of my father dressed in a white tuxedo and a bow tie. This picture had helped me idealize my father as a gallant, intelligent, witty, and youthful man, and it fixed his image in my mind as if he were frozen in time. I tried to reach into the future and added, "But he must have changed a great deal."

Before the Japanese gentlemen left to board their next plane to the interior of China, they helped me call Kwang Yi, my cousin's wife at her engineering office. I was happy that they found her at work. They gave me the receiver, but Kwang Yi's English was faltering, so I gave the receiver to the girl attendant at the front desk. She in turn related the message Kwang Yi gave her to the Japanese gentleman who could speak Chinese fairly well. He translated it to me thus, "Kwang Yi is coming by bus and will meet you here in an hour."

The Japanese gentlemen were relieved that I was able to contact Kwang Yi. But just in case I needed assistance, the younger man gave me two business cards, one with his name and Tokyo address, and the other with his company's name and address in Beijing. He wrote a message in Japanese on the back of one of the cards for me to present to one of the several individuals listed on the card, if I ran into some trouble. After this, we said goodbye, and they were off on their particular mission.

I paced around the hotel lobby, and then took the corridor to my right and noticed a small snack bar with tables and the sign "Coca-Cola" hung over the door. I went to visit the souvenir shop just outside the dining room. In the showcases were many Chinese curiosities such as vases, silk embroidered doilies, fans, and carvings, some of which reminded me of artifacts my mother had taken with her from China the year we departed, and which I had always seen adorning our various homes. Shortly afterwards, I went to sit in the parlor in front of the reception area, where many burgundy sofas and armchairs were protected by white doilies. As I sat, I watched the housekeeping crew go by several times, talking animatedly with one another. They were of both sexes and all of them wore white lab coats; they behaved like a group of high school teens meeting at school, and they seemed to be kidding one another constantly, but they would not speak to the guests unless spoken to. However, curious glances were cast my way, and I am sure they wondered about my presence there.

Across from me was a black doctor from Tanzania, dressed in dark trousers, white shirt, and sandals who spoke English very well.

"Have you been to downtown Beijing?" I asked to begin a conversation.

"No, I haven't. We will be going there later on by bus. I am returning from North Korea after six months of medical studies."

With his legs stretched out in front of him, I thought he looked bored and fatigued. I said, "You must be anxious to go home."

"Yes, I am looking forward to being home. The cold does not agree with me very much," he said in a thoughtful yet laconic manner.

The sun was shining brightly outside and sent a glow through the window, making me feel that all was normal. I decided to write some postcards I had purchased from the post office booth and then I studied some conversational Chinese while I waited for Kwang Yi.

Chapter 4

❀

Three Days in Beijing

The lobby's doors opened and Kwang Yi entered, bringing a burst of energy to the hotel's relaxed atmosphere. Her ready embrace and contagious smile were an omen of good fortune to me. She was a practical and energetic person with a welcoming and open manner, and our rapport was immediate. At the desk, she called the hotel downtown where I was going to stay and then engaged in a joyful conversation with the clerk, none of which I understood. Before we went to my room to pick up my luggage, she asked the clerk to call a taxi. Her English was poor, but we managed to exchange a few sentences without difficulty. At the room, I gave her the items Lou Xi Cheng had sent her. She was delighted to see his pictures and smiled with pleasure as she leafed through them, and then, without much ado, she put everything her husband had sent her and a few of my presents into her black vinyl zip-all bag. She insisted on carrying my heavy suitcase as we marched down the hall to the elevator and then the lobby to await the taxi.

In no time, the taxi driver came in and led us to the Japanese compact car waiting outside. He pulled down the meter and we sped through a long, straight, narrow boulevard studded with trees, with open fields on either side. The flatness and the brown winter hue of the soil reminded me of the landscape around Detroit. The driver took the center of the road, honking frequently as he passed a donkey cart, bikers, and an occasional truck. After twenty minutes, we found ourselves in the middle of downtown Beijing with a throng of bikers, billboards, and people all around us. We parked in front of the Chong Wen Men Hotel that stood at a corner of a solid city block, and I prepared to step out while the driver ripped some stubs from a booklet and gave them to me as a receipt.

Once inside the hotel, Kwang Yi learned that the attendant at the registration desk was out to lunch, so she ushered me into a nearby vestibule lined with chairs and separated from the main lobby by a privacy screen. She said, "Wait here. I will be back." I sat there, accompanied only by the filtered golden light that came through the old, tall, opaque windows. In a short space of time, Kwang Yi was back with two large loaves of sweetbread wrapped in wax paper, two cream-filled spiral cakes coated with sugar, and two bottles of a yellow soda. I ate the lunch with relish, but I could hardly consume it all, so I wrapped the remains in the wax paper and Kwang Yi stored it in her vinyl bag.

I registered at the hotel after lunch. Once again, I showed my passport and paid ninety-six yuans (seventy-two dollars) for a three-night stay. With all the paperwork settled, Kwang Yi and I took the elevator to the seventh floor where we asked for the key of room 701. It was the first room on a long corridor to the right of the elevators. The room was small, facing the street, and was packed with all the necessary furniture I had found in the airport hotel, plus a color television and an air conditioning system. The hotel was older, but nevertheless comfortable. I did not see any Western people around, so I assumed the hotel was reserved for Chinese and overseas Chinese people.

In the room, I tried to convey to Kwang Yi one of my concerns, saying, "Kwang Yi, I have to go to the ticket office of China Aviation to confirm my flight to Hangzhou on Thursday." I did not want anything to prevent me from seeing my dad at the appointed time.

She looked at me with a puzzled expression and said, "The children are at my house. They very much want to meet you. We go to my apartment."

"Kwang Yi, you don't understand me. I have to go to the ticket office; otherwise, I won't be able to fly to Hangzhou on Thursday," I said, worried about this necessary procedure.

She half-understood me, but she was anxious to take me to her house to meet the children who had stayed home from school. I repeated the request several times and showed her the word "ticket" in my *Chinese for Travelers* book. She finally yielded. We deposited the skeleton room key at the service center where several attendants waited (the key had to be deposited and retrieved each time we left the hotel) and proceeded down to the entrance.

While we were in the lobby, a man in shabby clothes entered from the street; he was holding onto a boy of about nine or ten. The two of them seemed out of place. I could tell the man was eager to talk to someone. His features bore the mark of hard work and weather exposure. He had large peasant hands and seemed to be holding something dear within his coat. Kwang Yi began to talk with him, and after a very lengthy explanation from him, she turned to me and said, "This man is going to America to see his mother, and he is bringing his son with him. They have also been separated for more than thirty years."

We looked at each other with understanding, and he showed us his passport with his picture and that of the boy, which he had taken from his coat pocket. They seemed unlikely candidates for an overseas trip, but then, life is never as it seems, and this humble peasant also had his story that paralleled mine.

Our escapade into the city took some time. I now had my first experience on Chinese buses and among the Chinese people. The buses were super-crowded, and the people were dressed simply. On our way into the bus, Kwang Yi had to purchase two tickets from the controller perched in a seat at the rear and protected from the crowds by a narrow counter. We stepped out near the China Aviation office, which I was surprised to find was located adjacent to another respectable hotel on a side street, but housed in what seemed like a dark underground parking structure. The workers were seated in cubicles separated by wooden panels with glass on top; they were busy talking with one another, so it took some time to draw their attention. One of the lady workers got up and came to the window, looked at my passport, and then stapled a small tab onto my flight ticket to Hangzhou. I was relieved that my ticket was thus confirmed, and now I was free to be at Kwang Yi's disposal. When I asked her whether it was possible for us to visit the Great Wall, she smiled and told me we would go there the following day.

Next, we went to a boarded booth at a busy street corner, not too far from the hotel where I was staying to purchase the bus tickets to the Great Wall. As we walked along the dusty pavements of a particularly busy intersection, I noticed large numbers of people walking by small vendors, who sold food from ambulatory carts, or passing by a repair man seated on a stool bent over an antiquated sewing machine fixing a black vinyl bag, the kind carried by virtually everyone to and from everywhere. At another sidewalk corner, a shoe repairman was putting small metal studs on shoe soles for a nominal fee. Some people gave me curious glances (due to my clothing and shoes), but most of them went about their business, shuffling along with the crowd. I saw a mother pull along her little toddler, a chubby child wearing a printed padded coat and pants that had a slit on the crotch (young toddlers in China do not wear diapers and the slit in the pants provides an avenue for the call of nature and much relief for mothers) and cloth shoes with rubber soles. Most of the men wore either the green army uniform trimmed in red or the blue or gray Mao suit with cap made of cotton and sometimes of wool, in varying degrees of neatness. Some of the younger ladies had perms while others wore their hair in a ponytail or loose over their shoulders, and many wore colorful acetate scarves around their necks, apparently the only adornment allowed. I did not see anyone wearing makeup or jewelry. Most of the women were dressed in dark polyester pants and jackets made from all sorts of materials. Most of the people's shoes were worn and dusty. Altogether, seeing all these people gave me the impression of humanity stripped to essentials, and busy acquiring the necessities of life.

During this walk through the city, we went to a couple of local stores to buy groceries. We entered a fruit and vegetable market, the doors of which were protected from the cold by heavily padded black vinyl curtains. The floors were bare cement and very dusty due to traffic from the streets. The produce lay in boxed tables, very much like what one would find in a farmer's market, yet I was astonished to find that in this particular store, the quality of the produce was very poor; the golden apples were marked with brown spots and the tomatoes were in part soft. The people, however, picked through these without being dismayed, choosing two or three fruits at a time to purchase. These were carefully weighed on a simple mechanical scale using weights, which were on a table nearby. Kwang Yi bought a few tomatoes and placed them inside her black vinyl bag. Wrapping paper was not provided at this store. Since this was my first view of China, I was taking it all in as a mystery unveiled. What I had failed to consider was that it was winter in Beijing, so acquiring and storing fresh produce was more difficult. No supermarkets yet.

After our errands in the city, Kwang Yi and I took a bus that dropped us off at the subway terminal's entrance, around the corner from my hotel. We went down a flight of stairs to the underground passage where Kwang Yi paid an entrance fee, and then proceeded to the well-lit platform below to await the train. The subway station was nothing extraordinary and could have been mistaken for one in Toronto, Chicago, or New York, except that all the passengers were Chinese and dressed in their customary garb. When a train arrived, we climbed onto a car with ease since the platform was not crowded. The cars, however, were loaded with people who looked very tired from their daily work, whatever it was, and there was not much talking going on. Soon a space was vacant, and Kwang Yi insisted I take it. Standing next to me was a boy of seven busily rotating a Rubik's Cube, probably made in Shanghai, with his father overlooking him in a protective manner. Even here, the fads of the young were pursued in a voracious manner. I was not surprised since the Chinese are known to love games, which challenge the player's mind and skill. Then I observed a confident young lady board our subway car with her wavy hair held back in a barrette, an over-the-shoulder handbag, a woolen black jacket, and neat black shoes. She impressed me as someone who knew what she was about and I envied her self-confidence.

The subway train sped rapidly through the darkened tunnels and stopped only briefly at various stations. I noticed that each time the train's automatic doors opened and closed, a tape-recorded message made by a woman with a sing-song quality to her voice was broadcast over the loudspeaker system. I could not understand one word she was saying; it seemed she was giving some kind of instruction that the passengers virtually ignored since they must have heard the same message hundreds of times.

Our station was approaching so Kwang Yi tugged at me. It had been a forty-minute ride on the subway to reach her neighborhood. Once back on the street level, we walked on an unpaved road to our right filled with pedestrians and bikers returning home from work. On either side of the road were a cluster of shabby houses, partially obstructed from view by makeshift fences and walls. At one point, I saw water drain out from the sides onto the earthen road.

"Do people live in these houses?" I asked Kwang Yi. She nodded affirmatively. For her it was commonplace, but for me it was a surprise, for I had forgotten about the poverty I had witnessed in Brazil. People live in shanties all over the world and this place was no different. The construction of these dwellings was sturdy enough, so they did not look like they would blow away very easily.

In about ten minutes, we came close to her apartment building, which was part of a huge complex of buildings five or six stories high. Near the entrance, a couple of children were playing ping-pong on a cement bench and another child was jumping rope. In the hallway of her building's ground floor were a number of parked bicycles. We went up five flights of stairs, and on each landing was a neat pile of round charcoal cakes with holes approximately five inches in diameter. The floors were not polished nor the walls maintained.

Kwang Yi lived in a modest apartment with two rooms, kitchen, bathroom, hallway, and front porch. I was ushered into the main bedroom that also served as a living room and dining room, and I sat in one of the two metal armchairs padded with vinyl near the door. It was a cozy and neat room with a large double bed, an enclosed bookcase with glass doors, and a small white refrigerator against the opposite wall from where I was sitting. Under the window facing the porch was an old, large desk, and between it and the bed was an old narrow bureau holding a black-and-white TV. Next to me was a glass-topped ashtray table with a small fish bowl that had two goldfish swimming in it. The rest of the space in front of the porch was filled with plants on shelves made of very coarse boards. The porch itself was used for storage and had an array of items.

As I sat there, feeling like I had stepped back in time and sensing the cold more than before (there was no central heating), Kwang Yi offered me some candy from a metal box and then handed me a couple of letters before she went to the kitchen for hot tea. One was a letter from my brother Wang Qian welcoming me to China that read:

Feb. 2, 1982. Hangzhou

My dear sister:

I got information from the letter you wrote to my father, that is, you arrive in Hangzhou on Feb. 11th, 5 p.m. We feel very happy and excited.

I want in this letter to tell you to decide and then tell us.

When you come, we'll greet you at airport.

How is your housing question? We want to bespeak a single room (including lavatory, air-conditioning equipment etc.) in Over Seas Chinese Hotel, which is situated by the side of the West Lake and also somewhat near in comparison with other hotels. Rent is about 16 yuans per day.

Can you eat Chinese food, dishes? or a mixture of Chinese food and foreign food, or to taste food cooked by us?

What do you want to bring back to U.S.? (for example, something for eating, for use, for decoration etc.)

I wait for your arrival. Embrace and kiss you warmly,

Your brother,

Goggeli

I was touched that I was greeted by a letter from my brother while I was still in

Beijing. All his questions baffled me some, but I suppose he wanted to make my stay as comfortable as possible considering their situation. Of one thing I was glad: they would be there to greet me at the airport.

The other letter was from Aunt Pei De (Kwang Yi's mother-in-law and mother of my cousin Lou Xi Cheng) who lived in Hunan Province with her daughter Aming, Xi Cheng's sister.

Jan. 6, 1982

Dear Marianne:

Your father has looked after your brother from childhood until grown up, he loves him so deeply; If your father does not allow your brother go abroad to U.S.A. for residence, our government also does not promise him to go.

We think your brother is better at first step to go for seeing your mother and looking for a chance to study. At the same time he should beg your father to allow him stay abroad forever.

We also think your brother is your father's only son. He also loves your brother deeply within his heart. Because of your father's mind is not so normal, he can't express his love in normal way. Your brother must discuss with your father heartily, unless he can't reach his aim.

Regard to your mother and all of your family,

Your Aunt and cousin

This letter caused me some consternation. I did not know how to take it. I knew my brother was planning to immigrate to the United States when it was possible, in about two years, but I did not know my father was vehemently opposed or that the family was taking sides about his decision. I folded the letter and put it in my purse, prepared to take everything as it came.

Soon Kwang Yi's children came in and greeted me with a mixture of shyness and excitement. I tried to talk in English with the youngsters but did not succeed very well (apparently children do not learn English in school, only teenagers). But I noticed at once that the younger boy of about eleven was very playful and coquettish, and loved to amuse and be amused. His sister, who had sensitive and intelligent eyes, was more subdued and exhibited a great deal of maturity. Their cousin, a lad of sixteen (my cousin Aming's son) whose English was good enough to convey some meaning, told me he was studying electrical engineering at a university in Beijing, so he was staying with Kwang Yi. We continued to exchange information in a halting manner, often with the help of a dictionary.

One of Kwang Yi's classmates from engineering school, who lived next door, came in to join us for dinner and helped everyone out with their English. Kwang Yi and she discussed Aunt Pei De's letter. I was surprised that family matters were brought out openly in the presence of a neighbor, even though this lady was a friend. She was a boastful sort of person with a teasing sense of humor. Because Kwang Yi had a hard time expressing herself in English, this lady said, "At school Kwang Yi was number one in English class, but when it comes to speaking, she needs the dictionary." Kwang Yi chuckled over this remark. I suppose they were good friends and they could afford to poke fun at each other: they both had gone to school together, they were neighbors, and they had sons the same age who also happened to be best friends.

When it was semi-dusk, the last of the evening light was coming through the filmed weathered glass pane. I looked over to the window and watched Kwang Yi's son put a tape in the recorder by the desk. Sousa's marches began to resound in the room, and as the day began to close in on us, I had a bewildering sense. Was this place here all along? Was it possible that China was isolated for more than thirty years, and that was why I found myself in such a different world? Could it be that these children were my relatives and I had never known of their existence or of their mode of living? Such were my thoughts and feelings at the time. I sat apart because of the sharp contrast to my accustomed way of life and because of my inability to speak Chinese, yet I began to discover a kinship with these people who were so kind to me, and to whom I was physically, if not mentally, related.

The children continued to entertain me with their questions and games. I noticed how carefully they took care of their prized possessions. A wicker basket under the bed contained most of the treasures their father had sent them through me. They began to display them with excitement and wonder. The young boy scrutinized the digital pen, the radios, and the markers. One of the biggest hits among them was the Rubik's Cube, which resulted in a small scuffle over who would play with it first. The cousin from Hunan had discovered the clue and could quickly rotate the cube's colors into place.

The porch's door was slightly ajar, and I began to feel very cold. Kwang Yi brought me my jacket, which I wore for the rest of the evening. Meantime, Kwang Yi's father had just arrived and came in to greet me. He was an affable, smiling man, who looked rather young and robust for his age. His cheeks wrinkled under his eyes and his good-looking teeth were exposed as he smiled. Kwang Yi took a couple of tomatoes from the refrigerator, and both of them retired to the kitchen to prepare dinner. Soon I could smell the marvelous aroma coming from the steamed kitchen, signaling that dinner was almost ready.

When I went to the bathroom to wash my hands, I had a passing view of the kitchen. Many pots and baskets hung from the wall, and there was a utility tub for washing dishes. They used a small gas stove perched on a table. The kitchen looked like a well-used and busy place. The bathroom had a bathtub filled with water, and strung between the walls were a couple of clotheslines on which hung some clothes and towels. On the floor were a number of washbasins. Of course, there was a toilet bowl and sink with a small mirror overhead.

Upon returning to the sitting room, I noticed the family had brought in the square wooden table from the hallway and many stools and chairs were placed around it. We were each given a small saucer, a bowl of rice, and chopsticks while "Grandpa" began to bring the many savory dishes, including a piping hot soup, and placed them in the table's center. The children waited to be served by their mother; then each of us helped ourselves from the many serving bowls and plates. I remember we were served chopped chicken, ham, fish, and aged eggs. Kwang Yi kept putting morsels on my small saucer and then asked, "Do you like the food?"

"Yes, everything is delicious," I said, proud of myself for managing the chopsticks so well. The only item I did not like was the translucent, aged green eggs, which were considered a delicacy in China. When Kwang Yi perceived my distaste for these, they were promptly removed. It was the strong ammonia taste at the end that I disliked. After dinner, we watched a program on TV called *Follow Me*. It was an English lesson given by a Chinese lady depicting a common situation in life, such as shopping or eating. It dealt with conversational English, and I could see how it entertained the family, for everyone joined in and repeated the various sentences, careful about their proper pronunciation, I think to impress me. At one point, the black-and-white TV was broadcasting somewhat fuzzy pictures, so Kwang Yi gave it the expert engineering touch with a couple of poundings.

Before leaving, I asked whether I could take some pictures of the family. Kwang Yi insisted that I be in some of them, so I showed her how to operate my pocket camera. Everyone smiled and was happy to be part of a remembrance photo. In the hallway, Kwang Yi's father was taking his supper alone. When I asked to take his picture, he obliged with his usual courteous smile.

Kwang Yi took me to the subway station on her bike, which was parked in the building's entrance hall. As I hopped on the luggage rack, I could hear some voices in the vicinity. Kwang Yi told me it was a film shown to residents at a nearby courtyard. After clearing the cemented walks between the apartment buildings, we were once more on the now darkened, unpaved road, where some people trickled by on foot or bike. At the subway station, Kwang Yi parked her bike in a bicycle lot, while a matronly woman placed a wooden tag on the handle and gave her a ticket. This was absolutely necessary because all the bikes were black and in about the same condition, so one would not be able to identify one's bike without such identification. A small fee had to be paid for this service.

I was so glad Kwang Yi was with me in the subway. I would never have guessed where to get off. At the hotel, she rode the elevator with me that was operated by a young lady who took her job very seriously, behaving as if she were steering a ship. On the seventh floor, after retrieving my key from the service room, Kwang Yi accompanied me to my room. I offered her some tea made from hot water in a thermos bottle that rested on the floor. Before we said goodnight, we agreed she would pick me up at eight the next morning.

Even though I was very tired, I decided to watch TV before going to sleep. The color TV on the table at the foot of the bed worked very well, so I watched a Chinese movie in color that was interrupted a few times by a Seiko watch commercial. Of course, I did not understand a word, but the characters and the setting gave me the impression that it was a love story. The young man was wooing his beloved and trying to gain her confidence, while at the same time trying to please his future mother-in-law. It seemed he was involved in some kind of scandal in the village and was trying desperately to justify himself before the enraged people who ran after him with accusatory gestures, carrying brooms and baskets. I did not see the movie's end since I fell asleep under the wonderful fluffy comforter.

The next morning, I was up at the time expected. When the phone rang, I thought it would be Kwang Yi. I could not understand the operator, but I told her I would be right down. I paced the lobby for a while but did not see Kwang Yi. So I walked through the front doors and watched the traffic in the streets. I was amazed at the solid mass of bicycles streaming by endlessly. The men and women on them wore dark clothes, and some had scarves, earmuffs, and gloves, while others did not; many wore white germ masks on their faces. A sense of admiration and pity came over me for all these people who had to brave the cold in this manner. The air was filled with the noise of bicycle bells and the horns of buses and trucks that cruised by this busy intersection.

I went inside where I met a young girl with a look of kinship on her face, but alas, I could not speak with her. Many attendants passed by with their enamel bowls, coming and going to and from breakfast. Each job at this hotel seemed to have many workers, and all went about their work with ease and self-assurance, chatting a great deal with their co-workers.

Shortly after eight, Kwang Yi arrived. "Sorry, I'm late. Did you have any breakfast?" she asked, as she emerged from the double doors, semi-breathless on account of her hurry.

"No, I haven't had breakfast, but it does not matter," I said, trying to reassure her, just in case we were short of time. I had not yet seen the hotel's dining room; nor had I tried to find it.

We went to a restaurant around the corner from the hotel where a few local people were having their meals. In the open kitchen were large vats containing some kind of gruel, a soupy rice mixed with brown beans ladled into china bowls and served with a long, fried twisted doughnut that was neither salty nor sweet. The patrons seemed to have all the time in the world as they sat at the round tables covered with white tablecloths, sipping their soup with their short china spoons and dunking their doughnuts in it with great relish. I could not eat all of the mixture, and I asked Kwang Yi whether I could have some tea. Apparently, tea was not served there, so Kwang Yi brought me some steaming hot water that she poured from bowl to bowl to cool it off. I drank the warm water, amazed at the new kind of breakfast I had been served.

The pavement was already warm with the sun's glow. We walked to the corner, across the street from the restaurant, and boarded a parked bus scheduled to leave shortly for the Great Wall. Kwang Yi and I took the front seat opposite the driver side, near the door. It was a modern spacious bus. The driver was a middle-aged man who seemed happy and confident, and who must have made this journey countless times. Next to the driver was a young girl who talked with him in an animated fashion; I thought she might be his daughter, but she turned out to be our guide.

Soon, local people and others who lived outside of Beijing settled into their seats, the last ones sitting on aisle seats that folded out from the main benches. Immediately, Kwang Yi made acquaintance with a man next to her who had come to Beijing on a visit from another province in China. A natural camaraderie followed among the passengers that I could not very well participate in because of my lack of knowledge of Chinese. I was left free to gaze out the window and watch the changing panorama before me. As we cruised through Beijing and began to approach its outskirts, I had a sense that it was like Mexico City, a blend of urban and rural, sometimes so intermixed that one could not tell where one ended and the other began. The big imposing buildings were replaced by small storefronts, which gradually gave way to open stalls and irregular clusters of dwellings with room for chickens and clotheslines. The city's dense congestion was alleviated, but one still encountered people on foot or on bikes, and a good number of pushcarts along the way.

Not too far from the city, I was surprised to see farming going on inside ingeniously built green houses made from bent bamboo reeds and clear plastic. I saw miles and miles of these vaulted structures, which were partly covered by straw mats. In the morning, one side of the mat was folded over to let in the sun; in the afternoon, the opposite side was uncovered, and in the evening, both sides were let down. It was interesting for me to watch a short, stout, peasant woman fold the mats with a bamboo stick in a manner oblivious to time's passing and that followed the rhythm of life itself. And so the feeding of millions went on in the dead of winter. I was witnessing China at work. The giant many thought dormant was really just readying itself for the opportunities to come.

We were deeper into the countryside now, and vast expanses of land opened themselves to the day's brilliance. Shortly, the bus crossed a bridge over a frozen river, where loose ice chips lay across the banks. Then the bus veered right and we were riding along a stately avenue lined with trees and huge stone statues leading to the Ming Tombs. A large parking lot was in front of the wall that surrounded the premises. Outside at a booth, I purchased several books of postcards and a map of Beijing. Kwang Yi facilitated the exchange, and I was happy to obtain pictures of the exotic places I was about to visit. After going through a small vaulted door in the wall, we were standing before magnificent buildings and grounds. The path to the main building was laid with blocks of fitted stone, intercepted on either side with beds of flowering bushes and pruned trees that in winter could only show their sinewy branches, barren and brown. There was, however, a great deal of color and brightness around us. Often we stopped to take pictures before some of the more embellished structures. One of these buildings impressed me in particular; it was painted in bright pink and towered over everything around it. It had a two-tiered roof upturned at the ends and made of fitted tiles. The walls just below the eaves were highly ornate, with a multi-colored design. Between the first and second roof was a small window, framed as if it were a picture, and which I think had symbolic significance because it permitted the spirits of the emperors buried beneath to look out into the world.

Because there were few visitors at the Ming Tombs that day, we had ample space and time to view everything. We went underground where the actual tombs of the emperors and empresses of the Ming and Qing dynasties were. The cave-like tunnels that led to the interior of the subterranean rooms were typically dark and empty. Some areas were guarded by metal railings that curved themselves around a few artifacts and tombstones. A particularly large urn caught my sight. It was beautifully decorated in blue, with a large dragon wrapped around its surface that stood in stark contrast to its milk-white background. I was sure I was before one of the prized treasures of the Ming and Qing dynasties, and so took several pictures of this vase that could hold a small child.

As we went up a cascade of steps outside at the grounds, I saw a small platform at the top landing erected for people to take pictures, furnished with a table and a vase with plastic flowers. Some young couples posed in stilted fashion behind this setting. Yes, it was a different world with a lot of catching up to do as far as modern manners and equipment.

Noon was fast approaching, so Kwang Yi and I went in search of somewhere to have our lunch. We took a circular walk made from blocks of natural stone and enclosed by a short wall made of large sand-colored bricks that had lovely openings at regular intervals. Beyond this wall, I could see a vast mountain range undulating endlessly into the distance. I felt like here was where the earth met the sky in timeless beauty. Kwang Yi led me to the side of a building set among many tall pine trees. It was very peaceful with not a soul in sight. I thought to myself, "Even in China, there is the possibility of solitude." I sat on a short cement step and Kwang Yi sat next to me. From her vinyl bag, she pulled out a couple of loaves of sweetbread and two apples. While I ate the bread, Kwang Yi proceeded to peel an apple in one continuous coil with her pocketknife, as if to break the coil were a sign of bad luck. I had seen some of these coils under park benches. I wondered why Chinese people peeled all their fruits; it was probably to avoid contamination. For the first time, Kwang Yi and I were able to converse in a leisurely manner.

"Do you miss your husband, Xi Cheng?" I asked, wondering how hard it was for her to live apart from him.

She smiled in a shy manner and said, "Yes, I do, but we write to each other every month. I also hope to go to America."

Kwang Yi, like her husband, was an electrical engineer, and she had applied to study at several major universities in the United States. It was now only a matter of time before a grant would be forthcoming.

"You know, my office give me permission to go. Now I have to wait for answer from United States. I go, my father stays in Beijing and take care of children. If I don't go, he goes back to my hometown and join my mother."

She had so much hope in her heart, and I knew she longed to join her husband from whom she had been separated for more than six years when he was banned to Inner Mongolia, during the Cultural Revolution.

"I hope you have a chance to go to the States, and when you come, I expect you at my house, and it will be my turn to show you around," I said, wishing I had more conclusive words.

"Did you ever meet my father?" I then asked with curiosity.

"No, I never meet your father. But I meet your brother; he come to Beijing with his wife and daughter when your grandfather died," she said, filling me in on what she knew about my family.

"Aunt Pei De, your mother-in-law, lives in the province of Hunan," I said. "I don't think I will be able to visit her since I am allowed to visit only three cities in China. I know she is concerned about my brother's intentions to live in America, but all of this will take some time to be arranged," I concluded, trying to settle the question in my own mind.

"Xi Cheng's mother live with me for many years. I like her very much. We get along very well," she said, proud of the state of her family.

"Not the typical mother-in-law, daughter-in-law relationship," I quipped with a laugh.

Kwang Yi was almost childlike in her expressions. Her high forehead and cheekbones gave her face an openness and friendly appearance. Her contagious smile parted her rounded lips and well-formed teeth, revealing a generous nature. At times, she appeared manly due to her assertiveness gained from years of hard work. However, she had a cheerful disposition that made her a wonderful companion for me in this distant land.

A bird flew in and rested on a branch of the pine tree in front of us. It felt rather warm in the sun, almost like springtime. We gathered our belongings and bounded back to the entrance.

Since this day was my first introduction to China, my birthplace, after so many years, I did not want to miss anything. And I was seeing some of China's great landmarks.

Soon we were all gathered back in the bus. When we were on the long avenue with the huge stone statues, I asked Kwang Yi whether I could step out and take a few pictures. The bus driver readily assented and he waited on the side of the road while I snapped a few hurried shots. The landscape became more rugged, and the bus, shifting to second gear, began to ascend the road on the mountainside. I saw some railroad tracks parallel to the road and soon a green passenger train went by. The houses were made from the mountain's rocks, mostly simple rectangular structures with walled-in yards. Some of them looked quite dilapidated, with a great many loose stones scattered about. Not too long after our rise into the mountains, we approached the area of the Great Wall. A small section of the Wall was visible from the bus, making us anxious to see it all. The bus parked in a small parking lot beside the mountainside. A time was set for our return, and then we were free to scout around the largest wall in the world, the only manmade structure visible from the moon.

The Great Wall runs through five provinces in China, more or less in a west-easterly direction. It was built as separate fortifications by ruling princes of several regions beginning in the fifth century B.C. It was linked up as one wall by the first emperor of the Ch'in dynasty who united the Chinese Empire in the second century B.C. It crawls along the northern mountain ridges in a serpentine fashion, extending itself as far as the eyes can see, hiding ultimately in the folds of the undulating terrain. It is approximately 2,500 miles long, and at one time was used by warriors to keep the northern Mongols from invading China.

Kwang Yi and I walked up to the first terrace and then took the steps that led to the Wall proper. The view was breathtaking, and a certain sense of awe overtook me. Here I was walking along the halls of this great architectural wonder, delineating on either side the straw green mountains that spread themselves beyond view. My hooded scarf was blowing like a flag, but I was not cold. While the sun was still high in the sky, I decided to take a few pictures and discovered that I only had three shots left in my camera, with no spare film in my pocket. I had wasted it on all those silly stone statues near the Ming Tombs. Kwang Yi and I stood at some strategic spots to include as much of the Wall as possible while we snapped my last pictures of each other. With my camera unloaded, all we had to do was roam the wall and enjoy the scenery.

After the flat part at the entrance, the climb up the Great Wall was very steep at either end. We went to the right, determined to make it all the way to the top of the watchtowers. Midway, we joined a few tired tourists sitting on the ledge. As I looked down, I could see that the Wall was made of large blocks of sand-colored stone and smaller bricks at the top that had square openings at regular intervals. It was about twenty feet high in most parts, except at the towers where the height was nearly doubled. We continued to climb the stairs that led to the tower, and there climbed an interior set of stairs that brought us out onto a terrace, much like the ones found in medieval castles. Once again, we stopped to gaze at this manmade structure that challenged Nature by embracing it with its outstretched arms. The original purpose of separation and protection was gone, and all I could see was harmony and unity between the works of men and the works of Nature. The Wall symbolized to me humankind's attempt to make a home for itself in this barren earth, claiming a part for itself, whether grandiose or small, and always in danger of losing its claim.

The descent was not so strenuous. The sun was still shining high over the Western hills. With all the exercise, Kwang Yi and I needed something to drink. We walked down to a gloomy looking building on the lower south end of the Wall. It had an old coal stove near the entrance that emitted smoke through a pipe that stuck out from the top of a window. Some men were seated at small square tables, smoking and chewing sunflower seeds, the husks of which covered the wooden planked floors. On one side was an encased glass counter displaying many food items such as fruits and sweets that one could buy. We did not stay here, probably because of its gloomy appearance. Closer to the Wall was a shed where hot tea was sold. Kwang Yi purchased a teapot filled with piping hot tea and we drank it from two cups after we sat on some round cement stools and tables nearby. A man was seated across from us enjoying his hot brew; we looked at each other with mutual curiosity. The tea we were drinking was a nearly clear green liquid with only a few leaves floating on top. Its warmth was comforting in this open, shaded spot where we were stung by the winter chill. We returned the porcelain teapot and cups, and then walked across the gravel yard, where there was a mound of rough coal probably used for heating stoves, and then reached the parking lot on the other side of the precarious mountain road. In a short time, the bus was nearly full; only one passenger was missing. The bus driver could not very well leave him stranded there, so far from the city. Everyone waited patiently, and lo and behold, after five minutes or so, a lonely figure was seen running hurriedly toward the bus. Everyone began to laugh, taking in this stray with great camaraderie, while he sat down on the last folded bench, a little ashamed and relieved.

As we traveled back to the city, I felt content viewing China's countryside. It gave me a chance to see my father's land, and the simple country folk scattered about here and there as they had been for a thousand years. This journey prepared me to meet my father. How could I understand him, if I did not have some knowledge, be it ever so slight, of the environment where he had spent most of his life? So the landscape had more than a visual appeal; it had an emotional appeal as well.

Again, a mixture of pushcarts, bicycles, three-wheel motorized vehicles, and primitive tractors moved by visible chains trudged along the road to Beijing. As we approached the heart of town, a donkey cart caught my attention; the driver, a sunburnt peasant, was frantically trying to avert the oncoming traffic while his helper was fast asleep on top of the load, quite oblivious to the increasing movement on the street. Suddenly, the avenues grew wider and the buildings became more impressive. Kwang Yi and I stepped out near Tiananmen Square, considered one of the largest urban squares in the world. We walked the wide square in the direction of the Forbidden City, or "Googung" as the Chinese call it, the estate that houses the Imperial Palaces, chatting amiably.

"Chinese people like Zhou," she said, pronouncing "Zhou," as Joe.

"Who is 'Joe'?" I asked, puzzled.

"Our leader after Mao. He die," she explained.

"Oh, you mean Zhou Enlai. Yes, we saw him on TV when President Nixon came to visit China. He seemed to be a sensitive man with a lot of character."

"He very good. We like him more than Mao Tse-tung. He very much for the people. When he die in 1978, this Square full of people. They come from everywhere to see his body kept in that building, The Hall of the People."

Near the end of Tiananmen Square, I saw a father flying a cluster of cellophane kites with two of his youngsters. Everyone looked up to the fluttering shapes of birds and butterflies, and for a moment, we shared in the happiness of the children who were oblivious of all else, except for the dancing colors in the breeze that were securely held in their hands.

After a considerable walk, we were in a business district where the streets were narrower and the buildings were unpolished stucco structures. Against the wall of one such building, I saw a pile of cabbages, and near another's entrance, some men were unloading baskets of produce into a dark storage garage. At the street corner, we entered a meat market that was very crowded. After we walked the store's entire length, Kwang Yi went to the counter on the left, and looking over her shoulder, said, "You go around and take a look."

"Okay, I will," I said pleased with the opportunity. In the center was a partitioned white tiled tub holding a variety of fish. Hanging above this enclosure were numerous kinds of poultry and game such as ducks and rabbits, all hanging limp from their necks and without feathers or fur. Near the end of the tub were a couple of scales. On either side of the shop were enclosed counters that sold other varieties of meat—salted, smoked, and plain. Then, after having gone around the store once, I lost sight of Kwang Yi. Panic struck me. How would I find my way back to the hotel or to Kwang Yi's apartment, lost in the middle of this multitude? I could not say a sensible sentence in Chinese, and they did not look like they could speak English. With a sigh of relief, I spotted Kwang Yi at the pork counter, behind a barrage of people, buying a small piece of loin with fat for dinner. Never was I so glad to see her than at that moment.

We took a bus to the subway station where we boarded the subway to Kwang Yi's place. The short sense of night within the subway compartment was alleviated by the gray daylight that hung over the city. When we arrived at her apartment, I immediately made myself at home by joining the grown children in preparing supper. On the menu was a special treat: Chinese steamed pork dumplings. So all pairs of hands were put to good use. First, the Chinese cabbage had to be chopped and put through the old-fashioned meat grinder attached to the square table in the hallway. Some ginger and green onions were added to the cabbage, and the whole mixture was wrung out through a cheesecloth. Kwang Yi's son and I took care of grinding the pork chunks. We attached the meat grinder to a stool while the rest of the family used the table to prepare the dough. The trouble was that the machine's grip on the stool was poor, so as I cranked away, the meat and grinder fell on the cement floor. Not much was lost, however, and we continued busily, making sure one of us held the grinder to avoid another mishap. After adding some warm water to the flour, Kwang Yi kneaded the dough until it was smooth and elastic. Then she cut it into strips that were rolled into fingerlike cylinders. These were cut into small morsels and then flattened into little circular pancakes with a narrow rolling pin. As Kwang Yi rolled out these pancakes with great manual dexterity, we filled them with the pork and cabbage mixture and added some soy sauce. At first, I had some difficulty shaping the dumplings because the corners had to be gathered and pressed together to form a crescent. Kwang Yi gave me a hand and so did her sixteen-year old nephew, Lu Qun. We began to fill three round bamboo trays that were brought to the kitchen either for boiling or steaming—I never did find out which. All I know is that our appetites were ravenous, and before long, we were seated around the table, feasting on the succulent Chinese dumplings that could be dipped in either soy sauce or vinegar, depending on one's taste. I ate so many that I could not eat the customary bowl of rice that came at the meal's end.

I was happy that this time Kwang Yi's father joined us for dinner; he had such a captivating smile. Kwang Yi had asked him to send my father and brother a telegram that afternoon, announcing my arrival in Hangzhou on Thursday. He diligently undertook the errand and was altogether such a kind and helpful man, even though we could only communicate with nods and smiles.

As the bowls were carried back to the kitchen, and the room restored to its original setting, Kwang Yi's daughter, Lou Chi-Jiang, brought me a couple of family albums. I was impressed by how well-kept and neat the books were; most of the pictures were small black-and-white snapshots with decorative edges and placed securely by corner fasteners. Chi-Jiang pointed to some of her baby pictures that were taken in her mother's arms. She was very proud of these. In the album, I also saw a few pictures of my grandfather and Aunt Pei De, Kwang Yi's mother-in-law. It was interesting to note that among the family pictures was also a picture of Mao Tse-tung, probably because my grandfather worked for the government in Beijing for many years.

After dinner, Kwang Yi and the children accompanied me to the hotel. In my room, Kwang Yi's son, Lou Yun-li, was fascinated with the color television set. It was wonderful to see this child's curiosity and the interplay between mother and son. Often, Kwang Yi would put her arms around her son and rock him in place in an affectionate manner; her son would smile, pleased with the attention, and be off to participate in some other fascinating antic. This evening, Kwang Yi wanted me to take a picture of her son while he placed himself erect on one of the room's red stuffed chairs. It was touching to see how docile and unpretentious this lad was. During the evening, he had worn Kwang Yi's jacket that was sent by his father. It did not bother him one bit that the jacket was meant for a lady. As he posed, I took several pictures, which pleased Kwang Yi immensely, for he was her youngest son. Before they left the hotel, we agreed that the whole family would participate in the following day's excursion.

Daybreak came quickly. We packed into a taxi waiting for us in front of the hotel. Because a policeman was directing traffic at the first busy intersection, Kwang Yi had to hide her son under her coat so it would appear only four occupants were in the car, instead of five. Soon we were out of danger and Yun-li could pop his head from under cover and watch the unfolding scenery. I could tell he was thrilled to be riding in a car, an adventure he seldom experienced. On a wide main avenue, Kwang Yi pointed to a gray house, explaining to me that it was my grandfather's home, where Xi Cheng, her husband, and my brother Wang Qian had spent two years together. My grandfather, Wang Sao-Ao, who was active in politics, and who for a time was Vice Minister of Finance for China, offered to take care of my brother shortly after our departure from Shanghai in the early 1950s. Later, my father reclaimed his son and took him back to Shanghai where he lived at the time. So I had a glimpse of the house where my brother spent part of his childhood.

The taxi was headed for the Summer Palace of the Ming and Qing dynasties. We passed the University of Beijing, which was totally enclosed within walls. Along the way in an open field, I saw some peasant people gathering dried sticks, probably to kindle fires for cooking and heating. Further on in an apple orchard, a man was pruning trees. I was surprised to find people working in the fields during the winter season.

In these short days while I was in Beijing, I began to feel the country's pulse. I could see that China was a less developed country than America, to the point where the wheel of time was rolled back some one hundred years, and where one could see people in great numbers going about taking care of their most basic needs with great resignation. Apart from the multitudes, I did observe a great deal of camaraderie among fellow workers, and much interaction among family members, so it appeared that the Chinese people had a great sense of belonging that gave them an air of self-assurance.

Contrary to yesterday's excursion, today we encountered a crowd of people visiting the same places we were. The Summer Palace is a complex of gardens, pavilions, and living quarters in Oriental style architecture that has long corridors and wraparound verandas overlooking Lake Kunming, where the Imperial family spent their summers. The last empress, Cixi, had the Summer Palace restored to its present day form, after it had been damaged in the early 1900s by the so-called Boxer Rebellion organized by anti-Imperial forces siding with the subjugated peasant population. She also built the famous marble boat that rests on the edge of the lake.

As we toured the grounds, I was amazed by the beautiful carved furniture and exquisite pottery that adorned the Summer Palace's rooms. We ascended to the various buildings built in typical Chinese style architecture that sat on the hillside at various levels. Each building was surrounded by a veranda and connected to others by means of passages and hallways. I peeked through some rooms that were supposedly the princes' quarters, and I was struck by the beauty and simplicity of it all. Every piece of furniture, every adornment, had its place, eliminating the possibility of clutter. It gave the spectator a sense of how important harmony, at least in the aesthetic sense, was to China's imperial families.

While Lu Qun, my cousin Aming's son from Hunan Province, held my purse (he insisted on carrying it throughout the day), I went into one of the main rooms on display to the public for a small fee; there I took pictures of the emperor's intricately carved throne that had on each side a large cloisonné stork made in aqua blue enamel and bronze. In another room, I had a glimpse of Dowager Empress Cixi, for on the wall hung a large oil painting showing her in all her silk finery.

Later, we walked through a huge covered arbor intricately painted with frescoes on the inside that led to the top of a hill where we had a magnificent view of many terraced buildings and the lake. Behind the buildings on the other side of the hill was a river on which three or four young men were playing hockey, very much like American youngsters would do in winter, except that their hockey sticks were merely tree branches and their pucks were ice slabs.

When we came down the hill, we walked on the frozen Lake Kunming and observed a pagoda looming in the distance. Nearby was the marble boat, which we inspected very carefully. It seemed to me an absurdity to have a boat carved out of marble, an anachronism to the order of things—but I guess the Empress wanted it to endure through history as a work of art more than she wanted it actually to float. It brought to mind the Greek legend of Icarus flying to the sun with wings of wax. Immortality cannot be won so easily.

The sun had been shining all day, and our senses were saturated with all the lovely scenery and artifacts we had seen this morning. We were tired from wandering about, so we took a rest and sat along the wall of an open pavilion while Kwang Yi served us lunch. Out of her now famous black vinyl bag came a few loaves of sweetbread and a few boiled eggs. As we partook of this simple lunch, I was touched by the children's courtesy; they were always mindful of the adults and made sure I had plenty of everything. We did not engage in long conversations because of our lack of knowledge of each other's language, but we acted like a family and were very comfortable with one another.

Before leaving the Summer Palace, I bought a beautiful silk kite in a gift shop near the entrance. It was shaped like a blue phoenix, one of China's mythological birds, and wrapped on a bamboo frame that folded neatly in a box. I knew my daughters would be delighted with my purchase; the only thing that astonished me was the price: twenty-two yuans or fifteen dollars, a bargain for such a beautiful item. I learned here that kites were used in the olden days to send messages to neighboring principalities.

Once more, we boarded a taxi that took us across the city to the Forbidden City or the Imperial Palace in the city proper. On our way, we dropped Lou Chi-Jiang, Kwang Yi's daughter, at her middle school where she was a boarder. When I watched her walk away with her small red scarf tied around her neck and her little purse hung over her shoulder, I felt a tinge of sadness from knowing I would not be seeing her again. The goodbyes were inevitable for someone on a short visit. As we cruised the city, Lu Qun pointed out to me Qing Hua University, where he studied engineering and was currently enrolled in the radio department. Before long, we arrived in front of the Imperial Palace's impressive outer walls.

Right outside a narrow portico, which served as the first entrance to the Forbidden City, were a few vendors selling an orange soft drink and other sweets. I wondered how the cherry-glazed fruit strung on a stick would taste. Lu Qun noticed my curiosity and bought us each a couple of sticks. They were tasty but rather tart because they were not cherries, but small crab apples. Past the portico to our right, a woman was making those delicious Chinese dumplings we had eaten the day before. A considerable crowd was gathered around the table, watching the preparation of these succulent delicacies that were either boiled or steamed in large pots. Knowing how much I had enjoyed last night's dumplings, Kwang Yi told us to go ahead into the palace while she tried to buy some of the dumplings, which were not yet ready; she would catch up with us inside the palace. So the two boys and I walked with the crowd toward a second wall, which separated this plaza from the palace grounds.

The crowd waiting to enter the Ming Palaces was very ordinary; I could not find any kind of distinction that would make one person stand out from another. The pajama-like suits and quilted jackets in muted colors were by now very familiar to me. A soldier with his long, oversized, green army coat and dusty shoes caught my attention. In almost every tourist place I had visited so far, there were a great number of these army clad young men. Apart from the sameness of people's outfits, what impressed me most was the tenderness family members bestowed on their young children, especially the fathers. I watched a young father run after his loose toddler and break into smiles when he scooped the youngster into his arms. Perhaps because of the government policy that each family could only have one child, so as to alleviate the staggering population problem, sternness was reserved for later years. Moving slowly through the crowd, a car pulled in front of the entrance and dropped off a foreign dignitary or tourist. He was the only foreigner there, beside myself, and all eyes were on him as if he had just arrived from the moon.

We began to scout the huge complex of buildings, beginning with the Great Halls of Supreme Harmony, Complete Harmony, and Preserving Harmony. These three halls had been used by the emperor for ceremonial and official purposes. Depending on the rank of a person admitted into the palace, he would be met either in the first, second, or third hall. For instance, if a scholar would arrive to partake of the Imperial Examinations, he would be greeted in the outer hall, whereas the princes and important personages of foreign lands were met in the inner halls. One hall had an exhibition for which we had to purchase a ticket, so one of the boys accompanied me inside. In this hall, I saw the most breathtaking artifacts made of gold, bronze, jade, and ceramics. Here I was able to take a picture of a terracotta soldier and horse excavated in 1977 from Xian (excavations began in 1974), a city in northern China, where archeologists found the burial place of a feudal prince. He had ordered that an army of such figures be buried with him, and the amazing thing was that each of these figures had a unique face and expression—quite a feat for artists who had to create 4,000 such sculptures.

Kwang Yi joined us later, empty-handed and disappointed at being unable to get the dumplings; they had been all claimed before it was her turn. Together, we paraded before the glass-enclosed imperial treasures at another exhibition hall. At one point, we stopped in front of a large, intricately carved golden urn. Kwang Yi looked at me, pointed to the urn, and then pointed to her head. "Ah," I exclaimed, "the Empress' head is stored in the urn." She began to laugh uncontrollably, and it dawned on me that she had meant the Empress' hair, not her head. So I began to laugh myself, hardly being able to stop on account of this severe mistake.

The place was vast: 9,000 rooms occupying 250 acres. It was impossible for us to see everything. We managed to see an exhibit of Chinese watercolor paintings and another exhibit of clocks from all over the world, many from England, Germany, and France. Apparently an emperor had made a collection of these treasures. Among the items exhibited were some ancient Chinese astronomy tools, globes cast in gold, and periscopes. Of special interest to visitors was a roped off room that could be seen from a veranda with all the imperial furniture in its original place. Once again, the carved tables and chairs were magnificent. Before leaving one of these exhibit halls, we took some pictures in front of one of the fierce golden lions that stood sentinel, exuding power and fear on us humble pilgrims.

We were a good way into the afternoon, yet we still had not seen the imperial private quarters. How could we leave the palace without gazing into the emperor's bedroom? Lu Qun took me on a quest for the bedroom, while Kwang Yi and her son Lou Yun Li rested on a bench. We traversed many corridors alongside buildings that were not open to the public. There were so many gates, pavilions, and gardens that we were virtually lost, but we never did find the emperor's bedroom. Luckily for us, we did find Kwang Yi and her son waiting serenely at the same spot where we had left them earlier. In this circular garden with benches, I saw another tourist from abroad, a tall Englishman who was examining a rock sculpture that his Chinese guide explained had been a fountain in earlier times.

On our way toward the exit gate, we stopped before the famous wall of the seven dragons made of tile. These mythological animals have great importance in Chinese history and culture: they symbolize superhuman powers derived from the gods, and therefore, are greatly venerated by the people. We crossed a moat that surrounds the imperial palace, going through a gate that placed us on a street outside the palace wall.

The afternoon was not yet spent when Kwang Yi decided to take me to a city park nearby. On our way, we met a toothless old woman seated at the top of a long row of steps. She was pleading to passersby, and Kwang Yi turned to me and said, "She has lost her son and wonders if we have seen him." I noticed how the passersby paid little attention to her. Millions cruised the streets everyday; why would the misfortune of one person be of concern to a stranger? Kwang Yi exchanged a few words with her and we went on. She was one of the old ladies whose feet had been bound and she was wearing a small cloth loafer.

From the top of the city park, we had a good view of many parts of Beijing, including the famous Behai Park with its picturesque lake. We decided not to visit Behai Park since it was too much of an undertaking so late in the afternoon for us weary visitors. A glimpse from the distance was good enough for us. The setting sun left a golden glow on the city, and I felt I had witnessed one day's worth of the spectacle in this part of the world, which had been obscured for so long.

Soon we were on the subway headed toward Kwang Yi's apartment for dinner. At the terminal, we hopped on two bikes and took the unpaved road toward the apartment complex. At dinner, we had fish, noodle soup, and bits of salted pork served with a bowl of hot rice that Grandfather had so kindly helped to prepare. During dinner, Kwang Yi was very careful in placing all the items on my small plate with her chopsticks.

Immediately after dinner, the whole family walked me to the building's entrance where we said our last goodbyes. I can still remember the friendly figures in subdued lighting, and especially that of Kwang Yi's father, waving goodbye as Kwang Yi and I rode off on her bike.

The night's darkness enveloped us, and we were soon moving with the subway's rhythm. Partly because of exhaustion and partly for the sake of economy, Kwang Yi bid me adieu at the subway platform; this way she did not have to purchase a return ticket home. I took the flight of stairs to my right and then crossed the street toward my hotel. It was good to be free for a short period of time and once again experience a sense of independence. Without much trouble, I got the key to my room on the seventh floor; in this instance, my memorizing Chinese numbers had paid off.

In the darkness of my room, I had a strange realization that I would be seeing my father the next day. The prospect seemed unreal, considering our thirty-two years apart. Never did I wish for a night to pass so quickly. I fell asleep lulled by the sound of the TV in the hallway where the attendants were watching their favorite show.

The next morning, I took a shower and watched all the dust I had acquired in Beijing swirl down the drain. I had to look my best for my father. Soon Kwang Yi knocked on my door. She had brought presents for me from her family: two glazed ceramic horses and a few silk scarves. Her generosity touched me. It was our last day together, and she took me shopping in the downtown area. First we went to the Friendship Store, a department store three stories high reserved for foreigners. On the second floor, I exchanged some of my travelers cheques into Chinese currency after filling out the appropriate forms, and then I joined Kwang Yi in browsing over the many items on sale. Everything was behind glass-encased counters, except for some bolts of silk cloth. Hardly any customers were in the store, so Kwang Yi and I had the place to ourselves. At one end of the store were toiletry items and some kitchenware. In an adjacent room were long glass-encased counters against the wall as well as in the center, displaying a variety of jewelry, ivory and jade carvings, and ceramics. The many rings and necklaces interested me, and I approached a saleslady, one of the many idle clerks dressed in white shirts and blue pants, waiting to serve the few customers who came by daily. I purchased two ceramic necklaces that she placed with great dexterity in a cushioned box. She was very efficient, but stern; she did not seem very willing to cater to a foreigner's indulgences. These luxury items were seldom, if ever, purchased by ordinary Chinese people. So here I had a keen sense of my bourgeois mentality. I could not resist the colorful cloisonné vases with their exquisite flower patterns imbedded in copper. In a shrewd manner, I asked Kwang Yi, "Is this the best place to buy such vases?"

"Yes, Beijing is the best place to buy this," she said in an enthusiastic tone.

So I proceeded to inspect several kinds of vases while a very patient lady showed us all the possible varieties. In the end, I purchased several pairs of vases with their carved stands together with matching jewelry boxes and ashtrays. The price I paid was small compared to what I would have paid in the U.S. for a similar item, so I knew it was the chance of a lifetime. Before leaving, I also purchased two lovely Chinese dolls to give to my younger daughters.

From the Friendship Store, we went by bus to a local department store in the crowded Wangfujing Street, the main shopping area in Beijing. As we moved along with the crowd and onto the department store's stairwell, we were crushed by people densely packed wall to wall. At the top of the stairs where the congestion was alleviated, I noticed a man dressed in army clothes, carrying his baby in a pink silk bunting trimmed with rabbit fur. I asked this man whether I could take a picture of him and his baby. He broke into an unforgettable smile that I have preserved in my photo album.

As we perused the store, I said, "Kwang Yi, I want to buy a present for your daughter and your son. Can you give me a suggestion?"

With a little reluctance, she accepted my proposal and said, "My daughter would like an album for her stamps."

We purchased the album for Lou Chi Jiang and then I had an idea and said, "I want to buy a soccer ball for Lou Yun Li."

She smiled with exhilaration, and after we had purchased the ball, ready to be carried in its own net, she said, "My son will be so happy! He will be playing this very day with his best friend in front of the projects."

In contrast to the Friendship Store, this general department store was packed with customers hovering over counters where everything from shoes and jackets to stationery and sports equipment was sold. To my astonishment, I even saw some jogging suits on display.

At noon, I was seated on a bench outside the China Aviation Office together with other passengers, awaiting the bus that would take us to the airport. The sun was shining brightly, adding to my sense of comfort and joy in going to the city where my father lived. Next to me sat a man whom I soon found out was also going to Hangzhou and who, as incredible as it may seem, knew my father, because he was a professor of engineering at Zhejiang University, the same university where my father had taught mathematics for more than twenty years. The man said to me, "I know Wang Fu Shih; he left the university because he was too old." I pondered his words, wondering how old my father really was. Was he older than this man with oily stretched hair and a gold tooth in front? The bus arrived and our new friend helped us climb aboard with my luggage.

At the airport, Kwang Yi and I stood in line waiting to have my luggage checked in and to obtain a boarding pass. Kwang Yi took care of all the details with great kindness and efficiency. I had to pay eleven yuans for excess luggage. After that was accomplished, Kwang Yi led me toward the departure gates and we said our goodbyes and thank yous. She could not follow me into the waiting area. Just a simple hug and then I was separated from this tireless and fervent soul.

Chapter 5

———— ✿ ————

Meeting My Father

I was seated in a modern sunlit glass paneled room with many Chinese citizens and some foreigners who were waiting to board the plane to Hangzhou. I had caught a cold and was slightly hoarse. With the excitement of the trip, I had quite forgotten that I had a touch of fever this morning. There was little talking in the waiting room and the time for boarding the plane had come. The boarding officer at the Jetway entrance asked me sternly in Chinese, "Piao?" I had learned the word *piao* (ticket) out of necessity, so I understood her request. Since the boarding pass was not enough, I quickly scrambled in my purse for the plane ticket, but she softened her stance and allowed me to board without it.

Once seated, I noted most of the plane's passengers were Chinese, except for a small party of men from Norway. I knew this because across the aisle from me was a Chinese man, approaching late middle age and with an uncanny European look, due perhaps to his receding hairline, who acted as their guide. He was a very communicative and enthusiastic person who explained everything at great length in French to the leader of the Norwegian entourage.

Next to me, seated near the window, was a gentleman from the People's Republic of China with whom I tried to make conversation. He was of meek disposition and did not know how to speak English. Through the aid of the English-Chinese book I was carrying, I was able to tell him I was going to Hangzhou to visit my father and brother after an absence of thirty-two years. In a strained give and take, he assured me that Hangzhou was a beautiful place, and I believe it was his hometown.

Throughout my trip, I had felt compelled to share my story with my traveling companions. It was as if I wanted to gain some sympathy and assurance; or perhaps, it was a way of including others in my plight who had led a more normal life, and to whom I reached out for affirmation and inclusion. Through a small remark about the chair not staying in place, I began a conversation with the portly Norwegian gentleman to my right. He was a middle-aged man who seemed accustomed to the niceties of life, but who made himself at home in any kind of circumstance. Our exchange in English was established easily on account of his congeniality. So I began to tell him about myself and the reasons why I was in China. "But you do not look very Chinese; of course, you are not dressed like one of them, so I thought you came from somewhere else," he said with interest.

"It must be the makeup that sets me apart; the Chinese do not ordinarily wear makeup. Also my mother is German," I said. I then summarized my whole life story for him and showed him my photographs.

After giving the pictures a long and careful look, he said, "This is all very interesting. You should keep a diary, and later write a story, even if it is just to leave it for your children."

"I do have a notebook, and now and then, I jot some things down," I assured him.

"And what does your father do in Hangzhou?" he asked with curiosity.

"He taught math at the Zhejiang University for twenty years," I answered. "He just retired."

"We are here representing a labor party from Norway. The Chinese government invited us to tour the country and visit the factories and similar organizations in various Chinese cities. It has been fascinating thus far," he explained.

Without my being aware of it, my good-natured Norwegian companion related my story in Norwegian to his friends seated behind me. Later, he said to me, "Your story is making quite a wave in our group. They are all speaking about you."

It surprised me that so many took an interest in my personal story. I tried to lighten the conversation by saying, "I have caught a cold, and my voice is getting hoarse."

"Take this Chinese cough drop," he said, opening a small packet taken from his coat pocket. "They say it is very good; it has Chinese medicine in it." I took the cough drop that tasted like a medicated licorice, pleased to have next to me a man with very few inhibitions.

During the three-hour flight south, the Chinese stewardess, whom I noticed wore makeup, presented us at different times with Chinese nail clippers, a Chinese magazine written in English, and fruit juice. After several hours, the small jet plane began its descent into Hangzhou's airport. When the plane touched ground, I noticed droplets of water running down the side windows, so I said to the Norwegian gentleman, "It looks like it is raining here."

"It may be condensation," he added, unsure of the weather's outlook.

But as soon as the plane was cruising down the runway, it was obvious to both of us that it was indeed raining. I became interested in this trivial event to grab a hold of something, for I was quite alone, and one of the most important events of my life was about to take place. As we waited in our seats to step into the aisle, the Norwegian man offered me a medicated piece of gum, and then he said seriously, "It may be quite difficult this meeting with your father after thirty-two years of separation. I think it may be hard to establish a relationship after so long a time."

After this remark, I nodded to him and we wished each other good luck.

I descended the steps of the plane, walked across the wet pavement, and saw a few people standing at the top of the stairs of the outside balcony. After ascending the multiple steps, I walked up to a family I had spotted earlier during my approach; it was a young woman holding a baby of about two, and a young man who held a black umbrella over them. I was quite sure this was my brother, his wife, and their young son. As I came near, my brother said politely, "Marianchen?" It was the same name I had been known by as a child, an endearing German diminutive for Marianne. His use of it touched a personal chord in me.

I nodded and smiled and saw that everyone was beaming with happiness. Immediately, I was introduced to everyone present, my niece Qion, a charming girl of thirteen, my cousin, a young man of about twenty, and a tall elderly gentleman of distinguished appearance, Uncle Lou. I had already sensed this man with erect posture and cotton white hair was not my father. So after we embraced and shook hands, I asked, "Where is my father?" They pointed to the interior of the building, so I knew he was waiting for me inside.

As I walked through the glass-paneled doors to the airport lobby, I noticed I was missing my flight bag; in the excitement, I had forgotten that my cousin was carrying it for me.

Then I came to a slight dark figure at the end of the hall. It was my father. He wore a long double-breasted navy blue raincoat and kept the hood over his head. He had a cane in his hand and was somewhat bent over. That he chose to meet me in this semi-hidden fashion was beyond my comprehension. I noticed at once that he had lost all his upper teeth, and he peered at me with glassy eyes through the round spectacles he had worn all his life.

I embraced him with tears and whispered, "My father!" He was short and frail; I could have easily taken him in my arms, even though he stood passively with the weight of the years. Then looking at him intently, I said, "My mother sends you her greeting." I was astonished to see a pained expression in his eyes, almost of guilt, which at the time I wrongly interpreted as a slight rejection. He looked me over very carefully, searching for that child he had lost long ago, while I too looked at him, trying to find my father in this hooded old man with a broken down appearance.

Then he said, "It is like a dream that a real daughter of mine comes to see me." It was as if he had rehearsed these lines and we were now acting out the play, for he said them in such a punctuated and dramatic fashion that I was caught off guard in want of something to say. Turning to my brother, he said, "Brother and sister from the same mother and father, yet two completely different persons." Then he added, "You look like a sportswoman."

I replied, "It must be because of this sports coat I'm wearing."

I could not tear my eyes off him. And he, in turn, looked at me with great curiosity. Then he said, "A van is waiting for us outside; otherwise, it would be very difficult the transport. This cousin here is going to get your luggage." He had a husky voice, but his English was good. Holding onto his cane, he led us to the van parked outside by the back door. As we walked, I realized that it must have been with some difficulty that they had managed to hire this large blue van with sliding doors, which could easily accommodate the entire family. I helped my father climb the tall step, and then he placed himself on the long seat next to the door. My brother and I sat on a seat adjacent to his, facing the front of the vehicle. When all were aboard with my suitcases, the van rolled off along the wet streets.

Wetness was all around us so I asked my father, "How long has it been raining?"

"Oh, it has been raining for over two weeks. But you are sure to have some sunny days because you are staying for three weeks," he replied.

"You know, I got this medicated gum from a Norwegian gentleman in the plane," I continued in a casual way.

"Did you get this gentleman's address?" he asked.

"No, I didn't," I said. "We just had a nice conversation."

My brother looked at me and was all smiles. He spoke something in Chinese to my father, so my father translated it to me, "Your brother is surprised you wear glasses."

"Yes, I have been wearing them for a long time because I am nearsighted," I explained.

As we cruised the wet streets of Hangzhou, they appeared to be getting narrower and had less vegetation compared to the avenues we had traversed earlier. The van stopped in front of an entranceway where the sidewalk was broken and muddy. We sidestepped the puddles and went through an old dilapidated metal door that remained always opened and served as the entrance to this compound. Once inside, we went through some dark corridors and courtyards, another shorter corridor made from the sides of two buildings, and then turned left onto a narrower path, along which some doors and windows opened. These enclosed walls extinguished the little light we experienced on our way in. At the end of this labyrinth was my brother's room, and I was ushered in with great courtesy. My father and I sat at the table near the door while relatives and friends sat on the beds and chairs available. I was given a sweet clear liquid to drink in a glass, and so remarked to my father, "This tea is very tasty."

"It is not tea; it is sugar water. You see, we are still celebrating the Chinese New Year so it is customary to drink sugar water," he explained. It pleased me to be part of a tradition.

My rosy-cheeked sister-in-law, Su Juan, peeked through the door and was aglow with joyful excitement. My father said, "She wants you to go to the kitchen to meet some of her friends." So I quickly obliged and walked outside and then into the kitchen; there a handful of ladies were hovering in a Spartan furnished room with cement floors, and my sister-in-law was preparing supper in a wok on a short ceramic coal stove. I shook everyone's hands and we shared the only language we had in common, the smile, which they gave to me readily and warmly. Then I returned to the room across from the kitchen where my father was sitting. They had moved the square wooden table to the center of the room and tied the dim hanging lamp over it with the aid of a clothesline. The rain, the dampness, the darkness, the gloomy quarters, and my father's old face gave this evening a Dickensian quality I cannot easily forget.

I sat facing the window and door while my father remained hunched over in the white wicker chair to my right. A great many dishes such as scrambled eggs, tossed greens, and chicken morsels were brought in bowls and placed in the table's center. My little nephew, Yun, wanted only to eat the roasted peanuts, which were delicately picked out for him by his aunt with chopsticks. I began to sample the many dishes before me, including the fish and soup, and I was happy to do very well with the chopsticks. My sister-in-law kept coming in from the kitchen and exchanging my bowl of rice for a warm one, so I was touched by her concern.

I continued my conversation with my father, since he was the only person who could speak English. Looking around me, I said to him, "You have a very large family."

He chuckled and said, "It only seems so. When you were a little child, just born in Chunking, your mother and I had a very small room. You slept in a small bed in the middle of the room, and when you cried, I often rocked you. It seems you had something with your heart. Do you still have trouble with your heart?"

"As far as I know, my heart is perfect," I said, listening intently to what he was saying. This little story moved me, and I kept trying to fathom the meaning of it all in the ember-like ambiance of this room crowded with people.

We continued to sit around the table after dinner; then my brother came in from outside and told my father something. He turned to me and said in a punctuated manner, "They need your passport to arrange for a hotel room. You see, the bathing conditions here are not very good, so we thought it best for you to stay at the Overseas Hotel. A car will be here shortly to pick you up. Your brother will come in the morning to show you the city."

I nodded in agreement, gave my passport to my brother, and asked, "But doesn't my brother have to go to work?"

"You see, you have been separated from your brother for so long, and now you come here, so he is given two weeks to be with his sister," my father explained.

I now thought it was time to show my father some pictures. I brought out the tattered leather box as I apologized to him, "I am sorry I have not put these pictures in an album like the other ones I have."

"Oh, it is better this way," he said, wanting no fuss.

"Aren't you handsome in this picture?" I said.

Looking at himself as a young man dressed in a tuxedo, he retorted, "I always liked to wear a bow tie." Perhaps I should have waited to show him these pictures at a later time when we had grown more accustomed to each other. But my feelings all poured out of me so quickly, wanting to establish a tangible bond. We passed the pictures around the room and everyone showed extreme interest. Some recognized a few pictures, of which my brother had duplicates.

Soon all the pictures had been looked at, and I asked my father, "Why did you travel to so many parts of the world with my mother before coming back to China?"

"It was 1941 during the war when we took the train from Munich to Istanbul with intentions to go to China," he explained. "But in Haifa, Israel, I met a friend in the Chinese Embassy and we discussed other possibilities. So your mother and I went to London, England to arrange for a research position in Canada. The research position was not forthcoming; we circumvented the war by stopping in Portugal, Egypt, Calcutta, and finally Chunking, all by ship and small two-engine planes."

"It would have been nice if you could have had the research position in Canada. Perhaps life would have been different for us," I said with some regret.

He replied with a solemn nod, "But it was good to come back to the motherland."

I felt a shadow of abandonment from this remark, and I had an irrational feeling that his country was more important to him than our life together.

When I saw my nephew prancing around the planked floors, I stood up, opened my small suitcase, and presented him with a large brown Teddy bear. He held it for a while until it was taken away by an aunt. He was happy just running about. I also gave him a nylon padded jacket that his mother put over his clothes and that he wore for the rest of the evening on account of the room's dampness. My father kept saying to me, "Marianne, come sit down and rest. You will have time for this later."

But I did not heed. The fount of presents was opened and I wanted to make everyone happy. Wang Yun got some more coloring books, crayons, and toy cars. To the ladies, I gave nylons, manicure sets, and toiletry items. To the men I gave pocketknives and disposable lighters, which they immediately began to try, for many of them smoked. I was not sure whether all these people were my relatives, but it did not matter; they all smiled gratefully. My father kept calling me to sit down, but I wanted to lighten my luggage anyway. To my father I gave a digital watch, some warm woolen socks, and some towels, all of which I placed near him on the bed. From my mother, he received a robe, a scarf, and some perfumed handkerchiefs tucked in one of the robe's pockets. He also got a supply of vitamins and diuretic pills prescribed by a doctor friend of mine, which I thought he might need. He thanked me for these and said, "I will take them later to my room."

Then, prompted perhaps by the bad lighting in the room and the encroaching darkness outside, I asked him with curiosity, "Do you have a window in your room?"

"Yes I do," he said, not surprised by the question.

"Life with a window is not so dismal, even in these simple quarters," I thought.

I continued to disperse the presents. My brother got a digital watch from my mother, and a tape recorder and calculator from my family, all of which he greatly appreciated. Then he called his wife from the kitchen, and I also gave her a golden digital watch similar to mine, a folding umbrella, and a great many bars of imported chocolates that she carefully tucked away. To my niece Qion, I gave a transistor radio, an electric curling brush, and a purse. Their smiles were worth every ounce of weight I had carried.

While I sat there talking to my father, Qion approached me with jovial familiarity, and my father said, "She wants to light some fireworks for you outside." The family and I went around the kitchen and down some steep cement steps that led to the small graveled bank of a canal. Shortly afterwards, my niece, with my brother's help, lit a Vesuvius of colors alongside the water. "What a lovely way to be greeted by my Chinese family," I thought.

Soon after we returned to the room, my father informed me that the car had arrived for them to take me to the hotel. Again, we walked through the compound's dark corridors with my suitcases. My brother, his wife Su Juan, and a friend climbed into a black, old-fashioned car. Before too long, we were in front of the Chinese Overseas Hotel that overlooked the famous West Lake. At the desk, I showed my passport and my brother filled in the forms for me. I was surprised he knew my age so well, thirty-seven. Then he wrote my Chinese name, Wang Kun, which I had never used. I was surprised he knew these intimate details of my life. I found out later that the name Wang Kun was given to me by my grandfather at my birth and recorded on my Chinese birth certificate.

When we were finished with these formalities, we walked up a broad set of stairs in the old hotel. My room was situated on the first hall to our right. It was somewhat musty and had more furniture than I would ever need, but it was comfortable. It had two single beds with tall spring mattresses and a cot; in one corner was a small round table with two wicker armchairs, and beside the window was a large oak desk. To the right of the door was a roomy bathroom with old fixtures and a shower.

Before my brother, his wife, and his wife's colleague left, I took some pictures of them, and to add some color, put some lipstick on my sister-in-law, which she found very amusing. My brother managed to convey that he would meet me at ten in the morning to show me the city. Soon, they were gone, and I was left alone to spend the night in peace.

I crawled in bed and felt I was burning with fever. The room's darkness seemed to be in my soul. I had missed my young father and I sobbed desperately. I was his child, but a child from a different universe…Brazil…America, and our full personalities and inner souls could not be revealed to each other in an instant. The last time I had seen my father, he was a man of thirty-eight, handsome and energetic, and I, a child of five. I remember sitting on his lap on the way to the Shanghai shipyard where my mother, stepfather, and I would depart from China. My father had been very quiet then, but I had not been sad. I had felt happy actually, thinking I was going to another world—to a fantasy place. Only when we had boarded the ship did I feel the slightest sadness. Little did I know that three decades would pass before I would see him again. My last image of them as I peered over the ship's railing, seeing my father tall and serious and my brother on his left with his head hung low, had never left me. Now words from his third letter to me crossed my mind: "So many years I was sick in heart as I had lost part of my heart." Was I really so much part of this man with whom I had shared so little of my life, and whom I came to see in his old age, when I was no longer a child? I was waging a war with time, trying to reconcile the past with the present. How successful I would be in bridging the gap, I did not know.

The next day I got up at eight. I still did not feel well, but I made an effort to be ready before my brother arrived. My throat was aching, so I walked down to the lobby to buy some lozenges. I exchanged some American Express checks, filling out the prescribed forms, and then asked the clerk, "Could you tell me where I can buy some medicine for my throat?" He pointed to a gentleman manning a booth near the doorway who could speak English. This man said, "You will find some on the second floor." I walked the whole length of the second floor, and down a wide back stairs, but found nothing.

Back again in the lobby, I looked around with interest. A local man approached me and asked, "Could you translate the novel *The Thorn Birds* into Chinese? You see, I work here at the hotel during the day, but at night, I go to English class." Of course, I could not translate the novel for him. I began to notice eagerness on the part of many who observed me to speak and learn English.

As I sat on a long black vinyl couch against the wall, a young Chinese man dressed in jeans joined me and said, "I came here from Hong Kong; I'm a tourist." I told him the purpose of my visit; then I looked out the glass doors and saw the wet pavement; cars used in the '50s were parked outside, while a few people crossed the premises with black bobbing umbrellas. It was another rainy, damp, and cold day in Hangzhou.

In a short time, my brother walked through the doors and closed his wet umbrella that dripped over his shoes. He wore the customary blue Mao suit, black shoes, and was about my height, 5'2". I greeted him with a hug, which I think caught him off guard, for he reciprocated stiffly. I was behaving like an American; the Chinese do not embrace as readily. He was handsome and gave me a broad smile, which made up for his short stature. Via my *Chinese for Travelers* book, I told him that I had a fever. I felt so bad this had to happen on our first day and I kept saying, "I'm so sorry."

He assured me with, "Nothing, nothing," and took me upstairs to the second floor. At the end of the hall, we went through a door with opaque textured glass panels, and I was inside a Chinese clinic. Two doctors dressed in white lab coats were seated at two large desks, facing each other. Built into the wall were glass cabinets filled with bottles of medicine. The doctor seated nearest the entrance was a slender middle-aged woman with delicate hands. After she put a thermometer in my mouth, she gave my brother some forms to fill out. They began to engage in a lengthy conversation. I learned that the stubby old doctor seated at the opposite desk was a man of over seventy years of age and proud to be working. I suppose they talked about the reason for my visit to China, and about my father who had recently retired on account of his bad health. Then the lady doctor told me to lie down on the examining table behind the privacy screen. Through gestures, I understood that I had a high fever, and she would be giving me a shot. She took a syringe out of a stainless steel container, broke an ampoule, and injected me on the buttocks, all the while deflecting the pain by lightly massaging the area around the needle with her indicator finger. As I lay on the cot, I noticed that the porch door was slightly ajar, and a man was seated outside at a school desk, working on something. It puzzled me that he was seated outside in the cold. Later, he came through the room, awkwardly, like a tall tree branch in the wrong place.

The doctor gave me several medications: a dark syrup or molasses for my cough, a bottle with yellow pills, and another with white pills. She told my brother I would have to continue with the shots for the next five days, twice a day, morning and evening.

We returned to my room, resigned that I would be confined for a few days. I began to take off my coat, but my brother insisted I keep it on. We sat on the wicker chairs, communicating with simple sentences, drawings, and gestures. I told him, "In the United States, the population is made up of all different races. In Detroit, there are people who are Polish, Italian, Irish, Oriental, Mexican, German, Arabic, and many other nationalities. They used to live in segregated communities, but now they are dispersed throughout the metropolitan area. The black people occupy the city proper, whereas the white people live in the surrounding suburbs."

Because I had made some drawing to explain to him what I was saying, he asked, "How many art classes you take?"

"I took six art classes, most of them in the evening. I enjoyed them very much. I had drawing, design, and one class of oil painting. When you paint, do you paint on paper, wood, or canvas?" I asked. I had a hard time making him understand the meaning of canvas, but the drawings helped. "What kind of work do you do in the shipbuilding factory?" I asked.

"I paint on pianos and make toys. I cannot take you to my factory because have sign: No Foreign People. But we go many other places," he said, eager to share with me much of his life and surroundings.

"Aunt Pei De wrote me a letter, which I received in Beijing. In it she told me that Father does not want you to go to America," I said, gently touching on a delicate subject.

"In the beginning, Father very angry. Oh, very angry. But now he agrees. I have decided I go, and he agrees," he said emphatically. Then he continued, "Su Juan one day wants to go, another time cannot go. Often change mind." Then shaking his head, he concluded, "Ah, very difficult."

Around noon, Su Juan arrived after her teaching duties at school. She made an expression that indicated to me she was very sorry I was sick. At the large desk, she corrected some children's notebooks that came out of her black vinyl bag. Later, she did some knitting, and carried on a conversation with my brother. Shortly thereafter, her sister arrived and brought some lunch in thermos containers. I had some *shi-fan*, soupy rice that is boiled a long time and is given to little children who have a stomachache or adults who are sick. Then Su Juan put some chicken in my bowl, which was promptly removed when my brother told her I had a cough. They discussed among themselves how chicken was not good for a cough. After my meal, everyone left and I had time to take a rest.

That afternoon, to my surprise, my father came to pay a visit with my niece Qion and one of the aunts. I had not expected him to come, nor even to be present at the airport on account of his recent bad health. He greeted me in the hallway with his hooded coat, twisted cane, and an emaciated, bespectacled face. He had that staccato greeting of an old man. I was so glad he had come; it made me feel welcomed. Little did I realize he had to squeeze through crowds to get on the buses.

As we sat on the wicker chairs by the window, I said, "I am so sorry to be sick on my first day in Hangzhou."

He replied in his husky voice, "Never mind, never mind, the main thing is for you to get better."

"I know you did not want my brother to go to the United States," I said, trying to let him know that I knew about this difficulty.

He looked away in silence, so I knew the question was settled. My brother was forty years old and could do as he liked.

"Would you like to come and live in the United States?" I asked precipitously.

"You see, I have been so long a Chinese, it would be hard for me to live in another country. Just as you got sick when you came here, I maybe get sick in your country. But I would like to come for a visit," he said in a slow and ponderous way.

We served him some sweet berry soup with whole boiled eggs that an aunt had brought in a thermos. He enjoyed the soup, and later, we had some tea. I showed him my wedding pictures that I had brought in a small album. I also showed him a copy of my birth certificate and that of my brother, written in Chinese. He certified their authenticity. After staying an hour or so, he left with one of the aunts.

In a short while, more people kept pouring into the room. They were Su Juan's mother, sister, uncles, and colleagues, all bringing dishes, cookies, and fruits. The beds were crowded with well-wishers smiling profusely at me. I showed them the pictures I had shown my father earlier. Around nine o'clock, everyone left and I felt relieved to be alone with my thoughts. I dismissed the idea of writing in my diary because I felt quite sick and feverish. I climbed into bed and covered myself with the thick quilts. I lingered in a semi-wakeful state for a long time, and many thoughts went through my mind. I still felt like a stranger to this place. I cried once more because I had missed thirty-two years of my father's life and he was now very old.

The next day, Saturday, February 13, 1982, I woke up at eight, and looked out the window that faced the back of the hotel. I could see the glare of a fire inside a room of the one-story building to my right. I supposed some of the servants were making breakfast. A large unit was on top of the building's roof directly in front of me, an air conditioning unit, perhaps. These structures were built close together, so I did not have much of a view; until now I had not seen the West Lake. An attendant came inside and mopped the unpolished wooden floors; another one came and cleaned the bathroom and left the door open. I could hear the clatter of teacups pushed around in a cart, and the lively conversation of many of the attendants going about their business. A young girl came in, changed the covered teacups, and gave me a fresh thermos with hot water.

Su Juan came early in the morning and brought me breakfast: some delicious spiral-shaped cakes and a can of sweetened evaporated milk. My brother arrived around ten and reminded me to take my medicine. Then he took me to the infirmary for my shot. When we returned to the room, he handed me a note written in English by a friend that read:

Dear Marianne:

I have several things to consult with you. Of all the following arrangements, if you find it suitable please check it.

Concerning Housing question:
Living in Overseas Chinese Hotel the advantage being it has air conditioner and hygienic facilities. It is situated by the side of the West Lake, but somewhat expensive, costing 23 yuans per day. And it will be more expensive if you have dinner here. It is a long distance from that hotel to our home.

Living at our home, so that we'll have a long time of contact, to further the understanding of each other after separation of 32 years, and you'll have a specific understanding of my wife, and of my father. For my part I'll have a chance to studying English with you. The atmosphere will be harmonious. It is convenient food which will be cooked by my wife. But my home in terms of its facilities is not so good as the hotel is: with no air conditioning and hygienic facilities. You will have to go to the bath house if you want to have a bath.

Concerning transportation:
We will take the trolley or bus; it is cheap. And we will try to avoid peak hours. It is also convenient.
Going by taxi although it is comfortable, it is also somewhat expensive.

Concerning shopping and sightseeing:
If you want to buy some Chinese local products (save those we will buy for you) it is desirable to make a list. And you tell us and we will buy such things for you.
If we have dinner outside we will pay money.
If you want to pay a visit to scenic spots, we will arrange it, because we are familiar with such places in Hangzhou.

If you have something to say to me, because of my insufficient ability to speak English and listen to English, then we may write on a slip of paper.

After I read the note, I turned to my brother who was seated on the wicker chair across from the table and said, "I don't want to give your little son a cough."

To which he quickly replied, "My son staying with mother-in-law. I stay with my mother-in-law, and you stay with my daughter and my wife." He seemed proud of this convenient arrangement. I was hesitant to agree right away because I did not want to be an imposition on the family. However, I was definitely happy they had invited me to stay with them; subconsciously, I had always wanted it that way and had felt put off when the hotel was mentioned.

My father came that afternoon with his daughter, my half-sister Jia Ming, and her three-and-a-half-year-old son. I greeted them cordially at the door to my room and asked them to come in. My half-sister handed me a box of cakes, and my father explained, "They come from her mother." I had not met my father's wife; I knew that relations between her and my brother were strained as well as with their respective families, so I suppose she stayed away, which I understood.

I gave Jia Ming a folding umbrella and some nylon stockings, and to her son, a toy car, some coloring books, and crayons. She smiled with her perfectly aligned teeth, and sat across from me on the bed, watching my father and me engage in conversation. Now and then, she would make a comment to my father and call him, "Baba." It was astonishing to me that this lady and I had the same father. She could call him by the familiar "Baba," but I could not. Some other relatives were in the room, including my brother and sister-in-law, but they were not on good terms with my half-sister or her mother, so they did not speak with each other. I guess the abuse she had bestowed on my brother when he was a child had taken its toll.

I served my father a cup of condensed milk, which I prepared from the can that had been placed on the windowsill and hot water from a thermos. "Is it too sweet?" I asked him as I watched him bend over and sip it from the cup.

"No, it's not too sweet," he said, drinking it down in larger swallows and cleaning his chin. He was in a convivial mood and said, "This morning, I wrote a letter to your mother, telling her of your safe arrival in Hangzhou, and that you have caught a cold."

I smiled at his fatherly interest in me and said, "In one of your letters, you mentioned the book *Sister Carrie* by Theodore Dreiser and advised that I should read it. I took it out of the library, but I only managed to read a few chapters before departure. So far I like the book very much. Some of Dreiser's descriptions are so vivid, especially the one in which he describes Carrie in a dream, about to be swallowed up in an abyss."

"So you can find the book *Sister Carrie* in the library," he replied. "It is about a young girl who is trying to find happiness." Then my father began to reenact some parts of the book as if he were the characters themselves. He continued, "Ames is sitting there with a special look in his face; it revealed man's longing for the truth. He speaks to Carrie: 'Someone expresses this longing in music, others in poetry, still others in drama. You express this longing in your face.'"

I listened to him with a sense of mystery, for I had not read the entire book, and said, "It is remarkable that you have found a book that echoes your own thoughts and feelings so well." He agreed with a wholehearted smile, revealing his toothless gums.

I showed my father the note my brother had handed to me earlier, and then I asked him, "Do you think I should stay with my brother? I don't want to be a burden to his family."

Weighing the question for a second, and considering my brother's desire to have me closer to the family, he said, "Yes, brother and sister separated for so long, it is better to live in the same house." Later, he saw my gaunt expression due to the illness and said, "But you stay in the hotel a few more days if you don't feel so well." Then he took his leave with his daughter, Jia Ming. In a strained protective gesture, I helped him button his overcoat out in the hallway.

A host of people came to visit me that evening. Some were Su Juan's colleagues from the elementary school where she taught, and others were Su Juan's brothers and sisters. Their familiarity puzzled me some, for I had come from a culture where a mere visit is preceded by a phone call. But I welcomed all the attention and the ambience of togetherness that all of this brought about. Su Juan bathed her child in the bathroom sink where he let out a loud wail. I helped her dry his hair, but he was afraid of my electric hairdryer. Then Su Juan took a shower, and I helped her dry and curl her hair. She was a pretty young woman with soft wavy hair that fell just below her shoulders and was brushed back off the temples in an undulating sweep. She was of petite stature and had wide almond eyes, revealing a vivacious personality. I began feeling quite at home with her.

Before my brother left that evening, he informed me that he would arrange for a car to take me from the hotel to his house at ten the next morning. He asked for the plastic card that identified my room as 218, so he could present it at the front desk. We searched the room high and low, but could not find the card. I noticed how worried Su Juan looked, and only later found out they had to pay two or three yuans for the card. I did find it the next week, tucked away in my notebook like a misplaced souvenir.

I slept a little better that night. I let the balm of sleep settle the struggles within me. By some kind of free association of the mind, I dreamt I had been adopted by my mother when I was very young, and she had to give me away.

When I got up on Sunday, I took a hot shower since I didn't know when I would take the next one. I was not feeling my 100 percent best, but I had enough strength to repack some things and get ready. At nine, I heard a knock on the door and thought it was my brother. Standing there was Uncle Lou, my cousin Xi Cheng's uncle, the tall elderly gentleman with a learned appearance I had met at Hangzhou's airport the afternoon I arrived. The wrinkles around his eyes made it seem like he was smiling even when he was not. He had a posture of extreme courtesy that intensified with embarrassment because I was still in my morning gown.

I uttered a few words in haste, "Wang Qian, my brother, is coming at ten."

Looking at his watch and somewhat ill at ease himself, he said, "Oh, I come back at ten."

My brother arrived promptly at ten, so I had no time to dry my hair. He helped me carry the heavy suitcase down the broad stairway toward the front entrance. As we walked out, I saw Uncle Lou by the hotel's curb on his bike. We greeted each other with a nod, and I felt touched by the kindness of this old man to see me off.

Chapter 6

Settling in the Family Compound

For more than two days, I had been confined in the hotel, so it was good to have a breath of fresh air and I was happy to see more of the city. As we climbed into the jeep, my brother introduced me to the man beside the driver who had arranged for the ride, Su Juan's brother-in-law. We placed the luggage in the space behind the backseat and then we were off. The jeep meandered through the city, often going down the middle of the road, passing bicycles and pushcarts with the aggressive toot of its horn. We were certainly at an advantage over the general populous in our privately driven motor vehicle. The sky was gray and overcast with only a faint promise of sunshine. After passing many grubby storefronts, the paved street became suddenly narrower and more deserted. The driver made a U-turn and parked on the sidewalk next to a high cement wall that enclosed the Foreign Police Bureau. My brother told me I would have to register here in order to stay at his home. At the time, very few foreigners visited China, and those who came were closely monitored in terms of where they could go and where they could stay. This monitoring by the government was done by the Foreign Police Bureau, an office I was about to visit. I was not surprised by this process since I was in a Communist country whose own citizens were closely controlled and where suspicion toward foreigners still lingered.

A soft drizzle began to shroud the city. So my brother and I quickly jumped off the jeep and headed toward the compound entrance where we approached a man dressed in ordinary clothes manning a booth. My brother spoke to him in Chinese, and the man in turn, in a sort of annoyed fashion, gestured for my brother to knock at the first door of the house behind us that had a long veranda. We walked up a few cement steps and went into the first room where we noticed an officer seated at his desk in a small office in the back. With proper civility, my brother explained the purpose of our visit. The officer immediately pranced on his feet and escorted us outside and into an adjacent room, which was apparently used to receive foreign guests, and then he went back to his office to get some papers. My brother and I had an opportunity to look around. The room seemed as if it were seldom used. A stack of papers was in front of a huge window blurred by dust. On the room's other side was a rack filled with copies of the English edition of the magazine *China Reconstructs*. I sat down on a long black vinyl couch; my brother sat on a high backed armchair. In front of us was a low coffee table covered with glass that had a crack in the corner. To soothe his nerves, my brother lit a cigarette and used the small ceramic ashtray on the table. Later, I understood my brother's nervousness in dealing with officials from the Chinese Government. It stemmed from his experiences in the Cultural Revolution and his fear and mistrust of them.

Soon the officer came in with hurried footsteps. He was tall and slender and appeared to be in his late forties. His pale face contrasted with his dark rimmed glasses and dark sleek hair combed to one side. His hands were delicate, almost feminine. Despite his soft exterior, I was sure I was encountering a man with an iron will. He began to interrogate me in perfect English, "How long do you intend to stay in Hangzhou?"

"I intend to stay here three weeks," I replied, adding, "I have returned to China after thirty-two years to see my father. I just found him last year. I was born in China in 1944, and I spent most of my early childhood in Shanghai."

"May I see your passport?" he asked, and as I handed it to him, he added, "How long have you been an American citizen?"

I honestly could not remember the year I had become a U.S. citizen and I had left my citizenship certificate in my bag in the jeep. So I excused myself and promptly went to get it. Upon my return, he scrutinized the document until we both learned I had become an American citizen in 1972. Never did I feel the importance of my citizenship so keenly as I did then. This man was the only Chinese official who interviewed me while I stayed in China. At first he was officious, but when we continued our conversation and I said, "My father has retired; he used to teach mathematics at Zhejiang University," he suddenly became cognizant of my case.

"Oh, I remember. I received a letter from the Chinese Embassy in Washington, and I am the one who went to the university in search of your father. So now you have come to see him. Your husband and children could not come?"

"No, the trip is very expensive and we could not afford it. Perhaps another time," I said, somewhat surprised at the ease with which he asked this question. Little did he realize that trips abroad are luxuries for the average American citizen.

"Do you intend to visit any other cities in China?"

"I will be going to Shanghai before I return to the States."

"If you desire to visit any other city in China, I can easily authorize it, and even extend your stay in China," he concluded in a friendly but formal fashion.

I thanked him profusely for his kindness while happy that the protocol was coming to an end, for I still felt lightheaded and weak from the influenza bug I had caught. After he wrote my name on a roster attached to a clipboard by the door, we left.

We hopped back on the jeep and headed toward the city's northeast corner where my brother lived. At the compound's gate, an old man had set up shop and was renting and selling paperback books from cardboard boxes set on a makeshift table. He was blind in one eye, but wore a smart Russian style hat and a jagged long brown overcoat. As I passed him carrying one of my suitcases, he gave me a very cordial smile. We walked once more through the corridors and courtyards. Many neighbors, who were outside the doors of their rooms or by the faucet washing clothes or vegetables, stopped to look at me—this strange intruder from America.

Now that daylight flooded the area, I was able to see that the two large courtyards in the compound were laid with large blocks of stone and not dirt floors as I had thought, and all the walks were cemented. The first corridor was very wide and dusty; it was made from the side of a building and the wall that separated this compound from the next. It was covered and there were rooms on the second floor. Against the wall was a stack of wooden cribs once used for a nursery. To one side of the corridor was a small enclosure with a bamboo-fenced area where chickens were kept and to which several rooms opened. In the first courtyard were two huge rectangular blocks of stone suspended on cinder blocks, which the tenants used to scrub their clothes, clean fish, and cut vegetables and fowl. The second corridor was narrower, again formed by the building's walls at the first courtyard's corner, and it began to the right of the first path. It opened to the second courtyard, formed by buildings of similar structure. Each building had two floors. The first floor had stucco walls, intercepted at intervals by round wooden beams, and onto which were attached rough planked doors. The second floor walls were thatched with straw mats with tall windows spaced evenly. Above the windows, clothes hung on bamboo frames. Also hanging near the windows were some dried meats hooked on wires, presumably preserved in this manner because of the lack of refrigeration. My father's room faced the faucet of this courtyard at the building's right-hand corner. Just before entering this short corridor lined with bicycles, old crockery and baskets, I noticed a broad stairway made of wood that led to the rooms on the second floor. Later, I found out one of my father's old cronies lived up there; they loved to play Chinese Chess (the board game *Go*) together. Perpendicular to this third corridor was a long and narrow path with gravel in the center and short cement walks along the buildings that enclosed it. My brother's room opened onto this narrow path as well as his kitchen. The kitchen was a short stucco structure made of beams and brick, which my brother built with the help of relatives and friends. The cement foundation had been built earlier, so he was able to add the kitchen to the existing building. The kitchen had two windows, one of which opened to a sluggish canal and provided a good view of the bank's other side, where stood a number of makeshift homes, some of stone and others of brick.

It was all a long cry from the living conditions to which I was accustomed. I had to adjust to the narrow confinement of these buildings with their shabby, damp, and dusty corridors. My American experience of wide-open spaces, trees, lawns, and comfortable homes had suddenly vanished. And I began to ask myself: "Am I a child of dilapidated walls and dark corners? I thought my father had come from a wealthy family and at least lived in a dignified environment. But this is China; even the learned have to grapple with the basic side of human existence." So began my experience with the cold, the wet, the dust, the fire, the smoke, and the darkness of simple humanity in pursuit of survival, and sometimes, I saw the extraordinary creep in and provide food for the soul. This experience I found during my conversations with my father.

We walked precariously through the last narrow corridor and deposited my luggage in the room. My brother turned to me and said, "I go to friend's house to get stove for the room." I understood he was getting a cast iron belly stove to heat the bedroom. Meanwhile, my father arrived in the kitchen across from the bedroom with a young woman. As I entered the kitchen, he stood at the entrance, wearing the dark blue woolen suit and wrinkled maroon scarf he wore from then on. With hands folded inside his sleeves and feet slightly apart to balance his frail body, he smiled at me and said, "I want you to meet another daughter of mine."

I looked at this smiling lady next to him. I was surprised he had another daughter, so I said, after greeting her warmly, "Is she a real daughter of yours?"

"No, not a real daughter," he said, dissipating my doubts about this matter. My directness did not disarm him; he almost expected it. He explained she was his stepdaughter and then said, "I want you to come with us to meet my wife. She expects us at her room," he added.

I followed them to the courtyard to a room two doors down from my father's room and directly behind my brother's room. The door was draped with a curtain, and as we stepped in, I was greeted by a large affable woman with tight facial skin who bore traces of former beauty. She was quiet, but gracious. Immediately, she offered me some red tea in a glass that had been stirred with sugar, which she placed on a stool in front of me. I think word got around that I liked red (black) tea with sugar for in Hangzhou, the Chinese drank mostly plain green tea. As I sat in the middle of the room, I noticed that everything was in neat order, and I thought to myself, "Can this be the same woman who tortured my brother while he was a young child?" I had heard that she was extremely cruel to him. Nothing seemed to be making sense at this point, and I felt cordial toward her. My father sat near the door with his stepdaughter, who never ceased to talk in an animated fashion with him. When he saw my puzzled look, he said, "She wants to invite you for dinner and is wondering if she should serve chicken? I told her she should go home and decide." Little did I know that chicken was an expensive item to be used with discretion.

My father's wife was cooking some fried sweet rolls in a wok placed on an iron coal stove elevated by a crate just in front of the window. As soon as the rolls were ready, she placed them on a plate in front of me. I took a few bites of the crunchy rolls and found they were filled with a sweetened almond paste that rendered them simply delicious! Later, I found out it was red bean paste rather than almond. As I raved about the taste, I asked, "How does your wife make these?" She walked to the bureau at the foot of the full canopy bed (everyone had a bed draped in gauze because of mosquitoes in the summer) and brought me a plate of round skins she had used for the dough. She spoke to me in Chinese, but I did not understand. I was not sure whether she made them or bought them in a store.

My father, noticing she had placed more of these freshly fried rolls on my plate, said, "You do not need to eat all of them; just eat those you like."

My stepsister, Wang Jia Xing, was anxious to take me home with her for dinner. Before I left with her, I went back to my brother's room to let him know where I was going. The relationship between my brother's family and that of his stepmother and sisters was strained, so I had to use the utmost diplomacy while I remained quite ignorant of the feud's cause or consequences, yet I believe Chinese honor was at stake here. When I arrived at my brother's quarters, he was on a wooden ladder, trying to remove the top glass panel from his bedroom window so the exhaust pipe could go through. I looked up at him and said, "I am going to stepsister's house for dinner, okay?" He looked at me with a sense of loss, but agreed, repeating my "okay." I wondered how he had hauled the heavy cast stove, whether on his bike or on top of a wheelbarrow. I never did find out.

We left the compound and I found myself walking along the main thoroughfare of this part of town with my newly acquired sister. She was a large person with a broad, freckled face and a ready smile that showed her perfectly aligned teeth. She did not look typically Chinese; her eyebrows were well-formed and her shoulder-length hair had a slight wave to it. She was happy to have me at her disposal, and I was glad her English was passable. She was energetic and warm and led me along the gray somber streets in a brisk pace. She kept saying to me, "My house much better than father's. He lives very poor place. My house more better."

When we passed a building set back from the street, she said, "This is the Post Office."

"Oh, can we go in? I have to mail a few postcards," I asked. When we went inside, she insisted she would pay for the stamps, but she soon realized that she had forgotten her change purse. "Never mind," I said. "I really want to mail these now and I can buy the stamps." A struggle ensued; she kept pulling my arms toward the door while I tried to move toward the counter. She won in the end because, not knowing how to speak Chinese, I could not make myself understood by the clerk. I had to give in to her imagined courtesy, albeit, reluctantly. This habit of the Chinese to pay for everything while in your company drove me crazy many times during my trip.

Wang Jia Xing continued to lead me along this business district with many small storefronts mixed in with people's homes that often did not amount to more than one or two rooms of a given building. Most of the buildings lining this street were two-stories high, with the typical thatched walls on the second floor. They all appeared to have been here for at least one hundred years. The sidewalk was broken and uneven, so we had to walk on the street a good portion of the time. Soon we veered right onto an old bridge suspended over a canal, which I later found out was the Grand Canal, the longest canal in the world (1795 kilometers), begun in 486 B.C. by the Wu dynasty and completed in 610 A.D. by the Sui dynasty; it connects Beijing in the north to Hangzhou in the southeast. While we were crossing the bridge, my stepsister pointed to a building on the left and said, "Su Juan's mother lives there."

On the bridge's other side, I saw that vegetables were sold on the sidewalk as well as in large interior stalls. Soon we were walking on a graveled side street onto which the door to her house opened. She lived in a row of white stucco buildings connected to each other with painted front doors.

We had walked a good twenty minutes, and now my stepsister was turning the key to her private home. As I walked in, I noticed that the entrance hall served as the kitchen. Against the left wall was a cage with two live chickens, and on the other side was a table, stove, and wok, with many wicker baskets hanging from the ceiling. We walked up one step and were in her dining room, which had a dark square table with chairs on one side and a china/food cabinet on the other. This room opened up to a back room that served as the living room and bedroom. The furniture here was dark and antiquated, but she had a stuffed chair, a black-and-white TV set, an old fashioned sewing machine, a bookcase, a wardrobe, and a storage trunk.

As I sat on the armchair between the bed and a table, her son, a boy of about nine, was nestled under some heavy comforters, just waking up from a nap. He was surprised to see me in the room, but he gave me a shy smile. Immediately, his mother helped him put on another layer of padded clothing because the house was not heated and the damp cold was very penetrating. In a half-serious and half-coaxing manner, she admonished him to do his homework. The boy whined and pleaded because he wanted to watch cartoons on TV. She turned to me and smiled, "Are your children naughty like this? He does not want to do schoolwork, just watch TV."

"Yes, my children are the same. They would much rather watch TV than do their homework," I replied, happy to share a common plight of mothers.

Wang Jia Xing then left the room with her son and returned shortly with a hot water bottle for my lap and a hot cup of tea. The warmth was very comforting because I was cold and puzzled by the newness of my surroundings. She also offered me some hard candy wrapped in decorative paper from a flat square can. This kind of guest welcome I would experience many times in many of the Chinese households I visited.

My stepsister was an energetic, accommodating person with a pleasant smile. She sat on the bed with a notebook she used for the English lessons she followed on TV every evening. It was the same series *Follow Me* that was also broadcast in Beijing. It started to become apparent to me that there was a general eagerness for people to learn English. Their isolation from the West for more than thirty years spurred the people's curiosity. The United States was opening up to them, and they were ready to leap out of their confinement and embrace the opportunity. "I study English every day, but sometimes I lazy; therefore, my English not so good," she said, proud of her accomplishments even if expressed in a self-deprecating manner. I often found that the Chinese would not boast of an achievement unless it was veiled in some kind of humbling gesture. It was as if they had a hidden rule that said, "Do not put yourself above your fellow man."

When she showed me her notebook, I was impressed with the lessons' level of difficulty. Then she continued, "We do not have book; next year will have book. Now

I must copy lesson."

"You do very well. What kind of work do you do during the day?" I asked, curious about her profession.

"I am a doctor. I work at the clinic in the same shipbuilding factory where your brother works," she replied.

"What is your specialty?" I asked. She did not understand the word "specialty," so she took the dictionary out of the bookcase.

After she translated the word, she said, "I am a general doctor. I see many different kind patients. I went to Zhejiang University. But during the Cultural Revolution, I work in countryside. Every doctor go to countryside." Then she added, "Your father go to prison for two years. It was very bad."

To illustrate her point, she drew the picture of a man wearing a double plaque, one in front and one in the back, like a living sign. He would be paraded in front of students and spectators in this manner.

Because of my weak state and the stress of the past few days, I broke out into tears from thinking about this situation. I could not envision my father so humiliated, and all I could say was, "Thirty-two years is a long time, a long time." My stepsister could not hold back her tears either, so we cried together.

She continued, "Your father was very good to me when I was a child."

I thought, "How different our experiences were. My father, her stepfather, was good to her, while my stepfather was evil to me." What a reversal of roles. I did not receive my father's love; she had taken my place, yet I was glad to know he was a good man and had treated her with kindness.

All this upheaval of the Cultural Revolution was very nebulous to me. I could not imagine the displacement of so many people from factories and schools to prisons and to the countryside to administer and to share in the labor of the peasants. I guess I had never understood about class struggle, but it was real here. To be an intellectual, especially one who studied abroad, was to be in a precarious state. Mao's anti-intellectualism seeped through every strata of society, making the learned man appear to be an enemy to the people, and above all, to the peasant population, which was considered by China's Communist philosophy to be the equalizing force or the status quo. Thus, my father had suffered.

After a few deep sighs, we continued our conversation. She became very interested in my American life, so she asked me a multitude of questions. "What does your house look like? Do you have a car?" I drew a picture of my colonial home with an attached garage, explaining to her the layout as best I could. She was fascinated that I had a car and such a spacious house, although by American standards, they were considered modest.

Then looking at me, she remarked, "Your daughters are very beautiful."

"So you must have seen the pictures I have sent my father," I replied. "Yes, they give me a lot of work, but they grow up very fast," I said, trying to bridge the vast gulf of cultural differences that separated us.

Meanwhile, her husband came home from work, a fragile, nervous, spectacled person, with a few large rolls of paper under his arms. He came into the room and greeted me with a mixture of shyness and anxiety. I learned that he worked as an architect for the same shipbuilding factory where his wife and my brother worked; therefore, he carried the scrolls of drafting paper. He soon excused himself to go to the kitchen to cook dinner. His wife also excused herself for a while, but before she left, I expressed to her my need to use the bathroom. For a moment, she appeared flustered; then she pointed to an enamel commode with a wooden cover at the corner of the wardrobe by the door. I tried to make myself as inconspicuous as possible, and I found it odd that while I was relieving myself, her son was watching the cartoon *Kimba* on the black-and-white TV in the same room.

In a short space of time, supper was ready and we were called into the dining room. The table was moved to the room's center, and the four of us sat down to a dinner of chicken, roasted peanuts, Chinese vermicelli soup with vegetables, salted pork, and rice. The chicken was chopped into bite-size pieces, bone and all, so one had to be careful not to swallow any slivers. As we ate, I said, "I love this soup; how do you make it?" The husband lifted the pork leg hidden under the noodles and explained that it was for flavor. Then his wife went to the cabinet and showed me the transparent noodles that were used for the soup. Once again, the soup and rice came after the main course when I expected the opposite. We toasted the evening with some wine from a bottle opened especially for the occasion and served in lovely wine glasses; it had the taste of Cinzano, a wine I had tried at a neighbor's house when I was a kid. Somehow, all these experiences were bringing me back to my childhood in Brazil, some thirty years ago, because of the different level of progress I found here.

At eight o'clock, my niece Qion came for me. She stood at the entrance with her super long hair out of braids and looked particularly charming. I finished my wine so as not to be rude to my hosts and thanked them very much for the dinner. Qion was offered some wine, but she did not take any. On my way out of the kitchen, I noticed only one chicken was in the cage. It was not hard to guess what had happened to the other one.

It was cold and dark. My niece illuminated the way with a small bicycle light. We crossed the bridge over the canal, heading for the main street. There we took a bus home, which at this hour was relatively empty. After a few stops, it was our turn to step out. We walked the darkened corridors and courtyards wrapped in one scarf, which amused my niece. Just before taking one of the last corridors, we stopped at my father's door, which was slightly ajar. He came out and smiled to see us wrapped as one.

In my brother's room was a black-and-white TV borrowed from Su Juan's parents. The film of Tolstoy's *Anna Karenina* was on, dubbed in Chinese. In the meantime, Su Juan's sister took my temperature, which was below normal. My father came over and said, "They told me your temperature is very low, 95 degrees." So Su Juan's sister took my temperature again, and this time it had gone up half a degree. My father became somewhat worried, but relaxed later when I told him I was okay. He said, "Well, if you were in the hospital, it would be very serious, but the reason you are cold is because you walked by the river and absorbed all that dampness in your body." He repeated this remark a couple of times, either to reassure me or himself.

I did not understand what was going on in the movie. The beautiful Caucasian characters speaking in Chinese intrigued me. My American sense of efficiency popped up and I told my sister-in-law with gestures that the heat was escaping through the hole where the exhaust pipe went out. I just could not let all that warm air, which was brought into the room with such difficulty, escape so senselessly. She found some cardboard, and I gave her the scotch tape Aunt Jane had given me in San Francisco, so the hole was patched in no time. The movie began to bore most of the people in the room so the set was turned off and everyone retired for the night.

It was interesting to note that the TV was plugged into an outlet attached to the only electrical fixture in the room, a 20-watt light dangling from the ceiling on a long wire. In the process of unplugging the TV, Su Juan found herself holding the fixture minus the wire. We would have to wait until morning for my brother to reattach them.

I was ready to tuck myself in bed when Su Juan insisted I take the large double bed. I pleaded that one of them should sleep with me, and I suggested that I take Qion's bed instead, but it was to no avail. They refused adamantly. Both my sister-in law and my niece slept in Qion's narrow bed by the window while I occupied the large canopied bed that took up half the room. They gave me a basin of hot water to wash my feet and placed a hot water bag inside the comforters. And so began the nightly ritual that persisted throughout my stay. Every night, after I was wrapped in two thick quilts, one of them would release the drawn gauze netting and allow me to drift into sleep in the privacy of my own world. Seldom have I slept so well.

Chapter 7

=== ❀ ===

Beginning Conversations, and then to Temple, Hospital, and Dinner

When I woke up at eight the next morning, Su Juan and my niece Qion had already left for school. I dressed quickly, tidied up the room, and then went to the kitchen. My brother was waiting for me there, ready to serve me breakfast. He had come from his mother-in-law's, and he would be free from factory duties for the rest of the week because of my visit. He made a cup of tea for me from the hot water in the thermos, and I suggested we have the cakes his stepmother had sent me a few days earlier at the hotel. I went to the bedroom to fetch the box, and we had an amiable breakfast together.

"Next week, I go to painting class. Mommy give me money so I can take oil painting in Hangzhou's best school," he said with great anticipation, and added, "I want to make many good paintings for America."

"I am glad you will be able to take this class. You do love art so much. I remember the few pictures you sent Mommy through Aunt Wang Yuan (Aunt Jane). They were very good, even though you were only fourteen," I said, trying to join the past with the present, but having great difficulty. The face I studied now was that of an adult much different from the image of the young boy I had in my mind. I had fond memories of him from when we had lived in Shanghai, he with my father, and I with my mother, on account of our parents' divorce. He would come to spend the weekends with us, and a flood of memories was coming back to me during our visit of the time we had then spent together. I remembered how we played in the courtyard of my mother's apartment building with a bamboo pole, pretending we were riding on a bus; or we made paper boats, which we floated in a basin on my mother's terrace. We were scared of my Russian stepfather, especially when we heard him coughing and coming up the building's stairs. Yet with my brother, who was then two heads taller than I, I'd had a sense of being protected. More than once, he shielded me from bad treatment by rowdy children whom we encountered. Once I remember going to an open street market nearby where he bought me some sugarcane, which I chewed with great relish. On our way to our mother's apartment building, we had to pass the guard's booth. I was petrified of this man and would hide around the corner of the booth. But my brother would prod me, giving me enough courage to cross the threshold with him. And now, his letters had given me courage to cross the threshold into China and experience what I had felt missing all my life since.

It was hard for me to communicate with my brother. His English was not fluent enough for us to carry on a lengthy intelligent conversation. Our many years of separation and cultural differences did not help either. Yet, we felt bonded. As my father would often say, "Brother and sister, same mother, same father, yet two different people." Yes, indeed, we had come from the same source, and we had, therefore, a strong family bond, but our lives had taken opposite courses; we were now in the process of merging again, I with the East and he with the West, the two separate parts of our experiences.

My father came over this first morning in his rickety manner carrying a bamboo pole. When he entered the room, he was all smiles and said, "This is for you. Just as you gave me some presents when you came, I also give you some, but they have to be small because I am not a rich man. Take this to America. I think it will be very interesting."

I looked at him with surprise because of the gift's curious nature. My brother looked at him as if he were a foolish old man, making me take this ridiculous pole on the plane, when I was already packed to my teeth.

I held the pole in my hand, examining its shape. It was shallow and hollow on one side and smooth and curved on the other; on each end was a groove and a hump to prevent the bundles from sliding off. It felt very sturdy and had the musty look of age. I was sure it had been carved from a strong bamboo stem.

My father, seeing that I had taken an interest, continued, "You see, I have had this pole in my room for over ten years. I carried my university books on it. It can hold fifty pounds on each side."

At the time I did not see the symbolic significance of this Chinese yoke, with which my father was parting. Later, I realized it had meant a great deal to him. It had helped him carry his burden for many years, and he wanted to share with me his life's work, for I had not been there to witness it. But I did not take the pole, opting instead for practicality. I guess my brother's looks convinced me that it was quite impossible to bring on the airplane home with me. My father was disappointed that his first attempt to give me a gift was met with disinterest, but he was used to being considered a foolish old man. The import of it all did not dawn on me then or I would have taken it no matter how impractical to bring home. The bamboo pole stood in the corner of the room for a few days, and then my father carried it back to his room.

After lunch, my father said my brother would be taking me to see Lingyin Temple, one of the most important places of Buddhist worship in Hangzhou.

"Why don't you come with us?" I asked.

"No, it is quite impossible for an old man like myself. You see when I came to see you at the hotel, my daughter, her son, and I had to rent one of those three-wheel cars you see on the street; the buses were so overcrowded. On our way home, I told my grandson to jump over one of the puddles and he fell flat on his behind," he laughed, showing his gums and sipping the last of his green tea from a glass half-filled with leaves, some of which had dried on the glass' side.

Outside the compound, my brother and I waited for the bus. I wanted to talk with him, but I felt bound, as if we were strangers. A gulf had to be crossed, and I did not know quite how to begin. Past experiences, education, and our cultural outlooks were keeping us apart, making the meeting of heart and mind very difficult.

On the bus, we were squeezed almost to the point of not having standing room. Often, I looked at my brother and saw a man of small stature, handsome, dressed in the same Mao suit as all the others, fighting the crowd in a literal as well as symbolic way. I thought of the many questions about America he had asked me at the hotel: prices, life conditions, and the people in America. I had answered earnestly. To him, America held a promise of happiness, of a better life style, and of freedom. Above all, it was the place he would find his mother. On occasion, he would express openly his love for our mother. He told me once in the kitchen that no one could keep a mother and son separated. He was ready to overcome all difficulties for the realization of this union.

As we climbed up the winding mountain road to the Lingyin Temple, it was cold and overcast. I was surprised that I was not overjoyed to be with my brother at this time. The burden of his dependence on us weighed on me. At one point he turned to me and asked, "Does Mommy want me to come to America?"

"Yes, she does," I reassured him. "It will not be easy, but she will do anything in her power to help you come over."

Even though it was gray and gloomy, the lovely foliage surrounding us was fresh and green. The mountains in the distance enlarged one's vision of the world, as if mirroring the longings of one's soul: remote yet somewhat near, lovely and yet unattainable.

Our first stop was at the main temple, a mammoth building with huge red columns; its interior was The Great Hall of the Buddha, or main sanctuary, where a few groups of scattered people were talking and burning incense. Almost immediately, I was captivated by the immense grinning golden statue in the middle of the hall. I did not feel reverence or fear, just a sense of strangeness. Then we proceeded to walk through a narrower path with ascending steps and overshadowed by bamboo trees. At the very top, we entered a gazebo built in front of a mountain cave. In this cave was another image, and a few people were taking turns bowing to it with incense sticks. I looked at this experience as if it were very natural and familiar to me. The truth was I knew very little about Buddhism, or Eastern Religions for that matter.

We sat atop this hill, gazing at the distant mountains for a long time, enjoying the view and talking.

"I can make many pictures before I go to America. Maybe Aunt Wang Yuan help me make exhibit in San Francisco. She have many friends?"

"I don't know. If you have enough pictures, I'm sure you will be able to have an exhibit. In America, there is much interest in China and its people. I suggest you make paintings of typical Chinese scenery and of people doing their daily chores. Chinese life as it is lived now is very mysterious to the American public. They are eager to know more and find out the truth."

"You think my whole family can come America?" he asked with great hope.

"Yes, I think your visa will be ready in two years. We have to be patient. Sometimes, it is hard for artists to make a living in America. Many people are out of work now, and it is hard to find a job. Also, life in America is very expensive, but we will manage with a little luck." I told him all this, so he would not have too many illusions. Even with material wealth, life in America was hard.

We descended the mountain, realizing the difficulty of life ahead of us. At a vending booth at the foot of the mountain, I bought a few handkerchiefs depicting Hangzhou's scenic spots. Then we ran toward a departing bus jammed with people. We managed to squeeze through for the ride back to the city, crossing the bridge over West Lake. The downtown area was congested as usual with throngs of bicycles, pushcarts, and pedestrians going about their business. We walked through the middle of town to a bus stop to catch Bus #51. The Chinese buses were like two long buses attached to each other by a swivel mechanism and covered at this junction by an accordion kind of vinyl to allow them greater flexibility in the streets. I always marveled at how these caterpillar monsters would swerve in the narrow streets, overtaking bicycles and a myriad of other obstacles in their path with relative ease.

We arrived home before dark. My father came to the kitchen to inquire about our excursion. I was standing near the door when he came very close to me, scrutinizing my face through his glasses, and said, "They say you have my eyebrows. Yes, I think you do, these triangles," and he laughed.

Then he sat across from me, with his usual stoop, preparing a cigarette to put into his white cigarette holder. We had a cup of tea that my brother poured for us. In a joking sort of way, I said to my father, "I hope God does not look like Buddha; at least not like the one in the temple."

He did not laugh, but looked kind of sad over my taking the whole mystery of Buddhism so lightly. "You see," he said, "Buddha is for us the last expression of God. God expresses himself in many ways, and this is the last stage."

"It must be what Christ is for us," I thought. Then I asked, "Have you been a Buddhist all your life?"

"No, not all my life; only since I was sixteen."

"Strange," I thought, "I also had a religious conversion in my adolescence. In my questioning, matters of ultimate importance were fascinating to me. How much like my father I was." But these remained thoughts; somehow I could not bring myself to express my findings. As I watched my father drink his tea and smoke his cigarette with no sense of hurry, I noticed that his hands were similar to mine. Even his handwriting resembled mine. Could this be an illusion or a true mirage?

"So you must practice meditation," I said, wanting to know more about his faith.

"Yes, I close my eyes like this," he said, showing me. "Then I sit very still for a long time. Only when you forget yourself can you find the Truth. Only in renunciation can you find happiness."

"What is Truth?"

"God is Truth," he answered.

His answer pierced me like an arrow. I did not expect such wisdom. In a reflective way I said, "You know, very few people practice the essence of Christianity."

"I know, it is the same here."

Soon my brother, Su Juan, Qion, and I left for Su Juan's parents' home for dinner. We took the bus, even though the house was only a fifteen-minute walk along the main street. We arrived at a cluster of buildings that formed a narrow corridor and then a hallway onto which many rooms opened. As I entered the long dining room, I was greeted by a great many smiling faces, all Su Juan's brothers and sisters; she was the oldest of seven, and all of them lived at home except for her and her other married sister. They had been waiting for me all day and were ready to make merry. I was introduced to each one, including Su Juan's brother-in-law who had come and was helping in the kitchen. I recognized him because of his mustache; he had been in the jeep that took me to my brother's house the day before.

Su Juan's mother, a petite, energetic, and affable woman, with an apron over her gray padded jacket and pants, and very much in charge of the family, led me to the kitchen to see what was being prepared for dinner. They were cooking up a storm. Two woks imbedded in a counter of white tile contained a poached fish and roasted chicken, while Su Juan's brother-in-law hovered over another wok on the kitchen's other side glazing a whole duck. The whole place was filled with a spicy sweet aroma. The likes of such a feast I had never seen; it seemed like a Chinese Thanksgiving.

I noticed that the kitchen's back door opened to a small terrace with steep cement stairs leading to the bank of a busy canal. I asked my brother whether I could step outside. My brother explained to me that this was the Grand Canal that went all the way to the city of Nanjing, and in former days, all the way to Beijing. Just below the bridge, I watched a modern ferry go by and waved to a few foreigners on deck. I'm sure that for them I was part of the local scene. A great many *sampans* (flat-bottomed wooden boats) carrying a variety of things, from bricks to vegetables, floated in the waters nearby. There were also some houseboats, and I watched a man wash his rice bowl in the murky waters. A woman was steering her boat with a pole, trying to avoid the larger boats. It looked like a real traffic jam in the river.

As we waited for dinner, one of the brothers put a couple of records on an old turntable atop a bureau. The sound of waltzes and accordion music filled the room. As I listened to the music, I felt transported back about thirty years because the melodies were similar to those I had heard as a child in Brazil in the '50s. I began to dance with some of the others, and they were overjoyed with my expertise. They gladly took turns dancing with me, and we became an animated group in celebration. Our joviality was broken when the large round wooden cover had to be placed on the square table in order to accommodate everyone for dinner.

At least twelve varieties of dishes were brought to the table such as chicken, duck, smoked and poached fish, salted pork, roasted peanuts, translucent eggs, and fried fish. All of us began to pick from the serving bowls with our chopsticks. A great many questions were asked in simple English sentences. I began to learn that all the brothers and sisters had jobs except for one sister who stayed home, sewed, and minded Su Juan's two-year-old boy, Wang Yun. One of the brothers worked in a sewing factory and another in a noodle factory. Su Juan's youngest sister, who wore her hair in braids, was a charming girl of eighteen who worked in a lightbulb factory. This very pretty girl, who exhibited a great deal of self-confidence, gave me a hot towel toward the end of the meal for me to wipe my face and hands, and some lotion that had a marvelous scent.

Immediately after dinner, I took photos of the family in small groups with my instamatic camera, and everyone responded with cheer and enthusiasm. Su Juan's married sister asked that I take a picture of her husband, her seven-year-old daughter, and her seated on the bed, so I quickly obliged, acting like the perfect family photographer.

It was getting late, so Su Juan, my brother, my niece, and I bid everyone goodnight. We walked once more through the extremely dark and narrow exit corridor made from the sides of two buildings and large enough for only one body to go through at one time. When we reached the street, the shops were dimly lit. We joined a few people waiting for the trolley, and when it arrived, this time we did not have to fight for a seat. After we returned home, my brother excused himself and returned to his mother-in-law for the night. My niece gave me again the basin of hot water for my feet. They continued to refuse to share the large bed with me. Exhaustion brought me to a quick sleep.

The next morning, everyone had gone to school and I was alone at last. I felt as if I had been stashed away in a drawer, somewhere in the world, a place quite foreign to my usual surroundings. I found myself in this shabby environment wondering how all this was connected to me. A sort of vacuum existed within me that I was struggling to fill. The aching hollow of my perennial depression still permeated my soul. Here I was with my real father and brother, but in many ways, they seemed like strangers to me; I had to decipher their world, their language, their customs, and their manner of thinking in such a short time that I felt like a penguin in a desert, only the people were almost as plentiful as the sand. I spent some time writing letters to my husband Tony and my mother, and some postcards to friends. I told them how well my family had received me and how simple were my surroundings. I could not mail these at the nearby post office because it did not have the seventy-cent stamps required for postcards. Su Juan's brother brought me these stamps later from the post office downtown, and when I received them, I was surprised that they were not gummed. I remembered seeing a gooey tub with brushes on a corner table at the post office, and immediately devised its purpose. I used this tub later to paste all the stamps onto the postcards and envelopes. But for now, my brother showed me a trick in the kitchen; he mashed a few grains of rice onto a paper and used it as paste; and voila, it worked as well as any store-bought product. While my brother was showing me this procedure, my father remarked, "Now you can tell them at home how we seal our envelopes. An ancient method!"

That afternoon, my brother and I went to a hospital across Hangzhou's West Lake, to visit Uncle Lou, the same gentleman who had met me at the airport and later visited me at the Overseas Hotel. He was an uncle of my cousin Lou Xi Cheng (most likely from his father's side of the family) who as mentioned before was studying at M.I.T. in the United States. The downtown was crowded as usual and we were still pressed in the buses, without relief from the crowds. We passed many sites along the West Lake that by now had become quite familiar to me. We crossed the same bridge that we had crossed on our way to the Lingyin Temple, but we stepped off the bus at an earlier stop. The hospital was situated on the outskirts of town and had some pleasant grounds with trees and flowers. The building was old, but solid and spacious. We checked in at a small desk at the side of the lobby, and then we proceeded to find Uncle Lou's room down a corridor to our left. I was astonished to see some potted flowering plants on our way. "The cold temperature must be just right for growing these inside," I thought. Usually buildings were so devoid of any kind of adornment.

Uncle Lou was in his room playing checkers with his roommate. Upon seeing us, he quickly folded up the game and introduced us to his friend. Then he excused himself and went out to make a phone call. When he came back, he ushered us to a waiting room on the next floor; he also got a thermos bottle and made us some tea. Shortly thereafter, his wife joined us and presented me with some tangerines that we all shared. Later, I found out that giving tangerines during the Chinese New Year or Spring Festival was a sign of friendship that brought good fortune. We spoke haltingly about many subjects. Most of the time my brother spoke to them in Chinese in an animated fashion. Uncle Lou's wife turned to me and said, "Stepmother," so I understood he was talking about his relationship with his stepfamily. It was not the first time I had witnessed family matters discussed openly. Perhaps my brother was trying to justify to them his desire to go to America.

It was not long before Uncle Lou brought a doctor into the room, whom I believe he had called earlier. This young man had a husky voice, was of average height, and had a pleasant and attentive demeanor. He sat next to me in his opened white lab coat and said, "I am a surgeon specializing in the thorax; you know heart and lungs."

"I understand. I lost a baby boy of three months who was born with a heart defect. He had Tricuspid Atresia with transposition of the main vessels," I said, trying to level with him on his own grounds.

"Oh, I am sorry to hear this. How long ago did this happen?"

"Over seven years ago. So it has been a long time," I said.

"You know, I am due to go to America for studies in a hospital in California, but I haven't heard from my sponsors. Do you know a place named Corona?"

"I believe I have heard the name of this city. You speak English very well. Where did you learn it?" I asked, enjoying my conversation with this enthusiastic young fellow.

"You see, during the Cultural Revolution, I was sent to the country to take care of the peasants; in my spare time, I learned English. My wife and child live nearby. I would like very much for you to come over for dinner. Only we have a very small place. You know that every family in China can only afford one or two rooms," he said, apologetic of his situation.

"I will be glad to come one day," I said, pleased with his invitation.

"Now I have to leave and return to the ward," he said, shaking my hands with a slight bow.

It was time for dinner, so Uncle Lou and his wife led us down the hall and through a glass door that opened to a small light-filled room with one round table. Uncle Lou's wife brought in the food—a poached fish and some vegetables and rice—apologizing for the meal's simplicity. I enjoyed every bite.

We returned to the sitting room after dinner. A woman dressed in a black robe and slippers was strolling outside the hallway near the door. Uncle Lou invited her to come in. He said, "She was a very famous actress and teacher."

She denied it with a smile, swerving her body on her slippers in a graceful way. She had a very expressive face, and immediately, the group engaged in a lively conversation. As I watched them talk, I thought, "How wrong it is to think of the Chinese as passive and inexpressive people." I found them to be very talkative and at times rather exuberant. Given the opportunity, they would engage in endless conversations with one another, telling stories, anecdotes, ways to do this or that, and of course, gossiping. I wished I knew their language so I could catch some of their humor, and even some of their sarcasm. Because of this barrier, I found myself sitting on the outside, a world unto myself.

It was dark outside when we left the hospital. Uncle Lou and his wife accompanied us to the bus stop. I believe he was there for some tests and on the whole seemed to be very fit. Every time we were about to board a bus, it was too crowded for us to get on. We chose to walk to the next stop instead of waiting. Along the way, I gave them a living English lesson, naming everything in sight, from roots, to twigs, and shadows cast by streetlamps. The road in this part of town was rather deserted, and the air was fresh and filled with the aroma of flowers as we were near the mountains. I enjoyed this cold brisk walk in one of the more serene places in Hangzhou. At the foot of the hill, on the road's other side, I saw a house that might have been the former mansion of a rich family, but now was occupied by several families and had fallen into disrepair, a sign that luxury was rare in a Communist country.

Chapter 8

❁

Art Exhibit and More Conversations with My Father

Mid-morning, I heard my brother's short rapid footsteps along the walk near the kitchen. He appeared at the doorway and smiled. After he hung his black umbrella and black vinyl bag on the nail behind the door, we had a cup of hot tea. The weather was still damp and grim. As I wondered what we might do today, he informed me of our plans.

"You like go to art exhibit downtown? Chinese famous artists' pictures."

"Yes, I would love to go to the Chinese art exhibit very much. It should be very interesting," I said, enthusiastic about his plan.

The art exhibit was held in the Hall of the People, a very spacious modern building situated at the back of a wide-open square, where I often saw youngsters playing soccer. Wide-open spaces are few and far between for Hangzhou's youngsters, who live in very crowded conditions, so it was not surprising for me to see young people at play there.

We turned out to be the only visitors at the exhibit that morning. Three artists who were sitting on a ledge by the window approached us and introduced themselves with great eagerness. Among them was a woman artist, whom I thought wrongly at that time did the large oil crayon drawings hung in the hall's first section. These were emotionally powerful paintings based on "The New Year's Sacrifice," a famous Chinese short story by Lu Xun. They depicted the life and suffering of a servant girl who lost two husbands, her young son, and later her job and life due to fate and others' inability to understand her. The most striking picture of this series was that of a hollow-faced woman screaming in horror as she was engulfed by blue flames, symbolic of her hell and her pain's abyss. She was running homeless and gave her life stretched out in the snow.

While we were looking at the pictures, one of the Chinese gentlemen made it his job to explain painstakingly each picture to us, or should I say to my brother since I did not understand anything in Chinese. Consequently, I was impatient to

~ 247 ~

move on and happy to be escorted to the second set of pictures behind the partition. Later, I found out this man was Qiu Sha, the very artist who had painted and drawn all these pictures, illustrating two famous stories written by the celebrated Chinese writer, Lu Xun. The bulk of the paintings in this section were pencil and charcoal drawings of a villager in trouble with his landlords. Through these pictures, I had an opportunity to see some typical country scenery, life within households and particular village's streets. I was struck by the contrast of Americans' modern way of life with fast cars and self-sufficient homes compared to that of more rural China. Art here did not evolve into abstractions of space and color; the pictures told the story of human suffering and the need for mercy and forgiveness toward the simple and downgraded. Perhaps this art was the kind the Communists liked to display, but for me, it had a human appeal. It showed the wantonness of life and the human pathos for those who are held in its grip, awaiting some kind of deliverance, whether it be food, knowledge, or respect.

At home, I sat once again in the kitchen, waiting for dinner. My father came over from his room to inquire about my day. He sat across from me at the square table by the window, placing his cigarette in a white plastic holder and lighting it with the disposable lighter I had given him. He wore thin, knitted gloves, for it was cold, and his blue woolen suit with breast pockets, the wrinkled maroon scarf loosely looped around his neck, and a moth-eaten brimless brown cap. The hot tea we drank was comforting on this brisk damp day. I had noticed earlier that my father's shoes were worn right through in parts, so I said to him, "I'd like to take you to the city and buy you some shoes."

"No, it is not necessary. You see, I have such an unsteady walk that I need these comfortable shoes," he assured me.

I did not expect to be met with resistance on the question of buying new things, but I was. Then he told me he was unable to set the digital watch I had given him and went to his room to get it. When he returned, I toyed with the watch for a while, reading the directions over and over again, but I was unable to set it either; it just would not stay in one mode long enough, no matter how many buttons I pushed. I was so disappointed that the first gift I gave my father had to be a malfunctioning watch. I said to him, "Please, let me take you to the city and buy you a reliable Chinese watch."

"No, never mind; you take it back with you and then give it to me when I come. It is good that it is so; it is one more reason for me to visit you in your home," he said enjoying his conclusion.

"All right, you will be coming," I replied. "Do you remember me as a child in Shanghai? I remember when you took my brother and me to the zoo. We boarded a bus and you prevented me from sticking my arms out the window. On our way home, you carried me on your shoulders," I said, trying to find the bond that had existed between us long ago.

Again, I saw that sad expression in my father's face, as he said, "Yes, I remember you in Shanghai, but I did not visit you very often, so we spent very little time together."

"Do you remember my stepfather?" I asked, still trying to find common ground. "Do you know he did not treat me well?"

"Yes, I remember your stepfather. He was a sort of philosopher who drew pictures."

I expected my father to express some pity for my sufferings, but in this case, he did not, so I continued, "I wonder what made my mother choose such a man; he was twenty years older than she was."

"I know why she married him. It was her good heart. She felt sorry for an old man," he said.

"Did you ever meet the Russian family the Von Ulrichs? I believe, Lizochka, the mother, introduced my stepfather to Mommy," I said, probing his memory.

"No, I don't remember this family," he said, trying to search for something about which he knew nothing.

"Well, I became very close to this family. They left China in 1953 and came to live at our riding school for a few months. I was eight then, and Teddy, the youngest daughter, was sixteen, and we became very good friends. She was a young lady of extraordinary beauty and poetry. Her blond hair was long and silky and it framed her rounded features with her expressive blue eyes. What appealed most to me about Teddy was her sunny personality and her insatiable lust for life. During the day, we took long walks by the beach, witnessing some beautiful sunsets. We talked, laughed, prayed, and played, while we were always filled with great anticipation for the future. At the time, she shared with me things she had written in her diaries and I was sworn to secrecy. At nights, she would tuck me in bed with a new fairy tale each day, all told from memory. Some of these stories I can still remember vividly."

After a long pause, he said, "So you listened to all those stories flat on your back, just before you went to sleep?"

I laughed and said, "Yes, I did. Do you know that I just heard from Teddy last year; she lives in England now. I got her address from her brother Cyril who lives in Toronto and whom I met two years ago, after an absence of more than twenty-five years. The last time I had seen him was on his wedding day. He is the same person, only older, grayer, and with a twenty-one-year old son."

Then I continued, "Living by the sea was wonderful. When I was young, I used to run barefoot on the sand, collecting wildflowers and seashells. When I went to the boarding school, I still could gaze at the sea because my school was nestled on a hill overlooking the Atlantic. I often wondered if you and my brother were waiting for me on the other side."

"The waves came and went and you had no word from your father and brother," my father replied, adding, "You have had a very poetic childhood by the sea. You should write a book and gather all the beautiful experiences, and make it a gift to mankind. You see, it would be a very interesting story for people to read—a daughter meeting her father after thirty-two years. Not everyone has the opportunity to see China as you have. Most people who come to visit stay in the luxury hotels. But you have been living with us, sharing our food, our home, and moving freely about the people. No foreigner can do this. You are privileged."

His command for me to write this book was more than a passing fancy. It was an exhortation. During my stay, he would often comment on the book I was going to write. I was deeply honored because he believed in me and in my talent for writing. I think he was the first person I took seriously in this regard.

I continued my conversation with him, saying, "Do you know that when I was fourteen I wanted to be a religious sister? I was drawn by the beauty of the Gospels and the example of a sister at school who treated me like a daughter. And did you know that Tony wanted to be a priest, and that he spent five years in a seminary?"

"Ah! I know now why you and Tony got married. You wanted to be a sister and Tony wanted to be a priest. Somewhere in the heavens, your desires met and you got married," he said, giving me one of his precious conclusions.

"It is not simple with me and Tony. We have had some terrible fights. There was a time I thought of divorce," I told him, trying to be honest.

The word "divorce" had a terrible clang for him, so he said, "Oh, not divorce. It would be bad for the children," he said, fearing that the cycle of discord would touch yet one more generation.

Then, he concluded, "I think Tony loves you more than you love him."

It was true I felt that Tony and I were wrapped up in different worlds, unable to reach one another. When my father spoke of love, I was silent, knowing full well my internal struggle. At times, I felt Tony could not understand me; his world was more important to him, and I just drifted, awaiting my destiny to unfold. I had hope that we might still be able to touch one another.

I wondered when I would be able to call my father "Dad." Somehow, I couldn't bring myself to this level of familiarity. We had been apart for too long; we had shared so little of my thirty-seven years. As I sat across from my father, I had a feeling of proximity, but not intimacy. Our exchanges had been mainly verbal. How could he know me well—all my struggles and growing pains, and all that gave me joy and sorrow? To some extent, he continued to be an outsider looking in. And yet, at times, I thought he understood. I remembered he cared for me in a special way the first few days when I was sick; he watched my comings and goings with great interest, and he believed in my talent.

I finally said to him, "You know, I don't find you peculiar as some people had told me you were." (He had a reputation among the aunts and uncles of being an eccentric.)

He turned to me, stooping lower than he normally did, and said, "You don't find me peculiar because we have a special rapport, which is not possible to describe in words."

What was his peculiarity? He drank at times, he prayed a great deal, but what made him different was his faith. I think I met him at this level.

He felt uneasy listening to the difficulties I'd had in my life, yet I felt I had to share them with him, so I said, "It was not so easy for me to grow up. When I left Brazil, it was devastating for me; I had to leave behind everything I loved. My adolescence was filled with turmoil. Unable to reconcile myself with my life, I had to seek help. It was then that a priest helped me; he was like an angel of light illuminating the darkness of my world. He is still a friend of the family's, and on occasion, he comes over for dinner."

My father became interested in my priest friend, and said, "Would I meet this friend of yours at your home when I come?"

"Yes, you will. He is a very wise and interesting man. He is also a philosopher who has written some books on love and ethics," I said, elaborating on my friend.

"So it was very hard for you," my father repeated monosyllabically.

"Yes, it was also tough to lose my son. I have a story to tell you. On the way to the cemetery, I saw a seagull flying overhead and I heard a voice pierce me that said, 'I'm free.' I was sure then that it was my son Paul. This experience managed to uplift me," I said as if thinking out loud.

He felt my pain and said, "Your little baby's death was hard on you. But you will see him again; he is like an angel in heaven."

I began to feel a filial bond with my father as a result of these conversations. He had been there when I was born; he had rocked me in a cradle when I cried, and now I had come back to him. It had been necessary for me to come back so I could touch ground. For so long I had felt like a pebble cast aside, not really belonging to anyone. Now I did not feel so alone. I had come from a pile of rocks on the beach with similar traits. I was my father's daughter. Slowly, this realization was dawning on me.

Chapter 9

=========== ❀ ===========

The Bathhouse, Excursion to West Lake, and Daily Routine

The family compound had no bath facility. Apparently, a community toilet existed, but I never saw where it was, and I didn't care to find out since I had my own chamber pot. On Saturday when we visited the neighborhood bathhouse, it was raining heavily. The family persuaded my father to go, so he held onto my brother while I walked with Su Juan behind them. With opened umbrellas, we walked along the broken sidewalk, avoiding many puddles. The traffic was heavy on the street with buses, bicycles, and pedestrians, passing storefronts, factories, and dwellings. I noticed my father's unsteady gait, a sort of shuffle that swayed from side to side, with a bent posture so his body was ahead of his feet. I was glad he clutched firmly onto my brother's arms, thereby preventing an accident.

The bathhouse was located in a one-story stucco building of considerable age. It was set at a distance from the street, creating an ideal location for vendors and parked bikes, and for young men to congregate and talk. We went up some steps and Su Juan bought a couple of tickets at a booth in the lobby.

Around the corner was the ladies' bath. We went through a door into a vestibule and again through another door draped in heavy vinyl curtains that separated the ladies' bath from the hall. Inside, I saw a large number of Chinese women dressing or undressing for the bath. The room was lined with reclining beds with bare mattresses, which were assigned to different customers, and used for ladies to dress themselves and their children. The floors were bare cement and the windows were set high, shedding a considerable amount of light. At the end of this large room were some wooden covered bins where we could store our clothes. The attendant locked them with a key, a procedure that seemed unnecessary since I had been told the Chinese were so honest, especially toward foreigners. Some very good-humored ladies ran the place and were always kidding around with each other and talking to the customers.

We took all our clothes off, except for the last two inner garments. It was an endless procedure because I had at least four or five layers of clothing due to the dampness and the cold. We walked immediately to the adjacent shower room with two open showerheads and sinks that had no plumbing; the water would run through the hole to a cemented groove on the floor. Beyond the short wall where the sinks were attached was another shower room where the showers were enclosed in booths. The place was steaming and wet and much darker than the dressing room. I watched a woman inside, scrubbing and cleaning with a garden hose and brush. At the center on the cement floor, I saw a naked child seated on a stool inside a wooden tub, playing with the water. The mother had taken a shower, so she wiped herself with a wet towel and then proceeded to bathe the child.

The only time I thought I was faster than Su Juan was at the shower. After washing and rinsing my hair and body once, I was done. She practiced the habit of the Chinese women of washing themselves three or four times with the damp towel before they were finished. When I shared my shampoo and conditioner with her, she gave me a grateful smile. I also sprinkled some marvelously scented talcum on her, which she accepted with some reluctance.

After the shower, we felt so refreshed. As we were about to step out onto the street, Su Juan's mother came hurriedly with a pair of galoshes for me to wear. She lived nearby so she directed us to her house. We went across the street and again through the narrow corridor that led us to a coarse wooden door that opened into the hall of her domain. A precarious stairway led to the two bedrooms on the second floor. I sat in the living-dining room that also served as a bedroom. A big window opened to the river where I could see the bridge I had crossed earlier. It was in fact the Grand Canal and a busy thoroughfare. My brother told me that boats tooted their horns all night so he had a hard time sleeping here. As I sat by the window, I felt in some way quite alone, but at the same time very privileged to be sharing my family's intimate life without any restraint.

Immediately, Su Juan's mother placed a cup of hot tea before me, as well as a heap of roasted sunflower seeds in their husks and other nuts. Before I could drink my tea, Su Juan's sister Sho Bei, the one who tended my two-year-old nephew Yun, took me to the upper room so I could dry my hair with an electric dryer. The room had a large canopy bed with two neatly folded silk comforters, and embroidered ruffled pillows. Against the wall opposite the door was a stack of trunks. Under the window was an old desk with a wobbly swivel chair, and next to the door was a dark dresser with mirror. Su Juan's sister pulled over the swivel chair for me to sit on, and there I sat for a good twenty minutes drying my hair. As I went down, I noticed that the next room also had a canopy bed and trunks against the wall.

While I sat in the living room sipping the hot tea, my father came in with my brother. He too was refreshed after the bath. He said to me, "It is not always possible for me to go to the bathhouse. I need to go with someone, so I seldom go." The family had complained to me that my father would often refuse to go, so his going today was a rare event, perhaps in my honor. He too got some hot tea and began to talk with Su Juan's father, who did not often speak to anyone else. Su Juan's father was the only man in China I do not remember smiling. He sat across from me in a quiet manner and wore a black Russian style hat with the brim flaps tied in the center, forming a dome. He stood in contrast with his wife, who was an airy effusive person. She came in, waving some tickets in her hands and uttering words I could not understand. Later, I found out these were theater tickets for a Chinese show she had purchased for the family to attend. She was a very affable person who always talked Chinese with me, whether or not I understood it. She had slight protruding teeth and her short hair was parted in the middle and held back with bobby pins. She always wore a full-length gray apron over her dark blue clothes. Her warmth more than made up for her comely appearance. She was totally immersed in the family's affairs and looked after everyone's welfare.

Back home, I sat in the kitchen, watching Su Juan cook dinner in the wok over the hot coals. She was cooking a whole fish and glazing it with a soy sauce sugar mixture. Then she prepared stir-fried Chinese celery. The rice had already been cooked in an earthen crock that was placed in a covered wicker basket. I sat in this cold kitchen with frayed windows and shabby walls, somewhat dismayed at the simplicity of it all. I had been used to the comforts of home with soft couches, appliances, and heat, but here I was seated in a folding chair around a table with one other chair and a couple of stools, watching my sister-in-law draw water from a barrel, wash clothes in a basin, and store food in a homemade cabinet. How could such disparity exist in the same world where men have reached the moon and machines govern their very thinking? And yet it was the same human world, machines or no machines. I found in these people's hearts the same human longings, anxieties, hopes, jealousies, ambitions, displays of petty selfishness, hard work, and laziness. The human element was here in all its shame and glory.

The next day was Sunday so the whole family was free to go on an excursion. Su Juan and my niece had no school. We took a bus downtown, and from there, we walked to the banks of the West Lake. Then we boarded a ferry with standing room only to cross the lake toward the Island of Little Oceans situated in the middle of the lake. This artificial island was built circa 1600; it has embankments of flowering trees and crooked bridges suspended over its many ponds; in fact, three-fifths of the island's area is water, with many water lilies and lotus plants. Here we strolled unhurriedly, taking a great many pictures. The rains had stopped. It was beginning to be a lovely day with only a few hazy clouds overhead. After crossing one of the typical Chinese zigzag bridges, we sat in a gazebo overlooking one of the inlets. Su Juan had brought a plastic bag with nuts and candy, so we munched away, resting our not-so-weary feet. Here my brother met an acquaintance of his with whom he had taught middle school. They chatted amiably while the man's wife chased her two young children, who were very active. She guarded them so diligently to prevent them from falling in the water. Once again, I observed the tenderness the parents bestowed on their children. They tolerated their antics with much understanding.

In the middle of the island, I met a large group of foreign tourists with expensive cameras, fur coats, and jewelry. They looked like rich Americans, and they stood in stark contrast to the simply clad Chinese with their old-fashioned box cameras. One woman became rather incensed with the pressing crowd from whom we could not escape, even in this lovely place. My brother took a picture of my niece and me looking through an ornate circular opening in a wall.

From here, we went to a pavilion where they served tea and other aperitifs. Su Juan purchased four bowls of a lotus root porridge, a gooey substance eaten hot with coarse, crystallized sugar sprinkled on it. It tasted like cornstarch, but it was comforting in this chilly day. Then we walked along the embankments as if we were seeing the world for the first time. Some of the barren trees were opening their first buds, some pink, some white. The pools reflected the sun's shimmering rays—the first time the sun had shown its face for days. Amid all this beauty, I still felt like a stranger to this world and to my family. How lovely was nature here, and how difficult the people's daily lives. Few Chinese had personal gardens; they lived in crowded quarters with very little space to own pools and plants, but here in these public gardens, they could wander at ease and forget for a while their daily grind.

When I took pictures with my sister-in-law and brother, I always made sure she was next to my brother. I wanted to assure her that I had come not to separate them, but to unite them. So we stepped onto a rock in the water and I stood behind them with my hands over their shoulders while my niece Qion snapped the picture. She was such a gay, intelligent, helpful girl, with the doleful eyes of a dreamer. She had a wide mouth and pretty teeth and she was always smiling. Many have said that she looks like me. Perhaps there was a faint resemblance because she had my fat cheeks and the eyebrows I shared with my father. However, I have a small heart-shaped mouth and my eyes are not so happy.

On the island's opposite side from where we had arrived, and where many wooden boats were docked, three black poles were in the water with windows built on their knobs. At night, a candle would be placed inside these lanterns and the light's reflection on the water would give the impression of moonlight, which must have created a romantic scene with all the surrounding pagodas and weeping willows, but we were not about to wait for sunset to witness this phenomenon. The afternoon became hazy as we took the small, motorized boat back across the lake. The boat had padded seats and was operated by a woman who wore a heavy black vinyl covering because it could be very cold on the lake. I enjoyed this slow ride across the water where I could almost touch the lake's surface. It was good to be in a wide-open space far from the pressing crowd.

Once on shore, we boarded a bus, which to my surprise was rather empty; however, it filled to capacity when we approached the downtown area. My brother excused himself to go to the main post office to retrieve a parcel I had sent him three months ago. Su Juan, Qion, and I did some window-shopping through some silk and artist supply stores. Su Juan indicated to me that this was a good opportunity to buy some silk. I had forgotten my glasses, however, so we left the buying of silk for another day. We did go hunting for the cloth children shoes I had seen all over China. In a department store with cement floors and wooden counters, we found upstairs a couple of pairs of red corduroy tennis shoes that I thought would be fine for my daughters. My sister-in-law insisted on paying for these, and I had no recourse to convince her otherwise. It would be her gift to my children.

On our way to the bus stop along Hangzhou's main street, we went into a shoe store in search of women's silk slippers. All these Chinese stores looked old-fashioned, and one had to ask for the items from the salespeople who worked behind the counters; this process became quite tedious since the counters were very crowded. Nevertheless, there I bought four pairs of silk slippers of various colors, and again, I was prevented from paying for them. From then on, I hardly dared purchase anything from fear my relatives would pay for it. I hoped to make up for it by giving my brother some money for all the expenses they had incurred on my account.

Shortly after we returned to the family compound, my brother walked into the kitchen with the open parcel. He'd had to pay fifty-seven yuans duty fee, a month's salary for them. My mother had sent them seventy dollars for this purpose and I had given my brother 150 dollars earlier. Everyone was very eager to find out what was inside. As we were opening the package, my father arrived in the kitchen. He was also pleased with the gift box. I had put in mostly toiletry items such as soap, toothpaste, skin creams, pens, chocolate, and small plastic games. My father only took a can of shaving cream and a razor with blades. He said, "I usually shave myself with a switchblade. Few can master it nowadays." My brother was so amazed with the foam that came out of the can that he began shaving himself right away, looking at himself in the small mirror hanging on the wall by the window, and washing himself over an enamel basin held in a bamboo stand between the ceramic water barrel and the dish/food cabinet. Su Juan locked away all the other items in the bureau in the bedroom for safekeeping, another sign of her thrifty and resourceful nature. Earlier during my stay, she had bought a jar of jam for my breakfast, but lo and behold, thirteen-year-old Qion got ahold of it and ate the whole jar. I heard them argue about this incident into the evening, which brought a smile to my face.

I had been in China now for two weeks. At times, it seemed like an eternity! Everyone had been so kind to me, and yet I did feel alone. I missed the comforts of home, I missed my family, and above all, I missed the freedom to go where I pleased and the convenience of being understood by those around me. Here the simplest expressions could not be shared. One time my sister-in-law had lunch with me in the kitchen while my brother was at art school. We could not utter one intelligible sentence to each other. It was like being locked in my own thoughts. To alleviate the strain, she got up and went to the next-door neighbor whose daughter was a schoolteacher who spoke and taught English. This young woman came over and wrote on a piece of paper some of the thoughts Su Juan wanted to relate to me. This is what she said through translation, "I didn't know Wang Qian had asked his mother for money to attend the art course at the Institute. I did not know about the duty money." As it turned out, it was my father who had written to my mother about the duty fees. Su Juan turned to me and exclaimed, "I didn't know" in Russian, which I understood because of my brush with the language earlier in my childhood. I understood her concern because I think I would have felt the same way. It bothered her to see my brother so dependent on his mother. She was guarding her sense of pride and independence. Our discovery of each other had created a number of emotional obstacles that had to be overcome.

One time, I noticed Su Juan's vivacious sense of competitiveness. My brother and I were sitting at the kitchen table talking when Su Juan came in with a piece of paper. She was attempting to write something in English and asked my brother how to form a certain letter. I was surprised she did not know the alphabet and she noticed my dismay. She challenged me by giving me a Chinese character to copy. I did well only because my brother had taught me to make the strokes going from the outside to the inside. I could only copy since I did not know any Chinese characters. This lesson taught me how much I took for granted. Su Juan had taken Russian in high school but never had formal lessons in English. What was second nature to me was not necessarily so to her.

One morning, while I was in the bedroom writing a letter to Tony about my situation in China, I heard a knock on the door. It was Uncle Lou's wife with some of her friends. I ushered them into the bedroom and we sat around the table. Soon I found out that the gentleman whom she brought was a doctor specializing in gerontology. He was on his way to Canton to deliver a medical paper. In about three years, he would be joining a fellow doctor in the U.S. In the meantime, he was very interested in acquiring a good knowledge of English. The lady next to him was his wife. She looked like a young schoolgirl. They had brought an English textbook and some empty tape cassettes, and asked me, "Would you be so kind and tape the lessons so as to help me with my English?" At first I didn't understand what they wanted, so I began to tape the first lesson right there. Later, I understood that I could take my time in taping the whole book. My father came to the door, but when he saw that I had guests, he went back to his room. The doctor, a cheerful robust man with curly hair, told me he wanted to have me over for dinner as soon as he came back from Canton, but I never saw him again.

I did the taping in the mornings while everyone was working or in school. When I woke up around eight, I could hear the neighbor's radio bellowing a popular Chinese song from Hong Kong sung by a woman with a beautiful voice. I became very familiar with the inflections and tone of these songs. It made me feel that I was indeed in China. I would change quickly from my flannel pajamas and sweater into my clothes to avoid the morning chill; then I folded the comforters neatly on the bed and stacked up the embroidered pillows. Next, I went outside and into the kitchen to brush my teeth and wash my face with the ice-cold water I drew from the drum with an enamel mug. The procedure was refreshing, and I let the water run into the gravel ditch between the cement walk. Su Juan had prepared my milk and teacup. All I had to do was add some hot water from the many thermoses on top of a narrow table in the kitchen's corner. Sometimes she prepared some fried bread filled with bean paste, the Chinese French toast that was very tasty. Most of the time, I ate cakes or cookies left on the kitchen table.

One morning, I did some washing. I could not bear to watch Su Juan bend over a basin after dinner washing everyone's clothes. The lady next door, when she saw me washing clothes, came over and brought me a bucket of water from the courtyard faucet. She said something in Chinese I could not understand. She was a slight woman with delicate features who had been a schoolteacher formerly. I thanked her profusely for the water and continued with my chores. After I had washed my clothes, I hung them out to dry on a rack built outside the kitchen window facing the canal. I had to climb on the table and then onto the wide windowsill to put my clothes on bamboo hangers that opened into a cross shape with clips on the ends. The rack was high up near the roof, so I had to suspend the clothes with a pole. It took days for the clothes to dry on account of the dampness.

My neighbor's daughter, the middle school English teacher, came over sometimes in the evening to talk with me. Her English was very good. One day she asked me, "Do you think China is poor?" to which I replied, "Yes, I think China is poor compared to the United States." My answer bewildered her. She then presented me with a few books about famous cities in China. I liked this girl very much; she had a gentle and pleasing nature. Hearing that I was taping some lessons for others, she asked me whether I could also tape a few stories for her. She told me I had a golden voice. With this compliment, I was ready to oblige. Besides, I was glad to have something to do in the mornings. Writing in my diary was a rather impossible task for me at this point. My emotions were not sorted out, and I needed some time for reflection. I had to absorb so much in such a short period of time. The dampness had penetrated my very bones. Some days, nothing would make me feel warm.

Thus I began taping the stories given to me. One story was "The Necklace" by Guy de Maupassant. It was the story of a woman who spent her life trying to pay for a pearl necklace she had borrowed and lost, only to find out the necklace had not been made of real pearls. Another story I taped was about Karl Marx' habits when he lived in an apartment in England. I began to realize that the focus of learning in the schools was about the plight of the poor. Although, many stories were about "The Four Modernizations," the goals of Deng Xiaoping, who had come to power in 1978, but they had been introduced as early as 1963. Zhou Enlai in 1975 had made another pitch for "The Four Modernizations: Agriculture, Industry, National Defense, and Science and Technology." I found this focus in the literature and education of the Chinese to be very interesting and understandable, considering much of the poverty I witnessed.

Chapter 10

Sharing More with My Father; the Neighborhood and Letters

Only during the first week of my visit did my father come to see me in the mornings. One morning he came with a copy of Theodore Dreiser's book *Sister Carrie*. He had underlined the most important parts in red and began to read some of them to me. One of the passages read:

> Oh blind strivings of the human heart! Onward, onward, it saith, and where beauty leads there it follows. Whether it be the tinkle of a lone sheep bell o'er some quilt landscape, or the glimmer of beauty in sylvan places or the show of soul in some passing eye, the heart knows and makes answer, following. It is when the feet weary and hope seems vain that the heartaches and longing arise. Know, then, that for you is neither surfeit nor contentment. In your rocking chair, by your window dreaming, shall you dream alone. In your rocking chair, by your window shall you dream such happiness as you may never feel.

This passage was one of my father's favorites. It shed light on my father's personality and experience of life. He had seen the glory of youth but had many of his dreams broken, one by one. Now in his old age, he was confined to his room with plenty of time to wonder about life's meaning. Hopefully, he would not be dreaming alone, like Ames in Dreiser's story, but in unison with many who loved him. He wanted to lend me this book, but I told him I could easily get it at the library when I got home. He did, however, present me with a book he had in his room, Dostoyevsky's *The Insulted and the Humiliated*, which he later autographed simply: "Father gives Marianne for memory! Fu Shih." Was he telling me something about his life and experiences during the Cultural Revolution with the gift of this book? I don't know. It was perhaps just a favorite book that embodied his views of life.

Most of the time, my father came to visit me during lunchtime when my brother was there or at dinnertime. We sat across from each other in the dimly lit kitchen, talking about the many books we had read in common, such as *The Count of Monte Cristo, The Scarlet Letter, Jane Eyre,* and *Gone with the Wind.* He preferred to read novels in English, although he spoke fluent German. He said, "You see, English has a musical quality that I enjoy. For instance, the word *longing...*(he said it slowly) really does sound like *longing....*" Sometimes he read a Chinese translation of a novel that he obtained from the man who rented and sold books for pennies in front of the compound. He liked the Chinese version of *The Count of Monte Cristo* because in it Mercedes, the main heroine, is reunited with the Count.

I said to him, "Here you are in your little room in touch with the whole world through your books."

To which he replied, "Like a monk in a cottage."

I was surprised he did not know any of the famous movie actors and actresses of the last thirty years. He said, "Never mind, never mind, we will live to be one hundred," meaning there was plenty of time to catch up with information. He was surprised when he heard that the price of gold had doubled the year before (1981). These financial reports interested him.

One morning, Su Juan's sister, Sho Bei, came to pick me up to take pictures around the neighborhood. It was a brilliant day—perfect for snapshots! As we walked along the main avenue, the street was alive with picturesque scenes of typical Chinese life—a visual feast! A stream of pushcarts went by heavily loaded with sacks of grain. The men were bent over, with rope strapped to their shoulders, and their hands on the handle, straining to pull the weight. A woman was seated on a stool on the sidewalk, dressed in a blue polka dot padded jacket, sunning her baby, who was also colorfully clad with quilted clothes, sweater, and knitted red bonnet. She smiled pleasantly at me, and was the picture of health and happiness. Over the main bridge, I was able to take a number of pictures of the canal with its houseboats, sampans (flat wooden boats), canoes, and irregular houses that lined the banks. In the market district, I watched people buy vegetables such as Chinese celery, radishes, and spinach from open baskets and carry away live chickens and ducks, either by their legs, or tied securely to their bikes in a shopping net. Of course, the streets were crowded with bicycles and people. When we went back over the bridge, a man was having trouble pulling his oversized load across to the other side because of the incline. He repeatedly had to shout a warning to the oncoming bicycles. At a corner, a group of men were sitting idle in their pedicabs waiting for customers. I noticed that many of the vendors were young girls who wore their hair in braids and had protective sleeves over their padded jackets, and some wore aprons. Along the main road, I took pictures of storefronts, some of which had a rather gloomy appearance. I saw a row of meats drying on a clothesline, and bicycles and carts filled with cardboard parked outside while customers and passersby glanced at me with curiosity. At a street corner, a man was selling an assortment of sweets and candy. In an alley between two buildings, a woman was roasting sunflower seeds in a huge wok. I went into a couple of fabric stores, but I didn't buy anything since I was waiting for Su Juan's help.

We ended up at Su Juan's mother's house. There I saw my little nephew Yun, who was under his grandmother's care while Su Juan taught school. He was treated with great tenderness; Su Juan's mother and sister talked to him all day long. I could see he was a very happy boy who liked to run and dance around the room, repeating gleeful sounds. He knew forty Chinese characters, even though he had just turned two. Grandma took the flashcards out of a drawer and placed them in her apron pocket. Yun would proudly recite each word without looking at the picture as she showed him each card. I believe she taught him in this manner all day long. I was amazed because my daughter Sara, who was three, could not yet recognize all the letters of the alphabet. Once again, I had hot tea, candy, and sunflower seeds. Grandma talked to me constantly, and I nodded pleasantly as if I understood what she was saying. I think she told me China's entire history; I just wasn't sure. As we were leaving, Su Juan's mother gave her daughter a large fish in a basket to take to our house. Such exchanges of food were customary among relatives, my father told me; only it was a good idea to give something in return the next time. On the way home, I met Su Juan's best friend and fellow teacher, who had with her two young girls. I recognized her because of the gap in her front teeth and her warm personality. They obligingly posed for pictures.

During the time I was in China, I received letters from virtually every relative alive. Aunt Pei De from Hunan Province and her daughter Lou Ming sent me greetings once more via my father. She also mailed me some tangerines that I unfortunately forgot in my bag on my way to Hangzhou. Aunt Pei Yan, a medical doctor in Shanghai who witnessed my birth in Chungking in 1944, also sent me a letter and invited me to spend the weekend with her just before my return to the States. Kwang Yi sent me a letter from Beijing, telling me she had enjoyed my visit and that she thought China was my first motherland because I had been born here. My father's cousin sent him a letter congratulating him on our reunion. Another letter came from Uncle Fu Ming, my father's only brother who lived in Nanjing and worked as a mechanical engineer. He was six years younger than my father, and had also studied in the same university in Shanghai. In his letter, he announced he would arrive on the second Wednesday I would be in Hangzhou after his physical exam and treatment in Shanghai. He'd had a cancerous lung removed the previous year by Aunt Pei Yan's husband, Liu Tzu, who was a surgeon in a prominent hospital in Shanghai. Uncle Fu Ming got special treatment there because he was family.

Chapter 11

━━━━━ ❁ ━━━━━

Uncle Fu Ming's Arrival, Cultural Revolution Revelations, and My Father's Conviviality

U ncle Fu Ming sent us two telegrams announcing the time of his arrival on Wednesday, February 24, 1982, so we were able to obtain two tickets for entry into the train depot. As my brother and I approached the train station, I found it interesting to observe the people around the square in front of the station, many huddled around their luggage. The pedicabs had their own area, but unfortunately, they had very few customers. When I told my brother I wanted to ride in one of them, he said, "No, too expensive and too slow."

It was already getting dark. My brother finished his cigarette and tossed it to the curb since it was time to go inside the depot. The train from Shanghai was already approaching. I watched the passenger compartments pass us rapidly, wondering which one my uncle was in. To our surprise, Uncle Fu Ming came out of a compartment close to us. He was a slight man with a brisk walk. He wore a Chinese green padded jacket with the typical cloth buttons, a gray scarf, and a Mao cap. He smiled at me, peering through his glasses, and immediately assumed a very natural demeanor. I don't remember whether we embraced or shook hands, but we did greet each other amiably, and I could see he was excited to meet me after so long a time.

The three of us walked in a rapid pace toward the bus stop while my brother and uncle engaged in an animated conversation. Uncle Fu Ming was one of my brother's favorite people. I, on the other hand, hardly knew him. I did not know what to say; once more, I felt the strain of meeting a new relative. I asked him a few questions in English, which he understood and spoke well. He had a hoarse voice because of his lung operation, and I was concerned for him when we boarded a crowded bus. Yet, he was in good spirits and immediately began a conversation with passengers in the back when a seat opened up. I think he told them my story as they smiled at me in amazement.

Soon we descended the bus and walked along the darkened street. My uncle apologetically remarked, "The conditions in China are very poor. It isn't so in America?" When I asked him whether he had traveled abroad, he said, "In the '50s I was in Berlin, and in the '60s, I was in Moscow, representing China. I enjoyed these trips very much." Before long, we were in front of a humble-looking local hotel. It had no lobby; the door that led to the stairway opened to the street. We went upstairs where we encountered an attendant in a white lab coat at a desk on the first landing. She kept all the keys under lock in her desk. This hotel was only three yuans per night compared to the twenty-four yuans I had paid at the Overseas Hotel. My uncle had to show his identification and permit papers to obtain a room. At the time, one could not travel freely in China; an employer or the local authorities had to issue a permit. The attendant gave my uncle a key and he asked us to wait for him at the landing.

While we were waiting, a poor peasant man came in looking for a room. He was rejected because he did not have the necessary papers. Without much of a plea, he left dejected, but he smiled at us, resigned with this unfavorable condition. One could not buy a bus, train, or plane ticket or obtain a hotel room without the prized permit. Nevertheless, the train stations were always super-crowded, and multitudes of people did travel.

My father's compound wasn't too far away. After we entered the initial corridors that led to my brother's place in the back, we passed my father's room in the corner and my uncle looked in on him. My father came out in great excitement and embraced his brother, whom he had not seen in seven years. Immediately, the family was gathered around the dinner table, eating the many dishes Su Juan had prepared—scrambled eggs, fish, stir-fried Chinese celery, roasted peanuts, rice, and plenty of beer poured warm. My uncle asked whether he could take a few pictures. He had a 35mm camera with many attachments and told me that photography was one of his favorite hobbies. For the next two days, I became my uncle's favorite subject. I ran to the bedroom and got my Kodak instamatic and took a few pictures myself.

During the evening, the conversation became very animated when we touched upon the Cultural Revolution, something people did not speak of freely. I turned to my father and said, "Your stepdaughter told me of your imprisonment for two years. Did you do any hard labor?"

He answered, "No. I lived in a room with six or eight men. I don't remember exactly. We slept on the floor on mats and it was very cold. They took us outside to be shown to the students and we wore plaques in the front and the back."

My uncle remarked, "Like a sandwich!"

This time I revealed to my father, "I cried when I heard of your imprisonment."

And he responded, "Never mind, never mind! We shall live to be one hundred!" and then gave one of his hearty laughs. My father never volunteered any information. Everything he said was prompted by questions. I had learned he was imprisoned at Zhejiang University where he had taught math.

I also learned my father had to wear a special band around his arm after his release from prison. He said, "If I go to the barbershop and keep my head hung low, it would be all right."

During the conversation, the topic of learning Mao's quotations came up, and my father said, "Yes, I had to recite certain parts daily, by heart."

I learned more about my father's suffering while he was imprisoned at Zhejiang University from my cousin Sheldon (Xi Cheng) Lou's book, *Sparrows, Bedbugs, and Body Shadows*. It is his memoir about his life in China, and in it, he has a chapter about my dad. He recounts that in October, 1966, he and a group of students were given free rein to roam the country and visit other universities to learn from their revolutionary methods. They traveled south from Beijing to Hangzhou to examine the posters at Zhejiang University. He passed through the math department where my father taught and was astonished to see huge posters hung from the second and fourth floors that reached to the ground floor. Some crude images depicted my father with long hair, a beard, and sunglasses, and his name, Fu Shih, was crossed out with large X's reminiscent of government posters announcing executions.

My father was a Buddhist who did not hide his beliefs. There was a time he let his hair grow and acted as an eccentric, akin to an American Beatnik, grounded in Buddhist values, and this did not bode well with the Communist society. Posters with enormous characters read such slogans as, "Down with antirevolutionary Wang Fu Shih!!!" and "If Wang Fu Shih does not surrender, we will crush his dog head!!!" Another poster depicted my father with a gargantuan hammer bigger than his head, on which were inscribed the words, "The Great Proletariat Cultural Revolution." My father was accused of wanting the death of Chairman Mao while he was practicing Tai Chi. Someone claimed he heard my father say, "Down with Mao" when in reality he was calling out a movement in Tai Chi of "sweeping bamboo stems" that sounds like "Sweeping Mao." So a gigantic poster was made where only his head and feet were seen and an enormous hand clutched his body that had the slogan, "Revolutionary Masses," in red characters. Above his head was a red sun, representing Mao, and out of it radiated black daggers, one of which pierced his head with black droplets falling from the tip, representing the black blood of the anti-revolutionary. My mother was also mentioned in a few posters as Wang Fu Shih's ex-wife, who was a foreign spy who had fled before the liberation and to whom my father was passing on secrets of the motherland. My father acted meek throughout this ordeal, and it never led him to hate his country. My uncle had also had his trials during the Cultural Revolution. He said, "I spent two years as a laborer, working in the fields. I did not enjoy the hard labor of farm work or the isolation from my family."

Thus, the story of the Cultural Revolution unraveled and was revealed to me as a time of frenzy in the great Communist Society of China. My father agreed that the government went too far in its efforts for equalization in society. It did not want any social classes. The intellectuals emerged in the eyes of those in power as elites, threatening the self-worth of the peasants who formed the basis of the social as well as philosophical structure of Chinese society. So for ten years, from 1966 to 1976, Red guards burnt books, searched homes, imprisoned offenders who were mostly learned men and women, and sent many who worked in hospitals, schools, and factories to work far off in the countryside. Universities were closed and clinics were manned by trained peasants.

This revolution cost China many years of progress. Since then, the Chinese Government had softened its stance and made retribution to some who suffered. The Gang of Four, which included Mao Tse-tung's wife, Jiang Qing, had been tried and sent to prison for life. They were officially blamed for the worst excesses that ensued during the ten years of turmoil. Their downfall in a *coup d'etat* in October, 1976 brought an end to this turbulent era. Many small businesses were returned to their original owners and a limited degree of free enterprise was tolerated. Farmers who exceeded their quota could keep the profit they made from sale of extra produce. Chinese could now open bank accounts and save money. These changes helped to motivate people and push forward China's backward economy. (Of course, that was how I observed things in the 1980s, while today we know China is one of the world's leading economies.)

Once I remarked to my father, "Perhaps Communism was the only solution for China with such an enormous population. At least now everyone is fed; there are no beggars, and the utter destitution of former days is gone." Since I personally did not embrace the philosophy of Communism, I struggled with the question. Another time, I said to my father, "I think the poorest person in America is richer than the richest person in China."

He looked at me compassionately and said, "Everything has to be tried in history."

As our evening with Uncle Fu Ming continued, we talked about the past, the present, and the future. In regard to politics, I ultimately concluded, "There is always the question of human freedom." And we left it at that.

Pictures were shared during the evening. My uncle opened his wallet and showed me a picture taken in Shanghai of my brother and me at the ages of six and four. I had the same picture, but it had been cut to show just me; I had not known my brother was in the missing part. Later my uncle gave me this prized picture, which I reluctantly accepted; it was very symbolic of our reunion. Su Juan brought out a few pictures that the family highly treasured. They were kept in an envelope and locked in a bureau. There were old pictures of my mother and a group picture of my mother, brother, and me. Among these was a small passport picture of me that I had sent to Aunt Jane (my father's cousin) in 1962, who at the time was living in Hong Kong. I had written two identical letters and included the same picture of myself with the date on the back of 6/23/62, and sent them to two different addresses, hoping that one of these letters would reach her. One letter came back and the other did not. I had always wondered whether she had received this letter. Now I had proof that she had. My brother told me that the picture was sent to Aunt Pei Yan in Shanghai, who in turn sent it to my brother. That was twenty years ago. A surge of anger rose in my chest as I asked, "How is it possible that Aunt Jane never acknowledged receipt of this letter since she had been living in San Francisco since 1963. How could she keep mother and son, father and daughter apart for so long—for more than thirty-two years?"

My uncle responded, "You see, your grandfather held high political office at the time and had forbidden the family from communicating with you and your mother."

I recognized then that the social conditions in China were not favorable so my brother never received our address in Detroit. My brother told me that in 1979, he had written a letter to Aunt Jane, asking her to help him search for his mother. He showed me a letter my aunt wrote to Mercedes-Benz of Brazil, one of my mother's former employers, inquiring about my mother; the response was that they did not know of my mother's whereabouts. My aunt also wrote to a newspaper in San Francisco, asking them to help a lonely boy find his mother. She had mentioned that she believed my mother and I had immigrated to the United States. Apparently, she had lost our former address.

My father said, "When you see her in San Francisco, ask her in all honesty about the letter you sent her, for basically she is a woman with a good heart."

That night, I tossed and turned in bed. I could not imagine why my family had not wanted our reunion. Had my father also known about this letter and never tried to contact us? I felt somewhat rejected. The danger they would have faced if they had contacted us was not clear to me. After all the searching and the pain, the long separation was intensified further by unanswered letters. Did they want me now? Was I an intruder in their unique way of life? Thoughts like these passed through my mind, leaving me bewildered to say the least. I then remembered that my father had told me he had written a letter to Brazil searching for us, but this letter was returned. So my father and brother had tried to find us. Political and social conditions had kept us apart, and I had to forgive.

By morning, my anger had turned into a quiet acceptance. "Thy will be done." My father liked to repeat this phrase. He told me it came from Tolstoy. I had said it so many times in the *Our Father*. What cannot be changed, one has to live with, without getting bitter. A reason must exist for everything that is beyond our understanding; such situations makes us reach into the deep and let go of the trivia. They are a call to the heart.

I woke up at eight the next morning and walked across the pathway to the kitchen. My uncle was waiting for me and offered to make breakfast for me over the coal stove, but I convinced him we could eat some of the cakes left in the bedroom from an earlier time. We sat across from each other, sipping our hot tea, when he told me he had written in his notebook some facts about my father's life and wanted to share them with me. I listened attentively; then I thought I should write these facts in my notebook, word-for-word as they were spoken to me:

> Your father in his youth was very clever and full of imagination. When he was a freshman in Tungshi University in Shanghai, he developed a so-called secret radio telegraphic transmitter. From then on, the director of the university paid him high attention and sent him to Germany for further studies. He graduated from the Technical College of Munich with a doctorate degree in Electrical Engineering.
>
> In 1942, he came back to China with your mother, Agnes. He

worked as an engineer for the Economical Reconstruction Committee. According to his naïve idea, he thought he could put his ability to work to develop the Chinese Radio Industry. The Koumingtang Regime (against the Communists) did not pay attention to promoting economical reconstruction; they were only interested in civil war. So the authorities did not put your father in an important position. In 1943, your father, Wang Fu Shih, and I worked in a radio factory in Guilin. So your father and mother established a household in the famous scenic city. Not long after, the Japanese aggressor occupied the city. We left Guilin for Chungking, the world capital of the Kuomingtang Regime, in 1944. On the way to Chungking, your mother and father stopped at Liu Zhou. Your father lost several hundred books and papers he wrote in Germany; they were destroyed by the Japanese. It was a painful memory for him for a long time. It was very difficult to work without these technical books and papers.

In 1945, he went to Shanghai to set up a new Radio Communication Institute, but it was all in vain. This institute was forced to stop without any reason. Your father was disappointed once more. During the Kuomingtang Regime, inflation and prices skyrocketed. At that time, living for your parents was very difficult. There was no money to buy even a pack of cigarettes. Your father did everything possible to make money, but he failed, because he was an honest man. Your mother could not endure the hardship and the poverty. She couldn't but make the decision to divorce. It was very painful for your father. From then on, he was dispirited and less confident about establishing the new institute. He took a passive attitude.

After this, he worked as a professor in a technical college in Shanghai for five years. In 1958, he moved to Hangzhou and taught mathematics at the Zhejiang University. In the time of the Cultural Revolution, a great many intellectuals and cadres suffered from political persecution. Of course, your father and I were no exception. Recently, he has retired, and at the same time, he has found your mother and you. He is very happy. This is his greatest luck.

I did not know Uncle Fu Ming very well, but in some way, he knew me because he knew my link to my father and brother since he had been there at the beginning of my life. He was a quiet presence who came to bridge the link. I remember he was eager to make a good impression on me because he was aware that I would compare everything in China with the West, and that for a visitor, China appears poor and uncivilized and the individual person cannot stand out in the homogenized multitudes. On the very first day, he showed me his shaving kit and said he shaved everyday unlike my father or others who did not care about appearance. We spent the next two days together, visiting places and witnessing life together to seal our bond.

Shortly after my uncle gave me this account of my father, Su Juan arrived from school and the three of us went to my brother's art school. The sun was shining brightly, a welcome relief from the rain and gloomy days I had experienced the first two weeks of my visit. My uncle would be able to take many good pictures and concretize our reunion. Downtown, I saw a large band of women with towels on their heads, carrying umbrellas and bags. I imagined they had come from a commune in the country and were visiting the city. Closer to the second bus stop, a circle of kindergarten children played in an open field, attended by a couple of teachers. The sunshine enhanced their colorful clothes, and their merrymaking filled the air with a spirit of cheer. But my spirits did not soar too high before I was brought back down to earth. A man on a bike was having a violent argument with a woman at the bus' door. I thought he was ready to hit her while she rebuked him. It seems the bike had crossed her path and almost run her over.

Walls enclosed the art institute, so we waited for my brother at the guard station's gate. We could not go in for a while because classes were in session, so my uncle and I decided to go for a walk. We took a solitary street that led to the West Lake, and on the sidewalk, I saw two old men doing the ancient exercise of Tai Chi. They moved their arms and legs in a graceful slow motion, turning their bodies now and then in the opposite direction, and lifting one leg in the air. It was a pleasure to witness their exercise that beautiful morning. By the lakeshore was a lovely park lined with benches. It was very quiet and peaceful, with hardly a soul in sight, an unusual occurrence in Chinese cities. The lake was contained by cement walls. I stepped near the edge while my uncle took a number of pictures. The water was placid and reflected the surroundings with great depth.

When we returned to the art school, my brother was excited to greet us; he'd had an active morning and his hands were covered with oil paint. He was ready to show us the school campus, which occupied a good city block and contained various buildings, including student residential halls and workers' quarters, as evidenced by clotheslines and vegetable gardens. We entered a building for the more advanced students in drawing and painting. I noticed the building's unpolished state, with coal bricks on the stairwell for heating and cooking. I was given a grand tour of the classrooms, mostly for advanced drawing students. These exceptionally gifted students had come from different parts of China, and only five or six students were permitted in each class to study with the masters. One of the students served as my interpreter since he could speak English very well, although he had a nagging way of making everything sound like it came straight out of a textbook. When he asked my opinion of the drawings, I told him they were superb. Realism prevailed in all the drawings. I took a photograph of a drawing of an old man's face in two different poses. All of the students had drawn the same man's face, but I thought this picture was the most expressive.

Then we went out to another building where I saw a large exhibit of the teachers and students' watercolor paintings, including landscapes, portraits, and still lifes. I witnessed a variety of styles and a greater freedom of expression, and I'm sure experts would have considered some of them to be masterpieces. My overall impression was that the art school was technically advanced, but very rigid in its expectations of the students, so it limited the scope of experimentation and individual style. When I chatted with a few of the professors, they also asked for my opinion. I told them the United States was moving toward modified realism, but had been heretofore engaged in abstract art. They looked at me with skepticism, for this ultra-modern approach was neither within their reach, nor perhaps to their liking.

Su Juan, my uncle, and I left the art school bound for the parks on the south side of West Lake. My brother was to join us later. As we walked the street, I noticed two women fixing the street with a road crew. I thought, "The equality of labor is taken seriously here." After a short bus ride, we stepped out near the park entrance. A woman was selling segments of sugarcane from an arm basket covered with a wet towel. I love sugarcane! It reminds me of my youth both in China and in Brazil. We bought a few segments that made the lady very happy! We walked along the lovely avenue lined with trees, stopping now and then to take pictures. Su Juan bought tickets for us to enter the park proper, so we continued our leisurely stroll through the gardens with exotic trees, some of which were in bloom. A few people were feeding the goldfish, which swam to the surface by the bridge. My uncle never ceased to take pictures as I sat on rocks or stood in front of gazebos and flowering trees, all to please my uncle's zest for photography.

For lunch, we went to the park's restaurant pavilion. The place was crowded with families, and groups of young students and workers, all wearing the customary garb. My brother was to meet us there, but he was nowhere to be seen. The pavilion's covered veranda with square wooden tables was full, so we decided to go inside where there was some room on round tables with stools. Su Juan went to order the food and told us she would go look for my brother. When the food arrived at our table, my uncle went to get the rice, chopsticks, and extra bowls for the fish bones. He did not agree with the custom of spitting the bones on the table. My uncle suggested, "Let's start to eat as the food will get cold!" The sweet and sour fish was delicious! The scrambled eggs were also good. But the shrimp, mixed with some kind of cartilage, was spoiled as I later could attest to with a stomachache and cramps.

Su Juan returned, frustrated. She could not understand why her husband did not show up as expected. After lunch, we walked some more through the park, and then we went into a teahouse while Su Juan went once more to look for my brother. As we sipped tea, I caught sight of some interesting people. They were dressed in colorful clothes with headgear and sashes. My uncle said, "I think they are from Tibet." But we later found out they had come from the province of Qing Hai in the north of China. Just as they were leaving, I asked them whether I could take their picture. Two ladies gave me the most heartwarming smile. One was carrying a baby in a papoose on her back, while the grandmother with a gypsy appearance helped her with her precious bundle. It was great to see the individuality of this ethnic group preserved. I was grateful for their graciousness in granting me their picture.

While we were waiting for Su Juan, my uncle told me a story about my father, "Your father was in the countryside when a peasant man approached him with a medicinal herb in his hand. Your father bought this herb that was supposed to cure a multitude of ills for a good sum of money. When he got home, he found out this herb was nothing more than a potato stalk! He was fooled!" Perhaps my uncle told me this story to illustrate my father's trusting nature and good heart or his naiveté about culinary matters.

When Su Juan came back without any luck in finding my brother, we went to another pavilion and had some lotus root porridge. At the entrance, a man was selling apples and pears from a stand. He had a most interesting weighing instrument. It was a calibrated stick with a string. He would attach the fruit onto the string and somehow decide its weight according to the angle produced by the stick. Some customers would have him weigh their purchases two or more times. I had seen this measuring stick in a street in Hangzhou where peddlers were selling fish and vegetables.

From there, we took a boat across to an island in the middle of the lake. It amazed me how some of the women harpooned the boats close to shore with long poles, all the while chatting away confidently with their fellow workers. I always enjoy boat rides. They give me a sense of space and freedom. When we reached the other shore, Su Juan looked for my brother's bike in the bicycle lot. Since it wasn't there, we headed home without my brother.

As we passed through downtown, we went into a silk store where I saw the most beautiful brocades in all colors. I began to want a piece of each of the silks that most appealed to me, enough to make a blouse. My tastes collided with that of Su Juan. She wanted me to buy a certain kind for the best price. My uncle came to my aid, so I was able to convey to the saleslady my wishes. The bolts of silk were kept in recessed glass cabinets behind the counter. The saleslady cut about two yards of the materials I wanted and folded everything neatly in a package. My order was written and sent to a main office via a pulley system running along the ceiling. This store, like most, also used the abacus for its calculations.

My father, who at the beginning I had found so old, had gained by this time a youthful appearance as he was steadily gaining strength. The weather was getting warmer, and sometimes, he could take off his tattered brown skullcap. He had a bushel of white silver hair that complemented his two cheek dimples. He told me, "They say people with dimples have a weakness for the bottle." This was true for him, for he certainly enjoyed his wine, sometimes too much.

When I took several pictures of him in the kitchen, I asked, "Can you take off your *moutze* (hat—one of the handful of Chinese words I knew)?" He obliged, but he would not take off his glasses because they were part of his identity.

My uncle's visit and my own visit to my father had brought back a glow in his face. During conversations, he would often make jokes and laugh with abandon. One morning, he exclaimed, "I have just written a letter to Michelle (my daughter). Happy days are here, and in all the excitement, I had neglected to answer her letter." One of the signs he was feeling better was that he relinquished his cane. I never saw him use it again after he visited me in the hotel.

My father liked to kid around with his brother. Once he remarked, "Your uncle too has the triangular eyebrows." I looked at both of them and saw I shared the family trademark. My uncle brought out his electrical shaver made in Japan; it was cordless and rechargeable. It never needed a new blade. My father looked with amazement at these modern wonders and even shaved himself with it. Then I noticed that my father had some of his fingers bandaged with cloth. He said, "These are some sores from the cold." I went inside the bedroom and got a can of Band-Aids, together with a tube of Neosporin ointment. He was very grateful and shared some of the Band-Aids with his brother. It was touching to see grown men happy with so little. Earlier, I had given my uncle some film for his camera and nylons for his wife. Later, he reciprocated with gifts for my family.

At dinner, my uncle posed the question, "Would you like to come to Nanging for a few days to visit with my family? This will give you an opportunity to see the beautiful and ancient city of Nanging that once was the capital of China." After considering all the logistics of such a trip, my father suggested I decline. It would mean taking all my luggage on the train, and from there going to Shanghai, and arriving there a day later than expected. My father said, "A day in a place is as good as a vision or a picture." So my uncle accepted the situation as it was.

The next morning, we roamed downtown to buy gifts. When we entered a large department store, my uncle said, "I would like to buy you a pen and some other gifts for your family."

In an apologetic way, I said, "It is not necessary; I have so many pens."

Then he remarked, "I know. But this one will be from me in memory."

He went looking for a suitable pen, but none were to his liking. So he said, "I will buy it in Shanghai and leave it with Aunt Pei Yan." We were not able to find a battery for my watch either, so Su Juan lent me the one I had given her. From there, we went to a teashop where my uncle bought a package of fine aromatic tea and told me to give it to my mother, whom he had known well during her stay in China.

Su Juan went back to school, and my brother and I took my uncle to the train station where his train to Shanghai was to leave at 1:00 p.m. He would stop in Shanghai for more lung cancer treatment before proceeding to Nanging. It was a sunny and pleasant day, and the square in front of the station was crowded with people and their bundles. Many used the shoulder poles to move their bundles from place to place. A group of young men and women were traveling together and appeared very officious. Because of my uncle's desire to rise above the common crowd, my brother tried to change my uncle's ticket to the first class section reserved for foreigners and high officials, but he was unable to do so. We walked toward the general waiting room, which was packed, had hard benches, and was not too clean. My uncle decided to venture into the first class waiting room, which was virtually empty except for a couple of overseas Chinese. I showed the guard outside my passport, so he let us in. This large room was centrally located and furnished with comfortable stuffed chairs, magazine racks, and tables. It also had a normal bathroom, which I had not seen in weeks, so I promptly used it.

We did not stay long in this room before we had to go out to the platform through the inner door. My uncle still wanted to change his ticket and secure a better seat.

The conductors would not listen to him. Finally, a man inside the train pointed out to my uncle the commander of the first class, a tall handsome man with an air of authority. My uncle showed him his identification papers and explained to him that I had come from abroad. When I showed him my passport, with some trepidation, he granted my uncle a seat in the first class carriage. My uncle asked us to climb aboard with him. He took the compartment with the two overseas gentlemen dressed in Western suits. After he dropped off his little bag, he said, "We still have five minutes." We stood on the platform near the door. Then my uncle gave me a warm hug and said, "I will remember these days forever." I waved goodbye to him with tears in my eyes as the train moved away. For some reason, I had the feeling I would never see him again, even though he had told me he would try to come to Shanghai to see me off. And I had given him so little. I now thought I could have at least given him a fruit basket or a bag of the cookies being sold on the platform.

Chapter 12

Su Juan, Our Daily Routine, Family Gatherings, and the Silk Coat

In the family compound, I had a chance to observe as well as participate in the routine of my family's daily lives. As I said earlier, Su Juan was very energetic and worked very hard. She and my niece Qion rose at 6:30 a.m. Sometimes, I did not even hear them get up. One thing I learned from them was how to fold quilts properly. Up until then, I had folded quilts in four equal parts, but they would fold a quilt in three parts and then again in three parts, which gave them a very nice appearance. They had a reason for folding quilts in this manner. At night, they would slip into a quilt like one would go into a sleeping bag, having two layers on top, to use them with the utmost efficiency.

At noon, Su Juan would come home to make lunch for us, using the coal stove which had slow burning ambers that remained lit all day. The heat would intensify when a small stopper was removed from the lower part. Once, I asked my father, "How many coals are used each day?" He answered, "Because you are here, they use four. Usually, they use three." It never dawned on me that ordinarily Su Juan ate lunch at school, so lunch at home was an extra. First rice was made, and then some fish and vegetables. One fish swam for days in a basin on the floor before it was sliced with the blunt cleaver on a board that was placed on top of the water barrel. They had little silverware, just a good number of chopsticks placed in a hanging basket near the cupboard and a few spoons. A set of three pots hung on nails near the window. A narrow table, with bottles of condiments and jars of sugar and sea salt, was at a right angle to the other narrow tall table that held the thermos bottles. Under these tables, my brother kept the shoe polish and other necessary items. The kitchen was the picture of simplicity, but every corner was used with great efficiency.

In the evening, Su Juan would prepare dinner. I offered to help her, but she would not have it. Only once did she allow me to clean the celery stalks with her. Aside from the meals I have already mentioned, we often had some treats. Through conversation, my brother found out that I liked crab. More than once, he brought a string of river crabs for dinner or lunch. Su Juan showed me how to eat the eggs in the body once the shell was removed. As always, nothing went to waste. The fried shrimp, which they also knew I liked, were placed on a plate in pyramid fashion. While we ate, I mentioned that in America shrimp and other meat dishes were tossed in bean sprouts and other vegetables. Sure enough, the next day I had sprouts for dinner.

Nothing was too much for Su Juan to accomplish. While my father, brother, and I talked after dinner in the dimly lit kitchen, Su Juan sat on a stool close to the ground and washed clothes in a basin. She had already taken the dinner dishes to wash under the courtyard's faucet. When she was not washing or correcting children's notebooks, she was crocheting or knitting. She crocheted four bonnets for me to bring to my children. She also made beautiful paper cuttings with colored paper from stencils she had made or copied, some of which she gave me to take home. Every day, she mopped the bedroom floors and took out the toilet seat or *matum* (in China, it's like a small barrel cut in half with a wooden cover). These are placed in front of doors near the street to be picked up for use as fertilizer by the farmers. Behind the kitchen door was a kind of bamboo broom to use to clean these chamber pots once they were emptied. My brother was alarmed when I tried to use this brush for something else; giving Su Juan a strange look, he warned me not to touch it, so then I understood its purpose. Fortunately or unfortunately, I never found out where the bathroom was; I knew one was in the compound, but I never dared find out where. My niece or brother had warned me, "It is quite impossible!" I conjectured it might just be a room with a primitive trough where one would squat, so it was probably a very dirty and smelly place. I was lucky as they gave me my own potty made of enamel with real toilet paper. Most of them used the loose coarse sheets of brown paper made from recycled boxes.

The Saturday evening after Uncle Fu Ming's departure, Su Juan had her sisters and friends come over for "a girl's night." I was unaware that they were in the bedroom, munching away on sunflower seeds and having a lively conversation because I had been in the kitchen with my father, but he now urged me to join the ladies. Too bad I could not speak Chinese because I would have had a wonderful time with them. Qion began to sweep the floor (wooden planks), which was covered with husks. Suddenly, attention was focused on my coat. My brother, who had come in, remarked, "It is too thin! Feel mine, very different!" I felt his coat and it was thickly padded. As long as they were scrutinizing my coat, I said, "It is very dirty!" I had worn it every day since my arrival and had not brought a replacement. I showed them my sleeves that were covered with soot from the stove, caused by my resting them on the kitchen table. Someone suggested that I wash it, but I said, "It will never dry!" The dampness there was too penetrating, and even thin items took days to dry, hanging on the rack by the canal. So my brother brought me a coat to try on. It was too big and I really did not want to wear it. I said to them, "Never mind! I don't care that my coat is dirty." They all laughed. Then I told them, "What I really should do is buy a Chinese padded coat, something that is practical and warm." They agreed wholeheartedly with me. "What a mistake!" I thought, as they wanted to pay for it. They told me they would take me to a coat store and buy silk coats for my mother and for me. I told my brother, "I want to pay for these." He replied that I could settle it with him later, so I was at peace. The arrangement was that they would all pool their money, sisters and friends, to buy us the expensive silk coats. Su Juan, in a coquettish way, indicated to me that I would look mighty chic going to the U.S. in a silk Chinese coat.

Many preparations were made for purchases and gifts I should take back to America. Su Juan's married sister came one afternoon with a number of silk embroidered cloths, depicting some of Hangzhou's famous lake scenes. She asked me to choose a few. I told her, "I choose a few and pay for them." I think she understood, but she was embarrassed about accepting the money. Then I called for my father and he came in. I told him, "Please tell them there is a principle of fairness in America where one pays for what one buys." After he translated my statement, they understood. With Su Juan's help, I could compute the cost. Su Juan's sister had bought these silk cloths wholesale so I got them much cheaper than if I had to buy them in a store. At this time too, Su Juan gave me some silk fabric that she indicated would make a lovely dress. I also received more silk sceneries to give my mother and aunt. Gifts of candy, dried fruits, tea, lotus root powder, Chinese wine, and Chinese sweets kept pouring in. The dresser and reclining bamboo chair at the foot of the bed were filled with such packages. My suitcases would have no room for my clothes.

Su Juan wanted me to bring home two pig legs that were salted and smoked. I thought she was joking. But lo and behold, when I was at her mother's house after a visit to the bathhouse, she showed me the hams hanging from the ceiling. She was dead serious. I spared myself this extra load by explaining that I was forbidden to take animal products into the United States. When I told them I had too much to take, she indicated to me in gestures, "You can always load up your pockets." I had much to learn from my sister-in-law's practical sense.

For three days during this time, I became concerned that I was without my passport, and after a couple of days, I became very worried. I had given it to my brother, who in turn gave it to Su Juan's colleague at school, who was to obtain extra food coupons for us. On the second day, I told my brother, "I would like to have my passport." With all the stories one hears, I became anxious and added, "Without my passport, I cannot return home." He understood my concern. So that afternoon, we went to Su Juan's school. In the rain, we walked beyond Main Street to an unpaved alley with some open lots where construction was going on. Piles of bricks lined the road, and mounds of dirt were scattered about. We skipped over the puddles and came through the gates to the school, which was a new, two-story building, with a central courtyard. I could see some children lined up on the balcony, ready to go into the classroom.

We went to the teachers' office on the second floor and asked for the colleague who had my passport, but she was not in. We decided to wait for her to return, so I sat at Su Juan's desk, which had three or four more desks on either side of it. Here the teachers corrected papers and sipped their hot tea. The school was not heated, but everyone was warmly dressed in padded clothes. A naughty boy was ushered into the room by one of the teachers. He looked like a defiant little brat, but his face changed expression when he saw me. When he returned to his classroom, suddenly the whole school knew of my presence. Little faces started to peek through the door, and one child pushed another to have a better look. Soon, however, all the children were shooed into their classrooms. Su Juan came smiling into the office. She wanted me to meet some of her other colleagues. I had a couple of flashes with me so I took the teachers' picture, and then asked for permission to take pictures of the students. Su Juan took me to her room where she taught arithmetic. The children, upon learning I was going to take their picture, sat up straight in their old fashioned, double desks with their arms folded. They were a class of a little over thirty six- or seven-year olds. Some of them gave me beautiful smiles, while others stared in wonder at the flash and me. By the way, Su Juan's colleague returned my passport the next day.

My brother and I spent the rest of the afternoon in the kitchen doing a watercolor painting. He pressed a paper smoothly across a lapboard with some tacks we found on the wall near the window. He arranged a still life of an apple, a mug, and a bottle on the bare brown table. Then my brother pressed an assortment of watercolor tubes onto a tray. He told me the lighting was very poor so it would be difficult to get a sharp contrast of shades. I had taken an oil painting class the semester before, so I was familiar with some painting techniques, but because he was using watercolors, it was difficult to mix the colors and give the objects a clean appearance. My brother told me it was necessary first to make a small composition in the corner of the page. We both worked on our miniature arrangements, but I noticed my brother was doing it with more expertise. Because I had learned to see all colors in everything, my painting became something of a rainbow splash with the background indistinguishable from the objects. My brother's picture was much more subtle with each object distinct from the next one, and it was fun watching him do what he liked best. When I decided to paint just the apple for the larger picture, I was more successful. As we painted, my brother assumed the stance of a teacher who was totally immersed in art's techniques and meaning. He showed me how the contrast and variation of objects' position and direction were very important. And he concluded that there was some hope for me as an artist. I felt this activity helped to make up for all the times my brother and I should have played together and didn't.

During the next few days, my brother and I spent the afternoons together. My mother had written him, asking for some kind of document from the Chinese government that would be equivalent to his birth certificate. She needed proof that he was her son so she could begin filing the immigration papers with the Department of Immigration and Naturalization in the States. We traveled by bus to the office where documents are issued. Again, it was an enclosed compound with very little activity going on. We were ushered into a room that opened to a courtyard. An old man sat by a desk near the window. He was very serious and reserved at first. He told us to sit on the couches that faced each other. My brother offered him a cigarette, which he promptly refused. My brother commenced his long explanation about his needs as the man's stone face continued. Finally, when my brother finished, the man's posture relaxed and he took some documents from an old cabinet in the corner. These were copies of "Affidavit of Support" given to people who have sponsored Chinese citizens into the U.S. He insisted that first my mother would have to send him an "Affidavit of Support" endorsed by the American government, before the Chinese government would issue any kind of document or permit. This explanation took a good hour. I did not understand a word said, but I did copy the important facts of an "Affidavit of Support" so I could relate them to my mother. This document had to have the sponsor's financial status and a promise of support.

These kinds of visits to the Chinese authorities made me realize how controlled the life of a Chinese citizen really was. No one could travel without permission from his or her leaders. No one could move to another city or even change jobs without a permit. Any alteration of a citizen's current norms or status was obtained with great difficulty. But on the other hand, there seemed to be a lackadaisical attitude about work. A citizen found less pressure in his job. My uncle said that the Chinese government was trying to combat this problem of the "iron rice bowl." Because everyone was insured a job, people did not need to exert themselves a great deal. My uncle, however, did tell me that some favoritism did exist in China; with the right connection, one could obtain some favors.

This trip to the city also exposed me once more to the crowded conditions of the buses. Every bus stop was crowded with people, and when a bus arrived, it would already be super-full. Some people ventured to mount the back door's steps, and in this case, there was no courtesy. Whoever got there first would push himself in, sometimes fighting shoulder-to-shoulder. The bus door had to close before the bus could move away, so cries for squeezing in more closely were given, and the people on the outside would push the ones hanging out the door, so the door could be shut. I did not much enjoy this experience, and once I refused to board the bus and asked my brother to walk instead. He obliged and we had a good long walk in the rain. It gave me an opportunity to enjoy the city. We stopped for some hot chocolate and cake, the creamed rolls I so enjoyed. The cocoa was made with water since dairy products were not readily available. I observed some men at the corner having their dinner. One man got up and brought the whole boiled chicken in its soup to the table while another man was already feasting on a whole fish. The chopsticks were obtained from a dispenser on the wall.

The times we did board a bus, there was always an episode to remember. One time, a man was seated in a single seat toward the back of the bus. Around him were all his bundles and in his hand his shoulder pole. People were pressed about in every direction. When he reached his stop, he got a hold of his bundles and tried to squeeze through the crowd that kept pouring in. He managed to step out, but alas, a bundle remained by his seat—a white sack of rice, probably his month's ration. I felt so sorry for him, but I had no recourse to point out his loss since the bus was already moving. Another time when we stepped off the bus, two men were engaged in a shouting match. Other men stood around to watch the showdown. Fighting was a hopeless remedy for a perennial condition. One could not very well fly over the crowds. Now and then, someone would be pushed in a way he didn't like and a scuffle would arise. Once, I was standing near the bus' front door when in the rush of stepping out, a passenger dragged my purse out the door. Luckily for me, the straps were strong; otherwise, I would have lost passport, money, and all.

On my second Saturday in Hangzhou, I had an occasion to visit the Pagoda of Six Harmonies with my brother and niece. It was situated on the Qiantang River's northern bank, in a southern suburb of Hangzhou. When we approached the famous pagoda, I could see many shops lined the street to serve the many visitors. The pagoda was built in 970 A.D. during the Song dynasty. It has an octagonal shape, with thirteen stories on the outside and seven on the inside. We climbed every level, walking around the balconies and looking out the many windows. The higher we were, the better the view became. A long bridge for the passage of trains connected the wide river's banks. Many boats, some of them joined like the parts of a train, floated near the bridge. My brother expressed a desire to make a painting from the top of the pagoda where the many elements of the city and nature were brought together in such proximity. My niece and I enjoyed coming in and out of the spiral staircase that would end and begin in different places. The pagoda's central column was massive. No wonder this brick and wooden structure had lasted a millennium! It was fascinating to see the multi-level roofs and the upturned eaves. From on high, we saw a roller-skating rink and young people enjoying themselves going round and round. On the way out, my niece bought some sugarcoated berries that were sweet, sour, and salty—a new taste for me. Then we had some tea and I bought some turtles and bunnies carved from stone; I decided against buying some silk slippers, which I later regretted because one cannot have too many of those for gifts.

From the bus, I watched an old man collecting paper on the side of the road with his wicker baskets and shoulder pole. It was a sight that always moved me. He would get only a pittance for his findings, yet he seemed satisfied, as if it were his destiny to trod the earth, bend down, and pick up what others threw away. It was a lesson in humility and preservation.

When we returned to the lakefront downtown, we passed a building with glass showcases, exhibiting technological progress. In this vicinity, I saw a man selling bamboo whistles with which he was making bird noises. The whistles were operated by wet wads of cotton placed at the end of a wire, which was raised or lowered within the reed according to the note desired. It made a beautiful bird sound that reverberated throughout the area. The whistles were ten cents each, so I went up to the man and told him I wanted to buy ten. The man dug into his vinyl bag, trying to find the best reeds for me. This man's care and kindness lingered in my mind for a long time. He had large hands and a friendly wrinkled face, much like a clown. Whatever his motives he must have given joy to many a child. I was sure I had bought a toy that would amuse my kids and their neighbor friends for days.

When I returned "home," my father's wife invited me for supper with her family. The square table was brought to the center of the room and the family was gathered around it. My half-sister, Jia Ming, was there with her husband and her son, as was my stepsister Jia Xing with her nine-year-old son. Jia Ming gave me a beautiful carved fan of jasmine-scented wood and a silk scarf. My father's wife gave me a can of Chinese tea to bring to America. It was touching to see that my father's second family was trying to welcome me into their fold. I had no hard feelings toward them since I had not grown up here like my brother. For dinner, we had soup, chicken, and salted meats. For the first time, a fork was placed by my dish; heretofore, I had been using chopsticks with sufficient skill, but I think my father's wife wanted to be especially helpful and sensitive to my needs. I talked with my father's family through my father, who patiently translated everything. I told them about the whistles I had bought in the city that day. My half-sister called her son, who was playing outside, to show me the same whistle I had been so enchanted with. After dinner, I took some pictures of the family seated side-by-side on the bed's edge. I had to step outside to include everyone in the picture. Then I sat on a chair near the bed and watched my half-sister's son play with small multi-colored blocks with some help from his dad. Grandma kept these in a bureau near the bed. Then Jia Ming's husband asked my dad, "How much money does her husband make?" I answered in all honesty. I imagine they were horrified with the salary discrepancy between a worker in America and one in China. They did not realize how expensive it was to live in a highly technical and sophisticated society. After some cordial goodbyes, my father and I returned to my brother's quarters.

One evening, Su Juan was expecting guests for dinner—three of my brother's best friends. A square table that usually stood in the bedroom was exchanged for the kitchen's less sturdy one. As we were carrying this table over to the kitchen, a small drawer on the side of the table fell down, spilling all its contents, including a picture of my brother at age sixteen and a picture of his and Su Juan's first son, who had died when he was three after taking medicine for an illness. I asked Su Juan if I could keep these two pictures since I had seen many copies of them among her belongings. She happily gave them to me. It meant a great deal to me to have a few tracings of my brother's past. They helped me recreate and bridge those thirty-two long years of separation.

My brother's friends arrived in good cheer and eager to meet me. Unfortunately, none of them could speak English. By this time, my brother's English had improved considerably so we could carry on the semblance of a conversation. One of his friends, a portly but handsome man, was an art professor at the art institute in Hangzhou. Another was a young fellow, tall and good-looking, who worked with my brother in the shipbuilding factory, and also decorated items for sale. He had taken an oil painting class from my brother. The third fellow was a man with a more subdued nature, but who nevertheless displayed much gentleness; he worked as a teacher with Su Juan. The men talked animatedly with one another, and now and then, my brother would throw a question my way concerning art. I was surprised that they knew most of the modern painters such as Picasso, Cezanne, Renoir, Van Gogh, Mondrian, and Matisse. So I thought, "They are not totally isolated from the world." In my view, I think a person's heart longs to embrace the outer limits, and nothing can imprison him or her from reaching out. The usual dinner of fish, scrambled eggs, fried shrimp, peanuts, and stir-fried celery was served, and the men drank a lot of beer and smoked each other's cigarettes. The professor told us he was going to Shanghai to view a modern exposition of paintings from Europe and America. This confirmed my belief that the Chinese felt a real hunger for items from the West, whether they were books, paintings, technology, music, language, or even one's way of life.

Chapter 13

———— ✿ ————

The Grand Excursion and Dinner

The Sunday for our grand family excursion had arrived. One of Su Juan's older brothers, Zhi Ling, planned to take all of us to Hangzhou's best restaurant, situated in a park on the northeast side of the West Lake, where we would tour all day. Most of Su Juan's brothers and sisters (she was the oldest of seven) and their children were part of this Sunday outing. Near all the bus stops that day, I noticed that a new phenomenon had taken over the city: a host of young people with rags, brooms, and slogans were reciting speeches through megaphones "to keep China clean." The day before, I had seen a few schoolgirls with buckets and rags go to the neighbor's room, offering to clean her windows. I did not think that unusual—after all, they were some of her former students who wanted to be helpful, and she treated them to tea. But my brother said to me while we were waiting for the bus, "It's Cleaning Month for the whole of China." It was interesting to see so many youngsters involved in this national effort.

When we arrived downtown, we saw six teenage girls in colorful costumes perform a dance on the sidewalk that incorporated Oriental gestures with Western ballet. I especially liked when they shook their shoulders in a graceful manner. I was not used to these street movements, except in parades and ethnic festivals.

After the performance, we went to a small silk jacket store that catered mostly to Chinese customers. The clerk brought out a number of exquisite silk, padded jackets. I found it hard to make a choice. Each of the silk brocade jackets was reversible and had beautiful stitching on the edges and cloth button knots held by decorative Chinese loops. I chose a red jacket with a reversible light blue interior. The price was forty yuans or thirty dollars, approximately one-month's wages for an ordinary Chinese worker. My family chose a brown jacket with a royal blue interior for my mother. I definitely wanted to pay for these, but I was waiting for an opportune time. I could not override four family members who wanted to present us with these jackets.

One of Su Juan's sisters took the jackets home while the rest of us rode the bus toward the Solitary Hill Island Park. We stopped in an area where there were a number of pavilions and suspended bridges. I was glad the sun was shining brightly since it had rained a great deal the day before. It was the birthday of Su Juan's niece, a young girl of five or six, so the family asked me to take her picture. I had one roll of film left so I wanted to use it judiciously. I chose a spot by the lake where the golden sun was behind me and I could capture this young girl with ribbons in her hair and dressed in a lovely burgundy pantsuit.

Then we all crossed the street and took a path along the lake's edge where the Hangzhou Hotel was visible in the distance. This hotel was for the foreign tourist and, therefore, out of bounds for the average Chinese. The grounds were rather lovely and quite hilly. The kids skipped along and loved running up and down the hills. Most of the park's paths were carved out of the sides of the hills and laid with huge blocks of stones. Some of the paths were not quite done, and one could hear the workers chipping away with the chisel and hammer, hoping for a perfect fit. The Chinese took great pride in their public grounds, which were well-kept and rather well-attended, I must say. To promenade through the parks was a national pastime—a rather inexpensive way to spend your day off with the family. We made a big circle around the park and came out on the lake's opposite side where the famous Hangzhou Restaurant stood.

The Hangzhou Restaurant was a glass and concrete building of two or three stories. The family was proud to bring me here because the beloved Premier Zhou Enlai had eaten here while visiting Hangzhou a few years back. The restaurant had many huge rooms with the customary bare round or square tables filled with diners. We went up to the second floor and took our seats around a large round table in a smaller room bathed in sunlight. Near the window next to us, a group of Chinese men were toasting each other with glasses of beer, and having a decidedly roaring time. Su Juan's brother, Zhi Ling, placed the order, sparing nothing. He played the gallant host with a glow of satisfaction at pleasing all of us. He ordered a bottle of wine as well as beer. How much this all cost him I never found out. The dishes kept coming. I remember the Peking Duck was superb! It had been roasted in a unique fashion, then cut into small pieces and presented on a plate, retaining the shape of the duck with its head. We picked away with our chopsticks at the various dishes of whole fish, shrimp, and vegetables with great appetite. Conversation was a little strained. It was hard to have everything translated by my brother who had to struggle with English himself.

Our table had three empty seats, but not for long. A gentleman with his wife and mother sat with us. This man with gentle manners and docile eyes noticed me, but never let on. Only when I heard a little boy call out, "Mama!" and I remarked, "The word for mother is the same in English!" did this man interject in perfect English, "It is the same in the whole world, in every language." Then I began to speak with this man, who told me he taught English in the middle school. He asked me about America. I told him that in terms of technical progress, America was by far more advanced, but the Chinese had more social contact with others, adding,

"The Chinese are more gregarious!" He understood immediately and said, "Yes, individualism." This word summed it up. America was founded on individual rights that expressed itself in rugged individualism and self-reliance. After talking to this man, I began to realize what lay at the heart of our differences.

An interesting aspect of touring the park was visiting the pavilion that houses the Siling Seal Engraving Society. On display was a collection of ancient carved inscriptions on stones used for seals. Also displayed under glass counters was a large collection of brushes and ink stones used in Chinese calligraphy. I enjoyed purchasing some stone seals that I could later have engraved with my Chinese name. The Art of Chinese Calligraphy and ink strokes fascinated me. There was so much meaning, beauty, and simplicity in it all!

In a business district, I found a store with a sign that read, "Kodak sold here." I purchased a few rolls of 110 mm films for my Instamatic camera so I would have ammunition for the rest of my journey. It was getting warm, so we began to shed some outer layers of clothing and purchased some tea from a lady who sold it on the sidewalk from a large pot. We were now further from the lake but still in a grassy area with trees where some families were picnicking. After a considerable walk, we came upon a building that housed many exotic fish with fancy tails and bulging eyes. They were displayed in the inner courts in ceramic tubs and in glass aquariums. Some of the larger fish swam freely in the ponds created within the building and surrounded by viewing verandas.

Here we decided to have some lotus porridge and tea. Next to our table was an elderly American couple with a Chinese guide. The guide did not say much, and the couple remained quiet until Yun, my two-year-old nephew, amused them by running close to them repeating "Yu, yu, yu!" (fish). They smiled kindly on him and continued their reverie about this strange land. Yun continued his gleeful sounds while fascinated by the carp and goldfish that swam so close to us and came to the surface for a bite to eat. Before sunset, I wanted to take a picture of Yun in his royal blue Chinese jacket. We went to the rock garden where the sun was shining. But when I went to take the picture, the golden rays were gone, leaving only a gray dimness, and I had no flash. The sun was playing hide-and-seek behind the clouds. Yun had to relieve himself, which was promptly done through the slit in his pants in an appropriate corner, an ingenious Chinese method.

On our way out of this park, we followed a deserted road up a hill. My brother told me, "Zhejiang University is close by in that direction." I did not see the university buildings, but it pleased me to be close to where my father had spent so much of his life. I opted against asking the family to walk all the way to the university since we had journeyed all day. I was happy just to experience the surroundings for now. I saw a young man jogging, dressed in a jogging suit with a German shepherd running behind him. This brought me close enough to a collegiate atmosphere. Soon after, I saw a bamboo forest, the first one I had seen in China. The branches swayed with ease and elegance in the breeze, at times catching the sun's golden rays. Here I could truly believe I was in China. Bamboo is so intricately weaved into the Chinese's culture and way of life. The bamboo poles provided rods for beds, infant cradles, strollers and toys, brooms, baskets, bookcases, chairs, scaffolding for buildings, and inspiration for Chinese art. Even Chinese calligraphy seemed to be fashioned with the rhythm of a bamboo leaf. Bamboo is the frame that holds so much of Chinese life together.

To return home, we boarded a crowded bus. Yun fell asleep, and a man was kind enough to give his seat to Su Juan who was carrying him. Zhe Ling had us step off the bus early because he wanted to buy some wine for the dinner at his mother's house. We crossed through a less frequented part of town where the road was narrow and lined with simple, connected one-story houses. A woman, by her doorway, was washing her vegetables in a basin and later threw the water in the street. Through the doorway, I could see how simply people's rooms were furnished. They usually had a dark brown table with stools around it and an occasional chair. The framed beds I knew had a weaving of rope with a cotton pad for a mattress. A calendar or a poster decorated the walls; artwork was forbidden. The floors were made of cement or wooden planks. The lighting was always very dim. Only the more affluent could afford a stuffed chair, black-and-white TV, bookcases, and cabinets. Otherwise, the necessities of life were enough.

I thought how life in China went on as steady as a drum beat. Everyone knew what to do from morn to dusk. The ordinary and necessary tasks of everyday life were done with total resignation. The fetching of water, lighting the fire, chopping green vegetables, washing the clothes, and hanging them out to dry, carrying fish or chicken home, and caring for children. For a millennium, this image of smoke, water, greens, feet shuffling in the dust with baskets of goods had existed, and I was now a witness to it all.

We arrived at Su Juan's parents at dusk. Before we went in, Qion took me to the common bathroom made of stalls with pits in the center. This arrangement appalled me, but I had to accept that very few in the neighborhood could afford private bathrooms with flush toilets.

As we walked back to her grandparents' house, I asked Qion, "Would you like to come to America?"

She replied, "In America, I have grandmother; in China I have grandfather, so I don't know." The initial split was working itself into the next generation. The unification of my family was going to be a hard-won prize. It was in one such walk that she told me she wanted to be called Joan in America. The possibility of coming to America was hard at work in her mind and she was already making plans.

At Su Juan's mother's house, the sumptuous dinner began. Everyone was there. A small turtle turned upside down with its paws sticking up in the air was placed in a bowl right next to me. Su Juan's mother, with a wave of her hand, indicated that the turtle was for me. I had never eaten turtle before, so it felt like they had asked me to eat snake. I insisted that all should share the dish, but they all refused. So I was given the honor of ripping one of the turtles little paws, which to my astonishment had a small bone at its base. The turtle had been split in the center, and by digging into it with my chopsticks, I found out it had more blubber than meat, and it tasted like a rubbery boiled chicken. During the meal, I learned that the turtle was an expensive delicacy with health properties. I was glad when my brother and Su Juan helped me break the turtle apart and invited the whole family to partake of the celebrated dish. Soon the legs and thigh of a duck were placed on my plate and dinner continued with the customary assortment of dishes. I was embarrassed that I always received the best parts, yet I managed to slip a few pieces onto my brother's plate. When I finished eating, Su Juan's mother gave me a hot towel to wipe my hands and face. The ancient custom of hospitality had reached me in this happy home.

The conversations at dinner were more subdued than they had been during our first family gathering. Everyone was very tired from the day's excursion. Su Juan's youngest brother, a tall handsome young man who had not accompanied us during the day, was not affected by fatigue. He was very ebullient and enthusiastic, and through translation, he asked me many questions about my travels. With the help of a world map on the wall, I was able to trace for them my journey of 1949 by ship from China to Europe, around Africa, and stopping in Cape Town. We entered the Mediterranean and remained in Naples, Italy for six weeks. Then we crossed the Atlantic on another ship to Rio de Janeiro, Brazil. In 1961 we flew to America via New York and settled in Detroit, Michigan. And now I was in China, having crossed the Pacific to complete the circle. When someone asked me whether I liked Brazil, I said, "Brazil is in my heart because it is where I spent most of my youth." One of the sisters looked over at my brother and me and remarked that we looked like a picture they had of us when we were young. Perhaps a trace remained of our childhood presence, but time marches on and we were now adults with our own families. Our parenting was so dependent on the completion of ourselves. Contrary to what I had thought at one time, everyone needs a father and a mother as well as a country and an identity. Perhaps this visit would set my foot on the ground and make me realize how much a part of the world I really am.

That evening, we arrived at the family compound at 10:00 p.m. My father greeted us at the door of his room. He said, "Uncle Lou and his wife were here. They wanted to invite you for dinner and they waited a long time. Perhaps another day." And then he added in an emphatic tone, "You have been gone for thirteen hours, and you must be very tired." How he kept track of my comings and goings.

Chapter 14

═══════ ❀ ═══════

The Zoo and a Night at the Theater

It was my last week in Hangzhou. On Wednesday, I did not feel very well. I think I had a case of indigestion from all the dinners and poor hygienic facilities. Yet today we had big plans. Su Juan had taken the afternoon off so we could go to the Hangzhou Zoo on the city's outskirts. When we boarded the second bus, I saved a seat for my brother with my purse. This brought a smile to Su Juan's face, as if she were thinking, "She is really catching on!" Only a few days earlier, I had refused to board a bus, and now I was quick enough to push myself in and even ambitious enough to save a seat.

The zoo was situated at the foot of a mountain and built in levels. There were all kinds of birds and mammals, some of which I had never seen before. We walked around the tiger and bear dens and then went to watch the lions in their cages. I saw a lion devour a side of beef, crunching its bones and all as if it were a cookie. Now I knew why they called the lion the king of the beasts, for nothing tame could escape its ferocious jaws. It saddened me to see elephants with chains on their legs tied to the ground. Some animals do belong in the wild and we have no right to curtail their freedom.

We were about to leave the zoo when I said to my brother, "We did not see the panda bears!" Su Juan looked at my brother and almost desisted in walking all the way to the other side of the zoo to view a few pandas. But they did it for me. We had to hurry, however, for we were expected for dinner at Su Juan's married sister's house. I rushed along, trying to keep pace with Su Juan and my brother, who were more agile. They often kidded with me that all the driving in the States had made me a slow walker. When we arrived at the building housing the pandas, I saw one seated on its rump, chewing some leaves from a bamboo branch. They were bigger than I had expected and their fur coarser. At the moment, they preferred the indoors, and unfortunately, I did not have any flash. But it was enough that I had seen pandas in their native land.

We sat along a short wall by a dusty road where a multitude of people waited for the bus. The buses that came were filled to capacity. Su Juan bought a few pears from a vendor and peeled them with my brother's pocketknife. As I ate my pear, I wondered about the crowds. Where had all these people come from, and where were they going? On the fourth or fifth bus, we pushed ourselves in and got out in the downtown area where we boarded the customary bus #51. Su Juan's sister lived a little beyond our compound; to expedite matters, my brother rented a bike for us. I hopped on the luggage rack and we meandered through the narrow road, overtaking many pedestrians with the help of the bicycle bell.

Su Juan's sister lived in an apartment in a newer two-story building with a long front porch. We parked the bike there and had ascended a few steps when Su Juan's sister, Juan Juan, greeted us with plump rosy cheeks. She had been cooking up a storm. We were served tea and candy, and I played with her daughter, who was so happy to have me as her guest. Two rooms and a kitchen held ample furniture, including two stuffed chairs. By this time, Su Juan had joined us with her other sisters and dinner began on a round table in the center of the room.

This day, tea would have been sufficient for me. Yet I could not refuse to eat, considering the effort made for this gathering. Nothing was spared. Shrimp was placed in a dish in the form of a pyramid, a whole chicken was boiled flavored with ginger, and we had steamed fish, an assortment of salted meats, peanuts, and vegetables. Another day, I would have eaten everything with relish, but this evening, all I could do was sip on some hot chicken broth. How atrocious I felt to be such a seemingly ungrateful guest. I tried to explain to my brother that I was feeling ill and that I could not eat very much. He sort of understood. He asked his sister-in-law to scoop the fat from the chicken broth, which she immediately did in the kitchen. Then she put a few choice pieces of meat on my plate and I took a few bites to please her.

Su Juan's married sister was a chubby person with a pretty face, white teeth, and motherly manners. She was always smiling and exuded a sense of health and happiness. I felt bad I could not enjoy the dinner with more enthusiasm. But this did not stop her generosity. She opened the bureau in the dining room and gave Su Juan two bags of powdered milk for us to use for breakfast.

We could not remain at the table too long because we were expected at the theater for a night out with the whole family. We said our goodbyes, and I tried to ride the bike myself, but the bar was too high so I had to be very agile to overtake the pedestrians and avoid the oncoming bikes in this dark and narrow street. My brother took over and we met the whole family at the bus stop near Su Juan's mother's house. Her mother was all smiles with my nephew Yun in her arms. She had managed to pull off this evening a week earlier when she had excitedly waved the theater tickets at me. We boarded the first bus that came along. My brother would join us later after he returned the rented bike. The buses were not crowded in the evenings and everyone was adequately accommodated.

The Hangzhou Grand Theater was housed in the Exhibition Hall for the Performing Arts, a modern glass structure near the downtown area. We crossed the wide-open square and ascended the multiple stairs with many other people, curious about what we would see tonight. The ushers gave us back our ticket stubs, and then we found our reserved seats. The theater was dimly lit and ready to raise the curtain. Our family took up a good part of a center row. We were seated among ordinary Chinese citizens who were dressed in their ordinary Mao suits and padded jackets or green army uniforms. To dress otherwise would be considered bourgeois. It was easy to spot foreigners with their fur-trimmed coats, puffy hairdos, and makeup. I had been reduced to simplicity in China, which made me realize how manipulated by fashion we are in the West. A little fashion adds to color and freshness, but when all our resources and time are spent on being presentable, it appears foolish and shallow. While I was in Hangzhou, I gave up using makeup; it would have appeared ridiculous in the current environment.

By the time the performance began, my brother had found his seat next to mine. A very elegant lady dressed in a silk Chinese dress introduced the numbers with a cheerful formality. First was a medley of Chinese songs sung by several sopranos and mezzo-sopranos. Then a gentleman flutist played several solos. The entire cast of performers was Chinese, and it was interesting to note that the men wore Western suits and ties. The evening's highlight was a Tibetan ballet danced by a couple who portrayed two lovers' dream night in the bride's chamber with the give and take of a struggle embodying the groom's pursuit and the bride's denial and resistance to his love before the maiden's final acceptance. Toward the end, an ensemble played a medley of Western music, including "Jingle Bells." One act followed another relentlessly, with the same profusion in performance as there was in food. It was good to see this kind of release in a country that had frowned on all kinds of artistic expression only a few years earlier.

I took Su Juan's arm on our way home. My brother and she asked whether I missed my family. I answered in the affirmative. Yes, I was feeling the strain of having to assimilate to a whole different culture in such a short time. The many years, the language and social barriers all confronted me. I wanted desperately to reach out, but I felt bound in my own inadequacy. That night when we crossed the dark corridors and passageway in the compound, my father's door was shut. A dim light came through the window, but we did not want to disturb him. The next day, I would talk to him about the performances.

Again I was under the canopy of the huge bed, my daily refuge, rolled under two very warm comforters. Su Juan had placed two new coals in the pipe stove to reduce the night's chill. I could see a dim light filtering through the window from the kitchen where Su Juan was boiling water for the thermos bottles, a chore she had to do each night. My brother was with her, so they could spend some time alone and share mutual concerns. Tonight, I heard a heated argument going on. In another minute, Su Juan stormed into the room and threw down the 100 yuans I had given my brother earlier for the silk jackets. She absolutely did not want to be paid, and she made it known to me. I was in a real dilemma.

The next morning, I decided to speak to my father about all matters. When I showed him the silk jackets and told him their price, he confirmed, "You must pay for these jackets. They cannot afford to pay for them." My predicament was how to pay for the silk jackets without appearing that I was doing so. The long years of suffering, the habit of living in simplicity had made my father protective of the poor, which in this case was his own family. Occasionally, he had to remind me to be mindful of others. Once, I was eating a delicious bowl of soup made of transparent noodles and Chinese cabbage when he gently told me, "If you cannot eat all of it, you can share it with Qion." I had overlooked that Su Juan had made this soup for me only and the others had none.

When we went back to the kitchen, I told my father, "I enjoyed the performances last night. I was surprised to see that the men wore Western suits. The building was very modern, but they did not have normal bathrooms. How come the stalls had marble troughs with running water? At least in this modern building they should have normal bathrooms!" My father looked at me silently, taking in my complaint, but he made no comment. I was still trying to reconcile the East with the West, and the Chinese, according to what I saw, were trying to do the same.

Then he said, "The foreigners stay in luxury hotels and do not see this part of China." And looking at me in a half-convinced way, he continued, "And you are a foreigner for all practical purposes." These words resonated with me like they were a rusty hollow can. I did not find it very reassuring to be a foreigner to my own father. Emotions have a way of not heeding reason. I was hurt, but I know he did not mean to hurt me; he was simply pointing out the differences in our countries at this time in history, so diverse in their ways that difficulties were bound to arise.

Chapter 15

————— ❀ —————

My Last Impressions of My Surroundings and My Father's University

I n the mornings as I did some tape recording for my brother, I became accustomed to the sights and sounds around me. If a duck waddled into the kitchen, it did not surprise me.

Each morning, a man with two huge wicker baskets on a shoulder pole would walk through the narrow passageway between the buildings and go down to the canal bank to collect the vegetable peelings thrown there by the tenants. It seemed nothing went to waste in China; someone always found use for what was thrown out. This morning, I also went down to the canal bank, taking the cement steps beside the kitchen. This part of the canal was not used for the normal boat traffic, except an occasional canoe that would pull up to collect trash. Hearing the sound of a hammer and chisel nearby, I followed the noise to find a neighbor constructing a wall with scraps of stones to create for himself an alcove at the foot of the main building. The need for enclosure and privacy was exemplified by this man's effort. The wall was rather high and well built, considering the scarcity of building materials. As I stood by the canal, I could hear the grinding and churning of the chain factory located nearby. My brother told me the factory workers made all sorts of chains for machinery, including bicycle chains.

Across the bank, I saw a woman dropping a bucket into the water with a rope. She was having some trouble reaching the water from the walled embankment where she stood. Two cats were lounging on the roof of her house, which was made of rough stone. Another woman was washing a container directly on the canal. In these parts of town, running water was a scarce commodity. Only those who lived in modern apartment buildings had running water; otherwise, public faucets and water from the rivers and canals had to suffice. My father told me that the university had offered him a better dwelling place in one of these modern apartment buildings, and he also could have made arrangements for a gas stove, but he refused. He had lived in this room for so long—nearly twenty-two years—and he wanted to remain close to his family. The gas stove could pose some problems: he had heard it would not function well in winter because the channels would get clogged and the flow of gas would be poor. Also, my brother would have to haul the tank for refilling on his bike, a very precarious chore. So they decided to continue with their primitive ways and use the faithful coal stove that served as a heater in winter.

We were having lunch when Su Juan's brother Zhe Ling and her sister Juan Juan came over to take us on an excursion. Since we were eating and there was no room for them in the kitchen, they said they would come back later. I felt sorry that we could not accommodate them, especially because it was raining. My brother fetched my father's university identification so we could go to Zhejiang University to collect my father's pension that was 120 yuans per month. When he had been working, he made 180 yuans per month, a good sum by Chinese standards since most workers only made between forty and fifty yuans a month. Soon we were off, my brother and I taking the bus and Su Juan's brother and sister following by bike. We met in a silk store downtown. Zhe Ling, who had taken a special liking to me, wanted to give me a gift before I left. I felt somewhat uneasy, but accepted his generous gesture so he purchased for me 1½ yards of a silk material with a light blue background and delicate buds of pink flowers. With this material, I later made a slim line dress with spaghetti straps and pockets that I used for my brother's first art exhibit in the U.S.

Again we went our separate ways, they by bike and we by bus, heading toward Zhejiang University. At the bus stop, I noticed bamboo scaffolding around a building and some men placing tiles atop a wall that surrounded the compound in an uneven fashion. Across the street, I spotted a crippled man without legs propel himself forward on a homemade platform with wheels, a courageous act amidst the large throng of people. We walked down the street that led to the university, and my brother, who knew I loved sugarcane, purchased a stalk that the man proceeded to peel with a giant cleaver that had a slit very much like a potato peeler; then we all enjoyed the sweet segments.

I was glad to have a chance to see my father's university. A tall iron grating surrounded the university with a gate and a guard's booth. My brother asked us to wait while he went in. I told him that we should try to venture in with my passport. The guard looked at us with skeptical eyes, but he let us in with bikes and all. The campus looked typical of a university, with many buildings and exercise fields. My brother pointed out the building where my father had taught math. It stood to right of the cement path, totally visible, and revealing itself as a solid structure, four or five stories high, probably built in the early 1900s. I gazed at it with more than a passing curiosity, wondering what it must have been like to have my father as a teacher. Nor did I forget that my father had also been imprisoned at this university during the Cultural Revolution.

While my brother went to the administration building to collect my father's pension, we stood around a paved drive that ran through the center of campus. I observed a group of girls in a field just adjacent to us and partially obscured by some hedges. They were standing shoulder-to-shoulder in a relaxed manner while their teacher gave them directives in an enthusiastic fashion. They looked almost too young to be studying in a university. Soon, my brother returned and Juan Juan gave us each an apple out of her black vinyl bag. She peeled them with a pocketknife and threw the peelings on the curb. A woman appeared at the second story window of the building to admonish us for littering. My brother was very embarrassed. The woman reminded him that it was cleaning month, so he should join the effort to keep the streets clean.

As we walked further on, I saw a group of boys playing basketball in a court. Other than that, the campus was rather deserted. I was told that the university's enrollment was around 10,000 students and the competition for admission was fierce, considering China's large population.

Back at the covered bus stop with benches against the back wall, I enjoyed watching a grandmother chase a little child. Again, I witnessed the great tenderness the Chinese people bestowed on their children. Perhaps I focused on these displays because of their contrast with my own broken childhood. I looked on with satisfaction to see the glee in the grandmother and child's faces as he ran about with the customary slit in his pants, very happy and secure. Never while I was in China did I see any real reproaches or unrealistic demands put on a child. They were allowed to be children and people enjoyed their antics. Perhaps it was because of this family care received in childhood that, as I observed, the Chinese population exhibited great self-assurance. Whether they worked on the buses, in shops or hotels, or on the boat docks, they carried on their work with ease and related very well with the people around them, often engaging in considerable chatter.

We were now on our way to the Dragon Well Park. Along the way, I saw a good many tea plantations on inclined terraces and some workers in the fields. I did not know that tea grew on bushes and was picked at various stages of maturity. Most people in Hangzhou drink green tea, the leaves of which are not completely dry and have a bitter taste. Just as we were arriving at the intersection where my brother and I joined Juan Juan and Zhe Ling, a wedding procession went by. The bride and groom had their belongings on a handcart with the family trailing behind. I would not have known this was the case had my brother not pointed it out to me because the bridal couple were dressed in ordinary clothes.

We now turned onto a country lane where my brother encouraged me to ride the bike. I mounted it and took off, but then I realized Zhe Ling was running behind me. I slowed down so he could keep pace with me, but I wished he would not exert himself so for my sake. He continued to run behind me and was almost breathless when we reached the end of the road.

We parked the bikes on an island lot where a matronly lady put a numbered wooden plaque on them and gave us small tickets. The park was built at the foot of a hill and was surrounded by cement walls. We paid a small fee and strolled the grounds leisurely. Zhe Ling found the best spots to take pictures. I became a little self-conscious with all the attention while I could not take pictures because I had run out of flashes and the day was gray and gloomy. The park did indeed have a dragon, spouting water from the top of the hill into a deep pool. On another level was a gazebo where we ate another apple. I noticed that one of the gazebo's columns had a great many names written on it, so I carved my name Marianne on the wood with my brother's pocketknife. It was the only Western name among hundreds of Chinese characters.

Next, we went up steep stone steps to the very summit where stood another gazebo made entirely of bamboo. Zhe Ling, using my brother as interpreter, told me that this gazebo was built in honor of President Nixon's visit to China and these gardens in 1972. Ten years later, I was sitting in the same place, joining my long lost family. Perhaps Nixon had a great deal to do with my visit there, so I should be very grateful for his renewed diplomatic relations with China.

While we were at the gazebo, Zhe Ling very proudly asserted that Hangzhou is one of China's most beautiful cities with many scenic spots and its beautiful West Lake. I found this to be true and agreed wholeheartedly with him, touched by his allegiance to his hometown. On the way down, we stopped by a bamboo cove to see bamboo trees with a square reed. I did not find one, but I believed they might be there.

As we left the park, this time I rode on the luggage rack behind Zhe Ling. I jumped off near the bus stop. My brother and I attempted to board the buses that came by, but they were so full that people were hanging out their doors. It was that time of the afternoon—peak rush hour. Zhe Ling suggested I hop back on the bike and he would try to give me a ride all the way home. It was against the law to carry passengers on the luggage rack in busy streets, so I was glad we didn't encounter a traffic cop when we crossed a busy intersection. We took the back roads, which were largely unpaved, and ran alongside a canal. It was a bumpy ride, and I sure wished I had some sort of cushion. We meandered around pedestrians and other bikers. I admired Zhe Ling's skill, dodging all the obstacles before him, including crossing another busy street with a stream of bicycles coming toward us that made me close my eyes. He had to give a call of caution to the oncoming traffic, and ride with determination; otherwise, we would have been easily run over. Along the canal, I saw people picking over some trash spread out along a large area. I don't know what they were looking for, but as I've said, everything is recycled in China and nothing goes to waste. I wondered how long we would be cruising the back roads when Su Juan's brother dismounted the bike and told me to continue to be seated as he moved the bike along. Soon I became familiar with the surroundings, and when we passed the Chain Factory, I jumped off and told him it was not necessary for him to carry me thus. It was a compliment to be courted by this tall attractive gentleman, my relative, who was polite, determined, and resourceful. My brother and Juan Juan followed shortly thereafter.

Once we returned home, my brother found my father in his room and delivered his money, from which he received a portion. I knew my father divided the money four ways, giving one portion to his wife, another to his daughter, and still another to my brother.

Soon my father came into the kitchen, so I told him about the day's sights and experiences. I asked him, "Did you take the side roads by bike when you went to the University?"

He answered, "Yes, I did, and it took me approximately half an hour. I went three times a week when I had classes. But I cannot ride the bike anymore; it would be very dangerous for others! I could cause a traffic accident!" Then he laughed. "But I wish I could go to the Lingyin Temple, a trip I made many times."

Then I asked him, "Is it necessary for you to share your money as you have for so long?"

He responded with a sense of urgency, "Oh yes, otherwise your brother would be very poor, very poor; he would not be able to buy the paints necessary for his art work." My father saw my brother's potential as an artist. He said, "Your brother's portraits are not only good renditions of their subjects, but they have something of poetry." I agreed with him that my brother had a sensitive touch with his brush, and the human predicament was always portrayed in his paintings, sometimes with strength and gentility, and other times with sadness and joy.

At the time, I did not know all the social implications attached to my father's sharing of his wealth with his immediate family. But then, China had been a patriarchal society for as long as anyone could remember. Homes of two or three generations were quite common. A cluster of families would live together in one house or compound, and the family patriarch or eldest male would take care of the finances. Children were obligated to care for their aging parents, and parents had an obligation to see to their children's welfare. While smaller families were becoming more popular because the elderly received pensions from the government, the age-old loyalties remained. It was not uncommon to see grandparents taking care of their grandchildren while the parents led an active life in the fields or at the shop.

Chapter 16

Conversations with My Father and a Walk to a Nearby Park

The next evening, I talked with my father about many things, including religion. He asked me about the Trinity, adding, "You see, I am a Buddhist, but I am friendly with all religions. This is why I ask you about the Trinity. Your mother speaks about the Holy Spirit in her letters." "Yes," I replied as he listened attentively, "we believe God is made of three persons, Father, Son, and Holy Spirit unified in love. This is our expression of God." We didn't delve very much more into the mystery of God, even though I knew he was interested in spiritual entities and believed in an afterlife. We then turned to the subject of my children. He had heard that Michelle and Lisa were in the Girl Scouts. He said, "This is very good. When I was young, I was in the Boy Scouts. I can still remember their motto." With a pause, to get it just right, he recalled, "Wisdom, Mercy, and Courage." Perhaps today the motto is expressed differently, but underneath it all, the principles are the same—to build the character of a young boy or girl.

Daylight began to fade away through the kitchen window. We were sipping hot tea after dinner and gathered around the square table with a dim light overhead. Qion brought out the cassette recorder I had given the family. She wanted to hear the tape my children had made for my father, their grandfather. Everyone was delighted to hear the voices and music making. Lisa and Michelle played a duet on the piano. Suzy improvised a piece of her own, playing the piano with great virtuosity. Sara told the story of "Goldilocks and the Three Bears" and "Little Red Riding Hood." The family was amused by my children's candid expressions, especially Qion who often listened to the tapes in the bedroom while she was doing her homework; the bond with her cousins had been initiated and she longed to see them someday.

Then my brother put on his favorite tape: Beethoven's most popular compositions. This music was a link to his mother. When he was a child, he remembered coming to my mother's apartment and listening to the radio that broadcasted classical music and many of Beethoven's melodies. We sat through "Moonlight Sonata" and "The 1812 Overture" and some other pieces while carrying on the customary conversations. Then I wanted my father to hear some popular American music. I put on a Neil Diamond tape with the song "If You Go Away." My father's face lit up; I could tell he was enjoying these love songs, rendered with such emotional force and rhythm. He was surprised they did not sound like the usual rock 'n roll. He continued to listen to Neil Diamond when I left for the bathhouse with Su Juan.

By now, the bathhouse routine was familiar to me. One of the attendants had come to know me and began to speak Chinese with me, but alas, my simple phrases of "Thank you," "Goodbye," "I don't understand," and "How do you do?" did not get me very far. The language continued to be totally obscure to me. The bathhouse was filled with steam. Semi-clad women were dressing their children on the mattresses provided. In the shower area, the washing ritual commenced. Three of us took turns under the shower, scrubbing ourselves with wet towels, not once but three times or more—after all, it was a luxury to bathe. In the front room, we put on the three or four layers of clothing we had come with. I had to put on my long underwear, T-shirt, blouse, two vests, a sweater, and my jacket. My cheeks were red and my forehead was dripping with sweat. Outside, I welcomed the cool evening breeze.

We walked home on the darkened main street. Su Juan entered a pastry shop to buy a few cakes for the morning. Some of the youth hanging around the store stared at me with curiosity. In the street, my identity was camouflaged by the darkness, but here in the shop my clothing gave me away as a foreigner. In the street, Su Juan pointed out a two-story building where her grandmother lived. Now I understood her loyalty and that of her brothers and sisters to the city of Hangzhou. It was their ancestral home. My loyalty was toward Brazil, where I had spent my childhood and where my spirit was formed. I definitely understood the importance of place, having longed for one place to call home all my life, and I worried that Su Juan might feel the same longing if she were to leave with my brother.

Back in the kitchen, I tried to dry my hair with my mini-hairdryer. My father sat there sipping tea and smoking while we women prettied ourselves. Suddenly, the power went out. Neighbors were coming out of their doors, murmuring. I said to my father, "I think my hairdryer might have caused it." He answered, "Impossible, such a small instrument cannot cause this." But then I told him that it drew 1200 watts of power so he believed me. It had indeed blown a fuse. My brother went quickly to the fuse box and Su Juan lit a candle. We sat there by candlelight for a while, but soon light was restored. By then, my father had gone to his room and returned with an electrical instrument very much like a screwdriver that checks whether electrical sockets are charged. He checked the socket by the window where I had plugged the hairdryer. He said, "It's all right!" He had bought this instrument and other tools to make a toy motor for his grandson (my half-sister's son). "The instruments cost more than the toy," he told me. Then he asked me, "Would you like to have it?" I wondered what I would do with it, but I took it as if it were a magic wand symbolizing my father's expertise in the field of electronics. My brother and he had talked about putting together a TV set. "If Wang Qian really wanted a TV, I would help him put one together." But this effort never materialized. Suffice it to say,

I did not use my hairdryer again.

During these last days, my father and I shared the most with each other. He looked at me emotionally and said, "After three weeks, surely a goodbye must come. But we will live one hundred years, and we will see each other often. I shall be coming." I told him that in English shall is weaker than will and was used more often in writing than in speech. From then on, he would say, "I will be coming!" When Uncle Fu Ming had visited, he had told me, "Your father has a great wish to visit you in America. You will help him, won't you?" My response was a promise I knew I must keep.

I went to the bedroom to get my black notebook and then asked my father, "Can you give me a brief outline of your life?" I felt a little hesitant to ask, but he obliged with a short report:

I was born near the city of Suchow, December 14, 1912. I know I am a rat in the Chinese calendar, so the date must be correct. A nursemaid nursed me for two years. I moved to the city of Peking at the age of one and lived there till I was five. My mother died when I was five or six during childbirth. I do not remember her name. [This surprised me.] At the age of five, I moved back to Suchow area to a city named Tong Li. It was a fine time. I went to a primary school built by a rich American. It had fish ponds filled with goldfish with big tails. They built several gazebos, one on an artificial hill where I played the game "Go" or Chinese Chess with my friends. [So he too had a poetic childhood.] I moved to Tiensin at the age of nine. Those were my Boy Scout days. I loved camping and making fires in the open. My middle school received foundation money from America and my English teacher had studied in America. When I was sixteen, my family and I moved to Shanghai. My brother, my sisters, and I attended Tungshi University. There were many German professors there as it was a German founded university. I completed my bachelor's in engineering there. In 1934 at the age of twenty-two, I went to Munich, Germany to attend the Technical Institute. I lived in a rented room and enjoyed the German countryside. I could speak the Bavarian dialect quite well so that a pub owner once gave me free beer. I completed the doctorate program in electrical engineering in 1940. In 1941, I left Germany with your mother and we got married en route. We visited many countries because of the war and arrived in China in 1942. That year, your brother was born in the city of Chungking, and you were born there two years later.

I knew the rest of the story. Later my father said to me, "It would have been a good thing if I had gotten the research position in Canada. Life would have turned out different for us." But "Thy will be done," he would often repeat.

Somehow, my father and I got onto the subject of fairy tales and he was trying to mention a "well" in one story, but he had forgotten the word in English and was trying to come up with it. I knew he meant a word that had to do with water so I repeated several words, such as "fountain, river, brook, pond," but none of them applied. So he told me to follow him to the next courtyard. We went into a woman's kitchen where he removed a chair placed against the back door. When he opened this door, I saw a stone well in the middle of a small opened enclosure. "Oh, a well!" I exclaimed. Now I knew what he was talking about. He had read stories of magical wells. He also told me about China's sacred animals: the phoenix, the dragon, and the turtle. I remarked to him, "Only the turtle is a real animal." It appeared that he liked the realm of the imagination because everything was possible there. He wanted me to buy a silver ring with a dragon imprint, but I never found one. Soon my brother appeared in the kitchen after his trip to the post office to send a telegram to Aunt Pei Yan in Shanghai, advising her of our arrival on Saturday. He came for us so we could go to the China Aviation office downtown to confirm my ticket and buy his ticket to Shanghai. Before I left, I said to my father, "I would like to walk with you to a park to take some pictures since it is such a lovely day." He agreed and said, "I will be ready when you get back."

We returned from downtown later than expected. My father locked up his room with his padlock and key. I took his arm and we walked to the street. A few pushcarts went by. I said to him, "I'm amazed how a man can pull such heavy loads!" He knew these sights interested me, as well as the sights of old men and women carrying wicker baskets on shoulder poles, collecting paper and cigarette butts in the street. He said, "Such things are never seen in America!" As for the cart pullers he said, "They have very good teachers who teach them a safe technique of pulling the loads, and frequently, they make more money than a university professor!" The wind was rather cold, but the sun was still shining. As I held my father's arm, I noticed he was a little tense and his arm was very thin. I seldom showed him any sign of affection; only once, I gave him a peck on the cheek when I was going to bed. I told him, "You look much better than when I first arrived." He said, "This is because my daughter came to see me." We went left on the first intersection to a broad avenue. My father turned to my brother and said, "I want to go through the narrow city road because I want to show Marianne something." In this side road, we stopped before a well where a woman was drawing some water. Then he uttered in a joyful way, "Many believe that the waters of this well are connected to the ocean!" Perhaps this was the Buddhist coming out of him, but it was definitely something my father would say, and today it was all about the well. A well held some sort of symbolic significance for him: he related the fountain of water to the desire for Truth and unity in all things. In the Gospel of St. John, Jesus talked to the woman at the well and promised her living water. I'm sure my father would have related to this! As a mathematician and Buddhist, my father no longer saw things apart, but deduced meaning from the simplest things to arrive at some kind of synthesis.

We proceeded to the park at the corner of the side street and a main boulevard. A stone wall, with an iron grating at regular intervals, surrounded the park. The grating on the first opening of the wall was torn off so we climbed through and my brother and I helped my father negotiate the height. The park had many paths and even a crooked bridge with white cement railings over a stream that ran its whole length. I took pictures of my father and brother in front of a flowering tree, but my camera began to stick and I could not push the frames forward all the way. I just hoped these pictures would come out; most of them did, and only a few overlapped. My father took us around to the park's other side to show me a building, saying, "There I often took tea. They also kept some goldfish." But the building was closed and would not be open to the public until summer. We went inside a gazebo and took some more pictures. The sun left a reddish streak across the sky that could be seen through the bare tree branches. It was beginning to feel cold, and the place was almost deserted except for a couple of bikers who rode by.

We were about to leave the park when I said to my father, "We did not cross the bridge." He quickly remarked, "Oh, very important! How could we leave without crossing the bridge at the center of the park?" With my arm around my father, we sat on the bridge's low parapet, facing the sunset, while my brother offered to take our picture. We bridged the span of time and space in this lovely moment. We then went back by the same route, careful not to be in the way of the bikers coming our way. This excursion was the only one I made with my dad while I was in China. It was as if I were a child and he took me to the park to discover the world, his world.

Chapter 17

— ❀ —

My Last Full Day

I had met Lou Hun at the airport when I arrived in Hangzhou. He was the son of my cousin Lou Ming (Aunt Pei De's daughter and Xi Cheng Lou's sister), and he was studying mathematics at Zhejiang University. He now came by bike at the end of my visit to bid me adieu. He was a handsome youth of about twenty. He sat on a low stool in front of my father and me, who were at the table by the window. He was a little shy because he could not speak English very well. My father spoke to him in Mandarin, the official Chinese dialect, different from the Shanghai dialect spoken in Hangzhou. Lou Hun's mother had written from Hunan, thanking my father for helping Lou Hun with his studies at the university. My father said, "This is not quite the case. Lou Hun's efforts were all his own." My brother called me into the bedroom to ask me to give Lou Hun some toiletry items and pens I had brought from America. I was glad my brother returned to me a few of these items because I had exhausted my supply of gifts and Lou Hun appreciated them greatly. It was a matter of custom to exchange gifts with your relatives and friends while on visits from out of town. I asked Lou Hun, "Did you have a mustache before?" He smiled and said, "Yes, I had one." I kind of remembered it when he came to pick me up at the airport when I first arrived. He did not stay too long. He still had to ride back in the dark to the university dorms.

I also received a visit from the neighbor's son, a pleasant young lad who studied geology at the University of Hangzhou. He spoke some English so we were able to talk about his studies. His mother later came in with a package of tea, a present from her family. Her daughter had given me a book about the cities of China, and we had some more conversations about what life was like in America. I really did enjoy the company of these gentle and kind neighbors.

While saying goodbye to family and friends, my father and I continued with our conversations. He said to me, "You have a musical quality in your voice." Chinese, especially the Shanghai dialect, sounded very harsh. "The reason you have music in your voice is because you had an easy life. We cannot have music in our voices because we have a hard life. They should be very happy to have you teach at the university. I think your speech is better than the one I heard in England." This was all very flattering to me. He went on, "I think the people are very lucky in having you tape lessons for them. I think the doctor who asked you to tape a whole book for him was too imposing." He had a conversation with Su Juan, and they both agreed that the doctor was insensitive in asking me to do all this work when I was visiting my father after thirty-two years.

This last day, I spent some time reflecting about my father. My image of my father when he was young and I a child had now merged with the father I knew now. Sometimes, I was able to reconcile these two images, but sometimes, it was very difficult because it was hard for me to realize that the old man before me and the young man I remembered were the same person. A new relationship had to be forged. When I was young, I was spontaneous and uninhibited—it was nothing to call after my father and throw my arms around him. Now I was more calculating and wondering whether I was really perceived as family by him and the others. Did I really belong? It had been such a long time! With much conversation, we had come to know each other better, yet at times, a feeling of uneasiness existed between us because of our long separation. At other times, we felt quite comfortable with each other, listening to each other's stories with great interest. My father had a special concern for my undertakings, more so than an ordinary friend would. The bond was there, but the insecurities built over the years made the silence between us awkward. I tried so hard to explain myself to him, yet I wondered whether it was within his grasp. Time had made honesty a shallow mirror of the past. Events almost did not count; it was the person who was all-important.

Often my father surprised me with his perceptiveness. He encouraged me to write. No one had done so before with such persistence. I trusted his judgment and thought he had a special gift of focusing on matters of importance. After we had visited the university, my father had come in while my brother's family and I were having dinner (he usually took dinner in his room, sometimes cooked by his wife, unless it was a special occasion and he was invited). He decided to take the short bamboo chair in the corner and sat in front of me. I looked at him and asked, "Did you like teaching at the university?" He paused a second, as if he were sorting out the truth. He looked at me with a penetrating gaze and said, "One cannot have such a mother feeling for an institution." Once more, I was struck down by his words, and I pondered the meaning of it all. Perhaps only he could interpret his own words since they carried the weight of his own life, not very happy at times in this place. I think he meant that the mother feeling or love was an inner experience that could not be fulfilled by institutions. Then I asked him, "Do you continue to have interest in mathematics?" "No," he answered. "Now I am interested in stories and I read books." He had left the realm of the impersonal and was living in that of the personal and individual human experience.

Friday was my last full day in Hangzhou. In the morning, I set my hair with my electric curling brush and packed my things. I put all the storybooks and pamphlets about China, bags of dried berries, Chinese candies and sweets, loads of tea, silk materials, slippers, and a host of other gifts together with some of my clothing into two suitcases. The dolls, kite, and cloisonné vases had to go inside a nylon net I had purchased in the street. I was all set for my return. Su Juan came home from school to prepare lunch. That afternoon, my brother, sister-in-law, and I went to the Foreign Police Bureau to sign me off the register. The same gentleman who had signed me in came to greet us. He ushered us into the sitting room with the vinyl couch and glass-topped table. Since he spoke English very well, we had an animated conversation. He asked, "How do Americans feel about Taiwan and China?"

I said, "I think Americans feel that China is China even though they recognize the vast difference in methods of government between China and Taiwan."

Then he said, "How about the Chinese Americans. How do they feel?"

I added, "Well I suppose the Taiwanese side with Taiwan."

He continued, "You know that China welcomes all overseas Chinese and many people from Taiwan come to visit China."

I made known to him that I was not very interested in politics and my main interest was literature and people's personal lives. He wished that I would come to China again soon to learn something about Chinese literature. He wondered whether I worked in America. I said, "I am a housewife since I have four children, but I am qualified to teach English in high school." The question of Taiwan was foremost in his mind so he mentioned to me that President Reagan had sold warplanes to the island, which had violated the Shanghai Communiqué signed by President Nixon. He asked me, "Do you get together with many Chinese people in the U.S.?" I explained, "Since my mother is German and I do not speak Chinese, I know very few Chinese families." Then I asked, "Can I help my brother with the necessary papers needed for his immigration to the U.S.?" He said, "Go back to the Document Office and ask the clerk to give you the specific names of the documents needed. I don't think you can obtain an original birth certificate from Chungking since so much was destroyed by war." We shook hands amiably, but I was glad to be off, considering the sensitive political issue of Taiwan.

We walked to the Document Office on foot. A soft drizzle shrouded the city. My brother walked in front with his huge umbrella while Su Juan and I shared one. When we arrived at the Document Headquarters, the elderly gentleman who handled the papers was not in. My brother engaged in a lengthy conversation while Su Juan and I looked on. Well, the matter of a birth certificate and paper of release was unclear. We did not know which paper would be honored by the U.S. or which government would issue the first papers. Perhaps we would settle this question in Shanghai with Aunt Pei Yan, whom my mother had asked to write an affidavit about my brother's birth.

Before we went home, we did some shopping. I wanted to leave my father a few gifts. My brother suggested I buy him some tea, so in a tea store downtown, we looked at the different qualities of tea inside a glass display case. The most expensive was eleven yuans a pound. My brother thought I should wait and buy the tea at a store near his house. In another store, I bought some chopsticks. My brother wondered whether I wanted to take home some chinaware, but I declined since it might all break. We went once more to the Friendship Store where only foreigners with passports were admitted with their escorts. I saw beautiful inlaid tables, stone carvings, and a room divider, things that would interest foreigners such as myself. Su Juan, who was very thrifty, prevented me from buying any kind of expensive jade carvings such as the beautiful butterflies, so I settled for silk embroidered coverlets to put under a vase or a lamp. When we passed in front of a store that sold manufactured goods, I told my brother I wanted to buy the game "Go" that my father was so fond of playing with his buddies. I wanted to go inside this store, but Su Juan said they would not have the game.

When we stepped out in front of the compound, we went to the teashop. I bought my father one pound of the best tea, which unfortunately, was wrapped in newspaper. I wanted to buy him some cigarettes. But for this, my brother would have to get some coupons. Cigarettes, rice, flour, cotton, oil, and sugar were rationed. Once at the compound, my father came around from his room and gave me a few presents to give my children. He had bought some storybooks from the man who rented books outside the compound and had written my children's names on each book. To Sara, my littlest one, he gave a small rubber bunny with a squeak. He asked me, "It was not possible for you to bring Sara with you?" I answered, "No, it was not possible." He also gave me a couple of cigarette holders for my mother and Tony. I gave my father the package of tea, which pleased him very much. He did not want me to give him cigarettes. The malfunctioning watch I had given him prompted him to say, "This is good. This will give me an opportunity to visit you in America."

Then I had my last dinner with the family. My father sat before me on a short stool. It was dusk and a faint light came through the window. He turned to me with tears in his eyes and said, "You know that your mother still loves me. We had hard times together. But it must not have been so bad because she kept all those pictures. It was good that you had your mother; otherwise, it would have been very difficult." I was touched by my father's show of emotions. Ordinarily, it would have been very difficult for him to speak like this. Su Juan was preparing the dinner in the wok over the coal stove. Her mother had sent a duck all washed and clean in a basket early that morning that Su Juan boiled for half an hour at lunchtime. Now she was glazing the chopped pieces in a glaze of sugar, soy sauce, and spices. She was preparing my favorite dishes: roasted duck, bean sprouts, noodle soup with vegetables, fish (that was also sent by her mother and that I had seen swimming in a basin on the kitchen floor), and of course, rice prepared earlier and kept in a crock and wicker basket. The dinner was delicious, and my father also commented on how good everything tasted.

After dinner, I told my father about the game "Go" that I wanted to purchase to show my children. He went to his room and showed me his set. There were two boxes, one for the black stones and one for the white stones as well as an old plastic sheet for a board. I asked him whether he would like to play the game with me. He declined. A game could take two or three hours. Perhaps I wanted to be the little girl who wanted to have playtime with her father.

We continued to share some stories. He told me the story of The Count of Monte Cristo and I told him the story of The Little Princess that Teddy had told me when I was eight and which meant a great deal to me. My father enjoyed the story because it dealt with the separation of a father from his daughter and he liked stories with a happy ending. In fact, my father believed in Utopia. He thought that one day men would live in peace because a gold mine would be found somewhere to satisfy everyone's needs. I could only take this idea symbolically since otherwise it sounded too naïve. The struggle of good and evil goes on in every facet of life, in every nation, and surely in the heart of each man and woman. Later when my father would visit me in America, he said, "Everyone is born with potential and anyone who thwarts this potential, especially the powerful who have the charge of many, will be judged and punished." A great deal of discernment and suffering goes on before victory can be attained, as these stories portray. We chatted some more about trivial matters and then I turned myself in for the night.

Qion prepared the basin of hot water for my feet. She was always so helpful. She gave me a painting she had done for my mother, her grandmother. She also wanted me to give my mother a couple of pictures of herself when she was four or five. Then she insisted I take two small teapots, one in the shape of a goat for my mother and another made of brown clay with a movable dragon's tongue on its spout for me. Also included in her gifts was a miniature figure of a Buddha on a vessel with legs. I did not have any room in my luggage, but I managed to place these fragile items in my flight bag, which Su Juan wrapped carefully with some rags. These were Qion's mementos that I could not leave behind.

Chapter 18

───── ✿ ─────

The Farewell

Morning came quickly. Su Juan and Qion did not go to school this Saturday. I dressed myself with the clothes I had laid out for the journey. On the bed, I left the pajamas and the sweater folded as if I were to spend another night next to the pillows and folded quilt. Then I gave Qion my tennis shoes and Su Juan some items of clothing I was not taking back. I left all the toiletry items, towels, and hairdryer. They were very grateful for my gifts.

As I walked into the kitchen, my brother was shaving. His mood was cheerful. He was excited about going to Shanghai with me. He told me he was determined to go to America. No one could keep mother and son separated. His longing to see our mother was overwhelming. It was the force that moved his life at this time. He went to the bedroom to change into a pair of clean trousers and jacket. My father joined us this morning. He wanted to say something to me, but he could only say it in German since there was no translation for it in English, "Die Upshied und Viederzehen sint immer zusser!" I understood what it meant: "The goodbyes and the seeing again are always sweeter!" This confirmed that the possibility of us seeing each other again soon was at hand, and we certainly would see each other again in our lifetime. Then in an earnest way, as if to dissipate all my worries, he added, "But I will only accept the ticket to the U.S. if you are rich." He thought that my writing a book might bring in some money. He wanted to make the task simpler for me, so in a cajoling way he would say, "Just write something each day on a piece of paper and put it in a box. You can call it Thirty-Two Years. It will be a gift to humanity." Little did he know that this effort would take almost a lifetime.

This last morning with my father, I felt like telling him about my arrival in America. I said, "You know that Mommy's second husband, Valerian Tmiro Khan Chestohin was a Russian Prince. His family, of Moslem descent, had ruled the small kingdom of Daghestan in a mountainous region in the south of Russia. They were exiled to Siberia and were allowed to breed horses and live in the region after captivity, as long as they did not maintain an army and lived in obscurity. My stepfather was born in this exile setting, but was well-treated by the Czar with whom he had an audience. He was educated in St. Petersburg in the military academy and reached the rank of captain. There too, he studied the art of drawing and painting. His family had turned Christian and he was baptized in the Russian Orthodox faith. After the Russian Revolution, he fled Russia on horseback and took his home in Tiensin, China, where he lived for years with his first wife and two children, Peter and Helen, before meeting Mommy in Shanghai. He continued to carry the title of prince and maintained it throughout his life. Thus when Mommy decided to immigrate to the U.S., word got around that she was a Russian princess. A limousine met us in New York and there was some press coverage in newspapers in Rio and Detroit. I enjoyed the royal treatment, but it bothered me to be called his daughter. I always called him 'Uncle,' never 'Father.'" I showed my father a picture of my mother that I had taken at the Empire State Building in New York.

He said, "Tell your mother she looks like a real princess in this picture, and that I enjoy the philosophical thoughts in her letters." Ordinarily, it would have been very tedious for my father to look at pictures and listen to someone read letters. Instead he said, "It is very important for me to see this picture. I don't remember seeing it before."

Then my father remembered something. He said, "You have not seen one of Hangzhou's most scenic places. It is where a river divides itself into seven streams and one walks barefoot from one stream to another, a sort of baptism of happiness. Oh, people come from faraway places to have this experience. I myself did not know about it till one night I was staying in an inn with your brother and a pilgrim told me about this wondrous stream."

I looked at him more like a mother than a child and said, "One leaves always something unseen…."

"Oh, but it is the most important place of all!" Then he looked at me intensely and said, "You know, I can still see you as a little girl. The image is vivid in my mind."

The image of my father as a young man was also burnt indelibly in my mind and it blended with the image of the old man before me. These two images superimposed each other, and there was no space or time in between, just these three weeks.

While we were in the kitchen, Su Juan's father, a very silent and serious man, came to visit me to say goodbye. I was surprised to see this old man, whom I had not seen utter a single word. He spoke mostly with a nod of the head. His coming was a sign of his friendship and respect. I made him some tea with hot water from the thermos, which he did not expect, but took graciously. Then he said something, which I did not understand. My father translated it to me. "He said for you to come again next year." Su Juan offered me some eggs in a sweet berry soup. With my father's help, I told her I did not want to eat too much before traveling. A biscuit would suffice. The old man did not eat the soup either because he was a vegetarian. I asked my father to inquire whether this was because he was a Buddhist? The old man assented. My brother ended up eating the soup for both of us. Soon Su Juan's father went home. I was touched by his quiet visit.

The time for my departure was approaching. My father said to me, "When you arrived in Hangzhou, I went to the airport to greet you. But now that you go away, I only go to the bus stop."

Then I asked my father, "Could you show me your room?" Because of my quiet and unobtrusive ways, I was unable to seek my father in his room before this. I wanted to see where he spent most of his time reading and meditating: like a monk in a cottage.

He agreed, and as we walked through the darkened corridors, he said, "My room is not very tidy." It did not matter to me. He opened the door and I went in. My father looked at me with a vulnerable affectionate look as if to say, "My daughter came to see my intimate quarters." I stood there for several moments looking around. In front of the window to the left of the door was a small table cluttered with books, writing paper, a clock, an ashtray, and an old teapot. In the middle of the room was a bamboo bookcase loaded with books. On the floor next to the bookcase was an array of bottles and containers and used teacups. Behind this bookcase was his bed, low to the ground, small in size, and draped with gauze netting. Against the wall to my right were a couple of more bookcases with books, his treasured possessions. He did not have a chair, just a stool. His room was not messy, but it had the appearance of being untouched for a long time. Dust had settled from the streets and the coal stoves, so it did not pay to be neat. It was here that a hazy secret in my mind was confirmed. I had a faint recollection that my mother had told me once that my father had had a daughter in Germany before he met her. We never mentioned it again, but here I saw a letter from this daughter on his desk with a picture. It was just a glance, and I did not utter a word about it. In later years, I mentioned it to my brother, who said he knew about this daughter. The thought did not hurt me because so many of my memories were remote and I was used to not claiming my father all to myself.

We returned to the kitchen and it was time to go. It was a gray day and rain was threatening at any moment. Su Juan's brothers and sisters came over and each took a piece of my luggage as we walked out of the compound. Many neighbors looked on. In the first courtyard, my father's wife came out of her room. I made it a point to walk up to her and shake her hand. I looked at her with kindness, hoping good will would issue forth from my visit and my father would be well cared for; perhaps he would regain his former dignity. As I passed the many people who were wishing me farewell, soft tears rolled down my cheek. Everyone had been so kind to me, and now I was going.

We weren't at the bus stop more than a few moments when the bus came. I turned to my father and gave him a warm embrace. This show of affection right in the street while tears were streaming down my face was completely unplanned and took my father by surprise. As the bus approached, I said to my father, "Thank you. Thank you." I could not say anything else. There was ample standing room in the bus. All my relatives climbed on the bus with me; only my father stood outside in his customary posture and gaze. We looked at each other through the transparencies before us—the windowpane, my tears, and his glasses. The bus moved away and soon I did not see him anymore. We traveled through streets that were familiar to me. Everyone was very quiet; it was not just another bus ride—it was a parting.

It was still overcast, almost raining. We got off near the China Aviation office. It was a modern glass building with visible steps leading to the second floor waiting room. We sat on the light wooden benches that were back-to-back on one side of the first floor, waiting for the bus that would take my brother and me to Hangzhou's airport. Little Yun was running around, making his rhythmic steps and singing his self-made songs while the adults looked on with admiration. I made him a paper airplane with a flyer I had in my purse and showed him how to fly it. This gift just added to his joyful mood, and he kept us entertained for a long time. I could not help wondering what would await this happy child in a world of so many separations, rifts, and dissent? Would he also leave his homeland and make his living in an alien world? Perhaps he would adjust much better than I had.

The airport bus had arrived and was parked in front of the building. The men took the luggage inside the bus and joined the family outside. My brother and I stepped on the bus and found a seat in the middle. I remained standing so I could see Su Juan and her family. Many had tears in their eyes, and I waved until I could not see them anymore.

The bus ride to the airport was relatively short. The avenues were wide and pleasant. The airport was built for President Nixon's visit to the city of Hangzhou in 1972. It was a steel and glass structure, not unlike some American buildings. We entered through the lower level and checked in our luggage, which was weighed; I had to pay twelve yuans for it being overweight. Then we went up a flight of stairs to the main lobby, which was flooded with light because of the glass panes. From there, we could see some military men hosing down the outside steps leading to the runway. The jets of water were so strong that some water seeped through under the door. Apparently, these men were part of the country's cleaning campaign. A clerk quickly mopped the wet floor. Some men on scaffolding were washing the glass panes on the first balcony where there was a restaurant. Just below the balcony was a huge mural of Mao Tze Tung's birthplace, which reminded me of the power and scope of Mao's regime, which had transformed China into the place it was during my visit. Only a handful of passengers were waiting around. The counter, where souvenirs and Chinese curios were sold, was not attended. My brother pointed out to me the chair where my father had sat while waiting for my arrival. It was near the door where I would walk in from the plane. I imagined how he had waited with apprehension, looking out to the runway and wondering how it all would be. Here in this airport I had met my father after thirty-two years of absence. Yes, it did seem like a dream. Now, I was leaving to join the life I had made for myself in another country with other people.

It was time for us to board the plane. The pavement was wet from all the washing. We climbed up the iron steps and were inside the small plane's interior. As we took our assigned seats, my brother began to exhibit the exhilaration of a young boy in an amusement park. This trip to Shanghai by plane was a thrill to him. I was not sure whether he had flown before. I knew he had traveled to Beijing to visit my grandfather and made several trips to Shanghai, but they all might have been by train. Air flight was very expensive for ordinary Chinese citizens, and I don't think many were allowed to fly. I knew he was enjoying every minute, so I acted as excited as if it were my first flight too. For him, it was the first leg of a liberating journey after so much repression and bondage from the government. Sometimes, I felt like the Chinese population was in a pressure cooker about to explode at any minute.

My brother had troubles with the seat-belt so I helped him fasten it. The stewardess stood in front of the captain's cabin and gave some instructions in Chinese. All the passengers were Chinese so there was no need for translation; only I remained in the dark as usual. In front of us sat a young couple who were recently married and probably on their honeymoon. The young man was demonstrating open affection to his bride. He caressed her hair, kissed her on the cheek, showed her the view, and talked about it. Only once before in China, on a park bench, had I seen two young people embrace. In China, amorous displays were seldom seen, except toward young children, so it was refreshing for me to see this couple in love. Sometimes, a young lad would put his arms around another male friend, and they would stroll down the street in that fashion. Otherwise, signs of affection among adults were limited to handshakes, and of course, the ever present smile.

My brother, who was seated by the window, looked out with satisfaction. We were flying below the clouds over a lot of farmland. I could see a river twisting itself through the landscape. The stewardess, a shy pretty young lady who wore makeup, passed out a few gifts: a small address book, candy, and gum. We took these presents as if they were gold. Soon we landed and the plane came to a halt. We descended the steps and walked toward a small side building next to the main terminal, which handled short duration flights, such as this flight from Hangzhou that had taken a half-hour.

Chapter 19

Shanghai

Just as we walked into the airport terminal, a warm lady with a broad smile, dressed in a black woolen coat and scarf, greeted us. It was Aunt Pei Yan, a medical doctor who had presided over my birth thirty-seven years earlier in Chungking. She recognized my brother immediately and shook my hands with a determined welcome. She was accompanied by her daughter, Yun Yun, a computer engineer who worked in Shanghai's Computer Center. My cousin exchanged a few words in English with me, but most of the time, she spoke in Chinese with my brother, telling him the car was waiting outside. My cousin continued to smile at me, pleased with my arrival. A light blue Chevy from the '50s was parked in the parking lot behind the building, a few steps from the back door. As soon as the chauffeur opened the door, I noticed the costumed covers on the seats and curtains on the windows. The car was in excellent condition and we had moved up a notch on the social scale!

In the car, my aunt had a good look at me and then said to my brother, "Your sister looks more like mother and you look more like father." Yet I had heard the opposite many times. It was true my brother's eyes were more slanted than mine, but I could see some of my mother's features in him, around his jaw line, nose, and mouth.

As we now traveled through the streets of Shanghai, for me it was a homecoming! I had lived here during my early childhood, so perhaps I had traversed these same streets before. For the first time in China, I felt I was in a more sophisticated metropolis. The appearance of the buildings were more kept up and the streets cleaner. I did not see as many bicycles and pushcarts as in Hangzhou or Beijing. My aunt pointed out the French and German consulates, housed in large mansions with enclosed gardens.

Soon the chauffeur entered the tree-studded courtyard of a large apartment building. It appeared to be an old brick structure with many entrances and several balconies on each floor. Later, my cousin Yi Dien (Aunt Pei Yan's son), also a medical doctor specializing in surgery at the Second Medical School in Shanghai, pointed out to me that all doctors lived in this building and Communist leaders lived in the next building. We went in the first entrance and up one flight of stairs. My aunt and family lived on the second floor in a very spacious apartment that was very nicely furnished. The walls were freshly painted and the parquet floors were beautifully polished, a stark contrast from the living conditions I had experienced in Hangzhou with my brother and father, who lived in simple rooms with the bare essentials. This family's affluence was attributed to there being three doctors and one engineer in the family, all drawing the highest possible salary: 250 yuans or more for each, a sizeable sum by Chinese standards. Uncle Liu Tzu, Aunt Pei Yan's husband was the chief of staff in a prestigious hospital in Shanghai. He had operated on Uncle Fu Ming's cancerous lung.

We sat down to a delicious lunch in the dining room. One of my favorites was served: fried rice and pork chops prepared in an exquisite manner. I asked Aunt Pei Yan, "How do you prepare these pork chops? They are so delicious!" She did not know. The cooking was done by her mother-in-law, who lived with them, and a young servant girl. She showed me a couple of trays on the window of the dining room filled with sweet and salty egg rolls. They were smaller than the ones made in the West, and I knew they were delicious since I had eaten a few in my father's wife's room. Aunt Pei Yan said, "They are for dinner." It pleased her that I liked them.

After lunch, my brother, my cousin Yun Yun, and I went about town. My aunt excused herself, "I will be busy about the house while you young people enjoy yourselves!" Our aim was to go to my mother's former penthouse apartment, which was close by. At first, we went along the narrow street bordering the apartment that had very little traffic or even pedestrians. It led to a main street with shops and considerable movement, the old Lafayette Street, where my mother's apartment had been just a fifteen-minute walk from my aunt's place. I was excited to see this place, which I remembered well. We went through a passageway in a building that led to a courtyard, which faced several buildings. My mother's apartment building was directly in the back of the yard, facing the throughway. I remember playing in this courtyard alone and with my brother.

The building looked disheveled and run down, as if it had not been kept up for more than thirty years. We went inside the entrance and proceeded to climb the many flights of stairs. It seemed like forever! As a child, I climbed these steps in nothing flat and it never tired me. I held on to the wooden banister attached to a fancy metal railing, hoping to make it all the way to the fifth floor. I noticed that the stairs were not waxed or polished, and the walls bore holes like they had witnessed a war. At the top of the stairs to our left, we knocked at the door of my mother's apartment, but there was no answer. To the side was a silver metal double door I did not remember. The wall running along the terrace had been knocked out and replaced by this door. It had many dents and the doorknob was missing, so we could peer through the hole. It looked like my mother's large terrace had been converted into rooms with a small porch. When we knocked on this door, a lady inside answered but did not open the door. My cousin carried on a conversation with her from the hallway; we soon found out that the apartment we wanted to see was vacant, but we could try again later when the manager was in. It was a disappointment for me not to see my mother's actual apartment, but I had peered through the side door, overlooking the former terrace, and seen that nothing was the same, so the apartment itself might have been changed to accommodate several families. However, I was satisfied. I saw the building, the courtyard, and the throughway that held so many early memories and gave my early life substance.

Soon we were on a bus headed downtown. It was apparent to me from here on that Shanghai was super-crowded, especially the business districts near the center of town. We came out on Nanjing Road, Shanghai's main shopping area. The sky was overcast and it soon began to rain. Yun Yun politely sheltered me with her umbrella. We entered a watch shop to see whether it had batteries for my watch. A tall man with light eyes but Chinese features told me in English that they only carried batteries for Chinese watches. His manner was curt, which was not surprising considering the pressing crowds. My cousin wanted to buy me a pair of baby cloth shoes that my sister-in-law in America was expecting. My brother had told her I had looked for such shoes in Hangzhou but could not find any. We went into a department store that carried children's clothes, but these shoes were not available. On the sidewalk, I saw a young child licking a Popsicle. I mentioned to my brother and cousin that I wanted some bingjiling (ice cream), one of the few words I remembered from my childhood. I would have been content with a Popsicle bought on a street corner, but my cousin led us into a café that served pastries, coffee, and ice cream. We went to an upper room that was heated and had small square tables covered with tablecloths. We took our seats in a cozy corner and my cousin ordered a chocolate sundae, custard pie, a sweet roll, and coffee for each of us. This experience would not have seemed unusual anywhere else but China, where coffee is hardly ever served, so it was additional proof to me that Shanghai had a more cosmopolitan atmosphere. We took the pie and cakes home in a bag since we could hardly eat all that was offered.

Back at my aunt's apartment, I met the rest of the family. Uncle Liu Tzu, Aunt Pei Yan's husband, a robust man in his sixties, hugged me warmly. I shook hands with my cousin Yi Dien. At this time too, I met one of my father's cousins. Just as I walked into the apartment, a tall man of about sixty and dressed in a Mao suit greeted me by the door. He looked at me as if he knew me and introduced himself as an uncle of mine. He had a gentle and perceptive demeanor. My cousin Yi Dien watched me from afar with a rather impartial look. Soon, however, drawn perhaps by my openness and sincerity, he began to address me with interest and concern. We sat in the living room on soft couches and chairs; next to me sat Aunt Pei Ron, my father's youngest sister, known to the family as "Mimi." My grandfather had had three wives, not all at once mind you, but during the course of his life. His first wife bore him a daughter, Aunt Pei De, whom I did not meet; my father, Fu Shih; and my uncle, Fu Ming. My father's mother died in childbirth when my father was four or five, and my grandfather took a second wife, a Japanese lady whom he met while studying economics and political science in Japan. Aunt Pei Yan was the child of this marriage. The family teased her for being part Japanese, especially her son Yi Dien, but all in good humor, indicating that her eyes were pulled a certain way. My grandfather's last wife was a kind sweet lady who stood by him till his death in 1978. They had one daughter, Aunt Pei Ron, who in her younger days was a beautiful girl who did some modeling and worked in the theater.

Aunt Pei Ron greeted me warmly. She had lost her upper teeth and her gums made her look older than her years. She had a decisive and dramatic personality that made up for her simple appearance. Her voice was deep and husky. We chatted for a while and I showed her some of my family's pictures, which the rest of the family shared. She asked me, "Can I keep some of these pictures with your children, husband, and mother?" I gladly gave her some. She took out of her pocket a little cloisonné jewelry box and gave it to me. I wasn't prepared for all these gifts, so I wondered what I could give her. I went into the bedroom and brought out a few things I found in my suitcase. To Aunt Pei Yan, I gave my nylon quilted blue robe; to my cousin Yun Yun, I gave a pair of knitted slippers with vinyl soles; and to Aunt Pei Ron, I gave a pair of brand new shoes with rubber soles. They were all delighted with their gifts. Aunt Pei Ron commented, "In China, they have not learned to make this kind of rubber soles." I was glad I found something to share since my bounty of gifts had been depleted in Hangzhou.

Soon we were called for dinner and were served many Chinese delicacies, some of which I had eaten before, such as aged eggs, steamed fish, shrimp, and chicken. Aunt Pei Yan informed me, "None of us have an infectious disease, and so we can all take from the common bowls." Such was the custom in China. While we were eating, Aunt Pei Ron's two teenage sons and two teenage daughters walked into the living room to greet me. They stood at the doorway between the dining room and living room, smiling shyly. They did not stay long because they were on their way to a Saturday night outing. After I shook their hands, they left. Aunt Pei Ron turned to me and said, "When you have four, you wind up with eight and then sixteen." This was a foreshadowing to me since I also had four young children. Then she continued, "I have so many children because our leader Mao Tze Tung wanted people to have more and more children." It is well to note here that Aunt Pei Ron wore a black band around her arm. He mother-in-law had died, so she was in mourning. The cremation would take place the next day. She said, "My husband excuses himself from our company because of this sorrow." I quite understood.

After dinner, my brother, my cousin Yi Dien, and I went to visit my brother's favorite relative, my father's second cousin, Qian Jia Jun, whom he called "Uncle," and who also was an artist. As we walked to the bus stop, my cousin began to chat, "I used to play with your brother when he lived in Shanghai. Once your father took me to a restaurant when I was a young boy and ordered some yogurt for himself, but did not allow me to have any. He said it was rotten milk and only for grown-ups. I got very angry." And then he began to laugh. I began to sense that this cousin had a wry sense of humor. Then he went on, "The students at your father's university adored him. He was a prominent professor with a great following." From what was said, I gleaned that my father was a kind of hippy professor with long hair who did not just teach math but dabbled in the mystery and magic of life.

The buses at this hour were not very crowded. I had a seat while my brother and cousin stood in the aisle next to me. My brother, prompted by my cousin, asked me, "Where would you like to go tomorrow?"

I thought for a while and then said, "I would like to see the ocean."

My brother shook his head, "Oh, the ocean is very far away. It is two or three hours from here."

I explained to him, "I have a desire to see the port from where we left China."

Now he understood, "Oh, it is possible! Not too far!" This port was not by the sea as I had thought, but by the Huang Pu River, not very far from the downtown area.

It was about 8:30 p.m. and the bus was dimly lit. We traversed a broad avenue with many high-rise buildings, some of which looked like they had been recently built. We stopped in front of one such apartment complex. The entrance was dark and bicycles were on each landing. We went up a couple of flights of stairs and then walked along a balcony onto which the doors opened. My brother was not sure of the exact address of this favorite uncle, so he knocked on several doors. A lady pointed out the last door. He rapped at this door and called out in Chinese. A man of short stature, already in his pajamas, opened the door. He was pleasantly surprised. With all due respect, his face was the closest thing to a jester or clown that I had ever seen. He was bald in the center with bushy silver hair on the sides. He had twinkling, kind eyes, and his wide smile was etched in his face. He ushered us into his small living room, picking up the newspapers that were spread out on a bed in the corner. He made some hot tea for us. My brother talked at length with him. I understood very little, but enjoyed the expressions in their faces; they were having a wonderful time. Although I could not remember his name for a long time, I obtained it recently: Qian Jia Jun. I do know he was an artist, and probably this is why he and my brother connected so well, so I always think of this man as "the artist uncle." Before the evening was over, I met his wife, a pleasant woman in her late forties, and his shy daughter of fourteen. After this, we took our leave, planning to get together with him in the morning for an excursion through the city and lunch.

The ride back to the apartment was peaceful. The shops were closed and the buses were empty. My journey to China was drawing to a close. I had seen, touched, smelt, and heard so much. I would not be the same again. All these experiences gave me a new insight into the human condition—how vulnerable we are and how difficult it is to attain happiness in this world. We may look different, but we are all made of the same stuff. Life and time push forward, leaving in their wake a humanity hungry for essentials as well as nonessentials. Therein lies the dilemma! How can there be progress without compassion? Human individuality and community walk hand-in-hand, expecting nurturing from each other; offspring, one generation after another, carve out for themselves new paths, yet need the security that only mother, father, and family can give. So I went forth, finding a link with my family with a renewed sense of identity.

By the time we arrived back at the apartment, it was 10:00 p.m. The family was watching a swimming competition on their colored TV. I joined them for a while until my aunt asked me whether I would like to take a bath. I declined because I did not want to cause any kind of inconvenience. They did not have a water heater so a lot of water would need to be boiled. My aunt showed me the basins and thermos flasks I could use to wash my feet and face and the appropriate towels in the large bathroom. After I was all washed up, I went to bed on a cot set up for me in my cousin Yun Yun's room. When I tucked myself into the quilt, folded like a sleeping bag, I found a hot water bottle placed there by my kind aunt, Pei Yan. I looked around the darkened room and saw that my cousin and her grandmother were sharing a large bed, each in their respective quilts. I soon drifted into a beautiful sound sleep.

It was almost nine o'clock in the morning before I was all washed up and dressed. The two uncles I had met the day before had already arrived and were chatting in the living room. The night before, my cousin Yi Dien had bought some cakes because my brother had told everyone I liked cakes for breakfast. My brother and I sat in the dining room and had our tea and cakes. Soon after, seven of us were walking along the sidewalk to the bus stop, three blocks away.

My three uncles, two cousins, my brother and I squeezed into the same bus. First, we went to visit the Revolutionary Peasant Army's headquarters at the museum that housed China's First Communist Party Congress. These revolutionaries came long before Mao and used to meet in a private residence and gardens near Shanghai's center. These gardens were surrounded by tall walls that had a dragon with two heads resting at the top edge. The gardens had large stone sculptures and walkways similar to the ones I had seen in Hangzhou. The pavilions' architecture was also familiar to me now, with the latticed doors and windows, red columns and upturned eaves. Only everything was much more compact. The walkways, bridges, and porches of the several exhibition buildings were crowded with people. In one of the exhibition halls, we saw some swords encased in glass urns that were used around 1925 by the peasant revolutionary army to fight the lords and the imperialists who subdued the people. On the walls of these halls were pictures, illustrating the battles that had taken place. One picture in particular stands out in my mind. It was the picture of one of the first peasant leaders, leading a troop of peasants, carrying their weapons with a posture of war; they wore red sashes about their heads and had captured one of the imperialist landlords. It was new information to me to find out that the Peasant Revolutionary Movement had begun long ago and only gained momentum and total victory with Mao.

A long walk through the old shopping district in Shanghai followed the visit to this garden. The density of the crowds increased abruptly. Bicycles and cars were barred from this area, but thousands of shoppers were strolling by, sometimes tugging along a little child and carrying all forms of bags, nets, and packages. Vendors in the streets were selling all sorts of treats such as ice cream, fried puffs, drinks, and fruits. As I walked with my relatives, pressed by the crowds from all sides, I felt a sense of amusement. The sights, sounds, and smells fascinated me. The only thing that comes close to such an experience in America are the fairs and country festivals. The difference here was that it was a daily occurrence. Through a glass pane, I could see workers preparing dumplings, a Chinese favorite, for the consumption of the multitudes. We went into a wicker shop where Uncle Liu Tzu asked me to choose a gift. I chose a set of straw mats; they were inexpensive, but I had no desire to be extravagant. At every store, my uncle asked me what I wanted. He wanted to give me a porcelain vase, but I told him it would break. We passed in front of all kinds of shops for porcelain figurines, intricate carvings, embroidery and silk, paintings, and printing gadgets. In a toy store, my brother tried to find a harmonica suitable for his needs. My cousin helped me look for a game of "Go," but we could not find any.

We wound up in a former Buddhist temple that had been turned into a huge marketplace. It was so crowded that policemen and women were perched on high stools with megaphones, overlooking the crowd. Cousin Yi Dien apologized to me, saying: "Here one can only come to see crowds." The square directly in front of the temple was less crowded, so we were able to take a few group pictures. It was overcast, but Yi Dien had a good 35 mm Japanese camera, and I had my Kodak instamatic. Then Uncle Liu Tzu bought me a bag of Chinese fried puffs. They were simply delicious! We shed our adult formal ways and were like children enjoying an outing together in Shanghai, the city of my early childhood. Just before leaving this district, I saw a Western restaurant with a neon sign depicting a cocktail. Some graciousness of living existed here!

It was quite a trick to fit all seven of us in the same bus leading to the Huang Pu River. We let a few buses go by, opting for a less crowded one. Once aboard the bus, we trailed along the city's lower east side. Soon the river was in full view and we crossed a large bolted steel and concrete bridge. I could see that the river was very wide and held back by a walled embankment that ran alongside a park where a huge crowd strolled about. Some people were going down cement steps to an area where they could take boat rides. Then the bus veered away from the center of town into a narrow boulevard that looked rather deserted, where large warehouses to our right and gray weathered buildings to our left obstructed the view to the river.

We got off at a stoplight onto a narrow street that led to the port. Uncle Liu Tzu informed me, "This is the very place where you and your mother left Shanghai so long ago." I felt a sense of nostalgia. Both my brother and I remembered that day very well, and its images had haunted us all of our lives. I looked for the large covered area where my family had stood waiting to board the Wooster Victory, a United Nations chartered ship, to take refugees from China. I did not see this place. All I saw were a few people sitting around near a shed with their belongings. A few pedicabs went by, taking customers back to town. At the end of this road, we went through a gate and bought tickets to take the boat across the river. We stood on the pier for quite some time. I searched for the place where my father and brother had stood while I looked down from the ship. I was not sure where it could be. Some large ships were docked on the next pier while other ships floated in the nearby waters. Only this small docking place was open to the public. The other areas of the pier were fenced in by tall meshed wire and steel bars. But near the water, everything was in plain view. It looked like a busy port. I understood that Shanghai is China's main port, trading with almost every country on the globe. The river is very suited for this traffic because it is very deep and wide.

As I stood at the water's edge, I wondered whether this was really the place where I saw my father and brother for the last time. We opted not to take the ferry across the river. Instead, we took some pictures at this historical sight, taking in the water, the ships, and the steel cranes, and my brother and I, standing side-by-side thirty-two years later. It was good to be here again. The breeze blew softly as I beheld the place that had made all the difference in my life: the point of severance in my childhood. Yet I had returned, defying the cruel currents of destiny.

As we walked slowly back to the bus stop, I felt a sense of satisfaction and completion, and I knew my uncles and cousins and brother shared my joy. We stepped out at the park on the Huang Pu River's bank that I had seen earlier. My cousin pointed to one of Shanghai's landmarks, a building with a clock in its tower that my mother would certainly recognize. The people were swarming alongside the embankment wall, enjoying their Sunday strolls. Uncle Liu Tzu bought us all Popsicles, the Chinese bingjiling, from a lady vendor on the sidewalk. Another uncle bought us tangerines. I asked my cousin Yi Dien if I could walk alongside the wall to have another look at the river. Everyone then waited patiently for me while I was still trying to recapture something of my past. Then we crossed the sturdy steel bridge and I watched a trail of connected sampans streaming down the river, a sight I think is typical of the Orient.

Still with tangerines in hand, we sat in the backseat of a very slow bus. The bus driver was obviously engaged in an interesting conversation with the ticket bearer, so he was in no hurry. We cruised along at a slow pace of 15 m.p.h. We were due for lunch at the house of the kindly artist uncle, Qian Jia Jun, but we just had to be patient with this state of affairs. At least the bus was not crowded, so I had a good view of the city. We came to a wide arbored avenue, a newer section of Shanghai, with high-rise residential quarters. Next to this uncle's apartment house was a two-story modern department store. My cousin Yi Dien and my brother went into this department store in search of the "Go" game. They came out empty-handed because the one they found had pebbles made of plastic. They would try again later.

When we arrived, everyone was already packed into the small living room. Aunt Pei Yan sat with me on the sofa bed and I offered her some tangerine. The uncles were helping set up the table in the center, and soon, we were asked to take a place. We were eight or more persons, but well-accommodated around a square table filled with savory dishes that the artist uncle kept bringing out of the kitchen. They were all prepared by his mother-in-law, a petite woman with short gray hair and large working hands. She did not take lunch with us, but she was at everyone's service. We had pork, chicken, fish, and appetizers, all prepared in a unique way. I was touched by the host uncle's eagerness to please all of us, passing the food to one and then to another. An uncle remarked, "We thought of having this lunch in a restaurant, but it is better here as we can talk freely," and everyone agreed. I was perhaps the first person from the West with whom they could share their experiences. They had much to unburden themselves of concerning the Cultural Revolution. There was no conceit here; all that had gone a long time ago. All these people had been brought down to their knees during the Cultural Revolution when they had spent time in prison or in farm communes. It was translated to me that Qian Jia Jun, the artist uncle, had spent four years in prison, yet they all marveled that he had not spent that time idly; instead, he took it upon himself to learn the principles of mathematics. All his valuables, antiques, and a room full of books were destroyed; he saw some of them go up in flames. I understood that the whole nation had gone into a state of paranoia and engaged in persecuting the educated elite at this time. The elite had to be reeducated into Chairman Mao's peasant Communist philosophy, as summarized in his The Little Red Book of Quotations. The government now recognized its mistake and many who had suffered had been repaid with reparation money. Mao was no longer a god, but seen as a man with fallacies. In fact, Premier Zhou Enlai was more beloved by the Chinese now than Mao.

During the meal, we talked about the many difficulties each of us had encountered in our private lives, including how hard it had been for my brother to grow up without a mother. I mentioned how my stepfather had treated me cruelly when I was a child, but that he was kinder to me at the end of his life. My cousin Yun Yun asked me, "Why?" so I said, "Because he was old and sick and had mellowed in his ways."

Aunt Pei Yan remarked to me, "You are a very active person. Your father was also very active in his youth when he studied at the Tungshi University of Shanghai. Then she added, "Now he is a very old man who sits in his room meditating." I replied, "Like a monk in a cottage." Aunt Pei Yan wanted me to bring my father to America and relieve him of his poverty. His family considered my father something of an eccentric. He preferred simplicity to riches and the solitude of his room to social engagements.

When the meal was over, Uncle Liu Tzu and his daughter Yun Yun excused themselves from our company to go downtown to do some shopping. Aunt Pei Yan returned home. Uncle Henry Lou, my father's cousin, and the artist uncle would meet us later in the evening at Aunt Pei Yan's for dinner. That left my brother, my cousin Yi Dien, and I free for the afternoon.

We went once more to the apartment house where my mother and I used to live. This time, a pleasant and very feminine young lady opened the double metal doors at the top of the stairs. She allowed us into the balcony area, which made me realize my mother's huge terrace had been partitioned into many rooms and only a small balcony remained. Or had these rooms been hidden from sight by a bamboo fence my mother had at one end of the terrace? I could not really tell as we never did go into the former apartment to verify the change. I was glad that my cousin took a battery of pictures with his sophisticated camera because it was too dark and hazy for me to use my camera. When we were in the courtyard in front of the building, I said to my cousin, "My brother and I used to play here, and there used to be an old dilapidated car behind the building to our right." I went to see whether the car was still there, but it was not. The sentinel's booth was still in the passageway that led to the street. It was made of wood and looked weathered and beaten, but otherwise, structurally the same. The only difference was that it was placed on the opposite side. My brother also remembered it on the other side.

Once more, we took the bus downtown and braved the crowds. At the corner of Nanjing Road, the crowds were spilling over to the street despite the metal railings. A policeman supervised the pedestrian traffic at this intersection, so it was impossible to dodge the crowds by walking in the street instead of on the enclosed walk. The crowds moved slowly, and I kept my eye on my brother and cousin, determined not to lose sight of them in this dense mass of people. On a less-crowded side street, filled with parked bicycles, we found a sports equipment store that carried the "Go" game. My cousin was satisfied with the quality of this one—two sturdy boxes were filled with two hundred glass pebbles each—so he purchased it for me. I thanked my cousin for his generosity; the game had sentimental value to me because my father had played it since he was a young boy. I had so little of my father that any reminder of his life gave me joy.

My cousin asked me, "Do you play this game?"

I said, "No, I don't, but I want to learn. It is a reminder of my father."

"I also do not play it; it is very difficult."

I knew full well that these boxes were going to be a burden to my luggage, not to mention my arms, so I wondered how we would carry the boxes home. My cousin very gallantly took a thin net out of his pocket and said, "I come prepared."

After my brother purchased a harmonica, we rode the bus back to the apartment and then walked. On the way, I said to my cousin, "I find Shanghai very clean."

"You know it is cleaning month and the streets are swept more than usual," he replied.

Earlier that afternoon when we had crossed a wide boulevard with landscaped islands, I had seen young people seated at tables with people hovering about them. My cousin had said, "The young people are offering services free of charge such as sewing and mending shoes." I understood that this was a way they could show their dedication to the community. All this caught my attention, and I felt edified by this kind of solidarity of spirit.

Back at the apartment, everyone was expecting us. My father's cousin, Henry Lu, approached me with his black vinyl bag. Out of it he took a pair of baby slippers and gave them to me. He also took out two beautiful lined silk vests and said, "Please, can you mail one of these vests to my niece in New Jersey. You keep one." I could not understand all this generosity, but I could not refuse this gentle and perceptive man's offerings. He was tall and his gray hair was thinned, but he was not bald. His hands were expressive and his eyes deep and kind. He asked me, almost in a whisper, "Would you like to have a scroll with an old Chinese poem on it?"

I said, "I would like it if you want me to have it."

He went into the next room and brought back with him a scroll with a Chinese poem written by a famous Chinese poet. I asked him, "What does the poem say?" I did not expect it to be difficult for him.

He said, "I don't know because it is written in ancient symbols that are no longer used today." So he and the other uncles began translating the poem for me with the use of a few dictionaries of Chinese literature.

Then Uncle Liu Tzu called me over because his daughter and he had a few things to present to me. Out of a small brown bag came two pairs of baby slippers. They had all gone about town to buy me these slippers they knew I wanted, and now I had three pairs. It was an extraordinary sight to see Uncle Liu Tzu, a robust man accustomed to deal with things of importance, handling a tiny pair of slippers to give to this niece who had appeared on his doorstep after thirty-two years. He acted in a grandfatherly manner and asked me to come to the bedroom to choose a piece of silk material for my mother, for Aunt Jane in San Francisco, and for myself. The materials were of exquisite quality and taste, suitable for making dresses. I told them, "They are so beautiful that I cannot choose." Then he said, "Pack them and make the decision later."

After I spent some time in the bedroom arranging my luggage, I joined the family in the living room. My brother was about to play the harmonica for all of us while cousin Yi Dien taped him with his stereo cassette recorder. I did not know my brother could play the harmonica so well; he filled the place with such music that we couldn't help but break out in dance. I took turns swirling around with Aunt Pei Yan, Aunt Pei Ron, and one of my uncles. Even their white cat got into the act. Aunt Pei Ron took the cat in her arms and danced with it around the room. Luckily, the place was large enough and high enough to take all our romping. We had a swell time! I had not been there but a day, and already, we were dancing and laughing like old friends.

While Aunt Pei Ron and I were dancing, she slipped into my hand a jade ring that looked very much like a circle for a curtain rod. It had belonged to her mother and she wanted me to have it. This crowned my sense of being a part of this family. I even had in my possession an heirloom that I would treasure for the rest of my life. This jade band represented to me total inclusion in a family I had missed for more than three decades. It sealed our bond.

By then, Uncle Henry Lou and the artist uncle had finished translating the ancient poem on the scroll. This is the translation he wrote in my black notebook:

The gully is deep,
The pine tree is old,
Let us forget the glory or the fall;
The sky is wide,
The cloud is lazy,
Let books at ease.

So I went home with this lovely Chinese poem that had a mystical quality of blending feelings with nature's beauty and summoned us to look at the passage of time, letting go of whatever happened, and beholding the beauty of the moment. My uncles were proud of their achievement in translating this poem. I could see it in their faces.

The family decided to make a tape for my mother with songs and messages from everyone present. Some wrote their messages first on paper and gave them to me to correct while others rehearsed what they were going to say. I acted as the script director and my cousin Yi Dien acted as the stage director, giving each person the cue when it was his or her turn on the tape. My brother went first:

Dearest Mommy,

I think about you very much. Today my sister Marianchen and I went to the old house. I have many memories. Hope to see you soon in America. I will play the harmonica for you to express my deep love.

He then played three beautiful melodies: "La Paloma," and two other Chinese compositions with a lively dance rhythm. I thought, "How talented my brother is." His love for music went deeper than mere appreciation; he was able to blow a mouthful without a single formal lesson. He was an artist in the genuine sense of the word. He expressed himself in painting with color and visual impressions, and now with music made by his own breath.

Then other members of the family followed:

I am your old friend Wang Pei Yan. My dearest Agnes, I think of you. I will sing now a Germany song for you.

She proceeded to sing the song in German. It was very touching since half of the song was almost spoken. Both she and her husband were graduates of the Tungshi University Medical School, a German-founded institution where they both learned German.

Next was Liu Yi Den's message:

Dear Aunt,

I am your nephew. My name is Liu Yi Dien and my mother is Wang Pei Yan. When I was a baby in Shentu, you may have seen me in my aunt Pei De's family. When I was a child I often played with Goggeli (my brother's nickname). Since I have understood the world, I always wished my cousin Goggeli could see his mother, you, as soon as possible. Today, I'm very glad to see my cousin, Marianchen. I believe Goggeli can go to America to see you soon. I wish you will be very happy. Now I am a surgeon and I do post-graduate work in Shanghai Second Medical College. My teacher is a famous surgeon who is visiting America. I hope I shall go to America to study. When I do, I certainly will see you. See you in America.

Uncle Liu Tzu delivered his message in German. Here is a translation:

Dearest Agnes,

How are you? Now Marianchen and her brother are here with our family. We have not seen each other for over forty years. Pei Yan and I are filled with joy over the reunion of Marianchen and her brother in China. We wish that our beloved Agnes and Marianne would visit Shanghai again in a short period of time.

In a low measured but heartfelt voice, uncle Henry Lu said:

Dear Agnes,
I'm Henry Lu speaking to you. Perhaps you remember I met you first in Chungking, the World Capital of China, forty years ago when you just arrived from Germany with my cousin Fu Shih. I am now sixty years old and shall retire from work next week. I am very healthy. Congratulations for your family reunion! I'm sure you must be very very happy. Please give my regards to my cousin Jane when you meet her. My brother Homer who you know well also gives you his best regards. He is very well too. Good-bye and good luck.

My cousin Yun Yun also wrote her message and read it:

Dear Aunt,
I am your niece. My name is Liu Yun Yun. My mother is Wang Pei Yan [Chinese brides keep their family name]. My father is Liu Tzu. Today I am very glad to see my cousin Marianne. Now I am a computer engineer and I work in the Computer Center in Shanghai Training Committee. I hope I shall go to America to study. See you in America. I wish you will be very happy.

Aunt Pei Ron spoke her lines in a candid and moving manner:

Dear Agnes,
I am Wang Pei Ron. I was thinking very much always but cannot to see you. Very glad meeting Marianchen in Shanghai. So I love you. My love with Marianchen go on to you. Kiss you, Agnes. Goodbye and good luck.

The formal part of the tape was ended with another German song sung by Aunt Pei Yan. My brother continued to play the harmonica and Aunt Pei Ron and I danced a few more rounds. She was a fun person with a dramatic personality. She said, "I remember rocking you to sleep when you were very young, but you would not go to sleep." My stubborn nature was already apparent then.

We had our last dinner. Aunt Pei Yan said, "I'm so sorry you only stay in Shanghai two days." I was rather quiet during this supper. We were served the accustomed meat dishes, vegetables, and apéritifs. Some chose to drink beer, but Aunt Pei Yan knew my preference and brought me a carbonated soda from the refrigerator. I listened to my brother, who was very animated and probably speaking about his desire to go to America. I was glad everyone was more relaxed and didn't have to make a tremendous effort to speak English with me. We understood each other with simple sentences while everything was said in the eyes, smiles, and wishes.

The white furry cat meowed and pawed my lap. She wanted something to eat. I tore a piece of chicken from my plate and tossed it on the floor. The cat smelled it and went away. Aunt Pei Ron, who was seated next to me, noticed the cat's refusal and said in a deep emphatic tone, "She likes fish." Cousin Yi Dien, in a joking way, added, "The cat is neither a she nor a he; it is an it." He had the honor of neutralizing her.

Now I had to think about how to carry all the gifts that kept on coming. Uncle Liu Tzu gave me a couple of colorful hemp rugs, one of which I squeezed into my large suitcase, and the other I folded into the hand-net I was going to carry. In this net, I also had a large Chinese calendar, a few of my brother's paintings rolled into a cylinder, together with the dolls, kite, etcetera, etcetera. There wasn't another inch of space. I wondered how I would carry all this onto the plane when I also had a flight bag and a purse filled to the brim. Chinese generosity and hospitality did not limit itself to the twelve-course dinners served to guests on festive occasions, but it extended itself to an unreasonable number of gifts given to the celebrated person.

I should note here that Uncle Wang Fu Ming never was able to come to Shanghai to see me off, but he had left some gifts for my family with Aunt Pei Yan. He had bought me an ink pen and a silk-covered diary that I later used to write my Brazilian memories that furnished material for this book. My husband, Tony, received a carved pipe with this inscription on the box: "In everlasting memory, Uncle Fu Ming." My uncle had also managed to develop all the black-and-white pictures he'd taken and had them waiting for me there. He asked in a note if I would be so kind as to develop the colored film because the process was difficult in China and very expensive. I gave my brother one of the pictures of myself to give my father and on the back I wrote: "In Memory, to Father, Marianne." My father was still on my mind.

The next morning after breakfast, my brother and I took a walk to the American Consulate, situated across the street from my mother's old apartment on the corner of the block. My brother was happy that we would have some immigration questions settled. We walked briskly on this partially sunny day, and in no time, we were in front of the American Consulate's gates, a mansion in former years, surrounded by cement walls. A Chinese guard, lean and short, barred my brother's entrance, but he allowed me in because I had an American passport. Inside, a Chinese receptionist, with a more sophisticated appearance than I normally encountered in China, greeted me with perfect English, asking me to sign the register and sit in the next room. I went through carved wooden double doors and sat in front of a wide, polished wooden counter. A handsome man in his middle thirties, dressed in a white shirt and tie, ushered me to his office by the counter while his secretary, a charming American lady, sorted out papers nearby.

As I sat in front of the desk of this pleasant gentleman with a reddish mustache, I said, "I came to China to see my father and brother whom I hadn't seen in thirty-two years. I am now an America citizen, but was born in Chunking, China in 1944. My brother is waiting outside. He is a Chinese citizen and has intentions of immigrating

Marianne Campagna

to the U.S. with his family. My German mother is also an American citizen and is sponsoring my brother. We are having trouble obtaining an official birth certificate to prove to the authorities in the U.S. that my brother is indeed my mother's son." Then I showed him some pictures of my father, mother, and my brother taken thirty-eight years ago in Guilin, China.

He looked at the pictures with concern and listened attentively to everything I had to say before he remarked, "I'm not surprised that you are having troubles obtaining the proper documents. All I do in this Shanghai office is dig up the last forty years. The pictures and your aunt's affidavit of your brother's birth will serve quite well as a record of birth." Then he asked me, "Would you like to draw up an affidavit of support for your brother at this office?"

I explained, "I'm leaving China this afternoon and so have very little time. My mother will be drafting an affidavit of support when I return."

The light came softly through the grated, leaded windows where some greenery could be seen. It was good to be here talking to a man who treated me with the utmost courtesy. It was good to speak English again without restraint or the burden of translation. I realized here how American I really was. More than twenty years of living in America had shaped my spirit, and there was no denying I was an American at heart as well as on paper. When I took my leave from this kind and well-mannered gentleman, he handed me his business card, saying, "Please contact me if I can be of any help."

I looked at the gold-rimmed card and realized he was the Consul himself. I felt honored to have had this meeting.

When I returned outside, my brother was waiting for me at the curb. I said, "The pictures and Aunt Pei Yan's affidavit will be good in the U.S."

He was once more reassured. We passed once more in front of my mother's apartment for the last time. My brother turned to me and said, "Perhaps Mommy, you, and I can come together to visit old place some day."

I smiled and said, "Yes, it will be possible!" This place also held for him cherished memories, and I wondered whether the same family bond could be reestablished.

The family gathered at Aunt Pei Yan's for my farewell lunch. Aunt Pei Ron and cousins Yi Dien and Yun Yun had taken the day off from work. Uncle Liu Tzu would be coming soon from the hospital to join us. Aunt Pei Yan asked me to sit at the head of the table since Uncle Liu Tzu would be late. I declined and sat on the side next to my brother. We chatted about trivial matters, comparing a Chinese lunch with an American lunch. Yi Dien said, "I would like to come to your house to eat salad and a sandwich. If I become a famous surgeon, I would like to invite your family to Shanghai." Aunt Pei Ron commented, "The ordinary Chinese family has to be very economical with food. They do not eat bingu (apple) or cakes every day. They have to make due with very little at times." I sensed she wanted to give me a more realistic view of people's lives. Uncle Liu Tzu now arrived and joined us at the table.

Earlier, Aunt Pei Ron had shown me an old family album. In it was a picture of my mother and father taken with Aunt Pei De's family when my mother lived with them in Shentu during her first year in China. It was very interesting for me to see these pictures of the past. I also saw a great many pictures of my grandfather, Wang Sao Ao, and his last wife. At this point, Aunt Pei Ron gave me a picture of my grandfather and his wife taken when they were swimming at a beach. She leaned over to me and said, "Your grandfather was very fond of you." I was proud to have this picture, and I do have a faint recollection of his round face and his short-cropped hair. She then said, "Your grandfather kept a family group picture in his living room for many years with you and your mother in the picture." It pleased me that we were so included, and her words contradicted the earlier impression I'd had that my grandfather had wanted us cut off from the family.

My luggage was piled up in the living room next to the couch. Uncle Liu Tzu and cousin Yi Dien gave me a few more things to put in my already bulging hand-net: a few scrolls and some books to be given to a friend in San Francisco. Then each of us took a piece of the luggage and went downstairs. I said goodbye to Uncle Liu Tzu's mother, a short, stout, peaceful person, and the young maid who had cooked the delicious meals. As they stood by the entrance, I said, "Xie xie nie" ("Thank you" in Mandarin). They replied, "Nie how bu how, bu how." ("Don't mention it; don't mention it.")

In the courtyard, we waited for the light blue Chevy that belonged to the hospital to take us to the airport. I took one last look at the surroundings, and my cousin pointed out the building across the street where Aunt Wang Yuan (my father's cousin in San Francisco) used to live. I could see some clothes hanging on a clothesline between the trees and a middle-aged woman doing her daily Tai Chi exercises. In a few moments, I would not see these sights anymore.

I was glad the sun was shining so I could use the film in my camera for the last pictures. I took everyone's picture in small groups, and I got some beautiful smiles. Uncle Liu Tzu stood by his wife as I snapped their picture. Aunt Pei Ron embraced my brother and said, "Please take a picture of my favorite nephew and me. You are lucky to have such a nice brother!" Inside, I felt a sudden shade of jealousy; my brother had been part of this family all his life. I had been celebrated for these two days, but in many ways, it was mainly cosmetic. I could not share their lives the way my brother had.

For a moment, I worried that the car would not come in time and I would miss the plane. I thought, "I should be at the airport by twelve because the Pan Am flight is leaving at 1:00 p.m." But my worries were soon dispelled when I saw the blue Chevy pull into the yard. Uncle Liu Tzu and Aunt Pei Ron bid me adieu with warm embraces because they were returning to work. Aunt Pei Yan, cousins Yi Dien and Yun Yun, my brother, and I slid into the car seats. The chauffeur, a courteous gentleman, drove us to the outskirts of town to the Hung Qiao area where the Shanghai airport was located; he took the old Lafayette Street, just like my mother had when she took me to the boarding school by rickshaw. The boarding school was in the Hung Qiao area, so my relatives in the car helped me to spot it. The car stopped in front of a brick building that they thought might be the boarding school. I said, "I remember a large garden around the building and it was set in a ways from the street." This could not be the building since it was facing directly onto the street and looked like it had been built in the last ten years. Well, I never did see my first boarding school, and it was just as well, for my memories remained pristine as I had experienced them, tinged with much sadness for being away from my mother.

At the airport, in front of the main building, I helped take my luggage out of the trunk and gave my brother his black vinyl bag. Then I said, "I will pay for your flight back to Hangzhou." He refused. He would take the train with jammed cabins, a four-hour ride from Shanghai. My relatives were barred entrance beyond the small vestibule just inside the airport door. My brother was allowed to accompany me to the ticket counter. I waved goodbye to my aunt and cousins. For the first time in one month, I was among many American tourists returning home. They were sophisticated people, and my brother was fascinated with the way they spoke English. He pointed to a lady he thought spoke English very well. He had a preview of what was to come for him in America, and I wondered, "Would he be happy in America?"

At the ticket counter, I obtained a boarding pass while two ticket agents helped each other fill out the necessary tags for my luggage. I would be boarding four planes to reach Detroit, so the luggage had to be marked with the appropriate abbreviations and numbers. I had to pay fifteen yuans in taxes, so I had to ask my brother for some of the Chinese money I had given him. Then my brother got a cart and I put my luggage on it. I still had to go through another checkpoint. My brother could not follow me beyond this place. I embraced him and said, "I hope to see you soon in America. Thank you for everything, and tell Father I think of him and wish him much happiness." I did not have to wait in line with the other tourists, so I proceeded with the cart to the customs area. My brother told me he would wait in the lobby in case I had difficulty with any item I was taking to America. I did not have any difficulty, so I did not return.

I parked my cart in front of a tall and handsome official who spoke English very well. He asked me for my customs declaration that I had filled out on my way into Beijing and for my passport. I told him, "I was born in China and my father lived in China all his life, teaching mathematics at Zhejiang University."

A smile broke out on his face and he said, "So you are half-Chinese."

Sensing a chance of benevolence I said, "Is it possible for me to be refunded the taxes I had to pay for a watch I am bringing back to America because of malfunction?"

He scoffed at my impudence and said emphatically, "Impossible." He told me to open my large suitcase, but he did not find anything of importance. The family had worried that the antique scroll with the poem would be confiscated, but luckily, I had put it in the small suitcase. He opened the scrolls my cousin was sending to his friend in San Francisco and also my brother's paintings that were rolled up and sticking out of the net.

So now I was free to go to the waiting area, a large comfortable space bathed in light with modern seats. Then I heard a man remark, "This isn't exactly what you call a bustling airport."

A woman retorted, "No, it doesn't have the madness of a Los Angeles Terminal."

A few people were scattered here and there. A young black woman, probably with diplomatic status, sat at one end with her toddler, who still sucked a pacifier. A businessman paced the aisles impatiently. I rested my things on a seat and saw a tall lean Chinese man of humble appearance, dressed in the usual Mao suit, standing close by. I approached him and we started a conversation. I told him my story. His English was not very good, but he made me understand that he was going to Los Angeles to visit his mother and brother whom he had not seen in thirty-four years. The consul had been right; many people were in my predicament, who only now were able to pick up the pieces of their lives after more than thirty years of interruption. Our lives had been tossed about by the waves of history, torn apart, changed, separated for more than one generation, and now we were trying to juggle everything back together. This was not an easy task, considering the distance, the influence of time, and the difference of language and mode of living. But one thing remained: the human heart seeks that which is its own. This man was just beginning his journey to see his mother and brother after so long a separation, and I was just completing mine.

Chapter 20

———— ❀ ————

Flight Home

Soon my flight to Tokyo/San Francisco was called. The handful of passengers in the waiting area went through the glass doors, harboring with them the lingering images of Chinese citizens with their faces pressed against the glass panes, trying to catch a last glimpse of their loved ones who were able to travel to freedom. We walked silently toward the parked plane on the tarmac, realizing the importance of having walked in this once forbidden land. The Chinese man whom I had just spoken with helped me with one of my hand pieces. He had a slight limp, short cropped hair, and large teeth, but he was a gentleman through and through. The stewardess directed us to our seats, mine being a window seat on the third row, just behind the wing that gave me a clear view.

We took off shortly after boarding. As the plane ascended, I could see peasants working in the vegetable plots near the airport and rows and rows of typical Chinese hot houses. Then the ground took on an aspect of subdivisions of land where there were some long houses and small villages. Gradually, we were over the clouds that looked as vast as snow. As I looked out again, waves of mist passed the plane's wings, and we were leaving behind more and more land. Soon we were over China's coast, and I could see where the water met the land. My eyes followed the coastline. I was about to leave the huge country of China, which from up here looked like a sleeping giant, but which I knew was bustling with life and vitality. No one was in the seat next to mine, so I was able to slide my filled hand-net with its odds and ends under the seat in front of me. Whether I would be able to pull it out again was another question. My flight bag was next to my feet.

I felt comfortable and relaxed, with a sense of having experienced life. The last few hectic weeks were now behind me, and I soon would settle into the role of a suburban mom, albeit sometimes terribly monotonous.

I looked out again and saw that we were flying over an island that looked very rugged and uninhabitable. All I could see was a large expanse of undulating mountain ridges of a greenish brown color. We cruised over the ocean some more and sometimes the clouds that appeared like vast fields of snow would transform themselves into fluffy cotton candy, becoming less dense. As we approached Japan, I could see the sun through the shutters of the wings. It was low in the sky and left a warm glow that almost made the wings look like they were on fire.

We arrived in Tokyo at about 4 p.m., but with the time change, we had lost an hour so it was 5 p.m. The stewardess ordered everyone to deplane and take his/her belongings. Since I had so much to drag along, I asked her whether I could leave some of my things in the plane. She called down to the main desk at the terminal and found out that everyone would be reseated, so it was safer to take everything with me. A host of new people would be coming into the plane, so reluctantly, I pulled everything from under the seat. At the terminal, we stood in line for the new boarding pass. I saw two American youths, a man and woman, who looked like they had been in China for a long time. I talked to the young man, who had a red beard and the air of an adventurer. Knowing full well the inconveniences of living in China for a Westerner—lack of private bathrooms and constant crowds—I said to him, "You must be glad to be going home!"

"Well, I am really a masochist," he replied. "A company is paying me a lot of money to go back next month." The young lady who accompanied him around the airport wore boots and looked somewhat unkempt. They looked like they were returning from the Third World, where life had been reduced to the essentials, and they were now entering a world where fashion and appearance counted for something, it being the priority of many. The departure gate began to fill up with more and more Japanese people with modern clothes and haircuts, bowing and chatting politely with one another. A very beautiful American lady, dressed in a black suit and expensive rings, was stretched out on a bench taking a nap. She succumbed to sleep, oblivious of the crowds.

This time I got a seat near the window just in front of the wings. And wouldn't you know it, next to me sat the female American student I had met in the terminal. We began a conversation almost immediately.

"I have been studying in Beijing for the last year," she told me, "and I take part in a conclave of foreigners at the University of Beijing who are experts in political science and world affairs. However, I plan to switch my major to Chinese language and culture and teach English in China in future years. I have mixed feelings about China, but I want to return nevertheless. In China, I felt the happiest and the saddest. The place has this gut level way of gripping your feelings. I saw cruelty as well as kindness during my many travels by train through the different parts of China."

The ambiguity of the two worlds, America and China, remained in me as well as in her. She told me she felt uneasy with American superficiality and arrogance. I told her about my experiences with my family, which in many ways were different from those of a student. We were two people trying to embrace two worlds.

For dinner, I found the steak, strawberries, and roasted potatoes particularly delicious because I had not eaten Western food for over a month. Then as night fell, and with the shutters drawn, we tried to rest the best we could. Somewhere over the Pacific, we crossed the International Date Line, so I would be arriving in San Francisco at the same hour I had departed Shanghai, but exactly a day later. A couple of hours before landing, the stewardess handed out the Customs Declaration forms. Each of us was allowed 300 dollars worth of items free of duty. From the receipts in my wallet, I could see that I had a little more than 300 dollars, so I had to itemize the gifts I was bringing into the States. I also had to include the dried berries that were given to me by my brother's family since all animal and plant products were checked very carefully to avoid spreading disease. All this took time. I did not want to be in any kind of trouble because of trivialities. The student fellow traveler had to declare only one item: a 400 dollar silk rug she had bought for her mother.

As we flew over San Francisco Bay, I could see a contour of hills overlooking the water. A thin haze partly veiled the Golden Gate Bridge. It was warm, sunny, and green in San Francisco. When I disembarked, I saw Aunt Jane waiting for me on the other side of the glass. She waved to me, indicating she would wait for me outside the Customs area. I had to walk through a very long corridor almost to the terminal's opposite end. My arms and hands were killing me under the weight of all the packages and bags. In the Customs area, a friendly chap asked me about the berries so I opened the large suitcase and showed them to him. He let me go without having to pay any excess duty. I could leave the suitcases in the corner for further processing.

Aunt Jane was outside the door waiting for me. She was elegantly dressed with becoming jewelry. We'd had so little time to chat when I had met her before my flight to Tokyo, but there was ample time now since my flight to Denver did not leave for another hour and a half. Aunt Jane had been my mother's only link to my father and brother over the years. Their relationship was based on mutual gain. My mother's outpouring of friendship toward Aunt Jane kept her informed about "Goggeli" (my brother's nickname since childhood), and Aunt Jane in turn had felt a sense of power from being the only point of contact. In their letters, they would often refer to gifts and favors to keep the communication lines open.

Aunt Jane often had appeared conflicted over the years, knowing she was treading on dangerous grounds; the family wanted silence, especially my grandfather. If the authorities discovered any communication with the West, any member of the family could be charged with treason and placed in labor camps, if not worse. Knowledge that my brother had a German mother was a known part of his history, so he and all the family had to be careful not to incite suspicion. In one letter, Aunt Jane had stated, "One cannot ride two horses at the same time, especially if they are both going in different directions." Was she referring to my mother or to herself? Yet, they had their secret plot, if only on paper. In another letter, Jane had suggested that my brother could be smuggled out through the island of Macao, a former Portuguese colony on China's coast. Yet Aunt Jane was also stricken with fear of the authorities, her own husband having been imprisoned for years, and according to her, he had died in prison. My brother, however, told me he had not died, but she had left China anyway, via Hong Kong, to escape the Communist oppression. She eventually moved to San Francisco where she married a wealthy American. In my mother's papers, I came across a typewritten letter, supposedly from my father, but unsigned, that stated simply, "Your son is fine. Do not write. Wang Fu Shih." Later, I compared that letter with another Jane had sent and found that the water markings on both matched. I was sure she had sent that warning to my mother because my father would have had no access to such paper or a similar typewriter and he would have written the letter in German. Another factor that might have motivated Jane was that in her youth she had been in love with my father, even though he was her first cousin. I knew all this context when I met her in San Francisco.

She said, "I would like to take you to Chinatown for lunch. We could have Peking Duck together, but there is so little time." Food was the last item on my mind. They had fed us so well on the plane. My aunt helped me with some of my hand pieces, and then we boarded the shuttle bus to the United Airlines terminal.

I said, "You know, no one wears makeup in China."

This seemed strange even to her, a lady who had lived in China most of her life, so she replied, "Oh, I would look awful without makeup. I am eager to hear about your experiences with your father and brother, and especially about your experiences with your aunts and uncles in Shanghai, my old stomping grounds."

"I found Shanghai to be very modern. The buses were, of course, another matter. They were super-crowded."

"That is why in the old days the ladies wore tight-fitting silk dresses, so they could slide easily through the crowds." We both laughed.

At the domestic terminal, I obtained a cart and we sat down in the waiting area for the gate for my next flight. I handed Aunt Jane all of her presents from the family and from me, as well as the scrolls, books, and embroidered blouses she was to give to family and friends around San Francisco. She said, "Lucky, I come well-prepared," and out came a black silk bag from her purse. A kind couple across from us gave me a cup of tea. While I was sipping it, I noticed that my hands were trembling. My aunt knew the cause immediately, "With all that you had to carry out of the plane, it is no wonder your hands are trembling." I was glad I was able to lighten my load with her.

Before I could feel totally comfortable with her, I had to mention the picture I had sent her some twenty years earlier. "You know, I found a picture of myself I had sent you in 1962 among other pictures in my brother's house. He said Aunt Pei Yan from Shanghai had sent it to him; she had received it from you." She was startled with the revelation. I just had to find out the truth, although I had no intentions of unearthing the past for the sake of friction or revenge. Her explanations were more than reasonable to me.

She told me, "The social conditions in China were so precarious at the time that no one dared communicate with the West. When I was on the border of China and Hong Kong, my knees were trembling when an official confronted me. We were so afraid then." She dissipated the rumors that it was my grandfather who ordered silence for all these years.

With this matter behind us, I showed her all the pictures Uncle Fu Ming had taken in Hangzhou and also the old treasured pictures of my father, my brother, and

I when we were young that I had kept in the tattered leather box. She did not know I had all these ancient pictures of my father. From the current pictures, she could see that my father looked quite well. She said, "You performed a miracle. You brought new life to this old man who not too long ago was close to death."

I replied, "I enjoyed my father's company. He was filled with philosophical ideas and interesting stories." Then I recited the Boy Scout motto my father remembered well: "wisdom, mercy, and courage." She could not remember my father being quite this way.

Now it was time for my flight for Denver. I said goodbye to Aunt Jane and then boarded the plane. I realized it was broad daylight, but I hadn't had a full night's sleep. Next to me was a handsome young man named Peter who was going to Denver to start a new job. His wife would follow him shortly. I was somewhat spaced out and glassy eyed, but I tried to make as much sense of my environment as possible. The American experience was again dawning on me, and I was trying to blend the two experiences, China and America, with ease. It was pleasant to see the beautiful blond stewardesses with their gracious manners. This was indeed a more sophisticated and comfortable world. But behind the luscious façade, I knew pain also existed—pain brought about by fierce competition in the workforce, criticism caused by the demands of high standards, and above all, the pain of isolation created by a highly technical, self-sufficient, and pluralistic society where the family was fragmented and people had little time for one another. Nevertheless, there were also joys here. It was a freer world where the individual was paramount. The opportunities for creative and fulfilling work were endless. And here, like anywhere else, we had to face each hour and carve out for ourselves meaningful and productive moments with courage and endurance.

As the plane flew over the Rockies, I was surprised to see that Denver was located on a plateau rather than nestled in the mountains as I had first imagined. When we arrived in Denver, Peter, the suave and attentive gentleman who sat next to me, helped me carry my heavy hand-net to the waiting area where I would board the plane to Detroit. I thanked him and wished him luck in his new job. Then I sat down, relieved to be almost home. I went to a phone booth and called home to announce my arrival. When I heard Michelle's voice through the receiver, tears welled up in my eyes. I had been gone for so long, but it had been necessary. My mother said, "I'm here with the children. Tony is in Chicago on a business trip. Sam (my father-in-law) and Angie (my sister-in-law) will pick you up at the airport. Everyone is excited and cannot wait till you get home." When I sat down again, I watched young people dressed in jeans and feathered hairdos go by. Yes, I was in America.

On the flight to Detroit, a young well-dressed woman with an air of professional arrogance sat next to me. She was busy going over papers for some kind of seminar and did not have much to say. I looked out the window. The moon was shining, and I could see some stars. I was going into a second night in less than twelve hours. I thought of my father, "We shall see each other again for we shall live one hundred years." Everything had gone by so quickly. We were descending. I would be home with my mother and my kids. When the aircraft landed, I could see it was snowing.

The snow passed rapidly by as the plane moved forward toward the terminal.

When I stepped through the arrival gate, my father-in-law and sister-in-law were there to greet me with welcoming smiles. Angie had an extra coat in case I needed one. She said, "You look like you came from China. I see the people on TV carrying these fish nets." She was right. The net was unsightly with bulging rugs, scrolls, boxes, and packages. After I claimed my luggage from the conveyor belt, my father-in-law drove me home in the snow. I talked all the way, telling them how things were in China, especially the food and the crowds. The roads were peaceful. A three-inch blanket of snow covered the ground. Millions of particles of snow danced around streetlights. It felt like Christmas, even though it was March 8, 1982. I was coming home laden with surprise packages for happy children.

I walked to the door of my home, making footprints in the snow. I was here. I opened the door and Suzy rushed to my side with a startled and delighted look. Lisa and Michelle looked at me with surprise and happiness. They too were glad I was home. Each embraced me affectionately. My mother, who had been so kind to mind the kids while Tony was gone, had set the table for tea and was eager to hear all that I had to say about China, my father and brother. Sara, my youngest child, was sleeping, but was awakened. I carried her in my arms in her warm sleeper, while she rested her head on my shoulders. She was still half-asleep and did not know quite what to make of this homecoming. Of all my children, Sara suffered my absence the most. It was as if I had vanished from the earth and all her security and comfort were gone. We had to grow accustomed to one another again. She had a cough, and as I held her, I felt she had lost some weight.

Just as in China, I couldn't wait to give them all their presents. I read their notes and saw all the decorations they had made for me, including the "Welcome Home" sign. We did not have much time for tea. I gave my mother all her presents, and after the children went to bed, we had some time to talk. She listened to the tape my brother and family made in Shanghai. A torrent of memories swept her mind. She could not but have tears in her eyes. She was crying. She needed time to sort all of it out. Tony called from Chicago and told me he had followed my journey home, hour by hour. He was sorry he couldn't be with me, but he had left me a long letter he had written in haste during one of his escapades to a hamburger restaurant. The domestic scene with four children had proven to be a little much for him. He was glad I was home and that I could take charge of things and we could get on with our lives. A tinge of sadness came over me because he was not there to greet me. My mother had written me while I was in China, but Tony had not done so. Only now would I hear about all the difficulties he'd had with the children and that he was happy I was home.

Part V

Family Fate Unfolding

Chapter 1

=== ✿ ===

Intervening Years

I had found part of myself in my father, in China, but it was not enough. I still felt like an uprooted person and the sap of joy did not flow in my veins. I was unhappy and recognized it, but I could not single out the cause. It was true I was far from Brazil and the city I most loved, Rio de Janeiro, under whose mountain I basked and from where I drew sustenance and pleasure. Now I was living the monotonous life of a suburban housewife laden with domestic work, isolation, and above all, an unhappy marriage.

In the ensuing years, I worked desperately to break away from my depression and unhappy life. I was still searching for myself and my role in society. I had enrolled in art classes at Schoolcraft College before going to China, and with those credits, I was able to obtain a teaching certificate. But before I applied for a teaching job, I had to wait for Sara to enter kindergarten.

Meanwhile, I worked on my book about my experiences. At first I called it Going Home, Coming Home, and then I changed it to Longing, and finally, after looking deeply into my soul, I named it Reflections from Gavea. I would spend days and nights on the typewriter, recalling my trip to China. It wasn't until years later that I decided to include in the book my full story, realizing that if I left out Brazil and the U.S., as well as my parents' background, I would only paint part of the picture. But the story had taken years in the making and would take many more years in the writing, so I had to continue on with my life. I was plenty busy, and even though I had Sara at home, I felt at times that I wasn't present in her life. I remember writing a poem on March 26, 1984, entitled "The Magic of Your Day" that captured how I felt at the time:

Can I share in the
    magic of your day?
My skies no longer

palpitate with stars
Nor do grasshoppers
laugh
And butterflies
dance in the
breezy waves
Can I share your world
Where Teddy bears sleep
And hummingbirds
speak
While cat whiskers
caress your cheeks
Can I share in the
kneading of the dough
And the shaping of
     a crocodile
When there is no time
And all the pieces
have been pulled apart?
Someday I'll find the
     golden thread
Which joins your life
with mine
O child
Someday there will be time.

I had so many obligations and tasks to accomplish with the housework and then my career. To occupy herself, Sara had an imaginary friend, Manny. Sara would open the front door and ask me whether she could let Manny in; she also would save a space for Manny next to her at the table. Sometimes, Sara would go by herself around the block to visit her friend Ally and they would play Barbie dolls. But most of all, she liked to accompany Suzy when she went with Tim, their next-door neighbor friend, and his father, Jon, to visit his grandmother in Dearborn, a suburb of Detroit.

In 1984, I enrolled in several creative writing classes. The teachers were very enthusiastic about my book. I even sent a few chapters to prominent publishing houses, and some even had a meeting about my book, but in the end, it was rejected because it needed more editorial work than they could furnish at the time. So it remained shelved till I could get back to it. That same year, I decided to be a substitute teacher in the school districts surrounding Canton, where I lived. I was called early every morning and taught English, French, Spanish, German, and even math in the high schools and middle schools. I also had several assignments that lasted several weeks where I taught art and engaged the students in painting a wall in their classroom.

In March, 1984, my brother arrived from China. My mother went to meet him in San Francisco, and they were both overjoyed to see each other. At first, my brother stayed with my mother in her small flat in Redford, adjacent to Detroit. Through my connections with an art teacher in Ann Arbor, I was able to set up an art exhibit for him at the North Commons building, a student center at the University of Michigan. The art exhibit was a success and he made over 1,000 dollars. With this money, he was able to buy a table to open a modest office to practice acupuncture. One day, I came home to find my brother parked outside with an antique Cadillac he had purchased for 800 dollars. He was so proud of it! He showed me how the windows and even the seats moved with the touch of a button. But the joy was not to last—a few weeks later, he found his car vandalized and stripped to nothing, and he did not have insurance. He did not let this dishearten him. He took a part-time job at Trapper's Alley, a hip shopping center downtown, located in old renovated buildings, doing people's portraits, and thereby built up his acupuncture business to buy another car.

Sadly, just a few months after my brother's arrival, my mother suffered a stroke, due to untreated high blood pressure. She was very suspicious of Western medicine, so she had always been self-sufficient in treating all her and my ailments with her potions and herbs; therefore, she was not going to concede to taking pills this late in her life. The stroke left her unable to walk because she had lost her sense of balance. When she was in the hospital, I brought her homemade soup and papaya, for which she was very grateful. Once she called me close and said, "Mousie, open the drawer!" I opened the nightstand drawer and saw she had spilled all her pills in it. I was shocked to see the pills haphazardly lining the drawer's crevices, but now I understood why the doctors were befuddled that her blood pressure would not go down. I had no recourse but to tell Dr. Cecilia Hissong, a friend of mine who was taking care of her, that my mother had been throwing away her pills. The doctor confronted her, but that only resulted in my mother looking at me like she had been betrayed. I was no longer her partner-in-crime. My mother then went to a rehabilitation center; in six weeks, she was able to regain her gait with the aid of a cane. My brother also went to visit; in fact, I used this opportunity to teach him how to drive on the picturesque country road on the way to the Rehab Center at St. Joseph's Hospital.

By August of 1984, my mother had recovered almost completely and was able to drive and carry on her new life with my brother. Aunt Caroline and my cousin Hildegard came to visit from Germany to attend an anniversary of the Sisters of Mercy at Mercy College where my aunt had taught, as well as to meet my brother. My mother had a small gathering at her flat, and I, in turn, had another party at my house. All seemed relatively normal except that my mother became obsessed with my brother and did not give him much freedom. My brother then asked me whether he could spend some time with my family since he could not tolerate my mother smothering him. Later, he got a small apartment for himself near my mother's flat.

With my brother living nearby, my mother quit coming to see me and the children so often; before she had come every day after school to lend me a hand. On Mother's Day the following year, I had wanted to bring her some flowers, but she had told me she would not be home; she and Goggeli (my brother) were going to dinner in Windsor, Canada (across the bridge from downtown Detroit). I had felt somewhat crushed and cried. The mother who had been mine all along did not want to see me. I had lost her trust to a brother who was absent for thirty-four years. Yet, she went to Germany that summer with high blood pressure and all, and on her return, presented me with an amethyst ring she had received from her sister Maria.

On Thursday, May 16, 1986, I received a call in the morning from my brother, saying, "Mommy is sick. You must come to her apartment right away!" It was very unusual for him to ask for my help with regard to my mother since he was an acupuncturist and knew how to treat her. Apparently, my mother had called him and then asked him to call me. I knew it was serious so I went to see her immediately. She had moved to a senior citizen apartment complex with an inner landscaped courtyard after my brother had found himself a place. She had wanted to buy a place with him, but it was not to be. When I arrived at the apartment, I had to call the manager because I knew my mother was unable to open the door. I found her in bed, having bouts of pain and calling for my brother. I tried to hold her back and massage it. When the pain went away, she said, "You know Goggi was here and he did some 'cupping' (an old Chinese treatment using glass cups where a vacuum is created by a heat method, usually a candle, and placed on the patient's skin in various places, resulting in a strong suction that forces the blood to come to the surface and promotes healing by redistribution of body energy). I had a French lover in Shanghai who did the same for me." She had never spoken to me about a lover, so I was now surprised with her uninhibited openness. She also asked me to give her a sponge bath and told me where her underwear was. Then she said, "I have three thousand in the bank, so you share it with Goggi."

I was unable to convince her to go to the hospital, but she agreed to see my doctor friend, Cecilia Hissong, who had treated her two years ago at Oakwood Hospital when she had her first stroke. My mother was very charming and cordial when Dr. Hissong arrived, even joking with her. Amazingly, her blood pressure was normal, but not normal for her; hers was usually in the 200s range. Dr. Hissong said to me, "You can't force her to go to the hospital if she does not want to." By evening, I prepared her a potato soup complete with parsley, onions, and butter. When she tried it, I could see that her tongue was coated white. She said, "It needs salt."

My brother had come over by this time, and since we hadn't eaten, we went to a nearby Chinese restaurant for dinner. He told me our mother had been sick since Tuesday night. When we returned from dinner, my mother ordered me to go home. Our relationship had been strained of late, and perhaps she preferred to be with my brother. Anyway, she did not want my help. Reluctantly, I left, thinking she would be all right for the night. While I was visiting her the next morning, Tony stopped by and asked her, "Did you take your medicine?" She retorted, "Have you taken yours?" Tony, unable to handle her, left. With some gentle talk, I convinced her to go to the hospital where they might have the latest methods and equipment to help her. I called the Huron Ambulance, and when it arrived, she walked to the stretcher herself since they could not fit it through the doors. She greeted the attendees as if they were Dr. Hissong's brothers because previously I had told her a story about how the doctor's brother had received help in a hospital.

We drove thirty miles to St. Joseph's Hospital where my mother had been rehabilitated two years earlier. In the emergency room, when a nurse asked my mother who was next to her, she was able to say, "My daughter." But the question of where she was and what date it was she could not answer. Her oxygen level was very low, so she was whisked away quickly to the catheterization lab. Soon I received the report that all her main arteries were blocked and she had suffered a major heart attack. They had to intubate her, but they could not operate on her; it was too risky.

I was in a daze in the waiting room. A nun came to sit by me, but she was of no consolation. I kept saying, "This is not a good time for her to die. There is so much unfinished." This sickness had come at the most inopportune time, I thought. I went to ICU to see my mother. She was on a respirator but conscious. She gave me the most haunting of looks, and through gestures, asked me to take off her rings, which I did with the help of some Vaseline. From then on when I came in, she would not look at me and was turned to one side asleep. When I came the next day, the nurse told me she had attempted to take off the tubes twice the night before, so they'd had to restrain her hands. After the doctors and I had a discussion, I wanted to relieve her from the intubation, but my brother still held out some hope. When my daughter, Michelle, went to visit her, my mother turned her face and looked at her.

The next day, I came to visit my mother in tears, asking her to let us know whether she wanted the tubes. My friend, Father Toner, came that afternoon to give her the Last Rites. She protested vehemently by turning and grunting in her bed. In the evening when she was partially seated, I saw a stream of tears running through her face, so I knew she did not want to leave us. After the tubes were taken out, she lasted one day. On Thursday, May 22, 1986, my mother expired. I had been in the waiting room with my friend Fadia, who had brought a bouquet of flowers. The nurse called us and I went in. My mother appeared peaceful with her eyes open. I closed them and bid my mother farewell.

Memorial Day weekend was coming up, so the funeral arrangements had to be made quickly. I went to my mother's apartment. When I looked at her slippers on the floor, I felt her presence. I chose a colorful dress, and the hairdresser, a German lady at the funeral home, asked for a picture so she could approximate her hairdo. Aunt Fe (Felicia) and her husband Pancho came from Mobile, Alabama, and my cousin Erich came from Toronto. On Saturday morning, the funeral director took me to the cemetery where I chose a plot close to my son Paul's grave. He also drove me to a religious store to print the cards. There was no time for a fancy card, so I chose what was available: the pictures of different saints, to which I inscribed an old English prayer my mother had tucked in her address book that summed her up well:

Give us, Lord, a bit o' sun,

A bit o' work and a bit o' fun;
Give us in all the struggle and sputter
Our daily bread and a bit o' butter;
Give us health, our keep to make
    An' a bit to spare for others' sake;
    Give us, too a bit of song
    And a tale, and a book to help us along.
    Give us, Lord, a chance to be
    Our goodly best, brave, wise and free
    Our goodly best for ourself,
    And others.

For the gravestone, I had the stonemason carve the shape of an ancient cross used in my grandparents Schuetzinger tombstone, together with a long stem rose with the saying, Mit Gott, that I found written in one of her ledger notebooks and with this inscription: Agnes Tmiro Chestohin, April 20, 1916—May 22, 1986.

Aunt Fe paid for the plot with a gift of 1,000 dollars. The money my mother left in the bank I used for the casket and wake held on Friday. Many friends and neighbors came and Father Toner conducted a simple ceremony. After the funeral mass on Saturday, the cars were lined up outside the funeral home circle to proceed to the cemetery. On the lawn in the island, I saw a black dog with a long dark snake in its mouth, looking sideways furtively. Tony saw the same dog and looked at me as if to say, "I'm sure you will make something of this." I did ponder the meaning of such an image and thought it symbolized some struggle yet to come that might involve Tony.

At the cemetery, as my mother was lowered into the ground and a couple of shovels of dirt were thrown in, Father Toner extended his hand to mine, understanding my sorrow.

Strangely enough, the sustained depression I had suffered all these years lifted from me one day shortly after the funeral when I was driving on the same road to the hospital where my mother had died. Then a few years after my mother's death, my daughter consulted a psychic at a party who told her, "You have a grandmother, but you don't call her grandma; you call her 'Oma' ("Grandma" in German), and her name is Agnes. She wants you and your family to pray to her as she is with you and is concerned about you."

My mother had made my children's lives magical. Michelle and Lisa recounted her taking them on many visits to the animals (ceramic-like zoo animals that a neighbor had made for children and that were scattered in his yard) and to the chocolate shop where they could choose anything, and they always came out with the largest chocolate lollipop. She also took them swimming at Kensington, driving erratically, so that Lisa, Michelle, and their friend Renee had to cower, with their eyes closed, in the backseat, with babushkas tied around their heads to prevent them from catching a cold. Suzy and Sara remembered her rallying them to clean the house and making them the captain of the rugs or of their room. And when all was clean, we had our tea and chocolates, sometimes apple pancakes or just sugar crepes we called rollups, and on the weekends, a roast with potato dumplings topped off with strawberries and real whipped cream. For birthdays, she made her famous coffee/rum torte, and on special occasions, we made apple strudel. She left real traditions that will be passed on to my children's children. She was a lady with simple pleasures.

The same year my mother died, I became desperate to find a job. We wanted to move to a bigger house, and we had found one to our liking, but we were short a few hundred dollars a month to afford the mortgage. I searched for work for weeks and eventually interviewed for cleaning jobs because teaching jobs were scarce. Working in hotels or airports appealed to me because they would give me a brush with adventure and travel, which I missed having in my life. A Hilton Hotel gave me a job cleaning rooms. One of the cleaning ladies trained me and showed me how to make the bed, dust, and pass the vacuum only in one direction. When she got two clean glasses and placed ice in them, I thought she was preparing for our lunch. Instead, it was for another cleaning lady, her friend. We went to service a room that was occupied by an Indian couple. The husband was a university professor and the wife gave us orders without even looking at us. I knew now what it was to be a servant. This job only lasted three days because the cook quit, so the management decided to close the hotel for renovations. Since the hotel had offered lunch as part of our employment package, the day the cook fled, they gave us the bread with the bacon drippings they had used for breakfast.

Soon after, I found a teaching job at St. Agatha High School. I taught English to juniors and seniors, and I found the workload overwhelming due to the steady stream of papers to correct and lesson preparation. While I lasted at St. Agatha for two years, I don't think I was a very good teacher due to that same sense of uprootedness and a feeling of not belonging that had plagued my life for so long. Perhaps it was all too much, as I also took a part-time job at this time as an English instructor at Schoolcraft College, which I held until 1992. I liked teaching college because the preliminary English classes I taught were filled with adults who wanted to learn and had struggled in life. When I left St. Agatha in 1988, I dabbled in real estate and liked it because it felt more like real life. I was relatively successful and able to pay my car note and insurance, even though the interest rates were around 10 percent. I also tried to make cloth purses from placemats, and I wallpapered other people's houses for a while, so I could have some money of my own.

In March, 1987, my brother returned to China to retrieve his family—his wife, Su Juan, and his children, Joan and Yun. They had finally obtained the residency visas they had applied for back in 1982 when I had gone to China. My father decided to accompany them and stay with my family for one year. They went by train from Hangzhou to Hong Kong and then flew to the U.S., a long journey for a frail old man. They said they were very scared at the Hong Kong border because reunification with China had not yet taken place. Once we knew my father was coming, Tony and I worked to fix up a room for him in the basement of our new house. On our first morning together after my father arrived, with tears in my eyes, I told him about my mother's death and how I had kept my mother's main jewelry but given Su Juan the remainder. He said, "It's okay. You are your mother's daughter." Yes, and I was also his daughter. If I had any doubts before, it was all dissipated. He had come to seal our bond. Earlier, he had given me three stone blocks with my Chinese name, Wang Kun (signifying feminine power), in Chinese characters carved in them, and one of these he carved himself and he wanted me to know that. These Chinese seals were dipped in wax or red ink to stamp letters and documents for time immemorial. This gift represented my identity in this family. He was happy to stay with us and often wanted to teach us Tai Chi, but he gave up because each of us was always coming and going, so he realized he could not gather the family. My father also had a reversed schedule. He had been accustomed in Hangzhou to read at night when the temperatures were cooler and when he would not be bothered with the traffic nearby the compound. So he adopted the same schedule here, making his meals in the microwave, consisting of scrambled eggs and hot dogs, and bringing it all to his room. He also asked for some wine, which I reluctantly bought for him in jugs— inadvertently, helping him with his circulation. Once he helped me make Chinese dumplings and told me that I could mash garlic and salt together for future use. I did that, but the garlic turned green even though I placed it in a ceramic crock, so I threw it out.

During that time, I had a big party for my father and he entertained my friends with his Tai Chi on the wooden deck in our backyard. They were amazed to see this old man doing these slow graceful movements with so much balance. My father was very happy to meet Father Toner who also came to the party. When they met at the foyer of the house, my father looked at him intently and with a smile said, "I am so happy to meet you." He knew how important Father Toner was to me.

In his basement room, my father liked to be busy, so one day he asked me to buy him some ether so he could make his own lighter and some rings so he could perform a magic show. I got him these items and wondered what kind of magic he was going to perform. He actually never completed the act because something was missing, perhaps glycerin. Anyway, I was glad he did not produce an explosion that might have cost my house. Most nights, he would be busy reading or working on a paper titled "Boolean Algebra Logic." He used formulas to determine the truth of problems with many variables. He wanted me to send this paper to a publisher, which I did, but it was not published.

For reading material, I took him to the University of Michigan graduate library where they have a large collection of Chinese books in the stacks. Because I taught at Schoolcraft College, I was given a courtesy pass so I could retrieve books. We made the trip to the library several times so he had plenty of reading material.

We went on several excursions while he was visiting. During the Detroit Grand Prix, I took him, my kids, and my brother's family downtown to watch the cars zip by. We also visited the Renaissance Center and went to the seventy-seventh floor to see the view across to Canada in the building's revolving tower. We tried to take my father for a picnic across the Detroit River to Windsor, Canada, but he was barred entrance at the Ambassador Bridge because he did not have a visa in his passport. On a visit to my brother and Su Juan, he dove into their above-ground pool and came out shaken but proud to have attempted this feat. Because he liked to test his prowess, he attempted to ride one of the children's bikes. On one outing, I took my father to Holy Sepulcher Cemetery where my mother and son are buried. He stood a long time before my mother's grave and then bent over and cleaned the stone with a small tissue. He had the same reverence at my son's grave.

My father's health was good during this time despite his chain smoking, which caused a perennial cough. Tony was concerned about my father's cough and the air quality for all of us, so he placed an air purifier in my father's room. So as not to awaken us at night, my father used a tall can rather than go to the bathroom on the next floor. Tony did not like this arrangement and crushed his can by stepping on it when my father was not in the room; he had become annoyed with my father's habits of smoking and sleeping all day, and it now culminated in much anger. The next day, my father was in the workroom trying to unbend his chamber can.

One day in October when I came home from teaching school shortly after the above incident, my father approached me in the kitchen and said, "You are my daughter, so father and daughter can speak freely. I would like to return to China. You see, the leaves do not fall far from the tree, and I want to return to the motherland." I understood he missed the comfort of his own place where he could do what he pleased. Before his departure, however, he told me he wanted to gather the family so he could tell them his philosophy, his view of the world. I gathered my fidgety kids who could not stop laughing. But we did listen to this seemingly foolish old man. I'll paraphrase here what I remember him saying: "You see, I am a Buddhist, but I am friendly with all religions. They are windows to the same reality. All religions have angels, the beings of light. Now all things have potential for life. A child has more potential because it is becoming, and woe to the powerful and those who were entrusted with their charge who thwart their potential." I came out of this mini-talk with a feeling that my father had great reverence for life, and therefore, was merciful.

Before he left, I also remember Michelle took him to her high school junior class where he was taped demonstrating Tai Chi: the circular one and the one with the sword. I watched the tape and heard him define Tai Chi as meditation in movement, a means of attaining harmony. He asked, "What is harmony? Then he was silent as if he were stumped by his own question. Then he said, "In mathematics, we have a principle: complete, something is complete. Harmony is completeness. I am just a junior, you see. A beggar in the street could be a master."

After we arranged for a ticket for my father's return to China, I packed his Tai Chi sword diagonally in one of his suitcases with many clothes he could use in China. He gave Tony his woolen Mao hat and went home with an American baseball cap. He departed in October 1987, having stayed with us for seven months.

My father came again to visit in 1990. This time, he stayed at my brother's place because he was more comfortable there. The episode with his chamber can had left some unpleasant feelings and he did not want to be a burden to Tony. That year I had a hysterectomy, so he came to visit me at home, showing me great concern but also optimism. Before he left, he had three requests for me: he wanted to go to the circus, go bowling, and find sweet olives. We went to all the ethnic food stores in the neighborhood, but we could not find the sweet olives he had tasted in Turkey. He said, "You see, only the rich person could afford the sweet olives because they are very expensive." His other wishes we were able to fulfill. We went to the Barnum and Bailey Circus in Joe Louis Arena; my father was very impressed by the performance with the tigers. When we took him bowling, he rolled the ball down the lane with both hands, causing my children to laugh as he remembered the time he bowled in Germany on the lawn of some farm. I also took him to Greenfield Village and the Ford Museum with all the cars, planes, and trains, by myself. It was as if I were a child going to work with my father. He explained to me the function of the conveyor belts and the lathe. He was most enthralled in Edison's Laboratory because, as an electrical engineer, he saw tangibly the beginning of his field. We had lunch in the spacious cafeteria, and he tolerated this strenuous outing quite well. Again, he returned to China and we said goodbye to him as he walked down the Jetway wearing a Tigers baseball cap.

Meanwhile, my marriage with Tony was not going well, and we had had several severe outbursts. I went to counselors with Tony and alone, but nothing seemed to help. Then I thought, "If we went to Brazil together, perhaps Tony would understand me better." Tony agreed to go with me to Brazil in the summer of 1988. I had not been back to Brazil since 1967, a span of twenty-one years! By then, I had been working long enough that I had saved up money for the trip.

The passengers applauded when we flew into Rio! I gladly shared the general elation at arriving in the most beautiful city in the world. I was home at last. My friends Virginia and Harumi were at the airport to greet us. Virginia looked older, with gray strands in her hair, but it took less than a second for us to connect as before. With her winning smile and a hug, she said in Portuguese, "Welcome back. Harumi is there to drive you to your hotel." I saw Harumi, who was all smiles and ready to take over the scene. She said, "I will take you to your hotel, but I thought you would like to look around first, so I will drive you to the old neighborhood." I could smell the musty Rio smell in this less than modern airport made of raw cement, but I was filled with anticipation. We hopped into her compact car and drove off the Ilha do Governador (Governor's Island) in Guanabara Bay where the airport is located and onto the viaducts extending over the center of town toward the picturesque boroughs of Flamengo and Botafogo, still overlooking the Guanabara Bay and flanked by the Sugarloaf Mountain. Then we veered inwards and drove along Lake Rodrigo de Freitas that led us to the mouth of a tunnel, constructed during my absence from Brazil; it would lead us to my neighborhood of Gavea/Sao Conrado. Before we entered the tunnel, Harumi pointed to the massive subsidized housing built on the rock for the favelas dwellers, a project speared by *Dom* Hélder *Câmara*, a Bishop in Rio known for his concern for the poor. When we came out on the other side, I was surprised that the square in front of Rocinha Mountain, home to the world's largest urban slum, was surrounded by high-rises, a virtual cement city that had not been there when I was growing up. The open spaces near the sea had been turned into a shopping center of many levels. The apartment building, the first in the area and where I had last lived, was sandwiched between these buildings; I would have missed it had Harumi not slowed down.

I wondered how Tony felt about taking in all the sites. He appeared to be enjoying this escapade into my old neighborhood as he smiled with satisfaction when he saw the mountains, the sea, and some beautiful homes past the congestion of the buildings. Apparently, it had not yet become a culture shock since so far, all he had needed to do was take it in with his eyes. The interaction with my friends and the population would come later.

The single road had been replaced by a multi-lane highway that stretched itself into Gavea Mountain. When we drove on the straightaway between the greens of the Gavea Golf Course, I could see the contour of the mountain, Pedra da Gavea, and I felt filled by its presence. We passed in front of my old house that now had a massive wooden door covering its arched entrance. I felt grateful to Harumi for bringing us here on the first day. We took the old road into the mountain and passed in front of Harumi's house and then to the Joa Restaurant perched on the rock overlooking the sea, which was a favorite for romantics and where my mother would dine with a friend. Then we descended the mountain, seeing some beautiful homes surrounded by wrought iron fences and stonewalls. We left the Gavea area by the avenue along the Sao Conrado beach where we saw some luxury apartment buildings and the International Hotel beyond the Gavea Golf Course Greens. Harumi chose to go along the Atlantic Avenue, passing Ipanema, and then into Copacabana where we would stay at the Hotel Excelsior. Harumi said we would be in touch to arrange other outings.

I could not believe I was back in Rio, listening to the sounds of the streets and breathing the damp ocean breeze. Near the elevator, an attendant asked me in Portuguese, "Are you Brazilian?" He didn't say, "Where do you come from?" a question I was often asked elsewhere. Yes, indeed, I was home.

That evening, we met up with some of my mother's old friends, the Friedlanders, at Mario's, a famous Rio Barbecue. I remember having Maltzbeer (a dark sweet beer sold in Rio), watercress salad, and creamed avocado for dessert, as well as the many grilled meats sliced fresh from a skewer. Tony enjoyed the company of my mother's old friends who could speak English, and he loved the food, which was outstanding. Back at the hotel, I had many messages from friends. Virginia had come by the hotel and dropped off some fruit that had been my favorite: fruta de Conde (sugar apples). My friend Alzira also stopped by; she was with her daughter, Claudia, buying clothes for her boutique in Vitoria, Espirito Santo where she lived. We met for breakfast at our hotel, and then Tony and I accompanied her to a wholesale outfit in Copacabana to buy dresses. I tried out a few and was able to buy some chic ones using her account. Before we parted, Alzira turned to me and said, "What took you so long to come back?" I really did not know the answer. I made the excuse of "money and kids to raise." Because she had to return to Vitoria, we would not see each other again until my next trip to Brazil.

Before long, Harumi gave me a call and arranged to pick us up for dinner at her sister Terumi's house in Barra da Tijuca to meet the whole family. As I climbed out of the car in Terumi's neighborhood, I saw walking toward me a familiar figure. It was Nega, the eldest daughter of the Lopes family, who had lived next door to our riding school when we were young. She walked slowly in her yellow sweatshirt and sandals. I saw tears in her eyes that drew the same from mine. We embraced. This was my childhood friend in whose eyes I was who I was. We had shared our youth and she had witnessed my antics. I had heard her describe me to others as intelligent, daring, and adventurous, but she had also witnessed my tight moments with my cruel stepfather as well as my joy in being called home from her house by my loving mother. To see these friends again was an indescribable moment for me. I met Terumi, her husband Renato, and her three children, as well as Cazu, his wife, and his three children. Nao, I believe, was on a trip with his wife. Inside I met Toki, Harumi's mother, Coimbra, Harumi's boyfriend, and Tuninho, Nega's husband. We shared many memories. I felt like the prodigal daughter who had come home. After dinner, Harumi pointed to the caramelized Brazilian flan on the table and said, "You taught me how to do this flan; don't you remember?" No, I didn't remember.

That evening, we drove to visit the Lopes family in Jacarepagua. I met Dona Linda and her husband, Senhor Joao, who was sick with kidney failure. He looked at me with tears in his eyes, making a gesture, elevating his hand three feet above the ground, to say that he had known me since I was small. I met all the brothers and sisters with whom I played so vigorously those many years ago, and who were indeed my family. There was Bisuca, the twins, Miuda and Grande, Ana, Wanda, Joaozinho, Tadeu, as well as those not born in Sao Conrado, Tarcizio, Rosaria, and Rita. Paulo could not come, however, because he was tending the store. Tony stood by the door, giving me signals that we should go. He became very irritated and did not share my joy in being with these people. The culture shock and the language barrier he was experiencing were becoming apparent to me. When I parted, Dona Linda gave me a warm embrace and said, "I hope this lasts till you come back."

At the hotel, I received a phone call from my friend Maria Clara who said she lived one block away on Avenida Nossa Senhora de Copacabana. Tony and I went to visit this exuberant friend, who was now married to a Brazilian military general and doctor, Hugomar Vieira. Her house was filled with carved furniture and tapestries she was able to import from China when her husband was stationed in Paraguay. Tony and she had a wonderful rapport and he presented her with a crystal owl we bought at a shopping center. They sent a chauffeured car to take us on a tour of Sugar Loaf Mountain where we boarded the famous cable car to the various peaks, and where we strolled leisurely, taking in all the panoramic views of Rio from various angles, including of Gavea Mountain nestled between the sea and the other mountains that adorned Rio.

Virginia and her mom took us to the Corcovado (Christ figure) overlooking Rio. We boarded the famous train that runs up the mountain, penetrating the Atlantic forest, the largest in an urban area, to reach the summit. The view was breathtaking! When we reached the imposing white statue of Christ, I was moved by how simple yet magnificent it was. I had never seen it on a clear day, and I was stunned by it, set against Rio's beauty.

We had many more invitations to fulfill. Harumi drove us to the Tijuca Forest where we dined in an elegant lodge by the fireplace, tasting typical Brazilian foods— pulled sun-dried meat, pumpkin, black beans, rice, sautéed collard greens, and my favorite soft drink, Guarana. Virginia nicknamed me "Guarana" because that was what I would drink when given a choice. Virginia's mom, Gladys, invited us for tea at her high-rise overlooking Lake Rodrigo de Freitas and the Jockey Club. Here, my friends and I spoke in Portuguese about old times and shared photos and viewed yearbooks. We spoke animatedly and our enthusiasm made us forget Tony, who by now was becoming visibly annoyed. Virginia's mom noticed and tried to engage him in conversation, but it was hard for her because of her poor English. Tony, who was always a great talker, felt pent up and out of touch being unable to participate in the conversation.

Virginia drove us to my school, Stella Maris, and I noted, from an open veranda in the new school building overlooking the sea and the mountains, that the houses in the favelas at the foot of the hill were now made of raw brick rather than boards as in the past. Virginia also drove us through some mountain roads that were quite dangerous due to the rains that had washed out large sections of pavement. But she was my adventure companion, so she knew I would be thrilled to be traveling the back roads of Rio's mountains.

Through a travel agency, we booked a flight to Iguacu Falls on the border with Argentina and Paraguay, and to Belo Horizonte to visit Madre Euridyna. At the falls, we had a wonderful time, sipping sugarcane juice and meeting an Indian man (from whom I bought a carved face of Christ) who said he was three nationalities because he was born in the intersection of all three countries: Brazil, Argentina, and Paraguay. We crossed over to Argentina by taxi and ate at a modest outdoor café. The taxi driver said that if we had been English, we would have been barred entrance to Argentina because of the Falkland Islands War waged with England a few years earlier. We were able to go to Paraguay's open market (where all sorts of Oriental exports were sold) only by foot over the Friendship Bridge; we had tried to take a taxi but were turned away from lack of a visa. On our way back, we took a local bus to escape scrutiny by the officials.

My first evening in Belo Horizonte, I visited Madre Euridyna at the convent by myself and had a heart-to-heart talk with her, while Tony stayed at the Othon Hotel and then meandered the streets by himself, surprised to see so many soldiers guarding public squares and buildings. Tony became concerned; he felt insecure and missed me since I was the only one who could speak Portuguese and could reassure him. He called Maria Clara in Rio to get the convent's phone number. Madre Luiza, who had been my math teacher, promptly drove me to the hotel and all was well. Tony and I then went to the hotel's top floor restaurant for a bite to eat. We were encased in glass, overlooking a panorama of city lights. A man played old Brazilian songs on his guitar, many of which I knew. He made me feel so special because we were the only customers, so it felt like he was serenading me.

In the morning, we went to pick up Madre Euridyna in a tourist van with another English couple and headed toward the famous colonial city of Ouro Preto, famous for its Baroque churches and cobblestone streets. Shortly before this trip, I had written a letter to Madre Euridyna about my problems with Tony, so now she could see firsthand how temperamental he could be. He became irate when the driver stopped at a restaurant to give us a coffee break midway; he felt the driver was wasting our time with these stops. While visiting the churches, Tony walked ahead of us as if he were a person apart from our group. On our way back, he criticized the driver for taking the van on a steep ramp or some other maneuver that prompted the driver to say in Portuguese, "This is a furious man." I was embarrassed by Tony's display of anger. Suffice it to say, my visit with Tony to Brazil was not a success in improving our relationship, but he was able to experience Brazil firsthand, and for the most part, he enjoyed it. Here in Ouro Preto, we did enjoy the gold leafed interior of the churches made from gold extracted from that region, as well as the intricate wood carvings by the famous artist Aleijadinho (meaning "The Cripple," because he was a paraplegic). It was interesting to see the jail and the many instruments of torture used on slaves and other inmates. Colonial times were not a pleasant period in Brazilian history, due to slavery, whose repercussions are still felt today.

To close our stay in Rio, Virginia invited all our friends to her house in Piratininga on the other side of Guanabara Bay for a typical Brazilian barbecue. Maria Clara and her husband, Hugomar, drove us there, crossing the long Rio-Niteroi Bridge. Once on the other side, we got lost since Hugomar did not know quite how to negotiate the mountains toward Piratininga. I saw young barefoot boys playing soccer in the street, and I enjoyed the less affluent local scene. We arrived before dark and were able to visit a Portuguese fishing village dating back to colonial times and a church near the beach, over five hundred years old, with walls that spanned several feet. At the house, we ate grilled meats prepared expertly by Virginia's husband, Edson, who was a gaucho (someone from the Pampas) from the southern state of Rio Grande do Sul, where the Brazilian barbecue originated. We had many memories to share and stories to tell. Hugomar told us how Maria Clara and he had visited this beach when a young lad came by selling these cookie puffs. Hugomar did not have the right change and was reluctant to buy them when the boy said, "No problem, Senhor; I can arrange change." He took the fifty reais and ran to the other side, leaving Hugomar with his stack of cookies. Needless to say, the boy did not return, and Hugomar stood there with the tall stack of puffed cookies encased in clear plastic, wondering whether he would become the next cookie seller. I enjoyed these exchanges with my friends, but I did not quite realize the tedium Tony was experiencing from not understanding the language and having to sit through photo albums and school memories. However, he did enjoy my good friends' company, and they did everything to make him feel comfortable.

During this visit, I became very aware of the changing atmosphere between the social classes in Brazil. It became apparent when Tony and I visited travel agencies to exchange money because the exchange rates at banks were not good. Tony would return to the hotel with money stuffed in his pockets because Brazil was suffering from 30 percent inflation per month at the time. Inflation was running rampant and the economy was on a downward spiral after the country emerged from two decades of military rule into a shaky democracy with the corrupt presidency of Fernando Collor de Melo who governed from 1990 to 1992, then resigned to avoid impeachment. My visit was just prior to his presidency, and I heard about Rio suffering from an epidemic of street assaults and house robberies and where gangs of boys combed the beaches for petty theft opportunities. The police and government recommended that people dress simply and not wear gold or carry cameras in the open. This reality was brought about due to the vast differences between the rich and the poor and the encroachment of the favelas or slums present everywhere on the city's hillsides. It was estimated that Rio had over 1,000 favelas scattered in all its neighborhoods. A welfare system did not exist, and educational opportunities for children were scarce. Gangs of street children could be seen, some of them begging, others resorting to selling boxes of chewing gum or peanuts or even juggling with painted faces before stopped cars at a light in order to get some donations. Virginia told me of a time when a gold chain was ripped from her neck when she was stopped at a light in Rio's affluent neighborhood of Leblon. Maria Clara remembered once walking in Copacabana when a man asked for her gold wedding band. Edson, Virginia's husband, had to chase a robber out of the house at gunpoint and tried to prosecute him. On the night we went to Virginia's house, Maria Clara's son Ricardo had his car stolen at gunpoint. The thief brazenly asked for Ricardo's car keys and left him sitting on the curb with only enough change to take the bus. Most people, to protect themselves, had built tall walls around their houses and had dogs to ward off intruders. Buildings in the city had wrought iron fences and were often guarded. Drug cartels had infiltrated the slums and sometimes even engaged in fighting between the various leaders. The police tried to maintain order, but were overpowered by the criminals, so it did not surprise me when Maria Clara spoke of installing a steel door that could withstand gunfire, or when I saw dogs at the houses of my various friends. I did take a second look when Hugomar placed a gun in the bin beside him when we went off by car to deserted areas. Fortunately during this visit, I myself did not experience any assaults or other unpleasant situations. And I'm happy to say that since that time, many social programs have been instituted in the favelas and the standard of life has improved for many over the years.

Since Maria Clara and Hugomar lived so close to our hotel, we spent many evenings together sipping beer along Copacabana's shore or rummaging through open markets nearby as well as attending a samba festival at a theater called Plataforma Um, where they had a spectacle of all types of Brazilian dancing, especially Carnival Samba with the ladies decked out in extravagant feathered costumes. The music and the dancing were intoxicating! Once, Maria Clara and Hugomar drove us to Grumari, an area on the southern end of Rio where there had not yet been urban intrusion and where the beaches and Atlantic forests were still virgin. The view was breathtaking as we meandered through these deserted undulating mountain roads, catching every hue of green that opened to the sea and that sometimes was shrouded with a lingering mist as evening approached. Maria Clara called it, "Deslumbrante!" ("Magnificent!")

When we drove back through the Sao Conrado area, we stopped at my old house, still covered with ivy, with heavy wooden doors in the arched entrance and square ones that led to the side gardens. A caretaker let us in. As I walked upstairs, I felt it was smaller than I remembered. The caretaker's family was having a barbecue on the grounds. I noticed it was no longer a riding school, but rather a summer home. In the back was a pool and another one-story house. However, the simple hibiscus bushes remained, where in my childhood I saw countless hummingbirds sipping nectar from their flowers. As a taxi driver had said to me earlier with the typical Brazilian expression, "Voce veio para matar a saudade!" ("You came to kill the longing.") Yes, it was so.

Tony and I flew home. He now knew the place I loved and my Brazilian friends who were so important to me. I suppose that on one level, the trip had made us connect better; we had an important shared experience. But in fact, his experience was his own and he couldn't quite embrace my experience, which reached back in time and had a deeper dimension. Our marriage stumbled along. I stayed focused on the housework, teaching at the Community College, and becoming a Real Estate agent while Tony put all his effort and time into his job as a pharmaceutical representative. Our emotions were still quite separate, and I continued to long to return to Brazil to be close to the people who understood me.

After this visit to Brazil, I could not wait another twenty-one years to return, so I went back by myself in 1991. At that time, I had earned some money so I could afford this trip without depending on Tony, and I also made some connections that led to my returning there. I had been teaching Portuguese to a Ford executive, Bob Rennard, and his wife, Ann. He was going to Brazil for three years to be the head of Auto Latina, a subsidiary of Ford in Brazil. He had agreed to keep me on as his teacher, so I had a chance to visit Brazil for six weeks. As it turned out, when he went to Brazil, the company had arranged for his tutoring with its own people so I was no longer needed. However, I had already bought my ticket, so I decided to go anyway for the six weeks I had planned. It was for the best, as I was able to spend time with my friends in Rio and elsewhere and not have to be restricted to Sao Paulo, a city I did not know and where Bob would be stationed; however, I did go to Sao Paulo to visit my friend Sonia Fonseca and I met Ann Rennard for lunch. The rest of the time, I divided between my childhood friends, Virginia, Maria Clara, and Harumi, with side trips to Nega's family and an excursion to see Madre Euridyna in Belo Horizonte. I definitely satiated my hunger. The need to be in Brazil among my friends was no longer a dream, but something concrete I could realize more frequently.

When I returned to Detroit, I began my studies for a Master's in Social Work at the University of Michigan. I poured over books and studied diligently, writing countless papers on various subjects and completing practicum in an adolescent treatment center in Ann Arbor and at Providence Hospital. I graduated in December 1992, and in June 1993, I obtained a job as a psychiatric social worker at a downtown Detroit psychiatric facility, Michigan Health Center. For the next eight years, I would work in two different psychiatric hospitals, run by the same company. I learned the ropes quickly and had to work at a fast pace since patients came and went quickly because the insurance companies did not allow for idle treatment time. I had to do the initial psychosocial assessments for admitted patients, daily group treatment meetings, and discharge planning with the many referrals to drug treatment centers and adult foster care homes, as well as write countless reports to facilitate patients' treatments in long-term facilities.

This experience made me first fully realize how each individual is a person with his or her own story; at first, I was unable to characterize the patients as mentally ill because I so strongly felt their uniqueness and presence. It was as if I witnessed pained humanity passing before me, so I had to do my best to help them. I remember a black woman whose face had been blown off by a bullet from an ex-boyfriend. She was blind so I tried to connect her with an institute for the blind. When her son, a boy of fourteen, came to visit her from a youth reform center, I observed how she spoke to him and touched his face, and how pleased they were to see each other. The bond of love was palpable. The woman spoke of her ordeal without bitterness and I marveled at her endurance. I also remember the quiet dignity of a mentally ill homeless middle-aged black man with a graying beard who showed up occasionally at our facility with worn clothes and shoes. He demanded nothing, but appeared grateful when given some clothes and a chance to take a bath. There were also the angry, delusional, some who were plagued with hallucinations, the manipulative drug abusers, the depressed, and the mentally challenged. Most remained in their chronic state, so we could offer only temporary bandages. A few were able to improve and find a better life.

By 1997, I had saved enough money to be able to take my four daughters, Lisa, Michelle, Suzy, and Sara to Brazil, the dream place of my youth. By then Sara had graduated from high school and Suzy turned twenty-one on June 13, 1997, the day before our departure. Lisa and Michelle were twenty-six and twenty-seven respectively. We went to Chicago and boarded an American Airlines plane to Miami, arriving at 8:30 p.m. The American Airlines counter in the Miami airport was in a state of mayhem. The plane was overbooked and people were demanding seats on the plane. A Brazilian "Popeye," an American Airlines attendant with wrestling arms, was chasing away irate customers and even exchanged obscenities with one, "No, you go to hell!" He ripped the assigned seat cards the other clerk had given me. At an appropriate time, I approached him quietly and spoke to him in Portuguese saying, "I am a mother who was raised in Brazil and am taking my four daughters there for the first time." I don't know whether it was charm or luck, but close to departure time, around 11:30, he gave us our seat tickets—three for first class and two for business class. We couldn't believe our eyes. Michelle and I had seat numbers 4 and 5. The stewardess treated us with extraordinary courtesy, taking our coats and asking whether we wanted our orange juice refreshed. We were served caviar, champagne, truffles, smoked salmon, lobster, and Chateaubriand wine. For dessert, we chose raspberry mousse on ice cream! All this served on real linen and with silverware! She brought us hot towels to clean up and a leather pouch as a gift. We had our own video center, so we were luxuriating in comfort with our plush, totally reclinable seats, with ample room to fit another body. Michelle and I laughed a lot and couldn't believe our luck; we tried to act "rich" with English accents, asking the stewardess to take our picture. Lisa sat nearby beside a Japanese guy who slept and was silent. She ordered her own video movies and feasted on the same amenities. Suzy and Sara were in business class and had essentially the same experience except the caviar and appetizers. Before long and after a good sleep, we noticed the sun was rising and below us we saw a vast range of undulating mountains. The captain announced that we would be in Rio in a half-hour. We arrived shortly after 7 a.m.

Once we passed through Customs without any trouble, we found Harumi, Virginia, and Coimbra in the lobby waiting for us. We kissed and Harumi said in Portuguese, "They have enough luggage for a year!" Michelle took a picture of the "three little pigs" as Harumi called Virginia, me, and herself, due to the weight we had put on over the years. The luggage almost didn't fit in the two cars and Harumi thought we might have to call a taxi. However, we put the last two pieces in the seat next to Suzy and Sara and we were off to Leme, the borough next to Copacabana where I had rented Alzira's aunt's apartment for two weeks.

Alzira, my best friend in high school, was unable to come and greet us because her sister Heloisa was hospitalized with a malignant brain tumor. I had not seen her in 1991 because I could not pull myself away from Rio. She told me over the phone, "I forbid you to come to Brazil and not see me." In subsequent visits, I made sure to go to Vitoria in the state of Espirito Santo and spend some days with her.

Anyway, when we arrived at Alzira's apartment, Senhor Augusto, who for thirty-six years had managed the apartment building, opened the gates and showed us to the apartment, after we piled up in a tiny antiquated elevator made for skinny people. The apartment doors were narrow, but we managed to squeeze in with our luggage. The smell was musty and the furniture looked like it had been there for half a century. The kitchen and the bedrooms were small, but the living room was spacious with a veranda overlooking Copacabana Avenue. We could see the heavy traffic of buses and cars veering onto Pricesa Isabel Avenue that led to the Tunnel toward the boroughs of Botafogo and Flamengo along Guanabara Bay.

Michelle and I entertained the guests while Lisa, Suzy, and Sara went to take a nap in the bedrooms. Around 1:00 p.m., we all went to a nearby Brazilian buffet for lunch. We paid by weight, approximately 10 dollars per plate from a large assortment of dishes including grilled meats, fried bananas, palmetto (heart of palm), pigeon eggs, and salads; everything was very fresh and delicious, accompanied by fresh cheese rolls and the famous Brazilian soft drink, Guarana. We walked back to the apartment by Atlantic Avenue along Copacabana Beach. The movement of the city, the intermingling of rich and poor people and buildings, and the sounds of the Portuguese language overwhelmed the girls. But we did not have much time to rest because we were invited to a party in our honor at Dona Linda's house in Jacarepagua, a suburb southwest of the city, about an hour away.

Harumi drove us along the coast, passing Stella Maris School on the mountain's ledge and then the Sao Conrado neighborhood where I had lived. Our house at the riding school was knocked down, replaced by expensive apartment buildings where an apartment sold for 400,000 dollars, according to Harumi. So my childhood home was gone, but they could never take away Gavea Mountain and the sea, which surpassed all else. On our way, while crossing the district of Barra da Tijuca, the girls saw three-fourths of a dead horse with its legs turned upward on a sidewalk. Michelle later remarked, "What a road kill!" Without the order of lanes, a traffic frenzy of buses and cars squeezed through the narrowest of spaces in a haphazard fashion, allowing through only astute drivers. It was a feast for the eyes for my American daughters, who were accustomed to the quiet order of the Detroit suburbs. We soon arrived at the Lopes family home. I met Dona Linda and Nega on the porch and quickly realized that the whole house and backyard were decorated with streamers, balloons, and a banner that said in Portuguese, "Welcome Marianne and daughters!" Inside were all of the family's sons and daughters, grandchildren, and great-grandchildren—over twenty-five people altogether, including us.

That night, we danced to Brazilian music while food was passed around on the covered back porch and shish kebab prepared on the grill in the backyard. A bonfire roared in the back on this dark night, combining our arrival with the festivities to celebrate the Feast of St. John, held in Brazil around the time of the summer solstice. We watched Marcello, Dona Linda's great grandson, dressed in a cowboy suit, dance the limbo and make funny faces. Michelle asked how to prepare a spongy coconut dessert she enjoyed. The others tried to dance and mingle the best they could. We talked and looked at each other with amazement over how the years had passed and now I was bringing my four daughters for a visit.

Before we left, I sat with Dona Linda in a small room to pray the Ave Maria as she passed around the customary glass of water. I said to her, "I came here with my four daughters to receive your blessing." She replied, "You are blessed." I had heard that her eldest son, Paulo, still came every morning before work to receive his mother's blessing as he and his siblings had done as children when they left the house. Before we returned to our apartment, we stopped at the home of Terumi, Harumi's sister, for a delicious fruit salad and passion fruit ice cream. Then we went next door to the home of Cazu, Harumi's brother, where he showed a video of his daughter Patricia riding horseback and taking part in a jumping competition. Sara made friends with Miriam, Terumi's daughter, who wanted to take her biking through the mountains, and Renato, Terumi's husband, invited us to go for a ride on his yacht before our vacation was over.

We were back at the apartment by eleven o'clock and went to the nearby Meridien Hotel to make phone calls home. On the way, we saw a poor boy sleeping on the sidewalk without covers. It was winter in Rio and the nights could be cold. The girls had to get used to these new surroundings, which for them definitely caused culture shock. The cot in the maid's room fell apart, so Sara had to share a bed with Suzy in one bedroom while Lisa and Michelle took the other bedroom. I slept on the couch in the living room, which was very comfortable. Right away, I had to show the girls how to light the wall furnace in the shower for hot water. They did this with much caution and holding their breath because the unit lit up with an explosion. The worst was when Suzy started to yell because she saw something run across the bathroom floor, which appeared to be a mouse, but turned out to be a giant cockroach. In the morning, I managed to prepare breakfast with the supplies Harumi had brought us. Lisa could not dry her hair since we had forgotten to bring an electrical adapter, so she had to wear a hat on our way to the morning's outing. Next to the bus stop, fortunately, we found a hardware store and bought an electrical adaptor.

Before long, we were on our first bus ride to Pao de Acucar (Sugarloaf Mountain) where we stepped out near the entrance to buy tickets to board the cable cars. The first cable car took us to the first peak where we could walk around and view Rio's magnificent panorama. We also saw some small monkeys with funny owl-like faces looking at us perched on trees. Every time I saw Gavea Mountain, I would exclaim, "That's my mountain! There's my mountain!" to the point where the girls got tired of my enthusiasm. Then we took the second cable car to a higher peak and gazed at Rio's panoramic view from a terrace where we ordered cheeseburgers and beer for the girls and Guarana for me. We made acquaintance with a California couple and began an animated conversation. I noticed a bee kept sipping my Guarana. I chased it away a few times and continued to talk. When I took my next sip, the bee was inside the can and stung the tip of my tongue. I spat him out and took out the stinger with tears in my eyes from the pain. Suzy remarked, "Oh no, the only one who can speak Portuguese, and now her tongue is stung by a bee!" Lisa got me some ice in a cup from the refreshment counter, and the pain began to subside slowly. It sure silenced me! Who else could say a bee had stung her at the summit of Sugar Loaf Mountain and on the tip of her tongue at that? We returned by bus for some rest and then some shopping at the nearby mall, Shopping Sul. Near the tunnel, we saw the Church of St. Theresa where I had gone to Mass when I was a teenager. In a courtyard adjacent to the church, we saw many people lighting candles and refrained from taking pictures because it would be disrespectful. When we got home, Marcus, Virginia's son, who was a couple of years older than Lisa, paid us a visit. He took English classes next door to our building and lived in an apartment a couple of blocks away, close to the tunnel we had crossed earlier. He offered to chauffeur us around and would come back tomorrow evening to take the girls out.

In the mornings, we went to the beach, a block away, armed with towels, sheets, and tanning lotion. The girls chose to park our things in front of the Copacabana Palace Hotel. Sara chose to jog on the sidewalk while the other girls sunned themselves. I walked to the shoreline where I saw a beautiful young girl with long, curly hair wading in the water. I approached her and we began a conversation. She told me in Portuguese, "I left my purse and camera with the young ladies up there."

"Oh, those are my daughters; they will be glad to watch your things," I said, happy to have someone with whom I could speak Portuguese. Then I asked, "What do you do?" wondering how she had time to come to the beach in the mornings.

She said, "My name is Simone and I do night programs." In my naiveté, I thought she gave tourists tours at night. Soon I realized she was a prostitute, and before long, I had her whole story. She used to work in a bakery having to scrub floors hours before dawn, making hardly any money. Then her boyfriend introduced her to "night programs," and he was okay with her participating in them since she always used protection. Her boyfriend did cocaine, but she didn't. Her father and stepmother lived a couple of hours from Rio, and when they visited her, she had to hide her strawberries and chocolate from her stepmother, who didn't like her. On the whole, she said she was happy. When we went to sit by the girls, she waved to a transvestite who came to the beach without a bra and in a very short skirt. She told me she was friends with all these unusual people and they looked out for each other. I had a mixture of sympathy and admiration for this young lady, whose story was not too different from many I had heard from patients in the mental hospital. Before she left, she took a few pictures of us and we of her.

Another morning when we came to the Copacabana beach, we saw a string of people bending down and picking up something by the water's edge. I thought they were clamming or picking up little crabs or other small crustaceans. It turned out that they were picking up coins and even jewelry that had been thrown in the ocean during past New Year's celebrations. The waves were very strong and had dredged these coins up, most of which were obsolete now because of Brazil's frequent currency changes. My daughters and I quickly joined in the search. Some coin finders only kept coins that were current, so we received coins from them by the handfuls. A man gave Lisa a silver medallion, and I got a silver Paraguayan coin. A woman found gold rings and pendants, and I found a chain that appeared to be gold. A man named Gaston, whom we met several times while at the beach, told me, "I spend four hours a day finding treasures; most coins I throw back as they are no use, but you can have them as souvenirs." I thought, "How wonderful that we are receiving these obsolete treasures churned up by the sea and picked by these perfect strangers, who do not know how much this all means to us."

The girls continued to explore Copacabana's Atlantic Avenue. They walked toward Fort Copacabana where vendors set up their booths in the afternoons for the sale of typical Brazilian artifacts; they bought stone trees, birds, chimes, jewelry, and key chains. They also liked to explore the souvenir shops in the neighborhood with their beautiful carved-stone items. We ate at the sidewalk of Maxim's right across from the Excelsior where Tony and I had stayed, but it was now covered in plastic for renovations. I also took them to Mario's Churrascaria (Brazilian barbecue) where the meats were grilled whole, brought to the table in skewers, and sliced to order for each guest. Unfortunately, the girls were not very hungry and turned the card on the table from the green to the red side, indicating to the waiter not to bring any more meat. I guess I was pushing too much on them. They found their own ways to enjoy the city. I found out much later that Lisa and Sara, on one of their evening jogs along the beach, accepted an invitation from a gay man who hung around the kiosk near the Copacabana Palace and could speak English. He took them to a Drag Queen show, which they found spectacular! I had told them never to go with strangers and to be very careful in Rio, but this one time, they did not listen. We never did encounter any trouble during our stay.

Of course, we could not leave Rio without seeing its most famous landmark, the 125-foot statue of Christ on the granite peak of Corcovado Mountain, which in 2007 would be declared one of the New Seven Wonders of the World. We took the bus to the Cosme Velho/Laranjeiras region and at the mountain's foot took a train up through the forest and toward the peak where we had a magnificent view of Rio. Everyone enjoyed this excursion, especially Sara, whom I saw seated on a ledge in an alcove in a pensive state. Certainly, the towering white statue and the all mesmerizing panorama of Rio nestled in the mountains and the sea could certainly place one in a world apart. We went down by escalator and then took the same train to the entrance.

We went back to the apartment by bus, encircling the city from the other side, via the Jockey Club. Suzy could not get over how crazy the bus drivers were. They would zip along through any opening as if they were racecar drivers; passengers had to hold on for their lives, especially on curves and after a stop. It was rush hour now, so it took us longer to get home.

Marcus came one evening to take the girls to Rock in Rio Café and "Mama" was invited. He took us to his apartment near the tunnel; from there, we squeezed into his small car and meandered the city toward Barra da Tijuca Shopping Mall where the Café was located. It was an ultra-modern setting with tubular décor, complete with strobe lights, balcony pods, a large screen, and a dance floor. The girls had to show their passports, and then we went upstairs and sat at a table with computerized beer taps that amazed me. We danced to rock music, sipping beer that quite agreed with my American girls, leaving the bar around 2:00 a.m. We took the coast roads and stopped to see the waves break on the rocks, having a good view of Leblon and Ipanema, very near where I had gone to school. Marcus took us along Ipanema and Copacabana Beaches. As we approached our neighborhood, I noticed that the city streets and the buildings were dark. Apparently there was a blackout in our part of town. We went up to our apartment on the third floor in the dark with the help of a lighter. We also gave Marcus a lighter for when he got home; he later said he was grateful for it since he had to climb seventeen flights of stairs and it was the only way he could have found his apartment number.

My daughters also had an opportunity to share the friendship bonds that were central to my life. Madre Euridyna had written them each a card and mailed them to our apartment. The words were filled with welcome, blessings, and love. As a group, we went to Stella Maris School twice. The first time, Michelle videotaped us as we met teachers and went to the kindergarten class in session. We met Madre Gloria, a nun who had been the superior when I was in the first and second grades. She said she did not want to be thought of as old, but only in the culmination of her youth. The girls walked through the entire school, including the attic and onto the new building's veranda, which faced the ocean and part of the mountains where the favelas could be seen. Before we left, we bought the Stella Maris T-shirt that was part of the students' current uniform.

Our second visit to Stella Maris was to meet Madre Euridyna, who had come to Rio from Belo Horizonte. Harumi, Maria Clara, and Hugomar accompanied us. Madre Euridyna was delighted to meet three of my daughters, Lisa, Suzy, and Sara (Michelle had already flown back to the States because she only had a week off from work). The nuns, many of whom I knew, offered us some refreshments at their indoor patio while the girls sat there awkwardly, mainly listening to the conversation in Portuguese that was quite foreign to them. Of course, theirs was a different world and their visit was only an approximation of mine. They felt quite close to Harumi, with whom we had many more meetings and excursions. While we were with the nuns, Harumi turned to Maria Clara and said, "Marianne should have brought the girls a long time ago so they would feel more a part of her life."

Harumi bent over backwards to make my daughters feel at home. The first time we went for lunch at her house, we took longer than expected to get there because we took the bus along the coast, the same bus ride I had taken so many times to Sao Conrado. We stepped out at the square by the Sao Conrado Church where I had made my First Communion. We tried to go in the church, but the porter said it would not open until 2:00 p.m. The girls and I took a leisurely walk up the road toward Harumi's house, stopping frequently to take pictures with Gavea Mountain before us. By then, they knew this was my mountain and my neighborhood, and we basked in its presence. When we arrived at Harumi's, the Chinese dinner she had ordered was still encased in its delivery pack and she said, "You see, I sweated a great deal to make this dinner for you." We ate the dinner with gusto, and then Sara and I went exploring; we climbed the back steep stairs, which were usually off limits to guests because they were in disrepair and overgrown with vegetation. However, the experience made us feel like we were climbing Gavea Mountain, even though these were mere cement stairs literally carved into the foot of the mountain where the bare rock was visible.

After much joking and laughter, we piled into Harumi and Terumi's cars and went to the beach and to take pictures in front of the building where our riding school should have stood. We also went back to the church, which was now open; I felt delighted to see my daughters go up and down the church's zigzag ramp that meant so much to me. Next, we opted to go to Barra Shopping since to drive up the mountain, which they knew I would have preferred to do, could be quite dangerous at this hour. At the mall, the girls did some shopping, including buying Rock in Rio T-shirts, and took a leisurely stroll through a Bonsai exhibit that had five-hundred-year-old trees and azaleas in bloom. Then we were off to a vegetable market that had artichokes with footlong stems.

On Saturday, Marcus came around 10:30 a.m. to take us for a barbecue at his mother's house in Piratininga, near Niteroi. We passed near the port where my mother and I had first arrived from China. Then, we crossed the long Rio Niteroi Bridge that spans just over eight miles of Guanabara Bay, connecting Rio to Niteroi. Marcus stopped at the Contemporary Art Museum in the shape of a huge white saucer that hung over the water, but it wouldn't open until 1:00 p.m. so we proceeded to the Parque da Cidade (city park) which had a high enough elevation for paragliding or parasailing to the beaches. The small car with all of us packed inside had a hard time climbing to the summit. Huffing and puffing over the cobblestones, the car finally took us to the top plateau without dying. There we had the most magnificent view of Rio and witnessed various people parasailing off the mountain. We even saw a woman with her pet parrot on her hand. "How Brazilian can we get?" I thought. I was so thrilled that my girls had these authentic experiences.

At Virginia's, we had a wonderful Churrasco (Brazilian barbecue) prepared by her husband, Edson, and we met the rest of their family and friends. Harumi and Coimbra were there, and she had brought a bag of pictures for us to share. The weather was clear, beautiful, and hot, so we cooled off in the pool and the girls socialized with Virginia's daughter, Lenka, and her cousins Ilam and Marcela, as well as Virginia's mother Gladys, who was always so warm and welcoming and won us over with her million dollar smile. Toward the evening's end, we formed a caravan of three cars and went to see the surrounding beaches and a magnificent sunset. Michelle had to be taken to the airport since she only had one week off from work, so Harumi drove her there. When we embraced, Michelle began to cry, but she made it up by returning to Rio many years later with her husband David. Just as for me, Rio had become one of the magical places in my daughter's heart.

Later, we all went to a typical Brazilian bar in the Arcos da Lapa, an area of Rio known for its nightlife and offering regional music. In the bar, musicians played the Chorinho, music typically played in Brazil's northeast. We danced and drank Caipirinha, made with cachaca, a type of Brazilian rum, sugar, lime, and ice; it was potent enough to light a fire.

One morning, we got a call from Maria Clara who said she had just returned from Brasilia where she and Hugomar had been stationed for the last six years. They were home and would like to meet us in the evening. But before we could play, we had to do some housekeeping. The girls and I traipsed along the fashionable Copacabana Avenue with black garbage bags filled with our dirty clothes and headed toward the only laundromat we knew. There we dealt with an Argentinean manager who helped us load the machines and then stuff our clothes back into the garbage bags and file back into the Copacabana Avenue traffic toward our apartment with Suzy in the lead. It was a sight to behold!

By evening, we were presentable, so Maria Clara, Hugomar, and Marcus took us to the Sindicato do Chopp, an open bar and grill at the Copacabana Atlantic strip, which was very popular with tourists and residents alike. We had some beers and fried cassava root or manioc that was enjoyed by all. Maria Clara, as always, was dressed to kill, filled with wonderful stories, and very happy to meet my daughters.

One evening, Marcus brought his English teacher, Ron, to meet us. He talked like a machine, glad to be in an American's company. Ron was from Racine, Wisconsin, but had lived in Managua, Nicaragua, and now in Rio. He lived six months in a favela in the city of Sao Paulo, Brazil with a friend who was very philanthropic. Ron used to be a seminarian and wanted to be a Franciscan Capuchin monk. He had visited the Capuchin monastery in Detroit and worked in their soup kitchen downtown, with which I was familiar. He was finishing his doctorate in political science and writing about human rights within a democracy such as Brazil. He stated, "Brazil has the greatest gap between the rich and the poor in the Western Hemisphere." We visited his apartment in Ipanema, and he gave us his phone number and email. I was glad to meet a young man with deep concern for the poor since we shared his sensibilities.

During our visit, my daughters had a chance to see the fate of some of Rio's poor. On the beach, they saw some homeless youths. At a kiosk where we had some refreshments, a black girl of twelve or thirteen socialized in a playful manner with the locals; late at night, we saw her lying on a mattress someone had given her in our neighborhood. Sometimes we saw whole families lying on newspaper in a doorway. One particular teenage boy broke my heart. I had gone to a local restaurant to buy pizza for the girls when I saw this very pale youth of mixed race coughing nearby. He approached me and asked for some money to buy food. I gave him some money to buy one or two meals, but not enough to sustain him. I wish I had done more. Suzy was more practical. When we encountered a poor family in the streets and I wanted to give them alms, she would caution me and say, "There are too many, Mom, and they will all begin to follow us."

Harumi and her family entertained us for the rest of our visit. On Sunday, Terumi and her husband, Renato, took us to the Naval Club in Niteroi where Renato docked his yacht. We had a tour of the place, including his yacht, which he hesitated to take out because of the weather. It was a record 95° F, considering it was winter in Rio. But there was a heat wave due to an El Nino. After a buffet dinner inside the air-conditioned dining room, the girls swam in the pool and lay out while Terumi and I talked. Before we left, Renato presented each of us with a T-shirt with the insignia Charitas, the name of the club.

On our way home, we visited an open market in Ipanema and had some ice cream on a street corner, reminiscent of the times when I had come to the movies there in my youth. Miriam, Terumi's daughter, came the next day to take us to Barra Beach and meet up with Harumi, who made sandwiches. The day was glorious and the sea was calm. The girls lay out and I took pictures of a local fishing boat that was bobbing on the waves near the shore, which I later intended to paint.

The next morning we had one of our most memorable trips to the beach when Miriam took us to Grumari Beach, which was beyond Barra da Tijuca and Recreio dos Bandeirantes, in a more remote area on Rio's southern coast, which looked like paradise—perhaps like Hawaii. We stopped in an area with a small beach where a rustic restaurant was nestled in the rocks below and the waters were crystal clear, but then we decided to go to the larger beach that had better access, even though the stairs going down were precarious. Harumi and Coimbra brought fried chicken and accompaniments, and Terumi shared pictures of her son and daughter's wedding while I talked about my niece Joan's wedding in Hawaii. Miriam, in her underwater suit, swam to an island nearby and harpooned a small fish. Meanwhile, the girls and I explored the region, deciding to climb a large rock protruding out of the water that we could reach only with the help of someone's strong hands, and the only way down was to jump some twenty feet into the water. Of course, I had to do it. Up on the rock, I engaged in conversation with two young Brazilian men who marveled at my courage to jump off the rock.

Later, Lisa and I walked on the road above the beach, and near a parapet, we saw a very tanned old man with a boy, showing some of the fish he had caught that day. We gazed with wonderment at the basket of fish. I was so glad to be sharing this local scene with Lisa, who since her youth had wondered what my life was like in Rio. She was not disappointed.

A few days before our departure, Harumi invited Marcus and us for a sumptuous Sushi dinner at her house to make up for the previous Chinese take-out. She employed the help of Cazu's children, who had taken a Japanese cooking class with her. When we arrived, Harumi was fast at work completing the dinner. Soon a couple of tables were colorfully decked with a variety of sushi, shrimp tempura, sashimi, crab, various rolls, and radish salad. She had certainly outdone herself this time. The whole family was there, including Terumi, Cazu, their children, and Mama Toki with her dog, Yuki ("Dirty Snow" as she called him).

Our stay in Rio had now come to an end. As we returned home, I felt my girls had given me so much pleasure by letting me show them the place I considered home. When we returned, Sara wrote a piece for school entitled, "Waiting for the Sun." In it, she said that when she was small, I had sat her in my lap and promised to take her to a place where the mountains meet the sea and give way to a jungle and where there is perpetual sunshine. She thought she was going that day, but it did not happen until she was eighteen. She loved going to the mountaintops and seeing her mother's Rio, the places where I had told her I had danced, attended school, swam, and the beaches where I had dreamed. She was delighted to learn about my culture that had become her own. She said it took her one year to learn her mother's name, but eighteen to know what it contained. Even though she did not understand one thing I said when I spoke Portuguese to friends and strangers, instead of being offended, she was suddenly enchanted. She said she wanted to learn Portuguese because it is such an expressive and positive language. While in Brazil, she saw so many, exotic, beautiful faces, but the best face of all, she said, "was my mother's; her happiness was filled with many smiles because she was able to fulfill her lifelong promise to me."

Chapter 2

Trip to China: October 2000

In the year 2000, I again traveled to Brazil and China, the places that held my soul, one because I lived there and the other because of my father. By mid-October, Tony and I prepared to leave for China for two weeks, arriving first in Beijing. My brother left for China before us and had gone directly to Hangzhou, where my father and his wife's family lived. But I wanted to show Tony the sights and sounds of the Imperial City of Beijing.

Once we landed and cleared Customs, we found ourselves in the airport lobby in need of a taxi to the Taiwan Hotel, situated in a modern shopping district, where we were staying. Immediately, a man approached us who represented a transport service. After we paid him 380 yuans (fifty-six dollars), he told us to follow a second man who took us over a few medians to a plain old car without a taxi sign, driven by a third man, who was rather young and disheveled. He had a hard time putting our luggage in the trunk, which was littered with soft drink bottles, so he ended up putting a few pieces in the front passenger seat. He was in a hurry, but on the way out of the airport, an official stopped the car. The driver had to park the car in a precarious curve at a freeway entrance and run out with some documents. Tony and I looked at each other, convinced we had made a mistake. This car reeked of tobacco and urine, the doors rattled like sheets in the wind, and now the driver wasn't even legitimate. But he did return, apologizing, and sped through the freeway. At the tollbooth, he muttered something, but we refused to pay the toll fee as we had already paid his boss. All I could hear in my mind was my niece Joan's warning, "Beware of swindlers; China has changed." But it was too late.

What used to be a two-lane highway lined with trees, connecting the airport to the city, had turned into a wide expressway that, when it approached the city, branched out to many other multi-lane throughways and boulevards. It was the five o'clock rush hour; the roads were packed with cars and buses, and only the daring and clever made headway. Suddenly, our driver veered away from the main avenue, and we found ourselves in a narrow dark alley where our driver dodged a woman emptying a basin of water, and the two exchanged some choice words. A man on a bike watched the near accident as the car continued to snake around pedestrians, cyclists, and vendors huddled in dark doorways. I wondered, "Where is this man taking us?" and I said to Tony, "I think we have been kidnapped." Before long, however, the driver was back on the main boulevard and drove into the well-lit circular drive of our luxurious hotel. When we left him, he was very pleased with his tip.

In the evening after dinner, we walked around the city near the Taiwan Hotel. It was very cold, but the surroundings were pleasant. We saw a beautifully lit Romanesque Catholic Church with a statue of St. Joseph in the park-like yard in front and a rose garden on the side. I asked Tony, "Do you think this is a Catholic Church?" I was surprised to find one in China. We tried to enter, but the doors were locked. However, we saw posted a schedule of morning services. I thought, "Things have definitely changed in China." The ideology as well as people's way of life appeared transformed. On an adjacent street with modern high-rises, we witnessed the set up of a bungee seat in which three teenagers whirled in the air, bouncing and turning upside down with screams of delight and fear. Not too far away, we walked through a food fair where shish kebab, corn on the cob, noodles, and dumplings were served to family groups, all talking in loud exchanges. Then we decided to walk through a beautiful modern mall, complete with layered floors, reached by escalators and glass elevators with views of the modern courtyard below. The shops sold modern leather goods and men and women's apparel. We walked through a luggage store where the prices were excellent. However, I was a bargain hunter and headed for the shopping stalls across from our hotel. I bought some silk Chinese vests for my daughters and many silk scarves for my friends. One thing I learned from experience in these open markets was, "Never settle for the first quoted price." I bought a silk Chinese pajama outfit for my niece's baby Maya for twenty-five dollars that I could have bought for seven in another booth.

The next day, we headed to the Great Wall and the Ming Tombs. A large tourist van with other Chinese tourists from Hong Kong, Taiwan, and other parts of China picked us up. Brandon, our guide, relished the opportunity to speak English with us, the only English-speaking tourists on the van. Soon we stopped at a jade workshop where we observed workers rotate a wet piece of jade on machine-driven file bits. We were told the jade was from the mountain range nearby. We were also warned about fake jade. Real jade scratches glass without scratching itself, and also has a cloudy appearance when held up to the light; when tapped, it has a musical resonance rather than the flat sound characteristic of the glass reproductions. Needless to say, I bought a few trinkets aided by a masterful salesman who spoke perfect English.

Then we were off to the Ming Tombs. This time, I did not see the road lined with mythical animals as I had in 1982. Brandon took us to the main tomb of the emperor who had built the Forbidden City. The building that houses the tomb is magnificent with carved and painted ceilings and a blue tiled roof. Inside, we saw the emperor and empress' ceremonial garb. The tomb itself had never been excavated. On my way out of the building, I saw two men digging a ditch. They had just unearthed the bust of a statue so they were smiling with delight. On a mound of dirt nearby, I found a shard of yellow tile from a roof or wall and asked a man, "Can I have this?" The man smiled with approval. So now I had a piece of the Ming Tombs.

Brandon, aside from being a wonderful guide, was also a shrewd salesman. He took us to the Institute for Traditional Chinese Medicine. After seeing plaques with Mao Tse-tung and Zhou Enlai's handwriting, testifying to the greatness of this institute as well as samples of gallstones taken from various patients, the group was ushered into a small classroom with about fifteen desks. A slender woman, with delicate hands and wearing a lab coat, introduced herself in Chinese and then English as a doctor versed in Chinese Medicine. She spoke about the principle of Chi, the life force, as well as about acupuncture and Chinese herbs. Then she introduced a man, also dressed in a lab coat, who was a master in Chi Gung. Before long, this man was in a state of high concentration or meditation. He held two ends of an electrical cord that had a socket in the middle. The slender doctor showed us an electrical bulb and screwed it onto the socket. Lo and behold, the light flickered and then the bulb was fully lit from the energy emanating from this man. Then the doctor told all the tourists to hold hands. The Chi Gung Master was on one end, and immediately, we could feel a current passing through our hands that intensified and then diminished. It was true magic—I was impressed! At the session's end, a scurry of doctors and nurses entered the room to offer free pulse readings. Of course, Tony and I submitted. One matronly doctor with soft gentle eyes placed three fingers on Tony's wrist and asked him to show his tongue. The diagnosis was not good. Tony needed five bottles of herbal medicine. He was to take fifteen round pellets either before or after every meal. I was prescribed three bottles. We settled for three bottles for Tony and two for me with a price of roughly 300 dollars. They were happy to take my debit Visa card. Later, upon reflection, I thought I had been taken. In Hangzhou, I called my bank to cancel my purchase, but it was too late—the transaction had long been processed.

After lunch at a large Chinese restaurant with mainly Chinese customers, we had a simple but delicious lunch. One of our fellow tourists was especially solicitous and kept filling our plates and brought a round of Chinese beer to toast our meeting and journey. It was then I learned a little about our fellow passengers and realized that Chinese people who lived in other parts of the world were just as interested in the motherland as I was.

The mountain range became closer as we approached the Great Wall at a place named Bah-dah-Ling. The sun was high in the sky and it was a clear glorious day. The van parked in a gravel parking lot reserved for tourist buses. Brandon asked us whether we would like to take a lift halfway up to the first tower of the Great Wall. Everyone thought this was a good idea. We would show our stamina and heroic qualities when we dared climb to the second tower. We gave Brandon the money for our tickets and then had to be careful not to be lost in the maze of buses and vendors hidden in alcoves. Before long, we spotted Brandon waving our tickets and summoning us to an area where we lined up along pipe railings as if waiting for an amusement ride. Little did we know that it would indeed be an amusement ride!

What I thought would be a chairlift turned out to be individual saucers with one lever in the center. Each of us climbed into our "saucer" (Tony, because of his size, sat in one backwards as suggested by Brandon to mitigate the climb's impact). The saucers were grabbed at their bottoms by some kind of chain. Slowly, but surely, we were transported to the top. It took four men to lift Tony out of his "saucer."

We climbed a series of steps that opened to the main aisle of the Great Wall. Groups of people were taking pictures and some headed for the second tower's one hundred-plus steps. The panorama was breathtaking. I had to take my sweater off and tie it to my waist because the sun was so intense. I saw the dark green trees turning into granite patches that wrinkled and faded into the distance. I followed the Great Wall up and down some peaks and valleys, undulating like a man-made spine on the world's back. I felt I wanted to capture it all—all five thousand miles of the Great Wall, but it all came in pieces and the rest was hidden from sight.

I climbed to the top of the second tower and looked through the ammunition windows. I wanted to linger there for a while and let my hair catch the breeze and my mind float onto the vast ranges beyond. The Great Wall continued rising to the third tower, and some dared climb it; however, I was out of breath. Tony, who had recently had a heart attack, waved safely from the ramp as I climbed down the knee-high stone steps. Luckily for us, we had bought some water bottles.

We then climbed back into our roller coaster saucers, situated discretely behind the Great Wall. This time it was a freefall through a winding aluminum chute covered with light green plastic. We quickly discovered that the lever between our legs was not just for holding, but actually controlled the speed of our saucers when we pulled it forward or backward. We zipped down as if in a bobsled, careful not to spill over the sides by bringing it to an andante pace. How delightful! I actually can say I bobsledded down the Great Wall of China. Before boarding the van, I bought one souvenir for my dad—a dark blue baseball cap with the inscription: The Great Wall (in English and Chinese symbols in red).

The next day, we walked to the Forbidden City (Goo Gung as the Chinese know it), which was a little over a mile from our hotel. At the desk, the clerk said, "Take a right and walk several blocks and you will reach the Forbidden City." So we did. It was gray and cold so the brisk walk did us some good, and it was interesting to see the many facades of buildings, local restaurants, and local shops geared for local customers rather than tourists.

After about twenty minutes, we came upon a tall red stucco wall—we were outside the Forbidden City, but where was the entrance? I said, "Goo Gung!" to a pedestrian who gestured we were to go along the wall to the other side. This stretch could have very well been called, Barber's Lane, since I saw several barbers cutting customers' hair on the sidewalk. One particular individual caught my eye. He was a simple man who was absolutely ecstatic about getting his hair cut. He was smiling and talking animatedly with the older barber, who performed his task with ritualistic precision. They were oblivious to us intruders, who knew nothing of their world.

Shortly, through a side entrance, we found ourselves in the courtyard/parking lot in front of the main gate. A youthful man in an army green jacket approached us with an honest smile and asked us, "Would you like a guided tour and explanation of the highlights for 130 yuan or twenty dollars? We obliged. Our insightful, gentle guide was named John, and he had a wry sense of humor and a delightful smile, despite his stained teeth, probably from a combination of tobacco and tea. He had a pleasant gait made soft by his cloth and rubber-soled shoes. He spoke English fluently because his parents were English professors at Peking University. I found out later that he was born and raised in Beijing, but he had spent some time in another town during his adult years. Not only did he educate us, but he also entertained us regarding the mythical lions guarding the entrance. He asked, "Which one is the male or female?" Of course, we guessed wrong. He said, "The right one has a ball under its paw—it is the male. The left one has a baby lion under its paw—that is the female. She is not hurting the baby—she is just playful."

Through John, we learned that the first series of buildings before the first courtyard was for official business. There the twenty-four emperors who had lived here had conducted the business of the state and met with many dignitaries. The emperor was always carried on the shoulders of eunuchs in a covered sedan chair. The ride was always smooth because the poles were long and the servants learned to move in unison. The carved ramp made from one block of marble was brought from a distant region of China and could only be transported in winter when it could be slid on the ice. It was about fifty-four feet long, weighed two hundred tons, and was beautifully carved with intertwining dragons, the imperial symbol. The middle buildings were for the imperial family, the first wife, and one hundred or so concubines who had their individual quarters and stood outside their doors each night for the emperor's choosing. John told us that a lot of infighting and jealousies took place among the women, but the first wife ruled. We passed by the first wife's room with its exquisite carved furniture with canopied bed and tall blue cloisonné vases. It was here that the emperor's twenty-four seals were held.

In the back were various gardens with old trees whose branches had to be supported by wooden amulets. The empress' gazebo was strategically placed so she could have a perfect view from all sides and while away her time in painting, calligraphy, or music. Warm water was obtained from huge outside cauldrons that were heated by log fires; the water was then ladled into buckets and brought in for the emperor's bath. Meals were prepared daily by an army of chefs who cooked one hundred dishes. The emperor would eat a small morsel of each after official tasters tested it.

With so many concubines, each emperor usually had a few dozen kids. Who would succeed him? The emperor named his successor and placed his name behind a high tablet over his throne so it would remain out of sight and always be guarded. I was surprised that contrary to my first visit, we were not allowed inside the buildings. The carvings and exquisite artifacts, including the blue cloisonné cranes by the throne, had to be seen through doors and windows. The throngs of tourists forced officials to protect the antiquities.

Before long, we found ourselves outside the back gates. I refused to take a taxi, much to Tony's chagrin, since I thought Tiananmen Square could be reached easily. Well, I forced Tony on another long march, winding around the Forbidden City's wall, which seemed endless, just so I could have underfoot my father's land. We walked along the moat lined with weeping willows and saw an occasional pedestrian. At a particular bridge, a few men were fishing in the canal's murky waters with long bamboo poles. Someone pointed us in the direction of Tiananmen Square. We had gone full circle, perhaps two miles to the gate opposite to the one we had come in. Inside the tourist courtyard, we headed toward the front entrance that opened itself to Tiananmen Square. Once outside, we could see Mao's picture hanging over the entrance, fresh and ominous, but he no longer had a grip on the destiny of the Chinese people, who were feverishly engaged in surpassing the modern era. The Tiananmen Square Revolt of 1989 had made an impact, at least in terms of economic freedom: China appeared like any capitalist country struggling to survive, yet it differed in regards to speed and intensity of economic growth, a virtual race to the top. An underground tunnel took us under the busy avenue adjacent to Tiananmen Square, and we strolled through some gardens near the Chinese People's Museum, which was closed for remodeling. By all appearances, the Communist ideology seemed to have taken a backseat.

We did return to the hotel by taxi and took a well-deserved rest. That evening, we went to a Peking Duck Restaurant recommended by my niece Joan, who dined at this particular restaurant with her husband Curt, an American. The taxi dropped us off in front of a restaurant we thought was "the one." We sat down at the only vacant table when the hostess remarked, "We serve duck, but this is fast food." I noticed the food was served in paper plates with plastic silverware. A waiter gestured that we needed to go to the restaurant in the back. When we approached this restaurant, we saw a tour bus had just unloaded its passengers, and when we went in, we were placed on a waiting list. This restaurant was a large two-story building with wooden stairs in the center that led to the upper dining areas. In a glass enclosure, I saw dozens of ducks hanging on hooks, moving along a pipe, and then being placed in ovens. Apparently, the ducks needed to be inflated so the skin separated from the body, and then they were aired for twenty-four hours after being sprayed with sugar syrup. After we sat at our table, I saw chefs wheeling the whole roasted duck and carving it expertly at the customer's table. We ate ours with flat pancakes that we coated with thick soy sauce and sprinkled with green onions. In addition, we had vegetables and duck soup for about twenty-five dollars a piece.

The next day, after settling our account at the hotel (ninety-eight dollars for three days with breakfast—not bad), we summoned a taxi—this time a legitimate one. The driver was an animated man who made a mad dash through the city because he thought we were late for our plane to Hangzhou. He charged us the appropriate price of twenty-five dollars. Compared to my first visit in 1982, the airport was completely transformed. There were modern check-in counters for the various airlines and overhead electronic boards displaying the schedule for arrivals and departures. The one difficulty was that all signs were in Chinese, so we ended up standing behind people who were purchasing their tickets. We soon found out that we should go to an area behind the lobby for passengers with tickets where we could process our luggage. I thought to myself, "This is not the same China of 1982—where are the tissue paper tickets written over carbon paper and where is the abacus?" We stood behind a group of Chinese teachers and some Western tourists, who, I found out later, were headed to the Hangzhou International Expo due to open on Saturday. We waited a long time to board the plane. With the help of a computer furnished for customers near the gate, I was able to check the weather in Hangzhou. The forecast was rainy and cloudy for most of next week.

It was raining when we arrived in Hangzhou, just as it had during my first visit with my father in 1982. At the airport, I looked at the same stoop of stairs where my family had stood then, and where inside I had met my father after more than thirty-two years of absence. My brother, Wang Qian, and his brother-in-law Tze Ling (Su Juan's brother) were waiting outside the crowded baggage area ready to take us home, which would be the apartment of my brother's mother-in-law, Tze Ling's mother. I noticed the city's transformation with its many modern shops, high-rises, and wide boulevards. Tze Ling's car sped through the crowded streets, where in the interior of the city, bicycles, pedestrians, and motor vehicles competed for the same space. I watched the bustle of life with amazement.

When the car suddenly halted in front of an apartment building, my brother turned to me and said, "Let's go upstairs and see Father for a while. He is waiting. Tze Ling will wait here to take us to the family dinner."

I was glad to be able to see my father on my first day in the city, even though dinner was waiting in Tze Ling's mother's house. We walked up the mud-spattered pathway toward the entrance of a bare bones, project-like cement building with evidence of charcoal dust, grime, and years of neglect. We went up the stairs to an exterior hallway on the fourth floor, onto which opened many apartment doorways. My brother approached the first corner apartment and knocked on the frame of a metal door lined with a partially ripped screen.

"Mah!…Mah!….Mah!….Mah!" I could not understand the rest, for it was in Chinese, but I thought, "Is he calling his stepmother, Mom?"

After a few moments, my father's wife came to the door and gave us a look of resigned understanding. She knew the purpose of our visit and let us inside. It was dark except for the late afternoon light coming from the window of an adjacent bathroom where I saw my father seated and noticed his white hair in the amber glow. We had caught him off-guard, but he was excited and made an utterance of greeting. My father's wife ushered us into her bedroom and brought extra stools for Tony and my brother as I took a seat in an old wicker chair. I looked around as I waited for Father. The ambiance was simple, almost Dickensian. I felt an uneasy silence since I could not speak Chinese with my stepmother.

Soon, Father was presentable so we joined him in his room. He was seated in his canvas green-striped lawn chair between his bookcases and a catchall table. He had a look of satisfaction and anticipation. I bent down and gave him a kiss on the cheek, glad to see him again. He was emaciated and frail. His bony hands protruded from his blue fleece jacket and rested on his green corduroy pants.

"Hello, Father. How are you?"

"I'm all right. Did you have a good journey?" His voice sounded the same. Somewhat guttural, emphatic, husky, and with an urgency that bespoke a need to be present and share our news.

"Tony and I visited all the great sites in Beijing," I told him, "including the Ming Tombs, the Great Wall, and the Forbidden City."

"You saw the Great Wall?" The pace of his thoughts had a staccato and fragmented quality, but he listened attentively to all we had to say with probing and searching eyes.

"Yes, I bought you a hat at the Great Wall and I will bring it tomorrow." He was pleased.

"You know, the family is going to take us to all the important places in Hangzhou. You must remember that I visited the Ling Ying Temple, the West Lake, and the Pagoda of Six Harmonies when I came to see you many years ago. My brother will not come sightseeing with us because he intends to videotape surrounding picturesque towns and villages to make oil paintings later so he can have an exhibit."

"Where is he having the exhibit?" He asked with interest, glad to follow his son's career and success even from afar.

"I think it will be in New York. But first he has to paint fifty paintings…."

Then I asked, "How long have you lived here?"

"Oh…about three years."

To which my brother interjected, "No, it's closer to ten years. He was here the last few times I came to China."

This gave me a clue. Time did not have the same relevance for my dad. Ten years ago, or three years ago, it did not matter. What was important was that we were together. So many separations. So many memories. All we needed to do was to establish contact after so many years of distance. I wondered, "Are there traces of former mild strokes? Has his mind gone? Does he even recognize me? Am I Cordelia at King Lear's feet, gathering some pearls of wisdom from his scattered mind?"

Father began to enunciate carefully the name of each of my daughters, dispelling my doubts. He had met them on his two visits to the U.S. in 1987 and 1990, the year I last saw him.

"Lisa…Michelle…Suzy…Sara." He was pleased with his memory exercise.

"How is Lisa?" I think he was concerned about the time I asked him to pray for her surgery.

"Lisa is fine. She still works as a dental assistant; her boss is very pleased with her."

"And Michelle…?"

"She works like her father as a pharmaceutical representative, and she is engaged to be married. Her fiancé is a wonderful young man. His name is David."

"Suzy still rides?"

"Oh, yes. She loves to ride. She owns a horse, a dog, and a cat."

"And Sara studies…?"

"She wants to be a lawyer and is gifted in writing."

I bore the weight of the conversation since my father spent most of his days in silence and had to get used to speaking English again. However, he surprised me with many of his questions.

"Do you still have the dog?"

"Yes, Mimi, the 'Lion Pekingese' as you called her. She is fourteen years old now and has trouble climbing stairs."

"I remember going to the Edison Laboratory with you."

"Yes, you and I went to Greenfield Village and we saw Edison's famous laboratory." I knew this visit was significant to him as an electrical engineer and it had pleased him to see the beginnings of his field. We recounted some of the other outings we'd had when he was in Detroit.

As we continued our conversation, I said, "Tony's father died in March."

He had heard of Tony's father's bout with lung cancer. We had called him during the festival of the Chinese New Year from my brother's home in Detroit. At that time, he had suggested we take Tony's father to Dr. Schumann, a specialist in Germany. "He certainly could help." But now with the news of the death, he simply said, looking at each of us, "But he believes in Christ…he is Christian…he must be in himmel (heaven)." Then he said something in Chinese to my brother, and trying to impart hope as he always had, he told us, "We Buddhists believe in life again." Turning to Tony, "I remember your father liked to keep a garden."

"Yes, my father liked to grow his vegetables and tend to his tomato plants every year." Tony did not say much, gripped as he was by culture shock and fatigue.

While my father spoke in Chinese to my brother, I looked around the room. I saw cobwebs, faded walls, four bamboo bookcases filled with books—upright and orderly, but covered with a thick layer of dust—and some knick knacks such as a pipe in its case, a slide ruler, and a wooden chess box. I recognized some of the English paperback novels I had sent him such as Evergreen, The Thorn Birds, and Flowers in the Attic. By the window was a small desk with some weathered paper and some other clutter. I asked myself, "Was it here that he wrote his occasional letter where the greetings were more important than the content?"

A single bulb hung loosely from a wire draped from the ceiling to the wall. The window was partially covered by a grime-covered fan, which must have provided relief on hot summer days. I was seated on my father's bed, a wooden frame strung with weaved rope, on which was a thin pad and a small, faded white cotton comforter, soiled on the edges with urine, due to his incontinence. I also noticed on the table next to him an old tattered leather suitcase covered with a mound of papers and miscellaneous items. I wondered whether that suitcase contained some treasure from the past, some relic that would bring us closer together. I would never know since I never asked. The whole of China had undergone a modern transformation over the last few years, but my father still lived like a monk in a cave, undisturbed and holding on to another time.

My brother continued to speak animatedly with my father and then turned to us, speaking in English, "Father says grandfather is born again. He is alive in China." He laughed with surprise and humor. "Life again…everybody has life again. Father also says Agnes lives downstairs. She lives downstairs with her Hungarian servant."

"But Father," I said, believing I could convince him of the truth, "Mommy died in America in 1986 of a heart attack."

He looked directly at me, "No, Agnes is not in Brazil or America. Agnes went to Germany and saw Dr. Schumann and was cured of her cancer. And now she lives downstairs."

There was no convincing him. He looked toward the doorway in a fixed gaze, lifted his hand, brought his walker in front of him, and slowly, in a partially bent posture, got up and was ready to visit his beloved Agnes, his first wife, my mother, downstairs. He took a few halted steps, but we could not allow him to go any further because the outside cement steps were steep and not made for a frail, bent over old man with a walker. Quickly, to remedy the situation, my brother told my father he would go look for Agnes and report back. He left the apartment and went downstairs, returning shortly thereafter.

"Father, Agnes moved away. The neighbors do not know where she went. She did not leave an address." My brother repeated the same information as father inquired some more.

His wishes had come up empty. With a slight tilt of the head and disappointed eyes, he said in an almost inaudible tone, "Ah…but then the problem cannot be solved!" His words might have been lost to the others, but not to me. He wanted to reunite our family.

After visiting my father, Tze Ling took us to his mother's house for a banquet of crabs, fish, turtle, chicken, and assorted vegetables cooked by his younger brother, Tze Jwing. As I mentioned before, Su Juan, my brother's wife, had six brothers and sisters, who in one way or another made sure that our visit to Hanzhou was enjoyable. Mama's apartment was small but comfortable and on the fourth floor of a large apartment complex. It had light pecan wood floors throughout with a matching dining room table and chairs as well as floor-to-ceiling closets of the same color on almost every wall. The main bedroom extended itself into a glass-enclosed balcony that ran the room's full width. It held more closets, a desk made of the same wood as the floor, and a sewing machine. In the corner stood a covered washing machine that was used occasionally. We were offered this master bedroom with a king-size bed and a headboard matching the color of the closets. It appeared very comfortable, but Tony felt he was sleeping on boards since the bed was a frame weaved with rope, like most Chinese beds. However, each of us got a fluffy cotton comforter most adequate for the damp weather we encountered. I describe this apartment to contrast it with the old dwellings the families had lived in when I visited them in 1982.

All rooms opened to the dining room, including the bathroom that had a hand-held shower, but no curtains. To take a shower in the morning, I had to tell Do Bei, the oldest sister who lived with her mother, so she could plug in an appliance in the wall above the toilet that displayed the water temperature in red numbers on a luminous panel. Of course, after the shower, the whole bathroom would get wet and the interlocked wooden mats had to be dried each time. Once, Su Juan's mother slipped on one of the mats, hitting her jaw on the toilet seat and knocking a couple of teeth out of her dentures. We ran to her rescue. She was okay, but shaken. Tze Ling had the dentures repaired the next day. My brother took the smaller front bedroom that faced the street. Sometimes, he complained he could not sleep because the street vendors would start arguing at four o'clock in the morning, each claiming the other's space.

Mama and Do Bei relinquished their apartment for us. They slept in one of the brothers' apartments nearby. However, they came faithfully each morning, worked until night, and left only after we went to bed. They offered us peeled apples, tea, a multi-course breakfast and lunch. We would have steamed rolls, green onion fried pancakes that we called "Chinese Pizza," and an assortment of bean and berry soups. They always tried to find out what we liked. Mama talked to me as she had during my first visit, as if I understood every word. When my brother came home in the evenings after his excursions to the towns he intended to paint, he would translate some of the conversation.

When we heard Mama and Do Bei come in the early morning, Tony would say, "Our keepers are here." They would not rest till we were clean, fed, and doctored. A household custom was that whenever we entered the apartment, we were immediately furnished with rubber slippers of different sizes kept in a built-in cabinet near the front door. We were never allowed in the kitchen. Mama and Do Bei changed slippers when entering the kitchen so as not to track grease or water through the house. Needless to say, the house was impeccable. It fit the common saying: There is a place for everything and everything is in its place.

We went to Ling Ying Temple with Do Bei. On the mountain ledge along the path, it was misty and wet with lush greenery everywhere. A small stream ran alongside the mountain wall that had a slippery stone-studded footpath. Do Bei motioned to us that we should stay clear of it because it was too dangerous. I saw some grottos and some huge images of Buddha carved right out of the mountain's face. Inside the main temple, I saw a giant golden Buddha with an area cordoned off where a few Buddhist monks prayed and rolled their beads through their fingers. One monk stood behind a counter, taking prayers and requests from penitents who wrote them in a book or on a piece of paper. We then moved to the Hall of One Thousand Buddhas. These were life-size golden human statues with all kinds of expressions and poses, representing all different personalities and walks of life. It was a real study of the multi-faceted aspects of life. When we went outside, I saw a large iron kettle, onto which the prayerful placed incense sticks, and then they bowed several times respectfully. The rituals were not too different from the ones I had experienced while growing up Catholic: incense, candles, shrines, beads, petitions, and statues, all with the purpose of elevating the soul to a higher, more merciful plane. In the midst of the devout was also a crowd of tourists. Some guides carried electronic bullhorns to keep their groups together. We returned home, crossing the downtown area via bus and taxi.

Other trips included a visit to the Pagoda of the Six Harmonies, overlooking the Hangtang River where we could see the first railcar bridge built in China. We managed to climb to the pagoda's fourteenth floor to view the scenery from the various windows and ask for blessings.

At the entrance of a glassed building downtown, I met Hue Juan, Tze Ling's wife, who was one of the most wonderful people I ever met in China. She had a natural magnetic beauty, coupled with self-assurance and a loving, vivacious spirit. When she met me, she embraced me and made it her job to guide me upstairs. At first, I did not know who she was so I asked my brother, "Who is she?" He answered, "Oh, she is Tze Ling's wife. She will take you upstairs while Tze Ling waits for his daughter Tcha Tcha (her nickname)." As I looked at Hue Juan, I saw she had dancing eyes, filled with curiosity and appreciation, and dark and slightly undulating hair. She had laughing folds, not around her mouth, but around her rather large eyes that shone like black pearls. Her voice was deep and melodious, always involved and engaging. There on the eighth floor, totally encased in glass, we were to have dinner with Tze Ling's family and other guests. We could also watch the fireworks display scheduled to go off later in the evening and furnished by several countries to commemorate Hangzhou's International Expo.

At dinner, Tze Ling was a charmer. He liked to entertain, tease, and sometimes flirt with me. He was seated beside me, and in one of his flirtatious moves, with his chopsticks he proceeded to place in my mouth one of the delicacies on the table. I was taken by surprise and did not know whether he'd had too much to drink. By the same token, he was mindful of everyone's comfort. He took special care of my brother, who in 1993 had had a stroke and experienced weakness in his right hand. Wang Qian could not use chopsticks with dexterity, so Tze Ling made sure his plate was always full from the various dishes on the Lazy Susan. He was the one who provided my brother with a car and a chauffeur (a relative of Hue Juan) for his daily excursions to the countryside and nearby towns for material for his future paintings. Tze Ling was well positioned, being an executive in a steel business. He was accustomed to taking customers out to lunch or dinner, much like a businessman would do in the States. He always wore a suit and carried a cellular phone and leather pouch.

Tze Ling was frustrated that we could not understand each other, so he often turned to humor, saying, "Hello, okay, goodbye, thank you," and then he would throw in a Chinese phrase I didn't understand, but that would turn out to mean "so and so is ugly." When I would laugh and nod my head, it would spur more laughter because unknowingly, I had agreed with his foolish remarks. Tcha Tcha, his fifteen-year-old daughter, sat near Tony and spoke decent English. She sang for us Mariah Carey's song "Be My Hero," which moved us all. After dinner, we watched the fireworks and I heard the common, "Awwwwww…. Ahhhhhh…!!!!" with every luminous explosion.

Returning home that evening was a nightmare! It seemed that all of Hangzhou was in the downtown area and Tze Ling had to inch along surrounded by a throng of people on foot and walking their bikes. It felt like being lost in an anthill. I had to close my eyes for fear someone would get hurt. We were free at last after thirty minutes of stop-and-go traffic that took us less than a mile.

Sunday was another busy day. Tze Ling dropped us off at the zoo and Hue Juan was our guide. We all shared an umbrella because it was drizzling. We couldn't converse, but I indicated to her the direction where I thought the pandas were. "Yes, Yes…" she said, and then we went past snake pits, monkey cages, the lion's den, an elephant stall, the bird sanctuary, and finally around a bend and up a ledge, we came to the panda house. A large panda was on her back with her paws frolicking in the air. I was preparing to take a picture when an attendant from inside the cage motioned to us while he gave the panda a few slices of apple. Hue Juan understood and paid the man twenty yuans for us to enter the cage and take a picture with the panda. When we entered, the panda was seated on her rump, so we filed behind her. I was able to touch her fur from behind ever so lightly, cautious not to cause a disturbance because I had heard that pandas could be quite dangerous, but not this one. I was surprised that the fur felt quite coarse and not smooth as I had imagined. Many who saw the picture later swore she was stuffed. On our path back to the zoo's entrance, we came across a small arena where spectators, mostly families, were watching acrobats, monkeys, and bears perform tricks. I wanted to stay for the spectacle and join the audience, which was applauding with glee, but Hue Juan received a phone call from Tze Ling, who was waiting for us at the zoo's entrance.

Tze Ling took us to eat at an eighth floor downtown restaurant; this time, we sat down with a doctor anesthesiologist and her husband. Both spoke English and were invited by Tze Ling to be our translators. The fare at the restaurant was unusual—we had barbecued snake served on a platter with tropical flowers. It tasted like fish, but it was a little tougher, with many more bones. After lunch, we took a pedicab ride to the West Lake. Ever since my first trip to China, I had wanted to ride in one of these bicycle-driven carriages and Tze Ling had read my mind.

Once we reached West Lake, it was drizzling and wet, but this did not prevent us from boarding a covered rowboat. The rain began to blow inside the boat, so I furnished my umbrella to Tze Ling, which immediately spurred some conversation. "Where was it made?" The tag said, "Made in China." So were my shoes, my trench coat, my leather purse and my slacks—all bought in the U.S.A. What did this reveal about China's booming manufacturing economy and link with the West? The floodgates were opened and there was no turning back. As we cruised the misty, peaceful waters of the West Lake, I remembered that this was an ancient site where emperors from the Tang and Song dynasties often visited and may have seen, like us, the charming internal islands with their many pools, bridges, and man-made rock formations, typical of Chinese gardens.

In the next few days, Sho Bei, Su Juan's middle sister, took us to the Silk and Tea Museums in the forested hills of Hangzhou. She came with a car and driver, furnished by her husband, and we picked up Kent, a young Chinese man of twenty-six who owned an advertising company in downtown Hangzhou and who was to be our guide and translator. In the Silk Museum, we learned about the history of silk, how it was made, and the history of its trading, dating back four thousand years. I saw thousands of white larvae on bamboo trays eating mulberry leaves. Later, they were transferred to wire mesh screens where they made the cocoons. These were then boiled and pulled into threads placed on looms to make various fabrics. The fabrics were placed in vats of natural die and dried. Some were embroidered into famous garments for kings and townspeople.

Before proceeding to the Tea Museum, we had lunch at the famous Hangzhou Noodle Restaurant. Sho Bei and Kent ordered for Tony and me the most expensive dish—noodles with prawns, exquisite mushrooms, and Chinese greens. It was delicious and a welcome relief from the twenty-course dinners. We spent some of the afternoon strolling through Hangzhou Silk Warehouse District with blocks and blocks of stalls, selling every possible kind of silk product at the most affordable prices. I had learned from previous experiences not to dare buy any item because Sho Bei would insist on paying for it. She did buy me a beautiful silk blouse for five dollars and silk scarves, three for one dollar. Under other circumstances, I would definitely have waited to buy silk here in Hangzhou, where the Chinese themselves buy it in big bundles that they transport to other cities like Beijing and Shanghai.

At the Tea Museum, we learned that tea had first been medicinal and made into cakes, and only later ritualized as a social drink with the more familiar infusion process and poured into vessels, some of which could be seen in the museum. In Hangzhou, many artifacts of jade and porcelain had also been unearthed and were on display. Nearby, we saw a reproduction of an old room where tea would have been served. To top it off, we had green tea in a charming tea room overlooking the gardens. Here I had an opportunity to chat with Kent. He said, "It is important to enjoy life. It is a Chinese motto that many follow. Money is not enough." It seemed he wanted to hold on to these simple and true values as China was swept into a wave of rapid economical development.

Little did we know the family was preparing a farewell dinner for us. It took place in a private room of a famous Hangzhou restaurant lined with lanterns in the West Lake district. Black lacquered chairs inlaid with mother of pearl surrounded a similarly adorned huge round table. We were given appetizers and drinks while we waited for my brother to come from Tongli (my father's birthplace), a town near Suchou, west of Shanghai. Once my brother arrived, we were served a twenty-course dinner, including wild duck, West Lake fish, and eggplant on a bed of fried breadcrumbs.

As we chatted, Kent's wife, a charming red-haired young Chinese woman with keen intelligence and a winning smile, told me she had been to Germany, but not to the U.S. She explained, "It is hard for young Chinese to obtain visiting visas as immigrating officials believe that they may stay." When I told her about my experience at the Chinese Clinic in Beijing, she laughed with sympathy and said, "You are too trusting!" We exchanged email addresses.

On our way out of the restaurant, we discovered that Kent's leather portfolio was missing from the car. It contained 500 dollars, which he had saved to give his brother, who was coming home from Seattle, Washington, where he had been studying. A frenzied search took place to see whether any of us had inadvertently taken it with our packages. But it did not turn up. Tony remembered that when we had entered the Tea Museum, the car's back windows were partly rolled down, and Kent thought he had left it in the backseat.

While in Hangzhou, I saw my father five times. We returned to his apartment on Sunday after our West Lake tour. I had an armful of gifts for him, his wife, my half-sister Jia Ming, and my stepsister Jia Ching (who was not present). Jia Ming's husband, Wang Shing Juan, prepared dinner in the wok in the simple kitchen by the entrance. As I understood from the family's conversation, he was the one who cleaned up after my father when he had an accident. Father was sitting in his usual green-striped lawn chair in his room. I unpacked the gifts of chocolates, simple electronic games, and a beautiful weaved cotton blanket with an angel that had outstretched wings to give to him. I knew my father was partial to angels. He had once told me that angels were in every religion and they were the bearers of mercy. To his wife, I gave another blanket of an angel caressing a child. Since she was my father's principal caretaker, I could not show too much partiality. She was included in the family circle even though memories of cruel deeds against my young brother might have dictated otherwise. All the others received chocolates and cologne, my standard gifts. I helped my father play electronic solitaire while he proudly wore his blue baseball cap from the Great Wall. My brother exclaimed, "Toys for children; that's good!" referring to my father as a grown child.

Jia Ming, my half-sister, was more beautiful than I remembered her. She wore a black suit with a gray blouse and pumps that were very becoming. She had a short wedge haircut, long and brushed back in front, and wore earth-tone lipstick, appearing very much like the professional accountant she was since she worked downtown for a large firm in Hangzhou. Her cheeks were rosy as she brought out the many dishes cooked by her husband. Her son, Chang Chang (nickname), sat at the table near me, and I learned he was a computer engineer and the family was very proud of him. I had seen him last when he was a young boy. A myriad of bowls were placed on the round wooden table: fish balls, Chinese dumplings, and green vegetables, and of course, many bottles of Chinese beer. Jia Ming helped me crack some river crabs that were spread in groups on the bare table, and I dipped the meat in the ginger vinegar or soy sauce. Father joined us at the table, sitting in the wicker chair brought in for him. I offered him a dumpling, but Jia Ming exclaimed, "No, No!" Nevertheless, my father went to the forbidden bowl and helped himself to several mouthfuls. When he finished eating, he retired back to his room, using his walker. I tried to stay with him, but he said, "Go join the others." He had grown accustomed to being an observer, and he enjoyed the glow of the evening—both his families joined as one.

Chang Chang, my nephew, had a meeting in town and excused himself to me in rather formal English. To his father, who had joined us after cooking the last dumplings, he gave a spontaneous, affectionate hug and they had a few friendly exchanges that I, of course, could not understand. The dichotomy before us could not be missed—the barrier of language, time, and place that we were trying to bridge. I found my brother-in-law, Wang Shing Juan, to be a handsome, sturdy man, and he appeared to be a hands-on kind of worker. His hands were stained as he lit a cigarette and puffed away. The topic of my father's incontinence came up. My brother translated that Wang Shing Juan was saying that Father would soil his clothes and bedding often, and he was tired of cleaning after him. The problem was overwhelming to him and the family, so they wanted to restrict his evening intake of food and tea. I suggested adult diapers that I would try to find.

After we said goodnight to everyone, on the street below, my brother stopped at a vendor because he was impressed with his organically grown Fuji apples neatly packed in Styrofoam sleeves. After he bought the whole crate, I asked him, "How are we going to carry it?" He answered, "Oh, I will." We walked all the way home, bouncing the crate between us in the sparsely lit street that connected the main avenues. We had to dodge construction, litter, and traffic when the sidewalks disappeared.

The next day, Tony was not feeling well. The banquets had finally taken their toll and he woke up with intense back pain and made frequent visits to the "throne." Mama and Do Bei were very worried, and with many gestures and drawings of crosses, asked whether Tony needed to go to the hospital. I made them understand that it was not necessary. While Tony rested, Do Bei and I took a walk to my father's apartment. At the corner, I went into a sort of convenience store and searched for diapers and antibiotics, but I found neither. I just bought some bottled milk for Father. We walked the mile-and-a-half to Father's apartment through a ramshackle avenue; it had a bridge that went over a partially-filled canal that had makeshift worker dwellings made of brick. A hole on the street wall revealed workers playing cards and clothes drying on a line. All around us, we saw construction. Some tall apartment buildings, painted white with pink trim and modern windows, were finished but empty. I saw a gardener hoeing a flowerbed in a building's interior courtyard. My brother had told me that the old neighborhood was gone, and with it, the old compound by the canal where my father had lived. Further down, the street narrowed, causing some congestion among cyclists, pedestrians, and cars. At a busy street corner by my father's apartment, we went into a huge two-story supermarket, complete with escalators, lockers, and a Kentucky Fried Chicken restaurant. Again I looked for antibiotics and diapers, but I did not find any.

Father was waiting for us in his room, sitting in his lawn chair. He had asked me to visit in the morning. After Do Bei spoke to him, he said, "I hear Tony is not feeling so well and she asks if Tony needs to go to the hospital?"

"No, I think Tony will be okay," I replied.

Father drank the milk I brought and carefully unwrapped a Little Debbie chocolate wafer, cleaning his hands on an old Kleenex. I showed him the box of Wet Ones I had brought earlier. When he looked toward the door, I knew what was on his mind and said, "You think Agnes lives downstairs."

"Yes, she lives downstairs. You go down and speak to her neighbor. He knows her."

I could not refuse. I went downstairs and was confronted by closed doors. After waiting a little while, I went back upstairs and told him, "Father, the man told me that Agnes left some time ago, but he does not know where."

"What is his name?"

I had to think quickly. How could I lie to my father? Perhaps I could give him the name of Jesus or of an archangel.

I said, "His name is Michael."

And so Father said, "Tell him to come upstairs. I want to talk to him."

It had been a long time since I had played the game of pretend, but I went downstairs once more. The latch closed behind me and I had to knock to get back into the apartment. My stepmother was intrigued. Why was I going out and coming back?

"Father," I said when I returned, "Michael stepped out. He went shopping."

Father picked up his walker. I asked, "You want to go out?"

"Yes."

I helped Father while he placed the walker carefully in front of him one step at a time. His jacket was covered with white hair, which I tried to brush away, thinking, "His shock of white hair is finally thinning out." I held the outside door as he placed the walker on the cement floor just clear of the shallow step. He walked to the balcony where he had a clear view of the street. He lingered for a while, looking with intensity, as if waking up from a dream, or like someone who for the first time had stepped out of his cell after years of imprisonment. Then he proceeded slowly to return. He looked down the stairwell, halted, and cried out loud:

"Agnes!...Agnes!"

My stepmother was holding the door. I looked at her, hoping she would understand. However, her look of puzzlement made me think they shared the same language, but not the language of the heart.

When I returned to the apartment, Tony was feeling better, having rested all morning. But Mama had been contacting her resources; Tze Ling could come at any moment to take Tony to the clinic. When the phone rang, she answered, then handed it to me, saying, "Jia Ming, Jia Ming." I realized it was my half-sister, but we could not speak to each other except to say, "I don't understand," so I gave the phone back to Mama. Through gestures and a few familiar words and pointing to the clock, I was given to understand that Jia Ming, her husband, and Jia Ching, my stepsister, were coming soon. When they arrived, Jia Ching, a medical doctor, confirmed with Tony that his stomach was making gurgling sounds, and she handed him the stethoscope so he could hear his own sounds. She recommended plenty of water, but hesitated to give Tony the antibiotics she had brought in her bag, giving it to him anyway if he needed it. He and I understood they should be taken twice a day. She was slimmer and her dark curly hair had thinned out and had some gray. She appeared talkative, but we had to talk aided by a dictionary. I said to her, "I remember you studied English. What happened?"

"Oh, no time to study," she retorted. She told us her son was in Shanghai and was a salesman for a soft drink company. She planned to retire as a psychiatrist at sixty and was currently building a house. I wanted to ask her about her experiences as a psychiatrist since I worked as a social worker in an inner city psychiatric hospital, but the language barrier prevented it. We exchanged minimal information about common medications used for schizophrenia and depression. Ordinarily, my father's family would not come to visit my brother's in-laws, but today was different. We had a friendly exchange. Jia Ching was very interested in the apartment's hardwood floors and cabinetry due to the construction of her new house. Before she left, she gave me a beautiful silk tablecloth and Jia Ming gave me satiny socks. I never saw these family members again.

Our stay in Hangzhou was drawing to a close. The day before our departure, Tony and I took the familiar walk to father's apartment. On our way, I bought my father some bananas, tangerines, and a few sweet potatoes baked in an iron barrel at the street corner. My father inquired about Tony's condition, "Are you feeling all right?"

"So, so. But much better than yesterday," Tony replied.

"Did my daughter come to see you and give you some medicine?"

"Yes, she did. It was very kind of her."

"You will be all right!" Father ate a tangerine and threw the peels in the wastebasket near him. He was neat in his own way. I asked Father whether he had been doing some reading, noticing the newspaper on the small table nearby. He picked up the paper and said, "I only read the headlines." Turning the page, he saw a picture of a person and exclaimed, "Oh, this is an African man from Africa." This most likely evoked memories of his journeys through Africa with my mother.

"So you don't wear glasses anymore?" I asked.

"No, I don't. I see well."

I then looked at him and asked him the central question, "Are you happy?"

He looked at me and answered with a whimsical resigned smile, "I am happy that you are here."

That was enough for me. I would not probe any further. I knew that growing old was not easy and that he felt confined and a burden to his family. The waning years were at hand. On our way out, my stepmother handed me several packages of Chinese-roasted walnuts saying, "Jia Ming." So I knew they were from my half-sister.

Back at Mama's, we had lunch and then Tze Ling sent a driver for us. My brother had spent the night in Zangzhou, a town built around canals 100 miles west of Shanghai, near Suchou, an area where my father spent his childhood. My brother and the driver came back early from his videotaping excursion, so all of us could go to Tze Ling's apartment for tea and later back to Mama's for dinner with the whole family.

It had been raining off and on for seven days, but nothing could dampen the vitality, charm, and hospitality of the Lou family. Hue Juan opened the door to her apartment on the twenty-second floor of a luxury building. She ushered us in with her customary smile and gave us each a pair of slippers in exchange for our wet shoes. The apartment was spacious and elegantly furnished. The pecan hardwood floors and cabinetry reminded me of Mama's apartment. Before we could settle into the green leather couches, Hue Juan gave us a tour. Her daughter Tcha Tcha's room had a small balcony. The master bedroom had a private bath, and in every room were built-in closets and everything was very orderly. There was even a washing machine in a small laundry room/dispensary. While we waited for Tze Ling to arrive, Hue Juan offered us green tea, an assortment of cut fruits with toothpicks, and sunflower seeds and other nuts. I took a walk to the breakfast alcove and could see the city of Hangzhou spread out before my eyes. The family did indeed live in comfort in a modern apartment, complete with a wide-screen projection TV.

By now, Tze Ling had arrived. He motioned for us to come near the cabinetry. He climbed on a chair and took out a couple of boxes from the glass enclosed cabinet and presented us with a special Chinese wine and the best green tea in China—Longing tea. He told my brother that not too many Chinese people could afford such an apartment. He made some jokes with Tony about the wine and found a flight bag to put the presents in and then we said goodbye.

At Mama's, Tze Jwing was busy making our twenty-course last supper. Some family dropped by and we had a little conversation. I had picked up a few words and they were ready to teach me more. I knew how to count from one to ten and say: hat, pants, chopsticks, ice cream, hello, goodbye, and thank you. I asked one of the brothers, "How do you say beautiful?"

He said, "Pearlean. Marianne is pearlean."

I was slightly embarrassed, but I could see that I did not need to make an effort on my part. I was completely accepted and found to be beautiful.

For dinner, we had an assortment of duck, chicken, fish, shrimp, vegetables, and fish ball soup. We exchanged more gifts. By now, I had six cans of Longing green tea. The older brother, his wife, and son visited from next door; they gave Tony a beautiful dark green silk shirt. They all had heard of Tony's illness. Before Hue Juan left, she gave Tony boxes of small adhesive magnets to be placed behind the ear that would help him sleep. She asked me to bring my daughters to China next time. When the apartment was quiet, my brother gave Do Bei some acupuncture for arm mobility due to an earlier lymph node operation she'd had. Tony rested and I packed to be ready for our departure.

In the morning, my brother did Tai Chi on the outside landing of the apartment building. Tony still did not feel well, so my brother gave him some acupuncture and ordered him to rest while we went to visit Father.

Father was sitting in his chair and knew it was our last day there. I told him, "Tze Ling is sending a driver to take us to Shanghai. We will meet our cousin Yi Dien there; he has arranged for our stay in a hotel. Then on Saturday, we fly to Detroit." My father listened attentively to everything and watched my brother, who was about to give him some acupuncture. He rolled up my father's slacks, revealing his spindly legs. He measured a distance from the knees and placed a needle on the side, near the ankle of both legs, exclaiming, "This is for long life!" Father submitted to all the poking and probing with satisfaction. My brother commented, "Father has a strong heart. I take his pulse and notice a strong beat." My father was pleased. He had not drank or smoked in a couple of years. We declared that he was in optimal health.

I gave Father a keychain with a crystal stone from Brazil, which he held securely. We accompanied him for his last walk to the balcony. He took careful deliberate steps with his walker and looked out for a few moments and then returned. He knew my brother would stay for another week, but I was going. I bent down, teary-eyed, and gave him a kiss, saying, "I wish you very well, Father."

He looked up at me and said, "I wish you, very, very, very, very well!"

Still clutching the keychain, he watched us leave until we were out of sight. I pondered in my heart why he had repeated, "Very, very well."

We took a quick lunch, and before long, the driver was in front of the apartment. We said a hurried goodbye to Mama and Do Bei, who helped us with the luggage and gave us a supply of fruits and bottled water for the journey. My brother translated what they said, "Please come again, and excuse any inconvenience."

We were off to Shanghai. I had expected a two-way highway, but to my amazement, we were on a modern expressway all the way there. We saw the multi-colored farmhouses with towers and steeples, four or five stories high, which were used as rentals and had made many farmers rich; they dotted the landscape, giving it a Disney-like quality. Among the fields, we also saw some rural scenes with older buildings and some country lanes with people on bicycles and pulling carts. As we approached Shanghai, the expressway was lined with bushes and flowers for miles and miles. The buildings became denser, and we were literally immersed in a sea of high rises, all well landscaped.

About four o'clock, we found ourselves in a traffic jam. As we were in a standstill, with traffic pouring in from all sides, we witnessed an incident of road rage. Two men, who had inadvertently bumped their cars into each other, got out of their vehicles and started moving toward each other with flailing arms and fierce verbal attacks. They began wrestling with each other until the bystanders separated them. We did not see the outcome since the traffic started moving again. Tony would say later, "I never met a rude person in China except for this incident."

When we entered Shanghai, the driver made a few turns, trying to find Yi Dien's apartment, which he did with my brother's help. It was dark by now, but I realized I was in the same apartment building where I had visited Yi Dien and his family in 1982. Yi Dien and his wife Gloria asked us to change our shoes into slippers. They had an older apartment with high ceilings, recently remodeled, and elegantly furnished. I noticed a Jacuzzi in one of the bathrooms. Yi Dien was now head of the household since his father, Liu Tzu, a surgeon, had died two years ago. His mother, Aunt Pei Yan, sat in a back bedroom watching TV with an attendant. She had become petite and frail and had suffered a stroke. She also had Parkinson's and was unable to control her right arm and had hand tremors. Yi Dien placed his mother's arm on the armrest and tweaked her nose, saying, "Mama, Tony and Marianne are here to see you."

She looked up at me with amazingly youthful eyes and said slowly, "Marianne" with a German pronunciation. When I said, "I'm glad to see you," she formed the words, "Thank you." She recognized that I couldn't speak Chinese, another family affirmation I tucked away for safekeeping.

Gloria was an extraordinarily beautiful Chinese lady in her thirties. She had long flowing black hair and carried herself with elegance. She wore a black leather vest with a sheer black blouse that was very becoming. By the time she was ready to serve dinner, Aunt Pei Ron, the youngest of my father's sisters, had arrived. She had a bag of apples and apologized for her humble offerings in return for the scarf and chocolates I gave her.

During dinner, Gloria's potato salad was a hit. As we took our second helping, she explained that she made it with two kinds of mayonnaise, sweet and sour, and added, "I will show you the jars when we pass by the market."

After dinner, Aunt Pei Ron had fun with her two favorite nephews who did not stop teasing her. She turned to me and said, "I love Goggeli (my brother's nickname given by my mother). You see, I saw him grow up. You look very different from your brother. I think you look like your mother and Goggeli looks like his father. I only saw you very few times." She punctuated the differences and the distance that had caused me pain and could not be ignored. I recalled her saying she had held me a few times when I was crying as a baby.

The conversation then turned to politics and I became aware of what they were talking about when she said in English, "I do not like this modern selfishness. Me, Me, Me. Only Me. In Mao's time, we think about each other. I respect that."

Of course, Yi Dien and my brother disagreed. They continued joking and Yi Dien said, "Old people are stuck in their old ways."

Aunt Pei Ron still lived in her father's house. The same house my father and mother had lived in during the beginning of their stay in Shanghai when they fled Japanese-torn Chungking, my birthplace. I never got the chance to visit this house.

I turned to Tony and said, "Aunt Pei Ron used to be an actress in the theater."

"Oh, that was so long ago," she said.

"And a very good one," Yi Dien added.

"Aunt Pei Ron, do you remember you gave me a jade ring when we were dancing during my first visit in 1982?" I asked.

"Oh, I can't remember. I am getting very old and forgetful!" More laughter ensued. Words had a dramatic playful tone when she was around.

When it was time to go, we said our goodbyes and then drove to the hotel, which was complete with brass door handles, mirrored walls, and chandeliers. The rooms had two full beds, complete with bathroom and balcony, and all for a very good price. My brother and the driver had a room separate from Tony's and mine. We had a restful sleep in the city of my early childhood.

We rose early and we all met in front of the hotel. The driver, guided by Yi Dien, took us to a local fast food restaurant where we had Chinese braided fried bread, sweet soymilk, and delicious sesame cakes. Then we were off to see the city. I asked Yi Dien whether I could see the Huang Pu River. As we crisscrossed overpasses in search for an opening to the river, the city proved itself a feast for the eyes and senses—a veritable forest of spectacular buildings and architectural wonders that passed before us. We found a deserted cobblestone street with a guardhouse and gate at the end where the security guard let us leave the car. Then we entered the Huang Pu River Park, walking along the flagstone path, passing round marble tables and stools, and beautifully landscaped gardens throughout. Yi Dien turned to me and said, "You left China from the dock across the river where that ship is standing." I tried to recreate my first departure, but I was not sure whether any of the buildings were the same. Yi Dien said, "This is the first time I come here. This park opened recently, so I'm learning where everything is." As we walked along the path, I saw a class of colorful preschool children seated in a circle on the grass while their teachers served them a picnic lunch. Then we came to a focal point—a terrace with club-like tables and umbrellas where Chinese families and businessmen were enjoying their lunch. In the background, I could see the twin domes of the International Convention Center, the Broadcast Tower, and Shanghai's tallest building with eighty-eight floors. The sun was shining brightly, bathing the newly transformed city that could truly be called the "Jewel of the East."

Yi Dien sensed that we would like to climb to the top of the highest building. Before long, he was buying tickets to the summit. Once we were up there, Shanghai appeared endless in all directions. I would guess Shanghai was five times the size of New York and ten times the size of Chicago. We had lunch across the street from the tall building in a glass-paneled restaurant and ordered a bowl of noodles. We had some pleasant conversation, cousin style. I asked Yi Dien, "How long did you live in the U.S.?" (Tony had helped him obtain a visiting Visa and he had come to Detroit for a visit in the '80s.

Yi Dien said, "I was in Berkeley for about four years. I had to work in a restaurant to make money. Then I got married, but my wife took everything and I lost my visa, so I returned to China. Life is good here. I got married again, and my wife and I own two businesses: a software business and a coffee business. I buy a portion of coffee beans from a lady in New York who imports them from Brazil. I roast them here and supply area restaurants. I have a computer genius working for me, and I hope to make a breakthrough in the software business."

I was astonished with my cousin's vitality and optimism. I asked, "Did you know our cousin Xi Cheng is writing a book? He called me from Hong Kong, but I was unable to get hold of him then. I think he wanted to ask me some questions about my life."

"No, I did not know about his book. He does not talk to us too often. I hear he is a professor at a University in California. Goggeli and I are closer. We grew up together and we understand each other. We all suffered, but we bounce back. I like to try many new things." Then he recounted the yogurt story he had told me before when my father took him out to a restaurant, but did not offer him any yogurt, saying that it was for grown-ups. Beware what you give or withhold from children; it may last a lifetime in their memories!

We were going to spend the afternoon shopping, but instead, we returned to the hotel, saying goodbye to my brother and his driver at 3:30 p.m. Yi Dien suggested we take a nap and then he would be back to take us for supper. We took a short, refreshing rest, and then at 4:30 p.m., Tony and I watched the stream of bikes and cars passing in front of the hotel. I said, "Tony, look at that beautiful Chinese girl on that bike!" Then I saw Yi Dien on his bike and realized the beautiful girl was Gloria, so I exclaimed, "It's them!" They parked their bikes in the back and we were off to peruse the neighborhood on foot.

We walked past my mother's former apartment building. I recognized the entranceway and courtyard where my brother and I had played. The guardhouse was no longer the wooden booth I had feared as a child; it had been replaced by a brick structure built on the opposite wall. We entered the doorway of the back building where we had lived. I noticed the walls had a fresh coat of paint and the windows cast a pleasant light. As I went up the stairwell, I saw that the ornate wrought iron banisters and wood railings were the same all the way to the top. My mother had lived in the penthouse apartment on the sixth floor. I did not bother to knock on the door because I knew from my last visit that the apartment did not exist anymore. They had added rooms on the terrace to accommodate more families. It was nevertheless nostalgic for me since the outside doors were still the same. I told my brother, "I have a special bond with Shanghai." He replied, "Of course—the first five years of your life." I lingered a bit, taking in the surroundings one last time. It was dusk and we stepped onto the busy sidewalk outside. I asked Yi Dien, "Which direction is Hong Qiao?" He said, "It is to the right." I had thought so. That was the direction my mother took me by rickshaw to the boarding school when I was four.

Yi Dien had prepared a treat for us. We were on the way to a Brazilian steakhouse nearby. Along the street, just a few doors from the apartment archway, I saw a gift shop. I went in to buy a small trinket for remembrance, but Yi Dien insisted on buying the gifts for me: red rice bowls and accompanying porcelain chalices with spoons. These had to be packed for travel, so Gloria told us to go with her to the restaurant so we would not lose our reservation. Later, Yi Dien came to our table and said, "The store is for marriage gifts. It is to wish couples happiness. For you and your daughters!" Tony and I looked at each other, knowing the gift would probably go to our daughter Michelle, who was engaged to be married—a little present from her grandmother's haunts.

How ironic it was that I was seated in a Brazilian Churrascaria in my old Shanghai neighborhood. I listened to Brazilian music and helped myself to the excellent salad and fruit bar. The waiters carried fire-brazen meats on skewers and sliced beef, chicken, and sausage until you said, "Enough!" As we listened to the samba beat, I asked Gloria, "Do you like to dance?"

"Yes, very much. I want Yi Dien to come dancing with me, but he does not like to," she said.

"It is the same with me. Tony and I took some lessons, but I am the enthusiast. I guess the Latin soul beats in me."

The small storefront restaurant was filled to capacity—the marriage of Brazilian and the Chinese palates was a success. But then, we were in Shanghai, a city that boasted a cosmopolitan flavor. Yi Dien told us we were in the diplomatic district, an upscale neighborhood. We walked down a block and looked across the street to see the gates of the American Embassy. I remembered when I had entered there to plead my brother's case so he could come to America. We continued to stroll leisurely, passing many other embassies on this balmy autumn evening. Gloria wanted to show me the mayonnaise she used for her potato salad. We found a convenience store, very much like one we could find in any city in the West. On a shelf by the refrigerator, Gloria found the jars of sweet and salty mayonnaise and said, "They are made in Japan." As we continued walking, I saw the roots of trees protruding from their trunks, bespeaking their age. This was indeed an old neighborhood that had seen many changes of the guards, some oppressive and some more liberal, letting freedom ring in their citizens' hearts. It was apparent everywhere that people were savoring the manifestations of life, culture, and foreign exchanges. Shanghai was a vibrant city and I was glad to be there.

On our last day, Yi Dien came by bike around 7:30 a.m. to meet us at the hotel. He hailed a taxi and gave us breakfast in a paper bag. I thought, "How considerate of my cousin!" The milk and Chinese cakes were delicious! It was a forty-five-minute ride to the International Airport. We passed a group of senior citizens doing Tai Chi at a downtown square. Then the road opened to the freeway and we saw many warehouses and advertising billboards. Yi Dien said, "That is like the Sam's Club; we have many in the city. This afternoon, Gloria and I are going to look for a large screen TV."

"I hope you find a bargain," I said.

Once at the airport, we had to pass many security checkpoints. While we stood in line, Yi Dien paid the airport taxes. Then we said goodbye and moved on to a secure area for those in transit. We forgot to fill out a departure slip so we remained in the back of the line. We were nervous as we heard for the third time, "Last call for Northwest flight to Detroit." We went down an escalator and rushed through a long hall to the gate with our boarding passes in hand. We were finally in the aircraft and settled into our seats beside a window behind the plane's wing. The plane had close to four hundred passengers, many being Chinese families with babies. A fussy baby across the aisle from us did not want to stay in the bassinet attached to the wall. I saw a young father bending over, trying to appease the baby, which made me wonder about the destinies of all these people, their hellos and goodbyes.

Chapter 3

—— ✿ ——

My Father's Death

Back in Detroit, Tony and I settled into our respective routines. I went every day to my social work job at the Aurora Psychiatric Hospital in downtown Detroit, and shared with my colleagues and friends about my Chinese trip.

On Sunday, December 3, 2000, around 11:30 p.m., I got a call from my brother.

"Marianne, Jia Ming called and they are taking Father to the hospital. I told her I would call her back as it is cheaper to call from the U.S. She said, "Father would not get out of bed for three days and has difficulty breathing."

"Call me back as soon as you can." I imagined them taking my father's frail body down the cement steps and onto their car. He was very ill, perhaps unconscious.

It was around 3:30 a.m. that I heard the phone ring again, but it stopped right away. I thought, "Perhaps it is my brother," but I waited till the morning to call him back. I feared the inevitable. I got into work and told my co-workers my father was very ill so I had to go into my office to call my brother.

It was 9:00 a.m. When I called, Su Juan answered and immediately put my brother on the phone.

"Father died," he told me. "They took him to the hospital and tried to revive him nineteen times."

Tears rolled down my cheeks. I was given a three-day leave and went home. In mourning, I went through the process of trying to internalize my father. I gathered his letters, his pictures, and I invited my family to remember him. I made a memorial card with the most handsome picture of my dad I could find.

Suzy and Sara came from college. Lisa, Michelle, and her fiancé, David, drove over. My niece Joan, her husband Curt, and her daughter Maya also arrived. Shortly thereafter, my brother and Su Juan walked in. My friend Fadia dropped off some food.

We went downstairs to the family room, near the basement room my father had occupied during his visit in 1987, and we shared our memories.

We watched a video of my father, taped in 1987, when he taught a group of high school students how to do Tai Chi. He was seventy-five then, but still limber and could move with amazing grace. As he came a little too close with his sword, a student moved back in fear and he said, "Never mind."

At the end, he was asked, "What is the central idea in Tai Chi?"

My father thought and said, "It is meditation in movement. This is what I say, you see. It represents the earth's four elements: Fire, Water, Wood, and Gold." Then he did the movements and said, "You need to make only these four movements and it will be okay."

Then he added, "It is harmonious. What is harmonious?" There is a long pause. He cannot answer his own question. There is some laughter. Then he says, "In mathematics there is a concept....Harmonious means complete."

He was friendly with all religions and considered them as windows to reality. He had passed to the great beyond. It was complete.

At the memorial gathering, my niece Joan asked me, "Did you give him a hat?"

"Yes, I got one at the Great Wall," I replied.

With tears in her eyes, she said, "The family in China told us he was cremated wearing that hat." It moved me to know that my father had worn the hat I had given him to the end.

My father had walked the seasons and passed through all the stages. He gave me the gift of life, love, and understanding. I could see a book on his shelf, *Thank You for Smoking*, so I grappled also with tolerance and I heard him say:

"I wish you very, very, very, very well."

Epilogue

Parasailing Off Gavea Mountain

In April 2006, I returned to Brazil and made my usual visits to old friends. Then I told them I would like to parasail or glide off Gavea Mountain.

My friends thought I was crazy and cautioned me not to do it. Harumi cited that a woman had died recently when the wind drove her sail against the mountain's rocky face. Later, Maria Clara and Hugomar confirmed that someone had died, but she had employed a poor guide who had faulty equipment. Maria Clara actually voiced a desire to come with me. When I visited Virginia in Piratininga, she was amused that I had these plans. Her son Marcus had a glider in the carport and had sailed off Rio's mountains many times, so this activity was not strange to her. When I told it to Nega, she smiled with that twinkle in her eye, knowing full well that the daredevil in me would do it. While in Vitoria, my friend Alzira thought my plans were a distinct possibility. However, when I was in Belo Horizonte visiting Madre Euridyna, she said, "It is very dangerous. You know you are not getting any younger."

Yet I was spurred on despite my fears. I thought, "If seventy-two-year-old ladies I met at the Tango Club in Detroit could fly off Gavea Mountain while visiting Rio, so could I."

My last full week in Rio, I was staying at Harumi's apartment in Botafogo. Tatiana, a Russian friend I had met in dance class in Detroit, joined me for that week after Easter. Being a good sport, she was game to procure a flight guide for our jump. On Friday, we took the bus to Harumi's house in Sao Conrado, at the base of Gavea Mountain, and found out that the Parasailing and Gliding Headquarters was at the end of the beach across the road from Harumi's house. We braved crossing the busy multi-lane highway and reached the Flight Center. We approached a bronzed, middle-aged man, Ron Torres, who exuded fitness, and I said to him in Portuguese, "Sir, my friend and I would like to fly off the mountain. Is it possible?"

"Yes, it is possible. Only we're not flying today because the winds are not favorable."

"When do you think the winds will be favorable? Tatiana is leaving tomorrow night and I am leaving Tuesday night."

"Oh, we expect the wind to change direction in the next few days. You see the wind has to blow toward the mountain; otherwise it could be dangerous."

"So, you'll call when you are ready to take us? My friend Harumi lives right across the street from you and we should be there."

"Yes, absolutely. We'll pick you up at your friend's house; I know where it is."

"Do you think Tatiana might have a problem since she is a little heavier?"

"No, there is no problem. We just have to wait for the right wind."

"In your opinion should we parasail or hang glide? What is your recommendation?"

"Well, both are safe and comfortable. It is up to you. In hang gliding, you hold the bar and maintain the flight posture, whereas in parasailing, you sit. Perhaps for you ladies, parasailing might be preferable."

"How much will it cost for each of us?"

"The charge is eighty dollars."

"We'll be awaiting your call. Thank you very much for giving us this chance. We're scared, but we will do it."

"Oh, you'll do fine. Most people are scared at first, but it dissipates quickly."

We left our phone number and he gave us his business card.

Tatiana's enthusiasm was infectious. I needed the reassurance of friends, but she just needed the opportunity to fly. Granted she was forty-five years old, while I was sixty-one. The next day, Saturday, we appeared at Harumi's once more, wondering whether it would be the day. We met with Ron at the Flight Center, but he said, "Today, the winds are not right for takeoff." Tatiana was very disappointed since it was her last day in Rio. But we enjoyed ourselves anyway, spending the whole day frolicking in the water and basking in the sun beneath my beloved Gavea.

Sunday, I was alone in Harumi's apartment and decided to sleep in. Around 1:00 p.m., I received a call from Ron.

"Marianne, tomorrow the weather forecast is great and I can take you! The wind will be perfect! It will be clear so you will be able to see everything!"

"Oh, that's wonderful! You know Gavea Mountain and its valley mean so much to me. My stepfather had a riding school there, and I grew up in Sao Conrado and have so many memories."

"You're not the first person I will take who has ties to this place. I can relate to you." He proceeded to tell me the story of various people he had taken parasailing, and how grateful they were to be given a chance to fly over Gavea.

"I'm so sorry your friend had to leave before it was right to fly. I will pick you up around noon tomorrow at your friend Harumi's house. Wear tennis shoes, jeans, and a T-shirt. You may want to bring a light jacket since it can get cold up there."

"I will be ready. Thank you so much!"

Monday, I showed up at Harumi's around 11:30 a.m. I felt a mixture of excitement and fear. In fact, I had so much fear that I had been running a fever since early morning. Harumi feared for me as well; she offered me some food, but I could not eat. She had invited her whole family for lunch and kept busy to distract herself from worrying about me.

Ron showed up at the appointed hour in a small red convertible buggy driven by a portly, middle-aged, blond man from Switzerland. Ron jumped in the back near a luggage rack holding two huge black plastic bundles. I sat in front near the Swiss man who told me, "I want to visit Switzerland this year, but I am very happy here." He had lived at the Favela da Rocinha (one of Rio's largest slums adjacent to the Gavea valley) for ten years and had been parasailing for some time. We spoke in German as I told him about my roots in Sao Conrado and my parentage. We had an easy rapport.

Just before we reached the single steeple, whitewashed church of Sao Conrado, we veered left and I could hear the rumble of the tires gripping the cobblestone road. As we ascended, I saw to our right a cluster of raw brick dwellings, part of a favela. The Swiss man turned to me and said, "They make here the best beef stew ever!" As we curved around the mountain, I saw some impatiens growing out of the rock's face and remembered that in Portuguese, these flowers are called sem vergonha ("without shame") because they pop up in any little moist space. I felt very much at home with the flowers, the vegetation, the rock, and even with the stranger next to me who embodied a life I envied. Before I knew it, we were turning left and going up a dirt road leading to a place called Pedra Bonita (Beautiful Rock) where the jumps took place. At the top was a paved area for cars and another dirt area for open gliders. Below was a small, covered observation deck with benches followed by the jumping ramp.

Ron had a few assistants spread out our blue sail by the ramp. He gave me a few papers to sign, and while we walked, he said, "I am very careful now. To tell you honestly, a while ago I had an accident and we flew into some trees. So I only take people when the wind is perfect, so this is why we had to wait." His words actually made me feel reassured that I was flying with a pro, who did not take chances. I walked around and stood in front of some armed gliders and took some pictures. Then I walked down to the observation deck and marveled at the magnificent view as I watched Ron and the men spread out our sail, and I asked myself, "Will I have the courage?"

An assistant gave me a helmet and began to fit me into the harness, so I asked him, "What do I do in the beginning?"

"You run as fast as you can!"

Ron placed himself behind me and we were ready. I tried to run, but I couldn't. I was tied in place and had a flashing thought, "We will fall; I did something wrong and we will not fly." Just then, I heard a series of flapping sounds and knew the sails were filling up with air and my feet were off the ramp—and we were flying! I held the harness with all my strength and felt a cool mist touch my face. What an exhilarating feeling! I was flying over the forest and could see the whole valley and sea beyond. I told myself, "You don't have to hold so tightly. Just relax and enjoy!" We floated in the quiet breeze with the sun illuminating my childhood home.

Ron said, "There is where your riding school stood."

I looked over to where he was pointing. Besides the golf course to the left, I saw a cluster of high rises lining the beach. Ron took some pictures with my camera. The silence was good. It was twenty minutes of bliss as we coasted along. I felt one with this place that was bathed with my memories. I felt born again from the womb of Gavea Mountain that had helped me conquer my fears and embrace the present.

The buildings began to come closer, so we veered right and passed over Harumi's house. I was hoping to see someone wave at me, but no one was watching. Ron said, "I will land on the beach, and when you touch the sand, just run." However, he landed on the grass and I just sat and was dragged on my butt.

He asked, "Are you all right?" He knew people could injure their feet on the landing.

"I'm fine!" I thanked him. I was so grateful to have accomplished my dream. With a full heart, I took pictures with Ron and the young black lad who folded the parasail.

So I have come to the end of this journey. I gather within me all the people and places that have meant something to me. Even though, at times, I felt very much alone in my life, I was never alone.

From my mother, I embraced her courage, her resolve in the face of danger and the unknown, and her simple grace and capacity to enjoy nature and the fleeting company of friends.

From my father, I received his playful wisdom and optimism and the resignation that all will be all right. I can hear him say, "We'll live one hundred years!" I share his faith in the completeness of life, even as we suffer losses and humiliation.

From Madre Euridyna, I received her delight in beauty and the quiet presence of God. In 2003 I visited her, filled with turmoil, having aborted my divorce from Tony and wondering whether I had made a mistake. She knew I loved precious and semi-precious Brazilian stones in their crude form. She got a small, unpolished amethyst from her desk, and showing it to me, she said, "In the Apocalypse, the angel speaks of precious stones. The amethyst is the blue of Truth and the red of Love." When I left, she gave me a note in an envelope and told me to read it on my way back to Rio. I read it on the bus when the mountains formed a magnificent landscape. In it was a quote from Isaiah she meant for me, "I will hold you by your hand and I will help you."

I did divorce Tony in 2005. From then on, I wore an amethyst ring given to me by my mother. I lost that ring in a store once, but someone found it and turned it in so I got it back. However, I lost it again preparing a Christmas dinner for my family in 2009, and never found it again. I guess the heart has to be given to that which cannot be lost or destroyed.

Father Toner was a beacon of light for me. He was there for me in my darkest hours. When I felt ugly and abused and bent in shame, he said, "Your life is like a puzzle that makes a beautiful picture. Even the bad fits in the picture, but it does not make you ugly." I relied on his love and wisdom. He died in June of 1999, not quite witnessing the passage of the millennium. We had a picnic one late afternoon in

September, the year before his death, in a park not far from his Jesuit Residence for the elderly priests. He enjoyed watching a Mexican family interact lovingly toward each other and their baby. He wanted nothing more for me than my happiness.

From Gavea, I take the strength and beauty of this mountain where there is a special presence, and where the birds soar at its summit and the sun shines on the waves below that never cease to lap the beach with the moist balm of its waters. It is like the landscape of the soul, always changing and transformed and longing to partake of this world.

From China, the place of my birth and early childhood, my father's motherland, I also take sustenance. Here I found the face of humanity in all its myriad forms, hungry and thirsty to unfold and be born again. It was here I found my father, who gave me a sense of completeness or what he would call "harmony." We had been apart for thirty-two years, but it did not matter anymore, for space and time had little relevance as all became unified in the heart.

I am here in America, a place I had found unfamiliar, alien, and cold. I have been thrust into this place for so many years and now I have grown roots. Here too, I find meaning. It offers its space, its possibilities of freedom and connectivity with the whole world.

The past has given me meaning, but I must embrace the present. I find myself in a lovely condo, able to visit my daughters and babysit my grandchildren with whom I have a special bond. On February 5, 2011, my daughter Sara got married to Jake Manteuffel in Cabo San Lucas, Mexico. She wanted to be married at a beach to approximate the life I had in Gavea. I went to Mexico with my family and close friends, armed with sixty Brazilian rock trees made with chips of semi-precious stones that in Brazil are called Arvore da Felicidade (Tree of Happiness) that would be given to the wedding guests. My friend, Maria Clara, bought them from a rock warehouse in Rio and chose each one with much love. They are a myriad of different colors and types, including amethyst, rose quartz, agate, and crystal. She placed them in a suitcase that was brought to me by a friend who recently visited Rio. Maria Clara also included a brochure that described the healing properties of the various stones, so they come with many well wishes. These trees symbolize our unity and how we are a part of each other—no matter how disparate our paths, we awaken in each other the God within.